Charles A. Hanna

Of this work one thousand copies have been printed from type, and the type destroyed.

G. P. Putnam's Sons

November, 1910.

The Trail through Shadow of Death Gap.
From a photograph made by the Author in September, 1909.

The Wilderness Trail

Or

The Ventures and Adventures of the Pennsylvania Traders on the Allegheny Path

With Some New Annals of the Old West, and the Records of Some Strong Men and Some Bad Ones

By

Charles A. Hanna

Author of
" The Scotch-Irish "

With Eighty Maps and Illustrations

In Two Volumes
Volume One

G. P. Putnam's Sons
New York and London
The Knickerbocker Press
1911

COPYRIGHT, 1911
BY
CHARLES A. HANNA

The Knickerbocker Press, New York

To

ELIZABETH HARRISON HANNA

CONTENTS

VOLUME I

CHAPTER	PAGE
I.—The Debatable Land	1
II.—The Iroquoians of the Susquehanna	26
III.—The Petticoat Indians of Petticoat Land	88
IV.—The Shawnees	119
V.—The Early Traders of Conestoga, Donegal, and Paxtang	161
VI.—The Young Red Man Goes West	182
VII.—The Shamokin Traders and the Shamokin Path	192
VIII.—Andrew Montour, "The Half Indian"	223
IX.—The Frankstown Path	247
X.—The Raystown Path	274
XI.—The Traders at Allegheny on the Main Path; with Some Annals of Kittanning and Chartier's Town	290
XII.—The Ohio Mingoes of the White River and the Wendats	315
XIII.—Kuskuskies on the Beaver	340
XIV.—Logstown on the Ohio	352

MAPS AND ILLUSTRATIONS

VOLUME I

	FACING PAGE
THE TRAIL THROUGH SHADOW OF DEATH GAP	*Frontispiece*
ONA INDIANS IN ACTION	1
A SUSQUEHANNA IROQUOIS OF THE STONE AGE	26
STONE AGE AMERICANS OF THE PRESENT DAY	28
ATTACK ON AN IROQUOIS FORT	30
THE SITE OF THE "FORT DEMOLISHED" OF 1688	36
LOOKING WEST FROM THE SITE OF THE FORT DEMOLISHED	38
THE MOUTH OF OCTORARA CREEK	40
ARCHÆOLOGICAL RELICS OF THE SUSQUEHANNOCKS	42, 44
THE SUSQUEHANNOCK FORT OF 1670	46
THE SITE OF THE SUSQUEHANNOCK FORT OF 1670	48
LOOKING EAST FROM THE SUSQUEHANNOCK FORT OF 1670	50
HERRMAN'S 1670 MAP OF MARYLAND	54
THOMAS CRESAP'S FORT OF 1730	56
MAP OF THE IROQUOIS CASTLES IN 1681	58
SUSQUEHANNOCK PICTURE WRITINGS ON ROCKS IN SUSQUEHANNA RIVER	60, 62, 64
THE SITE OF THE CONESTOGA INDIAN TOWN OF 1700	78
DE L'ISLE'S 1718 MAP OF LOUISIANA	122

Maps and Illustrations

	FACING PAGE
THE SITE OF FORT ST. LOUIS	124, 126
MINISINK FLATS AND MINISINK ISLAND	140
SHAWNEE ISLAND AND THE SITE OF PECHOQUEALIN TOWN	142
PAHAQUALONG, OR DELAWARE WATER GAP, FROM THE SITE OF PECHOQUEALIN TOWN	144
THE MOUTH OF PEQUEA CREEK	150
INDIAN POINT, ON CONESTOGA CREEK	152
MAYO'S MAP OF THE POTOMAC SHAWNEE TOWNS, 1737	156
PETER BEZALLION'S GRAVE	170
THE SITE OF THE SHAWNEE TOWN OF WYOMING	186
THE SITE OF THE SHAWNEE TOWN OF CHILLISQUAQUE	190
TAYLOR'S MAP OF SHAMOKIN AND VICINITY, ABOUT 1727	192
CONRAD WEISER	196
TIOGA POINT	206
HOWELL'S 1792 MAP OF PENNSYLVANIA	220
SHADOW OF DEATH GAP	248
BLACK LOG GAP	250
THE SITE OF AUGHWICK TOWN	252
JACK'S NARROWS	254
WATER STREET	256, 258, 260
KITTANNING GAP	261
THE SITE OF KISKIMINETAS TOWN	264
McKEE'S ROCK	270, 272
ALLIQUIPPA'S GAP, FROM THE EAST	280
THE SITE OF SAGUIN'S TRADING HOUSE ON THE CUYAHOGA	334
THE SITE OF OLD KUSKUSKIES	340

Maps and Illustrations

	FACING PAGE
LOOKING DOWN BEAVER VALLEY FROM THE MOUTH OF MAHONING	342
THE SITE OF LOGSTOWN	356
BONNECAMPS'S 1749 MAP OF THE OHIO RIVER	360
THE OHIO COMPANY'S MAP OF THE FORKS OF OHIO, ABOUT 1750–52	372
THE OHIO RIVER FROM THE SITE OF LOGSTOWN	380
MAP OF THE WILDERNESS TRAILS	384

ACKNOWLEDGMENTS

ACKNOWLEDGMENTS are due to the following persons for their courtesy, suggestions, and assistance in furnishing material, information, and photographs for use in these volumes, and to the authors and publishers named for permission to use copyrighted matter from their publications:

To Mr. Charles William Burrows, and the Burrows Brothers Company, for transcripts from De Lery's *Journals* (manuscript) and the *Jesuit Relations*.

To Messrs. Charles Scribner's Sons, for transcripts from Richard Smith's *Journal*, in Halsey's *Four Great Rivers*.

To Col. J. Stoddard Johnston, for transcripts and notes from his *First Explorers of Kentucky*, relating to the travels of Walker and Gist in Kentucky.

To Dr. Reuben G. Thwaites, for transcript of Dr. Draper's manuscript account of John Finley.

To Dr. John W. Jordan, Jr., for transcripts of manuscript *Journals* and itineraries of Thomas Hutchins and Captain Harry Gordon.

To Messrs. Robert H. Kelby, A. T. Doughty, P. Lee Phillips, Frederick S. Dellenbaugh, William M. Beauchamp, and Wilberforce Eames, for numerous courtesies.

To Messrs. David H. Landis, Oscar J. Harvey, James Mooney, Frank R. Diffenderfer, and Archer B. Hulbert, for suggestions, criticisms, corrections, photographs, and data.

And to Mrs. Louise Welles Murray, Miss Frances G. Weiser Shiffner, Mrs. Henrietta H. Bodwell, Miss Sarah Cresson, Mrs. Mary Calhoon Taylor, Mr. Charles W. Furlong, Mr. Clark B. Jamison, Mr. Charles Starek, Mr. George F. Hunter, Mr. H. Frank Eshelman, Mr. J. C. Hommer, Mr. J. Ferd. Walther, Mr. Henry Houck, Mr. Thomas Lynch Montgomery, Mr. E. O. Randall, and the officers of the Maryland Historical, Society, for photographs, maps, books, information, material, and assistance furnished.

Ancient Civilization was spread among the Barbarians by the Trader and the Soldier.

Modern Civilization has been made known to the Far Nations by the Trader, the Soldier, and the Missionary.

Future Civilization will be carried to the Ends of the Earth by the Trader alone.

INTRODUCTION

THE American Indian has become familiar to the reading portion of mankind chiefly as a foremost exemplar of those two surviving arts of the savage in which he scarcely has been surpassed—war and oratory. The reputed speech of the half-breed Mingo warrior, Logan, even though its eloquence may have been largely that of John Gibson, his sister-in-law's "squaw-man," who wrote it down, will be declaimed by the American school-boy in ages to come, perhaps long after the stately and impassioned periods of a Webster or a Gladstone have been forgotten. In America to-day, the stories of Champlain and the Iroquois, of King Philip's War, of Braddock's Rout, of the Wyoming Massacre, of St. Clair's Defeat, and of Pontiac, Brant, Tecumseh, and Sitting Bull, are at least as well known as are the legends of Marathon and Syracuse, of Hastings and Orleans, of Blenheim and Waterloo. But as the arts of war and oratory are primarily arts of mischief and deceit, it is to be expected that the revelations which mediums of that nature afford of the life, sociology, and character both of the Red Man and the White Man should be distorted, one-sided, and incomplete—and the picture to a corresponding degree false.

Yet, with few exceptions, the writers of history, until a comparatively recent period, have written chiefly of wars and words, of soldiers and politicians, and have neglected the matters of more real moment to the seriously interested student of man—matters pertaining to his origin and development, to his daily life and pursuits, his migrations and colonies, his taboos, ceremonies, social culture, and religions. To such a student there is more value in one line of Cæsar relating to some peculiar custom of the ancient Britons than in two pages of the rhetorical harangue which Tacitus imagines Galgacus to have delivered to his warriors before a battle; and more merit in one page of a contemporary record of material facts than in a whole chapter of hypothetical philosophizing on the patriotic motives of politicians, or the logical continuity of cause and effect in the statesmanship of kings and the favor of princes; or in the mathematical analysis and explanation of the movements of two opposing mobs made up of men intent either on killing or running.

Introduction

History comprehends as many branches as there are phases in the activities of human life. It is trite to say that a complete history of a nation or a race would present the life of that nation or race in all its aspects—physical, geographical, social, economical, philological, commercial, recreational, intellectual, literary, artistic, sexual, religious, and spiritual; as well as political and military. The two latter aspects, while more spectacular, certainly are not so important as the others. Yet most of the writers of history have confined themselves to politics and battles alone. This is due, perhaps, to the innate fondness of immature humanity for noise and pageantry. There are still a few grown-up men living in the civilized world, who, out of sheer vanity, delight to dress themselves in bright colors, and, following a brass band, to parade before their fellow-men. At one time in the life of every man, nation, or race, the same thing has been universally true. Now-a-days, however, most men outgrow this weakness before they become men. But most of our histories have been written after ancient models which were designed to be read by the other kind of men. They were made to please and instruct men and nations who had reached the same period of intellectual development as the modern boy of ten, or the man of thirty, who still takes pleasure in wearing feathers.

It is for this reason, possibly, that most of the histories which have been written, have, sooner or later, taken the next place on our library shelves to the books of last year's sermons or the highly ornamented volumes containing a miscellaneous assortment of the "World's Famous Orations." Happily, the writing of this kind of historical fiction has ceased to be the work of serious minded men; and its field is now chiefly occupied by very young women novelists.

However, for those students and readers who insist on having the romantic in history, there is no field of reading which yields such abundant returns both in interest and knowledge as are afforded by the authentic records of the North American Indian in Colonial times. Parkman has demonstrated this with the greatest success in his highly interesting chronicles of the French Traders and French Missionaries. He first appreciated what has since become a recognized fact, that the most romantic and picturesque characters in American history have been the Latins, of both continents. Indeed, the careers of some of these have never been surpassed in romantic interest by those of any characters in European history. By his faithful and spirited narratives, the writer last named has made the whole world familiar with the stories of La Salle and Tonty, of the Jesuits and the Hurons, of Frontenac and La Verendrye.

Equally interesting, and in many respects more romantic, are the yet untold stories of the lives and vicissitudes of some of the French "squaw-men," and the French half-breeds, whose parents were partly Indian and partly white—such as the Joncaires, father and sons, the Chartiers, father and son, the Montours, father, daughter, and grandson, the Shekallamys, father and son, the Langlades, and others, the history of all of whom belongs chiefly to that of our own country.

The ancient historians who wrote of battles still have their lessons for us to learn, though, if not in one way, then in another. The harangues and fights, for instance, which form the substance of the literary remains of Thucydides, are not without their value even at this late day. They at least serve to show that the chief interest of the early Greeks for whom he wrote, like that of all races in their primitive days, was the savage's love for battles and talk. While we of to-day have largely outgrown, even if our historians have not, the blood-thirsty attributes of the savage, we still have his fondness for many pow-wows. Nevertheless, the evil of too much talk is not wholly an unmixed evil, for it serves men as a vent for excess of spleen, which, if held too long confined might cause even more disastrous results than the unrestrained output of words.

As war, or the effort to gain power by force, is no longer the chief business of men, neither can the record of plotting for political power, or power by craft, be regarded seriously as the most important branch of history. The falsity of Freeman's conception, that history is past politics and politics present history, is fully illustrated by the fate of his own historical work, the political part of which has been superseded to a great extent by the work of newer historians of politics. It is on a line with Carlyle's dictum that true history is to be found only in the record of the lives of the world's heroes. Yet many of our histories are written on the assumption that both of these propositions are true.

Heroes and politicians still survive, to dazzle and bedevil our present day mankind; just as the moral uplifters of the ten-cent dreadful will always flourish—men who start in to make the world good, for a consideration, and then, like most other men, consider their work done when they have made it good to themselves. But there are few thinking people to-day who would credit any of these three classes as being typical or representative of our own or our country's life, activities, and ideals. Fortunately, there can be no long endurance of those men or principles that would make of government an end rather than a means.

The few soldiers and statesmen who have been truly great in American history, were so before, and not because they temporarily acted the parts of soldier and statesman. To mention the most familiar examples, Washington was a great general because he was first a great business-man and knew that secret of wealth—to run when other people stand still, and to stand still when other people run. In our present day he would be, and in the past he has been called a land-jobber. So Lincoln was a great President, because he was first a great lawyer, and possessed to a very high degree the homely wisdom called common-sense, or the faculty of seeing things as they are to common men. Franklin, likewise, was great as a public leader because he was first a great inventor, practical philosopher, and hard-headed man of business; and by precept and example taught his countrymen that man's first duty was to be thrifty.

Dead heroes, like dead kings, are seldom missed. No political soldier or oratorical statesman who ever lived can compare in industry, usefulness, integrity, or substantial patriotism with the higher class banker or business genius of to-day, a man whose type can be found in every large and almost every small community in this and other lands.

Another view of history is, that it should be so written as to show the working out of some one or more of the theories and precepts of the philosophers. This would be admirable if philosophy fulfilled its promise in such cases, and really led us to the goal of power by knowledge. But does it?

A favorite formula of the school-master is to the effect that history is philosophy teaching by example. The same thing might as well be said of the earthquake. While one is an understatement and the other an overstatement, both are alike misleading; for both history and earthquake have repeatedly tumbled the house of the philosopher down upon his head, as they will continue to do for an indefinite time in the future. And while it is not to be denied that history is the womb from which philosophy was born, and the mother from which it should draw its sustenance, the teachings of philosophy are always diametrically opposed to some of the examples of history, and often to one another. There is neither consistency nor continuity in the examples, and their only constant teaching is that men *do not* act in accordance with such teachings of philosophy, but in accordance with the always different conditions which confront them. To attempt to follow all the teachings drawn from the examples of history, on any one proposition, is exactly as impossible as to attempt to travel at the same time on four roads leading north, south, east, and west. Yet this conception of history has been elaborated and augmented to the point where some people, like the brilliant and pedantic Buckle—whose philosophy has largely turned to fustian—have undertaken seriously to fabricate history into an exact science. They attempt to analyze, dissect, classify, generalize, and draw morals from the record of the impulses, activities, and casualties of man—a record which furnishes the most vital examples for showing the fallacies and incompleteness of philosophy. In this they are at one with those who in recent years would make a counterfeit science of religion. Scarcely less fallacious, indeed, was the method of the ancient philosophical historians, whose narration of almost every event was prefaced with a description of the particular sign or portent which presaged it. No king could die until a comet had appeared in the sky; no battle was lost, by their side, until after a cow had given birth to a two-headed calf. The omen, of course, was always discovered after the event had happened. Their science was more exact but not much more ridiculous than that of those who would make a science of religion or of history. But men now call the science of portents superstition.

Written history at its best is nothing more than a tentative and cumulative record of those things which concern the environment and activities of men; in short, the record of human experience. But the secret influences which control the actions and determine the destiny of men, are entirely too subtle, complex, intangible, mixed, and remote to be even grasped by the human mind. We must be able to fathom the infinite before attempting to formulate them into principles of philosophy which will abide. The theory that history should be so written as to show the logical development, unfolding, and continuity of some divine plan of God, some law of Nature, or some principle of metaphysical philosophy, is simply a survival in another form of the ancient theological dogma which held that every good or evil happening in a man's life was either a reward for some virtue or a punishment for some sin, and that both were ordained and carried out solely for the enhancement of the glory of God.

Experience, of course, is our best teacher; but it must be our own experience, or no lesson is taught.

Philosophies, like religions, are largely made up from the imagination; and both tend to make romance of history and history of romance. Philosophy's truths, so fondly worshipped by their admirers, are necessarily half of them speculations, pure and simple, and as such they may or may not have the value which gives them permanence. The events of history do not take place from causes circumscribed by the limits of philosophy. On the contrary, the truths of philosophy are themselves more or less matured outgrowths from those events.

History cannot be developed into a science or made to serve as a handmaiden to philosophy, for the simple reason that the mental characteristics and susceptibilities of every human being are different from those of every other human being, and therefore, to the limited perception of man, *like causes*, in human affairs, *do not produce like effects*.

Written history should be a phonograph to lived history, which is a vaster thing than philosophy, because it comprehends both wisdom and folly, and something more besides, which philosophy cannot compass. The possibilities of man's life are too huge, and its history too kaleidoscopic for either to be fossilized by the labels and classifications of the precisian, or limited by the definitions of the philsopher.

As is naturally to be expected, among those who would make philosophy the chief purpose of history, we find a certain number of writers and critics—educated to a point where it may be said their intellects are either overtrained or undertrained—who affect to disparage the importance of facts in the writing of history, and who patronizingly inform us that history should not be concerned with the common things of every-day life, but only with life's great moments and crises; and that the first place should be given to the consideration of the workings of those immutable laws and eternal verities, whatever these may be, which (they say) have governed the whole course of human affairs from the beginnings of history.

Facts, it must be allowed, are stubborn and ofttimes unwelcome things. They are not permitted in poetry under any circumstances whatever; and they are given such an ungracious welcome, and apologized for in a footnote, as it were, when they chance to make their appearance in other fields of polite literature, that they have come to be regarded as interlopers. They are subordinated by the metaphysician; there is no welcome for them in the drama; and the artist runs away rather than meet them face to face. Yet the poet, the novelist, the philosopher, the playwright, and the artist all are, or at least all profess to be, zealous devotees at the shrine of truth.

Now, verified or verifiable facts, material or perceptible, are the stuff from which truth is made. Without venturing into the deep waters of metaphysical definition it may be said that truth is the result of the mind's correct analysis and generalization of those kinds of related facts. Some may go so far as to say that a fact is, potentially, a concrete truth, and that truth is, or should be, fact in the abstract.

Abstractions, however, are usually more than the naked truth. They are facts—bare realities—dressed up by the emotions, the imagination, and the intellect, and as such not free from fallacy; for the most brilliant intellects often take entirely diverse views of the same subjects, interpreting their facts into opposite conclusions. This being the case, it may not be unreasonable for common-sense to assert, as some of our modern practical philosophers seem to do, that, apart from the material facts or demonstrable principles on which it may be based, no such thing has yet been discovered as absolute or eternal truth; and that all abstract truths are relative, or conditional, or contingent, and in a process of growth and change. Christ's question to Pilate, "What is Truth?" has never been and never will be adequately answered. The so-called truths of the remote past, not wholly based on and synonymous with ascertained or anticipated facts, have all been modified or have died, just as we see that such truths of the recent past are to-day being increased or diminished, and as we feel assured that similar truths of the present will likewise be changed or abandoned in the future. What men call truths are really men's opinions about truth, and as such they are neither immutable nor eternal.

Hence, as facts accumulate, philosophies pass away, and the seeming truths of one generation become half-truths to the next. Facts are the only realities which abide, and a concrete truth in history, whether it be newly discovered or newly presented, is the only vital thing about history. It possesses a double interest, in that it serves to establish a new and truer point of view, as well as to destroy an old error.

The business of the common man's philosophy, therefore, is to seek the meaning of facts; not to fabricate them, as the writings of our philosophers might lead us to infer. But the business of the historian is simply to discover and record facts.

A recent observation of Mr. Taft on the subject of "Journalism" is so entirely applicable to the writing of history as well that it may be quoted with profit here: "The increase in the intelligence and discrimination of the people," he says, "has in one way largely modified the power of the press. The editorial writers have by no means such influence upon popular view as they had in days gone by. The newspapers are taken more for the news they contain than for the advice as to the lessons which should be drawn from it. The people make more allowance now for the bias of the paper than they ever did before."

So in the future will our histories be written and read more for the news they contain than for advice as to the lessons which should be drawn from it. And the accurate reporter of the events of history is bound to take a higher place as an authority than the moralizing professor, the brilliant rhetorician, or the idealistic philosopher. Who cares now what Macaulay thought of the Tories; or that Buckle ascribed Scotland's "lack" of progress to superstition and thunderstorms? And what permanent historical value has Carlyle's opinion, that "the history of what man has accomplished in this world is at bottom the history of the great men who have worked here"?

After all, the source and standards of ideals are the lives of men, and high ideals are only the examples set by the best for the others to follow. None of them are more important than the elemental virtue of simple moral and intellectual honesty. Yet this is an ideal that every common man can by example create, and leave behind him as a standard for others. If the historian would attain it, he must confine himself to the discovery and setting forth of pertinent facts.

The present age, as the natural heir of the past, is one where men gain power chiefly by industry, or by the sweat of the brow and the brain

—more or less value given for value received; which, being a cumulative and reciprocal process, may, as some believe, be the true means and end of power by knowledge. According to this view, men's desires drive them to work for their accomplishment, and their accomplishment brings knowledge, and leads to new desires, which require more work and result in further knowledge and produce further effort for more power. In this way knowledge may be said to grow with what it feeds upon; but the price paid for the food is always physical or mental labor. This seems alike true, whether the objects of desire be material, social, or spiritual—money, rank, authority, or wisdom; and even though inherited wealth and position are not always paid for by those who possess them.

There may be more wisdom than is conceived of by philosophy in the simple Bible allegory of the Garden of Eden, which suggests that the fruit of the tree of knowledge is the attainment of man's desire. But what a preposterous lie do we now perceive that part of it to be which teaches that work—man's one sure means to attain all things—is a punishment decreed by God's curse. Such a conception is incomprehensible to a civilized intelligence, which regards creative or productive work for a definite end as the highest privilege and blessing of life; though the study of the Indian, as of all other savage races, shows that to look on labor as a curse is the natural attitude of the mind of primitive man. Indeed, the average Indian community in Colonial America was a Socialist's Utopia. There were no laws beyond those of Nature, and tribal customs. As a general thing, land was held in common. Such government as existed was that of a pure democracy, of the town-meeting style. The men had no other occupation than fishing and hunting, and making war and speeches; *and the women did all the work*.

Now, while our material civilization has been built up by the pick, the axe, the plough, the spinning-wheel, the steam-engine, and the historically ignoble Trader, rather than by, and notwithstanding, the war-club, the battle-axe, the Idealist, and the Talker, it has only recently occurred to men that there might be a better way to learn their own race history than by repeating unmeaning and ofttimes unmerited eulogies of soldiers, or attempting to analyze, classify, and draw lessons from the short-sighted and short-lived policies of opportunist statecraft, or prophesying the rise and fall of the stock market in times of peace, by citing causes for the high price of wheat during the Punic Wars or the Norman Conquest.

Some have, therefore, in late years, undertaken to apply the pick-axe and shovel method to the learning and teaching of history, and have done so, and with great success, both figuratively and literally. The archæologist in Europe has turned up the dirt of the Mediterranean countries, and discovered that the history of ancient civilization will have to be in large part rewritten, and that it must begin before Adam. The antiquarian has searched the charter chests of families and the private and state archives of his own and neighboring nations, and found that the story of his institutions and governments and people has never been truthfully told. As a result, we have the very interesting reports of what new excavations have unearthed in Greece and Italy, in Egypt, in Asia Minor, and in Mesopotamia; and the equally important discoveries made by students of ancient documents other than official papers, with the light they throw on the contemporaneous activities of man. We see, also, that in the writing of European history, what Walter Scott called the "big bow-wow style" has become well-nigh a thing of the past, and in its place we have the results of the careful, painstaking, minutely detailed, and illuminating researches of such men as Mommsen, Heitland, Lecky, Stubbs, and Gardiner, instead of the labored, brilliant, and intrinsically disappointing rhetoric of a Hume, a Macaulay, a Gibbon, a Froude, or a Carlyle.

The same thing is true in the treatment of the race history of the aboriginal American, whose period was much nearer our own than is the case of his prototype in Europe and Asia, and whose living descendants have not yet wholly emerged from barbarism. The archæological and philological investigations which have been carried on by the Bureau of Ethnology at Washington, and by many private investigators in various of the States, have revealed a wealth of material evidence that the prehistoric inhabitants of this continent were the natural and logical ancestors of the Indians living here to-day; and so have upset the finely elaborated theories so eloquently set forth by scores of writers on the subject of the Mound Builders in the past—writers who drew on their imaginations for ninety per cent. of their facts.

Since Lewis Morgan established the modern science of anthropology through his works illustrating the development of human society, from the study of the tribal relations of the Iroquois, each year has added a new stroke to the knell of the old romantic group of writers about America—a group which included Cooper (who frankly acknowledged his output to be fiction), Prescott, Schoolcraft, and both the Bancrofts. The historical value of the work of Albert Gallatin, in his comparative study of the Indian languages, of that of Morgan, in his *League of the Iroquois* and *Ancient Society*, of that of Mooney, and Gatschet, and Hale, and Parkman—whose books are so vital because he followed so literally his sources—is incomparably greater than, for example, the highly poetical bathos used by George Bancroft in telling of the Cherokee towns of Tennessee. As a writer of flowery literature and master of highfalutin, the latter might take a more exalted place than the others who have just been named; but in studying the Indian, in that department of letters, most people prefer Cooper; and as a faithful recorder of American frontier history, Bancroft is far surpassed by Butterfield.

The tendency of the intelligent student of history at the present day seems to be to require more facts, and not so much pseudo-philosophy; more documents, and not so many dissertations on the science of accidents; more early geography, and not so many classical comparisons; more economics, and not so much politics; more particulars, and less generalization; information instead of polemics.

Against this growing demand, the followers of the Oxford or classical tradition, in Chinese fashion, continue to set up in effect the old literary ideals of rhetoric, brilliancy, imagination, and style as the first essentials in the writing of history; as they sometimes are in literature and debate. Eloquence of style, naturally, was the chief shibboleth of the mediæval college, when the sole function of the college was to drill boys for pulpit oratory. But the business of the history writer is not like that of the orator, but rather like that of the judge. The work of either the judge or the historian, in which facts are sacrificed or subordinated to style, while it may be literary, is not judicial, or honest. For that reason, it lacks vitality. It is like that of the portrait-painter who idealizes his pictures. If he be talented, he produces a work of art, which may have a value as such, but it has no value as a correct likeness of the subject. Yet the writer is told that if he present only his facts and let his readers do their own assimilating, instead of giving the reader his own opinions, and theories, and illusions about the facts, he is doomed to be set on the shelf called dry-as-dust.

Unfortunately, this has been largely true in the past; for witness the publishers' axiom that the only histories which sell are those written in a popular style. This is equivalent to saying that the only history the public will buy is the one which is absolutely worthless to the historical student.

Such a conception of history, however, is not only false and shallow, but it also confirms serious men in their belief that the system of so-called education which fathers it is also false and shallow. It is of the same variety of mental millinery as that other highly artificial crop of blossoms from a pseudo-classical education, namely, the propagation of unmeaning and absurdly applied Greek and Latin place-names as place-names for American towns and cities, and, unfortunately, in many cases for towns and cities with the sites of which already were associated Indian place-names of greater beauty and having infinitely more historical significance. Unhappy exhibitions of this product of pedantic ignorance are to be found, sorry to say, in almost every county in America. Why, but for such a false education, should a city built near to what was for more than two hundred years the place of the Great

Council Fire of the Five Nations at Onondaga, be called "Syracuse, New York," instead of "Onondaga"; or a town at Tioga Point, the starting place for all the War Trails leading south from the Iroquois country, be called "Athens, Pa.," instead of "Tioga Point," or "Diahoga." Illiteracy, pure and simple, would be preferable to an education which produces such abortive results.

Of all who have written of the function of the historian, perhaps none have exceeded in truth, breadth, or good sense, the modest precept of the somewhat credulous Father of History himself, who wrote his facts and fictions together in simple language, distinguishing them as such, without exaggerating or subordinating one fact at the expense of another, and without grouping them together in one place and scattering them in another for the purpose of having them show his own or life's "unity of purpose." Old Herodotus wrote history more than two thousand years ago "in order that the actions of men might not be forgotten"; and that is the best and an all-sufficient standard in writing it to-day.

It is the accumulation and presentation of facts material to his subject, therefore, that the present writer believes to be the sole office of the modern historian; and it is in that spirit that the following pages have been written—to give some simple annals of a primitive race; to suggest the direction and extent of some of its early migrations; to present some further information on early American geography; as far as possible to permit the actors themselves to narrate some of the events in the drama which preceded the conquest of the central portion of this country by the axe and plough of the pioneer; to recall one or two of the causes which led up to the birth of a new nation; and to endeavor to brush aside and destroy some of the fictions which have been suffered to grow up and vitiate the record of these things.

In doing this, the writer does not undertake to guarantee the correctness of all the statements here presented as facts or seeming facts. Neither does he attempt consistency or uniformity in the spelling of Indian names. It is well known to students of early American history that all Indian names have from one to fifty or more synonyms, and that their spelling varies, according as to whether it was a Spaniard, an Englishman, a Frenchman, a Swede, a Dutchman, a German, or a well-educated official or a poorly educated Trader who wrote the word.

The sixty-year period of which this book mainly treats may be called the growing age of the American Colonies. It extended from 1692, when white men—twelve New York Traders, led by Arnold Viele—seem first to have reached the Ohio Valley, to 1752, when five of George Croghan's Traders were captured by the French Indians at the siege of Pickawillany. The boundary war which followed between England and France merely served to establish the British claim to the Ohio country, a country which had in this period been virtually won by the Pennsylvania Traders.

In these days of quickened political morality, it is interesting to note, as the following pages incidentally show, that during and for some years after this growing time, nearly all the prominent figures in early American political history—including William Penn and his sons, Washington, Franklin, most of the Colonial Governors, and all the politicians, were engaged in land or merchandise trading operations on a large scale; and that their efforts to push these operations to success were chiefly responsible for the resulting expansion and union of the Colonies.

C. A. H.

December 1, 1910.

The Wilderness Trail

Ona Indians in Action.
Published by permission of Charles Wellington Furlong.

The Wilderness Trail

CHAPTER I

THE DEBATABLE LAND

DURING the first quarter of the eighteenth century the largest extent of unoccupied and unexplored land in North America east of the Mississippi and south of the Great Lakes was the wilderness lying contiguous to the Ohio River and its tributaries. Before the close of the first quarter of the following century, that wilderness had been so far subdued as to witness the planting and growth of a small settlement at the heart of the great artery which gave it life, a settlement which, before the passing of another hundred years, was destined to become the most important center of the industrial activity of the world. But during the hundred years between, that land had been the scene of more terrible, more sanguinary, and more fatal battles than had ever been fought on the territories of the American Colonies before. That soil had been drenched with the blood of more slaughtered foes and massacred innocents, white and red, than perished by violence elsewhere within the bounds of those colonies in all the actual battles of Spanish and English, English and French, British and American, from the accession of Queen Anne to the death of George Washington.[1]

Like most other achievements by the race of mankind, the first attempts of the American colonists towards the conquest of the West were feeble and tentative. And as great inventors, great generals, and great statesmen often win their chief successes by wisely building on foundations laid by others, so was the ever conquering march of the pioneer towards the setting sun first preceded, guided, and led by a few score of brave but inglorious men, known as Indian Traders, the most of whom have passed into deep and, to judge their lives by modern standards

[1] For a computation of the number see Warren K. Moorehead's "Ohio Indian Tribes," in vol. vii., *Ohio Arch. Hist. Soc. Publications*, p. 108.

of conduct, well-merited oblivion. Yet the unforeseen results of the petty commerce of these men involved the bringing on of the Seven Years' War between England and France, and prepared the way for American Independence, and American Expansion.

These Indian Fur Traders of Colonial days, and particularly the Pennsylvania Traders, who formed the great proportion of the first English explorers west of the Alleghany Mountains, and who were the first among the English to "venture themselves and their goods farther than any person formerly did," were a class that was stigmatized by some of the Provincial governors as being made up largely of men who were not content to live by cheating the Indians among whom they traded, but must also often debauch their customers' wives in the bargain. Brave, cautious, mercenary, dissolute, adventurous, disloyal, chivalrous, cruel, generous, crafty, as individuals, these Traders undoubtedly were; just as a like number of men in any other so hazardous a calling would probably be. The perils of their trade, like those of the soldier's, made them at many times regardless of those ethics of conduct so essential to the well-being of a community; and, unlike the soldier, the many opportunities for illegal gain in their dealings, stimulated and developed their cupidity to such a point that many of the Traders did not scruple to cheat the Indians in the most outrageous manner. But the story of their lives and adventures, the trials they endured, the dangers they faced, the difficulties they passed through, and the final great catastrophe in which perished nearly all the Traders "in the Woods" at the outbreak of Pontiac's War, is a story most thrilling and one of the most instructive in the pages of American History.

The early trade carried on by the Dutch of New York with the Iroquois at Albany and along the Mohawk Valley for more than a hundred years before 1745 was of a peaceful, limited, and commonplace character. After that time, it was largely under the control of Colonel William Johnson, in whose hands it became an instrument for cementing a lasting alliance between the English and the Indian tribes known as the Five Nations; and thus secured the active co-operation of those tribes in the French War. The New York Traders, as a class, had but little enterprise, and after a fort was built and a trading-post established at Oswego, few of them ventured beyond that post. Their trade was principally in beaver skins; and the Indians with whom they dealt were induced to bring their peltries to Albany or Oswego, and there make an exchange for goods. In a "Review of the Trade and Affairs of the Indians in the Northern District of America," prepared for the British Lords of Trade by Sir William Johnson about the year 1767, that personage writes: "Before the war commenced in 1744, and until that which ended in the reduction of Canada, etc., the trade of the

Northern District, tho. limited and under many disadvantages, was not inconsiderable. Indeed, the circumstances of situation and other disadvantages prevented more than two of the colonies within that district from enjoying much of it. These two colonies were New York and Pennsylvania. If Virginia is admitted into the Northern District, it must likewise be admitted to have had a large share of trade, particularly in deer skins, etc., but excepting it out of this review, we shall consider the trade as principally possessed by the two before mentioned colonies, and of these two, New York had the greatest advantage from its occupying a post on Lake Ontario, to which there was a good water communication, with very little interruption, which enable them to get the most valuable furs.

"The Traders of Pennsylvania penetrated to sundry places on the Ohio, and many of them to the country of the Twightwees [on the Wabash and Miami], etc.; but their purchases being chiefly in deers' leather, transported by pack-horses, and having tedious journeys to make, their returns could not be equally beneficial. The Traders in both colonies were chiefly composed of the frontier inhabitants, who, having some acquaintance with the Indian language, and being necessitous, were the easier induced to such undertakings in a country where credit was easily had for goods. New York bade the fairest for being the principal, if not the only barcadier for the most valuable part of the fur trade, and certainly enjoyed a good deal of it; but to improve its advantages, other measures and other men should have been made use of than the ordinary Traders.

"Those who traded to Oswego were for the most part inhabitants of Albany, Schenectady, and the Mohawk River, the posterity of the Low Dutch, who, being very ignorant, and accustomed to the strictest parsimony in diet, clothing, and all other expenses, had no idea of extending the trade or bringing large cargoes, but contented themselves with a certain profit arising from a small quantity of goods, which they took care to trade off within the compass of three or four months, the issues of which maintained them in idleness for the remainder of the year."

The writer then proceeds to relate some instances of fraud on the part of the Traders at Albany, Schenectady, and Oswego, stating that "two of these instances were the occasion of our losing the trade and affections of some powerful tribes of the Ottawas, who were persuaded to come the length of Oswego to trade with us[1]; and the last instances caused the defection of the most powerful tribe of Senecas."

This indictment of Sir William Johnson against the Albany Traders

[1] See also *N. Y. Doc. Hist.*, i., 717.

was too sweeping, in so far as the lack of enterprise on the part of a few of them went, at least. In the course of an examination of Kakarriel, a Christian Mohawk prisoner from Canada, which took place at Fort James, in New York, August 31, 1687, the Indian related that in crossing Lake Ontario with a French and Indian War party they "met with a brigantine, in which Arnold Viele, the interpreter of Albany, was being taken prisoner, as he was going to Ottawa with the rest of his company a trading." Viele was possibly the leader of one of the parties of Major Patrick McGregory, who, with Captain Roseboom, of Albany, in the years 1685–86, had been given licences by Governor Dongan, for the purpose of trading, hunting, and exploring among the Far Nations of Indians to the southwest. "When the English had thus procured a peace for the French [with the Five Nations in 1684–85]" wrote Councillor Colden, in his Memorial on the Fur Trade, prepared for Governor Burnet in 1724, "they were therefore encouraged to send forty men with great quantities of goods, into the lakes, under the command of Major McGregory, to trade with the Far Nations. At this time [1687], Mr. DeNonville, Governor of Canada, was gathering together all the force of Canada, and of the Indians, enemies of the Five Nations, in order to surprise the Five Nations and destroy them at the time they thought themselves secure by the peace so lately made. Major McGregory and company were met by a French officer on Lake Erie, coming with a great number of men to the rendezvous of the French, and he, with all the English, were all made prisoners."

Arnold (or Arnout) Viele, the Albany interpreter, lived for many years among the Onondaga Indians, where he attended the councils of the Five Nations, as the representative of the New York government. His travels among the Indians of the Far Nations must have been extensive and varied. In the "Journal of Captain Arent Schuyler's Visit to the Minisinck Country" (what is now Montague Township, Sussex County, New Jersey), February 3 to 10, 1694, Captain Schuyler, who was sent from New York on a scouting expedition for news from the French, writes from Minisink under date of February 7th: "Enquireing further after news, they told me that six days agoe three Christians and two Shanwan Indians, who went about fifteen months agoe with Arnout Viele into the Shanwans' [Shawnee] country [then in the lower Ohio Valley], were passed by the Mennissinck going for Albany to fech powder for Arnout and his company; and further told them that sd. Arnout intended to be there with seaven hundred of ye said Shanwan Indians, loaden wth. beavor and peltries att ye time ye Indian coarn is about one foot high (which may be in the month of June.)"

Colonel William Johnson himself, very soon after his arrival in America in 1738, became largely interested in the Indian trade, and within a few years the management of Indian affairs was entrusted to him by the New York authorities. Cadwallader Colden, writing to Governor Clinton August 8, 1751, speaks of Colonel Johnson as the most considerable Trader with the western Indians, he sending more goods to Oswego than any other person. The Dutch Traders at Albany, jealous of his influence and more favorable opportunities, induced their friends in the Colonial Assembly to refuse supplies for Indian Affairs after the conclusion of peace in 1748; which caused Colonel Johnson to resign, the Assembly then owing him £2,000. Many other persons of high official position in the Colonies, like Colonel Johnson, carried on a prosperous trade with the Indians, by means of agents, whom they sent out with stocks of goods. Governor Dinwiddie, of Virginia, in company with Arthur Dobbs, Thomas Lee, George Mason, two brothers of George Washington, and others, in 1748, organized the Ohio (Land) Company, for the purpose of colonizing the western portion of Virginia, and carrying on a trade with the Indians. Thomas Lawrence, a member of the Governor's Council of Pennsylvania, was interested with George Croghan in his trading expeditions to the western Indians, as early as 1747, and for some years before the building of Fort Duquesne. In partnership with Edward Shippen at Lancaster, he carried on an extensive trade in supplying goods to adventurers at that point, to be carried into the wilderness and sold on joint account. The Pemberton Family of Philadelphia, for many years a ruling family of the Quaker oligarchy, was likewise, through some of its members, largely interested in the Indian trade in Pennsylvania during the middle of the eighteenth century. Excepting George Croghan, however, none of the individuals whose names have been mentioned, personally embarked in the actual business of carrying goods to trade with the Indians. The men who did this were usually borderers, of scant means and less education; men who were willing to take more than ordinary risks in hazarding their lives and fortunes in the far wilderness for the sake of bettering their condition; men of similar spirit and enterprise to those of the present day who resort in such large numbers to the Klondike and the Rand for gold.

A few of the early Indian Traders were men of literary attainments, and of these, two or three have written lengthy and more or less interesting accounts of their lives and adventures among the Indians. James Adair, a Scotsman, who traded among the Chickasaws in the Carolinas and Tennessee from 1735 to 1774, wrote a *History of the American Indians in the South*, which was printed in London in 1775. Alexander Henry, a native of New Brunswick, New Jersey, of Scottish descent, who was the first English Trader to establish himself among the Chippewas and Ottawas at Michillimackinac after its surrender by the French in 1761, also printed (New York, 1809), a history of his *Travels and*

Adventures in Canada and the Indian Territories Between the Years 1760 and 1776, relating to the Indians of the Northwest. Much of Henry's book has been used by Francis Parkman as the basis for the chapters on "Michillimackinac," in his *Conspiracy of Pontiac*. John Long's *Voyages and Travels of An Indian Interpreter and Trader, 1768–1782*, also treats of the author's life among the Canadian Indians. The *Short Biography of John Leeth, Giving a Brief Account of His Travels and Sufferings among the Indians for Eighteen Years* (Lancaster, Ohio, 1831), although not written by his own hand, was taken from his lips, like Filson's *Life of Daniel Boone*, and contains an account of Leeth's experience as a Trader among the Indians of Ohio and Detroit from 1774 to 1786.

The Pennsylvania Traders from 1725 to 1775 were by far the most numerous and enterprising of their class; the most noted among them being George Croghan, who was engaged in the Indian trade for over thirty years before the outbreak of the Revolutionary War. Aside from his journals and letters, few other memorials of the Pennsylvania Traders, of their own writing, have been preserved. Accordingly, in endeavoring to portray or understand their lives and experiences, one must have recourse to the numerous scattered documents and letters printed in the Pennsylvania and New York Archives and Colonial Records, and elsewhere; to the manuscript collections of New York State, of the Pennsylvania Historical Society, and of the Canadian Government; to the early maps; and to the brief and fragmentary journals and narrations of early travellers (usually captives of the Indians), and of armed expeditionary forces.

As to who were the prehistoric inhabitants of the Ohio River country, it is not the purpose of this book to conjecture. The volumes that have been published about a supposed enlightened and cultivated race called the "Mound Builders," have been many and marvellous. The wonderful theories that have been evolved, and the elaborate structures of past glories that have been, in fancy, reared over the remains of the graves, forts, totem symbols, and burial mounds of those who were really the not very remote ancestors of the Natchez, Cherokees, Shawnees, and other historic Indians, would do credit to the imagination, if not to the judgment, of the Divine Evangelist himself. From either a scientific or historic standpoint, nine-tenths of this output is absolutely valueless. It was time, indeed, that such a book on the subject of the "Mound Builders" should be issued, as has been recently prepared by Mr. Gerard Fowke,[1] and published by the Ohio Archæological and Historical Society. Would that this book should also cause the elimination for a time of the "Archæological" part of the Ohio Society's title; since so many crimes against good sense and proper historical research have

---

[1] *Archæological History of Ohio*, Columbus, 1902.

been committed in that word's name; while the rich collections of really valuable documentary material relating to the eighteenth century history of Western Pennsylvania and Ohio, to be found in the Manuscript Archives of the Canadian Government, among the French, the Bouquet, and the Haldimand Papers, have been entirely neglected.[1]

In 1615, Samuel Champlain, Lieutenant Governor of New France, ascended the Ottawa River from the St. Lawrence to the mouth of the Mattawan, thence to Lake Nippissing, and into Georgian Bay. He had with him three white companions and ten Indians, the party occupying two canoes. Paddling along the eastern coast of Georgian Bay, they landed on the southwestern shore of what is now called Matchedash Bay. Between this point and Lake Simcoe was the country of an Iroquois nation, to whom Champlain applied the name "Ochateguin," that being the name also of one of their chiefs. By the Iroquois of the Five Nations these Indians, at a later time, were called "Quatoghies," and by the French, according to Lalement (1639), in allusion to the stiff, bristly, boar's-head appearance of their scalp-locks, "Hurons." There were four septs or brotherhoods of this clan—those of the Bear, the Wolf, the Hawk, and the Heron. Two days' journey to the west of the Ochateguins dwelt another tribe of the same Iroquois race, known as the Tobacco tribe, or Nation du Petun, called later by the Iroquois of New York, "Tionnontates," or "Dionondadies," and sometimes written "Yonontadies." These also were called "Hurons" by the French. Both of these tribes had another name, "Owendats," or "Wendats," spelled by the French "Ouendats," and later, by the English, "Wyandots." The name "Tobacco Tribe," seems to have been applied by the early French Traders to the Tionnontates, from their habit of industriously cultivating the tobacco plant.[2] The Wyandot was the most ancient of the Iroquois tribes.[3]

Champlain does not seem to have been aware of the existence of Lake Erie. In his map of 1632, he depicts the Niagara River, somewhat elongated, leading from the outlet of Lake Huron (called by him, "Mer Douce") to Lake St. Louis (Ontario). On this map, he shows a tribe of Indians which he calls the Neutral Nation, seated along the southern shore of the Niagara River. This was another of the Iroquois-Wendat tribes, and by the Hurons proper they were called Attiwandarons.

[1] While Ohio has been completely dug over by the archæologists, the field of Pennsylvania archæology is still practically unbroken.

[2] "It is probable that wherever the name Chenango [or Shenango, or Venango] occurs in early times or on early maps, it indicates the site of a town of the Tobacco tribe—Wyandots—or of a place where Indian tobacco was cultivated."—Darlington, *Gist's Journals*, 108. Morgan and Beauchamp give the definition of *Chenango* as "bull thistles," (from the Onondaga word, *Ochenang*).

[3] *Penna. Col. Rec.*, viii., 431, 433.

Between them and the Hirocois (a term which Champlain limited to the Mohawks), were the Antouronons, or Onondagas.[1] South of the Hirocois, between the Delaware River and the head of Chesapeake Bay, were the "Carantouannais," a tribe afterwards known to the French as the "Gantastoges," or "Andastes," (the Conestogas of later Pennsylvania history), but visited by and known to Captain John Smith in 1608 as the Sasquesahanoughs (Susquehannocks), and by the Dutch of New Netherland, as early as 1614 by the name of "Minquas,"[2] (the Mengwes, overlords of the Delawares; not the Seneca Mingoes of the later English). This tribe also, was a clan of the Iroquois-Wendat-Huron race; and it was the same tribe which was so nearly exterminated by its kindred, the Iroquois of the Five Nations, between 1666 and 1676.[3] On April 23, 1701, at Philadelphia, William Penn made a formal treaty of alliance with Opessa, chief of the Shawnees, Weewhinjough, chief of the Ganawese, inhabiting at the head of Potomac, and Connoodaghtoh, "King of the Susquehanna Minquas or Conestogo Indians."

A fifth branch of the Iroquois Wendat-Petun-Neutral-Andastes tribes lived along the southeast shore of Lake Erie, and its members were called the "Erigas," "Erich-ronnon," "Erigheks," or "Eries." The name of the Erie, or Erighek, tribe, comes from the Iroquois (Onondaga) word, *tsho-eragak* (Zeisberger's spelling), meaning "raccoon." The same word, spelled *tchou-eragak*, is defined in the *Jesuit French Onondaga Dictionary of the Seventeenth Century* (Shea's edition) as *chat sauvage*, or wildcat.[4] The name was preserved so late as 1755 in that of a river in the original territory of the Eries, the Cherage River (now the Grand) shown on Lewis Evans's map of that year; and it exists to-day in a modified form, as Geauga, the name of an Ohio county in which one of the heads of this river has its source. By the French the Eries were called the Cat Nation, or Clan of the Cat. It may be that it was a true countertype of the Scottish clan of the same name, by having for its tribe totem, the cat, or the animal which went under that name, which was really the raccoon.[5] The Jesuit *Relation* for 1654–56, however, states that the tribe was so called for the following reason: "They [the Senecas] informed us that a fresh war had broken out against them and thrown them all into a state of alarm: that the Erieh-ronnons [*ronnon* is the Huron-Iroquois word for 'people'] were coming against them (these we call the Cat Nation, because of the prodigious number of wildcats in their country, two or three times as large as our domestic

[1] Butterfield, *Brule*, 38, 59; Parkman, however, identifies them with the Senecas.
[2] So-called on the Hendricksen maps of 1614 and 1616; on De Laet's map of 1630; etc.
[3] See Butterfield's *Brule*.
[4] The same French-Onondaga Dictionary gives *tchiougaragak* as the Onondaga word for *biche* (deer) and *elan* (elk).
[5] *Jesuit Relations*, Thwaites's edition, xxi., 315.

cats, but of a handsome and valuable fur)." Sagard, the Recollect missionary, who knew of the Eries as early as 1626, in his *History of Canada*, (1636) describes their nation as one "which we call the Cat Nation, by reason of their cats, [raccoons] a sort of small wolf or leopard [1] found there, from the skins of which the natives make robes, bordered and ornamented with tails." Father Brebeuf, who visited the Neutral Nation in 1640, found that tribe living mostly to the west of the Niagara River, and remarks that only four of their towns lay to the east of that stream, "which towns ranged from east to west towards the Eriehronnons, or Cats." "The Niagara River," he says, "falls first into Lake Erie, or of the Cat Tribe, and then it enters the Neutral ground." Bressani, in his *Short Relation* (1653), placed the Neutrals north of Lake Erie and the Eries south. The Jesuit *Relation* for 1648 also refers to them as the Eries, or Cat Nation, and states that they are of "the same language as the Hurons." Sanson calls the lake, "Erie, ou Du Chat," in his map of 1656. Crexius's map of 1660 designates the tribe as "Natio Felium," to the south of "Lacus Erius, seu Felis." On the Raffeix map of 1688, the lake is called "Lac Erie, ou Du Chat," and the same in Hennepin's map of 1697, the Erieckronois being seated between the Maumee and Sandusky rivers. La Hontan, in his map of 1703, calls it "Lac Errie, ou De Conti," and locates the Errieronons between the Sandusky River and the west side of the Maumee. This tribe was broken and scattered by the Iroquois of the Five Nations soon after the middle of the seventeenth century, principally in 1655; but it is not to be believed, as some writers assert, that the tribe was then entirely exterminated. Being a kindred people to the Hurons, the Wyandots, and the Susquehannocks, there can be little doubt that many of them fled northwards across the lake, and became affiliated with the Tobacco tribe, or Wyandots, living beyond its northwest coast; from whence their descendants returned to again occupy the Ohio country during the first half of the following century.

It is probable, also, that some of them made their way down the west branch of the Susquehanna and joined the Andastes, to be later decimated or adopted by the same terrible scourge from whom they had fled at the Lake. But the greater part of the survivors were carried as captives into the Seneca country.

Parkman (*Jesuits*, xlvi.) thought the Eries and the Carantouannais of Champlain were probably identical; and that the Neutrals were the "Kahkwas of Seneca tradition."[1] Several other writers, among them

[1] In his *Grand Voyage du Pays des Hurous*, p. 307, Sagard says the Huron name for this animal is *Tiron*.

[2] The following erroneous but often repeated statement occurs in the recently published *Diary of David McClure* (New York, 1899, p. 93). McClure was a Con-

being Mr. Lewis H. Morgan, identified the Eries with the Kahkwas. Of the Eries, Morgan wrote: "They were known to the Iroquois by the name *Gaguagaono*. They were an off-shoot of the Iroquois, and spoke a dialect of their language. It is a singular fact that the Neuter Nation, who dwelt on the banks of the Niagara River, and who were expelled by the Iroquois about the year 1643 [1651] were known among them as the *Jegosasa*, or Cat Nation."

Horatio Hale remarks that there is no reason for doubting the correctness of the statement of David Cusick, the Tuscarora historian, when he wrote that the Eries were an off-shoot of the Seneca tribe. And Hale also gives his own opinion of what became of the Eries after the war of 1655. "Those who suppose that the Hurons only survive in a few Wyandots," he writes, "and that the Eries, Attiwandaronks, and Andastes have utterly perished, are greatly mistaken. It is absolutely certain that of the twelve thousand Indians who now [in 1882; the number is much greater in 1909], in the United States and Canada, preserve the Iroquois name, the greater portion derive their descent, in whole or in part, from those conquered nations."

Father Jean de Lamberville, writing from Onondaga, June 18, 1676, says: "They [the Iroquois] are actually bringing fifty captives from a distance of 200 leagues from here, to whom they have granted their lives because they destine them to work in their fields."[1]

The author of the Jesuit *Relation* for 1656–57 writes of the Iroquois conquests "Nevertheless, these victories cause almost as much loss to them as to their enemies, and they have depopulated their own villages to such an extent, that they now contain more foreigners than natives of the country. Onnontaghe counts seven different nations, and there are as many as eleven in Sonnontouan [Seneca Land]."[2]

The *Relation* for 1659–60 in giving an estimate of the number of warriors belonging to the Five Nations, proceeds to describe the population of the various villages. "If any one should compute the number of pure-blooded Iroquois," the writer says, "he would have difficulty

---

gregational minister from New England, who visited the Ohio Indians at Muskingum as a missionary in the summer of 1772. In speaking of the location of the Delaware, Shawnee, and Wyandot tribes in the Ohio country, he writes: "These nations are tributary to the Six Nations, or the Iroquois. The latter claim the country south of Ontario and Erie, by conquest of the former inhabitants, the Catawbas; the remnant of which nation now live on the Catawba River, in the bounds of North Carolina."

The Catawba, or Issa Indians, are now known to have belonged to the Siouan stock, and to have lived on the Catawba River in South Carolina as early, at least, and continuously, since 1567. They were the same as the Ushery of Lederer (1670) and the Esaw of Lawson (1700). See Mooney's *Siouan Tribes of the East*, pp. 69–70.

[1] *Jesuit Relations*, xlv., 185.
[2] *Ibid.*, xliii., 265.

in finding more than twelve hundred of them in all the Five Nations, since these are, for the most part, only aggregations of the different tribes whom they have conquered,—as the Hurons; the Tionnontatehronnons, otherwise called the Tobacco Nation; the Atiwendaronk, called the Neutrals when they were still independent; the Riquehronnons, who are the Cat Nation; the Ontwagannhas, or Fire Nation; the Trakwaehronnons, and others,—who, utter foreigners although they are, form without doubt the largest and best part of the Iroquois."[1]

As late as 1773, there were two towns on the Chatahuchi River among the Lower Creeks, known as Sawokli, and inhabited by an adopted tribe who spoke the "stinkard" [*i. e.*, alien] tongue. Gatschet gives the meaning of *Sawokli* in Creek as Raccoon Town, from the Hitchiti *Sawi*, raccoon, and *ukli*, town. Whether there was any connection between them and the lost Raccoon or Cat Nation of Lake Erie, would be interesting to know. A Shawnee band from the South of the same name (Sawokli) settled on the Youghiogheny River about 1730.

In an anonymous French map without date (No. 3 of the Parkman Collection,[2]) but fully ten years later than Joliet's map of 1673 (and evidently confused by Marshall and Beauchamp with Coronelli's map of 1688), Lake Erie is called "Lac Teiocha-rontiong, dit communement Lac Erie," and in the legend accompanying the map it is stated that "the environs of this Lake and of the western extremity of Lake Frontenac [Ontario], are infested by the Gantastogeronnons, which keeps the Iroquois away. This lake is not the Lake Erie commonly so-called. Erie is a part of Chesapeake Bay, in Virginia, where the Ericchronons have always lived."[3]

In a letter of LaSalle, written to Abbe Bernou (?) August 22, 1682, (published by Margry in vol. ii., p. 243), the writer of the letter says, in referring to a map of some portions of New France and particularly of Lake Erie: "The river [Maumee] which you see marked on my map of the southern coast of this Lake and towards the extremity, called by the Iroquois 'Tiotontaraeton,' [Totontaraton?] is without doubt the passage into the Ohio, or Olighin Sipon, which is to say in Iroquois and in Ottawa, the Beautiful River."[4]

These citations and references suggest the queries, whether or not

---

[1] *Jesuit Relations*, xlv., 207.

[2] Reproduced by Winsor, iv., 215; also printed in Beauchamp's *History of the New York Iroquois* (p. 400) and called by him Coronelli's map of 1688.

[3] The writer of this observation had evidently seen the 1640–50 map of the so-called "Ottawa Route" (printed by Winsor, iv., 202), which locates Lake Erie at the head of Chesapeake Bay.

[4] *Collections Ohio Historical Society*, xii., 111. This statement of LaSalle also leads to the inference that he had explored no other branch of the Ohio than, possibly, the Wabash.

the Eries were all exterminated by the Five Nations in 1655 or thereabouts; whether they were not of the same race, and substantially identical with the Neutrals, the Hurons, the Tionnontates, or Wyandots, and the Andastes, or Susquehannocks; and whether the occupation of the valleys of the Maumee and Sandusky by the Wyandots from 1735 to 1750, was not virtually a return of some of these tribesmen to the land of their not very remote ancestors.

In the *Analysis* of his "Map of the Middle British Colonies in America," of 1755 Lewis Evans speaks of the Pennsylvania and Ohio Indians as they were known in his day. Inasmuch as his book is now one of the rarest issues of Benjamin Franklin's press, and as the few lines Evans wrote about those Indians are quite as instructive as any like number which have been written since, it is fitting that they should be reprinted. Of the Iroquois, the Delawares, the Susquehannocks, the Eries, the Wyandots, and the Shawnees, Evans writes:

"The Lenne Lenoppes, whom we usually call the Delaware and Minnesink Indians, they [the Iroquois Confederates] entirely subdued; and have therefore a right to their country as far as was not sold by the conquered before their subjection; but all from the sea to the Falls of the Delaware at Trenton they had conveyed to Peter Menevet [Minuit], commandant under Christina, Queen of Sweden. Their [the Confederates'] boundary extended thence westward to the Great Falls of Susquehanna, near the mouth of Conewago Creek. For though they gave the finishing stroke to the extermination of the Susquehannocks [in 1676], Bell [Ninian Beall], in the service of Maryland, at the fort whose remains are still standing on the east side of Susquehanna, about three miles below Wright's Ferry [Evans was mistaken about the site of the Fort], had given them [the Susquehannocks] a blow that they never recovered of, and for that reason the Confederates never claimed but to the Conewago Falls.

"The Erigas, who were of the same original stock with the Confederates [Iroquois] themselves, and partook also of the Tuscarora language, were seated on Ohio and its branches, from Beaver creek to the mouth of the Quiaaghtena [Wabash] river. The far greater part have been extirpated; some incorporated into the Senecas; and the rest have retired beyond the woodless plains over the Mississippi, and left the Confederates entire masters of all the country. From the ruins of the Eriga towns and fortresses, we suppose they were the most numerous of any in those parts of America.

"The Wiandots, or Junundats, had Tiiughsoghruntie [Detroit] for their seat, but by the superior forces of the Confederates, were compelled to abandon it, and at last obliged to sue for peace, after they had many years wandered beyond the Lakes. Upon this account, all that peninsula between the Lakes Michigan, Huron, and Erie, is become the property of the Confederates, and the Wiandots their subjects; and to preserve their fidelity and to afford them protection, their present seat was allotted them. The Delawares and these entered into an entire league of association in 1751. I think the Wiandots the same as the Foxes, or Outagamis. Their language discovers them of the original stock of the Erigas or Confederates.[1]

"The Shawnees, who were formerly one of the most considerable nations of these parts of America, whose seat extended from Kentucke southwestward to Mississippi, have been subdued by the Confederates, and the country since become their property. No nation held out with greater resolution or bravery; and though they have been scattered into all parts for a while, they are again collected in Ohio, under the dominion of the Confederates; which they bear with great reluctance, though all that is required of them is to acknowledge the others as braver men and partake of their protection.

"The Monacans, or Tuscaroras,[2] divided also into many tribes, occupied the branches of the James River from the Falls upward and the country thence southward [previous to their alliance with and settlement in the country of the Five Nations, in 1722]."[3]

The Jesuit *Relations* for 1659–60 and 1661–63 call the Eries the Riqueh-ronnons and the Rigue-ronnons. In this connection it may be of interest to refer to the suggestion made by the late Mr. William Darlington in his Introductory Memoir to *Christopher Gist's Journals*. Mr. Darlington writes of John Lederer's explorations in Virginia and Carolina in 1670. He says, that when Lederer went south from the "south branch of the James River," he came to Akenatzi, an Indian village on one of the islands at the junction of the Dan and Roanoke rivers. This place is called "Achonechy Town" by John Lawson in 1709; and "Occoneachy Islands" on Fry and Jefferson's map of 1751. Mr. Darlington proceeds:

Here he met four strange Indians, survivors of fifty who had come,

---

[1] The Jesuit *Relation* for the year 1648, in speaking of Lake Erie and the Indians who dwelt there, says: "The southern shores of this lake, called Erie, were formerly inhabited by certain tribes whom we call the Cat Nation, who have been compelled to retire far inland to get at a distance from their enemies, who are more to the west. These people of the Cat Nation have many permanent towns, for they cultivate the earth, and are of the same language as our Hurons."

For an instructive paper on the identity of the Erie and Huron Indians, see Russell Errett's article on "Indian Geographical Names" in the *Magazine of Western History* ii., 238. Equally instructive, but by no means so convincing in its argument, will be found to be C. C. Royce's paper on "The Indentity [with the Eries] and History of the Shawnee Indians," in the same volume, pp. 38–50.

[2] They were not identical. The former were of Siouan stock; the latter, Iroquoian.

[3] See the map in Donaldson's *Six Nations*, p. 24 (Washington, 1892); also, Hewitt's "Iroquoian Cosmology," in *Bur. Am. Eth. Report*, xxi., 133.

Lederer says "from some great land by the sea to the northwest" (probably the Great Lakes). He calls them Rickahickans, and states that "they were treacherously killed in the night by the Indians of Akenatzi."

These strange Indians, or Rickahickans, doubtless were fugitives of the tribe known as Eries, or the Nation of the Cat, whose country was on the south shore of Lake Erie. They were conquered and destroyed as a nation by the Iroquois in 1654–5.

The Fathers call the tribe Riguehronnons, or those of the Cat Nation. The considerable number of the defeated Eries, or Rickahickans appear to have reached Virginia in 1655, about which time the Iroquois completed their conquest. A special law was passed [in 1656], to remove by force "the new-come western and inland Indians drawn from the Mountains and lately set down near the falls of James River to the number of six or seven hundred."

Captain Edward Hill, at the head of one hundred men, assisted by Tottopottemen, king of the Pamunkies, with one hundred warriors, attacked the Rickahickans. The allies were defeated, Tottopottemen slain. Captain Hill was cashiered for his conduct and his estate charged with the cost of procuring a peace with the Rickahickans [Burk spells the name, Rechahecrian; Henning, Rickahecrian].

On Lederer's map of 1670, the Rickohockans are located west of Akenatzy, and beyond the Appalachian Mountains. Likewise, on Ogilby's map of 1671. What Lederer wrote was:

"At my arrival here I met four stranger Indians, whose bodies were painted in various colors, with figures of animals whose likeness I had never seen; and by some discourse and signs which passed between us, I gathered that they were the only survivors of fifty, who set out together in company from some great island, as I conjecture, to the northwest, for I understood that they crossed a great water in which most of their party perished by tempest, the rest dying in the marshes and mountains by famine and hard weather after a two months travel by land and water in quest of this island of Akenatzy. . . .

"I have heard several Indians testify that the nation of Rickohockans, who dwell not far to the westward of the Apalatcean Mountains, are seated upon a land, as they term it, of great waves, by which, I suppose, they mean the seashore.

"The next day after my arrival at Akenatzy, a Rickohockan ambassador, attended by five Indians, whose faces were colored with auripigmentum (in which mineral these parts do much abound), was received, and that night invited to a ball of their fashion; but in the height of their mirth and dancing, by a smoke contrived for that purpose, the room was suddenly darkened, and, for what cause I know not, the Rickohockan and his retinue barbarously murdered."

Mr. James Mooney, of the Bureau of American Ethnology, in his monograph on the *Siouan Tribes of the East*,¹ identifies the Rickohockans of Lederer with the Cherokees.

The suggestions made by Mr. Darlington and Mr. Mooney are interesting and it is possible that either one of them may be correct. They would be more important were it not for the fact that John White's 1586 map of the country around Sir Walter Raleigh's Colony on Roanoke Island (of which White himself later became Governor) shows a "Ricahokene" town on Albemarle Sound, near the site of the present Edenton, North Carolina. John Smith, also, in his *True Relation*, and John Pory, in Smith's *General History*, mention the Indian Towns of "Richkahauck" and "Rickahake."² The former Smith visited while exploring the Chickahominy; and the latter Pory describes as being situated between Chesapeake and Nansemond. Righkahauck is shown on Smith's map of Virginia, located on the right bank of the Chickahominy, near its head. In 1689 three chiefs of the Chickahominy Indians petitioned the Virginia Council for leave to remove to a place "called Rickahock," on the north side of Mattapony River. This locality could not have been many miles away from the original site of Smith's Righkahauck; and may possibly have been the battle-field of the encounter between Captain Edward Hill and the Rickohockans. Nevertheless, Mr. Mooney's identification of the Rickohockans with the Cherokees may be correct.

Some have thought that the Erigas, or Eries, and the Cherokees were identical. While possible, this is scarcely probable; although there is a similarity between *Tsaragi*, the word used by the Cherokees as their own tribal name, and *Tshoeragak* (meaning "raccoon," and translated by the French as *chat sauvage*, or "wild cat") the Onondaga word which was applied to the Eries as their tribal name. If such an identity could be established, it would go far towards solving the mystery both of the Eries and of the Ohio mounds.³

Campanius, in his account of New Sweden in 1643–48, states that the Swedes on the Delaware and Christina Creek at that time carried on no trade with any other Indians than the "Black and White Mengwes."

In a letter written by William Beeckman from Tinnekunk to Governor Peter Stuyvesant, December 23, 1662, it is stated: "On the 3d inst. five Minquas chiefs with their suite arrived here at Altena [now Wilmington] . . . The chiefs informed us among others, they were expecting shortly for their assistance 800 Black Minquas, and that 200

¹ Bureau of American Ethnology Publications, 1894.

² Reckonhacky, Reckowacky, Rechqua-akie, Reck-kouwhacky, were New York Indian names applied to Rockaway Point from 1639 to 1660, and meaning, "sandy land," from the Algonquin, *Rekau* (or *Lekau*), "sand," and *Hacki*, "land," or "place."

³ See Cyrus Thomas's *The Cherokees in pre-Columbian Times*.

of this Nation had already come in, so that they were fully resolved to go to war with the Sinnecas next Spring, and visit their fort." [1]

On Herrman's 1670 map of Virginia and Maryland[2] is a notice of a tribe of Indians called the Black Mincquas, living beyond the mountains on the large Black Mincqua River, possibly the Ohio. "Formerly, by means of a branch of this River which approached a branch of the Susquehanna above the Conestoga Fort [probably the West Branch, or the Juniata River] those Black Mincquas came over and as far as Delaware to trade, but the Sassquahana and Sinnicus Indians went over and destroyed that very great Nation."[3]

On August 22, 1681, the Governor and Council of Maryland held a conference at St. Mary's with two Northern Indians who had been brought in, one an Onondaga and the other a Cayuga. These Indians gave the Governor several items of information about the Five Nations and the Susquehanna Indians, one of which has already been cited. "They likewise say," runs the chronicle, "that another Nation, called the Black Mingoes [4] are joined with the Sinnondowannes, who are the right Senecas; that they were so informed by some New York Indians whom they met as they were coming down. They told them that the Black Mingoes, in their coming to the Sinniquos, were pursued by some Southern Indians, set upon and routed, several of them taken and bound, till the Sinniquos came unto their relief." [5]

On the Adrian Block Map of 1614,[6] three different tribes are located west of the Susquehanna, between the Senecas and the Minquas. They are called the *Gachoos*, the *Capitannasses*, and the *Ioteccas*. The first two of these names may be of Spanish origin. *Gacho* is a Spanish word, meaning "bent downward," and is applied to "black cattle having their horns bent downward." It has been suggested that this was an earlier name for the tribe which the Dutch and Swedes later called the Black Minquas.

These various statements, and the location given on Herrman's map, make it probable that these Black Minquas were the Carantouans of Champlain, or, possibly, the Eries, or a northern division of the Tuscaroras.

The wars of the Five Nations with the Hurons (1634–49) the Neutral

[1] *Penna. Archives*, Second Series, vii., 742.

[2] Published in the *Report and Accompanying Documents of the Virginia Commissioners on the Boundary Line between Maryland and Virginia*, Richmond, 1873, and reproduced in this volume.

[3] See Chapter III., Vol. II.

[4] This is the earliest use of the word "Mingo," for "Minqua," that has come under the writer's notice.

[5] *Md. Archives*, xvii., 5.

[6] *N. Y. Col. Doc.*, i., 10–14.

Nation (1651), the Eries (1654–56), and the Andastes and Shawnees (1660–76), may be studied at first hand in the Jesuit *Relations* covering those periods. They are summarized in part by Parkman in his *Jesuits in North America*. These wars gave the Iroquois Confederacy suzerainty or actual possession of a vast territory, which, in 1701, they claimed to hold by inheritance from their ancestors, who had acquired it by conquest from the Hurons. This territory embraced all the land between Lakes Huron and Erie, and westward to the eastern shore of Lake Michigan, and all the land to an indefinite extent lying south of Lake Erie. In 1726, the chiefs of the Senecas, Cayugas, and Onandagas executed a deed in trust to the King of England for a portion of this land, extending from what is now known as the Salmon River, in Oswego County, New York, to the Cuyahoga River, in Ohio, and sixty miles to the southward along the whole of this line.[1] In 1763, Sir William Johnson, then Superintendent of Indian Affairs, for the Northern Colonies, in a letter to the Lords of Trade, wrote: "The Six Nations claimed, by right of conquest, all the country, including the Ohio, along the great ridge of the Blue Mountains at the back of Virginia; thence to the head of Kentucky and down the same to the Ohio above the rifts; thence northerly to the south end of Lake Michigan; then along the East shore to Missillimackinack; thence easterly across the northern end of Lake Huron to Ottawa River and Island of Montreal. Their claim to the Ohio and thence to the Lakes is not in the least disputed by the Shawnees, Delawares, and others, who never transacted any sales of land or other matters without their consent."

In a deposition made by George Croghan, Feb. 13, 1777,[2] he relates, that, while trading with the Shawnee Indians at the mouth of the Scioto in 1750–51, a band of Shawnees, with some fifty to sixty Cherokees who had just come over the mountains from the Cherokee country, represented to a Council, which had been convened, that the Cherokees desired the good offices of the Shawnees, Wyandots, Delawares, and Six Nation Indians there present, in helping them to make up a difference at that time existing between the Cherokees and Wyandots. After this matter had been presented, "The Cherokees addressed themselves to the Six Nations [to their representatives] and requested they might have liberty to hunt between the Allegheny [Cumberland] mountain and the Ohio for that season; as they knew the country belonged to them." Croghan further relates in this deposition, that some thirty or thirty-one years before 1777, a party of Shawnees, headed by a chief named Chartie (Chartier), having received permission from the chiefs of the Six Nations then residing in the Ohio country "took possession of and

[1] *Penna. Arch.*, Sec. Ser., xviii., 301; *Doc. Hist.*, N. Y., i., 773.
[2] *Virginia State Papers*, i., 276.

formed a settlement on a large river which falls into the Ohio, between the mouths of the Oubache [Wabash] on the west and the Tennessee or Cherokee River on the east side of the Ohio, which river was afterward called and known by the name of the Shawnese River" (now the Cumberland).[1]

The claims of the French to the Ohio country, while they did not culminate in acts of war until about 1750, had been frequently and persistently asserted for more than ten years before that date. Indeed, paper claims of the French to this particular territory had been in existence for nearly forty years before. Governor Burnet, of New York, in writing to the British Lords of Trade, Nov. 26, 1720, called attention to what he had observed in the "last mapps published at Paris, with *Privilege du Roy*, par M. de Lisle, in 1718, of Louisianna and part of Canada; that they are making new encroachments on the King's territories from what they pretended to in a former mapp published by the same author in 1703, of North America. Particularly, all Carolina is, in this new map, taken into the French country, and in words there said to belong to them; about fifty leagues all along the edge of Pennsylvania [including the 1670 site of the Susquehannock Fort], and this province taken into Canada, more than was in their former mapp."[2]

Father Mermet, a Jesuit missionary to the Illinois, wrote to Quebec in the summer of 1715, "respecting the encroachments of the English in the rivers Ouabache [this name was at that time often applied to include not only the Wabash proper, but also that part of the Ohio between the mouth of the Wabash and the Mississippi] and Mississippi; where they are building three forts." On October 31, 1725, M. de Longueuil writes to the Governor of Canada that he has learned "that the English of Carolina had built two houses and some stores on a little river that flows into the Ouabache, where they trade with the Miamis and the Ouyatanons, and other Indians of the Upper Country."

[1] It is evident that Croghan was mistaken in his belief that the stream known since 1750 as the Cumberland River, received its former name, the Shawnee, so late as 1746. In an address to six Shawnee chiefs, who held a council with Governor Penn at Philadelphia, July 27, 1739, Secretary James Logan reminded them that "forty years ago, a considerable number of families of your nation thought fit to remove from the great river that bears your name, where your principal correspondence was with the French nation, and, in 1699, applied to the Indians of Susquehanna to settle amongst them." In a French "Memoir on the Indians between Lake Erie and the Mississippi," of 1718, published in the *New York Colonial Documents*, ix., 885–892, the author, after describing the Ohio, the Wabash, and the Tennessee rivers, adds: "A great many other rivers come from the direction of the Flatheads [Cherokees], and also into the Mississippi but I am not acquainted with their names. One of them is called the Chaouenon" (the French name for Shawnee).

[2] A London edition (1721) of this new map was laid before the Provincial Council of Pennsylvania, Aug. 4, 1731. See *Penna. Col. Records*, vol. iii.

It was not until some years after 1725, however, that the French found it necessary actively to assert their claim to the country about the head waters of the Ohio.

The reason they did not do so earlier can be readily understood. There was practically no resident Indian population south of Lake Erie, or on either side of the Upper Ohio and its tributaries, during the first two decades of the eighteenth century, as there had been none during the closing decades of the century preceding. The Iroquois scourge had driven all other tribes away; and the Indians of the Five Nations themselves looked upon this only as their great hunting ground. They asserted supremacy and maintained possession of this territory for near half a century after 1675; and none of the conquered tribes who had been driven thence dared return to make it their home. The Iroquois themselves did not settle there, but traversed the waters and ridges of the Ohio country only on their hunting or war expeditions. The Eries and Hurons who were not adopted had been killed or had fled beyond Lake Erie; the Shawnees and the Flatheads had been driven to the extreme western part of what is now the state of Kentucky, or southwards beyond the Cumberland Mountains into the country of the Cherokees and Chickasaws; the Andastes of northern and northwestern Pennsylvania had been all but exterminated, the remnant retiring far down the Susquehanna to the vicinity of Chesapeake Bay. Even the Miamis and the Illinois south and west of Lake Michigan, had suffered from the dread attacks of the same terrible foe; the former, slightly; the latter, most severely. In 1701, the Confederates made the exaggerated claim of sovereignty over all the country for eight hundred miles to the westward of their Council fires in the Mohawk Valley, and from the Ottawa River four hundred miles south.

James Logan, Colonial Secretary of Pennsylvania, prepared a report on Indian Affairs for the use of Governor Keith in 1718, which the latter official transmitted to the London Ministry the following year. In his notes on that report, Secretary Logan observes: "The business of the forts being of very great importance, seems to require some further consideration:—That it is the interest of these Colonies to have forts as far back as practicable is very obvious; especially, on Lake Erie, where at present there are no Indians; and on Ontario, where the Five Nations are settled."[1]

The French Memoir on the Indians between Lake Erie and the Mississippi for the same year, after describing among others, the Wabash, the Miami (Maumee), and the Sandusky rivers, adds, significantly: "The River Ohio, or Beautiful River, is the route which the Iroquois

[1] Hazard's *Register of Penna.*, iii., 211.

take. It would be of importance that they should not have such intercourse, as it is very dangerous."

In the following chapters we shall see how the country of Ohio received a new Indian population from the east, the west, the north, and the south, between the years 1720 and 1750, accompanied and followed by a large and energetic advance guard of civilization in the way of numerous English and French Traders. We shall also be able better to understand why, after the decade, 1730 to 1740, such frequent and emphatic reiterations of the claim to the Ohio country on the part of the French governors of Canada came to be made. The substance of many of these claims is to be found in the records of the official correspondence between the French provincial authorities and the Paris Ministry, as published in volumes nine and ten of the *New York Colonial Documents*, and in volumes sixteen to eighteen of the *Wisconsin Historical Collections*. The bulk of the correspondence (unpublished), is recorded in the Canadian Archives at Ottawa and calendared in the annual reports of the Archivist. The "Memoir of M. DeNonville on the French Limits in North America,"[1] written in 1688, while significant from the fact that it does not claim that LaSalle discovered the Upper Ohio, does give a fairly complete calendar of the discoveries and conquests on which the French claims were based, down to that year. Their final expression before the outbreak of hostilities near Fort Duquesne is best summarized in the "Minute of Instructions to Marquis Duquesne," which were issued to that official by the Home Ministry in April, 1752. Of Duquesne's instructions, the following portions relate to the Ohio country:

> The River Ohio, otherwise called the Beautiful River, and its tributaries, belong indisputably to France, by virtue of its discovery by Sieur de la Salle; of the trading posts the French have had there since; and of possession; which is so much the more unquestionable, as it constitutes the most frequent communication from Canada to Louisana [by way of Lake Erie, the Maumee, and the Wabash]. It is only within a few years that the English have undertaken to trade there; and now they pretend to exclude us from it.
>
> They have not, up to the present time, however, maintained that these rivers [the tributaries of the Ohio] belong to them; they pretend only that the Iroquois are masters of them, and, being the sovereigns of these Indians, that they can exercise their rights. But 't is certain that these Indians have none; and that, besides, the pretended sovereignty of the English over them is a chimera.
>
> The Marquis de la Jonquiere has rendered an account of a solemn Council which was held on the 11th of July last, with the Onontagues of the Five Iroquois Nations. Two articles were discussed there, respecting which it is proper to give M. Duquesne particular orders.

[1] *N. Y. Col. Doc.*, ix., 377 to 384.

The first is relative to the lands on the River Ohio. The Onontagues asserted in their speech that these lands are the property of the Five Nations. The Marquis de la Jonquiere has unadvisedly answered them so as to countenance that pretension, by giving them to understand that the French would not settle on those lands without their permission.
'T is necessary to disabuse them on this head. They have, in fact, as has been already observed, no right to the River Ohio. We had discovered it long before they themselves had known it; [a mis-statement of fact, of course, as La Salle's first knowledge of the Ohio River came from the Senecas who visited him at La Chine in 1669]; and we have resorted to it when no other Indians were there but the Chaouanons [Shawnees], with whom they were at war, and who have always been our friends.

The English claim to the Ohio country at the time the foregoing was written rested upon much stronger grounds than that of the French. It was grounded on the fact of their actual possession of the disputed territory. Since some twenty-five years before, the Pennsylvania Traders had been carrying their goods across the Alleghanies, and each succeeding year penetrating a little farther to the west of the Ohio Forks; until, by 1750, they had acquired for the English, by peaceable means, virtual possession of a great empire, which needed only to be protected in order to insure its eventual absorption into the territories of the existing colonies. Its extent is shown on the map of Dr. John Mitchell, published in London a few years later, after the English, through the fatuous obstinacy and incredible and short-sighted selfishness of the Quaker Assembly of Pennsylvania, had lost this country. Mitchell's map shows English trading posts and blacksmiths' forges (Mitchell calls them "factories") established at the Indian towns of Logstown ("built and settled by the English some years ago") and Kuskuskies ("chief town of the Six Nations on the Ohio"), in the present counties of Beaver and Lawrence; at Muskingum, in what is now Coshocton County, Ohio; at Lower Shawnee Town, near what is now the city of Portsmouth, Scioto County, Ohio; and at Pickawillany, near the present town of Piqua, in Miami County, Ohio, at which last named point, located on the west bank of the Great Miami River, Mitchell says, an English (Traders') fort was established in 1748, being the western limit of the English "settlements." "Allegheny," and "Old Shawnee Town," (located on both sides of the Allegheny River a little south of the mouth of Kiskiminetas River, and near what is now Tarentum, Allegheny County) Mitchell states (in 1755), "was settled by the English thirty years ago."

The nature and extent of the English trade to the westward of the Alleghanies, and the circumstances attending its loss and that of the territories in which it was conducted, through the neglect of the theocratic oligarchy controlling the Assembly of the Quaker Province, are set forth in a "Detail of Indian Affairs, 1752–1754," prepared for the use of Governor Morris about the beginning of the year 1755. After enumerating the disputes between the Pennsylvania Assembly and the former governors, this report concludes as follows:

During the Spanish and French War, the Indian Trade was very considerably enlarged by means of ye Shawnesse, Delawares, and Six Nation Indians, who, from the quick increase of ye English in ye Colonies, quitted their old places of residence, for want of game or korn, and removed to Allegheny. They were greatly encouraged by ye Twightwees and other nations inhabiting beyond ye Ohio, as they draw our Traders after them.

Croghan and others had stores on ye Lake Erie, all along ye Ohio from Bar[?], and other storehouses on the Lake Erie, all along ye Miami river, and up and down all that fine country, watered by ye branches of ye Miamis, Scioto, and Muskingham rivers, and upon the Ohio from Bockaloons, an Indian town near its head, to below ye mouth of the Miami river, an extent of 500 miles, on one of the most beautiful rivers in ye world, yn. they traded all along the river.

Great quantities of goods were vended in the towns of the Twightwees at their own pressing instances. Several nations, Twightwees, Picts, Tacons, Piankkishaws, and Owendats, entered into an intimate friendship with the scattered tribes of Shawenese, Delawares, and Six Nation Indians, and, pressing to enter into an alliance, they were, on ye recommendation of ye Six Nations, Shawenese, and Delawares, admitted in ye summer of 1748.

The Peace was concluded 7th 8br. 1748, at Aix-la-Chapelle, and in Novr., Governor Hamilton arrived. Care was taken to make ye new Gvr. acquainted with ye accession of the Twightwees and Owendats into ye English Alliance, wth. yr. good disposition towards ye English, and ye flourishing state of ye Indians' Trade, and ye great interest his Majty. had wth. numerous nations of Indians beyond ye Ohio.

When the Indians perceived by the French proceedings and preparations that they not only contended for a sole and exclusive trade, but for the possession of the country lying on ye borders of the Ohio, they gave us timely notice, entreated us to build forts, continue our trade, and make head against them, and to be expeditious and resolute.[1] When they saw

---

[1] George Croghan's "Journal" of a conference with the chiefs of the Six Nations at Logstown, May 29, 1751, gives a message from those chiefs to the Pennsylvania authorities, which concludes as follows: "We expect that you our brother, will build a strong house on the River Ohio, that if we should be obliged to engage in a war, that we should have a place to secure our wives and children, likewise, to secure our brothers that come to trade with us; for without our brothers supply us with goods, we cannot live. Now, brothers, we will take two months to consider and choose out a place fit for that purpose, and then we will send you word. We hope, brothers, as soon as you receive our message, you will order such a house to be built. Brothers: That you may consider well the necessity of building such a place of security to strengthen our arms, and that this, our first request of that kind, may have a good effect on your minds, we send you this belt of wampum."—*Penna. Col. Records*, v., 538. See, also, in the same volume, pp. 437, 497, 498, 515, 529, 547, 609, 755, 764; *Penna. Archives*, iv., 452.

no fruits arising from their sevl. solicitations, and noticed neither forces nor workmen to help them build forts, they nevertheless repeated their applications, and offered to join us. We heard them patiently, continued to send unarmed Traders with great quantities of valuable goods, wch. fell from time to time into the hands of the French. The Traders were seized and carried prisoners to Canada without the least struggle or opposition. The Gvt. of Virginia sent Mr. Washington to summon ye French commander on the River B———, and on his haughty answer, raised a few forces, expecting ye Province of Pennsylvania woud. have either sent men or given a large sum to inlist such as woud. enter volunteers; but found yt instead of affording assistance, they fell into disputes wth. their Gvr., and seemed to espouse the French claims to these countries.

In short, we irritated the French, dispirited the Indian allies, and gave the enemy by our weak and small efforts, such immense advantages as are beyond conception.

The criminal folly of the Quaker politicians in charge of the public purse led to all the deplorable consequences which the sensible members of the Pennsylvania government had foreseen. These self-sufficient incompetents are without doubt chargeable with the calamities which came upon the frontiers of their Province after the French had established themselves, unopposed, at Fort Duquesne. They deserted their allies and betrayed their fellow subjects by refusing to heed the warnings so frequently sent to them. They deliberately neglected and contemned all attempts to prevent the invasion of their western frontiers which followed the defeat of Washington at Great Meadows. They were brave as lions when their own hold on political power was threatened, but mild as doves when their far neighbors were being killed.

That manly and vigorous action on their part, in the protection of the Province, would have given an entirely different reading to the history of the French Boundary War, requires no more eloquent or convincing proof than that afforded by the woful letter of the Acting Governor of Canada to his superiors, written nearly a year after the request by the Six Nation chiefs on the Ohio, for a Strong House, for protection, had been made to and rejected by the Pennsylvania Assembly, and bearing a date but little later than that of the "Instructions" to the Marquis Duquesne, who superseded him. This letter of the Baron de Longueuil to the Ministry in 1752, after enumerating at length the different ills which had befallen nearly all the various French posts in the West, proceeds:

You are fully informed, my lord, by the detail that I have just had the honor to submit to you:

1st. That the expedition which M. de Celoron was ordered to get up [against the Ohio Indians on the Miami River], did not take place.

2nd. That the promises the Indians [of Detroit] had made to the late M. de la Jonquiere were feigned, and that they are more in favor of our rebels than of us.

3rd. That the attack of the Nepissings [against the Miamis of La Demoiselle's band at Pickawillany] has only rendered our rebels more dangerous.

4th. That the Miamis have scalped two soldiers.

5th. That the Pianguichas have killed seven Frenchmen and two slaves.

6th. That the same nation had, shortly before, killed another Frenchman and two slaves.

7th. That, according to what has been stated to M. de Joncaire, the Flatheads have scalped three Frenchmen and taken a fourth, whom they delivered to the English with said scalps.

8th. That we are threatened with a general conspiracy.

9th. That we must fear even for Toronto.

10th. That the English are the indirect authors of the murder of the French.

11th. That famine at Detroit and its dependencies is quite certain.

12th. That small-pox is ravaging the whole of that continent.

You perceive, my lord, the sorrowful condition of the entire of that Upper Country. I am invested, by the death of the Marquis de la Jonquiere, with the government of Canada, under very unfortunate circumstances. I lay before your eyes the blood of the French of that Colony, of which you are the powerful protector. . . . Though I overcome, at first, certain obstacles, I am always met by the insufficiency of provisions, canoes, and time, which prevents me guaranteeing that I shall make peace succeed the vigorous war.

Here, then, we find the conclusion of the indictment against the Quaker oligarchy of that day.

Contrary to the generally received opinion, Pennsylvania did not have a democratic or popular form of government at this time; nor indeed at any time between the years 1730 and 1776. The three original Quaker counties of Philadelphia, Chester, and Bucks, were entitled, under the Constitution of 1701, to be represented in the Assembly by eight members each, and the city of Philadelphia, by two. As new counties were formed (and no new counties were formed, so long as it was possible to defer their organization), only a partial representation in the Assembly was given to such counties. This was done in order that the control of the three original Quaker counties in the Assembly should never be overthrown. In 1760, when Philadelphia City and the five counties of Lancaster, York, Cumberland, Berks, and Northampton contained sixty per cent. of the total population, and paid nearly sixty per cent. of the total taxes of the Province, they were allowed only twelve members in an Assembly composed of thirty-six; while the three Quaker counties of Philadelphia (exclusive of the city), Chester, and Bucks, which contained but forty per cent. of the total population, and paid but little more than forty per cent. of the total taxes, retained the whole of the twenty-four seats in the Assembly with which they had started a few years after 1701.

Unfortunately, through an alliance with the German population which had come to Pennsylvania from the Rhine provinces to escape military duty and military oppression, the Quakers succeeded in perpetuating their unfair control of the Government, through the French War, and clear down to the beginning of the Revolution; and the fact of that control seems not only to have retarded the natural development and advance of the Province during the remainder of that century, but also to have brought additional troubles on the heads of a great many of those who protested against it.

The murder of the Conestoga Indians by the "Paxtang Boys," at Lancaster was an instance. That affair must always be a matter of reproach to the Scotch-Irish of the Susquehanna Valley. But a study of the causes which led up to it cannot wholly absolve from responsibility therefor the leaders of the sect which was then in control of the Government. These same people, who in 1764, so loudly condemned the action of the Paxtang lynchers, had been, by refusing to permit the construction of a fort at the Ohio Forks thirteen years before, chiefly responsible for the murder and rapine from which the frontier people suffered at the hands of the Assembly's former wards. And they had been, also, for the same reason, responsible for the alienation of these former wards to the French interest at Allegheny, after the French occupied that region in 1754.

Hence, without attempting to palliate the barbarous action of the Paxtang Boys, it may be inferred that much of their blind rage was really inspired by hatred of that Quaker government which took no voluntary steps to save its own citizens or its own wards from destruction.

Serious as must be our condemnation of the proceedings of the Paxtang Rangers on that occasion, it must also seem to many who study the shortcomings of their rulers, that these men and their neighbors are subject to another serious reproach. At least, if not a reproach, it is a matter of great wonder that these Scotch-Irish of the Pennsylvania frontier did not organize themselves into a lynching party nine years before the Conestoga massacre, as Provost William Smith suggested at that time; that they did not then, as they unsuccessfully attempted to do in 1764, and succeeded in doing in 1776, march to Philadelphia and overthrow and forever destroy the Quaker government—a government which as early as 1751 had forfeited its right to existence by coolly inviting the sacrifice of the lives and fortunes of hundreds of its subjects, in order that the safely protected and over-righteous members of its own little clique might escape taxation for military purposes, and better the supposed chances for the salvation of their own tiny, pinched, and self-magnified souls.

CHAPTER II

THE IROQUOIANS OF THE SUSQUEHANNA

IN the latter part of July, 1608, Captain John Smith sailed from Jamestown, Virginia, on a voyage of discovery. He went in an open barge of less than three tons burden, taking with him twelve men. The vessel entered Chesapeake Bay, and the party spent seven weeks in exploring its shores, returning to Jamestown on the 7th of the following September. After Smith reached the head of the Bay, on the Tockwogh (Sassafras) River he met the Tockwogh Indians. Here he found "many hatchets, knives, and peeces of yron and brasse, which they reported to have from the Sasquesahanockes, a mighty people, and mortal enimies with the Massawomeckes." Smith "prevailed with the Interpreter to take with him another interpreter, to perswade the Sasquesahanocks to come to visit us, for their language are different." Later, sixty of the Sasquesahanocks came to the discoverers, "with skins, bowes, arrowes, targets [shields], beads, swords, and tobacco pipes for presents. Such great and well proportioned men are seldom seene, for they seemed like Giants to the English, yea, and to the neighbours; yet seemed of an honest and simple disposition, with much adoe restrained from adoring the discoverers as Gods. These are the most strange people of all those Countries, both in language and attire; for their language it may well beseeme their proportions, sounding from them as it were a great voice in a vault, or cave, as an Eccho. Their attire is the skinnes of Beares and Woolves; some have Cassacks made of Beares heads and skinnes, that a man's necke goes through the skinnes neck, and the eares of the beare fastned to his shoulders behind, the nose and teeth hanging downe his breast, and at the end of the nose hung a Beares Pawe: the halfe sleeves coming to the elbowes were the neckes of Beares, and the armes through the mouth, with pawes hanging at their noses. . . . They can make neere 600 able and mighty men, and are pallisadoed in their Townes to defend them from the Massawomekes, their mortall enimies. . . . They are seated [on the Susquehanna River] 2 daies higher than was passage for the discoverers' barge" [or "two days higher than our barge could pass for the rocks"].

A Susquehanna Iroquois of the Stone Age.
From John Smith's Map of Virginia, 1612.

These Susquehanna Indians, or Susquehannocks, as they are usually called, are clearly identified as the Andastes of the French by a passage in Governor de Courcelles's narrative of his voyage to Lake Ontario in June, 1671, wherein he relates that the young men of the larger villages of the Five Nations (during the time war was raging between them and the Susquehannocks) "were on the eve of setting out on a war expedition against the Indians of New Sweden, called the Antastouez [a French synonym for Andaste]." In common with other Iroquois tribes, they were called "Minquas" by the Dutch of New Netherland. Besides "Andastes," or "Andastoguez," the French also called them "Gandastogues," etc.[1] They were a very war-like people, and at times made attacks on the neighboring Indians of the Delaware, known as River Indians, afterwards the Delawares, or Lenni Lenape, whom they terrorized and subjected. Smith, in his *Map and Description of Virginia*, (Oxford, 1612), locates the Susquehannocks as having a village on the right bank of the river bearing their name, not far above Smith's Falls (now probably Amos' Falls at the mouth of Octorara Creek). The remains of one of their forts, situated in what is now Manor Township, Lancaster County, Pennsylvania, three miles below Wright's Ferry, were in existence as late as 1755, according to the statement of Lewis Evans, in the *Analysis* of his map of that year.[2] In 1614, Captain Cornelius Hendricksen ransomed from the Susquehanna Indians, whom he calls Minquaes, three Dutch captives, employes of the New Netherland Company, engaged in trade with the Mohawks and Mohicans.[3] The Susquehannocks told Etienne Brule of these prisoners while he sojourned with them during the winter of 1615–16.

When Samuel de Champlain was at the Huron village of Cahiague, near the lower end of Lake Simcoe, in August, 1615, preparing to lead a war party of the Hurons against the Onondagas of the Five Nations, he found that the Hurons had "received intelligence that a certain

[1] They were called "Mengwe" by the Lenape and Swedes of the Delaware. Mr. James Mooney (*Siouan Tribes of the East*) identifies this word with "Mangoac," *stealthy ones*, the name applied by the Algonquian tribes of Albemarle Sound in 1585 to their Iroquoian neighbors on the West, and later used by Captain John Smith in referring to the same tribes.

[2] This is shown as a "Fort demolished" on a map of a survey made by Benjamin Chambers in 1688–89, of which a copy is printed in Smith's *History of Delaware County*. Another and possibly an earlier fort of the Susquehannocks was at the mouth of Octorara Creek, shown on a map of 1740 printed in *Penna. Archives*, Second Series, vol. xvi.

[3] See *N. Y. Col. Doc.*, i., 10–15. Mr. Butterfield, in his *Brule's Discoveries*, gives this date as 1616, thus making it appear that two parties of Dutch Traders were captured. He falls into the error of taking the date of Captain Hendricksen's report for the date of his voyage. Hendricksen's explorations, as stated in the letter of Gerrit Witsen, covered a period beginning three years before 1616.

nation of their allies, dwelling three good days' journey beyond the Entouhonorons [Onondagas[1]], on whom the Iroquois also make war, desired to assist them in this expedition with five hundred good men; also to form an alliance and establish a friendship with us [the French], that we might all engage in the war together; moreover, that they greatly desired to see us and give expression to the pleasure they would have in making our acquaintance.

"I was glad to find this opportunity for gratifying my desire of obtaining a knowledge of their country. It is situated only seven days from where the Dutch go to traffic, on the fortieth degree. The savages there [the Mohawks], assisted by the Dutch, make war upon them [the Hurons' allies], take them prisoners, and cruelly put them to death; and indeed, they told us that the preceding year [1614], while making war, they captured three of the Dutch, who were assisting their enemies, as we do the Attigouautans [Hurons], and while in action one of their own men was killed. Nevertheless, they did not fail to send back the three Dutch prisoners, without doing them any harm, supposing that they belonged to our party, since they had no knowledge of us except by hearsay, never having seen a Christian; otherwise, they said, these three prisoners would not have got off so easily, and would not escape again should they surprise and take them. This nation is very warlike, as those of the nation of the Attigouautans maintain. They have only three villages, which are in the midst of more than twenty others, on which they make war without assistance from their friends; for they [their friends, the Hurons] are obliged to pass through the thickly settled country of the Chouontouarouon [Senecas], or else they would have to make a very long circuit."

When the Hurons were all assembled and ready to march against the Onondagas, "it was decided," writes Champlain, "to choose some of the most resolute men to compose a party to go and give notice of our departure to those who were to assist us with five hundred men, that they might join us, and that we might appear together before the fort of the enemy. The decision having been made, they dispatched two canoes, with twelve of the most stalwart savages, and also with one of our [French] interpreters, who asked me to permit him to make the journey, which I readily accorded, inasmuch as he was led to do so of his own will, and as he might in this way see the country and get a knowledge of the people living there. The danger, however, was not small, since it was necessary to pass through the midst of enemies. They set out on the 8th of the month [September, 1615]."

[1] General John S. Clark thought the word *Entouhonorons* was a form of the name *Onkwehonwe* ("men-alone" or "the only men") which the Five Nations applied to themselves.

Stone Age Americans of the Present Day.
Ona Indians of the Land of Fire.
From photographs published by permission of Charles Wellington Furlong.

Champlain and his Huron warriors reached the country of the Onondagas in the early part of October, and on the 10th appeared before the Onondaga Fort, which seems to have been located in the present township of Fenner, Madison County, N. Y.[1] They made several fruitless attacks on this stronghold, and remained in camp until the sixteenth, waiting for the arrival of the 500 men under the leadership of Champlain's interpreter; but "after some days, seeing that the five hundred men did not come, they determined to depart and enter upon their retreat as soon as possible," Champlain having received two arrow wounds in the leg. On the 18th, they reached the shore of Lake Ontario, and Champlain returned with the savages to Cahiague before the end of the year, spending the winter with the Hurons. "On the 22d of the month of April [1616]," he writes, "we received news from our interpreter, who had gone to Carantouan [the village of the Hurons' allies], through those who had come from there. They told us that they had left him on the road, he having returned to the village for certain reasons."

Champlain returned to France without seeing his interpreter again; but came back to Canada in June, 1618. He left Quebec on July 5th and proceeded up the St. Lawrence to Three Rivers. Here he found a large party of his Huron allies, who had come down to make war against the Iroquois. He also met his former interpreter. Champlain wrote of this meeting:

Now there was with them [the Hurons], a man named Estienne Brule, one of our interpreters, who had been living with them for eight years, as well to pass his time as to see the country and learn their language and mode of life. He is the one whom I had despatched with orders to go in the direction of the Entouhonorons, to Carantouan, in order to bring with him the five hundred warriors they had promised to send to assist us in the war in which we were engaged against their enemies, a reference to which is made in the narrative of my previous book. I called this man, namely Estienne Brule, and asked him why he had not brought the assistance of the five hundred men, and what was the cause of the delay, and why he had not rendered me a report. Thereupon he gave me an account of the matter, a narrative of which it will not be out of place to give, as he is more to be pitied than blamed on account of the misfortunes which he experienced on this commission.

He proceeded to say that, after taking leave of me to go on his journey and execute his commission, he set out with the twelve savages whom I had given him for the purpose of showing the way, and to serve as an escort on account of the dangers which he might have to encounter. They were successful in reaching the place, Carantouan, but not without exposing themselves to risk, since they had to pass through the territories of their enemies, and, in order to avoid any evil design, pursued a more secure route through thick and impenetrable forests, wood and

[1] *Penna. Mag.*, ii., 103.

brush, marshy bogs, frightful and unfrequented places and wastes, all to avoid danger and a meeting with their enemies.

But in spite of this great care, Brule and his savage companions, while crossing a plain, encountered some hostile savages, who were returning to their village and who were surprised and worsted by our savages, four of the enemy being killed on the spot and two taken prisoners, whom Brule and his companions took to Carantouan, by the inhabitants of which place they were received with great affection, a cordial welcome, and good cheer, with the dances and banquets with which they are accustomed to entertain and honor strangers.

Some days were spent in this friendly reception; and, after Brule had told them his mission and explained to them the occasion of his journey, the savages of the place assembled in Council to deliberate and resolve in regard to sending the five hundred warriors asked for by Brule.

When the Council was ended and it was decided to send the men, orders were given to collect, prepare, and arm them, so as to go and join us where we were encamped before the fort and village of our enemies. This was only three short days' journey from Carantouan, which was provided with more than eight hundred warriors, and strongly fortified, after the manner of those described, which have high and strong palisades well bound together, the quarters being constructed in a similar fashion.

After it had been resolved by the inhabitants of Carantouan to send the five hundred men, these were very long in getting ready, although urged by Brule to make haste, who explained to them that if they delayed any longer they would not find us there. And in fact they did not succeed in arriving until two days after our departure from that place, which we were forced to abandon, since we were too weak and worn by the inclemency of the weather. This caused Brule and the five hundred men whom he brought, to withdraw and return to their village of Carantouan. After their return Brule was obliged to stay and spend the rest of the autumn and all the winter, for lack of company and escort home. While awaiting, he busied himself in exploring the country and visiting the tribes and territories adjacent to that place, and in making a tour along a river [the Susquehanna] that debouches in the direction of Florida, where are many powerful and war-like nations, carrying on wars against each other. The climate there is very temperate, and there are numbers of animals and abundance of small game. But to traverse and reach these regions requires patience, on account of the difficulties involved in passing the extensive wastes.

He continued his course along the river as far as the sea, and to islands and lands near them, which are inhabited by various tribes and large numbers of savages, who are well-disposed and love the French above all other nations. But those who know the Dutch complain severely of them, since they treat them very roughly. Among other things he observed that the winter was very temperate, that it snowed very rarely, and that when it did the snow was not a foot deep and melted immediately.

After traversing the country and observing what was note-worthy, he returned to the village of Carantouan, in order to find an escort for returning to our settlement. After some stay at Carantouan, five or six of the savages decided to make the journey with Brule.

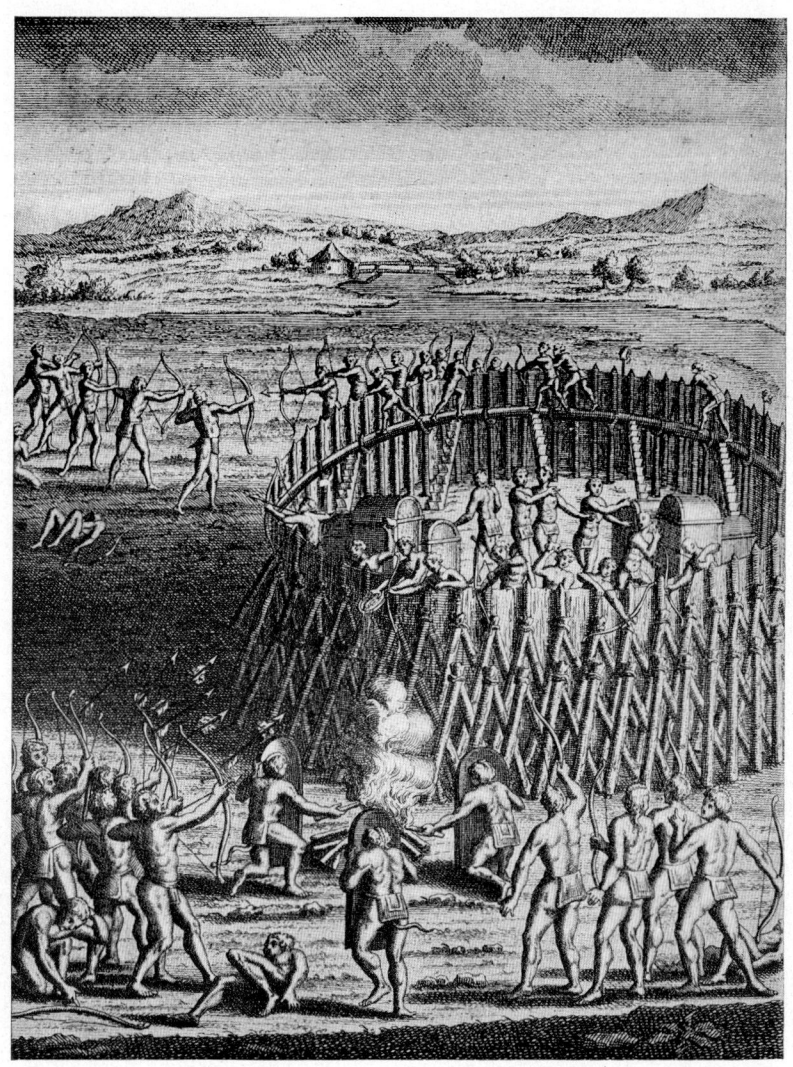

An Attack on an Iroquois Fort.
From Lafitau's *Mœurs des Sauvages*, 1724.

In Champlain's map of 1632 he locates the Carantouannais villages on what appears to be the head waters of the Delaware, but is really intended for the Susquehanna. In the description of this map, Champlain says that the "Carantounais is a nation to the south of the Antouhonorons [Onondagas], in a very beautiful and rich country, where they are strongly lodged, and are friends with all the other nations except the Antouhonorons, from whom they are only three days distant. They formerly took prisoners from the Dutch, whom they sent back without doing them any injury, believing they were Frenchmen."

Reference has already been made to the *Carte Figurative*, or Adrian Block's Dutch map of 1614 and 1616, of which reproductions of both copies are given in the first volume of the *New York Colonial Documents*. Near the center of the original map a legend is written in Dutch, of which the following is a translation:

Of what Kleynties and his comrades have communicated to me respecting the localities of the rivers, and the places of the tribes which they found in their expedition from the Maquas [Mohawks] into the interior, and along the New River downward to the Ogehage (to-wit, the enemies of the aforesaid northern tribes), I cannot at present find anything at hand except two rough drafts of maps relating thereto, accurately drawn in parts. And in deliberating how I can best reconcile this one with the rough drafts of the information, I find that the places of the tribes of the Senecas, Gachoos, Capitanesses, and Jottecas should be marked down considerably farther west in the country.

Kleynties and his companions were the three Hollanders of whom Captain Cornelius Hendricksen reported to the States General of the United Netherlands, August 18, 1616: "He also traded for and bought from the inhabitants, the Minquaes, three persons, being people belonging to this Company; which three persons were employed in the service of the Mohawks and Machicans; giving for them kettles, beads, and merchandise."

The sites of the three towns of the Carantouannais have been identified by Messrs. John S. Clark and David Craft, and their conclusions have generally been accepted as final. The principal town, Carantouan, where Brule went for re-enforcements, was possibly located near or on the top of what is now called Spanish Hill, in Athens Township, Bradford County, Pennsylvania, about five or six miles north of Tioga Point (the junction of the Tioga and Susquehanna Rivers), and within sight of the village of Waverly, New York. Rochefoucauld, who visited this place in 1795, wrote: "Near the confines of Pennsylvania a mountain rises from the bank of the River Tioga in the shape of a sugar-loaf, upon which are seen the remains of some entrenchments. These the inhabitants call the 'Spanish Ramparts,' but I rather judge them to have been thrown up against the Indians in the time of M. de Nonville. One perpendicular breast-work is yet remaining, which, though covered over with grass and bushes, plainly indicates that a parapet and a ditch have been constructed here."

A second town is thought to have been at the mouth of Sugar Creek, also, in Bradford County, above the present town of Towanda. The name, *Towanda*, was applied to the Creek, which is still known by that name, before 1737. It is shown on Lewis Evans's map of 1749 as Tynandaung Creek. Conrad Weiser, who first travelled down its valley in March, 1737, spelled it *Dewantaa*, and gives the meaning as "the fretful or tedious." Some students of Iroquois words have thought that it comes from the word *Attiwandaronk*, meaning "a people who speak a slightly different language"; and as such, marks the residence there of tribes kindred to the Iroquois of New York, which of course, the Carantouannais were. Sugar Creek, which enters the Susquehanna above Towanda Creek, was called by the Indians in 1737, according to Weiser's *Journal*, *Oscohu*, or "the fierce" (also written *Oscolui*[1]). At its mouth was a Carantouannais town, possibly of the same name.

Another town, later called *Gahontoto*, was at the mouth of Wyalusing Creek, and likewise in the present county of Bradford. In the early summer of 1750, Bishop Cammerhoff and David Zeisberger, two Moravian missionaries, journeyed from Wyoming up the North Branch of the Susquehanna to the Onondaga Council. On the 6th of July, they passed Wyalusing Falls, which Cammerhoff describes as "a dangerous cataract, extending across the whole Susquehanna. The water falls down as from a mountain, and makes the current very rapid. . . . On proceeding, we came to a place called *Gahontoto* by the Indians. It is said to be the site of an ancient Indian city, where a peculiar nation lived. The inhabitants were neither Delawares nor *Aquanoschioni* [Iroquois of the Five Nations], but had a language of their own, and were called *Te-ho-ti-tach-se*. We could still notice a few traces of this place in the old ruined corn-fields near. The Five Nations went to war against them, and finally completely extirpated them. The Cayugas for a time held a number captive, but the nation and the language are now exterminated and extinct. The Cayuga told us that these things had taken place before the Indians had any guns, and still went to war with bows and arrows."

Beauchamp gives the meaning of *Gahontoto* as a place where it was necessary to lift the canoe (*i. e.*, in order to pass the Wyalusing Rapids safely), and as such that name may have had no particular application to *Tehotitachse*, the ancient town which stood there.

The Dutch map of 1614, based in part on information furnished

[1] Spelled *Uskoho* in John Bartram's *Journal* of 1743.

by Kleynties and his comrades, shows the Susquehanna source to be a "fresh-water" lake, south of the country of the *Maquas*, or Mohawks, and north of that of the *Sennecas* (a name applied by the early Dutch to all the four other tribes of the Five Nations indiscriminately), whose villages are shown on a western tributary of the main river. Below them, on another branch from the west are the *Gachoos*. South of them, on a third western branch are the *Capitannasses;* and below them, the *Ioteccas*. Some distance below, and on the west side of the River, near its mouth, are located four villages of the *Minquaas* or *Ogehage;* and the same nation is indicated as controlling the country between the Susquehanna and Delaware. Between the Maquaas and the Sennecas are placed the *Canoomakers*.

While the names, *Gachoos* and *Capitannasses*, on these maps, seem to be of Spanish origin, it is possible they were merely Dutch attempts at spelling the Indian names of the tribes; and it is not altogether impossible that Gachoos, Capitannasses, and Ioteccas may have been meant for the names of the other three tribes composing the Five Nations, and as such, living not on the Susquehanna, but in the Lake country of New York.

John Smith's 1612 map of Virginia, also, shows a number of Indian villages in the interior of Pennsylvania. Besides the Town of *Sasquesahanough*, he locates on the east bank of the Susquehanna, near its head, *Tesinigh*, and about midway between these two, *Quadroque*, which is also on the east bank. Near the heads of two western tributaries of the same River he locates *Attaock*, and, some distance north, *Utchowig*. Mr. A. L. Guss, an intelligent and discriminating student of Indian History, was inclined to place Attaock as on the Juniata; Quadroque at or near the Forks of the North and West Branches; Tesinigh on the North Branch, towards Wyoming; and Utchowig on the West Branch near the Great Island. The name, *Utchowig*, Guss says, probably comes from the Powhatan word for wildcat, which Smith gives as *Utchunquoyes*, Purchas as *Vetchunquoyes*, and Strachey as *Utchoonggwai*. Following this thread, Mr. Guss suggests the probability of Utchowig having been a town of the Eries, or Cat Nation; although he admits that the "*chat*" of the Eries, from which they took their name, was, according to the Jesuit *Relations*, the raccoon; and gives the Powhatan word for raccoon as *rahaughoun, raugroughoun, arocun, aroughcun, rarowcun*, etc. Mr. Guss did not, however, as he might have done, attempt to show the possible derivation from the Powhatan word for raccoon the name, *Rickohockan*, which was applied by the Virginians in 1656 and by John Lederer in 1670 to those Indians who came over the mountains from the West to attack the Virginians, and whom Mr. William Darlington thought were the Eries (or Cat, or Raccoon, Nation), and Mr. James Mooney identifies with the Cherokees.

Ragueneau, in the Jesuit *Relation* for 1648 (vol. xxxiii., Thwaites's edition), writes that "Andastoe is a country beyond the Neutral Nation, distant from the Huron country about one hundred and fifty leagues [375 miles] in a straight line to the Southeast, a quarter South, from the Huron country—that is, Southward, a little toward the East; but the distance that has to be travelled to reach there is nearly two hundred leagues, owing to detours in the route. Those people speak the Huron language, and have always been the allies of our Hurons. They are very war-like, and in a single village they count thirteen hundred men capable of bearing arms. At the beginning of last year, 1647, two men of that nation came here, deputed by their Captains to tell our Hurons that, if they lost courage and felt too weak to contend against their enemies [the Five Nations], they should inform them."

The French, it will be remembered, applied the name Andastes (a variation of Kanostoge) to the Iroquois of the Susquehanna generally.

The Jesuit *Relation*, in the "Journal for 1652," states under date of June 4th and 5th: "We picked up in the islands of Lake St. Pierre two Algonquin women, escaped from *Anniene* [the Mohawk country], where they had been captives for two years. . . . The fugitives brought back the news . . . that the Iroquois, having gone during the winter in full force against the *Atra-kwa-e-ronnons* or *Andasto-e-ronnons*, had had the worst of it."

On July 3, 1652, the same "Journal of the Jesuits" contains the following entry: "As for news of the enemies: 1st. The capture of *Atra-kwa-e* by the Iroquois Nation to the number of a thousand. They have carried off 5 or 6 hundred—chiefly men. The *Annie-ronnons* [Mohawks] lost, in this expedition, ten men; the other cantons, some 20, some 30,—all together, 130."

This expedition may have been against the towns of the Carantouannais on the upper Susquehanna at and near Tioga Point; though it is possible that it was against those of the Andastes who lived farther down the River; because it was in that very year that the latter applied to the Maryland government for and entered into a treaty of peace and friendship. The carrying off of "five or six hundred men," however, would doubtless involve the destruction of numerous villages, and it is very probable that some of these villages were between Tioga Point and the mouth of the North Branch.

The Susquehanna Indians belonged to the Iroquois, racially and linguistically; though never taken into the Confederacy of the Five Nations except as a subject people. They were claimed by the Mohawks in 1675, however, as "their own offspring."[1] From 1661 to 1676

[1] See letters of Governor Andros to the Governor of Maryland, Oct. 21, and Dec. 15, 1675, in *Penna. Archives*, Second Series, vi., 706, 708.

they again carried on an intermittent warfare with that powerful aggregation of their kindred tribes known as the Five Nations; and though for some years victorious,[1] they lost many by small-pox and were at length subdued in 1673-74, and in 1677 a large number of their warriors were carried into the Cayuga country. Some years after their final subjection, the old men, women, children, and the few surviving warriors, removed from their old strongholds upon both banks of the Susquehanna River, to a new village which they built on the east side two or three miles inland.[2] Here they lived after William Penn's arrival in Pennsylvania, a broken and dismembered remnant, under the name of Conestogas—that name being a slight variation of their own tribal name *Kanostoge*[3] ("at the place of the immersed pole"), and of its French form, *Gantastogues* or *Andastogues*. Colonel John French, who visited a band of Tuscarora Indians recently come from the South, at Conestoga, June 8, 1710, expressly states that the Tuscaroras were "of the same race and language with our Senecas" (Conestogas). In 1728, the Conestoga chief reported to the Colonial Governor of Pennsylvania that they had lost nearly sixty of their men in a fight with the Seraws, near the Potomac.[4]

The first trade of the English with the Indians of Pennsylvania began with these Susquehannocks. In May, 1631, William Clayborne, or Claiborne, a member of the Virginia Company, obtained from Charles I. a license, authorizing him to trade for furs and other articles along all

---

[1] The Senecas and Oneidas made an alliance with the French in 1666, agreeing, if the latter would send them Traders and missionaries, that they would build forts to protect them against their common enemy, the Andastes. *N. Y. Col. Doc.*, iii., 125; ix., 45, 46, 110, 111, 227, 403, 601, 786.

[2] One of their forts was located in what is now Manor Township, Lancaster County, near the river, between Turkey Hill and Blue Rock. The town which they afterward occupied lay to the east of Turkey Hill about two miles west and north of Conestoga Creek, and one mile west of Little Conestoga. (Evans's *Lancaster County*, p. 950.)

[3] Shea gives the meaning of *Andasto*, as "cabin roof pole"; Sagard gives *Andasatey* as the Huron name for the gray fox; Bruyas defines the Mohawk word, *Gannasta* as "cabin poles."

[4] *Penna. Archives*, i., 239. An anonymous contributor to Dr. Egles's *Notes and Queries* (i., 421), writes of these Indians: "The terms, Andastes, Andastogue, Gandastogue, etc., as used in the Jesuit *Relations* and other French works at different dates, covered a wide field and a great number of tribes; certainly as far east as the Lower Susquehanna, as far north as the Carantowaunais, near Tioga Point; and as far west as the western extremity of Lake Erie. . . . Another of these tribes, Massomacks, the learned Gallatin and all modern writers confused with the Iroquois of New York. They are the same mentioned by Smith in 1608 as Massawomeks, west of the Susquehannocks, which term, as used by Smith, probably included the Eries, or a portion of them. These last are also mentioned in Captain Henry Fleet's Journal, 1632, (Neill's *Founders of Maryland*) as Hirechenes, who lived a three days' journey from the Mosticums, 'one of our confederate nations.' The Hirechenes were the Erichronons of the *Relations*." Gatschet thought the Hirechenes were the Iroquois proper.

the coasts "in or near about those parts of America for which there is not already a patent granted to others for sole trade." Subsequent to this date and before 1634, Clayborne had established a trading post on Kent Island, in the Chesapeake, and also (in 1638) one on Palmer's (now Garrett) Island, in the mouth of the Susquehanna. In a petition presented by him to the King, many years after the arrival in Maryland in 1634 of the first colonists under Lord Baltimore's charter, who attempted to dispossess Clayborne, the latter relates, that he and his partners, while acting under a commission from under his Majesty's hand, divers years past, discovered and planted the Island of Kent, in the Chesapeake, which island they bought of the kings of that country; that great hopes for trade of beavers and other commodities were likely to ensue by the petitioner's discoveries; and that "they had [also] discovered and settled a plantation and factory [forge?] upon a small island at the bottom [top] of said bay, in the Susquehannocks' country, at the Indians' desire, and purchased the same of them [Palmer's Island, in 1637 [1]]; by means whereof they were in great hopes to draw thither the trade of beavers and furs which the French then wholly enjoyed in the Grand Lake of Canada."

In his disputes with the Calverts over his land titles, Clayborne endeavored to stir up the Susquehannocks to making war against the early settlers under Baltimore; and for a time appears to have been successful.[2] Later, the invasion of their own country by the Five Nations in 1651-52 forced the Susquehanna Indians to seek and make an alliance for defense and offense, with the whites of [Baltimore's government. Accordingly, on the 5th of July, 1652, a treaty was made with them on the present site of Annapolis, by which the Indians ceded all their lands, extending from Patuxent River to Palmer's Island, on the western side of the Bay, and from the Choptank River to the Northeast Branch on the eastern side, "excepting the Isle of Kent and Palmer's Island, which belong to Capt. Clayborne." This treaty also provided that both parties were to be permitted to build a house or fort, for trade, on Palmer's Island.[3]

This Indian deed to the lands in Maryland was acknowledged as valid some ninety-two years later by the Six Nation deputies at the Lancaster Conference of 1744. Through Cannassatego, their speaker, the Iroquois then claimed dominion over all the lands of the Conestogas, by right of former conquest. "We have had your deeds [of 1652] interpreted to us," they told the Maryland Commissioners, "and we

[1] *Maryland Archives*, v., 231, 234.
[2] See the Journal of Captain Thomas Young, in *Fund Pub. Md. Hist. Soc.*, 9, 289; and *English Colonization of America*.
[3] *Maryland Council Proceedings*, i., 277.

The Site of the "Fort Demolished" of Chambers's 1688 Survey. Turkey Hill in the Distance.

From a photograph taken by the Author in June, 1910.

acknowledge them to be good and valid, and that the Conestogue or Susquehannah Indians had a right to sell those lands unto you, for they were then theirs; but since that time we have conquered them; and their [present] country now belongs to us."

In 1722, Sir William Keith, the Pennsylvania Governor, suggested to his Council "that some measures be taken to prevent the Five Nations from taking their war-like course through Pennsylvania to the southward. It was more necessary, because the Conestogoe Indians were formerly a part of the Five Nations, called Mingoes, and speak the same language to this day;[1] that they actually pay tribute to the Five Nations; and, either from natural affection or fear, are under their influence."

In his "Notes on the Indians of Lancaster County," written about 1841, and first published in Egle's *Notes and Queries*, Redmond Conyngham stated that "James Logan, in 1707, informed Governor Evans that the Conestoga Indians had paid tribute to the Five Nations twenty-one years." Thirty years would be nearer correct, if we assume that tribute began from the time that the Andastes were finally overthrown by the Iroquois of the Confederacy in 1676–77. That was the time when the Susquehannocks made peace with the Senecas.[2] It is certainly true that the Five Nations entered into negotiations with a view to deeding the Susquehanna lands to the English crown as early as 1679—twenty-eight years before 1707. The Nanticokes told Governor Evans at Pequehan in 1707 that they themselves had been at peace with the Five Nations—and hence their tributaries—for twenty-seven years.

In the preceding chapter is printed an extract from Lewis Evans's *Analysis* of his map of 1755, in which Mr. Evans wrote that the southern bounds of the Iroquois territories extended from the Delaware River "westward to the Great Falls of Susquehanna, near the mouth of Conewago Creek; for though they gave the finishing stroke to the extermination of the Susquehannocks, Bell, in the service of Maryland, at the fort whose remains are still standing [1755] on the east side of Susquehanna, about three miles below Wright's Ferry, had given them [the Susquehannocks] a blow that they never recovered of, and for that reason the Confederates never claimed but to the Conewago Falls."[3]

While the Susquehannocks did have a fort in the location to which Mr. Evans refers (shown as a "Fort Demolished" in Benjamin Chambers's 1688 survey of a line from Philadelphia to the mouth of Conestoga Creek),[4] there is some doubt as to whether or not it was their most

---

[1] From the vocabulary given by Campanius (1643–48), their language was most similar to that of the Onondagas.
[2] *Maryland Council Proceedings*, ii., 243.
[3] See *Penna. Archives*, Second Series, xvi., 710–12.
[4] Smith's *Delaware County*, 170.

ancient fort, and it certainly was not the fort which was attacked by Ninian Beall, as Evans states. Another fort of the Susquehannocks stood at the mouth of Octorara Creek, on the north side of that stream in what is now West Nottingham Township, Cecil County, Maryland.[1] These forts are referred to in the Maryland records as early as 1644. In Augustine Herrman's map of Virginia and Maryland (1670) he locates "the *present* Fort of the Sassquahana," on the *west* side of the River, below the "Falls." Herrman lived on Bohemia Manor in Cecil County, Maryland, and was familiar, of course, with the Lower Susquehanna at the time he made this map. The Fort in the reduction of which Evans says that Bell [Ninian Beall] took part was that near the mouth of Piscataway Creek, on the Potomac, which was besieged by the Marylanders in September and October, 1675.

The exact location of the site of the principal fort of the Susquehannocks was long a matter of bitter dispute and actual warfare between the heirs of Lord Baltimore and the children of William Penn; for the reason that the southern boundary of Penn's colony (now known as Mason and Dixon's Line) was supposed to be marked by it.

In 1658, Josias Cole, a member of the Society of Friends, and an associate of George Fox, its founder, had visited America and travelled among the Indians of Maryland. After his return to England, Fox and his supporters authorized him to treat with the Susquehanna Indians, with a view of securing from them a grant of land on which to plant a colony. He made a second visit to America in 1660, and in November of that year, Cole wrote Fox in regard to the matter:

DEAR GEORGE—As concerning Friends buying a piece of land of the Susquehanna Indians, I have spoken of it to them and told them what thou said concerning it; but their answer was, that there is no land that is habitable or fit for situation beyond Baltimore's Liberty till they come to or near the Susquehannas' Fort.[2]

Cole proceeds to tell Fox that nothing could be accomplished in the way of a land purchase, because the Indians were at war with one another, and William Fuller, a Maryland Quaker of much influence, was absent from home.[3]

In the negotiations William Penn carried on with the King's Council at Whitehall prior to the granting of his petition for the charter of his province, he was called before a meeting of the Committee of Trade and

[1] On John Smith's map of Virginia, of 1612, he locates the Sasquesahanough Town about twenty-five miles above the mouth of the River, which would place it some distance above Octorara.

[2] Bowden, *History of the Friends in America*, i., 389; *Proc. Md. Council*, i., 348–353.

[3] Fisher, *Pennsylvania*, p. 2.

Looking West from the Site of the "Fort Demolished," towards the Site of the Susquehanna Fort of 1670

From a photograph taken by the Author, in June, 1910.

The Iroquoians of the Susquehanna 39

Plantations June 25, 1680, and "told, that, it appearing by Sir John Werden's letter, the part of the territory desired by him is already possessed by the Duke of York, he must apply himself to His Royal Highness for adjusting their respective pretensions; and Mr. Penn being also acquainted with the matter of the letter from the Lord Baltemore's agents, he does agree that Susquehannough Fort shall be the bounds of the Lord Baltemore's Province."[1]

The history of the dispute between the Penns and Baltimore's heirs as to which Susquehanna Fort was meant in these negotiations fills more than one volume of the *Pennsylvania Archives;* and while the line, as finally run by Mason and Dixon, passes about five miles north of the mouth of Octorara, the temporary line run by Talbot (representing Baltimore) in 1683, was from the mouth of Namaan's Creek, in the northeastern corner of Delaware, to the mouth of Octorara Creek.[2]

The Penn Family's brief in their suit with Lord Baltimore over the boundary line is published in volume sixteen of the *Pennsylvania Archives* (Second Series). From this lengthy document the substance of three or four depositions made by Penn's witnesses may here be set forth.[3]

John Hans Steelman, or Stillman, the old Indian Trader of Cecil County, Maryland, of whom more will be related in the succeeding chapters, made a statement in the year 1740 to the effect that he was an Indian Trader, then aged eighty-five years; that he was acquainted with the greater part of Maryland and Pennsylvania, and well acquainted with the Bay of Chesapeake and the Susquehanna River. "He has frequently seen both Indian towns and Indian forts, and the difference between an Indian Town and an Indian Fort is, that an Indian Town is a number of houses or cabins built or set near together; and an Indian Fort is such a town fortified or surrounded with a breast-work of poles or stakes of wood set up, and a bank of earth thrown up about them. About forty or fifty years ago, he saw an Indian Town, wherein were Indians then residing, at the point of land at the upper side of and about half a mile from the mouth of Octorara Creek, which runs into Susquehanna River aforesaid. And at the side of, or near the said Town, this deponent then also saw an Indian Fort, consisting of a great number of poles or stakes of wood set up, and a bank of earth thrown up about the same, as herein before described, which the said Indians then told this deponent had been the Indian Fort. Says he also remembers that one Jacob Young [another early Indian Trader of Cecil County, whose name disappears from the records before 1700], did, before or about the same time, show this deponent the ruins of another Indian Fort which

[1] *Proceedings Maryland Council*, ii., 272; P. R. O. *Colonial Entry Book*, cvi., 178.
[2] See map in Johnston's *Cecil County; Penna. Archives*, Second Series, xvi., 530, 534.
[3] Pages 522–25; 710–12; see also, vol. vii., pp. 356, 357.

stood at about three-quarters of a mile from the said first mentioned Fort, and where the said Jacob Young then also showed this deponent several dead men's bones, and told him that a great battle had been fought there by the Indians."

Jacob Young, before 1687, lived at the head of Mill Creek, a short distance east of the present village of Port Deposit, Maryland. In 1695 he was a tavern-keeper at the mouth of the Susquehanna River opposite (east of) Palmer's Island, and operated a ferry across the River at that point.

The Penns' attorneys also submitted another deposition made in the year 1740 by James Hendricks, then seventy-three years of age, who stated that "near fifty years ago he saw about forty Indian cabins or houses upon the upper point of land which forms the mouth of Octorara Creek . . . which town had stakes of wood and a bank cast up round it. That the affirmant was then told by some of the Indians there residing, that they called the same place *Meanock*,[1] which, they said, in English, signified a fortification or fortified town. He has also seen the ruins of another such fortified town, on the east side of Susquehanna River aforesaid, opposite to a place where one Thomas Cresap lately dwelt. That the land there on both sides of the said River was formerly (called) Conajocula.[2] Further says, that the Indians who lived in the said last mentioned Town before he saw the same, were moved thence from lower down the said River to Conestoga. . . . That he knows the place on the said River called Conestoga, and that near fifty years ago (that must be 1690 or after), he and another person travelled to Conestoga, and this affirmant understanding the Indian language, inquired of several of the Indians there whether any Christian people had ever travelled so high up the said River as Conestoga aforesaid; and was informed by them that there had not; but that this affirmant and his companion were the first; for which reason this affirmant does believe no Christian people had ever, before that time, travelled so high up the said River." [3]

[1] This was a name given by the Delawares, from the Lenape, *Menachk*, a fence, or fort.

[2] James Logan reported to the Pennsylvania Council, June 6, 1706, that he had visited the Conestoga Town in October, 1705, and "that he, with the Company, had made a journey among the Ganaweese [Conoys], settled some miles above Conestogee at a place called Connejaghera [now Washington Borough], above the Fort."— *Pa. Col. Rec.*, ii., 255. Thomas Cresap lived on the York County side of the Susquehanna in what is still called Conejohela Valley.

[3] In harmony with Hendricks's deposition, and others, a record in the *Maryland Archives* (viii., 518), of a conference held by Governor Copley and his Council with some Susquehanna Indians at St. Mary's, April 11, 1693, establishes the fact that the principal town of the Susquehannocks at that time was not near the mouth of Octorara Creek. This record shows a request made by the Indians, "that they may have liberty

The Mouth of Octorara Creek, from the West.

Elizabeth Murphy and Margaret Allen, two daughters of Jonas Erskine, also deposed that about thirty years before (1710?) they lived with their father near the mouth of Octorara Creek, "where the remains of an ancient Indian Fort, a bank, and some part of the logs with which it had been surrounded, appeared," between the mouth of the Creek and the River. The former stated that, "when she saw the same, there appeared a large bank cast up round it, and the tops of the pallisadoes that had been there appeared to be rotted off, and the stumps of them remained in the ground; and says, that her father, who lived at the same place many years, by the license of the Indians, informed her there had been a great battle fought there, and showed her the bones of several persons buried in the cliffs of the rocks, which he said were the bones of Indians slain in that battle." Margaret Allen said "that she often heard her said father, and several Indians, who resided very near the same place, say that, at the same place there had formerly been an Indian Fort; and says that she saw there great numbers of human bones, which, her father informed her, had been [of those] slain in many battles fought there; and that she often pickt up great numbers of stone arrow points and stone hatchets there."

Samuel Preston, one of the Penn witnesses, was cross-examined by Baltimore's attorneys, during the progress of the case in 1740. He was then aged seventy-five, and "remembers when he was a boy to have heard that the Susquehanna Indians, near the River Susquehanna, as he believes, built a Fort, which was attackt and taken by some people from Maryland, under the command of one Colonel Bell; but how far the said Fort was from the mouth of the said River, knows not. Says that when he first heard of the said Fort, he was so young that he has but a faint remembrance of a rumour about it. But further says, that above twenty years ago, he rode over the River Susquehannah, above Conestoga Town, with Samuel Carpenter and Joseph Wood, and about a mile from the said River, on the west side thereof, saw a field with an

---

to come and settle upon their own land at the Susquehanough Fort"; to which the Maryland Council made answer, "That this Fort, as they call it, falling within the limits of another Government, as Pennsylvania, this Government can take no cognizance thereof."

So far as Hendricks's statement covers the question of white men having reached the Susquehanna at Conestoga Creek before 1690, it is probably incorrect; as Benjamin Chambers surveyed a line from Philadelphia to the "Fort Demolished" of the Susquehannocks under an order issued in July, 1688. It is a significant fact, however, that this survey of Chambers, the line of which passed two miles below the site of the Conestoga Indian Town, as known at present, shows no town to have been there when the survey was made; although it does show Indian paths between Philadelphia and the Susquehanna, and also mentions the "Fort Demolished" above the western end of the line. Watson gives 1700 as the date of Chambers's survey, but the document he cites is dated July 7, 1688.

apple-tree in it, and was told (by Joseph Wood, he believes) that, according to the description of one [Sylvester] Garland, an Indian Trader, he, the said Wood, believed that was the place where the Susquehannah Indians forted themselves in when they were pursued by Colonel Bell [Ninian Beall] from Maryland; but says, he believes the said Wood knew nothing more of the place than by hearsay. Has heard, and believes, that the Susquehannah Indians aforesaid had killed some people upon Patapsco in Maryland, and, to secure themselves, built the Fort as aforesaid; and that the before-mentioned Colonel Bell, with some men from Maryland, pursued them, besieged their Fort, and obstructed their receiving any provision into it, by which means the Indians were obliged to leave it, and by force rushed thro' the said Bell's men."[1]

[1] After the first proofs of this chapter were printed, Mr. Frank R. Diffenderfer placed in the writer's hands a copy of a paper on the *Susquehannock Fort*, prepared by Mr. David H. Landis of Lancaster County and read by him before the Lancaster County Historical Society, March 4, 1910. Mr. Landis's paper is the most complete and satisfactory history of the Susquehanna Forts that has yet appeared. He locates the site of the fort on the west bank (shown on Herrman's map of 1670), as on the lands of John Haines and Samuel R. Kocher; and thinks that after the destruction of this fort by the Senecas (in 1673 or 1674) and the defeat of the Susquehannocks at their Potomac Fort by the Virginia and Maryland militia in 1675, the remnant of the tribe returned to the east bank of the Susquehanna, above Turkey Hill, and (about 1676) built near the fort, shown on Benjamin Chambers's survey map of 1688–89 as "Fort Demolished." The site of this fort was on the fields of H. G. Witmer and Charles Heise, "just east of and around where the old Anchor Tavern spring is located, which the Indians probably used; although Indian skeletons and many Indian curios of various kinds have been found within several hundred yards on either side of this point." (Letter from Mr. Landis.)

In his paper Mr. Landis refers to the archæological proofs of the long continued occupation of the region between the mouth of Conewago and Conestoga Creeks. "The Indian graves of that section," he says, "contain articles which the above early records [of Father White, Alsop, Campanius, and others] tell us the Susquehannocks received at peace treaties, and as truck from Traders in exchange for their valuable peltry. These consist of small copper kettles, brass bells, bronze whistles, iron hatchets, knives, hoes and guns, clay pipes, thimbles, scissors, jews' harps, buttons, lead bullets, cast-iron cannon balls, etc., and a great variety of glass beads. Among these, pottery and implements and ornaments of stone of Indian make are also found. If we had no other records, this alone would be ample proof that the locality was the location of Susquehannock towns during the early Trader period. . . .

"In this section, designated above, between Safe Harbor and Bainbridge, we find four Indian village sites conspicuously marked by the large quantities of "Trader truck" found there in the past, and no doubt much more still remains underground.

"One of these Indian town sites is located about two miles south of Bainbridge, known as Locust Grove. . . . Dr. Haldeman states that this was where the Conoys lived [after removing from their former village at Dekanoagah, near the site of the present Washington Borough, or of Columbia].

"Another interesting village site is on the property of John Stehman, at Washington Borough. Just east of his dwelling several Indian graves were found within the last

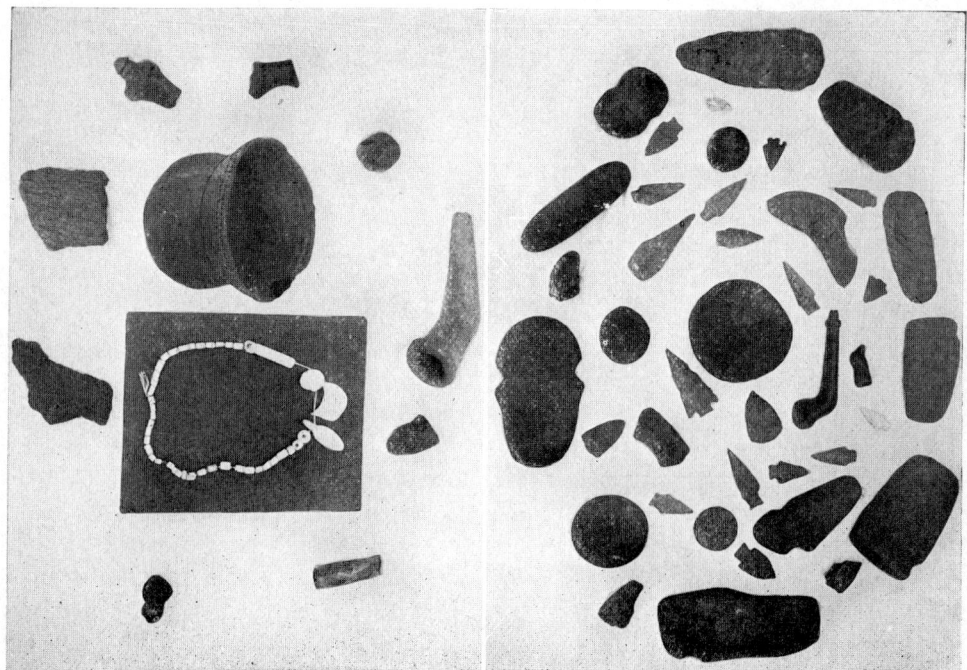

Articles of European Manufacture, Indian Pottery and Images, and Stone Implements, Found in Indian Graves near the Fort Demolished, Dekanoagah, and the Site of the Susquehannock Fort of 1670.
From photographs of a portion of his collection, furnished by Mr. David H. Landis.

A treaty of peace and friendship between the Government of Maryland and the Susquehannocks was entered into July 5, 1652. This was signed, on the part of the Indians, by five chiefs, who are described as war-captains and councillors. Their names were as follows:

Sawahegeh, Treasurer.
Aurotaurogh.
Scarhuhadigh.
Ruthcuhogah.
Wathetdianeh.

A second treaty of peace and amity was made May 16, 1661, between Governor Philip Calvert, of Maryland, his Council, and the Susquehanna Indians, and from the preamble of this instrument we get one of the earliest lists of the chiefs and clan (or tribal) names of these Indians, who were then known to the French as the Andastes. The Indian signers of this treaty were as follows:

Dahadaghesa, of the Great Torripine [Terrapin] Family.
Sarangararo, of the Wolf Family.

---

several years, containing a flint-lock gun, iron hatchets, some vermillion, glass beads, wampum, etc. . . .

"On Taylor's map of Conestoga Manor of 1717 the site which is now the Stehman property is the location of Martin Chartier's trading post. The Shawanese and Ganawese Indians were also located there at [before] this period. . . .

"Among the Indian graves which have been found on this property by Mr. Stehman, one was a most unusual one, which was uncovered in 1873. . . . Besides portions of a skeleton, it contained an iron helmet (see Egle's *Penna.*, 818–19), a cutlass, an iron hatchet and hoe, several 2¼ inch cannon balls, and a bowl. . . . One can only come to one conclusion concerning this grave and that is, that this was a European buried with Indian rites. . . .

"About one mile down the River from Chartier's trading post, Taylor's map marks a fort on where now the H. G. Witmer property is located, which is especially noted for the quantity and variety of Indian Trader articles found there, especially glass beads, also copper kettles, brass bells, buttons, clay pipes, jews' harps, scissors, thimbles, rings, whistles, etc. . . .

"The fourth site which I refer to as being conspicuous for the abundance of Traders' articles found there is just opposite Washington Borough, in York County. . . . This site is a few hundred yards north of where Cresap had his fort, where he defended Maryland's northern boundary from 1731 to 1735. . . . Copper kettles, a very old flint-lock gun barrel, iron tomahawks, and a variety of glass beads have been plowed up there, accompanied by Indian pottery, stone arrow points, tomahawks, and other Indian articles. . . .

"That this site was the location of Susquehannock Fort as recognized by the Indians and Europeans of 1680, when William Penn consented to Lord Baltimore's request that it should mark their boundary, there can be no room for doubt whatever.. . .

"Neither is there any evidence to-day, nor had there been two centuries ago that the recognized Susquehannock Fort was located at the Octorara Creek, as it can be seen by the evidence given by Mrs. Murphy and Mrs. Allen that about 1700 their father plowed up only implements of stone, which shows that that fort site was not

Waskanecqua, of the Ohongeoguena Nation.
Kagoragaho, of the Unquhiett Nation.
Saraqundett, of the Kaiquarioga-haga [or] Nation.
Uwhanhierelera, of the Usququ-haga [Snake?] Nation.
Wadonhago, of the Sconondi-haga [Deer?] Nation.

One of the conditions of this treaty was, that the English should send up to the Susquehanna Fort fifty men, to help defend the fort.

In accordance with this agreement, Captain John Odber was commissioned, on May 18th, to take command of fifty soldiers, with provisions and ammunition, and to "sett forth with them in this march to the Sasquesahannough Forte." He was instructed "to demand the assistance of the Sasquesahannoughs to fetch tymber and other necessaryes for the fortificacon, according to articles now concluded between us, and further, to cause some spurrs or flankers to be layd out for the defence of the Indian forte, whome you are upon all occasions to assist against the assaults of their enemies."

According to the Council Records, Captain Odber failed to carry out his commission to build this Fort, at least in the year 1661.

In a note to his observation that William Penn agreed that the Sasquehannough Fort should mark his southern boundary, Mr. William Hand Browne, editor of the *Maryland Archives* remarks (v., vi.): "This was the fort or block-house built by the Maryland militia for the Susquehannoughs in 1661, and placed exactly on the 40th parallel of latitude, as Herrman's map (1670) shows. We thus see that the plea that Penn understood the southern and not the northern limit of the 40th degree to be his boundary was an afterthought."

The point here raised by Mr. Browne was covered in the Penn Family's *Breviate* of 1742, where a copy of Lord Baltimore's map of 1635 was produced, on which the line of 40° had been placed by Lord Baltimore "precisely at the head of Chesepeake Bay, and 23 miles south of every part of Philadelphia." See *Penna. Archives*, Second Series, xvi., 653, and the 1740 map in the front part of the same volume, showing the location of Lord Baltimore's north line of 1635 to be south of the

---

inhabited since the Trader period, or glass beads and articles of iron and copper would also have been found there."

At the time the present writer took the photographs of the site of the "Fort Demolished" on the Witmer farm, which are printed in this volume, he picked up several stone implements of Indian use, including a scraper, a pestle, and two hammer heads. Such articles can be found on this site by the hundred; and the fact that many hundreds of similar finds have been made there in the past lead to the inference that this spot was inhabited as an Indian village for a very long period of time—probably from before 1608 until 1652, or later—before it became the "Fort Demolished" which Benjamin Chambers found there in 1688.

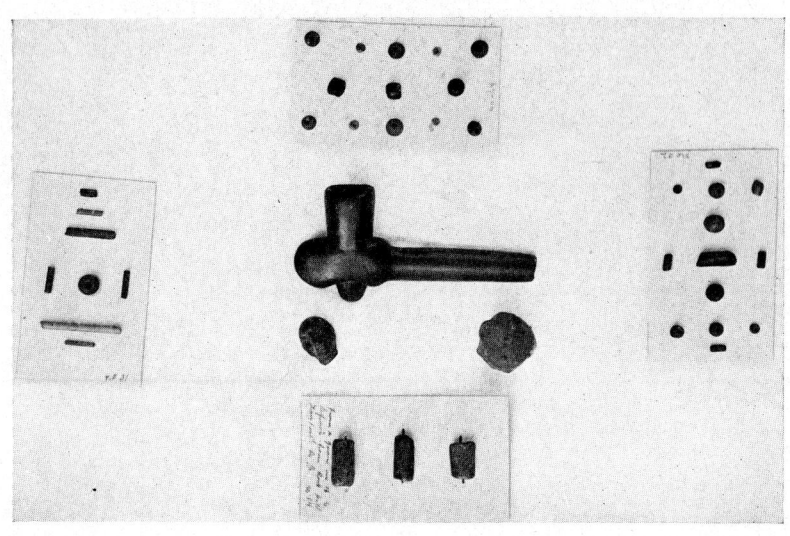
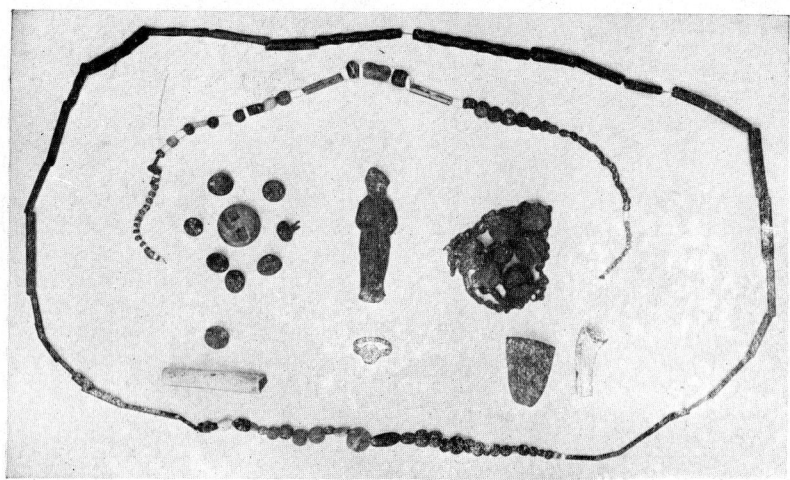

Archæological Relics of the Susquehannocks and Shawnees, from Indian Graves in the Vicinity of Indian Point and the Fort Demolished.
From photographs of a portion of his collection, furnished by Mr. David H. Landis.

mouth of Octorara Creek.¹ Baltimore copied this error from John Smith's map of 1612.

In Plowden's *Description of New Albion* (1648) reprinted in Force's *Tracts*, the author states that "the Susquehannock's *new town* is also a rare, healthy, and rich place, with it a chrystal broad river, but some *falls below* hinder navigation." These "falls below" could hardly have been Conewago Falls, but may have been the rapids at the mouth of Conestoga, or Amos's Falls near Port Deposit; unless indeed the *new town* of the Susquehannocks in 1648 was farther up the river than latitude 40°.

Campanius states in his history of New Sweden that the Mengwes had a fort (about 1645) "on a high mountain, about twelve miles from New Sweden [now Wilmington]." Twelve Swedish miles would be equivalent to nearly eighty English miles. However, Lindstrom, the Swedish engineer who came to the Delaware with Governor Rising in 1654, in his map of New Sweden, printed in Campanius's book, uses the German mile as the unit of measurement, one of which is equal to 4.611 English miles.

In the instructions issued by the Maryland Government to Colonel Henry Coursey April 30, 1677, preceding his departure for Albany to arrange a treaty with the Five Nations and the Susquehannocks, it is set forth as a complaint to be made against the Susquehannocks, that "some (if not all) of their great men present assaulted the house of Randall Hanson, standing within three miles of their fort." The Fort here referred to was the Fort located on the Potomac and the one in the reduction of which Ninian Beall took part.²

Lalemant writes in the Jesuit *Relation* for 1662–63 of an expedition which left the Iroquois country in April, 1663, to wage war against the Susquehannocks. "The three other Iroquois nations [the Senecas, Cayuagas, and Onondagas]," he says, "had no better success in an expedition undertaken by them against the Andastogue-ronnons, savages of New Sweden, with whom war broke out some years ago. Raising, accordingly, an army of eight hundred men, they embarked on Lake Ontario toward the beginning of last April [Lalemant's letter was written

---

¹ For a further discussion of this subject, see *Penna. Magazine*, ix., 241; and G. W. Archer's "Dismemberment of Maryland," in *Md. Hist. Soc. Fund Pub.*, No. 30. For a complete bibliography of the subject see Edward Bennett Mathews's "History of the Boundary Dispute" in *Report on the Resurvey of the Mason and Dixon Line*. Harrisburg, 1909.

² On July 22, 1699, the Maryland Legislature passed an act entitled "An Act of Gratitude to Col. Ninian Beall, viz., for his Services upon all incursions and disturbances of the neighboring Indians, seventy-five pounds sterling, to be laid out for three serviceable negroes, to him and his wife during their lives, and afterwards to their children." See Bacon's *Laws*, 1699, chap. xx.

in September, 1663, or later], and directed their course toward the extremity of that beautiful Lake, to a great river, very much like our St. Lawrence, leading without rapids and without falls to the very gates of the village of Andastogue. [This description, which is probably inaccurate, makes it appear (like Plowden's description of 1648) that the village was above Conewago Falls in 1663]. There our warriors arrived, after journeying more than a hundred leagues on that beautiful River. Camping in the most advantageous positions, they prepared to make a general assault, planning, as is their wont, to sack the whole village and return home at the earliest moment, loaded with glory and with captives. But they saw that this village was defended on one side by the stream, on whose banks it was situated, and on the opposite, by a double curtain of large trees, flanked by two bastions erected in the European manner, and even supplied with some pieces of artillery.[1] Surprised at finding defenses so well-planned, the Iroquois abandoned their projected assault, and, after some slight skirmishes, resorted to their customary subtlety, in order to gain by trickery what they could not accomplish by force. Making, then, overtures for a parley, they offered to enter the besieged town to the number of twenty-five, partly to treat for peace, as they declared, and partly to buy provisions for their return journey. The gates were opened to them and they went in, but were immediately siezed and, without further delay, made to mount scaffolds where, in sight of their own army, they were burned alive. . . . The Iroquois, more humiliated by this insult than can be imagined, disbanded, and prepared to adopt the defensive."[2]

The Dutch account of this attack on the Susquehannocks is contained in two letters written from Altena and New Amstel (now Wilmington and Newcastle) to Director-General Peter Stuyvesant at New Amsterdam. The first letter, from Andries Hudde, bears date May 29, 1663, and informs Governor Stuyvesant that, "News have been brought from the English by one Harmon Roynderson, living in the Colony of New Amstel. They were there communicated to him by Jacob [Clawson, or Young?], my friend, to inform us here, that the Sinnecus, 1600 men strong, with wives and children are on a march to the Minquas, and they were at that time only two days' march from the Minquas' Fort. The Minquas were mostly at home, except eighty men, who were still outside. There were also one hundred of the River Indians here in their Fort."

William Beeckman wrote from New Amstel, June 6, 1663: "Arriving at New Amstel on the last of May, I found there a great excitement,

[1] Plowden's *New Albion* (1648) states that "the Swedes hired out three of their soldiers to the Susquehannocks, and have taught them the use of our arms and fights.'
[2] *Jesuit Relations*, Thwaites's edition, xlviii., 77–79.

TWEEDE BOEK:

136

The Susquehannock Fort of 1670.
An Amsterdam view. From Montanus's *Nieuwe Weereld*, 1671.

and all had joined to repair the Fort, because the Minquas were besieged in their Fort by the Sinnecus, who are said to be about eight hundred men strong. Upon the arrival of the Sinnecus, three or four men were sent into the Minquas' Fort with presents and offers to make peace, and the whole force kept concealed at a distance. But a Minqua returning from hunting tracked the Sinnecus, and thus they were discovered; and the next days they of the Fort went out and met troops of twenty or thirty men; and finally, the Minquas made a sally in force, drove away and pursued the Senecas for two days, capturing ten prisoners and killing a number, according to the report of two Minquas, arrived at New Amstel on the 2d. inst."[1]

On July 28, 1663, the Maryland Governor ordered Captain Thomas Stockett to deliver to "Civility [Harignera] and the other Susquehanna Indians," two barrels of powder, two hundred-weight of lead, and a small cannon from the house of Colonel Vyte (Utie).[2]

Civility is referred to by Captain Stockett in 1664, as being the principal man of the Susquehannocks.

The Maryland treaty of 1661 was renewed on June 29, 1666, by two war-captains of the Susquehannocks, who stated that the Senecas were resolved to storm the Susquehanna Fort in August next. The chiefs signing the new treaty were:

Wastahunda-Hariguera [Harignera] of the Terrapin Family.[3]

Goswein-querackqua, of the Fox Family.

In 1671, the Susquehannocks were reduced to about three hundred warriors by the ravages of the small-pox, their wars with the Five Nations during the past ten years having proven less fatal to them than the destructive effects of this disease.

Count Frontenac met a number of the chiefs, warriors, and families of the Five Nations at Katarakoui (now Kingston) in July, 1673. On the 18th, "they earnestly exhorted Onontio [the French Governor] to assist them against the Andastoguez, the sole enemies remaining on their hands, as he had told them to live in peace with all the other tribes, and it would be a shame for him to allow his children to be crushed, as they saw themselves about to be; the Andastoguez being strongly fortified with men and cannon, and they not having the means of going to attack them in their fort, which was very strong; nor even of de-

---

[1] *N. Y. Col. Doc.*, xii., 430–31.

[2] His house stood on Spesutia Island, a short distance below the present Havre de Grace.

William Beeckman, in a letter from Altena to Governor Stuyvesant, dated September 1, 1663, writes: "The Governor of Maryland assisted lately the Minquas with a quantity of powder and lead, also with two pieces of artillery and four men to manage them."

[3] He was probably the chief then known to the English as Civility.

fending themselves if the others came to attack them in their villages."[1]

La Salle wrote Frontenac from Techirogen, in the Onondaga country (at the foot of Oneida Lake) August 10, 1673: "I have just learned that the eight *coureurs de bois* [Traders] who had fled on your arrival have returned from the Dutch to join the Ottawas. As this is of consequence for the future, and that, not being content to have created terrible confusion here, two have gone to war with the Andastoguez, which will extremely expose the Fathers, whom they have spared up to this time, I have considered it my duty to advise you of this," etc.

The campaign of that summer (1673) in which these two French Traders took part was probably the one in which the Five Nations inflicted a decisive defeat upon the Susquehannocks.

While there are no records extant relating to the final battle between the New York Iroquois and the Susquehannocks at the Fort of the latter near Conestoga Creek, it is probable that one took place in the latter part of 1673 or the spring of 1674, which resulted in the complete destruction of the fortified village of the Susquehannocks on the west bank of the River. It is certain that during these two years the New York Iroquois pressed them so hard that they were obliged to leave the Susquehanna and flee for protection towards the Piscataway Indians on the Potomac. On June 1, 1674, both houses of the Maryland Assembly voted "that a peace be by the Governor made with the said Cynicoes [Senecas] Indians, and forasmuch as that peace may bring a war with the Susquehannoughs, this House, for the security of the Province, do vote that an Act of Assembly be drawn up to empower the Governor and Council to make war, even without the Province." On the 19th of February, 1675, the Upper House of the Assembly desired to be informed by the Lower House, "what they conceive is fit to be done with the Susquehannah Indians, who are said to be now at Patuxent River." Two days later, the Upper House admitted Harignera and others of the Susquehanna chiefs into the Assembly, "and being asked their business, they desired to know what part of the Province should be allotted them to live upon." The Lower House, on being consulted, expressed its opinion that if the Susquehannas should be permitted to take up their residence with the friendly Indians, it might be of dangerous consequence to the Province. The House feared that the design of the Susquehannas in coming among the English and claiming protection from the Senecas, might be for the purpose of discovering the strength of the Province; that the Susquehannas and Senecas were suspected of having private correspondence together, notwithstanding the seeming war between them; and even if they were the absolute enemies of the

[1] Margry, i., 228.

The Site of the Susquehannock Fort of 1670.
From a photograph furnished by Mr. David H. Landis.

Senecas, it would so exasperate the latter for Maryland to entertain the Susquehannas, that should a war occur between the two tribes the ensuing year, the whole Province must of necessity suffer.

It was then proposed to the Lower House and agreed to, that if the Susquehannas should refuse to remove to such a place as the Governor should appoint for them, two or three days' journey above the Falls of Potomac, they should be forced by war to remove. The Interpreter was finally instructed, "to let Harignera, the great man of the Susquehannahs, know, that when he was at Mattapanie with the Governor, he then told the Governor he would be contented if the English would let him and the Susquehannahs live at the Falls of Patowmack; that the Governor hath moved the Assembly to permit them to live *above* the Falls . . . but are not willing to let them plant corn nearer the English, lest the English and Susquehannahs fall out and fight." After some discussion the Susquehannas agreed to remove as far as the head of the Potomac. They failed to do this, apparently, for by the end of the summer they were gathered in an abandoned Fort of the Piscataways, which stood on the Lower Potomac, either at Piscataway Creek or in the Zachaiah Swamp (both opposite the site of Mount Vernon[1]).

In the summer of 1675, a white man was murdered by Indians on the Virginia side of the Potomac. A party of Virginia militia killed fourteen of the Susquehannock and Doeg Indians in retaliation. This was followed shortly afterwards by several other murders on both sides of the River, some of them being at the house of Mr. Randall Hanson. The Virginians organized several companies of militia, which were led by Colonel John Washington, great-grandfather of George Washington. On September 14th, the Maryland Governor received a letter from Colonel Washington and Major Isaac Alderton, requesting the assistance of Maryland in pursuing and punishing the murderers. The Maryland Government immediately authorized the raising of a regiment of horse, to consist of five troops of fifty men each, "for the purpose of assisting the Virginia forces now preparing to pursue the Susquehanough Indians." Major Thomas Truman was appointed commander of this force, and instructed to meet the Virginia militia at the mouth of Piscataway Creek, on the north side, for offensive operation against the Indians. For his conduct in killing his prisoners in this campaign, Major Truman was impeached by the General Assembly when it next met, in May and June following. From the proceedings at Truman's trial we get most of our information about the details of the campaign. On May 15, 1676, it was, by the Maryland Upper House, "ordered that Ninion Beale doe with all expedicon make his appearance before the Rt. Honoble. Lord Proprietary and his Honoble. Council, sitting in Assembly, to

[1] *Md. Assem. Proc.*, ii., 476; *Council Proc.*, iv., 359.

testifie the truth of his knowledge touching the barbarous and inhumane murder of five Susquehan Indians." Beall, who lived on Patuxent River, was lieutenant for Charles County, in which the Potomac Fort of the Susquehannocks was situated.

Captain John Allen, John Shankes, and a number of other witnesses were also summoned. Ninian Beall did not appear before the Assembly, but two of the others did. The questions which the Council agreed should be put to John Shankes included the following:

"1st. Whether Major Truman with the forces under his command was at the north side of Puscattuway Creek [in September, 1675], and did there expect and meet the Virginians. 2dly. Whether the said Major consulted with his officers and those of Virginia before he held any discourse or treaty with those Susquehannough Indians which came out of the Fort. . . . 8ly. Did Major Truman stay at the north side of Puscattuway Creek till the Virginians came thither to him; or did he there treat with them concerning the management of the war against the Susquehannoughs?"

John Shankes was examined by the Council on May 19th, and in his deposition said, that, "being at the Fort of the Susquehannoughs on the Sabbath day, he was sent up to the Fort to desire one of the great men, by name Harignera, to come and speak with Major Truman; and the said Harignera being dead, this deponent desired some other great men to come and speak with the said Major; upon which message of his there came out three or four of them. . . . In the morning following, the Susquehannoughs' great men, being at the place of meeting . . . were taxed again by the Virginians more highly of the injuries done by them in Maryland and Virginia, and they utterly denied the same; and thereupon this deponent was commanded to declare to them that they should be bound."

On May 20th, Captain John Allen was examined by the Council. He stated that "about the 25 or 26 of September [1675], on Sunday morning, the Maryland forces appeared before the Fort under the command of Major Truman, who, sending Hugh French and another to the Fort, there came out two or three of the Indians, and more after to the number of thirty or forty; and the Major examined them concerning the mischief that was done to Mr. Hanson and others; and if they knew what Indians they were. And they told them it was the Senecas. During which discourse between the Major and them came over Coll. Wasshington, Coll. [George] Mason, and Major Alderton, and they likewise taxed them with the murders done on their side. . . . On Monday morning early, the Major commanded Mr. Cood and two or three ranks of men, whereof himself was one, to go to the house of Mr. Randolph Hanson, to see if the Indians had plundered it, which

Looking East from the Site of the Susquehannock Fort of 1670. Turkey Hill on the Left, beyond the Susquehanna

accordingly they did; and after [coming] back to the Fort, the deponent saw six Indians guarded with the Marylanders and Virginians, and the Major with the Virginia officers sitting upon a tree some distance from them. And after some while they all rose and came towards the Indians, and caused them to be bound. And after some time they talked again, and the Virginia officers would have knocked them on the head in the place presently; and particularly Colonel Washington said, 'What, should we keep them any longer; let us knock them on the head; we shall get the Forte to-day.' But the said deponent saith that the Major would not admit of it, but was overswayed by the Virginia officers; and after further discourse, the said Indians were carried forth from the place where they were bound, and they knocked them on the head."[1]

The anonymous *Narrative* of Bacon's Rebellion, written by "T[homas] M[athews]" in 1705, which was copied and furnished to Thomas Jefferson in 1803 by the American Minister at London, states that those of the Conestogas who escaped from the Potomac Fort were responsible for bringing on Bacon's Rebellion in Virginia in 1676. The author of this *Narrative* relates that Virginia and Maryland raised an army of one thousand men, "upon whose coming before the Fort, the Indians sent out four of their great men, who asked the reason of that hostile appearance. . . . But our two commanders caused them to be instantly slain; after which the Indians made an obstinate resistance, shooting many of our men, and making frequent fierce and bloody sallies; and when they were called to, or offered parley, gave no other answer than, 'Where are our four Cockarouses?' *i. e.*, great men.

"At the end of the six weeks marched out seventy-five Indians, with their women, children, &c., who, by moonlight passed our guards, halloaing and firing at them without opposition, having [leaving] three or four decrepits in the Fort. . . .

"These escaped Indians, forsaking Maryland, took their route over the head of that River, and thence over the heads of Rappahanock and York Rivers, killing whom they found of the upmost plantations, until they came to the head of James River, where (with Bacon and others) they slew Mr. Bacon's overseer, whom he much loved, and one of his servants, whose blood he vowed to revenge, if possible."[2]

The Conestogas are said to have found refuge with the Occaneechi Indians on the Islands at the Forks of the Roanoke. Here they were followed by Bacon and his men in May, 1676, and attacked by the English[3] in conjunction with the Occaneechi. The Conestogas then re-

[1] *Md. Assembly Proc.*, ii., 425, 429, 450, 476, 482.
[2] See also *Virginia Magazine*, iv., 119.
[3] Some accounts say the attack was made near the site of Richmond.

treated to the Susquehanna[1] and soon afterwards yielded to the Cayugas and Onondagas. A number of them were taken as prisoners or adopted subjects into the country of the Five Nations in the Spring of 1677,[2] but afterwards a few were suffered to return.

Governor Edmund Andros wrote to the Governor of Maryland from New York, December 10, 1675: "I have received yours of the 4th past, of your progress against the Indians, which I wish may have ended it, but am sorry the Susquehannahs were concerned, having always (as the Maques [Mohawks] to this) having the repute of being perfect friends to the Christians, particularly Maryland, and being off-springs of the Maques, though by the Sinnekes engaged in war."

On June 2 and 3, 1676, Governor Andros had an interview at the Fort in New York with Conacheoweede and Sneedo, two sachems of the Susquehannocks, "from Delaware and the head of ye bays and those parts." The minutes of these interviews are preserved in the New York colonial manuscripts at Albany. They state that the Susquehanna sachems speak the Mohawk tongue; that the Governor proposed that he would "take care the Maques and Sinnekes shall be at peace with them, and will also make peace for them with Virginia and Maryland"; "that the Maques shall do them no hurt, for he hath spoken with the Maques about them already, and they have promised it, calling them their brethren and children, and if they will, they may go and live with them." The two chiefs replied that they would go back to the South River, to the rest of the people, and tell them what the Governor said, and would return with an answer.

At a meeting of the New York Council held July 28, 1676, a letter was read from Captain Cantwell, of Delaware, about the coming in of the Susquehanna Indians. It was agreed that the Governor should write to Captain Cantwell, "to encourage the coming in of those Indians, till when not to promise or engage anything to them; but if they desire it, the Governor will endeavor a composure of all things in Maryland, and perfect a peace with the Maques and Sinnekes, after which the said Indians may return to their land, as they shall think good."

September 25th following, Governor Andros wrote to the Deputy Governor of Maryland, "concerning the Suscohanes; this is the same occasion, upon their coming near to Delaware and offering all assurance for their future comport, and not any ways to injure any English; finding if some course be not speedily taken, they must all necessarily submit to the Maques and Sinnekes, which passionately desire it, but might prove of a bad consequence, I have therefore dispatched the bearer,

[1] *Proc. Maryland Council*, ii., 135; *Md. Archives*, xv., 120.
[2] Hazard's *Annals of Penna.*, 423; Smith's *Delaware County*, 109.

Capt. John Collier, express to you, desiring you 'll by him let me know your resolucons; if I may be serviceable to you therein, and whether you judge the late peace with the Susquehanas sufficient, and their continuing or being removed from these parts best."

During the session of the Maryland Assembly, May 15 to June 15, 1676, the members voted, on May 24th, "that match-coats, corne, powder, and shott be purchased and forthwith delivered to the friend Indians, by way of gratification for the services done by the said Indians in the late warre against the Susquehannough Indians; and that the said match-coats be distributed to the number and in the manner as followeth, viz., to Puscataway, 80; to Chapticoe, 30; to Mattawoman and Pamunkie, 30; to Nangemy, 10; in all, 150."

Governor Thomas Notley wrote from Maryland to the Governor of Virginia, August 6, 1676: "We have lately received intelligence from the Head of the Bay, that the Susquehannough Indians have resided at their old Fort, *about sixty miles above Palmer's Island* for so many months that they have now corn fit to roast; that they shortly expect the remainder of their troops, and as many of the Western Indians near or beyond the mountains as they have been able to persuade to come and live with them. We are further informed, that, by means of Colonel Andrews, the Governor of New York, a peace was made last summer between them and their old enemies, the Cinigos [Senecas]; so that now they are at ease, and out of our reach."[1]

The chiefs of the Piscataway and Mattawoman Indians (tribes in alliance with Maryland) met Governor Notley and his Council in conference eleven days after this letter was written. It was proposed to the Indians that peace be made with the Susquehannocks. But the chiefs were unwilling that peace should be made, even though they were included in it. They were then asked "whether they will march with the English to the *new* Fort they [the Susquehannocks] have built, or otherwise to pursue the Indians." The two chiefs answered that they were ready to march with their warriors. A few months later, however, they informed the Council that they were willing to make peace.

It will be seen by referring to the section of Herrman's 1670 map of Maryland, reproduced in this volume, that "the present Sassquahana Indian Fort" is located on the west side of the Susquehanna River, exactly on the fortieth degree of latitude, a few miles below "Canoage," or Conewago, Falls, and about forty miles farther north than the mouth of that River. This was in the same locality as that which Governor Notley, on August 6, 1676, called "their old Fort, about sixty miles above Palmer's Island," and on August 17th, "the new Fort which they

[1] *Maryland Council Proc.*, iv., 122. The Marylanders applied the name, Seneca, to all the tribes of the Five Nations.

have built"; although it is possible that the "Old Fort" referred to the site of their 1670 stronghold, and the "New Fort" to a fort above Turkey Hill, on the opposite side of the River. The legend on Herrman's map relating to the Susquehanna reads as follows: "The great Sassquahana River runs up northerly to the Sinnicus, above 200 miles, with Divers Rivers and Branches on both sides, to the East and West, full of falls and Isles, untill about 10 or 12 miles above the Sassquahana Fort, and then it runs cleare, but Downwards not Navigable but with great danger, with Indian Canoos, by Indian Pilots."

On August 2, 1684, the sachems of the Cayugas and Onondagas at Albany informed Governor Dongan, of New York, and Governor Howard, of Virginia, that "Wee have putt all our land and our selfs under the protection of the great Duke of York, the brother of your great Sachim; We have given the Susquehanne River, which we wonn with the sword, to this Government [in 1679, as they told William Penn's agents during 1683]. . . . We do putt the Susquehanne River above the *Washinta*, or Falls, and all the rest of our land under the Great Duke of York." This extract shows, as Lewis Evans wrote in 1755, that the Five Nations only claimed as far south as to Conewago Falls; and it also indicates that they respected the claim of Maryland, so far as it may have extended north, to the country south of the Falls, by reason of that Province having defeated the Susquehannocks so completely in 1675 at the Susquehannock Fort on the Potomac.

Upon the whole, the evidence seems preponderatingly, though not entirely conclusive, in favor of the contention of Lord Baltimore, that the Susquehanna Fort which was to limit the northern extent of his Province was one of those between the Conewago and the Conestoga, and not, as William Penn asserted, the one at the mouth of the Octorara. The whole history of the controversy also leads inevitably to the conclusion that William Penn was a shrewd, unscrupulous, evasive, and somewhat tricky trader in his land operations, and that he and his sons outwitted and gained an advantage over the more honest but less resourceful members of the Calvert family.

The site of the 1670 Fort on the west side of the Susquehanna River was in the Conejohera (Iroquois pronunciation) or Conejohela (Algonquin pronunciation) Valley, opposite the present borough of Washington, and in what is now Lower Windsor Township, York County. In the *Archæological Report* of the Dauphin County Historical Society for 1898, Dr. William Bigler, of York County, locates a village site in this township, four miles south of Wrightsville, on a stream called the Cabin Branch, and within one mile of the village of East Prospect. "The Indian Fort," he says, "was located on the River, near the mouths of the Cabin Branch and Conejacula corruption of Conejohela] Creeks, about

The North Half of Herrman's 1670 Map of Virginia and Maryland.
From the copy in the Library of Congress.

The Iroquoians of the Susquehanna 55

one mile from the Village Site, which was hidden behind the hills, and at that time difficult of access." [1]

Thomas Cresap, an agent of Lord Baltimore, settled here about 1729, claiming the land as within the bounds of Maryland. [2]

It is stated above, that on Herrman's map of Maryland (1670), "the present Fort of the Sassquahana" is located on the west side of that River, at the "Falls"; and that this was at the same location which Governor Notley called, on August 6, 1676, "their Old Fort," and August 17th, "the New Fort they have built." The "New Fort," of the Susquehannocks in 1676, however, may have been on the east side of the River, near Turkey Hill.

But the "blow" which Maryland gave them, and which Lewis Evans, in 1755, said was given by Ninian Beall, "in the service of Maryland, at the Fort whose remains are still standing on the east side of the Susquehanna, three miles below Wright's Ferry [*i. e.*, the "Fort Demolished],"[3] seems to have been given them, not by Beall, but by the Maryland militia under Major Thomas Truman, and the Virginia militia under John Washington and another officer, and it was given them, not at the Fort on the Susquehanna, but at the Susquehannock Fort which stood near the banks of the Potomac and the mouth of Piscataway Creek, or at the site of the old Fort of the Piscataways. This was in September, 1675. Ninian Beall was commander of the militia for Charles County, Maryland, within the bounds of which this Fort was situated. He did take part in the campaign under Truman; but there is no mention in the Maryland records showing that he ever led any troops as far north as the Susquehanna River; and no probability, in view of the records cited above, that he ever saw the sites of the Susquehanna forts on both sides of that River, between Conewago Falls and the Conestoga.

The correspondence between the Governors of New York and Maryland later in 1675–76 seems to have resulted in a conclusion to leave

[1] Mr. David H. Landis, in his paper on the *Susquehannock Fort*, read before the Lancaster County Historical Society March 4, 1910, states that the site of the fort on the west bank of the river was directly opposite Washington Borough, on the present properties of John Haines and Samuel R. Kocher, a few hundred yards north of where Cresap afterwards built his fort. In another paper, Mr. Landis states that the walls of Cresap's Fort (built in 1729) are still standing, and used as the basement for the dwelling of Mr. B. C. Gnaw, of Lower Windsor Township, York County.

[2] For further information about the Indian occupation and Cresap's settlement, see *Penna. Arch.*, i., 295, 364; *ibid.*, Sec. Ser., xvi., 711.

[3] Evans's statement was probably based on the tradition given in the depositions of Samuel Preston and Patrick Maugher about 1740, which are printed in the Penn-Baltimore Boundary Dispute papers in *Penna. Archives*, Second Series, xvi., 710. Maugher thought that Beall attacked the Fort when Francis Nicholson was Governor of Maryland (1694). Preston's statement has been given in this chapter.

the Susquehanna Indians to their fate; and during the Fall and Winter of 1676-77, they submitted to the Five Nations and became their tributaries.

A minute in the records of the court at Upland, on the Delaware (now Chester, Penna.), dated March 13, 1677, recites that, "Att a meeting held by ye Commander and Justices at Upland, upon the news of the Sinneco Indians coming down to fetch the Susquehanno that were amonghst the River [Lenape] Indians, etc., March the 13th, annoq. Dom. 1676-77: Itt was concluded, uppon the motion of Rinowehan, the Indian Sachomore, for the most quiet of the River, viz., That Captn. Collier and Justice Israell Helm goe up to Sachamexin [the site of Philadelphia], where att present a great number of Sinnico and other Indians are; and that they endeavor to prswaede the Sinnecus, the Sasquehannos, and these River Indians to send each a Sachomore or Deputy to his honor the Governor att New Yorke." The conference with the Indians was accordingly held at Shackamaxon from the 14th to the 18th of the same month, at a cost of 250 guilders to Upland District, "for the expenses of the Commander, Justices, and Indians." The records of this conference have not been preserved. If they had been they would in all probability show that the Susquehannahs and Delawares had submitted formally to the Five Nations during the time the representatives of the latter were at Shackamaxon.

On April 6, 1677, the New York Council issued the following order to Captain Collier: "If the Susquehannes in any part of ye Government your way, will come hither (as was told them last year), and resolve to leave off ye warre, they shall have a convenient place assigned them to their content; or, may goe and live with ye Maques, or any other our Indyans. If they doe not like it, then they have liberty to go back where they will; but are not to live in ye South [Delaware] River, it not being safe for them; and therefore ye River Indyans are to have notice not to suffer their continuance there amongst them, it being dangerous to both."

On the last day of the same month, the Governor and Council of Maryland commissioned Colonel Henry Coursey to proceed to Albany and endeavor to arrange a peace between that Province, the Five Nations, and the Susquehannas. Coursey's commission recites, among other things, that, "whereas, the said Susquesahannohs have sithence and lately desired to come to a treaty of peace with his said Lordship [Baltimore], and have (as I am informed since the said overture) submitted themselves to and putt themselves under the protection of the Cinnigos [Senecas, *i. e.*, the Five Nations] or some other nations of Indians resideing to the northward of this Province," etc. In his *Instructions*, Colonel Coursey was ordered to proceed to New York by way of New-

Cresap's Fort, near Site of the Susquehannock Fort of 1670.

Cresap's Fort, marking the north line of Maryland as originally granted, and confirmed in 1680' forms the basement of the dwelling. From a photograph furnished by Mr. David H. Landis.

castle, and while at the latter place to inform himself from Captain Collier and others of the true state of the Susquehannas; what number they are; upon what terms they are received by the Senecas; and whether there be any of them that are not submitted to the "Cinnigos."

Colonel Coursey met Jacob Young of Cecil County at or above Newcastle on May 20th, and from him received an account of the Susquehannas which he transmitted to Maryland two days later. In this letter he relates that "them that kild Richard Milton's family were eight Susquehanoes, and upon that immediately fled to the Senuques; and that all the mischief that hath been done hath been by their severall troops as they come out of Virginia; and them two this year shot by two Susquahanoes, that came with that troop of Senuques that carried the Susquihanoes from this place; since which, the same troop took the chiefe warriours in the Susquihanoes River, being 30 in number, who had then been a hunting, to make a present to you for peace. . . . Here is 26 of them left here still. I purpose to persuade them to go with me to New York. . . . Hee [Jacob Young] tells me that the Senuques, having marched about two days, then fell at some difference among themselves how to divide them Susquahanoes they had with them— they being of two severall forts; and upon the division the Susquahanoes were very much displeased, and some of them got away; the rest they bound and carried with them, but it is judged not to hurt them, for every one of the forts strive what they can to get them to themselves, and Governor Androes to get them to the Masoques [Mohawks], for it was told me by Capt. Delavall that if they had them they would make war immediately with the French."

Colonel Coursey also relates that on "this 23d instant came to me 4 Susquahanoes, and with them the Emperor of the Delaware Bay Indians, and upon discourse with them, I find them all inclining to a peace."

From what has been given in these citations, it will be seen that the Susquehanna Indians made a peace with the Five Nations in the winter or spring of 1677; that the negotiations were concluded at Shackamaxon on or about March 13th of that year, and that these were followed by the departure of many of the Susquehanna warriors to the country of the Five Nations.

It is also reasonable to conclude that at the conference at Shackamaxon in March, 1677, the Delaware Indians likewise formally submitted to and placed themselves under the protection of the Five Nations.

From the Delaware River Colonel Coursey proceeded to New York, and met the chiefs of the Five Nations at Albany during the months of July and August, where he entered into mutual agreements of peace and friendship between them and the Province of Maryland and its Indians. The Onondaga chiefs, however, informed him that four castles of the Senecas were still on the war-path against the Susquehannas; and the Oneidas stated that twenty of their men had gone to fight against the Maryland Indians. The Mohawks, on their part, thanked the Maryland Commissioner for having released the two sons of one of their chiefs, and likewise, for having beheaded the sachem of the Susquehannas, named Achnaetsachawey, who was the cause of their having been taken prisoners.[1]

One of the interpreters at these conferences was Arnold Cornelius Viele, the Albany Trader.

On June 30, 1681, Captain Randolph Brandt wrote Lord Baltimore from Charles County: "I have little to offer your Lordship but the enclosed paper, it being a rude draught of what I have received from an Indian formerly taken by the Quiaquos [Cayugas], and now come from them. . . . This description is given from an Indian called Jackanapes, taken by the Quiaquos the first day of January last past (which said Indian did belong to the Mattawoma Fort and was seen by the subscriber at the Zachaiah Fort the 18th of this instant, when the peace was made) and since made his escape, as he sayeth."[2]

This rude map of the Five Nations' country in 1681 is printed in this volume. It is valuable chiefly for the information it gives as to the number and disposition of the captured Susquehannocks among the towns of the Five Nations. According to the map, there were then of the captives among the Cayugas, eight Susquehannocks; among the Oneidas, seventeen; and among the Onondagas, fourteen.

The Governor of Maryland and his Council met in conference at St. Mary's, August 22, 1681, two Northern Indians, an Onondaga and a Cayuga. These Indians told the Governor, among other things, that there were then living in the villages of the Five Nations about one hundred of the fighting men of the Susquehannocks; some of whom were among the Senecas proper; fourteen with the Oneidas; seven with the Onondagas; "but the chiefe [part] of them are among the Quiagoes [Cayugas]."[3]

On May 30, 1690, Captain Jacob Young wrote from the head of the Bay to the Commander-in-Chief of Maryland, that there were then at his house fourteen Senecas, who had come from their own country in the latter part of April with the intention of settling among the Susquehanna Indians.

On April 11, 1693, Colonel Casparus Herman and Jacob Young, of Cecil County, brought a number of Susquehanna Indians before the Maryland Council, who stated, that "being reduced to a small number,

[1] *Proceedings Maryland Council*, ii., 243–250. Hazard's *Annals of Penna.*, 423–4.
[2] *Maryland Archives*, xv., 383.
[3] *Ibid.*, xvii., 5.

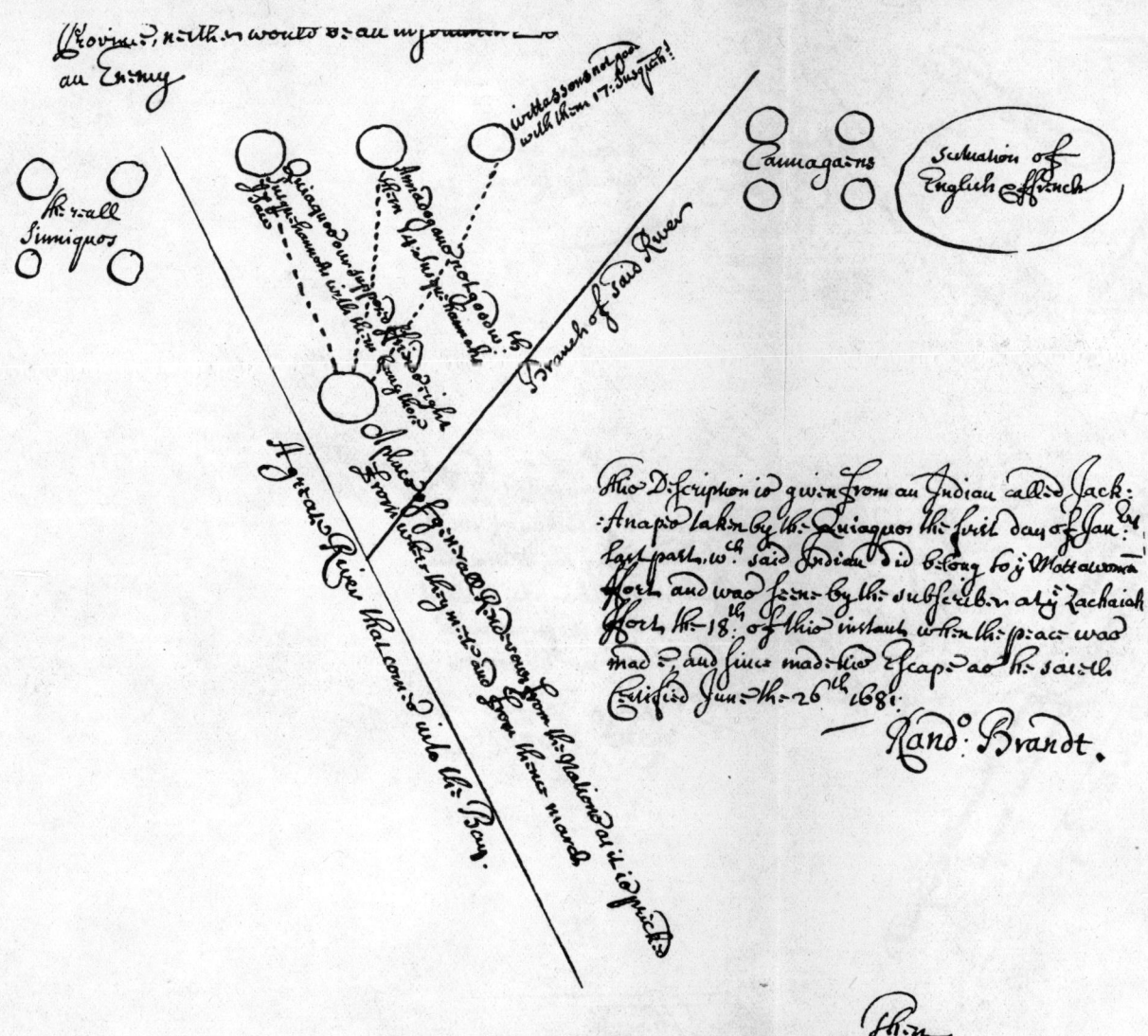

Map of the Iroquois Castles and Susquehanna River in 1681.
From the original in the Maryland Council Journals, in possession of the Maryland Historical Society.

Map of the Iroquois Castles and Susquehanna River in 1681.
From the original in the Maryland Council Journals, in possession of the Maryland Historical Society.

and, as it were, newly grown up, they desire the favor of the Governor and Council, that they may have liberty to come and settle upon their own land at the Susquehanna Fort and to be taken and treated as friends." The Council replied to the Indians that "their Fort, as they call it, falling within the limits of another Government, as Pennsylvania, this Government can take no cognizance thereof"; and after a private discussion by the Council, it was decided that, as for the Susquehanna Indians, "they may continue at their Fort, and if they are inclined to enter into a league with us, there may some of their great men come down to confirm the same, and shall be kindly treated; and then also they may make choice of some great man to preside over them, as Civility formerly did, and as they now desire."

In the treaty made at Philadelphia, April 23, 1701, between William Penn and the chiefs of "the Sasquehanna Minquays, or Conestogas," the Shawnees, and the Ganawese, by which the Conestogas confirmed to Penn the 1700 sale of some of their lands on the Susquehanna, a representative of the Five Nations was also a party to and one of the signers of this agreement. He is described in the Minutes of the Pennsylvania Council as "Ahookassoongh, brother to the emperor or great king of the Onondagoes of the Five Nations."[1] This chief may possibly have been the vice-regent of the Iroquois Confederacy, and then living in the Conestoga town.

Besides the names of the Susquehanna chiefs which have been given, the following names are also found on the New York records before the time of Penn's settlement in Pennsylvania:

On March 29, 1639, Peter Minuit, who had come from Sweden to establish the colony of New Sweden on the Delaware, purchased from Mitatsimint and four others, chiefs of the Minquas, that part of the western shore of the Delaware lying between Minquas Kill (Christina Creek) and Boomtiens Hoeck (Bombay Hook).

Two Minquaas chiefs, Aquarichque and Quadickhe, held a conference with Governor Stuyvesant at Fort Amsterdam in New Netherland, July 13, 1647.

Four Delaware chiefs conveyed to Governor Peter Stuyvesant on July 19, 1655, their lands on the Delaware River lying north of Minquaas Kill (Christina Creek), and extending westward as far to the "bounds and limits of the Minquaas' country." This deed was executed "in the presence of the undernamed witnesses, sachems of the Minquas, to-wit: Jonnay and Tonnahoorn, Pimadaase and Cannowa Rocquaes." On the 9th of July, 1654, the Delaware chiefs who executed this deed had told Governor Stuyvesant at Fort Nassau, "that they were the great

[1] *Penna. Col. Rec.*, ii., 9.

chiefs and proprietors of the lands, both by ownership and by descent and appointment of Minquaas and River Indians."

Naaman, a chief who lived near what is to this day called Naaman's Creek, is mentioned in one of the records of the year 1654. Ferris states that he was a Minqua chief.[1]

The Relation of Bagnall, Powell, and Todkill, in John Smith's *General Historie of Virginia*, gives us the earliest information about trade being carried on by the Susquehanna Iroquois with the white men. This account is found in the sixth chapter of Smith's book, which relates to "what happened the second voyage in discovering the [Chesapeake] Bay":

The 24 of July [1608], Captaine Smith set forward to finish the discovery, with twelve men. . . .

Entering the River of Tockwogh [now Sassafras River, on the Eastern Shore of Maryland], the salvages all armed, in a fleete of boats, after their barbarous manner, round environed us; so it chanced one of them could speake the language of Powhatan, who perswaded the rest to a friendly parley. But when they saw us furnished with the Massawomeks' [Smith's name for the Iroquois of the Five Nations and possibly also the Eries] weapons, and we faining to have taken them perforce, they conducted us to their pallizadoed towne, mantelled with the barkes of trees, with scaffolds like mounts, brested about with brests very formally. Their men, women, and children, with daunces, songs, fruits, furres, and what they had, kindly welcommed us, spreading mats for us to sit on, stretching their best abilities to express their loves.

Many hatchets, knives, peeces of iron, and brasse, we saw amongst them, which they reported to have from the Sasquesahanocks, a mightie people and mortall enemies with the Massawomeks. The Sasquesahanocks inhabit upon the chiefe spring of these foure branches of the Baye's head, two dayes journey higher than our barge could passe for rocks; yet we prevailed with the interpreter to take with him another interpreter, to perswade the Sasquesahanocks to come to visit us, for their language are different. Three or foure dayes we expected their returne, then sixtie of those gyant-like people came downe, with presents of venison, tobacco-pipes three foot in length, baskets, targets, bowes and arrowes. Five of their chief Werowances came boldly aboord us to crosse the Bay for Tockwogh, leaving their men and canowes; the wind being so high they durst not passe.

Our order was daily to have prayer, with a psalme, at which solemnitie the poore salvages much wondred; our prayers being done, a while they were busied with a consultation till they had contrived their businesse. Then they began in a most passionate manner to hold up their hands to the Sunne, with a most fearefull song; then embracing our Captaine, they began to adore him in like manner: though he rebuked them, yet they proceeded till their song was finished: which done, with a most strange furious action, and a hellish voyce, began an oration of their loves; that ended, with a great painted beare's skin they covered

---

[1] *Original Settlements on the Delaware*, p. 134.

Susquehannock Picture Writing on Rocks near their Forts.

These rocks are in the Susquehanna River, between Turkey Hill and the mouth of Conestoga Creek, south of Neff's Island, and a short distance below Creswell. From photographs taken by Mr. Landis in the fall of 1906.

him: then one ready with a great chayne of white beads, weighing at least six or seven pounds, hung it about his necke; the others had 18 mantels, made of divers sorts of skinnes sowed together; all these with many other toyes they laid at his feete, stroking their ceremonious hands about his necke for his creation to be their Governour and Protector, promising their aydes, victualls, or what they had, to be his, if he would stay with them, to defend and revenge them of the Massawomeks. But we left them at Tockwogh, sorrowing for our departure, yet we promised the next yeare againe to visit them. Many descriptions and discourses they made us, of Atquanachuck, Massawomek, & other people, signifying they inhabit upon a great water beyond the mountaines, which we understood to be some great lake, or the River of Canada; and from the French to have their commodities by trade. These know no more of the territories of Powhatan than his name, and he as little of them; but the Atquanachuks are on the Ocean Sea [probably the Lenape of what is now New Jersey].

These passages from Smith's *Historie* have always been interpreted to mean that the hatchets, knives, pieces of iron, and brass, which Smith found among the Tockwoghs, who got them from the Susquehannocks, had been obtained by the latter in barter with the French of Canada. A careful reading of the paragraphs, however, will show that the writers may have meant to say that the Massawomeks, who were mortal enemies of the Susquehannocks, got *their* commodities by trade from the French. Certainly, the Susquehannocks did not get *their* articles of European manufacture that way. The Massawomeks, their "mortal enemies," occupied the country between themselves and the French, who were then at the mouth of the St. Lawrence; and such of the Huron-Iroquois as were in contact with the French were likewise mortal enemies of the New York Iroquois. The latter were probably the particular tribes of the Massawomeks who made war on the Iroquois of the Susquehanna, as well as on the Hurons; and while the last two branches of the family were not enemies to one another, they were effectually separated by the barrier of the Five Nations in what is now the State of New York.

Taking these things into consideration, it is necessary, therefore, to inquire in another direction for the source of the European supplies which Smith found among the Indians at the head of Chesapeake Bay in 1608. That source has been pointed out to the writer by Mr. James Mooney, of the Bureau of American Ethnology. Mr. Mooney has suggested that a certain "Report of the Board of Accounts on New Netherland for the year 1644," a document which has been in print since 1856, and is included in the first volume of the *New York Colonial Documents* (page 149), contains the solution of the mystery as to where the iron weapons and implements of the Susquehanna Indians came from before 1608. This report begins as follows: "New Netherland, situate in

America, between English Virginia and New England, extending from the South River, lying in 34½ degrees, to Cape Malabar, in the latitude of 41½ degrees, was first frequented by the inhabitants of this country [Holland] in the year 1598, and especially by those of the Greenland Company, but without making any fixed settlements, only as a shelter in the winter. For which purpose they erected on the North [now Hudson's] and South [now Delaware] Rivers there, two little forts against the incursions of the Indians. A charter was afterwards, on the 11th October, 1614, granted by their High Mightinesses," etc.

It is probable, therefore, that the articles of European manufacture which John Smith found among the tribes at the head of Chesapeake Bay were obtained by them from the Dutch whalers, or others, who visited the coasts of New Jersey and Delaware before 1608.

Captain Henry Fleet, one of the later Jamestown settlers, who had been captured by the Nacostine Indians on the Potomac in 1621 and remained among them as a prisoner for several years, after his return to England, made a number of trading voyages to Chesapeake Bay, and carried back cargoes of furs. He was there in 1632, and sailed up the Potomac to the head of navigation. In his *Journal*[1] Fleet states, that "the Emperor [of the Powhatans?] is fearful to punish the Nacostines, because they are protected by the Massomacks, or Cannyda Indians, who have used to convey all such English truck as cometh into the River [Potomac] to the Massomacks. . . . I find that the Indians of that populous place [the Massomack country] are governed by four kings, whose towns are of several names, Tonhoga, Mosticum, Shaunetowa, and Usserahak, reported above 30,000 [?] persons, and that they have palisades about the towns, made with great trees, and with scaffolds upon the walls."

From Yowaccomoco (afterwards St. Mary's) Fleet had sent his brother, Edward, "to the Emperor, being three days' journey towards the Falls," on May 26th. Proceeding up the Potomac himself, until within six miles of the Falls, Captain Fleet remained there until the 2d of July, when his brother returned "with the two Indians . . . in which journey they were seven days going and five days coming back to this place. They all did affirm that in one palisade, and that being the last of thirty, there were more than three hundred houses, and in every house forty skins at least, in bundles and piles."

On the 11th of July Fleet received a visit from "seven lusty men, with strange attire," who called themselves Mosticums, but whom Fleet afterwards learned "were of a people three days' journey from there [Mosticum], and were called Herecheenes, who, with their own beaver, and what they got of those who do adjoin upon them, do drive

---

[1] Neill's *Founders of Maryland*, Albany, 1876.

Susquehannock Picture Writing on the Little Indian Rocks.

Susquehannock Picture Writings on the Big Indian Rock.
Big Indian rock is located in the Susquehanna River, about 240 rods below the mouth of Conestoga Creek.

a trade in Cannida at the plantation [of the French], which is fifteen days' journey from this place."

In an interesting article on these passages in Fleet's *Journal*,[1] Mr. Albert S. Gatschet suggests the similarity of the name of one of the Massomack towns, *Tonhoga*, with *Tongoria*, Colden's name for the Eries; and with *Touguenha*, the name of that tribe of whom the Senecas told La Salle in 1669, that they lived on the Ohio River, and of whom Gallinee states that they spake a corrupt Algonquin, meaning, probably, the tribe of the Shawnees. The *Shaunetowa* town of the Massomacks, Gatschet identifies with *Sonnontouan*, or Seneca. Gatschet thought the seven days' journey of Edward Fleet and his Indian guides was toward the country of the Massomacks. This is rather doubtful.

Probably the first Trader settled among the Susquehannocks was Captain William Claiborne, the first Governor of Kent Island, to whom the chiefs of the Susquehanna Indians granted Palmer's Island in the mouth of the Susquehanna River in April or May, 1637.[2] Claiborne had begun trading on Kent Island in 1632, and had associated with him as assistants or partners, George Scouell, Richard Thompson, John Butler, and others. He built a fort and houses on Palmer's Island, but was not permitted to remain there long, his settlement being broken up by order of Lord Baltimore in 1638.

Among other Traders in Chesapeake Bay at this time was Captain Henry Fleet, the Virginian, who as already stated, had been captured by the Indians near the site of Washington in 1621, spent several years among them as a captive, and after his release continued to trade and treat with them until 1644 or later. He was licensed as a Trader in Maryland by Lord Baltimore in 1637 and 1638. His Journal of 1632 is printed in Neill's *Founders of Maryland*. Fleet mentions Charles Harman as being another Indian Trader along the Chesapeake at that time.

James Coughton, Andrew Chappell, and Thomas Morris were also licensed to trade with the Indians in Maryland in 1638.

William Brainthwait was licensed in 1639. He was a Counsellor of the Province and Commander of Kent Island in 1645. Colonel Nathaniel Utie, who had been made a member of the Council in 1657, was licensed as an Indian Trader in 1658. John Bateman was also licensed at the same time. He was made a member of the Council in 1660.

William Hollingsworth was licensed as a Trader in 1659, and again in 1661; John Nuttall, Francis Wright, —— Clanson (Jacob Clauson?), William Calvert, Vincent Atcheson, Captain William Boreman, and Robert Sley, in 1662.

[1] Peet's *American Antiquarian*, iii., 321.
[2] *Proc. Md. Council*, ii., 231.

The licenses of Boreman and Nuttall were renewed in 1663, and additional licenses issued to John Abington, Christopher Birkehead, and Abraham Birkehead. In 1664, George Richardson, Francis Armstrong, and James Jolly were licensed as Traders. John Nuttall's license was renewed in 1665, and John Lumbrozo licensed; John Edmondson and John Pitts, in 1666; Thomas Jones, Peter Groenendyck, and Harman Cornellinson in 1672; and Edward Fitzherbert, in 1673.

The Indian Trader who had, probably, the most intimate knowledge of and the most exciting experience with the early Susquehannocks was a Pennsylvania Dutchman (from Holland), named Jacob Young. In the *Relation* of Garret Van Swearingen concerning the settlement of the Delaware by the Dutch and Swedes, made by him at St. Mary's in 1684, that gentleman states that he (Van Swearingen) was one of the Council and Commissary General for the City of Amsterdam, at New Amstel (now Newcastle) on the Delaware, in the year 1659; and that Jacob Young was then interpreter at that place; and served in that capacity at a meeting between the Dutch authorities and some English deputies who had been sent there from Maryland.

On the 22d of September, 1661, Vice-Director William Beeckman wrote, "in haste," from Altena (or Altona), formerly Fort Christina on the Delaware, to the "Noble, Honorable, Very Worshipful, Wise, Prudent, Discreet Gentlemen," Director Peter Stuyvesant and his Council at New Amsterdam, as follows:

Gentlemen:—I was informed by Mr. Laers, the Swedish priest, yesterday, that his wife had eloped with one Jacop Jongh [Jacob Young], and departed with a canoe during the night, whereupon I have immediately written by an express to the Governor of Maryland and the Magistrate on the Sassafras River, and requested, in case the aforesaid persons might arrive there, to arrest them, and give us notice.

To-day, we learn from one of our Commissaries that Jacop Jongh has had with him a savage from Meggeckosiouw for two or three days; I presume, therefore, that it is more likely that he intends to follow the road of Captain Vuller, and escape by way of Long Island. I believe he has reached the Nevesins in company of Mr. Van Gezel.

A short time ago I delivered to this Jongh about 200 fl. worth of commodities, consisting of blankets, cloth, and other things, to purchase corn and maize for the garrison. He owes me too, on private account, since last winter, six beavers and about 100 fl. in wampum. He traded last year for Mr. d'Hinojossa about 200 schepels of maize. This year he had engaged to trade for us.

On the 26th of October, Beeckman wrote another letter to Director Stuyvesant, in which he said:

On the 24th of September I was at Upland [now Chester] to inquire after the effects of Jacob Jongh. I have found some of our commodities

Susquehannock Picture Writings on the Little Indian Rock.
This rock is located in the Susquehanna River, about 200 rods below the mouth of Conestoga Creek. From photographs taken by Mr. Landis in 1906 and 1907.

in his trunk; I received also from his landlord a certain open letter, wherein this Jongh writes me and specifies what goods and grain he had left for us in his trunk and chamber. But according to this statement we found only about one-fourth of the value. He gave also an order for four hogs, of which only two were acknowledged, the others being reported dead.

I suppose we shall be able to find a guaranty in his landlord, who, on the morning after the said Jongh had decamped during the night, had the audacity (without our knowledge, and in the absence of any Commissary, though some of them live at Upland) to open the room of Jacob Jongh with an axe, and finding the key inside, to examine the chest and everything. He has apparently purloined a part of the commodities. It is said that Jacob Jongh went to New England, for he has not been heard of in Maryland, as I learned from the letter received as answer from the Honble. Philip Calvert. . . .

The Minister, Dominie Laers, has earnestly requested consent by word of mouth on the 15th instant to marry again; he wanted to have the first proclamation (of bans) with a girl of 17 or 18 years made on the 16th, which I delayed until your Honours' approbation.

On the 8th of November, "Mr. Laers asks for advice from your Honble. Worships, whether he may now marry again, as his household requires it."

February 1, 1662, Governor Beeckman writes: "I have examined the case of Jacob Jongh on the 23d December, before the Council meeting. . . . I am afraid that it will prove injurious to Dom. Laers, as it has been partly discovered that he has opened the door with an axe and examined the said Jongh's chest and goods, and made an inventory of them, in the absence of the landlord. This fine priest demanded with great circumstantiality in the above-mentioned meeting a decree of divorce on account of his wife's flight, and received the same, subject to your Honours' approbation, on the 15th December. I have been informed yesterday, that he married himself again last Sunday; an act which, in my opinion (under correction), he has no right to do." Another letter, written May 12th, tells us that, "The Swedish priest, Dom. Laers, has been condemned by the Commissaries on the 14th of April, in the well-known case, to pay the balance of the 200 guilders which had been advanced to Jacob Jongh for account of the Honble. Company for the purchase of grain; also, 40 fl. in beavers which were due to Mr. Decker and me as balance of account with the said Jongh; furthermore, a fine of 40 guilders for usurpation of the authority of the Court. I have told the priest at the meeting to address himself to your Honble. Worships and ask for a decree of divorce, and that in the meantime his new marriage was considered illegal." The proceedings at the Court held by the Commissaries (Cocke, Harnse, and Stille) at Altena, April 14th, appear on the records of New Amsterdam as follows:

Honourable Vice-Director as Sheriff, plaintiff, versus Rev. Laers Carels, defendant:

The plaintiff concludes, as it is of notoriety and acknowledged by defendant, that on the 20th September, 1661, he, Minister Laers, committed the violence, in breaking the room open, and opening the trunk of the fugitive, Jacob Jongh, when said Jongh, the night before, absconded, and made an inventory of his property which he left behind, as is evident by his own handwriting; to which the defendant was not qualified, which ought to have been performed by the Vice Director and the Court; and that he usurped and suspended their authority, and vilified it;

Wherefore, he remains answerable and holden to make compensation to the Company of what was yet due the Company by said absconded Jongh, of which the residue amounts to 200 gl. in corn and 40 gl. in beaver, which is to be delivered; and besides this, a fine of 40 gl. for having vilified authority.

Defendant said, he came at that time to the house of Andreas Hendriessen, Finn, and asked him if his wife was with J. Jongh in his room; when the wife of Andreas, Finn, answered, that she did not know it, that her master might look at it; on which he took an axe and broke the door, and made an inventory of the goods.

The Commissioners having considered the case, command that Rev. Laers shall satisfy the demanded 200 gl., and pay for his insolence.

On the day aforesaid is communicated to aforesaid Rev. Laers Carels, by Vice Director Beeckman, that his marriage is declared null and void, as illegal; as he married himself, which is directly contrary to the orders sanctioned about marriage connections; that he before ought to have demanded and obtained from us the dissolution of his former marriage by letters of divorce, agreeably to the laws of our Fatherland, which ought to have been granted by the Court of Magistrates; and that by a further delay from his side, he shall be prosecuted.

The unfortunate Dominie, who had been not only ravished of his wife but also compelled to pay the ravisher's debts, wrote on the same day his appeal to New Amsterdam. In this he says that "the true state of the case was this: while I was searching for my wife I imagined she was concealing herself in that place, on which I broke it open, but found nothing but a few pairs of stockings, which the fugitive raptor of my wife left behind, of which I made an inventory."

Jacob Young, with the minister's wife, probably fled to the country of the Minquas, near the mouth of the Susquehanna; and he may have kept in the back country until after the Dutch Government was superseded by that of the English; as he afterwards returned to the Delaware, and was living again at Newcastle in 1675.

On August 6, 1676, Governor Notley and his Council wrote to the Governor of Virginia that the Susquehannough Indians, then residing at their "Old Fort, about sixty miles above Palmer's Island" (as distinguished from the New Fort on the Potomac, which they had occupied in the summer and fall of 1675), had come with Edmund Cantwell, Deputy Governor of Newcastle and "Jacob Young, *our old Interpreter*, to the house of Mrs. Margaret Penroy, at the Head of the Bay, near Palmer's Island, and from thence sent to desire a pass to come down to St. Marie's, to treat of a peace with the English in general. . . . We have sent them a safe conduct to come down and treat with us."

On the 22d of January, 1677, Governor Thomas Notley wrote from Wiccomonico, in Maryland, mentioning "the Sennico and Susquehannah Indians, who have had, the beginning of December last, a small encounter at Jacob Young's house." His house or camp, at that time, was probably in Cecil County, near the mouth of the Susquehanna.

In May, 1677, Colonel Henry Coursey was sent to Albany by Governor Notley, as a Commissioner from Maryland to treat with the chiefs of the Five Nations for a peace between them and the Piscataway Indians of Maryland. He wrote the Governor, either from Upland or Shackamaxon on the Delaware River on the 22d: "On the 19th I wrote you from Newcastle. . . . On the 20th came Jacob Young from Maryland. . . . I likewise find a necessity to carry Jacob Young along with me, without whom I can do nothing, and what truth is to be had is from him and none else." Coursey met the Five Nations deputies at Albany in July, and arranged a satisfactory peace. The Onondagas gave their answer to his propositions, promising that they would not in the future injure or do damage to the people of Maryland or Virginia; "but doe acknowledge that we have killed of your Christians and Indians formerly, whereof Jacob Young, als. my friend, was a great occasion thereof. . . . They doe again rehearse that Jacob Young was a great leader and captain against them, whereby the wars have been continued."

At a meeting of the Maryland Council, held June 13, 1678, a letter was read from Augustine Herrman, complaining that the Delaware Indians caused great damage and injury to the inhabitants of Baltimore and Cecil counties by driving away and killing their stock, claiming that the land in the upper part of those counties properly belonged to them. The Council authorized Mr. Herrman and Jacob Young to treat with these Indians, and ascertain what recompense they would require for a quit-claim deed to these lands. Jacob Young was also instructed to go to the Old Susquehannah Fort and treat with the great men of the Sinnequos Nations regarding a rumor that, "by instigation of the remaining part of the Susquehannoghs now amongst them," they designed to come down and make war against the Piscataway Indians of Maryland toward the latter end of the summer.

On the 29th day of August, in the same year, Jacob Young was ordered by the Council to be employed for the purpose of discovering the Indian murderers of the family of David Williams, in Somerset County.

On June 12, 1680, the Governor of New York issued a warrant to Sheriff Cantwell at Newcastle on the Delaware, requiring him to summon Jacob Young to appear personally before the Governor and Council of that Province, to answer for presuming to treat with the Indians in this Government without any authority, to the disturbance thereof.[1]

The Maryland Governor and Council issued a commission to Jacob Young on June 29, 1680, instructing him to lie in wait at the house of Anthony Demondidier for the coming of the Sinniquo Indians, who were expected to send one of their war parties down in July or August, and to let them know that the Proprietor desired to see and speak with some of their great men, and to renew the treaty of peace with them.

The Council met at St. Peter's June 17, 1681. A letter from Col. George Wells was read, dated May 29th, in which he reported that he had "this day received information from Jacob Young that there is about two hundred Sinniquo Indians now upon their voyage down to the Pascattoway Indians, and that they have to their guide the king of the Mattawomans, and intend by presents to draw the Pascattoways with them, but if they cannot, to destroy them where they light of them." A second letter was also read, from William Chandler, dated June 15th, stating that "the Sinniquos is come to Zachajack [Zachaiah] Fort [near the Potomac], and have taken some prisoners that was without the Fort . . . and that they desired to treat with some of the great men of the English."

Jacob Young appeared before the Council at St. Mary's August 22, 1681, accompanied by two Northern Indians, an Onondaga and an Oneida. These Indians, in behalf of their nations, told Lord Baltimore that he should not believe reports against them, circulated by evil minded Indians; that they had come down, to the number of three hundred, for the purpose of making an end of the Piscataways; and that they expected to be before the Zachaiah Fort on the 24th; and desired Jacob Young to accompany them to the Fort, in order to satisfy their party that the English were friendly. Jacob Young was ordered to demand of them what number of warriors they represented, and how many Susquehannohs were among their villages. "They answer, they are in all four forts (vizt.), Anondagoes, who consist of three hundred men; Onneydes, near one hundred and eighty; Quiagoes [Cayugas], three hundred; Mohaukes, als. Maques, at least three hundred; and amongst these four nations are some Susquehannohs, but how many they cannot tell; some are among the right Sinniquos; they believe were they all together they might make about a hundred fighting men; there are fourteen

[1] *Penna. Archives*, Second Series, v., 749; xvi., 339.

Susquehannohs with the Onneydes; seven with the Anondagoes; but the chief of them are among the Quiagoes. They likewise say that another nation, called the Black Mingoes, are joined with the Sinnondowannes, who are the right Sinniquos; that they were so informed by some New York Indians whom they met as they were coming down. They told them that the Black Mingoes, in their way coming to the Sinniquos, were pursued by some Southern Indians, set upon and routed, several of them taken and bound, till the Sinniquos come unto their relief."

On the next day Cols. Henry Coursey and William Stevens were appointed as Commissioners and instructed to proceed with Jacob Young to the Zachaiah Fort and endeavor to make a peace with the Northern Indians. The Journal of the Commissioners was presented to the Council a week later, in which they state that they reached the war party of the Five Nations before Zachaiah Fort and began negotiations with them on the 28th of August; but that before these negotiations were concluded, the Indians decamped during the night.

On May, 1682, Lord Baltimore issued a commission to Henry Coursey, a member of his Council, and Philemon Lloyd, Speaker of the Assembly, appointing them as agents for Maryland, and instructing them to proceed to Albany and effect a peace between the Christians and Indians of Maryland and the Five Nations. One item of the *Instructions* recites that "There hath been some discourse as if those Northern nations would be hired to cut off the remnant of the Susquehannohs. If you find any truth in that, fail not to pursue that point; and purchase the peace of the Province by extinguishing that Viper's Brood, that never fail to kill all English whenever they are the greater number in any party, and make us feel the effects of war, though they live under the shelter of nations that pretend a peace with us." The Commissioners accordingly proceeded to New York, in the early part of June, and reached Albany on the 23d. Here they remained for more than a month, and succeeded in concluding a peace with the Five Nations which would embrace the Piscataways, or Conoys, as well as the Christians of Maryland. On the 4th of August, at the close of the conferences, they were told by the Oneidas:

Since the gentlemen have so earnestly enquired of us what Christians have stirred us up to fight against the Piscataway Indians, we should not have told it if you had not made so sharp enquiry; we do say that about two years ago a troop of ten Oneydes were at the house of Jacob Young, who said unto them, "What do you here so few in number; you may get some mischief; but go home and fetch an army of your people, and warn me ten or twelve days before; we shall all be at arms, and then destroy them [the Piscataways] and deliver them into your hands; for we suffer great damages by these Indians because you make war upon them in our country." Whereupon, he presented us with a roll of Duffles.

This information was made part of the report which the two Commissioners carried back to Maryland, and upon its receipt, Lord Baltimore caused Jacob Young to be arrested. At the first meeting of the next Assembly, held at St. Mary's October 26th, the Proprietor's message informed the House "that some discoveries have been made of the evil practices of Jacob Young, that long disturber of our peace and quiet. I caused him to be apprehended and secured in irons, and do resolve he shall receive his trial this Assembly, that so you may all see the villainy of that ungrateful wretch; who not only hath made a trade of the spoils he received of the Indians that have yearly robbed us, but by their means hath also had the command of any man's life in this Province that he desired to have taken away."

Young's trial for treason by both houses of the legislature followed accordingly. Articles of impeachment were prepared and presented by the Assembly, which were in substance as follows:

1. That Jacob Young had taken to wife an Indian woman of the Susquehannah Nation, by whom he had several children.

2. That in the year 1675, and several other years since, he had given aid, succour, and assistance to the Susquehannahs and other Northern Indians when they were enemies, and in open hostility against the Province.

3. That the said Jacob had oft times declared that the Susquehannahs are an innocent and harmless people, and had not only excused and palliated their spoils and rapines, but had even justified the murders perpetrated by them.

4. That while he had been employed by Baltimore as an Interpreter and to aid in securing peace between the Northern Indians and the Piscataways, yet he had ungratefully and unfaithfully endeavored to keep on foot the animosities between these various tribes.

5. That the said Jacob, because the Piscataways would not assist the Susquehannahs in their late war against Maryland, had made it his business to stir up the Susquehannahs and other Northern Indians to make war upon the Piscataways; and to that end supplied the Susquehannahs and Northern Indians with corn and other provisions.

6. That the said Jacob, since his imprisonment, had threatened to be revenged on those who put him in irons, by means of the influence he had with the Susquehannahs.

Jacob Young presented his answer to these charges on November 15th. He denied having a Susquehanna wife or children, or even being interested in the Susquehanna Nation as against Maryland; and claimed that he did not live in Cecil County in 1675, but inhabited in Delaware until August, 1676, when he received requests from the Maryland Government to accompany the Susquehanna deputies to St. Mary's and to act as Interpreter for them. He said that he had received a letter from the Chancellor on the 29th of November in the same year, enclosing a third safe conduct for himself and the Susquehanna Indians, desiring them to continue at the head of the Bay for four months, until the winter was over and they could treat, and to persuade those of the Susquehannahs who had gone to the Delawares [at Shackamaxon], to return; and that he had received two commissions about the same time to the same effect.

"Pursuant to which orders, letters, and commissions, the said Young, with great hazard of his life, sought out the said Susquehannah Indians and found them, thinking therein that he had served the Lord Proprietary and the people of the Province; and that at that time the Bay was frozen, so that the said Young and Indians could not come down to St. Mary's according to the direction and orders aforesaid, and at that time and no other the said Young did succour and assist the Susquehannah Indians, who destroyed about twenty or thirty barrels of corn, besides meat;

"That the said Young hath likewise orders and instructions under the hand and seal of Coll. Coursey, bearing date the 12th of March, 1677, ordering him, the said Young, to find out and endeavor to speak with the Sinniquo Indians, . . . pursuant to which instructions, the said Young did find out and speak with the said Sinniquo Indians, but not without great hazard of life;

"And whereas, by one other commission, bearing date the 14th day of June, 1678, the said Jacob Young was ordered, that as soon as he should be informed that the Sinniquo Indians were come to the Old Susquehannah Fort, he should repair to them and know from them what their designs tended to; . . .

"And whereas, by one other Order of Council, bearing date 29th of June, 1680, the said Jacob Young was authorized and empowered, at what time he shall be certainly informed the Sinniquo Indians are upon their march, to lie in wait for them . . . and endeavor to speak with the said Indians, and let them know that his Lordship the Lord Proprietary of this Province, is very desirous to speak with the said Indians; . . .

"Which said Order, as well as all the before mentioned commissions, orders, and directions, the said Jacob Young justly, faithfully, and honestly performed. . . . And the said Jacob Young doth aver that the before mentioned letters, commissions, and orders, together with a strong inclination and desire to serve the Lord Proprietary and the good people of this Province were the only inducements that invited the said Jacob Young to come from his habitation in Delaware in the year 1676, and since to inhabit and dwell in this Province."

Mr. Young likewise denied having any knowledge of any robberies or murders committed in the Province by the Susquehannahs since the year 1676; claiming that he had tried in good faith to secure a peace between the Northern Indians and the Piscataways in 1677 and 1681; and that he had never stirred up the Susquehannahs and Sinniquos to make war upon the Maryland Indians; neither had he made threats of his intention to use his influence with the Susquehannahs in order to punish his enemies.

In answer to the charge made against him by the Oneida Indians at Albany, Young denied the imputations against his integrity, and stated that he had only once made them a gift, which was at the time he sent Evans Salisbury, with a present of two match-coats, to the Oneida Indians then staying at the Falls of the Susquehanna, desiring them to come down to Spesutia Island in order to treat with Colonel Wells and Captain Johnson.

The Upper House of the legislature agreed to postpone Young's trial until he could produce his witnesses; but on the 16th, he petitioned the Governor and Council for an immediate trial, agreeing to waive his right to produce witnesses, and giving as his reason that, "being now stricken in years and not able to endure so hard and strict an imprisonment as hitherto he hath suffered by being kept in irons in a room without fire, and all his provision cold before he can have it, all which hardships will now be augmented by a cold approaching winter to the death and destruction of your Petitioner." On the following day a *Relation* of one George Oldfield of Cecil County, was laid before the Assembly, which was to the effect that having been in Upland on the Delaware about the first of October, Lasey Cock, who lived at Schuylkill on the same river, had informed him that the neighboring Indians there, together with the Susquehannahs, who lived amongst them, were very much disturbed about the imprisonment of Jacob Young, and the Susquehannahs told him that whatever could be alleged against Young was false; "that he had always kept them from doing more mischief than they did, or else they would have killed many hundreds more in Maryland than they did; but that they were stopped through his means; and . . . that in case the life of the said Jacob Young be taken away, that they would have 500 lives more for him out of Maryland."

The Council decided to keep Jacob Young in prison until the next meeting of the Assembly. His trial took place on October 13, 1683. The Upper House decided that there was not enough evidence against him to justify taking away his life, but that there was sufficient to warrant his confinement. The Council suggested to the Lower House that a bill of attainder be drawn against the prisoner, and that he be kept confined during the pleasure of the Legislature. To this the Lower House replied that, as they had impeached and prosecuted the case, they did not conceive it fit that they should name the punishment. The Upper House therefore passed judgment on Young October 25th, requiring him to give bond for the penal sum of £1,000 with four sureties in double that amount for his personal appearance at every session of the Assembly to be held in the Province during the term of his natural life, so long as he remained in America, or until discharged by Lord Baltimore and both Houses.

This was cruel and unusual punishment, indeed!

The sheriff took the prisoner into custody again, to be detained until his security was furnished, and the charges and fees of his imprisonment paid. Anne Young, Jacob's wife, on the same day, petitioned the Lower House that it propose some way to satisfy the Sheriff's fees, as her husband's estate was entirely inadequate to do so; and, also, that his bond might be reduced; and his irons taken off. The Lower House gave as its answer, "That if this House can be assured that the said Jacob Young will forthwith depart this Province and go for Holland, or any other part of Europe, and first give good and sufficient security that he will never return into any part of America, that then this House will be willing to contribute toward the payment of his fees."

On November 3d, the Lower House further agreed, that if Young and his sureties would "stand obliged for his immediate transportation for Europe, or be confined to some credible house in this Country for some reasonable time until he can take shipping, not exceeding two months," then the Lower House, with the concurrence of the Upper House, would advance some tobacco toward the payment of Young's fees.

At the next meeting of the Assembly, in April, 1684, a deposition of one William Blankenstein was read, to the effect that Jacob Young was so sick and weak, "being all over his body broken out with boils and sores, that he is altogether uncapable of going or being carried upon any journey or voyage without apparent danger of his life." The House accepted Young's excuse for not appearing at that meeting of the Assembly.

The Assembly *Journals* for the next four years have not been preserved, and we cannot learn how Jacob Young escaped transportation; but that he did so and continued to live in Maryland for more than ten years thereafter, is apparent from the later records.

On the 10th of June, 1687, George Talbot, a connection of Baltimore's, deeded to Jacob Young a tract of land called "Clayfall," in Cecil County, in consideration for the "iron work of a Swedes' mill, 200 young apple trees now growing near the present dwelling-house of the said Young, and . . . ye seat of a mill that he formerly caused to be built at the head of Piny Creek, vulgarly called Mill Creek." This mill was on the stream still known as Mill Creek, near the village of Port Deposit; and it is probable that Jacob Young had settled at the head of that creek a number of years before.

Among the papers relating to the Maryland Associators' Assembly of 1689, still preserved, is an order concerning Jacob Young and the Indians, issued by that Assembly August 28, 1689. This recites that, "forasmuch as several overtures have been made by some of our late great officers and others popishly affected within this Province, to the Northern Indians, for the ruin and destruction of their Majesties' Protestant subjects here . . . ; and whereof, Jacob Young, formerly employed by this Province in affairs of this nature, as well-known and skilled in the language and customs of the said Indians, hath been deemed by this House a person most fit and capable to negotiate in the present juncture; . . . Voted and ordered in this House that immediate notice be hereby given to the said Jacob Young . . . to repair to this Assembly, if the same be then sitting or else to Captain John Cood or Nehemiah Blackiston at their houses in or near Pottomock River. . . . Hereby granting, promising, and assuring to the said Jacob Young, free and safe conduct, . . . speedy and effectual redress to all his just grievances and complaints, . . . and, also, full and sufficient satisfaction for his pains, trouble, and charge herein to be taken, sustained, and expended."

On May 30, 1690, Jacob Young wrote Captain Coode, sending him a report on Indian affairs at the head of the Bay. He says: "I have no great matter any further than at this time there is at my house 14 Cenockoes [Senecas] . . . these Cenockoes came from their own country about the last of April last past; their intent is to settle among the Susquahanough Indians here, upon the Susquahanough River, for there is some of every Fort of the Cenockes[1] come down to them, and they tell me that their great men will be down very shortly."

On May 26, 1692, Jacob Young was called before Governor Copley and the Council and asked to give his opinion about the strange Indians he had seen at the Piscataway Fort. "He declares them to be Sinequos, some of them to his knowledge have been out and stragglers this four or five years . . . but . . . the best and most certain intelligence can be expected, must be from Albany, for he can get nothing out of our

[1] As already stated, the Marylanders applied the name "Seneca" to any one or all of the Five Nations, indiscriminately.

Indians." At this meeting of the Council it was recorded that, "In consideration of many good services Mr. Jacob Young has done and performed to this Province, and his readiness always therein, also how much further serviceable he may yet be in the present juncture; Resolved, That the same may be by this Board recommended to the Assembly at the next laying the levy, and a suitable sum proposed for a gratuity to be made to the said Jacob Young. Power given also to JacobYoung to press boats and hands, &c., as by a former order of the Convention, April the 10th, 1692."

In a commission issued by Governor Copley to Thomas Blake and Casparus Herman, March 9, 1693, to treat with a party of strange Indians lately seated at the head of the Bay (the Shawnees from the South), the Commissioners were instructed "to persuade or press, and bring with you [to St. Mary's] Captain Jacob Young, of Cecil County, the ancient Interpreter, formerly and generally employed by the Government of this Province in such cases of treating with Foreign Indians." A warrant was also issued to Captain Young to attend and interpret for the Commissioners in treating with the "strange Indians lately seated on the said Herman's land" (Bohemia Manor). At a meeting of the Council held at St. Mary's April 11th, Captain Young accordingly appeared, with Colonel Herman, a Susquehannoh, the king of the Stabbernowle or Southern Indians, and one "Martin Shortive," a Frenchman who had come into the Province with the Strange Indians. An account of this conference will be given in the chapter on the Shawnees.

On October 17, 1695, "Came and appeared in Council Jacob Young and William York, living upon Susquehanna River, and its being proposed in Council the keeping a ferry and ordinary [an inn] upon each side the said River, William York on this [the western] side and Jacob Young on the other side, for which is settled upon them, one shilling sixpence for the passage of a horse and man, and one shilling for a footman, to which they both agreed . . . ordered, that the Justices of the County Courts where they live grant them license accordingly, they giving bond as the law in that case directs."

On January 25, 1796, the Council issued an order to William York and Jacob Young, persons authorized and appointed to keep a publichouse and ferry on each side the Susquehanna River, instructing them to "transport or ferry no person whatsoever over the said River but what shall come with good and legal passes; and that they take up all suspected persons travelling that way without such passes, and carry them before the next Justice of Peace."

This is the last appearance of Jacob Young's name on the records of Maryland Province. It is to be hoped that he passed peacefully the remainder of his days as an inn-keeper and ferryman at the mouth of the river on whose shores he had experienced so many vicissitudes during his long and eventful life as an Indian Trader.

Unlike the Indian trade in Maryland, which was in the hands of individual Traders, the most of whom were licensed by the Governor, the trade of the Swedish and Dutch colonies on the Delaware with the Indians, was largely in the hands of the Companies which had planted those colonies, and the natives were induced to come all the way to the forts with their peltries to trade.

In the *Report* of Governor Johan Printz, of New Sweden, for 1647, he writes:

"The Fort in Skylenkyll [Schuylkill], called Karsholm, is pretty nearly ready. . . . Further, to prejudice the trade of the Hollanders, I have built a fine house (called *Wasa*), on the other side of Karsholm, by the Road of the Minquas, so strong that four or five men, well provided with guns, balls, and powder, will be able to defend themselves there against the savages; seven freemen, sturdy fellows, have settled in that place. Again, a quarter of a mile [the Swedish mile is equal to 6.625 English miles] higher up, by the said Minquas' Road, I have built another strong house, five freemen settling there. This place I have called *Mondal*. . . . Now, when the great traders, the Minquas, travel to the Dutch trading place or house, Nassau [on the east bank of the Delaware], they are obliged to pass by those two places, which (please God) hereafter shall be provided with cargoes.

"Concerning trade, in the year 1644, when the ship *Fama* went from here, there was very little of the cargo left in store; and, as no cargo has been received since, not only has the Right Honorable Company suffered the great damage of losing 8,000 or 9,000 beavers, which have passed out of our hands, but also the Hollanders have moved the principal traders (the White and Black Minquas) to forsake us; and we shall not, without great difficulty, regain them. But, as soon as this vessel arrived, I dispatched Commissary Hindrick Hughen, with the Sergeant Gregorious van Dyk and eight soldiers, to the country of the Minquas, five German miles [equal to about twenty English miles] from hence, offering them all sorts of presents, by which means they were induced to negotiate, and we received assurance from them that they would trade with us as before. . . . If we are able to renew our friendly relations with the White and Black Minquas (as we are assured and may hope we shall) the trade with these will commence next April, and continue the whole summer until fall."

The *Report* of Andries Hudde, Commissary on the Delaware for the Dutch West India Company, dated November 1, 1645, gives the

Dutch view of the Swedish efforts to push their trade among the Minquas. He says:

"Further up the [Delaware] River about three miles, on the west shore, on a Creek called the Minquas Creek, so-named as it runs near the Minquas' Land, is another [Swedish] Fort named Christina. . . . In regard to the Schuylkill. . . . He [Governor Printz] . . . constructed there a Fort on a very convenient spot. . . . This Fort cannot, in any manner whatever, obtain any control on the [Delaware] River, but it has command over the whole [Schuylkill] Creek, while this Kill or Creek is the only remaining avenue for trade with the Minquas, and without this trade the River is of little value. At a little distance from this Fort was a Creek to the furthest distant wood, which place is named Kingsessing by the savages, which was before a certain and invariable resort for trade with the Minquas, but which is now opposed by the Swedes having there built a strong house."

In the *Journal* kept by Augustine Herrman of the "Dutch Embassy to Maryland," Mr. Herrman relates, under date of October 4, 1659, that his party sailed or rowed over the Severn River, on the western shore of Maryland, and lodged at the house of the father-in-law of Godtfried Harmer, the Indian Trader.

On November 11, 1665, after the English had captured New Amsterdam, Governor Richard Nicolls issued a trading license to Peter Alricks, of New York, permitting him to traffic with the Indians in and about Hoare Kills, in Delaware Bay.

On January 3, 1671, Governor Francis Lovelace, of New York granted a license to Mrs. Susanna Garland, "to trade to Delaware." On the 10th of March, 1672, the Governor issued a certificate to John Garland, stating that he had given "unto him or Susanah, his wife, a license to trade or traffic with the Indians at the Whorekill, or any other parts at Delaware."

The succession of the Conestoga chiefs from the time of their first treaty with William Penn seems to have been as follows:

Kekelappan of Opasiskunk, on October 10, 1683, deeded to Penn, "that half of all my lands betwixt Susquehanna and Delaware, which lyeth on ye Susquehanna side."

Machaloha, October 18, 1683, deeded to William Penn the lands between the Delaware and Susquehanna, from Chesapeake Bay to Susquehanna Falls.

There is nothing on the records to show the nationality of either of these chiefs, beyond what may be inferred from the location of the lands they purported to convey.

Connoodaghtoh, king, or chief sachem of the Susquehanna Indians, with Widaagh (alias Oretyagh), Koqueeash, and Andaggy-junkquagh (or Ojunco), chiefs, signed a treaty of peace and alliance with William Penn, April 23, 1701. Widaagh and Andaggy-junkquagh "kings or sachemas," had executed a deed to Penn some seven months earlier, conveying to him their lands on the Susquehanna.

Widaagh, or Oretyagh, with Kyanharre, both chiefs of the Conestogas, attended a conference at Philadelphia in July, 1694. Six years later, as already stated, Oretyagh and Ojunco, another Conestoga chief, conveyed to William Penn all the lands of the Conestogas on both sides of the Susquehanna. In October, 1701, Oretyagh came to Philadelphia with some of his people, and some Shawnees, to take leave of William Penn before his final departure for England. In May, 1704, Oretyagh is referred to in the Minutes of the Provincial Council, as "ye chief, now, of Conestogoe." Connoodaghtoh had evidently died since the time of the treaty of 1701.

Chief Andaggy-junkquagh, or Ojunco, visited Philadelphia June 4, 1706, and September 21, 1710. On the latter occasion he accompanied the "Queen," Connoodaghtoh's widow, who is recorded as having sent friendly messages to the Council from Conestoga as early as February, 1708. In 1711, she sent a message, desiring the Governor to visit Conestoga. This chieftainess is mentioned in July, 1712, as "the old Queen, Conguegos." On October 1, 1714, the Conestogas informed the Governor that "their old queen was dead."

Thomas Chalkley, a member of the Society of Friends, who travelled extensively in America during the first decade of the eighteenth century, visited the Conestoga Indians in 1706, and met their queen. The following description of his visit is given in Chalkley's *Journal:* "When I was travelling in those parts [Nottingham Township, Chester County, Pennsylvania], I had a conceit on my mind to visit the Indians near Susquehannah at Conestogoe. . . . We got an interpreter, and thirteen or fourteen of us travelled through the woods about fifty miles. . . . When we came, they received us kindly. . . . We treated about having a meeting with them in a religious way, upon which they called a council, in which they were very grave, and spoke one after another, without any heat or jarring. And some of the most esteemed of their women do sometimes speak in council. Our interpreter told me that they had not done anything for many years without the counsel of an ancient, grave woman, who, I observed spoke much in their council; for I was permitted to be present at it; and I asked what it was the woman said. He told me she was an empress; and they gave much heed to what she said among them. Here were two nations of them, the Senecas [Conestogas] and Shawanese. We had first a meeting with the Senecas." The Queen's counsel to her tribe was, to receive and welcome the missionaries, as they came on a good errand.

The Site of the Conestoga Indian Town Occupied from 1693 (or earlier) to 1763.
From a photograph taken by the Author in September, 1909.

Possibly one of the Conestoga chiefs of 1701 was the husband of "Queen Alliquippa," whom George Washington visited at the mouth of the Youghiogheny December 30, 1753.[1] On the 10th of June, 1754, Washington wrote to Governor Dinwiddie from his camp at Great Meadows: "Queen Alliquippa desired that her son, who is really a great warrior, might be taken into Council; as she was declining, and unfit for business; and that he should have an English name given him. I therefore called the Indians together, by the advice of Half-King, presented one of the medals, and desired him to wear it in remembrance of his great father, the King of England; and called him by the name of Colonel Fairfax, which he was told signified, 'the First in Council.' This gave him great pleasure." The son's name is variously given as Canachquasy, Cashuwayon, Kanuksusy, Ah Knoyis, Kosshoweyha, Cashiowayah, and Cashunyon.[2] He first appears in the colonial history of Pennsylvania as Canachquasy, the leader of a band of ten young Mingo warriors, whom he conducted from Kuskuskies to Philadelphia, arriving there November 11, 1747; and bringing the first authentic news from the West of the operations of the French in that quarter. In his speech to the Pennsylvania Council on this occasion, he stated that he and his companions were "of the Six Nations." He spent the winter of 1747-48 with the Nanticoke Indians, in their village at the mouth of the Juniata. In November, 1753, his name appears as one of the Mohawk chiefs, "now entrusted with the conduct of public affairs among the Six Nations."[3] At a meeting of the Council in Philadelphia, August 15, 1755, Governor Morris publicly thanked him, as one of the seven Indian chiefs who fought under General Braddock.[4] At a meeting of the Council held one week later, the Governor, "addressing himself to Kanuksusy, the son of Old Allaguipas, whose mother was now alive and living near Raystown, desired him to hearken; for he was going to give him an English name. 'In token of our affection for your parents, and in expectation of your being a useful man in these perilous times, I do, in the most solemn manner, adopt you, by the name of New Castle; and order you to be called hereafter by that name; which I have given you, because, in 1701, I am informed, that your parents presented you to the late Mr. William Penn, at Newcastle." Captain Newcastle died at Philadelphia of the small-pox, in November, 1756, after more

[1] See Chapter XIV.
[2] *Penna. Col. Rec.*, v., 146, 166, 212, 222; vi., 524, 588; vii., 6, 108; *Archives*, Second Series, ii., 600.
[3] *Penna. Col. Rec.*, v., 685.
[4] The names of the seven, as given in *Penna. Col. Rec.*, vi., 524, were Scarrooyady (or Skirooniata, or Scruneyattha, or Monacatoocha, or Great Arrow), Cashuwayon (New Castle), Kahuktodon, Attschechokatha, Froson, Kashwughdaniunte (or, the Belt of Wampum), and Dyioquario.

than a year's arduous and perilous duties as a messenger and spy for the Governor among the hostile tribes of the Upper Susquehanna.[1] His mother, Queen Alliquippa, is sometimes alluded to in contemporary and later records as a woman of the Delaware tribe; but this she was not.[2] On August 27, 1748, Conrad Weiser, on his way to Logstown, dined with her at her "Seneka town, where an old Seneka woman reigns with great authority." She was probably a Mohawk, for the son is mentioned as a chief of that tribe, in a list furnished by Conrad Weiser to the Pennsylvania Government about the first of November, 1753. Celoron also speaks of passing her town on his journey down the Ohio, August 7, 1749. "I re-embarked," he writes, "and visited the village which is called the 'Written Rock' [McKee's Rock, on the opposite side of the Ohio from where Alliquippa lived in 1752]. The Iroquois inhabit this place, and it is an old woman of this nation who governs it. She regards herself as sovereign; she is entirely devoted to the English." Alliquippa remained here until after May 30, 1752, on which date she was visited by the Virginia Commissioners Patton, Fry, and Lomax, on their way to treat with the Indians at Logstown. Her town was known as Lequeepees Town by the Pennsylvania Traders as early as 1731.[3] She lived at the mouth of the Youghiogheny when Washington visited her in December, 1753; and fled from there to the vicinity of Raystown (Bedford) after the defeat of Washington at Great Meadows in 1754.[4]

Sotayriote is mentioned as chief of the Conestogas at conferences which he attended at Philadelphia, in October, 1714; September, 1715; and July, 1716.

Taghuttalesse, Togatolessa, Tagodrancey, Togodhessah, or Civility, appears on the Pennsylvania records as "the Senneques' King," June 8, 1710; and on July 23, 1712, as a "War Captain and Chief." In June, 1713, he is spoken of as "the young Indian called Civility, now one of their chiefs." In October, 1714, he informed Governor Gookin of the death of the old queen of the Conestogas, "Conguegos," whom Thomas Chalkley had met at the Conestoga Town in 1706. In June, 1715, Civility is referred to in connection with Sotayoght, or Sotayriote, as "the chiefs of the Conestogoes." July 30, 1716, Sotayriote is called the chief, and Civility the captain, of the Conestogas. In June, 1718,

---

[1] See *Penna. Col. Rec.*, vii., 137–141; *Archives*, ii., 727.

[2] "Paxinosa, the Shawonese chief, interpreter for the Delawares, because Newcastle talks good Shawonese, and Paxinosa talks good Delaware."—Minutes of a Council at Tioga Point, May, 1756. *Penna. Col. Rec.*, vii., 139. Mr. James Mooney is the latest authoritative writer to repeat this error.

[3] *Penna. Archives* i., 301.

[4] Governor Morris, as stated above, announced that Queen Alliquippa was living in August, 1755. George Croghan wrote the Governor from Aughwick, Dec. 23, 1754, "Alequeapy, ye old Queen is dead, and left several children."—*Penna. Archives*, ii., 218.

Civility visited Philadelphia again, at which time he was called "the present chief or captain of the Conestogas." He then took with him Oneshanayan, "a near relative of their former king, whom they had lost in war, sometime before the Governor's arrival" in Pennsylvania, (Governor Keith arrived in 1717); and also, Soohavesse, or Sohais, the son of Connoodaghtoh or Conedechto, their king in 1701. Captain Civility then informed Governor Keith that the Conestogas had chosen Oneshanayan[1] to be their new king. Their visit to Philadelphia was repeated in July, 1720; and soon after that Civility seems to have become the ruling chief among the Conestogas; although in a conference held at their town May 26, 1728, Tawenna and two others are recorded with Civility as the chiefs of the Conestogas.

Tawenna had been present at conferences in Philadelphia between the Conestogas and William Penn in 1700–1701.

Another queen of the Conestogas is mentioned in the Minutes of a conference held at their town June 29, 1719, in the person of "Canatowa, Queen of the Mingoes."

Captain Civility's name disappears from the records for some years after 1731; but at a Council held with Thomas Penn at Philadelphia, some eighteen Iroquois chiefs informed him on October 14, 1736, that Civility of Conestoga had no power from them to sell any lands.

Tiorhaasery, a chief of the Conestogas, "that speak the Oneidas' language," represented his tribe at the Philadelphia conference of 1742, and at the Lancaster conference of 1744.

Some of the Conestoga tribe began moving up the Susquehanna Valley again as early as 1715. On Evans's maps of 1749 and 1755 a Conestoga Indian Fort is located near the mouth of Tiadachton (Lycoming) Creek, on the West Branch. This, however, may have been the site of one of their towns in the seventeenth century, and abandoned or destroyed during their wars with the Five Nations. It is probable that Queen Alliquippa, her son, and some of their people emigrated from Conestoga to the vicinity of what is now Bedford, Penna., and thence to the Allegheny Valley, before 1731.

Sohais, or Shahaise, son of Connoodaghtoh (the chief who signed the treaty with William Penn in 1701), appears as their chief in May, 1758, at which time a number of the tribe were reported to have gone to join the French. The members of the tribe living at Conestoga in 1763 were murdered in that year by the "Paxtang Boys."[2]

[1] The similarity of this name to "Cashunyon," one of the names given to Captain Newcastle, by Governor Morris in a passport issued to him in April, 1756, raises the question, whether or not the two individuals were identical.

[2] *Penna. Col. Rec.*, viii., 117, 122. According to a tract issued by Franklin at that time, Sohais or Shahaise was one of the victims.

Some recent writers on the Indian history of the Lower Susquehanna Valley have made erroneous statements to the effect that the Andastes or Minquas were entirely exterminated by the Iroquois in their wars which concluded in 1676. In their report on this subject (published in 1898) a committee of the Dauphin County Historical Society goes so far as to say: "At the time of the coming of William Penn, it is supposed there were scarcely half a dozen families [of the Susquehannocks] in existence, on the western borders of Maryland, where they had taken refuge. . . . In 1682 there was not one of the Susquehannocks dwelling on their ancient seats. Some few vagabond families of the Iroquois, however, remained, occupying the deserted towns of their conquered enemy. These were the individuals representing themselves as Conestogas; not by blood, but simply by occupation." Perhaps a sufficient refutation of this assumption has already been printed on a preceding page, in the report of Governor Keith to the Pennsylvania Council that the Conestoga Indians "actually pay tribute to the Five Nations." Before that date, James Logan had reported to the Council (June 20, 1721) the results of an interview held with the Conestogas at their town, regarding the claim of the Five Nations to their lands on the Susquehanna, in which he speaks of the Conestoga chief, Civility, as "a descendant of the ancient Susquehannah Indians, but now reputed as of Iroquois descent."

It has already been stated that the Susquehannocks, ancestors of these Conestoga Indians, were of a tribe known to the French as the Andastes or Gantastogues; and to the Dutch and Swedes as Minquas, or Mengwe. Under the latter name, Heckewelder, the Moravian missionary who lived among the Ohio Delawares during and after the time of the Revolutionary War, describes the Susquehannocks as the traditional enemies of the Delawares; and in that fabrication so largely the product of his own imagination, by him called a "History of the Indian Nations," Heckewelder details at some length the imaginary wanderings and wars of the Lenni Lenape (Delawares) and the Mengwe, on their way to the East from some remote place beyond the Mississippi. In Heckewelder's day, the name, "Mengwe," then generally called "Mingo," was applied to the New York Iroquois of the Five Nations, and as a rule to those of the Seneca tribe, living on or near the waters of the Ohio—the descendants of those who had subdued the Susquehannocks or early Mingoes, and who, without a conquest, had "made women" of the Delawares. But the Mengwe or Mingoes who first subdued and terrified the Delawares in the seventeenth century, were their own near neighbors on the west. They were those of Iroquois stock, known as Susquehannocks at the time when the Delawares themselves lived along both banks of the stream from which they took their English name. The absurdly exaggerated traditions of the Delaware Indians as related by Heckewelder, therefore, may have contained a germ of truth in so far as they were founded on the actual contests which really took place along the Delaware River between the Susquehannocks and the Lenni Lenape in Captain John Smith's time, and later.

Before passing from the subject of this chapter, another Iroquoian tribe which lived in Pennsylvania near the Susquehanna for a number of years, will be noticed.

These Indians were the Tuscaroras, who came to Pennsylvania from North Carolina.

In September, 1711, five hundred warriors, principally Tuscaroras, but including Indians from every tribe in North Carolina, assembled at Hancock's Town on the Cotechney, in that State, and having dispersed themselves in small bands through the white settlements, fell upon the planters on the morning of the 22d, and began a wholesale massacre of men, women, and children. They killed 130 persons within a few hours, and continued their work of murder and rapine for three days, finally returning to their Fort on the Cotechney with eighty women and children as captives. Colonel John Barnwell was given command of a body of militia, consisting of fifty white men and 366 Indians from South Carolina (Cherokees, Catawbas, Creeks, and Yamassees). He marched against the hostile Indians, and about the first of February, 1712, attacked them near New Bern, killing three hundred and taking more than a hundred prisoners. Later, he was re-inforced by 250 whites and together they made an attack on the Cotechney Fort (near the site of Snow Hill); but were driven off. A truce ensued, and the Indian auxiliaries of North Carolina withdrew. In December, before the truce had expired, Colonel James Moore arrived on the Neuse River from South Carolina, with a new army from that Colony, consisting of thirty-three whites and a thousand friendly Indians. The hostile Indians proceeded to fortify themselves in two strongholds—one, Cohunche on the Cotechney, and the other, Fort Nohoroco.[1] On March 20, 1713, Colonel Moore invested the latter fort, and subdued it after three days' vigorous fighting. His loss in killed and wounded was forty-six whites and ninety-one friendly Indians, while he took 392 prisoners and 192 scalps, and reported 200 more killed and burned within the Fort, and 166 killed or taken outside the Fort.

This attack broke the power of the Tuscaroras in the South forever, and they sued for peace, delivering up twenty of their chief men to Colonel Moore as hostages.[2]

As a result of this war, most of the Tuscaroras were forced to leave

[1] Ashe, *History of North Carolina*, i., 182.
[2] *Va. State Papers*, i., 165.

North Carolina. At their own request they were taken under the protection of the Five Nations; and some years later joined that Confederacy and lived in New York.

Historians generally have given the date of the removal of the Tuscaroras to New York as the years 1713 and 1714, immediately following their punishment by Colonel Moore.

As a matter of fact they began to move northward into Virginia and Pennsylvania as early as 1710, but did not seat themselves in New York until some ten years later. On the 16th of June in the year 1710, Governor Gookin laid before the Pennsylvania Council the minutes of a conference held at Conestoga by Col. John French and Henry Worley, eight days before, at which there were present Iwaagenst, Terrutawanaren, and Teonnottein, chiefs of the Tuscaroras, Civility, "the Seneques King," and four chiefs more of that [the Conestoga] nation, and Opessa, the Shawnee king.

The Indians were told that according to their request we were come from the Governor and Government, to hear what proposals they had to make anent a peace, according to the purport of their embassy from their own people.

They signified to us by a belt of wampum, which was sent from their old women, that those implored their friendship of the Christians and Indians of this Government, that without danger or trouble they might fetch wood and water.

The second belt was sent from their children born, and those yet in the womb, requesting that room to sport and play, without danger of slavery, might be allowed them.

The third belt was sent by their young men fit to hunt, that privilege to leave their towns and seek provision for their aged might be granted without fear of death or slavery.

The fourth was sent from the men of age, requesting that the wood, by a happy peace, might be as safe for them as their forts.

The fifth was sent from the whole Nation, requesting peace, that thereby they might have liberty to visit their neighbors.

The sixth was sent by the kings and chiefs, desiring a lasting peace with the Christians and Indians of this Government, that thereby they might be secured against those fearful apprehensions [of being sold into slavery—the frequent fate of the Tuscarora children] they have for these several years felt.

The seventh was sent in order to intreat a cessation from murdering and taking them, that by the allowance thereof they may not be afraid of a mouse or any other thing that ruffles the leaves.

The eighth was sent to declare, that as being hitherto strangers to this place, they now came as people blind, no Path nor communication being betwixt us and them; but now they hope we will take them by the hand and lead them, and then they will lift up their heads in the woods without danger or fear.

These belts (they say) are only sent as an introduction, and in order to break off hostilities till next Spring, for then their kings will come and sue for the peace they so much desire.

We acquainted them that . . . it would be very necessary to procure a certificate from the Government they leave to this, of their good behavior, and then they might be assured of a favorable reception.

The Seneques [Conestogas] return their hearty thanks to the Government for their trouble in sending to them, and acquainted us that by advice of a Council amongst them, it was determined to send these belts brought by the Tuscaroroes, to the Five Nations.

Pursuant to your Honour's and Council's orders, we went to Conestogo, where the forewritten contents were by the chiefs of the Tuscaroroes to us delivered; the sincerity of their intentions we cannot anywise doubt, *since they are of the same race and language with our Seneques* [Conestogas] who have always proved trusty, and have also for these many years been neighbors to a Government [North Carolina or Virginia] jealous of Indians, and yet not displeased with them.

At a meeting of the New York Council, held July 3, 1712, it was reported that the Tuscaroras were willing to settle among the Esopus Indians. The Council decided, however, that the Tuscaroras might "conditionally settle beyond the Blue Hills."

On January 25, 1720, Governor Alexander Spotswood, of Virginia, wrote the President of the New York Council concerning Indian affairs, and called attention to the depredations committed by the war parties of the Five Nations on the frontiers of Virginia. "In the years 1712 and 1713," he writes, "they were actually in these parts, assisting the Tuscarouroes, who had massacred in cold blood some hundreds of the English, and were then warring against us, and they have, at this very day, the chief murderers, with the greatest part of that Nation, seated under their protection near Susquehannah River, whither they removed them when they found they could no longer support them against the force which the English brought upon them in these parts."

On September 1, 1722, in a conference held by Governor Burnet with the Five Nations, at Albany, the speaker for the Indians told the Governor: "Three companies of our people are gone out to fight against the Flat-heads who have been our enemies for a long time. There are also two French Indians that lived in Cadarachqui, that went out a-fighting two years ago towards Virginia by way of Cayouga, and have their abode among *the Tuscarores that live near Virginia*, and go backwards and forwards."

Governor Spotswood, with a member of his Council and a Deputy from the House of Burgesses, was present in Albany at this time, and held three conferences with the Five Nations' chiefs, from August 29th to September 12th. The Iroquois addressed him as "Brother Assarigoe, the name of the Governors of Virginia, which signifies a Simeter or

Cutlas, which was given to the Lord Howard, anno. 1684, from the Dutch word, *Hower*, a Cutlas." They agreed to his proposition that their war parties, in passing through Virginia, should not pass the Potomac, nor the Great Ridge of mountains extending along the frontiers of Virginia back of the settled portion. They then added: "Brother Assarigoe: As you engaged for ten Nations, so do we, viz., for the Five Nations, and for the Tuskarores, Conestogoes, Chuanoes [Shawnees], Ochtaghquanawic-roones,[1] and Ostanghaes [2] which live upon Susquehana River." At the close of the conference on September 6th, "the Speaker of the Five Nations holding up the Coronet, they gave six shouts, five for the Five Nations, and one for a Castle of Tuscarores, *lately* seated between Oneyde and Onondage." After the conclusion of this treaty, Governor Burnet received in his chambers, on September 14th, "the ten chiefs of the Five Nations, being two from each, together with two others, said to be from the Tuscororoes."

The residence of the Tuscaroras in Pennsylvania for a greater part of the period between 1713 and 1722 must have been in those places where their name has been preserved, from that time to this. These places are indicated by the names, Tuscarora Mountain, which divides Franklin and Perry counties from Fulton, Huntingdon, and Juniata; by Tuscarora Path Valley (now Path Valley) in the western part of Franklin County at the eastern base of Tuscarora Mountain; and by Tuscarora Creek, which runs through the valley between Tuscarora and Shade mountains, this valley forming the greater part of Juniata County of the present day. In these places and their vicinity the Tuscaroras must have lived while in Pennsylvania; and the Tuscarora Path marks the route of their journeyings to and fro between North Carolina and Virginia on the south, and Pennsylvania and New York on the north.

They were certainly living in the Tuscarora Valley in 1762.[3]

Revs. Charles C. Beatty and George Duffield were in Tuscarora Valley in August, 1766, where they found eighty-four families of settlers living, who informed them that the valley was "about thirty-two miles in length, between six and seven miles broad in the middle, and about ten miles wide at the lower end, next to Juniata River." Mr. A. L. Guss, a resident of this valley and a first-rate authority on the early Indian history of interior Pennsylvania, has given a very full account of the supposed residence of the Tuscaroras in this and the neighboring valleys, in the first volume of Ellis's *History of the Susquehanna and*

---

[1] O'Callaghan and Beauchamp located the *Ochtaghquanawic-roones* at Oghquaga, in the present Broome County, New York.

[2] O'Callaghan thought the *Ostanghaes* were the Indians of Otzinachson, on the West Branch, above Shamokin; Beauchamp says the Delawares are meant.

[3] *Penna. Col. Rec.*, viii., 722.

The Iroquoians of the Susquehanna 87

Juniata Valleys. He locates an Indian village site in the present township of Beale, Juniata County.

A short distance west of the upper part of the Tuscarora Valley, and beyond Shade and Black Log mountains was the former Indian town of *Aughwick* (now the site of Shirley), on the creek of the same name. On the site of this old Indian Town, George Croghan settled when he was forced by impending bankruptcy to leave the Cumberland Valley in 1753. Croghan wrote of the place as "Aucquick Old Town," and "Aughick Old Town." Richard Peters wrote the name "Aucquick" in 1750; Governor Hamilton, "Auckquick" in 1754; and Charles Beatty, "Aughweek" in 1766. Heckewelder, whose authority is doubtful, said it was corrupted from a Delaware term, *Ach-week*, signifying brushy, or overgrown with brush. Zeisberger gives this term as *Acheweu* ("bushy"), which is far from Aughwick. The Moravian *Lenape-English Dictionary* gives *Achewen*, meaning "bushy," but the Lenape editor of that work expresses a doubt as to the correctness of the term. Beauchamp spells it "*Ach-wick*," and gives the meaning as "brushwood fishing-place."

While the name is evidently Algonquin, could the place itself have been a former town of the Tuscaroras?

NOTE.—After the types were set for this chapter, the publication, in Dr. Clayton Hall's *Narratives of Early Maryland* (New York, October, 1910), of a conference held between William Penn and Col. George Talbot in 1683, establishes conclusively the fact that Maryland's conquest of the Susquehannocks, referred to on page 55 of this volume, was the conquest of September and October, 1675, at the time of the siege of the Susquehannocks' Potomac Fort. The original manuscript account of this conference is in possession of the Maryland Historical Society, and it had already been printed in the *Maryland Historical Magazine* (iii., 21), before its publication in Dr. Hall's book. At this conference, Penn referred at length to the 1675 conquest of the Susquehannocks, by reason of which Maryland laid claim to the territories of that tribe.

CHAPTER III

THE PETTICOAT INDIANS OF PETTICOAT LAND

OF the Delaware or *Lenape* (*i.e.*, "a man of our tribe") Indians, according to the Moravian accounts (which must be taken with allowances, when written by Heckewelder), there seem to have been three principal clans, sub-tribes, or totems, namely: those of the Turtle totem, or the Unamis (*i.e.*, "people down the River"), who were the most enlightened, socially and politically; those of the Turkey totem, or the Wanamis or Unalachtigoes ("people living near the sea"); and those of the Wolf totem, or the Minsis ("people of the stony country"; sometimes corrupted to Muncies, or Monseys). Charles Thomson, the teacher of a Quaker school in Philadelphia, and afterwards Secretary of the first Continental Congress, in his book on the *Alienation of the Delawares and Shawanese* (1759), classifies the three Delaware clans as the Lenopi, the Wanami, and the Minisinks, or Munseys.[1]

The first chiefs of the Delaware River Indians whose names appear on record seem to have been Quesquakous, Ensanques, and Sickonesyns, who, at Manhattan Island, on the 30th day of July, 1630, executed a deed ratifying a sale of land made by them on the first of June of the preceding year, to Samuel Godyn. The land lay on the south (west) side of South River (Delaware) Bay, "extending in length from Cape Hindlop to the mouth of said [South, or Delaware] River, about eight large miles [Dutch long miles, equal to about 45 English miles] and landwards half a mile [2.8 miles]."

On May 5, 1631, Sannoowouno, Wiewit, Pemhacke, Mekowetick, Teehepeuwya, Mathemen, Sacoock, Anehoopoen, Janqueno, and Poka-

[1] In the Appendix to Jefferson's *Notes on Virginia*, Thomson divides them into five clans, as follows: (1) The Chihohocki, who dwelt on the west side of the Delaware; (2) The Wanami, who inhabited New Jersey; (3) The Munsey, above the Lehigh to the Kittatinny Mountains; (4) The Wabinga, or River Indians, or Mohickander, between the Delaware and the Hudson and from the Kittatinny Ridge to the Raritan; (5) The Mahiccon, or Manhattan, who occupied Staten Island, York Island, Long Island, and that part of New York and Connecticut between the Hudson and Connecticut, and south of the Highlands which are a continuation of the Kittatinny Ridge.

hake, "proprietors and inhabitants of the east side of Godyn's East Bay [Delaware Bay], called the Cape of May," for themselves and the other inhabitants, sold to Samuel Godyn and Samuel Bloemmaert a tract of land extending four miles (Dutch short miles, equivalent to sixteen English miles[1]) from Cape May along the east side of Delaware Bay, and the same distance inland.

On the 7th of January, 1633, while David De Vries was sailing up the Delaware River, he was visited by a sachem of the *Armewaninge*, who lived in what is now Camden County, New Jersey, opposite the site of Philadelphia. This chief's name is given by DeVries as Zeepentor.

In the same year, Arent Corssen, commander at Fort Nassau, on the east bank of the Delaware (on or near the site of Gloucester), purchased from the Indians a tract of land on the Schuylkill River, on which was afterwards erected a fort called Beversrede. This purchase was confirmed by a deed made in 1648, in which the grantors are named as "Amattehooren, Alebackinne, Sinquees, chiefs over the portions of the tracts of land lying about and on the Schuylkill, called Armenveruis." Two of these chiefs, Amattehooren and Sinquees, together with two others, Peminackan (or Pemmenatta) and Ackehoorn, on the 19th of July, 1655, made another deed to Stuyvesant confirming a sale made by them to him on July 9, 1651, of some land named Tinnecongh on the west bank of the Delaware River and the south side of the Minquaas Kill, extending westward "to the bounds and limits of the Minquaas' country."

In 1641, Peter Hollender, Governor of New Sweden, purchased from Wichusy, the chief sachem, a strip of land extending along the east bank of the Delaware, twelve German miles (47 English miles) northward from Cape May.

Andries Hudde, commissary at Fort Nassau on the Delaware in 1646, in the report of his conflicts with the Swedes, mentions a sachem, Wirakehan, whom he met near the first falls of the Delaware, on his way up the River to the Great Falls (now Trenton). He also states that another sachem, named Meerkeedt, resided near Tinnekonk. Hudde bought some land on the Schuylkill, on the site of Philadelphia, from the Indians in September, 1646, and made preparations to build some houses for the Dutch there in April, 1648, the land being formally surrendered by Maarte Hoock and Wissemenets, two of the chief sachems of the River Indians.

At Fort Nassau, on July 9, 1651, Chief Amattehoorn told Governor Peter Stuyvesant that three or four years before, the Swedish Governor had bought some land on the west shore of the Delaware, from Siscohoka and Mechekyralames, two Mantas Indians, of the eastern shore, " of

---

[1] *N. Y. Col. Doc.*, vii., 334.

which lands they were not the chiefs or proprietors, but one Kyckesycken, in our tongue, Live Turkey." The chief last named evidently belonged to the Turkey tribe of the Delawares.

Wappanghzewan (White Wampum?), a sachem, also deeded his lands to Stuyvesant on July 30, 1651, some on the east shore of the Delaware and some near the lands conveyed by the chiefs named above.

Naaman is mentioned by Lindstrom as one of the chiefs who attended a conference with Governor John Rising on Tinicum Island June 17, 1654. His name has been preserved to this day in that of Naaman's Creek, which enters the Delaware just south of the Pennsylvania line. Ferris, however, in his *Original Settlements on the Delaware*, speaks of Naaman as a Minqua chief.

In a letter written by Director William Beeckman from Altena (on Christina Creek) to Governor Stuyvesant January 14, 1661, he relates that the grave of Hoppemink, an Indian sachem who had been buried a short time before, had been robbed. In another letter, written November 15, 1663, Beeckman states that "at the urgent request of some chiefs above Meggeckesjouw, [now Trenton] the chief, Erwehongh, and others had gone there, to contribute for the assistance of the Esopus."

On August 3, 1663, a treaty of peace and amity was concluded at New Amstel between the Governor and Council of Maryland, and Hocpeckquomeck, Lennoswewigh, and Collaccameck, "kings of the Delaware Bay Indians." In a letter written by William Tom to Governor Francis Lovelace of New York, in December, 1671, he refers to the chief last named, whom he calls Colecooum, as "one of the greatest sachems."

At a meeting in the Council Chamber at Fort Amsterdam, March 6, 1664, were present, Oratam, chief of Hacingkesack, and with him the following "Menissinck chiefs: Memmesame, Meninger, Mamarikickan." "They state that the Sinnecus had threatened to come and kill the Menissincks, but that the Minquaes from the South River had allied themselves with the Menissincks, and if the Sinnecus were to come now, the Minquaes would also come, to assist the Menissincks."[1]

On September 10th, 1668, Philip Carteret issued a permit to Lucas Peterson to purchase from the Indians of the east side of Delaware River, a tract of land "over against Christeen Kill;" and in accordance therewith, Peterson bought a tract lying south of Swart-hook from Kerpenneming and Mattien-meke, two brothers.

On February 8, 1673, Sospenninck and Wicknaminck, of New Jersey, conveyed to Edmund Cantwell and John Dehaes a tract of land along the Delaware, between Jeremiah Kill and Finn's Creek.

At Newcastle, May 13, 1675, Governor Edmund Andros of New

[1] *N. Y. Col. Doc.*, xiii., 361.

York held a conference with the sachems of the east side of the Delaware (New Jersey). Their names were Renowewan of Sawkin, Ipankicken of Rancokes-kil, Ket-marius of Soup-napka, and Manickty of Rancokes-kil.

On September 23, 1675, the sachems, Mamarakiekan, Auricktan, Sackoquewan, and Mameckos, deeded to Governor Edmund Andros, of New York, a tract of land on the west side of the Delaware extending eight or nine miles above and the same distance below the Falls (Trenton Falls). The names of these chiefs as written in the signatures to this deed, are given as Sackoquenam, Mamakackickan, Anricktan, and Nanneckos. The consideration for this conveyance was sixty fathom of wampum, six coats of Duffles, six blankets, six coats of douzens, six shirts, half an ancker of powder, forty bars of lead, six guns, six kettles, thirty axes, fifty knives, two anckers of rum, fifty looking glasses, fifty combs, thirty hows, twenty pairs of stockings, ten pairs of shoes, one hundred tobacco pipes, one pound of paint, one hundred awls, and one hundred jews-harps.

On May 14, 1679, Mechaecksitt, sachem of Cohansink, conveyed to Peter Bayard of New York, Bompies Hook, lying on the west side of the Delaware above Duck Creek. The same sachem sold to Ephraim Herman November 21, 1680, a tract of land between Duck Creek and Appoquinimy Creek.

On September 18, 1679, Captain Edmund Cantwell wrote to Governor Andros regarding some surveys he had made on the west side of the Delaware, from the Falls (Trenton Falls) southward to the lower end of Orechton Island. Here Matapis and Ockenichan stopped him from proceeding farther, saying that they were the owners of the land below, and had not yet been paid for their titles.

On November 15, 1679, Ausawitt, Woappeck, and Jan Awieham sold to Hans Hoffman and others a tract of land on the east side of the Delaware near Maritties Hook.

In 1681 Parret, an Indian sachem acknowledged in the Sussex County court that he had sold to Henry Bowman and others a piece of land lying between Slaughter Bridge and Cedar Creek.

The Delaware clan named the Minsis lived north of the Unamis and the Unalachtigoes, in a situation exposed to the inroads of the Iroquois. This clan was more inclined to war and more savage than its kindred clans to the south. About the year 1677, after the power of the Susquehanocks had been broken by the Five Nations, all three of these Delaware clans became tributary to the Iroquois. The territory occupied by the Minsis at that time seems to have been on both sides of the Delaware River, about the Water Gap, on what have since been known as the Minisink Flats, in the eastern townships of Monroe and Pike counties, Pennsylvania, and the western townships of Warren and Sussex counties, New Jersey." The term, "Pechoquealin," or "Pahaqualong" (of which Pahaquarry is a later variation), was formerly applied to the Delaware Water Gap and also to the settlements of the Shawnee Indians in the southern part of the Minsi territory, in the present Pahaquarry Township, Warren County, New Jersey, and Lower Smithfield Township, Monroe County, Pennsylvania. Possibly, one Pechoquealin town was in what is now Pahaquarry Township, three miles below the mouth of Flat Brook,[1] and a second Shawnee town, which was also called Pechoquealin, stood on the west bank of the Delaware, at the mouth of Shawnee Run, and on and opposite Shawnee Island, in what is now Lower Smithfield Township. Both these towns were some miles south of the main settlement of the Minsis, which seems to have been about ten miles below the mouth of the Mahackamack or Neversink River and on and opposite Minisink Island.[2] Some writers locate a Pechoquealin Town in Bucks County at the Durham Furnace, following the *Penna. Colonial Records* for the year 1728, which speak of Pechoquealin as being near Durham Iron Works. While it is possible a Shawnee town may have been near the furnace, it is very doubtful. The principal settlement of the Shawnees was higher up the river, as indicated above.

The villages of the Minsis cannot be located with exactness. Vanderdonck's map of 1656 describes their district as "Minnessinck ofte t'Landt van Bacham," and gives them four villages: Schepinaikonck, Meoechkonck, Macharienkonck, and Schichtewacki. The first of these he places on the east bank of the Delaware, above the mouth of the present Neversink River; the second, on the north bank of the Neversink, some distance above its mouth; the third, on the west bank of the Delaware, opposite the mouth of the Neversink; and the fourth, some distance south of Macharienkonck, on the east bank of the Delaware.

Thomas Budd's *Good Order Established in Pennsylvania and New Jersey*, (1685), states that: "From the Falls of Delaware River [now Trenton] the Indians go in cannows up the said River to an Indian Town

[1] "On Nov. 6, 1718, Joseph Kirkbride located a tract of land on the Delaware River adjoining a branch of the same [on the north bank of Flat Brook, Walpack Township, Sussex County], about three miles above Pahaqualin, an Indian village."
—Snell, *History of Sussex and Warren Counties, New Jersey*, p. 316.

[2] "The earliest mention of the Minisink in our County records is in 1733. Nicholas De Pui, a Huguenot refugee, settled there in 1725, and in 1727 he purchased a tract of land from the Minsi Delawares, with two islands in the Delaware. In September, 1733, William Allen, who meanwhile had purchased this land from the Penns, confirmed the title to De Pui. There were six tracts in all, containing 647 acres, and in addition the three islands in the River contained 303 acres. These islands were Maw Wallamick, 126 acres, Great Shawnee, 146, and a third."—Davis, *Bucks County*, p. 583.

called Minisincks, which is accounted from the Falls about eighty miles; but this they perform by great labour in setting up against the stream. . . . I have been informed that about Minisincks by the river-side, both in New Jersey and Pennsylvania is great quantities of exceeding rich open land, which is occasioned by washing down of the leaves and soil in great rains from the mountains."

By the present River road from Trenton to Shawnee Island, just above the Delaware Water Gap, the distance is about seventy-nine miles. Some seventeen miles farther up the river lies Shapnack Island, which is twenty miles south of Port Jervis, or the mouth of Neversink River. Shapnack Island preserves the name and is doubtless the true site of the Schepinaik-onck Minsi village of Vanderdonck's map.

Johann B. Homann's map of Nova Anglia, without date, but made before his death in 1724, locates Schepinaykonk, Meoechkonk, Mecharienkonk, and Schichtewacki, on western tributaries of the Delaware; while it places the village of Pechquahock (another form of the Shawnee "Pechoquealin") on the east bank of the Delaware, near its proper location.

Claude J. Sauthier's map of New York and New Jersey (1777) locates the village of Minising on the east bank of the Delaware, some ten miles south of the mouth of Mahackamack or Neversink River, and opposite Minising Island. Minisink Island itself lies in the Delaware River, three to four miles south of the present village of Milford, Pennsylvania.

Minisink was visited by Captain Arent Schuyler in February, 1694, as already mentioned in the first chapter. In his *Journal* of this visit Captain Schuyler relates that "one of their sachems and other of their Indians were gone to fetch beaver and peltries which they had hunted; and having heard no news of them, are afraid that ye Sinneques have killed them for the lucre of the beaver or because ye Minnissinck Indians have not been with ye Sinneques as usual to pay their duty."

It is difficult to determine who of the Delaware chiefs mentioned in the early records of Penn's province belonged to the Minsi tribe. Perhaps "Oppemenyhook, at Lechay" (*i. e.*, between the Forks of the Lehigh and Delaware), was one. On July 26, 1701, the Council ordered a message to be sent to him and to the chiefs, Menangy, Hetcoquehan, and Owehela, on Christina (Creek), southern Delawares, asking them to come to Philadelphia before the sitting of the next Assembly, to be consulted with about passing a law for prohibiting all use of rum to the Indians of their nations." At a meeting of the New Jersey Council held May 30, 1709, when an expedition against Canada was under consideration, it was ordered that "Coll. Aron Schuyler do forthwith send for Mahwtatatt, (Matasit?) Cohevwichick, (Kakowatcheky), Ohwsilopp, Meshuhow and

Feetee, sachems of the Maninsincks and Shawhena Indians, to attend his Honor at Perth Amboy forthwith."

Three earlier chiefs of the "Northern Indians on Delaware" at the time of William Penn's arrival in 1682, are also named in a deed of confirmation and release signed by Manawkyhickon, Lappawinzoe, Teeshacomin, and Nootamis, August 25, 1737. Their names were Sayhoppy, or Shakahoppoh, who executed deeds in 1682, 1685,[1] and 1686; and Mayhkeerickkishsho and Taughhaughsey, who joined with Sayhoppy in the lost deed of 1686. On the deed last named was based the Walking Purchase claim, which the deed of 1737 was given to confirm, and the metes and bounds of this purchase were fixed by the heirs of William Penn in that year (1737); being fraudulently extended, so their Quaker mentors got the Indians to claim, in order to take in the greater part of the land along the Delaware lying north of the Lehigh Fork and south of Lackawaxen Creek. Whether or not these three chiefs of 1686 were of the Minsi tribe is uncertain; but if the deed which the Penns claimed these chiefs had signed in 1686, and which had been lost before 1737, was a conveyance of lands "between the Forks," then the signers were probably chiefs of the Minsis. The evidence as to the validity of this deed of 1686 was collated by a Committee of five members of the Governor's Council, and laid before the Council January 6th, 1758.[2] This evidence is conclusive enough at least to justify the Committee's assertion that the real cause of the alienation of the Delawares in 1755 was, that the Quaker Assembly, "though so frequently and earnestly requested to afford them (the Indians) protection, and give them the Hatchet, and to join and go out with them against the French," refused to concur with the Governor in giving them any encouragement or assistance whatsoever, until it was too late.

The names of two chiefs of the Minsis appear on the Pennsylvania records in 1728: Manawkyhickon (who signed the deed of release in 1737) and Kindassowa. In April, 1728, James Le Tort, a Trader living at Chenastry, on the West Branch of the Susquehanna, not far above Shamokin, came to Philadelphia and informed the Governor that he had intended "last Fall, to take a journey as far as the Miamis Indians, or Twechtweys [then living on the Wabash] to trade with them." But on consulting with Mrs. Montour, a Frenchwoman, wife of Carondowana, "she having lived amongst and having a sister married to one of that [Miami] nation," and with Manawkyhickon, "an Indian chief of note in those parts" (about Chenastry), Le Tort had learned that the Delaware Indians who were hunting at Allegheny had been called home; and that Manawkyhickon, "a near relation of Wequela, who was hanged last

[1] *Penna. Archives*, i., 47, 92.
[2] *Penna. Col. Records*, viii., 246–259; vii., 324, 54; vi., 692.

year in Jersey," much resented his death, and had "sent a black belt to the Five Nations, and that the Five Nations sent the same to the Miamis, with a message, desiring to know if they would lift up their axes and join with them against the Christians; to which they agreed."

Muncy Hills and Muncy Creek, on the southern border of the present county of Lycoming, doubtless mark the location of the settlement of Manawkyhickon and his band of Minsis before 1728. Manawkyhickon wrote to the Governor on May 1, 1728, from "Catawasse."[1] This was a town of the Conoy, or Piscataway, and Delaware Indians, at the mouth of Catawissa Creek, on the North Branch, not far east of Shamokin. It was called "Oskohary, Lapachpitton's Town," by Conrad Weiser in 1754; and is so designated on Scull's map of 1759. The Delaware chief, Lawpawpitton, was met by Weiser when he visited Sassoonan at Shamokin in 1743. In August, 1740, "Menakikickon" is styled "the King of the Minisincks." Another town of the Minsis in that year was Welagamika, or "Captain John's Town," situated in Nazareth Barony (now in Upper Nazareth Township), near the site of Nazareth, Northampton County. Where Nazareth now stands, the Reverend George Whitfield, in 1743, began the construction of a large stone building (since known as "Ephrata," or the "Whitfield House"),[2] which was completed in 1743, by the Moravians, after Whitfield had sold them the lands comprising the "Barony." "Captain John," himself, was a half-brother to Chief Teedyuscung, both being the sons of Captain John Harris, a Delaware Indian of the Turtle tribe.[3]

In October, 1755, David Zeisberger and Christian Seidel, two Moravian missionaries, visited "Lechaweke, the Minnissing town," above the mouth of the Lackawanna, near the site of the present city of Pittston. This place was identical with the "Indian town called Asserughney, twelve miles higher up the river" from Wyoming, which was visited by Andrew Montour and Scarrooyady in December, 1755, on their mission from Governor Morris to the Onondaga Council. On that occasion, the messengers found there "about twenty Indian Delawares, all violently against the English, to whom we said nothing, when we saw the badness of their disposition."

The name of another Minsi chief in 1728 was announced to the Governor and Council in Philadelphia by Sassoonan, in June of that year. Being asked about the death of Thomas Wright, who had been killed the fall before at the trading-house of John Burt in Snake Town near Pax-

---

[1] "The Piscatawese, or Gangawese, or Conoys, had a wigwam on the Catawese, at Catawese, now Catawissa, Northumberland County."—Redmond Conyngham, in Egle's *Notes and Queries*, Fourth Series, ii., 62.

[2] See *Frontier Forts of Penna.*, i., 251.

[3] See Reichel's *Memorials of the Moravian Church*, i., 217.

tang, by some of the Delaware Indians, Sassoonan and his companions answered: "That it was not done by any of their people; it was done by some of the Menysinck Indians; that the Menysincks live at the Forks of Sasquehannah, above Meehayomy [Wyoming], and that their king's name is Kindassowa." This is the only mention of this chief that has come under the notice of the writer.

The "Forks of Sasquehannah" above Wyoming may refer to the forks of the Tioga (or Chemung) and the Susquehanna, near what is now Athens, Bradford County, sometimes known as Tioga Point, and among the Iroquois of the eighteenth century, as Tiaoga, or Diahogo; although Mr. Oscar Harvey, in his *History of Wilkes-Barre*, says that it refers to Asserughney, the town at the junction of the Lackawanna and Susquehanna; and calls attention to the fact that Candowsa Indian Town is shown near this place on Kitchin's 1756 map of Pennsylvania.[1]

Egohohowen was chief of the Minsis above Tioga Point in 1758. He married a daughter of "French Margaret" Montour, and will be further referred to in the chapter relating to the Montours.

Conrad Weiser found a Mohican town at Tioga on his visit to Onondaga in 1737, but mentions no town at the mouth of the Lackawanna. In March, 1756, Teedyuscung and the Delawares of Wyoming removed to Tioga, and built a village near the Mohicans; followed at about the same time by the Shawnees then remaining at their town on the Shawnee Flats, now Plymouth, Luzerne County, under their old chief, Paxinosa. Some of the Minsis also appear to have settled at what has since been called the Monseytown Flats, on the West Branch of the Susquehanna, near the present town of Lockhaven, Clinton County.

On the west side of the Delaware River, between the Lehigh and Schuylkill, in 1683, much of the country was occupied by the Turtle and Turkey tribes of the Delawares; the settlements of the clan last named being originally toward the mouth of the Delaware, and later along the Schuylkill,[2] on both sides, from the Lehigh Hills to its mouth; while the Unamis, or people of the Turtle tribe, lived on the west of the Delaware, from the mouth of the Lehigh to nearly as far down as Minquas, or Christina Creek, where Wilmington now stands. The early name,

---

[1] Also, on Lewis Evans's map of 1755.

[2] "The Unalachtigo or Turkey totem [originally] had its principal seat on the affluents of the Delaware near where Wilmington now stands. About this point, Captain John Smith, on his map (1609) locates the *Chikahokin*. In later writers, this name is spelled *Chihohockies*, *Chiholacki*, and *Chikolacki*, and is stated by the historians, Proud and Smith, to be synonymous with Delawares. The correct form is *Chikelaki*, from *chikeno*, turkey, the modern form as given by Whipple (*Report*, 1855; the German form is *tsichenum*), and *aki*, land. The *n*, *l*, and *r*, were alternating letters in this dialect."—Brinton, *Lenape and their Legends*, 37.

"Minquas Kill," was given to Christina and White Clay creeks by the Dutch, who first settled there between 1627 and 1638. From the name, we may infer that the stream was within or near the borders of the territory occupied by those Iroquois Susquehannocks whom the Dutch called "Minquas." Swedish settlements at the mouth of Minquas Kill began in 1638. Then its name was changed to Christina (now Christiana), in honor of Queen Christina, daughter of Gustavus Adolphus.

On July 15, 1682, through his agent, Lieutenant-Governor Mark-William Penn bought of the "sachamakers," Idquahon, Ieanottowe, Idquoquequon, Sahoppe, Okonikon (or Ocomickon), Merkekowon, Orecton, Nannacussey, Shaurwaughon, Swanpisse, Nahoosey, Tomackhickon, Weskekitt, and Tohawsis, all the land between the Delaware and Neshaminey Creek lying southeast of a boundary line which connected the two streams a little above the site of what is now Wrightstown, Bucks County.

In June, 1683, William Penn bought the lands lying between Neshaminey and Pennypack Creeks, and backward into the country along Neshaminey two days' journey "with an horse," from the chiefs, Tamanen, Metamequan (alias Richard), Essepenaike, Swanpees, Okettarickon, and Wessapoat.

In July, 1683, Penn bought the lands between Pennypack Creek and the Schuylkill as far up the river as Conshohocken Hill (now Edge Hill), from the chiefs, Neneshickan, Malebore (alias Pendanoughhah), Neshanocks, and Osereneon. On the same day he also bought the lands between Chester Creek and the Schuylkill, as far up as Conshohocken, from the chiefs, Secane and Icquoquehan. The chief last named was also one of the parties to the deed of 1682.

On June 25, 1683, Penn bought from Chief Wingebone all his lands on the west side of the Schuylkill, above the first falls of that stream.

In December, 1683, Seketarius and Kalehickop sold to Penn their lands between Christina and Upland Creeks.

These purchases, with the two made from Kekelappan of Opasiskunk, and Machaloha, the Conestoga chiefs, of their lands on Susquehanna, referred to on a preceding page, were all the land transactions Penn had with the Indians in 1683, of which the conveyances have been recorded. In July, 1685, he bought from the chiefs, Shakhoppoh (who had joined in the deed of 1682), Secane and Malibor (both of whom had deeded lands in 1683), and Tangoras, the lands lying on both sides of the Schuylkill, between Chester and Pennypack (or Dublin) creeks, north of Conshohocken Hills, and "from thence northwesterly, back into ye woods, as far as a man can go in two days." In June, 1684, he had also bought the residue of the lands lying on both sides of Pennypack Creek from Richard Mettamicont; and from Maughoughsin, his lands lying along Perkiomen Creek. The last two purchases were made by Penn's agents.

On the 2d of October, 1685, William Penn's agent bought from a number of Indian chiefs, four of whom had previously conveyed to him other lands, "all the lands from Quing Quingus, called Duck Creek, unto Upland, called Chester Creek, all along by the west side of Delaware River, and so between the said creeks backwards, as far as a man can ride in two days with a horse." There is at this day a Duck Creek in Delaware, forming a part of the southern boundary of Newcastle County. Quing Quingus Creek, mentioned in this deed, refers either to that stream, or to Appoquinimink creek, which runs some distance north of Duck Creek. Appoquinimink is an Indian term, said to signify "wounded Duck." The chiefs mentioned in this deed, none of whom appear as signers thereof in the printed copy contained in the *Pennsylvania Archives*, were Lare, Packenah, Tareekham, Sickais, Pettquessitt, Tewis, Essepenaick, Petkhoy, Kekelappan, Feomus, Mackaloha, Melleonga, and Wissa Powey. The Indians whose names appear at the bottom of the printed deed were probably witnesses. Two day's horseback journey would extend to the Susquehanna; so that others of these chiefs besides Kekelappan and Mackaloha may have been Susquehannock Indians.

In June, 1692, Kings Taminent, Tangorus, Swampes, and Hickoqueon, gave a confirmatory deed of their former conveyances of lands lying between Neshaminey and Poquessing creeks, "upon the river Delaware, and extending backwards to the utmost bounds of the Province." Taminy, his brother, and his three sons, executed a second deed in confirmation of his former ones, on July 5, 1697, for his lands between Neshaminey and Pennypack, extending backwards from the Delaware, "so far as a horse can travel in two summer days."

In the deed last mentioned, the grantors are described as "Taminy, sachem, and Weheeland, my brother, and Weheequeckhon (alias Andrew), who is to be king after my death, Yaqueekhon (alias Nicholas), and Quenameckquid (alias Charles), my sons." The name of Taminy's brother, written Whehelan, is affixed as a witness to the deed made by Chief Wingebone in 1683. Whehelan may be the same as "Owehela, on Christina," who appears as chief of the Delawares in July, 1701; and of whom an account will be given later. Concerning Weheequeckhon, who was to succeed his father as king, on the death of the father, Mr. A. L. Guss, one of the most intelligent and well-read writers on Pennsylvania Indian history, states that this son of Taminy was none other than the celebrated Sassoonan or Allumapees, head chief of the Delawares from 1715 to 1747. Mr. Guss bases his conclusion upon what he states to be the fact that one of the names of Chief Sassoonan was Wikwikhon. He fails to cite any authority for this statement, however.

The first extended conference between the Pennsylvania authorities and the Indians, of which a record has been preserved, was held at Philadelphia, July 6, 1694. The Delaware chiefs, Hithquoquean (or Idquoquequon), Shakhuppo, Menanzes (afterwards written Menange), Mohocksey, Tamanee, Alemeon, and others, were present. Also, Kyanharro and Oriteo (Widaagh) two chiefs of the Susquehannock, or Conestoga Indians. Hithquoquean, in the name of the Delawares, took out and laid down a belt of wampum, which he said had been sent them by the Onondagas and Senecas with this message: "You Delaware Indians do nothing but stay at home and boil your pots, and are like women; while we Onondagas and Senecas go ahead and fight against the enemy." "The Senecas," said Hithquoquean, "would have us Delaware Indians to be partners with them, to fight against the French; but we, having always been a peaceable people, and resolving to live so, and being but weak and very few in number, cannot assist them; and having resolved amongst ourselves not to go, do intend to send back this their belt of wampum."

Mohocksey, a chief from the eastern bank of the Delaware, possibly a chief of the Minsis, then arose and said: "The former belt, sent by the Onondagas and Senecas is sent to us all, and we have acquainted one another with it; and though we live on the other side of the river, yet we reckon ourselves all one, because we drink one water. We have had a continued friendship with all the Christians and old inhabitants of this river since I was a young man, and are desirous to continue the same so long as we live."

Tamanee made a similar speech, adding, that "though sometimes a tree has fallen across the road, yet we have still removed it again, and kept the path clean."

Governor Markham told them that "if the Senecas send again to you, do you send to me, and I'll send an express to New York, and his Excellency will take care that the Senecas shall do you no injury."

Tamanen, Tamanent, or Taminy, was the head chief or sachem of the Unami or Turtle tribe of the Delawares, from before 1683 until 1697, or later. He lived and hunted along the Neshaminey, in what is now Bucks County. His death probably took place before 1701; for in July of that year Menangy, Hetcoquehan (written Idquoquequon and Icquoquehan in the deeds signed by him in 1682 and 1683), Owehela on Christina, and Oppemenyhook at Lechay, are named as the Delaware chiefs.

Owechela and Weheelan, Taminy's brother, probably were identical, and it is likely that the brother acted in some sort of a vice-regal capacity during the minority of Weheequeckhon, Taminy's son, whom Mr. Guss identified with Sassoonan or Allumapees.

Owhala, or Ocahale (Owechela) is called the King of the Delawares in the Maryland Council Records, in 1698 and 1700. He signed a treaty of amity and friendship with three Maryland Commissioners at John Hans Steelman's trading house in Cecil County, August 29, 1700.

Wequeala, an Indian chief living at Freehold, was hanged at Perth Amboy, in New Jersey, June 30, 1727, for the killing of Captain John Leonard of that town. At that time he is mentioned as having been a "near relative" of Manawkyhickon, a chief of the Minsis. He deeded lands in Cranberry and Manalpan creeks, New Jersey, in 1701 and 1702; and attended an Indian conference with the Governor and Council of New Jersey in 1709.

Could "Wequeala" be another spelling of the name "Owechela"?

The name "Owehela" first appears on the Pennsylvania Colonial records July 26, 1701, at which time the Governor's Council invited Manangy, Hetcoquehan, Owehela on Christina, Oppemenyhook at Lechay, and Indian Harry of Conestoga, to come to Philadelphia for the purpose of considering the question of prohibiting the sale of rum to the Indians of their respective nations. On July 25, 1709, Owechela visited Philadelphia in company with Passakassy, Sassoonan, and Skalitchy, all four of whom were then described as "chiefs of the Delaware Indians settled at Peshtang, above Conestogoe, and other adjacent places." They were also accompanied by chiefs of the Conestogas and the Ganawese, and by their interpreter, "Sam" (son of Essepenawick, one of Penn's grantors in 1683). On the day following their arrival, the Delawares, in a conference with the Governor and Council, were desired to tell the object of their errand. "Whereupon, by order of Owechela and Passakassy, ——————— [Skalitchy?] rising, laid on the board a belt of wampum, as a token to confirm what he had to speak, and then said: 'That this summer they had intended to wait upon the Five Nations, and had provided for their journey twenty-four belts of wampum, to be presented to them as their tribute, of which they thought themselves obliged to acquaint the Governor.'" The speaker added, that, for reasons which he explained, it would now be too late for them to make this journey and return before cold weather set in.

On July 18, 1717, the Susquehanna and Delaware Indians informed Governor Keith, at Conestoga Town, that some two months before, three sons of Owechela, a Delaware chief, had been hunting beyond the farthermost branch of the Potomac, where they had been attacked by a party of Christians and southern Indians, and one of them killed.

Whether or not Owechela was the ruling chief of the Delawares of the Turtle tribe from 1701 to 1709, the name of a new chief appears on the records in the latter year. This was Skalitchy, who, with Owechela, Passakassy, and Sassoonan, attended the conference at Philadelphia in

July, 1709. He attended another conference near Philadelphia, May 19, 1712, where he was the principal speaker. Accompanying him were two other Delaware chiefs, Sassoonan (called "their chief"), being the hereditary sachem, and Ealochelan. Of Sassoonan we shall speak farther on. The third chief, Ealochelan, is mentioned again, with the other two, as attending a conference on October 12th of the same year. His name, as there written, may be an incorrect transcription of the name of the chief Owechela, or of Weheelan, Taminy's brother (who may have been identical with Owechela). Skalitchy's name does not appear again on the records until 1715. On June 14th of that year, Sassoonan and other chiefs of the Delaware and Schuylkill Indians attended a great council at Philadelphia. They met the Governor and Council in the Court House, "Sassoonan being their head, and Opessah, ye late Shawnois king, with his companion, attending him; and then opening ye Calumet with great ceremony of their rattles and songs, it was offered by Sassoonan, the King, to the Governor, Council, and all others of ye English there met, and afterwards was also offered by him to all his Indians, and then, with ye same ceremony, was put up again." Sassoonan then began a very eloquent and friendly address, in the course of which he said, "that their late king, Skalitchi, desired of them that they would take care to keep a perfect peace with ye English." This statement serves to fix the date of Skalitchy's death as between 1712 and 1715.

A graphic picture of the condition of vassalage or subjection to which the Delawares had been reduced by the power or through fear of the terrible hand of the Iroquois is that afforded by the account of the proceedings at the Indian conference of May 19, 1712, in which Skalitchy took the most prominent part. This conference was held at the house of Edward Farmar in White Marsh (now in Montgomery County, Pennsylvania). The Governor and his Council had been summoned thither from Philadelphia to meet the chiefs, Scollitchy (Skalitchy), Sassoonan, and twelve other head men of the Delawares, who wished to confer with the Colonial authorities before setting out on their journey to the country of the Five Nations. The Governor and Council having arrived, and taken their seats before the Indians, Scollitchy, their speaker, arose, and, through Mr. Farmar, the interpreter, directed his speech to the Governor. He said: "Many years ago, being made tributaries to the Mingoes, or Five Nations, and being now about to visit them, they thought fit first to wait on the Governor and Council; to lay before them the collection they had made of their tribute to offer; and to have a conference with the Governor upon it." Thereupon, the Indians spread out upon the floor before the assemblage thirty-two belts of wampum, in which various figures and designs had been wrought by their women, together with a long and curiously constructed pipe, having a stone head and a cane shaft, to which were attached feathers arranged to resemble wings. This pipe the Indians called the Calumet.

They went on to relate that, at the time of making their submission to the Five Nations, when the latter had conquered and "made tributaries" of them, this Calumet had been given to them by the Five Nations, to be kept and shown to other nations among whom they might go, as a token of their subjection and allegiance to the Iroquois. They then proceeded to open their belts, and declared for what purpose and with what intention each particular belt was sent.

"The first belt," they said, "was sent by one, who at the time of their agreement or submission, was an infant and orphan, the son of a considerable man amongst them.

"The second belt was presented by one who was also the son of one then deceased but who desired to be taken in and accounted as one of the children to those of the Five Nations, that he might have a clear and free passage amongst them.

"The third belt is presented by another orphan, who desires the same.

"The fourth, by a son of one then living, and sends it so large to express his respect, as that it shall cover the pipe or calumet.

"The fifth is to inform, that though the principal of the family that sends it be dead, yet they continue their obedience and show their intention by this present.

"The sixth, sent by another, who desires to be regarded as a child of the Five Nations.

"The seventh, by a woman, who desires to be considered according to her sex; desires peace; that she may eat and drink in quiet; and is willing always to pay tribute.

"The eighth, by a woman, to the same purpose; desires she may make and keep fires in quiet.

"The ninth, by a woman, to the same purpose; that she may plant and reap in quiet.

"The tenth, by a woman, desires peace and ease, from ye rising of the sun to his going down."

Another belt was sent, "that formerly one of the chiefs of those nations came down and dwelt among them; that they regarded him always as their superior, and one of them."

Nineteen more of the belts were sent by women, also, accompanying similar messages to the Iroquois over-lords. The Delaware chiefs explained that so many belts (twenty-four out of thirty-two) were sent from women, because, "the paying of tribute becomes none but women and children." The last two belts, they added, had been given them, one by William Penn, eleven years before; and the other since sent to them by Governor Evans.

Is it not reasonable to suppose that the receipt of these belts from the women of the tribe by the Great Council of the Iroquois at Onondaga, and the probable receipt of similar belts and messages in earlier and later years, did much to confirm the tradition among the Five Nations that the Delaware Indians were but a nation of women?

On October 14, 1712, five months after the conference of the Delaware chiefs with the Governor at White Marsh, the same three chiefs appeared again, at another conference, to relate the result of their mission to the Senecas. Some of the Senecas accompanied them on this visit. They had brought back from the Seneca town two wampum belts, which they presented to the Governor. The first belt was sent from the son of one of the Seneca chiefs, "called Mechelokeety, who formerly had been here, and was kindly received, and hoped to return, but being prevented by death, now his son sends this, in hopes that when he comes he shall meet with the friendship his father had before him."

It is possible the chief, Mechelokeety, was the former over-lord sent by the Five Nations to sustain their authority over the Delawares; the same person to whom one of the Delaware belts had been sent in the previous May.[1] Could he have been Machaloha, Penn's grantor in 1683?

It is sometimes said that the Delawares were not made tributaries of the Five Nations until after the time of William Penn's coming to the Province.[2]

If that were the case, it must have been done then through fear and intimidation, rather than by war; for there is no record of any conquest after the time of Penn's arrival. There was, however, as we have seen, a much earlier reference to the tributary relation sustained by the Delawares towards the Five Nations, than that of 1712, given in the account above. This was announced during the conference held at Philadelphia, July 6, 1694, between Governor Markham and eight Indian chiefs, six of them Delawares, from both sides of the river, and two, Susquehannocks of Conestoga. Hithquoquean then told the Governor of the war-belt and message received by the Delawares from the Onondagas and Senecas, and that they had determined to return the belt and not send warriors to assist the Five Nations. The message had said: "You Delawares do nothing but stay at home and boil your pots, and are like women[3]; while we Onondagas and Senecas go abroad and fight against the enemy."

[1] The Mohawks informed Colonel Henry Coursey, a Maryland Commissioner, at Albany, August 4, 1682, that Wowler, a Mohawk, "goes now to Maryland [*i. e.*, to the Susquehannocks], to be interpreter there."—*N. Y. Col. Doc.*, iii., 328.

[2] King Beaver told Conrad Weiser at Aughwick, Sept. 4, 1754, that it was before Penn came. See, however, a conference between Governor Gordon and some Cayuga chiefs, July 3, 1727, *Penna. Col. Rec.*, iii.

[3] The word "women" was frequently applied to the Delawares as a term of

It would seem from the proceedings of the Delawares at this time that their fear of the Five Nations was not so strong in 1694 as it became some years later.

Sassoonan, or Allumapees, as we have seen, became chief sachem of the Delawares of the Turtle tribe about 1715, succeeding their former chief, Skalitchy, who died before June 14th of that year. As early as 1709 Sassoonan had been reported as living at Paxtang, "or other adjacent parts," at which time he is named as a chief. In September, 1718, he and the other Delaware chiefs signed a deed of release to the Penns for all "the land situated between the rivers Delaware and Susquehannah, from Duck Creek to the mountains on this side of Lechay." It is probable that after the execution of this deed Sassoonan removed to Shamokin (now Sunbury), where he continued to live during the greater part of his life. He visited the Governor at Philadelphia twice during the year 1728, and at other times in the years 1734, 1736, 1738, 1740, and 1742. On June 4, 1745, Bishop Spangenberg wrote: "We also visited Allummapees, the hereditary king of the [Delaware] Indians. His sister's sons are either dead or worthless,[1] hence it is not known on whom the kingdom will descend. He is very old, almost blind, and very poor; but withal has still power over and is beloved by his people; and he is a friend of the English." Conrad Weiser wrote from Tulpehocken, July 20, 1747: "Olumapies would have resigned his crown before now, but as he had the keeping of the public treasure (that is to say, the Council Bag), consisting of belts of wampum, for which he buys liquor, and has been drunk for these two or three years, almost constantly, and it is thought he won't die as long as there is one single wampum left in the bag. Lapapitton is the most fittest person to be his successor." Nine weeks later Weiser writes: "I understand Olumapies is dead, but I cannot say I am sure of it"; and again, on October 15th: "Olumapies is dead. Lapaghpitton is allowed to be the fittest to succeed him; but he declines."

Nettawatwees, or New Comer, in far off Ohio, afterwards succeeded to the hereditary chieftainship of the Turtle tribe, but his authority did not extend over the other two tribes.

Some of the early chiefs of the Turkey tribe of the Delawares, probably, were those whose names are affixed to the deed of 1685, conveying

---

contempt, by the Five Nations, from this time on; and accepted by the former without any protest, until after the events of 1755. See *Penna. Col. Rec.*, iv., 579; vi., 156, 363, 615; *Archives*, i., 329; iii., 505; *N. Y. Col. Doc.*, vii., 48, 119, 157, 307.

[1] Two of these sons, possibly, were Nettawatwees, or New Comer (who, with Sassoonan and other chiefs, signed a deed to William Penn in 1718), and Kelappama, who both removed to the Ohio country, and were living at New Comer's Town at the time of Bouquet's expedition in 1764. Nettawatwees was then hereditary sachem of the Turtle tribe, and continued as such until his death, at Fort Pitt, in 1776.

to William Penn the lands along the Schuylkill beyond Conshohocken Hill. Their names were Shakhoppoh, Secane, Malibor (or Malibone), and Tangoras. One of their contemporaries, who afterwards became the principal chief of this tribe, was Menangy, or Menanzees. His name first appears as a witness to one of the deeds of 1683, signed by Essepenaike and three other chiefs. On July 6, 1694, he attended the conference at Philadelphia, in which the Delawares announced the receipt of a warbelt from the Onondagas and Senecas. In July, 1701, he is mentioned as one of the four principal chiefs of all the Delawares. His name appears again during May, 1705, as the "Indian chief on Schuylkill."

How long Menangy lived, and who succeeded him as chief of the Schuylkill Indians, I cannot discover. In 1726, however, Lingahonoa was a Schuylkill chief. In May, 1726, certain chiefs conveyed to the Penns all the lands on both sides of Brandywine Creek, near its head. In September, 1732, Sassoonan, Elalapis, Ohopamen, Pesquetomen (of the Turkey tribe), Mayeenrol, Partridge, and Tepakoaset, sachem and chiefs of the Schuylkill Indians, conveyed to the Penns all the lands along the Schuylkill between the Lechay Hills and Kittochtinny Hills, from the branches of the Delaware to those of the Susquehanna. Lingahonoa was not present at the signing of these deeds; but ratified and confirmed them on July 12, 1742, acknowledging that he had received his proportion of the consideration. At that time, he is called a Delaware of Shamokin. Shingas, a chief of the Turkey tribe, living on the Ohio, was made head chief of the Delawares by the Six Nations at Logstown in 1752, and after his death, or abdication, was succeeded by his brother, King Beaver.

A lesser Delaware chief of this period was Checochinican, chief of the Delawares on Brandywine Creek about 1716.[1] His son, Nemacolin, is better known to readers of Colonial history. Nemacolin was the Indian who, in 1752, was employed, with others, by Christopher Gist and Colonel Thomas Cresap, acting for the Ohio Company, in blazing the most direct trail between Will's Creek (Cumberland, Md.), and the mouth of Redstone Creek on the Monongahela River. It followed the route of Gist's second journey from the Potomac to the Ohio in November, 1751, being several miles shorter than the path then used by the Virginia Traders travelling from the Potomac to the Ohio. This trail, afterwards known as Nemacolin's Path, was used by Washington and Gist in their journey to the Ohio in 1753, and, in 1754, by Washington's little army on its unsuccessful march against Fort Duquesne.[2] Braddock's route

[1] He had removed to the Susquehanna before June, 1718. *Penna. Archives*, i., 239, 266. *Col. Rec.*, ii., 643; iii., 36.

[2] See *Penna. Archives*, i., 239, 266; Darlington's *Gist*, 70, 140; Smith's *History of Delaware County, Penna.*, 235, 240; Hulbert's *Washington's Road*.

was partly over the same road; and it is now followed in part by the National Road between Cumberland and the Monongahela.

Campanius' *History of New Sweden* (1702) was written by a grandson of the Rev. John Campanius, who accompanied Governor Printz as chaplain when he came to the Christina settlement from Sweden in 1643. This history was based largely on the journals of that chaplain. Campanius located the Minquas of Printz's day as living in a hilly country twelve Swedish miles (equal to eighty English miles) from New Sweden. He described them as a very war-like people, who had forced the River Indians (Delawares) "who are not as war-like as the Minques," to fear them; "and made them subject, and tributary to them; so that they dare not stir; much less go to war against them." In the *Short History and Notes kept during Several Voyages*, of the early Dutch explorer, David Pietersen DeVries (published in 1655), that adventurous sea-captain tells how he had, in February, 1633, sailed up the Delaware River to near the mouth of the Schuylkill, where he found that the post, established by the Dutch on the east side of the Delaware in 1623, had been evacuated. At this point, the Minqua Indians made their appearance in unusually large numbers, and DeVries learned a few days later that a war was then raging between the River Indians and the "Minquas who dwell among the English in Virginia."[1] Three Armewamen fugitives, whose cabins had been destroyed and their neighbors killed, told DeVries that the Minquas had also killed ninety men of the Sankikans (the New Jersey Lenape).

When, in 1634, Captain Thomas Young explored the Delaware River, the few natives he found on the west side told him that the "Minquaos" had killed their people, burned their villages, and destroyed their crops, so that "the Indians had wholly left that side of the River which was next their enemies, and had retired themselves on the other side farre up into the woods."[2]

From these early narrations, it is evident that the Delaware River Indians of Algonquian stock had been conquered and reduced to the position of a subject tribe by the Iroquois of the Susquehanna River long before the power of the latter had been broken by the more potent arms of their kindred of the Five Nations. The wars which the Five Nations carried on with the Andastes in this territory doubtless embroiled the Delawares, who were subject to the Andastes (Susquehannocks). The result of these wars certainly left the Five Nations, during the last quarter of the seventeenth century, in the same relation with regard to the Dela-

---

[1] *N. Y. Hist. Soc. Coll.*, Sec. Ser., iii., 31. See also, Smith's *History of Delaware County, Penna.*, p. 52.

[2] *A Briefe Relation of the Voyage of Captayne Thomas Young*, in *Mass. Hist. Coll.*, 4th Series, ix., 119; also, *Md. Hist. Soc. Fund Pub.*, 9, 301.

wares as the Susquehannocks had occupied in the earlier decades of that century. We find no records of any conquest of the Delawares by the Iroquois after William Penn came to America in 1682. On September 26, 1683, nearly a year after Penn's arrival, in response to overtures made by his agents at Albany towards the purchase of the lands on the Susquehanna from the Five Nations, three Cayuga chiefs declined treating for these lands because they "think that the land [lying on the Susquehanna River] cannot be sold without Corlaer's [the Governor of New York] order; for we transferred it to this government four years ago. . . . The aforesaid land belongs to us, Cayugas and Onondagas, alone; the other three nations, vizt., the Sinnekes, Oneydes, and Maquas [Mohawks], have nothing to do with it."[1] On the 2d day of the following August (1684), the Onondaga and Cayuga sachems told the governors of New York and Virginia, at Albany, that they "have given the Susquehanna river, which we won with the sword, to this [the New York] government, and desire that it may be a branch of that great tree that grows here." Penn, it is true, had previously purchased some of the lands along the Schuylkill and the Delaware from the River Indians without consulting the Five Nations; but he and his heirs afterwards compensated the latter tribes in various ways for the loss of that portion of the lands of their suzerainty. Nearly sixty years after Penn's purchase of the Delaware lands, the representatives of certain of the Delawares made complaints of having been defrauded by the proprietaries in the purchase of these lands. Governor Thomas accordingly arranged for a conference with the chiefs of the Delawares and the Six Nations, which was held at Philadelphia in July, 1742. Canassatego, an Onondaga chief, spoke as the representative of the Iroquois over-lords there present. Addressing Nutimus and another Delaware chief from the towns "between the Forks," he said:

Cousins: Let this belt of wampum serve to chastise you. You ought to be taken by the hair of the head and shaked severely, till you recover your senses and become sober. You don't know what ground you stand on; nor what you are doing. . . .

We have seen with our eyes a deed signed by nine of your ancestors, above fifty years ago, for this very land; and a release signed not many years since by some of yourselves, and chiefs now living, to the number of fifteen and upwards.

But how came you to take upon you to sell land at all?

We conquered you; we made women of you; you know you are women; and can no more sell land than women.

Nor is it fit you should have the power of selling lands, since you abuse it. This land, that you claim, is gone through your guts. You have been furnished with clothes, and meat, and drink, by the goods

[1] *N. Y. Doc. Hist.*, i., 396.

paid you for it; and now you want it again, like children, as you are.

But what makes you sell land in the dark? Did you ever tell us that you had sold this land? Did we ever receive any part, even the value of a pipe-shank, from you for it? . . .

And for all these reasons, we charge you to remove instantly. We don't give you the liberty to think about it. You are women. Take the advice of a wise man, and remove immediately. You may return to the other side of Delaware, where you came from. But we don't know whether, considering how you have demeaned yourselves, you will be permitted to live there; or whether you have not swallowed that land down your throats as well as the land on this side. We therefore assign you two places to go—either to Wyoming or Shamokin. You may go to either of these places, and then we shall have you more under our eye, and shall see how you behave.

Don't deliberate; but move away; and take this belt of wampum.

The Delawares between and south of the Forks, accordingly, removed to Wyoming and beyond during the ensuing year, "taking with them several Jersey and Minisink Indians." Their fear of the dreaded Iroquois warriors was great, because it was an hereditary one having originated with their grandfathers and great-grandfathers, at the time of the wars between the Five Nations and the Susquehannocks, some seventy years before. In these wars the Delawares, as tributaries of the Susquehannocks, may have been embroiled more or less with the Five Nations; although no accounts of any direct conquest of the Delawares by the Five Nations have come down to us. Their subjection probably came as a natural result of the conquest and defeat of the Delawares' former over-lords, the Susquehannocks.

It would probably be very near the truth to say that the date of the Delaware submission was on or near March 13, 1677, at the time the chiefs and warriors of the Five Nations came to Shackamaxon for the purpose of carrying away the Susquehanna warriors.

That the Delawares had been subject to the Susquehannocks or Minquas in land sales more than a hundred years before 1742, seems probable from what has already been printed and from records of certain conveyances by the chiefs of their ancestors to the Dutch West India Company in 1633, 1648, and 1651, which are published in volume one of the New York *Colonial Documents* (pages 587 to 600). In the first of these deeds, executed to Arent Corsen, agent of the Dutch Company, an Indian chief named Amattehooren, and two other "sachems over the district of country called Armenverius, situate around and on the Schuylkill river," sign the conveyance, made in 1648, and confirm a former sale of 1633. In the second deed, made to Peter Stuyvesant, "Director General of Curacoa, New Netherland, and Chief Sachem of the Manhattans," July 19, 1651, Amattehooren and three other "sachems and right owners of the lands situate on the west shore of the South [Delaware] river of New Netherland," convey a certain portion of land named Tamencongh, lying on the west shore of the Delaware, beginning at the west point of the Minquaas Kill (White Clay and Christiana creeks) unto Canaresse, "and so far landward in as our right extends, to-wit: to the bounds and limits of the Minquaes country." Amattehooren had previously assured Governor Stuyvesant, who was then present at the mouth of the Schuylkill, and questioned the Indians as to their right to sell, that he and his fellow sachems "were great chiefs and proprietors of the lands, both by ownership and descent, and appointment of Minquaas and River Indians." This conveyance was made in the presence of four sachems of the Minquas, who signed as witnesses thereto.

A few years after this deed was executed, the Minquas engaged in their wars with the northern Iroquois of the Mohawk Valley, which lasted for some fifteen years; and as a result of those wars their power and most of their nation was forever destroyed; and their sovereignty over the Indians of the Delaware River passed to the Five Nations.

As we have seen, William Penn, through his agent, Governor Markham, in 1682, and when he himself was on the Delaware in 1683, and through his agents thereafter, purchased from other sachems of the River Indians such of their lands north and west of the Schuylkill and south of the Blue Mountains as had not been previously conveyed. Through Governor Dongan of New York, he later bought what he thought was the title of the "Senecas of the Susquehannah" to the lands wrested by the Five Nations from the Susquehanna Indians of the southern part of that river.[1] Excepting a small remnant who remained on the Brandywine until shortly after 1718, under a chief named Checochinican or Shenkokonichan (the father of Nemacolin), the two southern branches of the Delaware tribe gradually retreated northwestwardly along the Brandywine, to the Susquehanna (at Paxtang) and along the Schuylkill to and beyond Tulpehocken, as the white settlements in Pennsylvania increased. Probably before the time of William Penn's death most of them had crossed the Blue Hills and seated themselves along the North Branch of the Susquehanna, between Wyoming and Shamokin (now Sunbury). From Shamokin, the greater part of the Delawares, beginning in 1724 or thereabouts, crossed the Alleghanies and settled on the Allegheny river, building a town which they named Kittanning, on the site of the present borough of the same name. By the Six Nations, this town was called Adigo or Attique.[2] The residue of the Delawares remained in

[1] Dongan's deeds of 1696 are printed in *Penna. Archives*, i., 121–123.

[2] In a letter from the Senecas to Governor Gordon, July 29, 1735, it is called "Adjiego, or the Handsome River."—*Penna. Archives*, i., 454. From this, it is probable that Adjiego, Adigo, Attigue, and Attiga, are simply variations of the Iroquois word,

the vicinity of Shamokin, under their old chief, Sassoonan, or Allumapees, who died there in 1747. Some of his tribe afterwards lived with the Tuteloes under a chief called Lawpachpitton, whose town, Oskohary, or Skogary (located at the mouth of Catawissa Creek, in what is now Columbia County, Pennsylvania), was visited by Conrad Weiser in 1754.

The Delawares who were ordered to leave their lands between the Forks of the Lehigh and Delaware by the Six Nations in 1742, settled, with their chief, Nutimus, on the site of Wilkes-Barre, opposite Wyoming Town, and at "Niskebeckon," on the left bank of the North Branch of the Susquehanna, above the mouth of Nescopeck Creek, in what is now Luzerne County. "Lawpaughpeton's Town" and "Old King Neutimus' Town" are both shown on Scull's 1759 map of Pennsylvania.

As has been stated, the River Indians of the Delaware, Schuylkill, and Brandywine, after 1707 moved westward from these streams to the vicinity of Peixtan, on the Susquehanna, thence crossed the Blue Hills, and later seated themselves along the North Branch of the Susquehanna, near and west of Wyoming and at Shamokin. Here many of them lived under Sassoonan until his death in 1747. Shamokin itself, a Delaware town before 1728 and in 1743[1] had been for some time the seat of Shekallamy, an Oneida chief, who for twenty-one years after 1728, appears on the official records of Pennsylvania as the over-lord, deputy, or vice-regent in Pennsylvania of the Iroquois Confederacy. After Shekallamy's death in 1749, some of the Shamokin Delawares also settled at Tioga (now Athens, Bradford County, Pennsylvania), where, in 1756, they and the Delawares of the Minsi tribe, who had formerly been under the chiefs Manawkyhickon and Kindassowa, and were then under Eghohowen, chose as their "king" Teedyuscung.

The greater part of Allumapees' tribe, however, removed to the Ohio country during the twenty-five years following 1724. After his death in 1747, three brothers, of the Turkey tribe, succeeded him as sachems of the Ohio Delawares, among whom they lived. Their names were Shingas, Tamaque or King Beaver, and Pisquetomen,[2] of whom the chief sachem from 1752 to 1763 was Shingas. A conference was held by George Croghan and Andrew Montour, representing the Pennsylvania Government, with the Indians at Logstown, May 29, 1751. Beaver, the speaker for the Delawares, replied to a suggestion that his tribe should

---

O-hee-ye,—the Beautiful or Great River—the name which the Senecas applied to the Ohio and Allegheny, and from which comes our modern word, "Ohio." See Chapter X.

[1] See John Bartram's *Journal of his Travels to Onondaga*, July 10, 1743.

[2] *Penna. Col. Rec.*, iii., 430, 544; viii., 147, 174; *Archives*, i., 344; Washington's *Journal of 1754;* Post's *Journals of 1758;* Hugh Gibson's *Narrative in Mass. Hist. Coll.*, 3d Series, vi., 140 *et seq.*; also, Egle's *Notes and Queries*, iii., 244.

comply with the promise they had made the Governor, through Conrad Weiser, three years before, to choose a new chief to succeed Allumapees. He said, that, as all their wise men were not gathered together, it would take some time to consider in selecting a man who was fit to rule their nation; but that as soon as possible, they would make a full answer, which they hoped would give satisfaction to the English and the Six Nations. On June 11, 1752, at the time of the treaty between Patton, Fry, and Lomax, the three Virginia Commissioners, and the Indians at Logstown, Tanacharisson, the Half King, as the representative of the Six Nations, bestowed the sachemship of the Delawares upon Shingas.[1] In October, 1753, Shingas, chief sachem, with his brother Pisquetomen, and Delaware George, met Governor Hamilton's Commissioners in a conference at Carlisle. King Beaver was head chief of the Turkey tribe at the time of Bouquet's expedition to Ohio in October, 1764. What became of Chief Shingas, or when he died, is not known; though some writers have sought to identify him with Buckongehelas, a later Ohio chief, who was living after 1800.[2] It is not improbable that Shingas, King Beaver, and Pisquetomen were the nephews of Allumapees and sons of his sister.

The history of the Delawares on the Ohio will be followed in connection with that of an abler and more powerful tribe of Indians—the Shawnees—whose movements we shall next attempt to trace. Before doing this, however, another point, showing the state of subjection to which the Delawares had been reduced by the Five Nations, should be mentioned.

In a conference held by Conrad Weiser with the Ohio Mingoes, the Shawnees, and the Delawares at George Croghan's house at Aughwick, September 4, 1754, the Beaver, the speaker for the Delawares, stood up and directed his discourse to the chiefs of the Six Nations. "Uncle," he said, "I still remember the time when you first conquered us and made women of us, and told us that you took us under your protection, and that we must not meddle with wars; but stay in the house, and mind council affairs." Afterwards, addressing Weiser, as the representative of the Governor, he began: "Brother, the Governor of Pennsylvania: I must now go into the depth, and put you in mind of old histories, and our

[1] See *Virginia Magazine of Hist. and Biog.*, xiii., 167. Shingas was succeeded by his brother, who was known as King Beaver. A memorandum made by Jasper Yeates at Fort Pitt in 1776 recites that, "there are three tribes amongst the Delawares, the Wolf, the Turkey, and the Turtle tribe. Beaver was chief of the Turkey tribe, and was succeeded by Captain Johnny, or Straight Arm, White Eyes ruling it. Custaloga was chief of the Wolf tribe, and succeeded by Captain Pipe; and New Comer was chief of the Turtle tribe, and succeeded by Captain John Killbuck." (Egle's *Notes and Queries*, v., 349.)

[2] Taylor, *History of Ohio*, 544.

first acquaintance with you, when William Penn first appeared in his ship on our shores. We looked in his face and judged him to be our brother, and gave him a fast hold to tie his ship to; and we told him that a powerful people called the Five United Nations had placed us here, and established a fair and lasting friendship with us."

The Five Nations had not only conquered and "made women," of the Delawares, figuratively speaking, but, as we have seen, at times also rebuked them with that taunt. Sometimes, the Iroquois also spoke of having "put petticoats" on the Delawares.[1] In a message sent to the Governor in 1732 from the Shawnee chiefs at Allegheny, they state that some five years before, the Five Nations had told the Delawares and themselves, that "since you have not hearkened to us nor regarded what we have said, now we will put petticoats on you, and look upon you as women for the future, and not as men." This would fix the date of the complete subjection of the Delawares by the Iroquois as 1727; which seems to be confirmed by the fact that at about the same time Shekallamy or Swatane, the Oneida chief, removed from the Iroquois country and settled above Shamokin, where he acted as the over-lord of the Delawares and Shawnees living there. In the conference at Philadelphia in 1742, Cannassatego, the Iroquois chief, taunted in a similar manner the Delaware sachems then present, and bade them depart from the country between the Delaware Forks forever. Even so late as December, 1755, the Delawares at Tioga replied to Sir William Johnson's messenger, sent to inquire why they began hostilities against the settlers south of the Blue Mountains, that they did not know the cause of the quarrel; "'t is true, Brother, as you say, we are not at our own command, but under the direction of the Six Nations. We are women; our Uncle [the Iroquois] must say what we must do; he has the hatchet, and we must do as he says; we are poor women, and have got out of temper." In the

---

[1] The vices of the Greeks were common among nearly all the Indian tribes. Frequent references are found in the early records to a class of perverts among the savages, who, by the Traders, were usually called "hermaphrodites." These men wore the garb and performed all the functions of women save that of child-bearing. "Certain young men of the tribe," writes Dr. Brinton, "apparently vigorous and of normal development, were deprived of the accoutrements of the male sex, clothed like women, and assigned women's work to do. They neither went out to hunt nor on the war-path, and were treated as inferiors by their male associates. Whether this degradation arose from superstitious rites or sodomitic practices, it certainly carried to its victims the contempt of both sexes." In 1756 the Iroquois sent a belt to the Delawares with the most insulting message: "You will remember that you are our women; our forefathers made you so, and put a petticoat on you, and charged you to be true to us, and lie with no other man; but now you have become a common bawd." (Records of the Easton Conference, 1756, in Lib. Am. Philos. Soc.) See, also, Thwaites's *Hennepin*, 168, 653; and Thwaites's *Jesuit Relations*, lix., 309, 310.

The Petticoat Indians of Petticoat Land 113

spring of 1756, Sir William Johnson sent a message to the Delawares and Shawnees living at Otseningo, "on one of the western branches of the Susquehanna," desiring them to attend a conference at Onondaga. As a result of this, some of the Delawares and Shawnees came to Onondaga in July, 1756; but the greater part of the Delawares, living at Tioga, refused to attend, for reasons which will be stated hereafter. In the conference with those of both tribes who did attend, Colonel Johnson, as he wrote the Lords of Trade, "concluded this treaty by taking off the Petticoat, or that invidious name of Women, from the Delaware Nation (which hath been imposed on them by the Six Nations from the time they conquered them), in the name of the Great King of England, their father, and on behalf of all their brethren, the English, on this continent; and promised them I would use my influence and best endeavors to prevail with the Six Nations to follow my example. The deputies of the Six Nations who were present approved of this measure, but said they were not a sufficient number, nor properly authorized to do it on behalf of their constituents; however, they would make their report, and press it upon them."

Ten months afterwards, in a conference held at Lancaster between the Governor of Pennsylvania, George Croghan, and some of the Six Nation chiefs, one of the latter, in explaining the causes which gave rise to the quarrel between the English and the Delawares and Shawnees, said: "In former times, our forefathers conquered the Delawares, and put petticoats on them. A long time after that, they lived among you, our brothers; but upon some difference between you and them, we thought proper to remove them, giving them lands to plant and hunt on at Wyomen and Juniata on Susquehannah."

It has been stated above, that, in the conference held at Onondaga in July, 1756, but few of the Delawares attended, and especially few from the vicinity of Tioga. The messenger who carried Sir William Johnson's invitation for this conference to the Delawares and Shawnees at Otseningo and Tioga, reported to that official that one of the Indians living near Otseningo had applied to the Delawares at Tioga, asking them to accompany the others to Onondaga; "which they refused to do, saying that one, Thomas McGee [McKee],[1] who lives upon the Susquehanna, and is married to a Shawanese squaw, had told them that in ten days an army of the English would come and destroy them, and said to them farther, 'You cannot think that as you have murdered the English from Conestoga to Esopus [Kingston, N. Y.], that they will put up with it quietly; and Warraghiyagey [Sir William Johnson] may pretend to

---

[1] See Chapter VII.

make peace with you, but that is not in his power. The Governor of Pennsylvania is master this way, and will not listen to peace.'"

This messenger does not seem to have reported to Colonel Johnson all that really occurred during the conferences at Otseningo and Tioga between the Six Nation emissaries and the Delawares. At that time Teedyuscung was engaged in bringing about an alliance between the three tribes of the Delawares and those of the Shawnees, Nanticokes, and Hudson River Indians (Mohicans) of northeastern Pennsylvania, of which alliance he was made sachem. Little Abram, a Mohawk chief who attended the conference at Lancaster on May 13, 1757, told Governor Denny on that occasion, that when the Mohawks found that the Senecas, whose business it was to keep the Delawares in order "had neglected their offices, we [the Mohawks] took the affair in hands, and sent messengers to Otsaningo; and there a council was held, and the deputies we sent charged them to get sober, as we looked upon their actions as the actions of drunken men. . . . They returned for answer, that they looked upon themselves as men, and would acknowledge no superiority that any other nation had over them. 'We are men, and are determined not to be ruled any longer by you as women; and we are determined to cut off all the English, except those that may make their escape from us in ships; so say no more to us on that head, lest we castrate you, and make women of you, as you have done of us.' In the meantime, though they did not any longer acknowledge the Six Nations as their Uncles, yet they would listen to what the Seneca should say to them—him only they acknowledged as their Uncle. Notwithstanding this rash speech, they afterwards, at the instance of Sir William Johnson, agreed to a cessation of arms, to come to an interview with him and their Brother Onas [Penn]."

What caused this remarkable change in the character of the Delaware Indians? What led them to step out of the ignoble rôle to which they had been assigned long before by their scornful conquerors; and which they had been meekly content to fill during more than half a century afterwards? What made them defy those Iroquois conquerors in such a bold and hazardous manner at this time; and, casting aside forever the name and garb of "women," at once take up the warrior's hatchet, and fearlessly proclaim themselves the peers of the best of their former lords; nay, threaten the latter with direful consequences to themselves if they should even attempt to talk with them about making peace with the English?

Many answers have been given to these questions.

The Quakers tried to make the Indians themselves ascribe it to the Walking Purchase of 1737, in which they had been overreached; and to the hanging of the chief, Owechela, in New Jersey, in 1727. Both of these incidents were too remote in time from 1755 to be thought of by the Indians themselves; and Conrad Weiser showed that they were only brought forward at the suggestion of the Quaker politicians, after the Indians had committed their outrages, and when they were put to an excuse for extenuating them.[1]

George Croghan and Provost William Smith said, it was because the Quaker Assembly of 1751 had refused to build a "Strong-House" at the Forks of Ohio, when the Delawares and Shawnees there were all united in the English interest, and repeatedly asked that a fort be built.

The governors of the other colonies said, it was because, when Washington was defeated at Great Meadows in 1754, the Quaker Assembly would permit no help to be given in response to such plaintive appeals as were sent by the Indians at Allegheny to the Six Nations—the Delawares crying to them: "Uncles of the United Nations, we expect to be killed by the French, your father; we desire, therefore, that you will take off our petticoat, that we may fight for ourselves, our wives, and children; in the condition we are in [without adequate arms or ammunition] you know we can do nothing,"—the Shawnees pleading, "Brethren, the United Nations, hear us; the French, your father's hatchet is just over our heads, and we expect to be struck with it every moment; make haste, therefore, and come to our assistance as soon as possible; for if you stay till we are killed, you won't live much longer afterwards; but if you come soon, we shall be able to fight and conquer the French, our enemy. Grandfathers [to the Delawares], don't leave me [to remove eastward], but let us live and die together; and let our bones rest together; let us die in battle, like men, and fear not the French."

The Governor of Pennsylvania said, it was because, when Braddock was defeated, and when Scarrooyady, a chief of the Six Nations (after travelling up and down the Susquehanna Valley and receiving the strongest assurances from the Delawares and Shawnees there that they would hold together, and resist the French), had gone to Philadelphia, and, on November 8th, told the Governor and the Assembly, "that he was sent on purpose, by all the nations of Indians on Susquehanna, to renew their application and earnest request to us [the English], to give them the hatchet, and to aid, protect, and join with them against the French; and that he came to obtain our explicit answer, whether we would fight or not; and, after he had used many other arguments, he addressed himself to the Governor and Assembly in these words: 'Brethren, I must deal plainly with you, and tell you if you will not fight with us, we will go somewhere else; we never can or ever will put up with the affront'; . . . and though the Governor, at the close of that conference, after he had

[1] *Penna. Archives*, iii., 86, 257.

dismissed the Indians, did in the most pressing manner entreat the Speaker and Assembly to return to their House, to consider well what the Indians had said on that important occasion, and to strengthen his hands and enable him to make a proper answer to what they had then proposed and expected of us; and letting the House know that without their aid he could not do it; yet we find that nothing could prevail with the Assembly to agree to our giving the hatchet to the Indians, and joining them against the French; the consequence whereof was, that the Governor was obliged to let the Indians go away dissatisfied, and soon after the Delawares joined the enemy, and began to fall upon and destroy our frontier inhabitants."

Daniel Dulany, of Maryland, said, it was because of the fact that Benjamin Franklin's bitter hatred of Governor Morris[1] [together with his acute sense of thrift and the fear of losing the public printing] caused him to act the basely mercenary part he did in using his influence, as Clerk of the Assembly, against granting any money in response to the Governor's appeals, unless the grant was coupled with a provision for taxing the Proprietary estates; a provision which Franklin and the Assembly well knew the Governor had no power immediately to accept.

Edmund Burke said, it was because it was "an error to have placed so great a part of the Government in the hands of men who hold principles directly opposite to its end and design"; and that, "as a peaceable, industrious, honest people, the Quakers cannot be too much cherished; but surely they cannot themselves complain, that when, by their opinions, they make themselves sheep, they should not be entrusted with office, since they have not the nature of dogs."

Benjamin Franklin, one of the leaders of the Assembly, said, it was because "these public quarrels were all at bottom owing to the Proprietaries, our hereditary Governors, who, when any expense was to be incurred for the defence of their Province, with incredible meanness, instructed their Deputies to pass [approve] no act for levying the necessary taxes, unless their vast estates were in the same act expressly excused."

The members of the Assembly themselves said, it was because their warning had not been heeded, when, in August, 1751, a Committee of their House (of which Committee Franklin was a member) reported: "As the generous allowances [for the charge of Indian Affairs] lately made, amounting within four years past to near £5000 [£4568], have had the desired good effect of confirming our alliances with the Indians, the present opportunity seems to us very proper to enter into the consideration of the proportion the People should pay of the charges"; and when, following this report, the House voted unanimously as its opinion, "that

[1] See Dulany's letter of Dec. 9, 1755, *Penna. Magazine*, iii., 23.

the Proprietaries' interest will be so greatly advanced by keeping up a firm peace and friendly correspondence with the Indians, that they ought to bear a proportionable part of the charges expended upon all such treaties as tend to those good purposes."

The Mayor and citizens of Philadelphia said, it was because the same despicable body of politicians and poltroons, assuming a holier-than-thou attitude, turned deaf ears, as long as they dared, to appeals like that from the Mayor, the Aldermen, and the non-Quaker citizens of Philadelphia, who on November 24, 1755, addressed the Assembly, to remind its members that, "while you have been sitting, scarce a day has passed wherein you have not heard of the inhuman slaughter of your fellow-subjects, and been loudly called upon for that protection, which, by the most sacred ties you owe to the people. . . . While you have been deliberating, much innocent blood has been spilt, a great extent of our country laid waste, and the miserable inhabitants scattered abroad before the savage spoiler. We, therefore, in the most solemn manner, before God and in the name of our fellow-citizens, call upon you, adjure you, nay, we supplicate you, as you regard the lives of the people whom you represent, to give that legal protection to your bleeding country which ought to be the chief object of all government at such a perilous juncture as this; and let it no longer be said, that while we are daily hearing so much concerning privilege and right, we are in the meantime deprived of that most essential right and great first privilege (which God and Nature gave us) of defending our lives and protecting our families."[1]

The Minutes of the Pennsylvania Council for some five or six years *after* 1755 would seem to indicate that the cowardly braggart, Teedyuscung, a minor chief of the Delawares, had so impressed Israel Pemberton and some of his fellow Quakers by his oratory, that they apotheosized him as a martyr, a king, and a hero; practically paid him tribute during most of that time; and permitted him, unopposed, with a small band of drunken savages, to harass the northern frontiers of the Province, kill by scores the unprotected Germans of the outer settlements, browbeat and flout the Provincial authorities, and to acquire such power and influence among his immediate tribesmen that he was able to intimidate and

[1] This petition, following the riots which had broken out in the city, in which the lives of the Assemblymen were endangered, and on the news received in Philadelphia the same day, that 2,000 inhabitants of Chester County, and a considerable number from Berks County "were preparing to come to Philadelphia to compel the Assembly to agree to pass laws for the defence of the Province," together with the receipt of a letter from the Proprietary, agreeing to contribute £5000 for the defence of the frontiers, and the arrival in Philadelphia of 400 of the angry Germans from the frontier, finally forced the Assembly to pass a militia law; and such a law was accordingly presented the next day for the Governor's signature.—*Col. Rec.*, vi., 729 to 735; *Penna. Magazine*, iii., 24; Egle's *Dauphin County*, 43.

levy tribute on the whole Province for a number of years with impunity.

Perhaps all these things taken together do enable us to arrive at the true reason for the attacks of the Delawares of the Susquehanna on the white settlers in 1755 and 1756. That reason may have been, simply, that after Braddock's inglorious failure, the Delaware Indians had found Pennsylvania to be ruled by a race of men more base, abject, and womanly, than themselves—men who were willing to sacrifice their neighbors' lives to save their own souls and money—and who were not only willing but eager to put on and glorify themselves in wearing the petticoat which these Delaware Indians themselves had at last become manly enough to cast aside.[1]

[1] See Report of Committee of Governor's Council, *Penna. Col. Rec.*, vi., 727.

CHAPTER IV

THE SHAWNEES

WE first find the name by which this tribe was subsequently known in the earliest maps of the Dutch and Swedish navigators. The Dutch map of 1614, on which was based the *Carte Figurative*,[1] depicts a nation called "Sawwanew,"[2] living on the east bank of the Delaware, near its mouth. Johannes De Laet, in the 1640 edition of his *History of the New World*, enumerates the "Sawanoos" as one of the tribes of the Delaware River; and on Vanderdonck's map of New Netherland, made in 1656, the "Sauwanoos" are located as between the Upper Schuylkill (and westward therefrom) and the Delaware. Roggeveen's map of New Netherland (1676) also places them between these two rivers, but much lower down and nearly to the mouth of the Schuylkill, under the name "Sauno."[3]

In Joliet's early map of 1673–4, that explorer locates the "Chaouanons" (as the Shawnees were called by the French) on the east bank of the Mississippi, below the mouth of the Ohio, which latter stream Joliet then called the Wabash. In what is called Joliet's *Carte Generale*, published at Paris in 1681, Franquelin locates the "Chaouanone, fifteen villages," south of the Wabash-Ohio (extended) and a little west of south of the lower extremity of Lake Michigan.

The earliest mention of the Shawnee name in the Jesuit *Relations*, appears to be in the following passage in the *Relation* of 1647–48 [4]: "On the south shore of this fresh-water sea, or Lake of the Hurons, dwell the follow-

---

[1] Both accompany the report of Captain Hendricksen's discoveries along Delaware Bay during the three years before 1616, laid before the States General of Holland by the Directors of New Netherland, August 18–19, 1616.—*N. Y. Col. Doc.* i., 11 to 13.

[2] "The Shawnees are the only tribe I have met whose name was the same among all tribes, Choctaw, Huron, Iroquois, or Algonquin."—Shea, *Charlevoix*, iii., 175. See also D. G. Brinton's article, *Hist. Mag.*, x., 1.; C. C. Royce, *Mag. West. Hist.*, ii., 38.

[3] *Schawaneu* (Zeisberger's German spelling) is the Algonquin word for "southward" or "from the south," and it has been suggested that its use on the early Dutch and Swedish maps may have been only for the purpose of distinguishing the country of the Lower Delaware Indians from that of the tribes living along the Hudson or North River.

[4] Thwaites's edition, xxxiii., 151.

ing Algonquin tribes, . . . who are all allies of our Hurons. With these we have considerable intercourse, but not with the following, who dwell on the shores of the same Lake, farther toward the West, namely: the Ouchaouanag, who form part of the Nation of Fire," etc. The Fire Nation, or Mascoutin, was an Algonquin tribe living at that time in eastern Michigan. They were known to the Hurons as the Assistague-ronons and are located on Champlain's map of 1632, under that name, south of Lake Huron and west of the St. Clair River. The *Relation* for 1659-60 speaks of "Ontouagannha, or Fire Nation" as a tribe that had been conquered, with the Eries, by the Five Nations, and some of its members adopted by the latter.

In the *Relation* of 1661–62, Father Lalemant writing from Montreal in 1662, says: "Proceeding rather westerly than southerly, another band of Iroquois is going 400 leagues from here in pursuit of a nation whose only offence consists in its not being Iroquois. It is called *Ontoagannha* signifying 'the place where people cannot speak'—because of the corrupt Algonquin in use there. Furthermore, if we believe our Iroquois who have returned thence, and the slaves whom they have brought thence, it is a country which has none of the severity of our winter, but enjoys a climate which is always temperate—a continual spring and summer, as it were. . . . Their villages are situated along a Beautiful River, which serves to carry people down to the Great Lake (for they so call the sea), where they trade with Europeans who pray as we do. From their account, we suppose these Europeans to be Spaniards." At that time, as at present, the Iroquois regarded the Ohio, or Great River, as including that part of the Mississippi below the mouth of the Ohio.

Father Julien Garnier, writing from among the Senecas in July, 1672, says: "God has shown great mercy to some baptized adults, among others, a captive Ontouagaunha, or Chaouanong, decrepit with age. Ordinarily, only young men are brought captive from such distant nations."

These passages may indicate that the Shawnees originally formed a part of the Mascoutin tribe; or, possibly, nothing more than that both tribes were *Ontouagannha*, *i. e.*, of "the place where people cannot speak" good Algonquin. In 1762–65 the Mascoutins were reported as being a clan of the Miami tribe.

Father Marquette, writing in 1670 from La Pointe, on the southern shore of Lake Superior, speaks of having talked with a party of Illinois Indians, who had visited La Pointe. They told him, he states, that "they were visited last summer by a nation whom they call Chaouanon, and who live to the east-southeast of their country. The young man who teaches me the Illinois language saw them, and says they had glass beads, which proves that they had communication with Europeans.

They had made a journey of thirty days to reach the country of the Illinois."

In mentioning the Ohio, as he noted it on his voyage down the Mississippi in 1673, Marquette remarks: "This river comes from the country on the east, inhabited by the people called Chaouanons, in such numbers that they reckon twenty-three villages in one district, and fifteen in another, lying quite near each other: they are by no means warlike, and are the people the Iroquois go far to seek in order to wage an unprovoked war upon them."

Nicholas Perrot, who lived among the Miamis, Foxes, and other western tribes from about 1664 until after 1700, in his *Memoire* (followed by La Potherie in 1722, by Charlevoix in 1744, and by Colden in 1746), relates that the Iroquois had their original home about the site of Montreal and Three Rivers; that they fled from their Algonquin enemies to the vicinity of Lake Erie, "where lived the Chaouanons"; that after many years of war against the Chaouanons and their allies, the latter were driven towards Carolina, where they were living in the time of the writer.

La Potherie gives an account of the capture of a canoe load of Iroquois by the Pottawattomies near Michillimackinack, which took place about the middle of the decade, 1660–1670. These Iroquois had just returned from an expedition against the Chaouanons, near Carolina, and had brought with them one captive to burn. The captive was released, and put in charge of some Sacs, to whom he related that his village was only five days' journey from the South Sea, and "was near a great river, which, coming from the country of the Illinois, empties into this sea."

The captive Shawnee, released from the Iroquois by the Pottawattomies, returned home;[1] and some time later a party of forty of his countrymen set out to visit his liberators, who were then living at the Baye des Puants. This party of forty may have been the same party of which Marquette heard in 1670; although it would seem from La Potherie's account of their visit that it may have occurred as late as 1672.

There is, in the *Relation* of the Abbé Galinee (1669–70), as given by Margry, another statement that refers to the Shawnees, and indicates the locality of a part of the tribe at that time. Speaking of the commencement of La Salle's journey to the southwest, and the reason for it, Galinee writes: "Our fleet consisted of seven canoes, each with three men, which departed from Montreal the sixth day of July, 1669, under the guidance of two canoes of Iroquois Sonnontoueronons [Senecas], who had come to Montreal in the autumn of the year 1668 to do their hunting

[1] La Potherie's account of this incident is reprinted in *Wisconsin Historical Collections*, xvi., 48.

and trading. These people, while here, had stayed quite a long time at M. de la Salle's, and had told him so many marvels of the River Ohio, with which they said they were thoroughly acquainted, that they inflamed in him more than ever the desire to go to see it. They told him that this river took its rise three days' journey from Sonnontouan, and that after a month's travel one came upon the Honniasontkeronons and the Chiouanons, and, that after having passed the latter, and a great cataract or water-fall that there is in this river, one found the Outagame and the country of the Iskousogos."

Father Jacques Gravier sailed from the Illinois, down to the mouth of the Mississippi, in 1700. His narrative is printed by Shea, from manuscript. Arriving at the mouth of the Ohio, which had been called the Ouabache by La Salle, in 1683, he writes of this stream: "It has three branches; one coming from the northeast, and flowing behind the country of the Oumiamis, is called by us, the St. Joseph, but by the savages, the Oubachie; the second comes from the country of the Iroquois, and this is called the Ohio; the third, on which the Chaouanoua live [the Cumberland], comes from the south-southwest. The stream formed by the junction of the three flows into the Mississippi, under the name of the Ouabachi."

These prehistoric Shawnee villages along the Cumberland and lower Ohio will be considered in the chapters on the Ohio Valley.

In Robert Morden's map of Carolina and Virginia (London, 1687), the "Sauna" are located in Upper South Carolina beyond the head waters of the Broad and Wateree rivers.

In John Lederer's map of his travels through Virginia and Carolina in the summer of 1670, he calls the Roanoke the "Rorenock or Shawan" River. Ogilby's map of 1670 copies that of Lederer in part and places the "Sauna" nation west of the forks of the Roanoke.[1] These names as used by Lederer, Ogilby, and Morden probably referred to the Chowans.

De l'Isle's map of North America, made in 1700, delineates the country of the "Ontouaganha" (Shawnees) as about the head waters of the Carolina and Georgia rivers, and the same locations are marked on the Senex map of 1710 as occupied by villages of "Chaouanons." In his 1700 map, De l'Isle also places the "Chaouanons" on the Ohio River about the mouth of the Wabash. On his 1718 map of Louisiana[2] he designates the Cumberland as the "*Riviere des anciens Chaouanons*," because the Chaouanons formerly lived there; and he calls the Savannah, the "*Riviere des Chaouanos ou d'Ediscou*," locating a Chaouanon village on the east side of the river opposite the site of Augusta. He also

---

[1] Both maps are reproduced in Hawk's *History of North Carolina*.

[2] Erroneously dated as of 1703 in Winsor's *Nar. and Crit. Hist.*, ii., 295; and as of 1707 in French's *Hist. Coll. Louisiana*, ii.

places a Shawnee settlement half way between the source and the mouth of the Alabama. In his 1703 map of Mexico and Florida the same cartographer locates a Shawnee village at the head of the Cumberland, and "villages des Chaouenons" at the head of the rivers of South Carolina. In Van Keulen's map of 1719, the Shawnee country is located about the head waters of the Tennessee (called *Caskinampo*), the Alabama, and the Appalachicola rivers; while Moll, in his map of 1720, places a "Savannah Old Settlement" at the mouth of the Cumberland. Van Keulen, Senex, Moll, and Homann all seem to have obtained most of their information from the maps of De l'Isle.

The Senex 1721 map of Louisiana, following that of Guillame de l'Isle published in 1718, shows the Savannah River as the "River Chaouanos or Ediscou,"[1] and locates a Chaouanona village on its eastern bank, southeast of the towns of the Catawbas and Cherokees. The Cumberland River is called the "River of the Ancient Chaouanons, so-called because formerly inhabited by the Chaouanons."

"Penicaut's *Relation* states that in 1713 Bienville located some Taensas, who had fled from the Mississippi, on Mobile Bay, at the place formerly occupied by the Chaouanons and Taouatchas, two leagues distant from the Fort."—(French, *Hist. Col. Louisiana*, New Series, i., 126.)

Margry's version of Penicaut, however, makes no mention of the Chaouanons in this passage.

"Sawanogi, or Shawanos, a town settled by Shawano-Algonkins, but belonging to the Creek confederacy, stood on the left or southern side of Tallapoosa River, three miles below Likasa Creek. The inhabitants in 1799 retained the customs and language of their countrymen in the southwest."—(Gatschet, *Migration Legend of the Creek Indians*, i., 143.) This may have been the site of the settlement of the Shawnees who left Mobile Bay before 1713; or it may have been a later settlement.

The "War Map of South Carolina 1711–1715" reproduced in Winsor's *Narrative and Critical History* (v., 347) shows the Savannah River as the "Sawano"; and even so late as 1739, De l'Isle's map in the *Atlas Nonveau* gives to that stream, or to the Edisto, the name "Riviere des Chaouanons," and locates a village of the Chaouanons on its banks, midway between the source and mouth.

The truth seems to be, that when the Shawnees were first known to the French, they were living in what is now western Kentucky and along

[1] "But the English, who have built on its banks the City of St. George or New London, have again changed the name to Edisto, and it is marked in some of our maps, River des Chaouanons":—Charlevoix, i., 136. Fort King George was built about 1720, by order of George I., on the Altamaha River, near the confluence of the Oconee and Ocmulgee.

the lower Ohio, the Cumberland (which stream was formerly called the "Shawnee" River by the English), and the Tennessee. Between 1665 and 1685 they appear to have made their way up the Tennessee, the Cumberland, and the Kentucky, across the mountains, into Tennessee and Carolina. They likewise went into the country of the Miamis and the Illinois near the southern shore of Lake Michigan. From these places, between 1690 and 1710, most of them, as we shall see, were driven from the west and south into eastern Pennsylvania by the wars waged against them by the Miamis, by the Iroquois, and by the Catawbas, Chickasaws, Cherokees, and other southern tribes in Tennessee and the Carolinas.

Some Shawnees were with the Illinois in 1680. Readers of Parkman's *La Salle* will remember that when a great war party of five hundred Iroquois, accompanied by a hundred Miamis,[1] approached the principal Illinois village in September, 1680, the news of their coming was first brought to the Illinois by a friendly Shawnee, who had lived with the Illinois, and who, on setting out to return home, discovered the Iroquois army advancing westward.[2]

La Hontan gives an account of a conference held by Governor La Barre with the Onondagas near the south shore of Lake Ontario in 1684, at which these Iroquois gave as one of the reasons why they had fallen upon and eaten the Illinois and Miamis, that those nations "have brought the Satanas [Shawnees] into their country to take part with them, and armed them, after they had concerted ill designs against us."[3]

This was a fact, for in the spring of 1681, "a Shawano chief, who commanded one hundred and fifty warriors, and who lived on the borders of a great river flowing into the Ohio, having learned that the Sieur de la Salle was in the country of the Miamis, sent to him to have the protection of the king. La Salle replied that the chief's country was inaccessible to the French, by reason of its great distance; but if he would come and join La Salle at the end of the year, and aid him to discover the mouth of the Mississippi, he could then be sure of the protection of the king, and aid against the Iroquois and other enemies. The chief agreed to this proposition and promised to be at the mouth of the River of the Miamis [St. Joseph River] by the end of autumn."[4] This migration does not appear to have been made, however, until after La Salle had started on his journey down the Mississippi. Upon his return, in the summer of 1682, he brought about an alliance between the Illinois and the Miamis, Shawnees, and Mascoutins, for common defence against the Iroquois.

[1] The *Relation des Decouvertes* says, five hundred Iroquois and one hundred Shawnees. Membre says that the allies were Miamis.
[2] Margry, i., 584.
[3] Colden, chapter iv.
[4] Margry, i., 529, 570, 612–13; ii., 143.

The Site of Fort St. Louis on the Illinois.
From a photograph furnished by Mr. Ferdinand Walther.

He also directed Tonty to construct a fort at the portage of the Illinois River, to protect the village of Shawnees that he had drawn to him and had united with the Miamis.

On April 2, 1683, La Salle wrote to the Governor of Canada, Le Febre de la Barre, from Fort St. Louis, in the Illinois country, telling him, "that the Chouenons, Chaskpe [Kiskopo?], and Ouabans [Wabanaki?], have, at his [La Salle's] solicitation, abandoned the Spanish trade, and also nine or ten villages they occupied, for the purpose of becoming French, and settling near Fort St. Louis, which he is about to have built."[1] This fort, which had been begun by La Salle and Tonty in December, 1682, was located on the Illinois River, about ninety-four miles southwest of the mouth of the Chicago River, and on a rock near the site of the present village of Utica, La Salle County, Illinois, some six or seven miles below Ottawa, the county seat. In the vicinity of this timber fort the intrepid Frenchman soon gathered many settlements of Indians of various nations. The Illinois and Shawnees were the first, and they were followed later by the Miamis and others. La Salle reported the total number of warriors to be about four thousand. On Franquelin's map of 1684, reproduced in this book, the numbers of warriors of the different nations are set down as follows: Illinois, 1,200; Miamis (or Twightwees), 1,300; Shawnees, 200; Ouiatanons, 500: Piankeshaws, 150; Pepikokias, 160; Kilaticas, 300; and the Ouabans, 70; 3,880 in all. Franquelin's map of 1688, reproduced in Winsor's *Narrative and Critical History* (iv., 231), shows the location of five villages of some of these tribes, clustered around the fort. They were those of the Illinois, the Shawnees, the Ouabans, the Ouiatanons, and the Chaskpes.

Joutel, the companion of La Salle on his last voyage, says, in speaking of the Shawnees of Illinois: "They have been there only since they were drawn thither by M. de La Salle; formerly they lived on the borders of Virginia and the English Colonies."[2]

The Marquis De Nonville, who succeeded La Barre as Governor of Canada in 1685, wrote to the Ministry at home, August 25, 1687: "M. de la Salle has made grants at Fort St. Louis to several Frenchmen who reside there since many years, without desiring to return. This has given rise to infinite disorders and abominations. Those to whom M. de la Salle has given grants are all young men without any means of cultivating the soil; every eight days they marry squaws after the Indian fashion of that country, whom they purchase from the parents at the expense of the merchants. Those fellows, pretending to be independent, and masters on their distant lands, everything is in disorder. This year, ten plotted

[1] *N. Y. Col. Doc.*, ix., 799.
[2] Margry, iii., 502.

to go off to the English, and conduct them to the Micissipy. The war arrested that."

Fort St. Louis stood on the south, or left bank of the Illinois River. The Shawnee village of two hundred warriors (and perhaps six or eight hundred souls) is located in Franquelin's map of 1684, as being on the south side of the river, behind the fort, while according to the map of 1688 it stood on the opposite, or north side of the river, near the fort.

If the present writer is correct in his reading of the colonial records of New York, Maryland, and Pennsylvania of the latter part of the seventeenth century, the earliest migration of the Shawnees into Pennsylvania known to history, came, in part at least, from this Shawnee village, built under the guns of La Salle's Fort of St. Louis. Their leader certainly came from there.

A meeting of the Maryland Council was held at St. Mary's in Anne Arundel County, August 16, 1692, presided over by Lionel Copley, Governor of the Province. At this meeting the Governor produced and read a number of letters received from Nicholas Greenberry and others.[1] Greenberry's letter was dated July 25th, and referred to an earlier letter on the same subject, written to the Governor one week before. The letters gave varying accounts of the coming of a number of strange Indians into the Colony, who had seated themselves near the mouth of the Susquehanna. Greenberry states that there are seventy-two men and one hundred women and children in the party.

After these letters were read, a Frenchman, who had come into the Province with this party of strange Indians at the head of the bay, and had been "taken up for a spie, or party concerned with them in designs of mischief," was ordered to be brought before the Council, and examined, through an interpreter.[2]

Having declared himself to have been formerly an inhabitant of Canada, from whence he had run away and taken up his habitation with the Indians, he was questioned by the Council and replied as follows :

He had left Canada eight years ago [1684?]. His reason for leaving Canada was, that he had once "gone away without leave of the Governor to some Indians that owed him some beaver; and when he came back to the town again, the Governor put him in prison, and in irons, where he continued several months; but at last got loose, made his escape, and ever since hath used the Woods." He had served three years in Canada as an apprentice to a house carpenter.

When asked if he had been amongst "those Indians" during all the eight years since he had left Canada, he replied that "He hath been ever

[1] *Maryland Council Proceedings*, iii., 341–350.
[2] *Ibid.*, p. 345.

The Site of Fort St. Louis, from the South.

since constantly with those Indians, chiefly at a Fort called St. Louis." The reason why he and those Indians with him came to desert that fort was, that "While he was with them there, it happened that about two years since [1690?], they went away; and some time after, about August, he resolved to follow them, and took a canoe and went after them, three hundred leagues in length; was forty days going; hunted for his victuals, which, as he got, he roasted; and found water in all places."

In explaining how he came to find the Indians again, he stated that he "guessed the way, and was guided by the course of the river; and when he came to them, they made him very welcome; having also amongst them five other Indians, called Wolf Indians [*i. e.*, either Minsi Delawares, or Hudson River Mohicans], which had formerly come to those thirty Indians that left the Fort abovesaid, and invited them to come and live among them."

He added that the party to which he belonged had with them six Catakoy (Catogui, *i. e.*, Cherokee?) Indians, who were prisoners; and that some of the Indians called him "Father."

After the examination of two others, who had been concerned in the capture of the Frenchman, a party of Indians that had been found in the back-woods of Anne Arundel County was brought before the Council for examination. Being asked if the strange Indians in the Frenchman's party were of the Naked Indians, they replied: "No, nor are they Senecas. There are, they say, seven forts of them—one fort of Naked Indians—and some French joined with them."[1] Another Frenchman was with them, who was free, was married, and had been among them for years. The Indians added that, some two or three days before, they had met a party of about sixteen of the Naked Indians, going after the New York Indians who had recently created some disturbance in the Province.

The Frenchman was placed in the custody of the sheriff of St. Mary's County, with whom he remained a prisoner until October 29th following, when he was released by order of the Council.

On February 15, 1693, Charles James wrote to the Governor from Cecil County, to the effect that the supposed king of the Indians, together with the Frenchman, had been received by Colonel Casparus Herman and were now residing upon his Manor (Bohemia Manor, on the south bank of the lower Elk River).[2] Their followers, also, had erected their wigwams, or "fabrics," on the same lands. The Frenchman, he was informed, had an Indian woman for his wife, and had been seen during the winter in a coat lined with rich fur; while one of his Indian followers had

---

[1] This was a correct description of the Indian towns clustered about La Salle's Fort St. Louis.

[2] See Johnston's *Cecil County, Maryland*, p. 4.

been seen naked on a bitter cold day—indicating that he must belong to the dreaded tribe of the Naked Indians. The Frenchman had informed Colonel Herman that he had been a captain in Canada, and for some misdemeanor had fled from that country. Colonel Herman stated that he was a man of excellent parts, and spoke several languages. The writer of the letter had been informed by one, Robert Drury, and by another, who had been a prisoner with the Canadian Indians after one of their descents on the Penobscot settlements in Maine, that they suspected this Frenchman to be none other than Monsieur (Saint) Castine, who had led the attack on the Maine settlements. The Frenchman's Indian wife, Drury had seen, and knew her to be the wife of Castine.

An affidavit from Drury accompanied this letter, in which these statements were again duly set forth.[1]

At a meeting of the Maryland Council held on the 8th of April, 1693, two more depositions relating to the Strange Indians at the head of the Bay, were read to the members. Henry Thompson, on March 4th, is reported to have declared that the Frenchman, "who lives at Col. Herman's, upon the Manor . . . is marked with the letters, 'M. C.,' upon his breast; he married two Indian squaws; hath one daughter aged sixteen." Robert Drury, in a second deposition, taken March 9th, stated, that "When he was brought to the sight of the French Indian who was supposed to be Monsr. Castine, of Penobscot, beyond Pemaquid, upon oath, saith, that he is not Monsr. Castine, but some other person."[2]

Three days later (April 11th), Robert Drury appeared before the Council in person, at a meeting held at St. Mary's; and was examined in regard to the discrepancies appearing in his two depositions about the Frenchman. He explained that his first affidavit was made before he had seen the suspected person, but the second was made after a sight of him. He knew that the Frenchman was not Monsieur Castine, whom he had known very well; but he had been informed by Mr. Thompson, from New England, that the Frenchman was a mate or associate of Castine, and that his name was "Martin Shortive" [Martin Chartier.] He added that he knew the Frenchman's wife to be the same woman whom he had known as the wife of Monsieur Castine, and that a French [Labadist] minister living in Cecil County had also told him the same thing. The minister had likewise informed Colonel Herman that the Frenchman had formerly lived at a place called "Asopris [Esopus?], between Albany and Canada," and that the Indians now with him were Southern Indians.[2]

Colonel Casparus Herman and Captain Jacob Young had been summoned to attend this same meeting of the Council, and they brought with

[1] *Maryland Council Proceedings*, iii., 458–469.
[2] *Ibid.*, 486–7.
[3] *Ibid.*, 517.

them from Cecil County, Martin Shortive, or Chartier, the Frenchman under suspicion, together with the king or chief of the Strange Southern Indians, and some Susquehannock Indians. These persons were examined after Mr. Drury.

Colonel Herman stated that the Susquehannock Indians whom he had now brought down with him declare "that they know those other Indians at the head of the Bay to come from the Southward; and that they are called the Stabbernowles; and that generally all the Indians in their parts know them to be the same."

The Frenchman, the Indian chief of the "Stabbernowles," and one of the Susquehannock Indians were then examined. The latter was asked how long the Frenchman had been among them. He replied, "That when those Strange Indians went away from the Twitteway [Twightwee or Miami] Indians to the northward, then this Frenchman came to them; that they were two years travelling towards the southward before they found a convenient place of sitting down, and there they lived three years [1689-92?]; the Sinniquo [Seneca] woman told him that this Frenchman about five years since [1687?] run away from the Twittawees to these Southern Indians."

Being asked later by the interpreter as to what was his opinion concerning those Strange Indians, and to what nation they belonged, the Susquehannock replied: "There are two parties of them; one gone to the northward, design to join with the Sinniquos in their war; and these here have desire to set down among us and be at peace. They are called the Stabbernowle Indians."[1]

The Frenchman who had led these Indians into Maryland, disguised in the pages of the Maryland records as "Martin Shortive," was of course, none other than Martin Chartier, afterwards well-known as the Indian Trader among the Shawnees of Pequea, in what is now Lancaster County, Pennsylvania; whose wife, according to the Pennsylvania authorities, was a Shawnee squaw. The Indians, called by the Susquehannocks, "Stabbernowles," were the same whom William Penn found a few years later, settled at Pequea Creek on the lands of the Susquehannocks, or Conestogas, and taken under their protection. In the present account, therefore, is given for the first time the true history and time of the coming of the Shawnees into Pennsylvania.

Captain John Hans Steelman (he is called John Hance Tillman, or Tilghman, in the Maryland records), an Indian Trader of Cecil County, who lived near the mouth of Susquehanna, was called before a joint

---

[1] *Proceedings Maryland Council*, iii., 517–18. From 1696 to 1700 the name appears on the Maryland records as Shevanoe, Shavanole, Shevanor, Shavanolls, etc., all synonyms for Shawano or Shawnee.

conference of the Maryland Council and Assembly, June 1, 1697, and asked to give an account of what he had done in pursuance of the late order of the Council relating to the Susquehannock and other Indians at the head of Chesapeake Bay. He reported that he had visited these Indians and made an enumeration of the different tribes, as the Council had directed. He said, that "at Canistauga, the Susquehanna and Seneca Indians have about forty lusty young men, besides women and children; that the Shevanor [Shawnee] Indians, being about thirty men, besides women and children, live within four miles of Canistauga, lower down, and submit themselves and pay tribute to the Susquehannas and Senecas; that the Delaware Indians live at Minguannan, nine miles from the head of Elk River, and fifteen miles from Christeen, and about thirty miles from Susquehanna River; are about three hundred red men, and are tributary to the Senecas and Susquehannas; fifty of them living at Minguanon, the rest upon Brandywine, and Upland Creeks."[1]

It would seem from this, that the Shawnees had followed the Susquehannocks in removing farther up the river between the years 1692 and 1697; for we have already seen from the deposition of John Hans Steelman, printed in the preceding chapter, that some of the Susquehannocks, about 1690 ("fifty years before 1740," the date of his deposition), were living in their lower village at the mouth of Octorara Creek.

On May 26, 1698, a conference was held at Steelman's trading-house between John Thompson and two other commissioners, sent by the Governor of Maryland, and the chiefs of the Susquehannocks, the Shawnees, and the Delawares. Penascok, or Penascoh, a minor chief, represented the Shawnees at the beginning of the conference; Connetectah (Connoodaghtoh), the sachem of the Susquehannocks, represented his tribe; and Owhalla (Owechela), the Delawares. The record in the minutes of the Maryland Council adds: "In the evening came Meaurroway, king of the Shawaneles, brought on horseback, by reason of his great age, together with one of his great men, and one, Martin Shartee, a Frenchman, resident and married among them."[2]

John Lawson, in his *New Voyage to Carolina* (London, 1714; Raleigh, 1860), refers to the settlement of these Shawnees on the Susquehanna. He writes: "And to this day they [the Indians in general] are a shifting, wandering people; for I know some Indian Nations that have changed their settlements many hundred miles; sometimes, no less than a thousand; as is proved by the Savanna Indians, who formerly lived on [near] the banks of the Mississippi, and removed thence to the head of one of the rivers of South Carolina; since which (for some dislike),

---
[1] *Proceedings Maryland Assembly*, v., 519.
[2] *Ibid.*, v., 428.

most of them are removed to live in the quarters of the Iroquois or Sinnegars [Senecas], which are on the heads of the rivers that disgorge themselves into the Bay of Chesapeake."

The main body of the Shawnees that did not migrate to Illinois, or to Pennsylvania, seems to have remained for some time in the valley of the Cumberland. Ramsey states in his *Annals of Tennessee*, without citing his authorities, that "M. Charleville, a French trader from Crozat's colony at New Orleans, came, in 1714, among the Shawnees, then inhabiting the country on the Cumberland River; and traded with them. His store was built on a mound, near the present site of Nashville." Here, says Ramsey, the Shawnees had "forted themselves, and maintained a protracted war for the possession of their country" until they were expelled by the allied Chickasaws and Cherokees. "A few years later, in 1714, when Monsieur Charleville opened a store where Nashville now is, he occupied this fort of the Shawnees as his dwelling."[1]

Penicaut writes that in 1714, he "found, among the Natchez, some slaves belonging to the nation of the Chaouanans, who had been captured by a strong party of Chicaschas, Yazous, and Natchez, who, under pretext of visiting their village for the purpose of dancing the calumet of peace, had attacked them in the most base and treacherous manner, and killed their grand chief, with most of his family, took eleven prisoners, among whom was the wife of the chief, and brought them to the Natchez."[2]

Some of the descendants of those Shawnees of La Salle's establishment on the Illinois who did not accompany the party with whom Martin Chartier came to the Susquehanna, are said by General Force to have removed west of the Missouri about a century later, where Baron de Carondelet, the Spanish Governor, subsequently, in 1793, made them a grant of land, on which they lived until they were removed by the United States Government to a reservation in the Indian Territory.[3]

It will be remembered that in Martin Chartier's examination before the Governor and Council of Maryland, August 16, 1692, he stated that he had left Canada eight years before, and had been with the Shawnees of his party ever since that time, "chiefly at a Fort called St. Louis."

In La Salle's letter of September 29, 1682 (1681?), written to the Abbe Bernou in France, he refers to certain charges which had been made against him at Quebec by some deserters from his Fort of Crevecœur on the Illinois, whom he had captured at Frontenac (killing two of their companions), while on their way back to Montreal. Of these charges La Salle writes: "The twenty-two men who deserted and robbed

---

[1] *Annals of Tennessee*, 45, 79.
[2] French's *Historical Collections of Louisiana and Florida*, New Series, p. 123.
[3] *American State Papers*, vi, 11., 591; cited by Force, *Indians of Ohio*, 26.

me [in the spring of 1680, while La Salle was on his way to Montreal, and Tonty, his lieutenant, had gone up the river to begin the construction of Fort St. Louis], are not to be believed on their word, deserters and thieves as they are. They are ready enough to find some pretext for their crime; and it needs as unjust a judge as the Intendant to prompt such rascals to enter complaints against a person to whom he had given a warrant to arrest them. But, to show the falsity of these charges, Martin Chartier, who was one of these who incited the rest to do as they did, was never with me at all; and the rest had made their plot [to kill La Salle at Fort Frontenac] before seeing me."[1]

These charges against him, to which La Salle referred, were contained in a "Declaration," made before the Sieur du Chesneau, Intendant of Canada, by Moyse Hillaret, ship carpenter, "late in the service of Sieur de la Salle." This paper is dated August 17, 1680, and reads as follows[2]:

Hillaret says that he wintered at Fort Crevecœur with the said Sieur de la Salle, Sieur Tonty, Fathers Gabriel, Louis [Hennepin], and Zenobe [Membre], Recollet friars, and La Rose, carpenter, Petitbled, Boisdardennes, Jean le Meilleur, *alias* La Forge, Jacques Messier, sawyer, Jean le Mire, Jacques Richon, Lesperance, lackey to the said Sieur de la Salle, le Parisien, Boisrondelle, Michel Accault, le Picard, d'Autray, Andre Henault, la Violette, Colin, the Wolf Indian [a Mohican] and Martin Chartier, Duplessis, Jacques Montjault, la Rousseliere, Baribault, and La Croix; from which place the last six named deserted about the time of Epiphany [January 6th] last, because the said Sieur de la Salle wanted them to build sleighs to draw his goods and personal effects as far as the village of the Illinois [the site of the proposed Fort St. Louis].

On the 28th February, Father Louis, Recollet, and the said Accault and Picard went to trade at the Sejoux.

On the 2nd of March, the said Sieur de la Salle left the said Fort for Fort Frontenac, with the said Henault, la Violette, Dautray, Colin, and the Wolf; and on his way, being near the River Tinticy, otherwise called Chicacou, he met la Chapelle and Noel le Blanc, whom the said Sieur de la Salle had sent to Michilimaquinac, to await the return of his barque, in which was between twelve and thirteen thousand livres worth of furs and four thousand livres worth of goods. The said Leblanc told the said Sieur de la Salle that he had learned that Fort Frontenac had been seized by Sieur Guiton and his creditors.

The said Leblanc then came to Fort Crevecœur, and repeated all that he had said to the said Sieur de la Salle; that he was a ruined man; that he would never come back to Fort Crevecœur; and that it was necessary to consider what should be done. The said Leblanc, Laforge, and Hillaret decided to leave; and as there was due them nearly three years'

---

[1] Margry, ii., 225.

[2] *Canadian Archives*, Moreau's *Memoirs of Canada, 1540–1759*, F. 176, p. 152; Margry, ii., 104, 108.

wages, at 800 livres per annum, making 2400 livres, and to the said Laforge, 1,000 livres at the end of July last, they took with them six packs of beaver, six robes, four axes, two guns, eight pairs of over-stockings, eight pounds of powder, ten pounds of shot, two dozen flint-stones, one canoe, nineteen otters, four pounds of sewing thread, and an old kettle, a memoranda of the whole of which they left with the said Larose. [The whole conformably to what Montjault, Lacroix, and Petitbled have said. And he has produced a note of the said Sieur de la Salle as to what he owes to the said Moyse, carpenter.]

It would seem from the Intendant's note at the bottom of this statement that at least two of the five who had deserted from Fort Crevecœur with Martin Chartier in January, were in Quebec at the time the examination of Moyse Hillaret took place. Martin Chartier may have been there too. The men concerned in the second desertion made their way to Michillimackinac, where they may have met the first party. Here, they received some re-enforcements, seized a quantity of furs belonging to La Salle, and, twenty in number, started in canoes for Fort Frontenac where they intended to surprise and kill him. On reaching Niagara, they plundered the magazine there, and the party separated, eight of them taking the south shore of Lake Ontario, bound for Albany, while the others, in three canoes, kept along the north shore of the lake, headed for La Salle's post of Frontenac. He intercepted them near that fort, killed two of them, and captured the remainder, whom he sent to Quebec, as prisoners.

Whether Chartier was with one of the parties on Lake Ontario, or whether he fled southward and took refuge with the Shawnees at the time of the desertion, or first joined his five companions at the time of their arrival at Michillimackinac, the writer has not been able to ascertain.[1] From his familiarity with Fort St. Louis, however, which was not built by La Salle and Tonty until the winter of 1682–83, it is possible that he returned to the Illinois country again and afterwards departed from there with a part of the Shawnee band which had settled at the site of Fort St. Louis in 1682.

Governor La Barre, an enemy of La Salle, sent the Chevalier de Baugis with a detachment of men, to take possession of Fort St. Louis, in the fall of 1683. He also sent numerous Traders and canoes of goods, the most of which were seized by the Iroquois. De Baugis reached the fort after La Salle had left, on his way to France; and superceded Tonty, who remained at the fort as the representative of his employer.

[1] There is in the cabinet of the Chicago Historical Society an original trade agreement signed by one Pierre Chartier, dated at Michillimackinac, July 20, 1691. He may have been a relative of Martin Chartier; as the latter, by his Shawnee wife, afterwards had a son, notorious in later Pennsylvania history as Peter Chartier.

The command was restored to Tonty, by order of the King, in the latter part of 1684. Possibly Chartier may have returned for a time while De Baugis was there, and have gone away with the Shawnees when he left. If the statement of the former is to be believed, however, he lived with the Shawnees near Fort St. Louis for some years after 1684.[1]

On April 11, 1693, Lionel Copley, Governor of Maryland, wrote to Benjamin Fletcher and Edmund Andros, Governors of New York and Virginia, telling them of the results of his interviews with Martin Chartier and the Shawnee chiefs examined by him that day. "The Indians," he proceeds, "declare themselves a sort of people or nation called the Stabbernowles, formerly driven away by another nation to the westward, called the Twittaweese, and forced far to the southward, where, for a considerable time, they have lived; and now come, as they pretend, in the way of peace, to live under our protection; but what credit to give them, or how far to trust them, we are at a stand, and not yet resolved."[2]

Copley was succeeded as Governor of Maryland by Francis Nicholson, in 1694. The latter wrote to the British Board of Trade, March 27, 1697, in regard to "the foreign Indians, which are mentioned in a certain message from the House of Burgesses to myself and His Majesty's Council." "Those Indians which come from the southward," he writes, "are supposed to inhabit upon the River Oheo, or Spirito Santo,[3] which runs into the Bay of Mexico, and upon which, 't is reported, the French have two or three settlements. The names which we know the Indians by are the Wittowees, Twistwees [both are names for the same tribe, *i.e.*, the Twightwees, or Miamis], and Naked Indians (but the Indians of one nation are called by diverse names, both by the English and other Indians). The exact point of the compass which their country lies from us is not yet known; but it's supposed to be westward of the South. Sometimes they come down to the Falls of Potomack, and Susquehannah Rivers, between which places the ranging is kept by our two parties of Rangers, consisting of a captain, lieutenant, and eight private troopers."[4]

Governor Nicholson wrote again to the Board of Trade, August 20, 1698, as follows: "Upon inquiry, I had an account from some Chaovonon Indians whose country lies to the southwest of South Carolina, and a Frenchman that came with them, *and was with Monsieur de la Salle that journey that he was killed;* that the French have some settlements west southerly not above two hundred miles from the Falls of Potomack.

---

[1] Joutel found some of the Shawnees still living at Fort St. Louis in the winter of 1687–88.
[2] *Proceedings Maryland Council*, iii., 525.
[3] The Spanish name for the Mississippi, and the French name for the Mobile.
[4] *Proceedings Maryland Council*, v., 84.

One of the chief of those Indians I got to chalk out the way to those settlements, and so to the River Maschasipi, to the parts adjacent, and down to the Bay of Mexico. I had one, with the help of the Frenchman, make a small rude draught with a pen, which I find in some sort to agree with Hennapin's maps."[1] It is probable that Chartier lied in saying that he had been with La Salle in 1687.

The first reference to these Shawnees to be found in the Provincial records of Pennsylvania is probably in the deposition made before the Provincial Council, December 19, 1693, by Polycarpus Rose against the loyalty of Madame Ann Le Tort, her husband, Jacques Le Tort, and other early resident French Traders among the Delaware Indians of Philadelphia and Chester counties, whom Rose accused of carrying on a treasonable correspondence with the French in Canada. One item of his charges was to the effect "that about a year since, there was a packet of letters sent from Philadelphia, from Peter Basilion, Captain DuBrois, and Madame Le Tort, to the strange Indians, called 'Shallna-rooners,' [*roona* or *ronon*, is the Huron word for "people"] sealed up in a blue linen cloth, and was left at James Stanfield's plantation by Richard Basilion's servant, who then run away, and the letters being there three days, James, the Frenchman, came and carried them away." At the examination of Madame Le Tort, which took place in the following February, she explained that the blue linen packet was simply her account book containing a record of what the Indians owed her husband. Shakhuppo, "an Indian king," of the Delawares, said that he had seen some Strange Indians come to trade with Madame Le Tort, "but that he neither knew them nor understood their language." Captain Cock, the interpreter, gave as his opinion of the transactions, "that he believes our Indians are only afraid that the Strange Indians will come and surprise them." The Shallnarooners were one of the bands of Shawnees that had come into Maryland with Martin Chartier and had probably made a temporary stop in Chester County, on their way either to the Delaware Forks or to Pequea Creek.

Reference has already been made to a treaty of peace and alliance entered into at Philadelphia on April 23, 1701, between William Penn and the chiefs of the Susquehanna Minquas, the Potomac Ganawese (otherwise, Conoys, Canoise, or Piscataways),[2] and Opessa (properly Opeththa, as the Shawnees did not use the sibilant), king or sachem of the

---

[1] *Proceedings Maryland Council*, v., 500.

[2] The Ganawese informed Governor Evans at their town above Conestoga in June, 1707, that their tribe had been at peace and tributary to the Five Nations for twenty-seven years past. In June of the preceding year, they had shown him the peace belt, delivered to them by the Onondagas at the time they were made tributaries to the Five Nations.

Shawnees, together with Lemoytungh and Pemoyajooagh, two chiefs of that tribe. Opessa, with some sixty families of his tribe, was said by James Logan to have come into Pennsylvania from the South about 1697–98, and by permission of the Minquas, or Conestogas, to have seated themselves on the east bank of the Susquehanna near the mouth of the Pequea Creek[1] (so-called because some of the Peckawee or Piqua clan of the Shawnees then settled there), in what is now Lancaster County. As has been already stated, these Shawnees were none other than the "Stabbernowles," who, under the leadership of Martin Chartier, had first seated themselves on Bohemia Manor in Cecil County, Maryland, during the summer of 1692. Their town in Pennsylvania was a few miles below that of the remnant of the Minquas, which was then on the north side of Conestoga Creek.

A record in the *Minutes* of the Provincial Council, dated May 18, 1704, would indicate that at that time the Five Nations were not at peace with the Shawnees. "Peter Bezalion, ye French Trader, coming to town, and being sent for, informed ye Board that he had heard that those of ye Five Nations who intended shortly down this way, had a design of carrying off the Shawanah Indians, both those settled near Conestoga and those near Lechay, they being colonies of a nation that were their enemies." The Council accordingly sent messages accompanied by belts of wampum to the Five Nations, in behalf of the Shawnees, "our friends and allies." During the following August, eight or nine chiefs of the Five Nations visited Philadelphia, in response to these messages, and a new treaty, favorable to the Shawnees, was made between them and the Provincial Government.

Reference has been made to the examination of Martin Chartier by the Maryland Council, August 16, 1692, and to the examination of some Maryland Indians at the same time. The native Indians reported that they had recently met a party of about sixteen of the Naked Indians, who were going northward after the New York Indians who had recently made a foray into the Province. The Susequhannock Indian who was examined before the Council, April 11, 1693, also stated that a part of the Strange Indians had gone north to join the Senecas.

As early as 1691, the representatives of Albany and Esopus had urged in the General Assembly of New York, that communications be opened and peace be made with the Far Nations of Indians, with a view to in-

---

[1] Rupp's *Lancaster County*, p. 46; John Hans Steelman's Report of June 1, 1697, already cited. A minute in the records of the Board of Property under date of Feb. 2, 1718, refers to the "Old Sawannah Town" and "Sawannah Old Fields," near the *head* of Pequea Creek, which were on that day granted to Col. John French. (*Penna. Arch.*, 2d. Ser., xix., 625, 681.) This may have been their residence some time between 1692 and 1697.

creasing the fur and peltry business at the two points named, which were then the centres of the fur trade in the Province. The Assembly agreed with the representatives from Albany and Esopus, and ordered that Albany should send six Christians, and Esopus six Christians and twenty-five native Indians, to treat with the Far Nations.[1]

In August, 1692, word was brought to Major Ingoldsby, then Commander-in-Chief of New York, that one hundred warriors of the Satanas (the Five Nations' name for the Shawnees) had arrived as far as to the Delaware River, on a mission to make peace with the Iroquois. At a council held at Fort William Henry, August 12th, the following action was taken:

The Commander-in-Chief being advised that the Sattanas Indians late in war with our Five Nations of Indians have, to the number of one hundred, travelled so far as Delaware River, coming hither to negotiate a peace with our Indians, which is agreed to contribute to their Majesties' interest in this Province, our Sinnequaes being much diverted and hindered in their efforts against Canada by reason of this war; Ordered, That Captain Arent Schuyler be forthwith dispatched to the said Indians, with two belts of Wampum, in order to conduct them safe hither, and that he have letters of credence to Mr. Thomas Lloyd, of Pennsylvania for his assistance.

Accordingly, on August 13th, Captain Schuyler started for the camp of these Indians, which was near the Delaware Falls. They had been conducted from their country by a chief and some warriors of the Minsi or Wolf Delawares and of the Mohicans (Loups). In all probability these Indians were a part of Martin Chartier's band which had seated itself at the head of Chesapeake Bay a few weeks before. Schuyler appears to have met them on August 15th, at which time he delivered two belts of wampum to the Indians, and gave them the acting Governor's message, inviting them to New York Town for a conference.

The Indians answered Captain Schuyler through Matasit, a Minsi sachem, as follows:

"FATHER CORLAER:

"We thank you for the great care which you have taken for us. My own brothers, the Mahikanders, have not done so much.

"When our brethren, about three years past [1689?], went from us to Albany, they left me; since which time I have been wandering, and came in Monsieur Tonty's Land [Fort St. Louis on the Illinois River], who inquired of me what I came to do there. 'Do you not know that your Father, Corlaer, is dead; for I have killed him, and burnt his country.

---

[1] *Minutes of the New York Provincial Council*, MSS., vi., 27.

Therefore, Sachem Matasit, become my child. There is my coat with silver lace.'

"Upon which I answered, 'That will not make me a sachem here, whilst all my old men, brethren, and my Father, Corlaer, are dead. Now I will go to my land to see where I shall make my fire; and if my people is not killed, I will make my fire there again.'

"Upon which Monsieur Tonty said to me: 'You have many nobilities—ye heart. You perhaps think that this is your land, or that you will govern over this people.'

"Upon which I answered: 'What shall I do with your land? I have land enough.'

"'Then,' said Monsieur Tonty, 'you have certainly some new design; but all the Indians that you take along to the Ssouwenas [Shawnees] will be killed, and yourself also.'

"Then I answered: 'Come, tomorrow I will depart for New York. If you can, kill me. I fear you not.'

"Then said the sachem of Ssouwena: 'If you go, I'll go along; and I shall stop Monsieur Tonty's ears'; and told me further, 'Now I'll go with you.'

"Then I answered: 'That is good; my land shall be your land.'

"Then the sachem of Ssouwena said: 'I am afraid for the Mohawks.'

"I answered him, 'Why are you afraid; the Dutch are my friends, and Corlaer is my Father?'

"Then the said Ssouwenee said: 'We have been everywhere, and could find no good land. Where is your land?'

"I answered, 'Menissinck is my land; there shall we live.'

"The Sachem of the Ssouwena: 'Where live ye brethren?'

"I answered, 'They live at New York.'

"The sachem of the Ssouwena asked: 'Your brethren, the Dutch, are they good?'

"I answered, 'For certain they are good. When you come there you shall see that they are good.'

"Then the sachem of the Ssouwenas said: 'If they are good, we will certainly all go thither.' "[1]

Captain Schuyler started with a number of these Indians for New York, where on August 18th they appeared before the Council. The following account of this conference appears in the Council *Minutes*:

Captain Arent Schuyler presented himself with the Far Indians called the Showannos Indians and some of the Sennequaes [?] that had been travelling amongst them nine years, the chief whereof was Matisit; who said, that in his return he met with Monsieur Tonty, Captain of a

---

[1] *New York Colonial MSS.*, xxxviii., 165.

French Castle at the head of the Lakes;—that Tonty asked him whither he was going. He replied, "To his country." Tonty said, "What need you return thither. I have killed your father, the Corlaer[1] (that is the Governor), your brethren, and relations, and burnt all the country. Tarry with me, and I will give you my laced coat. Matisit said he would first go to his country (meaning this Province), and see whether his father and brethren (to-wit, the Governor and the English) were alive or not; and brought with him the Sachem of these Far Nations, with his company, upon promise of protection.

They say they are now come to see the country and to open a way hither; but the next summer they will come with a greater number and more of the riches of their country and desire to have some Christians to accompany them; which Matisit sealed with his beaver coat.[2]

A few weeks after this meeting, the newly arrived Governor, Benjamin Fletcher, with his Council, held a conference at New York with some Hudson River Indians, who had been wandering in the West for some time, and lived among the Shawnees. They were doubtless the same Indians who had returned with Matasit and the Shawnees. They stated to the Governor that "they had long been absent from their native country, and did desire to be kindly received, as they in former days received the Christians, when they first came to America. They pray the same likewise in behalf of the Strange Indians they have brought along with them. They add, moreover, that they are now come to their own river, and those Far Indians have accompanied them by the Great God's protection. They are poor; but come to renew the covenant chain with Corlaer, the Mohawks, and Five Nations; and confirm it with the fruits of their far country, whither they intend to depart in twenty days."

A Minisink Indian, present at this conference, declared that the Minsis had accepted the Far Indians "as their friends and relations," and added, that his tribe, being very poor, intended to return with the Showanees and hunt in their country.[3]

Governor Fletcher suggested that the Shawnees should first make peace with the Five Nations and he would then take them under his protection. This suggestion seems to have been followed, for in July of the following year, the Five Nations told the Governor at Albany: "We are very glad that the Shawannoes, who were our enemies, did make their application to you last fall for protection, and that you sent them

---

[1] This name was applied by the Five Nations to all the English governors of New York, beginning with Andros. It was given them in honor of Arent Van Curler, or Corlaer, who came to the Colony in 1637, and was the chief founder of Schenectady (called after him, Corlaer, or Corlaer's Town, by the French and Indians) in 1661–62. He was drowned in Lake Champlain in 1667. See Jameson's *Narratives of New Netherland*, p. 317.

[2] *New York Council Minutes*, MSS., vi., 116–117.

[3] *Ibid.*, vi., 126.

thither to endeavor a peace with us"; and "also, that you have been pleased to send Christians along with them to their country to conduct them back again. We wish they were come to assist us against the common enemy [the French]."[1]

Who these Christians were will appear from the following record.

In February, 1694, Captain Arent Schuyler was sent by Governor Fletcher from New York on a scouting expedition to the Minisink country, a tract of flat lands lying on both sides of the Delaware River in the western part of Orange, Sussex, and Warren counties, in New York and New Jersey, and the eastern part of Monroe and Northampton counties, Pennsylvania. As Captain Schuyler's *Journal* of this expedition is brief, it is here given in its entirety:

May it Please Your Excell.:

In pursuance to your Excell: commands, I have been in the Minnissinck Country, of which I have kept the following journal, vizt.;

1693/4. Ye 3d of Feb. I departed from New York for East New Jersey, and came that night at Bergentown, where I hired two men and a guide.

Ye 4th, Sunday, morning. I went from Bergen, and travelled about ten English miles beyond Haghingsack, to an Indian place, called Peckwes.

Ye 5th, Monday, From Peckwes, north and by west, I went about thirty-two miles. Snowing and rainy weather.

Ye 6th, Thusday. I continued my journey to Maggaghkamieck [the Indian name of Neversink River, which falls into the Delaware a little south of Port Jervis, Orange County, N. Y.], and from thence to within half a day's journey of the Mennissinck.

Ye 7th, Wendsday. About eleven o'clock I arrived at the Minnissinck, and there I met with two of their sachems and several other Indians, of whom I enquired after some news; if the French or their Indians had sent for them, or been in the Mennissinck country. Upon which they answered, that no French nor any of the French Indians were nor had been in the Mennissinck country, nor thereabouts; and did promise it if ye French should happen to come, or yt they heard of it, that they will forthwith send a messenger, and give yr. Excellency notice thereof.

Inquiring further after news, they told me that six days ago, three Christians and two Shanwans Indians, who went about fifteen months ago with Arnout Vielle into the Shanwans country, were passed by the Mennissinck, going for Albany, to fetch powder for Arnout and his company; and further told them that said Arnout intended to be there with seven hundred of ye said Shanwans Indians, loaded with beaver and peltries, at ye time ye Indian corn is about one foot high (which may be in the month of June).

The Mennissinck sachems further said, that one of their sachems, and other of their Indians were gone to fetch beaver and peltries which they had hunted; and having heard no news of them, are afraid yt. ye

---

[1] *New York Col. Doc.*, iv., 43, 51, 90, 96; also, *Minutes of the New York Provincial Council*, MSS., vi., 115, 126.

Minisink Flats and Minisink Island, Looking East from the Pennsylvania Shore. From a photograph by W. H. Allerton

Sinneques have killed them for ye lucre of ye beaver, or because ye Mennissinck Indians have not been with ye Sinneques, as usual, to pay their duty; and therefore desire yt. your Excellency will be pleased to order yt. the Senneques may be told not to molest or hurt ye Mennissincks, they being willing to continue in amity with them.

In the afternoon I departed from ye Mennissincks; the 8th, the 9th, and 10th of Feb. I travelled, and came at Bergen in ye morning, and about noon arrived, at New York.

This, may it please your Excell., the humble report of your Excellency's most humble servant.

ARENT SCHUYLER.

In a conference with the Five Nations chiefs at Albany, held February 6, 1694, Major Peter Schuyler, in discussing plans for carrying on their war against the French, announced the arrival of the messengers who had passed through Minisink four days before. "It seems the Heavens are propitious unto us," he says, "for this day we have the forerunners of the Showannoes Far Indians come to town with one of our Christians that was sent thither, gave us an account that they are coming with seven nations of Indians, with women and children, in all a thousand souls, and are upon the way hither with Arnout [Viele], the interpreter."

In a letter to Governor Fletcher, written eight days later, Major Schuyler says, "In the interim that we were treating with them [the Five Nations], Gert. Luykasse with two of ye Far Indians called Showanoes, arrives, who brings ye news that Arnout ye interpreter, with a considerable number of those heathen will be here next summer, and good store of beaver."

Arnold Viele evidently reached the Delaware with a band of Shawnees in the summer of 1694, for on August 28th of that year a number of them, in company with some of the Mohicans, who had departed with Viele in the fall of 1692, met Governor Fletcher in a council at Esopus.

At this conference the sachem of the Mohicans addressed the Governor as follows:

"Father:

"You are Governor of this Province of New York. Some of your Christian people that went along this journey with us are killed by the way, by our enemies; for which we are very sorry. Some also of the Mahikanders, and some of the Far Indians are killed. I do now wipe off your tears for that loss."

He then gave two or three beavers.

"Father:

"We have had great sorrow for the loss of those men that were killed; which is now wiped off. We have had great difficulty to bring the Showannos and Far Indians to see your Excellency; and desire shelter under your wings, which will wipe all the sorrow off from us. We desire your protection."

He then gave some beaver.

"Father:

"We expected a great hunting, but have got little other than blows from an enemy that pursued us: and with a small share of what we have got, we come to renew the covenant chain of peace with you; and desire we may be as one heart, one blood, and one soul with the English, the Mohawks, Mahikanders, and all the Indians of this Government."

He then gave some more beaver.

The Governor condoled with them over the loss of the Christians and Indians, and admitted the Shawnees to the covenant chain. He also reminded the Mohicans that when they were last at Albany (in the fall of 1692), Major Schuyler had fitted them out for their long journey to the westward; and he now expected them to pay him for those supplies.

The Indians answered, "that, this time being so harassed with the enemy in this journey, to interrupt their hunting, they are not now able to pay Major Schuyler; but they expect three hundred Far Indians quickly to follow, and when they come up, they intend to repay him honestly for what he advanced."[1]

The Shawnees at Minisink are said to have built a town on the east side of the Delaware, in what is now Pahaquarry Township, Warren County, New Jersey, three miles south of the mouth of Flat Brook[2] (near Mill Brook), which was called Pechoquealin; and they certainly had another town on the west side of the river (either at the same time or later) which had the same name, and probably stood on or near the site of the present post-office of Shawnee,[3] at the mouth of Shawnee Run, and on and opposite Shawnee Island in the Delaware River, in what is now Lower Smithfield Township, Monroe County, Pennsylvania. Governor Gordon, however, spoke of Pechoquealin in 1728 as being "near Durham Iron Works," which are at the mouth of Durham Creek, in the northern part of Bucks County. He probably used the word "near" because Durham Iron Works was then the most remote white settlement on the north, and nearest to the Minisinks.[4]

[1] *New York Colonial MSS.*, xxxix., 188.

[2] See Sewell's *History of Sussex and Warren Counties, New Jersey*, p. 316 (Phila., 1881).

[3] See Thomson *Alienation of the Delawares and Shawnees*, p. 29 (reprint, Phila., 1867). See also pp. 92, 145, this volume.

[4] In Bradford's *American Weekly Mercury* for April 21, 1720, James Patterson, an

Shawnee Island and the Site of Pechoquealin Town in Pennsylvania, Looking West. Shawnee Island is at the Left of Centre. Mount Pocono in the Distance, at Left.

The Albany Dutchman, Arnold Cornelius Viele, interpreter and Trader, who had been captured on Lake Erie and carried to Montreal by the French while on a trading expedition to Michillimackinac in 1687; who, with Garret Luykasse and two other Christians, had been sent by Governor Fletcher in the fall of 1692 to accompany the Shawnees back to their home in the far west; and whose fellow travellers returned to Albany in February, 1694, leaving Viele in the Shawnee country, where he had been for nearly fifteen months previously; this man, and his companions, probably, were the first known white men to visit or explore the country between the Susquehanna and the Ohio, and the Ohio Valley.

The evidence as to La Salle having descended any other tributary of the Ohio than the Wabash[1] between the years 1669 and 1671, is very much less credible than is the strong presumption that Arnold Viele travelled and lived along its waters in 1692, 1693, and 1694; for, as we have seen, La Salle wrote in 1682 that the Maumee River portage to the Wabash was "without doubt the passage to the Allegheny": and it will require stronger evidence than anything that has yet been offered by Parkman and his successors to prove that the river La Salle possibly descended, "to the high fall," in 1669–70, was not the Wabash, or some other river, rather than the Ohio.

From what direction Arnold Viele's Shawnees came to the Minisink country may be inferred from what has been printed above. James Logan wrote that they came at about the same time that another party of Shawnees, from the South, came to Conestoga. This, he stated, was about the year 1697, but, as we have seen, it was really in the early summer of 1692 when they came to the mouth of the Susquehanna. It has been shown that the northern immigrants followed Garret Luykasse in 1694; though some of the earlier ones who had passed through the Minisinks on their way to New York in 1692 may have remained and settled at or near Pechoquealin on their return from New York.

One of the first white men known to have traded with the Shawnees who had settled above the Water Gap was the Maryland Dutchman or

---

Indian Trader at Pexton on Susquehanna, advertises for a runaway servant, who was last seen "at one Indian Town, called Pehoquellamen, on Delaware River." The town is called "Pechaquelly" in the *New York Weekly Journal* for Sept. 9, 1734.

"It is stated in a letter from James Logan to George Clark [Governor of New York] dated Aug. 4, 1737, that when the Shawanoe Indians came from the South in 1698 [they came in 1692], one party of them "was placed at Pechoqueolin, near Durham, to take care of the iron mines." Their village was probably on the high ground back of the lower end of Rieglesville, and near the furnace, where traces of an Indian town are still to be seen, and where arrowheads and other remains of the red man are picked up. . . . In 1715 there was an Indian town called 'Pahaqualing' above the Water Gap, on the New Jersey side of the Delaware."—Davis, *Bucks County*, 641.

[1] See Dr. Slocum's paper on "La Salle," *Ohio Historical Society Publications*, xii., 107.

Swede, John Hans Steelman,[1] who, as we have seen, made an enumeration of the Shawnees near Conestoga for the Maryland Government in 1697. Some of his goods, destined for his trading post at Lechay (Lehigh), were seized at Philadelphia by William Penn, April 2, 1701. Governor Penn represented to his Council, at a meeting held May 31st following, "that, whereas, there then is a law of this Govemt. prohibiting all persons to trade with the Indians in this Province, but such as dwell and reside therein, and have a license from the Govr. to that end; notwithstanding which, John Hans Steelman, represented to live in Maryland, and having no such license, had, ever since the enacting of said law [in May, 1700], followed a close trade with the Indians of the Province, not only at Conestoga, but had been endeavoring to settle a trade with them at Lechay, or ye Forks of Delaware, to the great prejudice of the trade of this Province in general; for which reason the Govr. has seized such of his goods as are going to Lechay, and taken security from him for such goods as he had bought and sold at Conestoga."

This action on the part of Governor Penn and his Council appears to have put a stop for a time to this trade with the Shawnees of Pechoquealin, as their town between the Lehigh and Delaware was called. In January, 1705, Governor John Evans, at Philadelphia, having been informed that two Indians from the "Shawannais upon Delaware, being lately arrived in town upon a message from their King," the messengers were called before the governor to give an account of their business. Thereupon the Shawnee emissaries "declared that considerable numbers of that and some other adjoining nations designed to come down hither to trade; they were sent to inquire whether they could be furnished with sufficient quantities of goods, and at what rates." The Indians were informed that the greater part of the goods last imported by the Philadelphia merchants, with the exception of powder and lead, had been sold; but that another supply was expected in the fall, and the Philadelphians would at all times be glad to trade with the Shawnees and their neighbors.

The names of some of the Shawnee and Minisink chiefs are given in the minutes of a meeting of the Provincial Council of New Jersey, held at Perth Amboy, May 30th, 1709. At this meeting, Colonel Aron [or Arent] Schuyler was ordered to send for Mahwtatatt (Matasit?), Cohevwichick [a misprint for Cokewichick, or Kakowatcheky], Ohwsilopp, Meshuhow, and Feetee, "sachems of the Manisincks and Shawhena

---

[1] In a deed executed by him in November, 1706, he is described as "John Hans Stellman, of Cecil County, Maryland." See Benjamin Ferris, *Original Settlements on the Delaware* (Wilmington, 1846), p. 177. Johnston intimates that he lived near the head of Elk River (*Cecil County*, 225). It rises in Chester County. Penna.

Pahaqualong, or the Mountain with a Hole in it (Delaware Water Gap), Looking South from the Site of Pechoquealin Town in Pennsylvania.

Indians, to attend his Honor at Perth Amboy, forthwith," for the purpose of organizing an expedition against the French of Canada.

The name of the Shawnee town near the forks of the Delaware in 1728 was Pechoquealin. Governor Gordon, in 1728, stated that it was "near Durham Iron Works," which are some thirty or forty miles below Delaware Water Gap. The same name, Pechoquealin, is said to have been applied to their town on the east side of the river, in New Jersey; while the town of the Shawnees who lived adjacent to the Conestogas on the lower Susquehanna was variously called Pequea, Pequehan, or, according to Redmond Conyngham (a writer who invented most of his facts, and distorted the rest), Pequehelah.[1] These names may possibly be identical, and if so, were either applied by the Shawnees to certain of their towns in common, as was the case, later, in Ohio; or else were different forms of the name of one clan of the tribe, namely, the Piqua or Peckawee, clan.

It seems more probable, however, that the word, *Pechoquealin*, comes from *Pahoqualing*, the name applied by the Lenape to the Delaware Water Gap, and meaning, "a mountain with a hole, or gap, in it." As such, the designation was territorial, and might have included all the Indian towns within that district. This would explain why the two Shawnee towns on either side of the Delaware, near Shawnee Island, were both called Pechoquealin and might also explain why the town near Durham Iron Works (if there was one there) bore the same name.

It seems probable that Peixtang, Pechstank, or Paxtang, the name of the Shawnee village which formerly stood on the site of Harrisburg, was another form of Pequea, or Piqua, its meaning being the town or place of the Pequeas (or Picks, as the Traders called them).

Other names used by the Shawnees to designate their towns were, "Chillicothe," "Maqueechaick" (or "Mecacheek," or "Maguck"), and "Kiskapoke."

After they had seated themselves in Ohio again, towards the middle of the eighteenth century, and later, the Shawnees had some seven or eight towns there, to which they gave the names, "Chillicothe," or "Piqua." In Daniel Boone's day, several "Chillicothe" towns were destroyed by the Kentuckians, and rebuilt again and again by the Shawnees, in different locations. The same thing was true of their "Piqua" towns. The principal town in Ohio before 1750, at the mouth

---

[1] See Redmond Conyngham's notes on Pequea, Egle's *Notes and Queries*, Fourth Series, ii., 85, 112. Zeisberger and Heckewelder give *Pockowalo* as meaning "a mountain with a hole in it," applied to the Delaware Water Gap. In Reading's *Journal*, printed in William Roome's *Early Surveys of East New Jersey* (Morristown, 1883), p. 28, Reading writes, under date of May 16, 1715: "We had sight of Pahackqualong, and of a cleft where the River Delaware passes through the same."

of the Scioto, was called Lower Shawnee Town by the Traders; but there is no record, in the writer's knowledge, showing what its Indian name was. Prior to November, 1758,[1] the Shawnees removed from thence, farther up the Scioto, and settled on both banks of that stream, near the site of the later village of Westfall on the west, and on the Pickaway Plains on the east, four miles below Circleville, in Pickaway County. This town was afterwards called Lower Shawnee Town (see Hutchins's map of 1764). On Crevecœur's map of 1787, it is called Kispoko. By the Kentuckians it was known as Chillicothe; and also, as Upper Chillicothe. The latter name may possibly have been used to distinguish it from the old town at the mouth of the Scioto (which had been destroyed by a flood, 1751-53, and rebuilt on the south bank of the Ohio or the east bank of the Scioto). If that was the case, then the original Lower Shawnee Town at the mouth of the Scioto was doubtless called by the Shawnees themselves, Chillicothe.

A second Chillicothe town stood on Paint Creek where now stands the village of Frankfort, Ross County. The Rev. David Jones visited this town in January, 1773; and also the Upper Town, which at that time was called "Kiskapookee"—another form, as given on Crevecœur's map of 1787, being "Kispoko."

Another and later Chillicothe town was located at or near the village of Oldtown, on the Little Miami, three miles north of Xenia, Greene County, Ohio.

According to Mr. R. W. McFarland, a fourth Chillicothe stood on the east side of the Scioto, three miles north of the present town of Chillicothe, the county-seat of Ross County, and on the site now occupied by the village of Hopetown.[2] I have not been able to find mention of any Chillicothe town at this point on the early maps, and have some doubt as to whether or not the location given by Mr. McFarland is correct. The town he refers to was probably the eastern half of that which stood on the site of and opposite a later white settlement called Westfall.

Another Chillicothe town was built near the site previously occupied (1747-52) by Pickawillany, on the Great Miami River, below the mouth of Loramie's Creek, about two miles north of the present city of Piqua, Miami County, Ohio. About 1780, the name of this town was changed to Piqua by the Shawnees, and its site is now known as Upper Piqua.

Pickawillany, the first Piqua town in Ohio, while originally not inhabited by many of the Shawnees of Lower Shawnee Town, was built

[1] See Croghan's *Journal* of that date (erroneously headed "Post's Journal") in *Penna. Arch.* iii., 560.
[2] *Ohio Arch. and Hist. Soc. Collections*, xi., 230.

at their suggestion, and with their help (and the help of the Pennsylvania Traders), for their friends and allies, the Twightwees or Miamis, who, about 1747, deserted the French interest, and abandoned their former town on the site of Fort Wayne, Indiana, seeking the protection of the Shawnees and English. Pickawillany is called "Tawixwti [Twightwee, *i. e.*, Miami] Town, or Picque Town," on Evans's map of 1755. The name was sometimes spelled Picqualline, and Pickwaylinee. It is obviously of Shawnee origin. This town was first destroyed by the French and Indians in 1752.

Other Piqua towns in Ohio were located, one, five or six miles west of what is now Springfield, in Clark County; and another, written "Pickaweeke," by the Rev. David Jones in 1773, on Deer Creek, about four miles southeast of the present village of Clarksburg, Ross County (near Carrie post-office).[1]

The resemblance of the words, "Pickawillany," "Pikkawalinna," "Pickawillanes," and "Picqualine," to "Pechoquealin," the latter the name of the Shawnee towns above the Forks of the Delaware, in Pennsylvania from 1694 to 1728, is so marked as to seem more than a resemblance. Possibly, they may have been other forms of the same word.

Pickawillany, in Ohio, was frequently called by the Traders, "Pick," or "Pict" Town; and, according to Dr. Lyman C. Draper, a town known among the Traders in 1753 as the Little Pict Town, was another Shawnee village, situated on Lulbegrud Creek, a tributary of the Red River branch of the Kentucky; and it was to the site of the latter Little Pict Town of the Shawnees, "where he had formerly traded with the Indians," that John Finley, the wilderness pilot, first led Daniel Boone and his companions on Boone's first visit to Kentucky in 1769. John Finley himself had been there seventeen years before, and carried on a trade with the inhabitants of Little Pict Town in the year 1752. This town is shown on Lewis Evans's map of 1755 as "Es-kip-pa-kith-i-ki,"[2] a word which may possibly be a variation of "Kis-ka-po-co-ke,"[3] the name applied to that sept of the Shawnees to which afterwards belonged the chieftain Tecumseh. "Kispoko," or "Kis-ka-poo-kee" Town on the Scioto, which has been referred to above, thus bore a name similar to that of the Shawnee town in Kentucky; while the latter town would appear to have been known by the names of two different clans of the Shawnee tribe.

[1] See Richard G. Lewis's map of the Indian Towns and Trails of Southwestern Ohio in Evans's *History of Scioto County*, p. 1214.

[3] Trumbull gives the meaning of the Shawnee locative *iki* as "place," or "country," Smith's *Armstrong County*, 156.

[2] Kispokotha is the form preferred by the American Bureau of Ethnology. Gatschet's Shawnee MS. gives Kispogogi. Other synonyms are Kespicotha, Kiscapocoke, Kiscopokes.

"Maguck," or "Macqueechaick," a town of Shawnee origin (occupied by ten Delaware families when Christopher Gist was there in 1750), stood on the east side of the Scioto, some three and a half miles below the present town of Circleville, Pickaway County. What are now known as the Pickaway Plains, in this county, were formerly called by the Indians and Traders, the Great Plain of Maguck.[1] Evans's map of 1755 locates the Delaware Town here on the *west* side of Scioto.

A second Maguck ("Macacheek") stood later near the site of West Liberty, in what is now Logan County, Ohio.

Colonel John Johnston, a Government Indian agent among the Ohio tribes from 1812 to 1842, in an article contributed by him to the American Antiquarian Society's *Collections* in 1820 (i., 275), states that the Shawnees have four clans or totems, as follows:

1. The Piqua tribe—meaning, "a man formed from ashes."
2. The Mequachake [Maguck, Maquichee, or Macqueechaick] tribe,—meaning, "a fat man well filled"; the tribe of the priest-hood, or medicine men.
3. The Kiskapocoke tribe—to which belonged Tecumseh.
4. The Chillicothe tribe—no definite meaning; applied to a place of residence.

Dr. Brinton, in his article on "The Shawnees and their Migrations," divides them into three clans or totems, namely, those of the Maquichee, Peckawee, and Chillicothe.

Whatever the original meanings of the words, "Chillicothe," "Piqua," "Kiskapocoke," and "Maguck" may be, it is certain that one or another of the four, or some variation thereof, was always applied to the name of every village of the Shawnees. On Crevecœur's 1787 map of the Scioto Plain as it was some years before, are shown the Shawnee towns of "Maqueechaick" (the Maguck of Gist), "Kispoko," "Pecowick," and "Chillicothe"; so that each one of the four septs of the Shawnee tribe is there represented as having a separate village. The Rev. David Jones, a Baptist missionary from New Jersey, visited three of these towns in January, 1773. In his *Journal* he names them as, Pickaweeke, Chillicaathee, and Kiskapookee. The word, "Pickaweeke," Mr. Jones explains, "signifies 'the place of the Picks'; the town taking its name from a nation of [Shawnee] Indians called Picks, some of them being the first settlers."

Chillisquaque Creek, entering the West Branch of the Susquehanna

---

[1] Mequachake seems to be the accepted form, although Gatschet's Shawnee MS. gives it as Menekutthegi. Hewitt gives the meaning as "red earth." Other synonyms given by Mooney include Machachac, Mackichac, Machachcek, Mackacheek, Magueck, Makostrake, and Maquichees.

River, in what is now Northumberland County, Pennsylvania, appears to have a name which may be a variation of the word "Chillicothe." It is certain that the district through which the creek flows was a former dwelling place of the Shawnees. Mr. James Mooney, however, is of the opinion that the two words are not synonymous Definite reference to this place, made by the Shawnees themselves in June, 1732, in their message to the Pennsylvania Governor will be found farther on.

The time of the arrival in Pennsylvania of the sixty families of Shawnees who came from the South to Cecil County, Maryland, in 1692, and from thence settled near the Conestoga Indians, is fixed approximately by numerous references thereto, found in the Pennsylvania *Colonial Records*, and *Archives*. In a message sent May 21, 1728, by Governor Gordon to Kakowatchy, or Kakowatcheky, chief of the Shawnees living in the Minsi country above the Delaware Forks, he informs that chief that at the time of William Penn's first treaty with the Indians in 1683, "the Shawnees were not then in this country; they came long afterwards and desired leave of the Conestogee Indians and of William Penn to settle in this country. They promised to live in peace and friendship with us, and the Conestogee Indians became their security." In September of the same year, Governor Gordon sent messengers to Shekallamy, the deputy of the Six Nations, who lived among the Pennsylvania Indians in the capacity of over-lord. Part of the instructions to these messengers were to the effect that they were to "tell Shekallamy particularly, that as he is set over the Shawnese Indians, I hope he can give a good account of them. They came to us only as strangers, about thirty years ago; they desired leave of this government to settle among us as strangers, and the Conestogee Indians became security for their good behavior. They are also under the protection of the Five Nations, who have set Shekallamy over them." Again, in December, 1731, Governor Gordon wrote to the chiefs of the Shawnees who had removed to Allegheny, as follows: "I find by our records, that about thirty-four years since, some numbers of your nation came to Sasquehannah and desired leave first of our brethren, the Conestogee Indians, and then of Col. Markham, who at that time was Governor under William Penn, that they might have leave to settle on Pecquea Creek, which was granted." In a conference held with six chiefs of the Six Nations at Philadelphia on August 26, 1732, these chiefs were told by the Governor and his Council "that the Shawnees who settled to the southward being made uneasie by their neighbors, about sixty families of them came up to Conestogee about thirty-five years since, and desired leave of the Susquehannah Indians who were planted there, to settle on that river; that those Susquehannah Indians applied to this government, that they might accordingly settle, and they would become answerable for their good behavior; that our late Proprietor arriving soon after, the chiefs of the Shawnees [at Pequehan] and of the Susquehannahs came to Philadelphia [in 1701] and renewed their application; that the Proprietor agreed to their settlement; and the Shawnees thereupon came under the protection of this Government; that from that time great numbers of the same Indians followed them, and settled on the Susquehanna and Delaware."

It will be shown later how the Shawnees of the Susquehanna left that river, about 1727, and removed to the Allegheny Valley. At a conference held with some of their chiefs from Allegheny who came to Philadelphia July 27, 1739, James Logan, the Provincial Secretary, reminded them of the manner in which their fathers and themselves had first been taken under the protection of the Quaker government. He said to them:

"Since your nation first left their settlement near Pextang, on the west side of the Susquehanna [before 1727 many of them from Pequea, Paxtang, and elsewhere had settled at what is now New Cumberland near the mouth of Yellow Breeches Creek, opposite Paxtang, a Shawnee town on or near the site of Harrisburg], and retired to so great a distance as the river Ohio or Allegheny, this Government has ever been desirous of a conference with some of your chiefs.

"Some of your older men may undoubtedly remember that about forty years ago a considerable number of families of your nation thought fit to remove from the great river that bears your name [since 1750 called the Cumberland] where your principal correspondence was with those of the French nation."

Governor John Evans visited the Shawnee Indians of Pequehan or Pequa, on the Susquehanna, in June, 1707. In a conference with Opessa, their chief, who had come with them from Maryland about ten years before, the chief told the Governor that his people were "happy to live in a country at peace, and not as in those parts where we formerly lived, for then, upon our return from hunting, we found our town surprised, and our women and children taken prisoners by our enemies." In his account of this visit to Pequea, the Governor states that while he was at that village "several of the Shawnee Indians from the southward came to settle here, and were admitted to so do by Opessah, with the Governor's consent; at the same time an Indian from a Shawnee town near Carolina came in, and gave an account that 450 of the Flat Head [Catawba or Creek] Indians had besieged them, and that in all probability the same was taken. Bezallion [a Trader, who acted as interpreter] informed the Governor that the Shawnees of Carolina, he was told, had killed several Christians; whereupon the government of that province had raised the said Flat Head Indians, and joined some Christians to

The Mouth of Pequea Creek, Looking West across Susquehanna.
From a photograph furnished by Mr. David H. Landis.

them, besieged, and have taken, as it is thought, the said Shawnee town." While among the Shawnees of Pequea at this time, Governor Evans visited another of their towns, further up the Susquehanna, called "Peixtan," on or near the site of the present city of Harrisburg.

This name, "Peixtan," as has been stated, was probably another form of "Piqua" or "Pequeas' Town" or "Place of the Piques," notwithstanding the fact that the word is usually given a different meaning, originated by Heckewelder.

Governor Evans also visited another Indian town when he was at Pequea in 1707. This was Dekanoagah, where lived some "Senequois," Shawnees, Conoys (or Piscatawese, or Ganawese), and Nanticokes (closely related to the Conoys). Dekanoagah, according to Governor Evans, was on the Susquehanna River, "nine miles above Pequehan." It almost certainly stood near the site of the present Washington Borough, Lancaster County. Here Martin Chartier had his trading post in 1717, and probably for some years before, after moving up the river from Pequehan, where his house stood in 1707.

James Logan visited the same locality in October, 1705. He then called it Connejaghera, and stated that it was "above the Fort," that is, the "Fort Demolished" of Chambers's 1688 survey. Lancaster County historians generally, but erroneously, locate Dekanoagah near the site of the present Bainbridge, at the mouth of Conoy Creek; but Governor Evans's location, of course, must be accepted as the correct one.

The Conoys told Thomas Cookson at his house in Lancaster County, April 11, 1743, that when they first came into Pennsylvania from their island in the Potomac (whence they had gone from Piscataway Creek), in William Penn's time (after the treaty of 1701), they built a town at Conejoholo; and that *later*, they removed higher up the Susquehanna, to what was called the Conoy Town in 1743. This was at the mouth of Conoy Creek, on or near the site of Locust Grove; which is a short distance below Bainbridge.[1] The Conoys were here before 1719.

The Connejaghera of James Logan in 1705, the Dekanoagah of Governor Evans in 1707, and the Conejoholo referred to by the Conoys in 1743, were all the same place, which was at Washington Borough of the present day, and directly across the river from that part of York County which is still called Conejohela, or Conjocula, Valley.

Dekanoagah may have the same meaning as *Decanohoge*, the name of one of the Mohawk castles in 1756. According to Beauchamp, Albert Cusick gave the meaning of the latter name as "where I live." A more probable meaning of both names, however, would be the same as that of Caughnawaga, or Canowaga, or Conewago, also a name for one of the early Mohawk towns, which meaning is, "at the rapids." In fact,

[1] *Penna. Col. Rec.*, iv., 657.

Dekanoagah is simply another form of Conewago, and its location was almost identical with that of the Conestoga Fort Demolished, though both were some distance down the river from Conewago Rapids.

The chiefs of the Shawnees who came from the South to Cecil County, Maryland, in 1692 and settled at Pequea Creek,[1] near the Conestogas, about 1697, as we have seen, were Meaurroway and Opessa. Mecallona, the name of another Shawnee chief, appears in a petition presented to William Penn, dated at Brandywine, May 1, 1700, which is printed in Hazard's *Pennsylvania Register* (ii., 71).

The name of a chief of those Shawnees who settled at Pechoquealin, in 1694, does not appear in the Pennsylvania *Colonial Records* until more than thirty years later, when, in 1728, we find Kakowatcheky (sometimes written Kakowatchey) to be their head man. Under the name "Cohevwickick" he is referred to in the New Jersey *Colonial Records*, May 30, 1709, as one of the sachems of the Shawhena Indians then with the "Maninsincks."

Opessa continued as chief of the Pequea Shawnees on the Lower Susquehanna until 1711, when he voluntarily abandoned both his chieftainship and his tribe, and sought a home among the Delawares of Sassoonan's clan. Later he removed to what in 1722 was called Opessa's Town, on the Potomac, now Old Town, Maryland.

On September 3, 1701, Shemekenwhoa, one of the chiefs of the Shawnees at Pequea, complained to the Governor that Sylvester Garland,

---

[1] Mr. David H. Landis, the best authority on Lancaster County Indian history, thinks that Pequehan village may have been at "Indian Point" (now Rock Hill), on the Conestoga, about two miles southeast of Conestoga Indian Town, and on land which was taken up by John Cartlidge, the Trader, about 1716. Here, from both the documentary and archæological sources, Mr. Landis has found very much more evidence of its location than at the mouth of Pequea Creek or elsewhere; and also, that Dekanoagah "nine miles from Pequehan," was on the site of the present town of Columbia rather than at Washington Borough. "Sawannah Old Fields," near the *head* of Pequea Creek, were conveyed to Col. John French by the Penns in 1718. This site was just south of The Gap, in Sadsbury Township, and was probably the temporary residence of either one of the bands of Shawnees which removed from Bohemia Manor to Pequehan and Pechoquealin between 1692 and 1697. When the road through Chester County to The Gap was laid out in August, 1719, its course was defined in part as "to the fording place at Octtoraro, at Old Shawana Town, thence over Octtoraro along the Indian Path" (Rupp, *Lancaster County*, p. 42). Futhey and Cope state, in their *History of Chester County*, that the Shawnees made a settlement in the vicinity of the present Steelville, in West Fallowfield Township, on the Octorara, and that they also had a large town near the present Doe Run post-office, on the Doe Run Branch of the Brandywine. One of these towns near The Gap may have been Minguanan, the Delaware village visited by John Hans Steelman in 1697, and reported by him as being "nine miles from the head of Elk River, and fifteen miles from Christeen, and about thirty miles from Susquehanna River."

Indian Point, on Conestoga Creek, from the South.
From photograph furnished by Mr. David H. Landis.

a Trader, had brought to their settlement 140 gallons of rum, made them drunk, and abused them.

On the first of October, 1714, three principal men of the Conestogas appeared before the Governor and Council at Philadelphia, to inform them that Opessa, the late king of their neighbors and friends, the Shawnees, had absented himself from his people for about three years, and refused to return, although repeatedly urged to do so. The Shawnees had therefore "elected" a new king, by the name of Cakundawanna, who had accompanied the Conestogas to Philadelphia, and was thereupon presented to the Council. Opessa had perhaps fled to the upper woods for fear of being held responsible by the Five Nations or the English for the killing by some of his young men in 1710 of Francis de la Tore and some other white men, all bond-servants of John Hans Steelman, the Trader. A traditionary account, probably invented by Redmond Conyngham, ascribes Opessa's desertion of his tribe and office to the influence of a Delaware squaw, of whom he was enamored, and who refused to leave her own people. Opessa really seems to have settled at what is still called Old (Shawnee) Town, on the Potomac, and which was known to the Marylanders so late as 1725, as Opessa's Town.[1]

Another Shawnee chief was present at a conference held in Philadelphia June 16, 1718, who was styled "Methawennah, chief of the Shawnois above Conestoga" (perhaps those of Peixtan).

Another chief, named Sevana, or Savannah, appeared at conferences held at Conestoga June 29, 1719, and March 21, 1721. He may have been identical with Cakundawanna; and was probably also the same chief who told Secretary Logan at Conestoga in July, 1720, how he came to be made chief. He said: "When their king, Opessah, who was then [1701] living, took the government upon him, and the people differed with him [1711], he left them. They had then no chief. Thereupon, some of them applied to him [the speaker] to take that charge upon him; but that he had only the name, without any authority, and could do nothing. He counselled them, but they would not obey; therefore, he cannot answer for them."

Governor Keith held a conference with the Shawnees and other Indians at Conestoga in July, 1717, at which time he asked them to explain their connection with an attack made by the Senecas on some Catawba Indians who were under the protection of Virginia. The Shawnee chief replied that six Shawnees had accompanied the war party of the Senecas on that expedition; but that none of these six were then present, their settlements being much higher up the Susquehanna River. These men

---

[1] See meeting of Pennsylvania Council, Nov. 19, 1722 (*Col. Rec.*, iii.) where it is spelled "Oppertus."

may have belonged to the clan of "Ocowellos, king of the Upper Shawanese," as he is described in the Council Minutes, May 23, 1723. At that time an address from him was read to the Council. He mentioned his past visits, and another shortly to be made, to the Governor of Canada, whom he styles his "Father." This was the same chief whom James Le Tort reported to the Council in November, 1731, as being then seated on the Conemaugh River, at "Allegheny," with two hundred men, and forty-five families, who occupied three villages on that stream.

As we have seen, the chief of the Shawnees at the Pechoquelin towns on one or both sides of the river, above the Delaware Water Gap, from before 1709 until after 1728, was Kakowatcheky. In the latter year, he and his clan removed to the Shawnee Flats on the North Branch of the Susquehanna (just below the present town of Plymouth), a settlement afterwards known as Wyoming. From there, in 1743, Kakowatcheky removed to Logstown, on the Ohio, where he was met by Weiser in 1748; and where he may have continued to live until 1755 (or later), that being the last year in which his name appears on the Pennsylvania records. Colonel James Patton of Virginia who visited Logstown in June, 1752, refers to him in his *Journal* as being then bed-ridden. If he was the chief who led the Shawnees from the Ohio Valley to the Minisink Flats, in 1694, under the guidance of Arnold Viele, then his chieftainship must have extended over a period of more than fifty years.

Heckewelder's account of the coming of the Shawnees into that part of Pennsylvania north of the Delaware Water Gap is one of the few passages in his so-called *History of the Indian Nations* where his story is corroborated by extraneous documentary proof; and as this proof has now been cited, these citations may be made clearer by taking them in connection with Heckewelder's traditionary account, which is as follows:

The Shawanos, or Sawanos.—The history of these people is here given, principally from the relations of old Indians of the Mohican tribe (the Shawanos call the Mohicans their Elder Brother), who say that they formerly inhabited the southern country, Savannah, in Georgia, and the Floridas [accurately speaking, parts of the country between Georgia and the mouth of the Cumberland]. They were a restless people, delighting in wars, in which they were constantly engaged with some of the neighboring nations. At last, their neighbors, tired of being continually harassed by them, formed a league for their destruction. The [southern] Shawanos, finding themselves thus dangerously situated, asked to be permitted to leave the country, which was granted to them; and they fled immediately to the Ohio [to the Illinois]. Here their main body settled, and sent messengers to their Elder Brother, the Mohicans, requesting them to intercede for them with their Grandfather, the Lenni

Lenape [the Minsis], that he might take them under his protection. This, the Mohicans willingly did, and even sent a body of their own people [in 1692] to conduct their younger brother into the country of the Delawares. The Shawanos, finding themselves safe under the protection of their Grandfather, did not choose to proceed farther to the eastward; but many of them remained on the Ohio; some of whom settled even as high up that river as the Long Island [probably not until after the Delawares, about 1724, had settled at Kittanning], above which the French afterwards built Fort Duquesne, now Pittsburgh. Those who proceeded farther [in 1694], were accompanied by their chief, named Gachgawatschiqua [Kakowatcheky, who is first mentioned on the Pennsylvania records in 1728; but to whom the Council of New Jersey sent a message as early as August 30, 1709, his name then written "Cowhevwichick," appearing in the Council Minutes, with the names of four others, as "sachems of the Maninsincks and Shawhena Indians"], and settled principally at and about the Forks of the Delaware, some few between that and the confluence of Delaware and Schuylkill, and some even on the spot where Philadelphia now stands [?]; others were conducted by the Mohicans into their own country where they intermarried with them [at Tioga, later], and became one people. When those settled near the Delaware had multiplied, they returned to Wyoming, on the Susquehanna, where they resided for a great number of years [from 1728 to 1743, when the greater part removed to and founded Logstown on the Ohio; another band, with Packsinosa as their chief, retiring northward from Wyoming about 1756 and settling for a time with the Mohicans at Tioga and Otseningo, on the Upper Susquehanna].

As amended above, this paragraph of Heckewelder may be allowed to stand as a partly accurate account of the first coming of some of the Shawnees into Pennsylvania.

Kakowatcheky was succeeded as chief at Wyoming, a few years after his departure from there in 1743, by Packsinosa. This chief joined with a number of others in executing a deed to the Penns, August 22, 1749, conveying the land between the Delaware and Susquehanna north of the Blue Mountains and south of Wyoming. He remained true to the English during the trying years from 1755 to 1758. In the early part of May of the latter year, he was met by Benjamin, a Mohican Indian of Bethlehem, near Tioga, with his entire family. He told Benjamin that, as he heard the English had very bad designs against the Indians, he was going with his family to his land at the Ohio, "where he was born."[1] At Fort Pitt, on August 12, 1760, he attended a conference held by General Monckton with the chiefs of the Six Nations, Twightwees, Delawares, Ottawas, Wyandots, and Shawnees. "Puckshenoses Town" is shown on Crevecœur's 1787 map of the Scioto Plains, reproduced in Volume II.

[1] *Penna. Col. Rec.*, vi., 35, 360; vii., 104, 108, 139, 187, 726; viii., 126; *Penna. Archives*, ii., 33, 34, 459, 491, 634; iii., 745; *N. Y. Col. Doc.*, vii., 17, 19, 20, 246, 316.

Its founder may have been Packsinosa, but more probably, he was Puckeeshano, or Packisheno, the father of Tecumseh.[1]

Besides the Shawnee settlements in Pennsylvania and New Jersey, which have already been noted, there was another of their clans seated on the North Branch of the Potomac, a short distance above the mouth of the South Branch, at what has ever since their departure been called Old Town, in Allegany County, Maryland. Captain Thomas Cresap settled here in 1741, at which time it was known as Shawnee Old Town, being then only the abandoned site of their former village, the inhabitants of which had, some time before 1732, removed to the Allegheny and Conemaugh valleys, below Kittanning, in western Pennsylvania. In 1729, Captain Civility, chief of the Conestogas, wrote to Governor Gordon that "about two months ago, the Southern Indians killed and took nine of the Shawaners, living on a branch of Potomac, near the Great Mountains; the which impute to their own fault, for settling so near their enemies." Opakethwa and Opakeita, two chiefs of the Potomac Shawnees from Ohio, visited Philadelphia in September, 1732, after they had abandoned their town on the North Branch of the Potomac and removed to the Allegheny. The Governor asked them why they had gone so far back into the woods as Allegheny. They replied, that "formerly they lived at Patowmack, where their king died; that, having lost him, they knew not what to do; that they then took their wives and children and went over the mountains [to Allegheny] to live."[2]

John Wray, the Trader, who had formerly traded at what was afterwards called Raystown (now Bedford), came down from Allegheny to Philadelphia with these Shawnee chiefs in September, 1732, to serve as interpreter. Prior to 1732, John Wray's trading was doubtless carried on with the Shawnees at their "Old Town," on the Potomac, and with the Conestogas and Mingoes who had settled at the original Allequippa's Town, very near the site of what was afterwards Raystown. Both of these Indian villages were on the Warrior's Path, which extended southwards from Frankstown to the Potomac; and they were but little more than thirty miles apart.

On November 2, 1722, Charles Anderson was sent by the Maryland Government to "the Shawan Town upon Potomack," with instructions to make a treaty with the Shawnee chiefs there, who were named Pockaseta and Oneakoopa.[3]

On May 20, 1725, John Powell was instructed by the Governor and

---

[1] A chief called *Buckshenoath*, is mentioned by Edward Shippen in the *Penna. Arch.*, (ii., 134) April 19, 1756.

[2] *Penna. Archives*, i., 241; *Col. Rec.*, iii., 492.

[3] *Maryland Archives*, viii., 394.

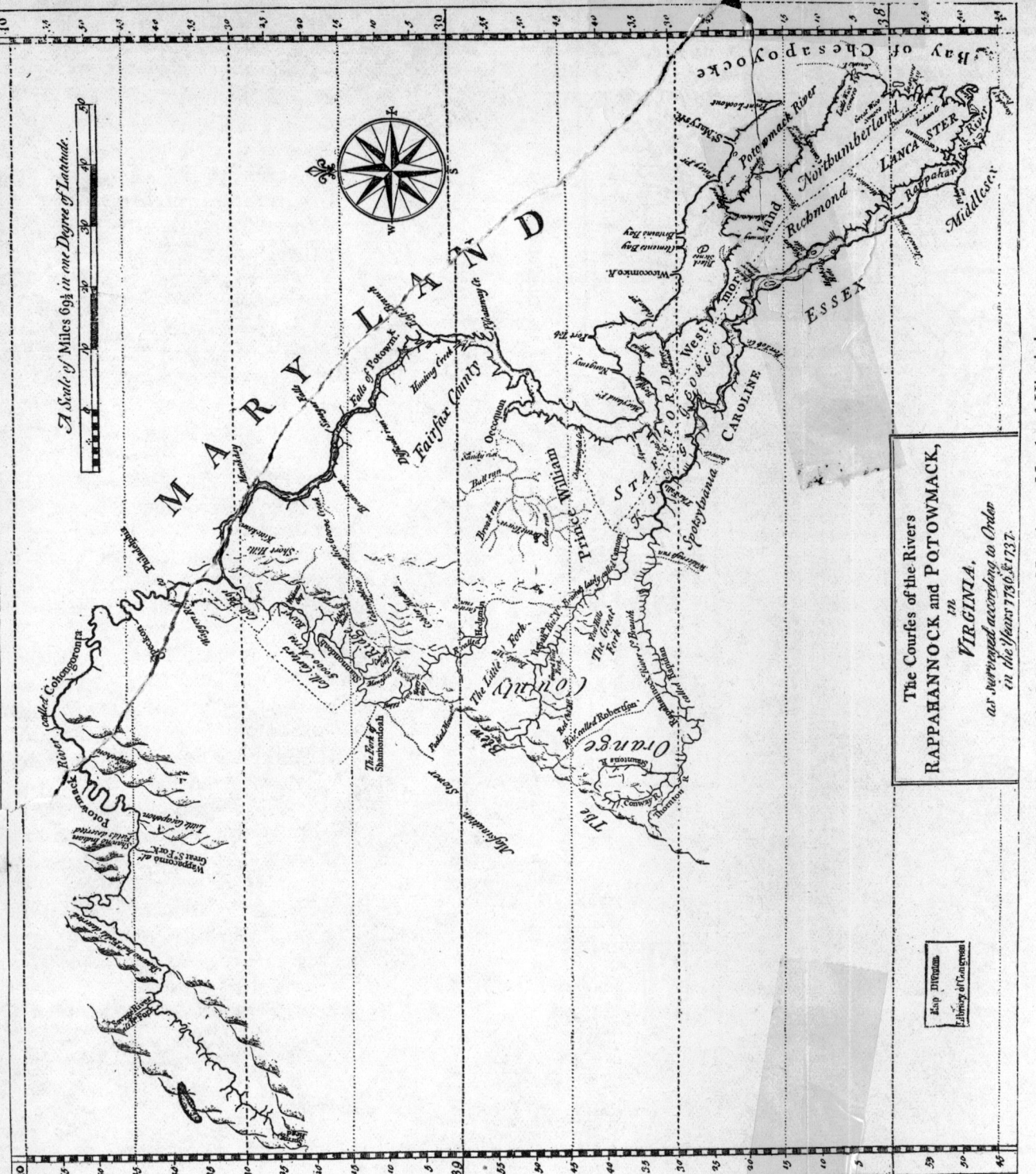

William Mayo's Map of the Northern Neck of Virginia.

Made for the Commissioners, William Byrd and others, in 1737. Showing the sites of two Shawnee villages on the Potomac.

Council of Maryland to carry a message to the "Shuano Town upon Potomack (commonly called Opessa's Town)" requesting the head men of the town to meet the Governor and some members of his Council at Charles Anderson's house near Monocacy Creek, in the early part of August following.[1] Opessa, it will be remembered, was the Shawnee chief from Pequea who joined the Conestoga and other chiefs in signing the treaty of amity with William Penn at Philadelphia in 1701. The Maryland Governor and his Council journeyed to the place of meeting, but the Shawnees failed to attend. A second messenger was dispatched, urging them to come down to a conference; but the Council records are silent as to what success this messenger had. A few years later, as we have seen, the Shawnees of Opessa's Town—the site of what is now Oldtown, Maryland,—were attacked by their Southern enemies (1729); and, their chief having died, they took their wives and children over the mountains to the Conemaugh and Allegheny.

Mayo's map in the Library of Congress (reproduced in this volume) entitled *The Courses of the Rivers Rappahannock and Pawtomack, as surveyed according to order in the years 1736 and 1737*, shows two Shawnee villages on the north bank of the Potomac, both marked "deserted." One was opposite the mouth of the South Branch of the Potomac; the other about fifteen miles further up the main stream. The first of these sites was on the flat now occupied in part by the village of Oldtown, Maryland (which was formerly called Shawnee Oldtown), and the second is shown on Fry and Jefferson's 1751 map of Virginia as "Shawnee Fields," on the flat lands now in part occupied by the west side of the city of Cumberland.

A much earlier reference than those given above to what may have been the beginning of the settlement of the Shawnees at or near Opessa's Town on the Potomac, is to be found in the *Minutes* of the Maryland Assembly for 1693. On June 1st of that year, at a meeting of a joint committee of the Council and the House of Burgesses, it was reported to the Assembly that, "This Committee are informed that the Strange Indians that are at the head of Potomack, near the mountains, do belong to and are part of a nation of Indians at the head of the Bay of the Susquahannahs, who are at peace and amity with us. Therefore, we propose, that caution may be given that king, either to call in the Indians, or be accountable and answerable for them in case of injuries." Accordingly, Major John Thompson and three others were instructed to confer with the Indians at the head of the Bay, and deliver to them the message from the Government.[2]

[1] *Maryland Archives*, viii., 443.

[2] In a letter from Joshua Lowe of Lancaster County, to the Governor of Pennsylvania, dated September 5, 1730, the writer refers to Opessa's Town and to a town near it called Augaluta. See *Penna. Archives*, i., 269.

We have seen that the Iroquois completed their conquest of the Eries about 1656, and expelled them from their home south of Lake Erie so completely that it remained practically an uninhabited country for nearly three-quarters of a century afterwards. Six years later, they turned their arms against the Shawnees and other tribes of the Ohio Valley, and waged an unrelenting war against them for more than a decade. Charlevoix says the Iroquois completed the conquest of the Shawnees in 1672; but the Onondaga chief, Outreouate, told Governor La Barre at Famine Bay in 1684, that one reason the Five Nations waged war against the Illinois and Miamis (in 1680), was, that "they have engaged the Chaouanons in their interest, and entertained them in their country." La Salle at La Chine in 1669 had been told by the Senecas that he might find the villages of the Honniasontkeronon and the Chaouanons on the Ohio, above "the Falls"; and he lighted a fire for some of the latter at his Fort of St. Louis on the Illinois in 1683. During the years between, it is probable that the Iroquois had succeeded in expelling the Shawnees from their earlier home in the Central Ohio Valley, and driven them to its mouth, up the Cumberland and Tennessee rivers, and across the Cumberland Gap into Carolina and Georgia, where they seem to have had two or more villages during most of the last quarter of the seventeenth century. From these villages the inhabitants moved into Maryland and Pennsylvania between the years 1692 and 1712, while others were drawn there from the remnants of the tribe still scattered through the Ohio Valley. They began to return to the Ohio country soon after 1725, and shortly after the middle of that century all but a small number had again seated themselves in the land of their ancestors.

From what has been written above it would seem that the Shawnees who first came into Pennsylvania were mostly from La Salle's settlement at Fort St. Louis on the Illinois, from whence they had gone with Martin Chartier up the Ohio or Cumberland to near the head of the latter stream, where they lived for a few years. Thence, either by way of the Virginia Valley, the Kanawha, or the Youghiogheny, they had travelled as far as the head of the Potomac, where a portion of them settled, and the remainder proceeded eastward to the Susquehanna. Here, a part seated themselves on Bohemia Manor, in Cecil County, Maryland (afterwards moving farther up the river to the banks of what was called, from their clan, Pequea Creek); and a part followed the Minsis and Mohicans who had led them from the Illinois country, visiting New York in the fall of 1692, and afterwards settling with the Delaware Minsis at Minisink. To the latter place a second band was conducted by Arnold Viele and his followers in 1694; who may have come from the Cumberland or the Ohio.

The "Chaouenons" located by De l'Isle and others on the Edisto and Savannah rivers about the year 1700, were known to the English as the Savannahs.[1] They are mentioned in Archdale's *Description of Carolina*, and Lawson describes them in 1709 as a "famous, friendly nation of Indians, living to the south end of the Ashly River." Gallatin thought they were identical with the Yamasees.

If many of these Shawnees ever lived in what is now the State of South Carolina, it is probable their stay there was but temporary; and their location in that country by the cartographers of the latter part of the seventeenth century may have been based upon the transitory residence there of Martin Chartier's band; or it may possibly have referred to the Chowan or Chawanoc Indians of North Carolina history; who may, themselves, have been Shawnees, under a slightly different name. This is improbable, however, as the Chowanocks lived in what was then Virginia in the days of Captain John Smith, and are mentioned by him under that name in his *General History of Virginia*.

They are first referred to in 1586 by Master Ralph Lane, commander-in-chief of Sir Walter Raleigh's colony on Roanoke Island, sent out from England in the preceding year. Lane states that, "to the northwest the farthest place of our discovery was to Chawanock, distant from

---

[1] In his introduction to the *Migration Legend of the Creek Indians*, Mr. Albert S. Gatschet, in writing of the Uchees, says: "Mr. William Bartram . . . calls them 'Uche or Savannuca,' which is the Creek 'Sawanogi,' or 'dwellers upon Savannah River.' This name, Savannuca, and many equally sounding names, have caused much confusion concerning a supposed immigration of the Shawano or Shawnee Indians (of the Algonkin race) into Georgia, among historians not posted in Indian languages. Sawanogi is derived from Savannah River, which is named after the prairies extending on both sides, these being called in Spanish *sabana*. *Sabana*, and *savane* in the Canadian French, designate a grassy plain, level country, prairies; also, in Spanish, pasture extending over a plain; from Latin, *sabana*, napkin. It still occurs in some local names of Canada and of Spanish America. But this term has nothing at all in common with the Algonkin word, *shawano*, south, from which are derived the tribal names: Shawano or Shawnee, once on Ohio and Cumberland rivers and their tributaries; Chowan in Southern Virginia; Siwoneys in Connecticut; Sawannoe in New Jersey (about 1616); Chaouanons, the southern division of the Illinois or Maskoutens." . . . These names cannot serve to prove the presence of the Shawano tribe in these eastern parts; but a settlement of Shawanos, also called Sawanogi, existed on Tallapoosa River, where they seem to have been mixed with the Yuchi" (pp. 23, 143; also, French, *Hist. Coll. Louisiana*, New Series, p. 126).

Notwithstanding what Mr. Gatschet says, Mr. James Mooney is of the opinion that "Savannuca" was a Creek name for the Shawnees.

John Lederer wrote in 1670 of his explorations in tide-water Virginia and Carolina: "The valleys [east of the Blue Ridge] feed numerous herds of deer and elks, larger than oxen; these valleys they [the Indians] call savanæ, being marish [marshy] grounds at the foot of the Apalataci, and yearly laid under water at the beginning of summer by floods of melted snow falling down from the mountains. . . . About the beginning of June . . . their verdure is wonderfully pleasant to the eye."

Roanoke about 130 miles." "Chawanock itself," he adds, "is the greatest province and seigniorie lying upon that River [the Chowan]; and the very town itself is able to put 700 fighting men into the field, besides the force of the province itself." The town of Chawanock[1] is shown on John White's map of 1586, which has been reproduced in the Messrs. Scribner's reprint of some of Hakluyt's *Voyages* (New York, 1906).[2]

[1] An entry in the Maryland *Council Records*, under date of July 23, 1698, states that "Capt. John Hans Tilman [Steelman], an Indian Trader att the head of the [Chesapeake] Bay, being asked concerned the Indians that live there, what nations they are, he says they are Chauhannauks, Susquehannahs, & Delaware; that the Chauhannauks are about forty men & live at a Town fifty miles of his house; the Susquehannahs are about fifty men, live two miles further up, at Caristauga [misprint for Canistauga, *i.e.*, Conestoga], and came from the Seneques; that the Delawares live at White Clay Creek; are about forty men." This statement, besides showing the similarity of the early names for the Shawnees and Chowans, would also seem to confirm Mr. Landis's belief that the Pequehan Town of the Shawnees, which Governor Evans visited in 1707, was at Indian Point, on the Conestoga, instead of at the mouth of Pequea Creek.

[2] Also, in DeBry's 1690 edition of John White's map, reprinted in Winsor's *Narrative and Critical History*, iii., 125.

CHAPTER V

THE EARLY TRADERS OF CONESTOGA, DONEGAL, AND PAXTANG

WHILE it is not the intention of the author to write at great length upon the Indian Traders of Eastern Pennsylvania in William Penn's time, yet, as many of these men and their sons afterwards became Traders on the Allegheny Path to the westward, it will enable us to have a better understanding of the situation of the various Indian tribes east of the Susquehanna at the time their movement westward began, if we devote some pages to an account of the Traders who dealt with them, after the time of Captain Jacob Young and his contemporaries.

During the greater part of the first two decades after 1700, that portion of Pennsylvania lying along the eastern side of the Susquehanna River, between its forks and the Maryland line, was regarded by the Provincial authorities as comprising four general districts, all of which took their names from the principal Indian towns located within their limits. These towns, which gave their names to the adjacent country, were: (1st), the Shawnee town of Pequea, near the mouth of Pequea Creek; (2d) the Susquehannock town of Conestoga, lying northwest of the creek of the same name, not far above its mouth; (3d) the Ganawese or Conoy town at Conejohela or Conejachera (called "Dekanoagah"[1] by Governor Evans in 1707), near the site of Washington Borough, in Manor Township; from whence that tribe removed up the river after 1707, locating a new town a mile or two below the mouth of Conoy Creek; and (4th) Peixtan or Peshtank (literally, Picts' Town; now written, Paxtang), on the creek of the same name, another Shawnee town, at the site of the present city of Harrisburg. Between 1735 and 1745 the Shawnees also had towns on Big (Halderman) Island at the mouth of the Juniata, and on the west shore of the Susquehanna opposite that island.

Prior to 1729, this territory was all included within the civil jurisdiction of Chester County; and so continued until the erection of Lancaster County in that year. White settlers (Swiss Mennonites) began to come into this country as early as 1710. Indian Traders had been there

[1] Nine miles above Pequea.—*Col. Rec. Penna.*, ii., 402.

for some twenty years before. In 1718, Conestoga Township was laid off, embracing all that part of what is now Lancaster County, between Octorara Creek and the main branch of the Conestoga. Early in the same year, 16,000 acres of land were surveyed by order of the Proprietary Government, lying between the west side of Conestoga Creek and the Susquehanna, under the name of Conestoga Manor. This included the Conestoga Indian Town; and now forms a portion of Manor Township, Lancaster County. In 1720, the township of West Conestoga was erected, embracing all the territory of Lancaster and Dauphin counties as at present limited, north of Pequea Creek. The following year, Pequea Township was erected, which included the white settlements along Upper Pequea Creek and its branches. In 1722, that portion of West Conestoga Township lying north of "Old Peter's Road" and Chiquesalunga (or Chickasalunga) Creek was erected into the township of Donegal, so-called on account of the great number of Scotch-Irish settlers from Donegal and other counties in the north of Ireland who, at the instance of Secretary James Logan, were then pouring into this district in large numbers.[1]

At the time of the erection of Lancaster County in 1729, the western boundaries of the townships bordering on the Susquehanna were as follows, beginning from the south: Drumore—from the Maryland line to the mouth of Muddy Run; Martock—from the mouth of Muddy Run to the mouth of Pequea Creek; Hempfield (including Conestoga Manor)—from the mouth of the Conestoga to the mouth of Chickasalunga Creek; Donegal—from the mouth of the Chickasalunga to the mouth of Conewago; Derry—from the mouth of Conewago to the mouth of the Swatara; Peshtank—from the mouth of Swatara to the foot of Kittochtinny Mountain. Upper Paxtang, although not definitely erected as a separate township until 1767, seems to have included the territory along the river from the mouth of Fishing Creek at the base of Kittochtinny Mountain to the mouth of the Mahanoy.

The following names are found on the first tax-list of Conestoga Township after its erection, in 1718, nearly all of the persons who bore

---

[1] "About that time [1720] considerable numbers of good, sober people came in from Ireland, who wanted to be settled. At the same time, also, it happened that we were under some apprehensions from ye Northern Indians. . . . I therefore thought it might be prudent to plant a settlement of such men as those who formerly had so bravely defended Londonderry and Inniskillen, as a frontier, in case of any disturbance. Accordingly, ye township of Donegal was settled, some few by warrants at ye certain price of 10s. per hundred [acres] but more so, without any. Those people, however, if kindly used, will I believe, be orderly, as they have hitherto been, and easily dealt with. They will also, I expect be a leading example to others."—Letter of Instructions on Provincial Affairs, James Logan to James Steel, Nov. 18, 1729. *Penna. Magazine*, xxiv., 495.

Traders of Conestoga, Donegal, and Paxtang 163

them being then engaged in trade with their Indian neighbors: Stephen Atkinson, Thomas Baldwin, Alexander Bense, Peter Bezaillion, Richard Carter, Edmund Cartlidge, John Cartlidge, Martin Chartier, Thomas Clark, William Clark, John Coombe (brother to Moses), Daniel Cookson, Richard Davis, Thomas Falkner, John Farrer, Thomas Gale, John Grist, James Hendricks, John Hendricks, Joseph Hickman, William Hughes, Morgan Jones, James Le Tort, John Linville, John McDaniel, Collum McQuair, Andrew Mason, John Millen, James Patterson, Joseph Roe, William Sherrill, John Taylor, Robert Wilkins, Francis Worley; freemen (mostly single men): Samuel Birchfield, Nathaniel Christopher, James Davis, Evan Evans, Richard Grice, John Harris, Thomas Jones, William Ludford, Robert Middleton, Thomas Perrin, David Priest, Thomas Wilkins. Other Traders, whose names first appear on the earliest tax-list of Donegal Township (1722), were: Peter Allen (who came about 1718), Henry Bailey (1718), John Burt, Jonas Davenport (1718–19), James Galbreath (1718), Gordon Howard, Robert McFarland, Owen O'Neill, Samuel Smith (1718), William Wilkins.

On July 25, 1684, the Pennsylvania Council ordered that Robert Terrill "be sent for, to appear before ye Govr. and Council, and all others that sell rum to ye Indians."

Jasper Farmar and Nicholas Scull, who lived in what is now Whitemarsh Township, Montgomery County, seem to have begun a trade with the Delawares as early as 1685. At least, in July of that year, some of the Indians along the Schuylkill complained to the Secretary of the Province that the servants of Farmar had supplied them with liquor, made them drunk, and then grossly abused them and debauched their wives. In August of the following year Nicholas Scull, a neighbor of Farmar's, complained to the Council that some Indians had entered his house, and carried off a portion of his goods. The Council, however, seems to have concluded that Mr. Scull himself was more to be reprimanded than the Indians; for they entered the record against him that he had, contrary to the law, first sold these same Indians rum, and made them drunk.

These three cases are the first recorded incidents of the beginnings of the retail trade of the Quaker colonists with the Indians. William Penn himself had begun earlier, in his land purchases; but Penn operated in what, in modern days, would be called a "higher sphere."

The sons of both Farmar and Scull learned the Indian languages, and frequently acted as interpreters in the conferences between the Delawares and the Governor. John Scull, and his brother, Nicholas Scull, Junior, carried on an extensive trade with the Indians both along the Schuylkill and, later, the Susquehanna. John Scull, after 1725, had a store on the east bank of the Susquehanna, above the mouth of Mahantango Creek. His brother afterwards became surveyor-general of the Province.

Jonas Askew is mentioned as an interpreter among the Conestogas in 1709; but there is no record of his trading transactions.

John Hans Steelman, or Stellman[1] a Marylander (naturalized in 1692), as we have seen, established a trade with the Shawnees at Pequea on the Susquehanna, and at Pechoquealin on the Delaware, before 1697. In 1701 William Penn caused his goods to be seized at Philadelphia while on their way to Lechay. William Penn wrote him a letter on April 12, 1701, notifying him of the seizure of these goods. The letter was addressed to "John Hans" but in Penn's report of the matter to his Council, the Trader's name is given as John Hans Steelman. His full name is signed as a witness to the treaty made between Penn and the Susquehannocks, April 23, 1701. James Logan visited the Indians at Conestoga in October, 1705, where he met the chief of the Conestogas, the Shawnees, and the Conoys. He told them "that he understood John Hans was building a log house, for trade amongst them, which made us [the Government's representatives] uneasy; and desired to know whether they [the Indians] encouraged it. To which they answered that they did not; and [they] were desired not to suffer any Christians to settle amongst them without the Govrs. leave." Doctor William H. Egle and some other historians of the Lower Susquehanna Valley have stated that the name, "John Hans," as printed in three places in the Pennsylvania *Archives* and *Colonial Records* covering the years 1705–11, is really a misprint for "John Harris," the Trader, who, some fifteen or twenty years later, was settled at what is now Harrisburg. These writers, however, do not explain why the surname "Steelman," follows the name, John Hans, in two other places in the *Colonial Records;* all of the references being to the same individual.[2] If that individual really was John Harris, Senior, father of the founder of Harrisburg, then he must share the odium for the murder of Francis de la Tore, who was killed by some of the young Shawnee warriors in 1710, or 1711, at the instigation of "John Hans."

[1] Ferris gives a very favorable account of him in his *Original Settlements on the Delaware*, pages 55 and 177. He donated £100 silver, in 1698, towards the building of the Swedes' Church in Wilmington.

[2] The name "John Hans," a misprint for "John Harris," signed to a deed of release, executed by the Delaware Indians to John, Thomas, and Richard Penn, at Philadelphia, August 25, 1737, I am inclined to believe, is the signature for an Indian bearing that name, notwithstanding the opinion of Dr. Egle and other Harrisburg historians to the contrary. The Indian who signed that deed seems to have been none other than "Captain John Harris," Sr., the father of Teedyuscung and of "Captain John," his brother. See *Penna. Archives*, i., 543; Reichel's *Memorials of the Moravian Church*, 217.

Governor Gookin visited Conestoga with four members of his Council in June, 1711, to investigate this murder; and while there, the Senecas gave him the following account of the affair: "That Opessa [chief of the Shawnees], being thereto solicited by John Hans Steelman, had sent out some of his people, either to bring back or kill Francis de la Tore and his company. Opessa, he affirms, was entirely innocent, for that John Hans came to his cabin, when he and his young people, who were then going a hunting, were in council; told him that some of his slaves and dogs (meaning La Tore and company) were fled; therefore desired him forthwith to send some of his people to bring them back or kill them, and take goods for their trouble. At which motion, Opessa, being surprised, told him that he ought by no means to discourse after that manner before young people who were going to the woods and might by accident meet these people; and therefore ordered him to desist, utterly denying his request."

Reference has already been made to Captain Jacques Le Tort, and his wife, Anne Le Tort, early Indian Traders near the Schuylkill, who in December, 1693, were wrongfully accused of carrying on treasonable correspondence with the Shallna-rooners [Shawnees] and the French of Canada. The first appearance of Le Tort's name on the Pennsylvania *Colonial Records* seems to have been on August 29, 1689, when the Governor laid a letter before the Council which he had received from "Capt. Le Tort, a Frenchman living up in the countrey." On May 22, 1690, a minute of the Council recites that "Capt. Le Tort, making his application to ye Council that he may have liberty to go for England; resolved, That he may, provided he performs the laws of Government in that case provided." The Le Torts were Huguenot refugees, who came to Pennsylvania from London in 1686.[1]

Col. Casparus Hermann informed the Maryland Council May 4, 1696, that "Peter Basilion does now live at St. Jones's [St. John's, in Chester County, Penna.]; but formerly lived thirty miles backwards from any inhabitants, where he treated with the Indians, and was then reported that he kept private correspondence with the Canida Indians and the French; and since, he [Hermann] has heard that he has a brother taken by the Mohages from Canada, to whom he was intended to go, in order to redeem him. That Capt. Le Tort, a Frenchman, does now live back in the woods in the same place where the said Basilion formerly lived, and trades with the Indians."[2]

A letter received from Governor William Markham of Pennsylvania

---

[1] Rupp's *Lancaster County, Penna.*, App. ii. Egle's *Notes and Queries*, Fourth Series, ii., 35.

[2] *Md. Arch.*, xx., 406.

in regard to Jacques Le Tort was laid before the Maryland Council, July 10, 1696. Governor Markham wrote: "Le Tort is a Protestant, who was sent over in the year 1686 with a considerable cargo and several French Protestants, of whom he had the charge, by Doctor Cox, Sir Mathias Vincent, and a third gentleman [Benjohan Furloy], to settle 30,000 acres of land up the Schuylkill, that they had bought of Mr. Penn; and that's the place he lives at."[1] While going to England in the ship with Governor Hamilton, Captain Le Tort was taken prisoner by the French and carried to Toulon where he narrowly escaped the galleys; but he finally succeeded in reaching England. There he made an agreement with the West Jersey Company to carry on a trade with the Indians for that Company's account, at his house on the Schuylkill,[2] which was located on the ancient path of the Minquas, leading from the mouth of the Schuylkill, up that river, up French Creek, and down Conestoga Creek to the Conestoga Town. The senior Le Tort seems to have begun trading at Conestoga and Octorara as early as 1695.

His son, James Le Tort ("son of James Le Tort"), with the consent of his mother, Anne Le Tort, bound himself to a five years' term of service to John King, a sea-captain, May 28, 1692.[3] It is recorded of him in June, 1703, that "James Le Tort, who about two years ago went out of this Province to Canada, and returned last spring, having been upon his return examined before several of ye Council and magistrates, and no great occasion found to suspect him of any evil designs against the Government, he having been bred in it from his infancy, had hitherto behaved himself inoffensively, and was seduced to depart in time of peace by the instigation of some others, without any evil intentions that could be made appear in himself; and being now in town, together with Peter Bezalion, another Frenchman and Indian Trader, it was judged necessary to call them both before Council, and for further satisfaction, to take security of them for their behavior towards the Government. Accordingly, they were sent for, and obliged each to give security in five hundred pounds sterling." A short time after these bonds were executed, James Le Tort was locked up as a prisoner in the common jail.

---

[1] This tract comprises the greater part of the present townships of East and West Vincent in Chester County. These two townships are divided by French Creek, which flows into the Schuylkill at Phœnixville, and probably took its name from this Huguenot settlement. On a map of Vincent Township made in 1773 one of the landmarks noted is "Bezalion's Cave" (named for Peter Bezaillion) which was located near the river, opposite the lower end of the island near Spring City. The tract is shown on Thomas Holme's map of Pennsylvania. (See Futhey and Cope's *Chester County*, 209, 210.)

[2] *Penna. Archives*, vi., 470.

[3] *Ibid.*, Second Series, ix., 179.

He was released, however, and continued trading with the Indians, his mother assisting him; and, apparently, she was the more business-like of the two. He was again imprisoned in 1711, because of his French descent. He was licensed to trade in January, 1713, by the Governor, and is referred to in the records of that year. In his petition in 1722 to the Chester County Court, for a renewal of his trading license, he asked for the renewal on the grounds that he had then been a Trader amongst the Indians "for the past twenty-five years." Governor Evans found James Le Tort to be a Trader among the Shawnees at Peixtan, when in July, 1707, he visited that town to arrest Nicole Godin. Five years later, Conguegoes, the old queen of the Conestogas, complained to the Governor that Madame Anne Le Tort did the Indians at Conestoga great damage by "keeping of hogs; and that twice she turned them into the Queen's corn in her own sight."

In March, 1704, Madame Anne Le Tort lived at Conestoga, from which place she wrote to Edward Farmar at Philadelphia, advising him of the killing of two families of Conestogas by the "Towittois" (Twightwees) Indians. In a letter written by Secretary James Logan to Isaac Taylor, the Surveyor for Chester County, November 4, 1719, instructing him to survey lands for Peter Bezaillion's wife, Martha, for Moses Coombe, her brother, and for Anne Le Tort, along the east bank of the Susquehanna, between Conewago and Chickasalunga creeks, Logan refers, probably, to Anne Le Tort in the following language: "I am very desirous the old gentlewoman should have some land, that she may be fixed, and leave something to her grandchildren. Pray see that it be laid out of a sufficient depth. I think a mile and a half, or a quarter at least, is little enough. . . . J. Le Tort is also to have 500 acres laid out in the same manner."

In accordance with this order, a tract of land was surveyed to her, lying along the east bank of the Susquehanna just below the mouth of Conewago Creek.

After this time, and probably after the death of his mother, James Le Tort settled at Le Tort's Spring, in Cumberland County, which took its name from him. He built a trading post at this place, which afterwards became the site of Carlisle. Between 1725 and 1727, or perhaps earlier, he had a store at the Forks of the Susquehanna, on the north side, where he carried on a trade with the Shawnees of Chillisquaque, at the mouth of the creek of the same name; as well as with the Mingoes and Delawares then living at Shamokin; with the Minsis under Manawkyhickon at Muncy Creek; and with the Indians of the Shawnee and other towns located on the West Branch between there and Great Island. In a conference at Philadelphia, July 4, 1727, between the Governor and Council and some chiefs of the Six Nations (they became the Six Nations about 1722), the Indians desired "that none of the Traders be allowed to carry any rum to the remoter parts where James Le Tort trades (that is, Allegheny, on the branches of Ohio)."

James Le Tort was one of the earliest, if not the first of the Shamokin Traders to follow the Delawares westward of the Alleghanies. The site of an old Indian town near the present village of Shelocta in Indiana County, was known as late as 1769 as "James Letort's Town."[1] This was probably the site of his trading post "at Allegheny" for some years after 1729. As early as 1728 he made preparations for a trading trip to the Twightwees' or Miamis' country, which was then between the southeastern shore of Lake Michigan and the head of the Maumee. Le Tort's Rapids, Le Tort's Creek, and Le Tort's Island (all now corrupted to "Letart's"), in the Ohio River, along the southern border of Meigs County, attest his presence in those parts at a very early day, when he traded with the Shawnees and Delawares at their towns there: one of which was at or near the mouth of what since before 1755 has been known as Le Tort's or Old Town Creek; and two below,—Kiskiminetas Old Town, on the west side of the Ohio, eight miles above the mouth of the Kanawha, and Shawnee Old Town, on the east bank of the Ohio, three miles north of the Great Kanawha.[2] He may have settled in the Ohio country permanently; but more probably continued making trips between Philadelphia and Allegheny until he became an old man. His name appears as a witness to a deed of release signed by the Delaware chiefs at Philadelphia, August 25, 1737. As late as July, 1742, Governor Thomas speaks of having received a letter from "Le Tort, the Indian trader at Allegheny," informing him that some Taway (Ottawa) Indians had passed through the Shawnee settlement there, having with them the scalps of two white persons whom they had slain. No later references to Le Tort appear in the records of Pennsylvania; although there was a James Le Tort with Washington at Great Meadows in 1754, a member of Captain Peter Hog's Company.[3]

Peter Bezaillion,[4] as we have seen, was also an early French Canadian Trader in what are now Delaware, Chester, and Lancaster counties, before 1696. His brother, Richard, was associated with him. Thomas Jenner and Polycarpus Rose, on December 19, 1693, accused them and the Le Torts before the Council of having carried on a secret correspondence with the "strange Indians called Shallnarooners" (Shawnees) the year

---

[1] See land application of George Campbell, in Caldwell's *Indiana County*, p. 132.

[2] Referred to in his *Journal* by George Washington, who visited its site in 1770, as "Old Shawna Town, which is about three miles up ye Ohio [from the mouth of Kanawha], just above the mouth of a Creek."

[3] Washington's *Journal of 1754*, Toner's edition, pp. 173, 192, 202, 217.

[4] His name is spelled Bezellon on his tombstone.

before. The latter of these informants swore, "that about a year since, there was a packet of letters sent from Philadelphia, from Peter Basilion, Capt. Dubrois, and Madame Le Tort, to the strange Indians called Shallnarooners, sealed up in a blue linen cloth, and was left at James Stanfield's plantation [in what is now Marple Township, Delaware County], by Richard Basilion's servant, who then run away; and the letters being there three days, James, the Frenchman, came and carried them away." In 1701, William Penn and the Council considered the case of "Louis [Michel?] and Peter Basailion, who have been suspected to be very dangerous persons in their traffic with the Indians, in this troublesome conjuncture of affairs." Accordingly, it was resolved, "that it was absolutely necessary the said two Frenchmen should be confined, and restrained from inhabiting or trading amongst the Indians." Two years later, both Peter Bezaillion and James Le Tort, Junior, were required by Council to give bonds in the amount of five hundred pounds each, that they would behave themselves as loyal subjects of Queen Anne. Le Tort was locked up in the common "gaol" for a time in 1704, and again in 1711; while Bezaillion also was imprisoned in 1711, at a time when his fidelity was again suspected.

It is quite possible that Bezaillion came over with Le Tort and the other French Protestants in 1686. In a letter written by William Markham, Governor of Pennsylvania, to the Governor of Maryland, June 26, 1696, Markham says: "Upon the copy of what Coll. Herman gave into your Excellency and Council, I shall require security for Le Tort [the father] and Basalion, tho' I know that will not satisfy the Coll. He still will be uneasy until he get all the Indian trade to himself. I have known Coll. Herman for a long time, and he that trades for him on Susquehanna (Amos Nicholls) is better known than trusted. I enclose to your Excellency what I found among castaway papers. Basalion was in equal partnership with Petit and Salvay, though it went in only their two names, Basalion coming in after the others had provided for the voyage, and after the voyage was overthrown, I divided the left cargo, and Basalion had one-third. But as to Le Tort he is a Protestant."

Peter Bezaillion at one time owned a plantation on the west side of the Schuylkill, referred to in the minutes of the Board of Property in February, 1718, as "the old plantation where Peter Bizalion formerly dwelt." From there he moved towards Conestoga; and eventually settled in East Caln Township, Chester County, where he made his permanent home a few miles east of the present site of St. John's Church. This church was built largely through the efforts and contribution of Bezaillion's wife, Martha Coombe, who was an Episcopalian. Bezaillion, himself, was referred to by the Governor in 1710, as a Frenchman, a Roman Catholic (which is doubtful), and a suspicious person generally, who traded with the Indians at Conestoga. He traded at Conestoga before 1696, and until the time of his imprisonment at Philadelphia in August, 1711. In November, 1708, the Property Commissioners gave him permission to erect a house and plant fields for his own use on the lands above Conestoga. He was licensed by the Governor in May, 1712, and in July of the same year the Governor told the Conestoga Indians that Bezaillion was the only Trader who had ever been allowed by the Government to settle amongst them. In 1714, he received a warrant from the Commissioners of Property, allowing him to "seat himself at Pashtang, or any other Indian town or place on Susquehanna, in this Province, and to erect such buildings as are necessary for his trade, and to enclose and improve such quantities of land as he shall think fit, for the accommodation of his family there." He acted as interpreter for the Delawares in a conference held at Conestoga, July 18, 1717. Two years later, 700 acres of land were surveyed for his wife on the east bank of the Susquehanna, between Chickasalunga and Conewago creeks, adjoining the Conoy Indian town.

In March, 1721, Bezaillion had a trading post near Paxtang, "about thirty-six miles higher up on Sasquehannah" than Conestoga; and in May, 1728, he acted with Nicholas and John Scull as interpreters at an Indian conference in Philadelphia. He was reported, as early as 1708, to have joined with James Le Tort and Martin Chartier in building cabins on the upper branches of Potomac (Antietam and Conococheague creeks, in what is now Franklin County, Penna.), and also had a trading post near Paxtang, as we have seen. Peter Bezaillion died in 1742, at the age of eighty.

His wife's brother, Moses Coombe, was also successfully engaged in the Indian trade, in Donegal Township, where he had a post on Conoy Creek before 1716. Mrs. Bezaillion had a nephew named John Hart. Possibly, he was an Indian Trader himself, and the son of that John Hart, one of the "Shamokin Traders," who was accidentally killed while hunting with the Indians on the Ohio, 1729–30.

Martin Chartier, another French Canadian, who was given such a bad character by La Salle in 1680, as we have seen, led the Shawnees from the West and South to the head of Chesapeake Bay in 1692, and when they removed to the banks of Pequea Creek, he continued to make his home among them. Here he lived until after August, 1707. He was examined by the Governor at Philadelphia, May 15, 1704, in regard to his relations with the Indians, he being "a Frenchman, who has lived long among the Shawanah Indians and upon Conestoga." In June, 1707, Governor Evans came to his trading house at Pequehan, and got Chartier to accompany him to Peixtan, where he went to arrest Nicole Godin. In February, 1708, he, with James Le Tort and Peter Bezaillion, was re-

Peter Bezallion's Grave.

From a photograph furnished by Mr. Frank R. Diffenderfer.

ported to have built houses upon the upper branches of Potomac (Conococheague?). These houses were probably trading posts where they carried on a trade with the Shawnee Indians at Opessa's Town and the other Shawnee Town on the Potomac. He acted as interpreter for the Shawnees at conferences held at Conestoga in 1711 and 1717. In 1717, he was granted a tract of land on the east side of the Susquehanna, about eight miles above the mouth of Conestoga Creek, including the site of the present borough of Washington, "where he had seated himself . . . including within the survey the improvement then made by him, for which he agreed, on behalf of his son, Peter Chartier . . . to pay for the same." Here he established his trading post and his home; and here he died in 1718.

He left an only son, Peter Chartier, who is said to have followed his father's example by marrying a Shawnee squaw. In the early part of 1718, on the application of his father, the Board of Property issued a warrant for 300 acres of land to be surveyed to Peter Chartier, "where his father is settled, on Susquehanna river." Peter Chartier traded for some years with the Shawnees, who had moved up the river from Pequea Creek, and established villages near the site of the present Washington Borough, in Lancaster County, and at Paxtang. Later, he settled at their town on the west side of the river, at the mouth of Shawnee (now Yellow Breeches) Creek, the site of the present town of New Cumberland. From thence he is said to have removed to the Conococheague. He was licensed as an Indian Trader by the Lancaster County Court, November 3, 1730; and about the same time began trading with the Shawnees on the Conemaugh. He removed to the Allegheny some time after 1734, at which place his later history will be considered in another chapter.

Sylvester Garland, of Newcastle, was a Trader among the Shawnees of Pequea within a short time after their arrival in the Province. On the 3rd of September, 1701, Shemekenwhoa, "one of the chiefs of the Shawanah Indians, solemnly declared and complained to the Govr. that Sylvester Garland had brought to the settlement of Indians of their nation several anchors of rum, to the quantity of about 140 gallons, and that to induce them to receive it and trade with him, he pretended he was sent by ye Govr., and gave one cask as a present from him; upon which, being entreated to drink, they were afterwards much abused." Mr. Garland was accordingly haled before the Council, and put under bonds to the amount of £100, that he would not sell any more rum to the natives. On September 17, 1702, Garland laid information before the Council that some of the Delaware and Conestoga Indians had recently brought from the southwards, where they had been on a hunting trip, articles of feminine apparel, which seemed to give rise to the belief that these Indians had murdered the owners of the articles. Garland's last appearance on the records as a Trader was in April, 1710, at which time he informed the Governor at Newcastle of some negotiations having been begun between the Five Nations and the Conestoga Indians.

Joseph Jessop and Nicole Godin were two more early French Traders among the Indians at Peixtan, both being there in 1707. Godin is mentioned as a Trader at Conestoga as early as May, 1704, in which month he brought news to Edward Farmar, at Philadelphia, of the attack made by some Carolina Indians upon those of Conestoga and the Potomac. Farmar laid the information before the Council, and took Godin before that body the following day, when he delivered a message from the Conestoga chief, complaining of the great quantities of rum brought to their town. On July 15, 1707, Governor Evans informed the Council that he had received information against "one, Nicole Godin, a Frenchman, a bold, active young fellow, who had long kept abroad in the woods amongst the Indians, and was with them in Philadelphia about three years ago; that he had been using endeavors to incense these people against the subjects of the Crown; and to join with our public enemy, the French, to our destruction." The Governor explained that this information came to him on the eve of his departure for a visit to the Conestoga and Shawnee Indian towns; and that he had resolved, before his return, to have Godin apprehended, "which after a tedious journey and considerable difficulties he had accordingly performed, and brought him a prisoner to Philadelphia, in the common gaol of which he now lies." A week later, Governor Evans laid before the Council the *Journal* of his trip to Conestoga, containing the account of the capture of Godin, which was as follows:

On Tuesday, 1st July [1707] we went to Conestoga [from Pequehan], and lay there that night, and the next morning proceeded on our journey, and arrived in the evening within three miles of an Indian village called Peixtan [on the site of Harrisburg]. The Governor had received information at Pequehan that one, Nicole, a French Indian Trader, was at that place, against whom great complaints had been made to the Governor; of which he acquainted the chief Indian of Peixtan, as also of his design to seize him; who willingly agreed to it, but advised the Governor to be very cautious in the manner; there being only young people at home, who perhaps might make some resistance if it were done without their first being told of it. For this reason, we lay short of the village that night; but early in the morning, we went within half a mile of the town, and, leaving our horses, marched afoot nearer the same; from whence the Governor sent Martine [Chartier] to the village, ordering him to tell Nicole that he had brought two cags of rum with him, which he left in the woods, for fear any Christians were there; and withal, to persuade Nicole to go with him and taste the rum. Martine returned with James Le Tort and Joseph Jessop, two Indian Traders, but could not prevail with Nicole. Upon this, Martine was sent back, with orders to bring down some of the Indians, and Nicole with them. Then we drew nearer the town, and laid ourselves in the bushes; and Martine returned with two Indians, whom the Governor acquainted with his intent of taking Nicole, telling at the same time he had spoken with the Uncle of one of them upon that head, who ordered the Indians to submit to the Governor's demand; with which they were contented, though we perceived too well the contrary by their inquiring how many we were, and how armed, and by the concern they seemed to be in when they found we were more men than they. But still Nicole was wanting. It was therefore resolved to try once more if he could be got into the woods. Accordingly Martine went again, and brought Nicole to the place where we lay concealed, and asking him to drink a dram, he seized him. But Nicole started from him and run for it. When immediately we started out and took him, and presently carried him to the village (through which we were obliged to pass). And there we found some Indians with guns in their hands who looked much displeased with what we had done; but we, being in a readiness against any surprise, they thought it not fit to attempt anything. Here we stayed about half an hour, and then started for Turpyhocken, having mounted Nicole upon a horse, and tied his legs under the belly. We got within a mile of Turpyhocken about two of ye clock, on Friday morning, and about seven the Governor went to the town. From thence we went to Manatawny that night; and the next day to Philadelphia.

Following the reading of this account to the Council, Edward Farmar appeared before that body the same day, and having long known Nicole, informed the Council that he had been told by the prisoner that he was born in London, although his father was a Frenchman. Godin himself, when brought before the Council, told them the same thing; whereupon the Council ordered that he should be tried as a subject of England for his treasonable correspondences.

Edmund and John Cartlidge, two brothers, were among the few Quakers who embarked in the Indian trade. Edmund Cartlidge owned land in Springfield Township, now in Delaware County, as early as 1702; while in 1712, his brother made application for a mill-site on the upper waters of Duck Creek. A warrant for 500 acres of land south of the Conestoga Indian town was issued to John Cartlidge under date of December 11, 1716; and one to his brother Edmund, bearing date October 1, 1717, for 400 acres, upon which he had erected a grist-mill, on "a branch of Conestoga."[1] One or both brothers were among the early Justice of Chester County, which then included Lancaster. Many of the conferences between the Provincial authorities and the Indians were carried on in the house of John Cartlidge between 1717 and 1722. In the year last named, while both the brothers were on a trading trip among the Potomac Indians who lived along Monocacy Creek, in Maryland, they were threatened by a Seneca Indian, who had drunk so much rum that he

[1] *Penna. Arch.*, Sec. Ser., xix., 569, 644.

became abusive and dangerous. When the Traders refused to give him more, he made an attack on them, and John Cartlidge killed him. Both brothers were imprisoned as a result of this affair; but were afterwards released, at the instance of the Five Nations. John Cartlidge died in 1726. His brother remained at Conestoga for some years afterwards. Edmund Cartlidge was one of the earliest Traders west of the Alleghanies, and made frequent trips to the Ohio country for many years after 1727. Edmund's Swamp, a noted landmark on the Ray's Town Trading Path, was named for him.

James Patterson located, in 1717, along the northern line of Conestoga Manor, about a mile east of Martin Chartier's post, and there established a trading house. He also took up a tract of land on the opposite side of the Susquehanna, in Conejohela Valley (in what is now York County), where he pastured the horses used by him to pack goods in his trading trips to the Indians of the Potomac. He was a licensed Trader in 1722, and died in 1735. The boundary troubles which began about 1730 between the Pennsylvania settlers and those of Maryland, led by Captain Thomas Cresap, entirely broke up Patterson's trade on the west side of the river, and entailed great loss upon him. His grandson, Captain William Patterson, (whose father, James, had settled on the Juniata, at the site of the present village of Mexico, before the French War), married a daughter of John Finley, another Indian Trader, who, late in his life (1769) piloted Daniel Boone into Kentucky. Susanna, daughter of James Patterson, Sr., married James Lowrey, another of the Donegal Traders. A second daughter, Sarah, married Benjamin Chambers, one of the founders of Chambersburg.

Robert Wilkins was another Trader who settled near the Conestoga Indians in 1718. In September of that year he obtained 318 acres of land, the site of the present town of Marietta. He had four sons, William, Peter, Thomas, and John, who also became Indian Traders. William Wilkins traded among the Indians of the Cumberland and Shenandoah valleys, and died in Donegal Township in 1734. In 1722, at the time of the trial of John and Edmund Cartlidge for the murder of the Seneca Indian at Monocacy, William Wilkins's presence was required, as he had been a witness to the killing, being then in the employ of John Cartlidge. He could not be summoned, however, as he was then "one hundred and fifty miles up Sasquehannah [above Conestoga], trading for his master." John Wilkins traded with the Indians at Ohio. He died in 1741, leaving a son, John, who became a Trader in what was then Cumberland County about 1763; and after the Revolution, settled in Pittsburgh. Peter Wilkins died in the Cumberland Valley in 1748; Thomas, in 1747.

Peter Allen was a Donegal Trader who settled on Chickasalunga Creek about 1718. In 1720 he lived near the site of Marietta, and traded with the Indians. Some ten years later, he had a trading post near the mouth of Fishing Creek, a few miles south of the hill which has since then been known as Peter's Mountain. He was living there until after 1735.

Isaac Miranda and his son, George, were Traders who settled on Conoy Creek, in what is now Lancaster County, about 1715. The father died in 1732, leaving to his heirs several thousand acres of land, and, among other personal property, twelve pack-horses, which he had formerly used in his Indian trade. His daughter married Governor James Hamilton. George Miranda, the son, was one of the most active Traders among the Shawnees at Allegheny between 1736 and 1740.

Jonas Davenport and Henry Bailey were two early Traders in Lancaster County, where they settled about 1718. In 1719 Davenport was granted a tract of land adjoining that of Bezaillion and Le Tort in Donegal Township. He was licensed as a Trader by the Chester County court in 1725. Davenport and Bailey, with Le Tort and Edmund Cartlidge, were the first of the Pennsylvania Traders to venture themselves and their goods as far west as the Allegheny River, where they began trading as early as 1727. Davenport lost much of his property through the assaults of hostile Indians; and died in poverty near the place where he had first settled.

James Galbraith, Jr., settled in Donegal Township, near Chickasalunga Creek, about 1718. He was an Indian Trader, and commanded a company of Rangers during the French War. He was a member of the Assembly for a number of years, a King's Justice, and, about 1742, Sheriff of Lancaster County. He died in 1787, aged eighty-three years. His son, John Galbraith, also established a trading post at the mouth of Conoy Creek, before 1760. He afterwards removed to the Cumberland Valley. John Galbraith's granddaughter, Dorcas Spear (daughter of Robert and Elizabeth Galbraith Spear) married William Patterson of Baltimore, and their daughter, Elizabeth Spear Patterson, married Jerome Bonaparte.

John Burt traded with the Indians of Conestoga before 1723. In that year he was licensed by the Governor. Later, he removed up the river to "Snaketown on the Susquehannah," where he established a trading post. This town was probably above Swatara Creek. In September, 1727, a number of drunken Indians, of the Minsi tribe, made an attack on Burt, who, after supplying them with rum, had foolishly insulted them. He escaped; but another man at the post, named Thomas Wright, was pursued and killed by the Indians. Burt fled from his trading post on the Susquehanna, and afterwards is said to have removed westward.

Samuel Smith came from the North of Ireland and settled in Donegal

Township, Lancaster County, about 1725, where he had a trading-post on Conewago Creek. He also erected a grist-mill and a saw-mill. He was Sheriff of Lancaster County 1735-37, and a member of the Assembly in 1737-38. Before 1750, he removed to the west side of the Susquehanna, and was appointed as one of the first Justices of Cumberland County, erected in that year. In a letter written by Conrad Weiser to Governor Hamilton, September 13, 1754, telling of his visit to the Indians of George Croghan's post at Aughwick, Weiser says: "It is a surprising thing that no means can be found to prevent the inhabitants in Cumberland County from selling strong liquor to the Indians. I am creditably informed that some of the magistrates of that county sell the most. Mr. Smith was at Aughwick, I suppose to gather some money for the liquor he sent. He is an old hypocrite."

John Harris, father of the founder of Harrisburg, removed from Philadelphia to Conestoga Township before 1718, his name occurring on the first tax-list of that township in this year. Before 1733, he had established a trading house on the Susquehanna, just above the mouth of Paxtang Creek, where he carried on a trade with the Shawnee and other Indians who then lived on the west side of the river, along Yellow Breeches and Conodoguinet creeks, and at the mouth of the Juniata. He died here in 1748. The account of Dr. Egle and others that he had seated himself and built a log-house on the Susquehanna as early as 1705 cannot be accepted as correct. These writers have mistaken John Hans Steelman for John Harris, and of course cannot contend that the two were identical. In June, 1733, Shekallamy complained to the Pennsylvania Council that John Harris had built a house and cleared fields at the mouth of Juniata. He was informed that Harris had built that house only for the purpose of carrying on his trade; that his plantation, on which were his houses, barns, and other improvements, at Paxtang, was his place of residence.

During the settlement of the Cumberland Valley by the Scotch-Irish, 1733-50, Harris's trading house on the Susquehanna, near the mouth of Paxtang Creek, became a place of great importance; and a ferry was established there by the owner, which was maintained by his son for many years after his death. John Harris, Jr., received a license for the ferry from the Governor in 1753. In the summer-time, the river was fordable at this point. Esther, wife of the first John Harris, assisted him in his trade with the Indians, and many incidents showing her courage and sagacity have been preserved in the local annals of Harrisburg. Her grandson related that on one occasion she rode on horseback nearly all the way from her home to Philadelphia in one day. At another time, while in charge of their trading house on Big Island, she learned of her absent husband's illness, when she immediately started down the river in a birch-bark canoe, so that she might join him and take care of him. Watson states that she was an expert swimmer, and could use firearms as well as a frontiersman. Of her children, Elizabeth, the eldest, married in 1744, John Finley, the Indian Trader who afterwards (1769) guided Daniel Boone and his party into Kentucky.

Lazarus Lowrey came from the North of Ireland and settled in Donegal Township, Lancaster County, about 1729. He took up 500 acres of land about two miles from the site of the present town of Marietta, where he established a trading house; and in 1730 was granted a license to trade with the Indians, and also to sell liquor "by the small." His dwelling-house is still standing. He was a man remarkable for his energy, industry, and courage. He made frequent trading trips to the Ohio country, and sometimes took his sons with him, five of whom became Indian Traders also. These were James, John, Daniel, Alexander, and Lazarus. The father died at Philadelphia in 1755.

John Lowrey made trading trips with his father west of the Alleghanies before 1740. Sometime in 1749[1] while in the Ohio country, he was seated near a keg of powder, to which an Indian applied a match. The explosion which followed blew Lowrey to pieces. His widow survived him, but they had no children.

James Lowrey, another son of Lazarus, married Susanna, daughter of James Patterson, also an Indian Trader. He took up a large tract of land on the Susquehanna above the site of Marietta, and made many trips to Ohio; acting with George Croghan to prevent the Indians there from going over to the French interest. The French Commandant at Detroit offered a reward for the scalps of these two Traders in 1750. In January, 1753, while trading in Kentucky, he was captured, with three of his men and four of Croghan's, by the French Mohawks, or Canawaugha Indians. Lowrey managed to make his escape within a few days; but his men were carried to Canada, and kept in captivity for some time by the Indians. A further account of this affair will be found in a later chapter. In a letter written by Captain Robert Stobo, while held a hostage at Fort Duquesne in July, 1754, he states that the Indians, under Mingo John, had made an attack upon Lowrey's Traders at the house of Christopher Gist and had taken prisoners, Andrew McBriar, Nehemiah Stevens, John Kennedy, and Elizabeth Williams. Several persons were killed. Kennedy was given to a wounded chief named The Owl, to wait upon him while his leg was curing. The others were sent to Canada. They were employes of James, Daniel, and Alexander Lowrey. Their goods were all confiscated. The losses he met with in these years proved so embarrassing to James Lowrey that he finally sold

[1] *Penna. Arch.*, ii., 39; *Col. Rec.*, v., 461.

his land in Donegal Township, and removed, after 1758, to what is now Blair County, Pennsylvania.

Alexander Lowrey, the most prominent of these five brothers, began trading with the Indians about 1744; although he had accompanied his father and older brothers to Ohio before that time. He acquired the language of several tribes, and could talk with his customers readily. At an early day in his career he formed an advantageous partnership with Edward Shippen and with a shrewd and successful Jew of Lancaster, named Joseph Simon. The latter alliance continued for about forty years, and through it, and his own courage and sagacity. Lowrey was enabled to acquire a respectable fortune for those days. He established trading posts at Carlisle, Logstown, and Fort Pitt, and employed a number of assistants in his trading enterprises. Although frequently among the Indians, he was never molested by them but once; and on that occasion saved his life by his nerve and his ability as a runner, In 1763, he is said to have met with the loss of a large quantity of goods by an attack on his train of laden pack-horses, by a party of Indians at "Bloody Run" (now Everett, Bedford County); although from the way his descendant, Mr. Samuel Evans, writes the story, there is a suspicion that the attacking party was the band of "Black Boys," organized by Col. James Smith in 1765, to prevent ammunition and supplies from being carried to the Indians so soon after the outrages committed by them during Pontiac's War. The Six Nations, in 1768, made a grant of a large tract of land covering the northwestern corner of the present State of West Virginia, to reimburse the Traders for their losses on that occasion, and in 1763.

John Kelly was an Indian Trader of Donegal Township, who traded at Allegheny as early as 1734. About 1740 he settled upon the land afterwards forming the western part of the site of Marietta, in Lancaster County. One of his descendants was the late Senator James K. Kelly, of Oregon.

Gordon Howard was an early and prominent Trader in Donegal from about 1722. In June, 1720, he applied to the Board of Property for 200 acres of land in Nottingham Township, Chester County; and in May, 1722, for 200 acres more, two miles north of Galbraith's Mills, and four miles east of the Susquehanna. Here he settled and lived, his post being about two miles west of what is now Mount Joy village. His sister, Susanna, married first, James Patterson, Sr., the Trader; second, Thomas Ewing; third, John Connolly; and became the mother of Dr. John Connolly the Loyalist.

Simon Girty, Sr., father of the notorious renegade of the same name was also an early Indian Trader of Donegal, located at one time on Conewago Creek. From there, he removed to Shearman's Creek, in what is now Perry County, where he was afterwards killed in a drunken brawl.

James and Thomas Harris were Traders in Lancaster County before 1730. The former had his trading post near James Le Tort's, about two miles west of what is now Maytown. The latter established himself on Conewago Creek, where the Conestoga and Paxtang path crossed. He became one of the wealthiest of the Traders. Before the Revolution he removed to Harford County, Maryland, and from thence to Baltimore. Some of his sons served as officers in the Revolutionary army.

James Hamilton, of Leacock Township, was also a Trader on Conewago Creek; and extended his operations to the Ohio.

John Fraser, or Frazier, lived in Paxtang Township, near the Susquehanna, in 1737. He removed to the Allegheny soon after that date, where he established a post at Venango. Here, and at another post at the mouth of Turtle Creek, he took a prominent part in the events preceding Braddock's defeat.

John Postlethwaite is mentioned as an Indian Trader of Conestoga in 1739.

William Dunlap kept a trading post on Swatara Creek as early as 1730.

John Kennedy, one of Lowrey's Traders in 1754, who was captured by the French at Gist's plantation in that year, after his escape from the Indians, raised and commanded a company of Rangers in the war that followed. He became a Trader on his own account, and lived in Lancaster County on the land upon which Maytown was afterwards built.

Thomas Perrin, a settler in Conestoga Township before 1718, was licensed as a Trader by the Governor in 1724.

Joseph Cloud, of Caln Township, petitioned the Chester County Court to recommend him for a Trader's license; and one was issued to him for the years 1724 and 1725.

The following additional persons petitioned the Chester County Court for licenses to trade, between 1730 and 1755; to all of whom such licenses were granted by the Governor: James Adams, 1743; Robert Anderson, 1743; William Black, 1738; Joseph Burgoin, 1733; Thomas Clark, 1754; George Conoll, 1749; Charles Conner, 1730; Samuel Cross, 1744; Matthew Dunlap, 1751; Richard Hall, 1753; Henry Hetherington, 1746; James Hunter, 1750; John McClure, 1743; Archibald McGee, 1730; Neal McLaughlin, 1749; Charles McMichael, 1742; James McMordie, 1751; George Mason, 1730; Samuel Mealy, 1750; John Millison, 1754; Terrence O'Neil, 1730; John Prince, 1755; Samuel Patterson, 1752; Alexander Richardson, 1730; James Rose, 1738; John Shaw, 1754; Daniel Stewart, 1742; John Swanner, 1742; Patrick Whinnery, 1749; William Young, 1730.

In their petitions to the Court, some assigned as reasons for desiring to become Traders, their advanced years of age, their loss of the use of a hand or arm, and other physical infirmities preventing them from hard manual labor. Others set forth that they had just arrived from abroad with large stocks of merchandise.

In the Lancaster County Court for November, 1730, the following named persons petitioned the Court to recommend them to the Governor for Indian Traders' licenses: James Patterson, a Trader for thirteen years past; Edmund Cartlidge, a Trader for thirteen years; Peter Chartier, an old Trader; John Lawrence, an old Trader; Jonas Davenport, an old Trader; Oliver Wallis; Patrick Boyd; Lazarus Lowrey; William Dunlap, an old Trader; William Beswick; John Wilkins, an old Trader; Thomas Perrin; John Harris, an old Trader.

One of the earliest Indian Paths leading from the Delaware to the Susquehanna which the white settlers in Pennsylvania used after William Penn's coming is indicated on the map of a survey made by Benjamin Chambers for the Proprietary in 1688–89. This survey was made in accordance with the terms of a deed from the chiefs, Shakkoppoh, Secane, Malebore, and Tangoras, to William Penn in 1685, granting him the lands lying between Pennypack and Chester creeks, and backwards into the woods as far as a man can go on a horse in two days. The southern line of the tract, as marked in this preliminary survey, extended from Clayton's Mill (adjoining Philadelphia on the west), westward sixty-six miles to a point on the Susquehanna about three miles above the mouth of Conestoga Creek, and about the same distance south of the "Fort Demolished" of the Conestogas, which is marked on the plat of this survey.[1] Thirty-eight miles west of Philadelphia, and two miles beyond the crossing of Doe Run, an Indian Path[2] is marked, which ran in a direction northwest by west from the mouth of Christina up White Clay Creek to the Pequea Valley, by way of "The Gap." This was undoubtedly one of the early routes taken by the Minquas to the Swedish settlement at the mouth of Christina Creek; and was the path afterwards followed by Sylvester Garland and other traders from Newcastle, in their trading trips to the Shawnees and Susquehannocks, or Minquas. A branch of this

---

[1] See also plat of original survey of Conestoga Manor, dated Feb. 1, 1718 (*Penna. Arch.*, 3d Ser., iv., map 11), which shows the exact location of Conestoga Town, and the approximate location of the Fort Demolished—1800 rods above the mouth of Conestoga Creek.

[2] Said by local historians to be identical with the Limestone Road, in Highland, West Fallowfield, Upper and Lower Oxford, and East Nottingham townships, Chester County; but more probably on the course now followed by the Gap and Newport turnpike through Mill Creek, New Garden, London Grove, Londonderry, West Fallowfield, and Sadsbury townships.

main path led from some point in Chester County, probably within what afterwards became Highland or Sadsbury township, eastward through Fallowfield and the Bradfords to the northern part of Thornbury Township, in Delaware County; thence diagonally over the whole extent of Delaware County, crossing Edgmont, Middletown, Nether Providence, Ridley, and Darby townships, and entering Philadelphia at the head of tidewater on Cobb's Creek, near the site of Swedes' Mill. Going westward from Sadsbury Township, Chester County, the path led by The Gap in almost a straight line to the Conestoga Indian town on Turkey Hill.[1]

The latter path, from Philadelphia westward, after crossing Delaware County, through the townships indicated above, and through East and West Bradford in Chester County, branched at Thomas Moore's Mill, in Chester Valley (now Downingtown), and the north fork led by way of The Compass (Compassville) into Lancaster County, thence along the dividing line between Earl and Leacock, Penn and Hempfield townships, by Old Donegal Church to Conoy Creek, near the Conoy Indian town. This path was followed by Peter Bezaillion in his trading trips between Philadelphia, Conoy Town, and Paxtang, and a portion of the route in Lancaster County is called to this day, "Old Peter's Road."

[1] Both roads are shown in part on the maps published in George Smith's *History of Delaware County, Penna.*, pp. 138, 582.

"In 1700, the main road westward from the little colony at Philadelphia was an Indian Trail, leaving what is now Market Street, passing through Westchester, The Gap, the Long Lane, past [John] Postlethwaite's [trading-post and tavern], crossing the Conestoga at Rock Hill, passing over the Hill and crossing the Little Conestoga at Dentlinger's Mill, then down the west side of the Creek and in the Indian Town Road to the Indian Town of Conestoga."—*Lancaster County Hist. Soc. Coll.*, xii., 146.

CHAPTER VI

THE YOUNG RED MAN GOES WEST[1]

THE trans-Alleghany movement of the Delawares of the Turtle and Turkey clans from the Forks of the Susquehanna to the Ohio began before 1724. They went chiefly from the vicinity of Shamokin (now Sunbury), or from the country to the east and southeast thereof Crossing the North Branch of the Susquehanna, at its mouth, they proceeded up the east side of the West Branch as far as Great Island (at the present town of Lock Haven), where they crossed, and on the south side of the river ascended the valley of Bald Eagle Creek to near where Milesburg now stands. From there they went almost directly west, along the north side of what is now called Marsh Creek, over Indian Grave Hill, near the sites of the present villages of Snow Shoe and Moshanon, across Moshanon Creek, and thence through the centre of the present townships of Morris, Graham, Bradford, and Lawrence, in Clearfield County, striking the West Branch again at Chingleclamouche, or Chinklaclamoose (now Clearfield, in the county of the same name). From there they went up the Susquehanna a few miles, thence up the present Anderson's Creek from its mouth, crossing the divide between that stream and the Mahoning in what is now Brady Township, Clearfield County; thence down the Mahoning Valley, through Punxsatawney (Jefferson County), to a point on the Allegheny some ten miles below the mouth of the Mahoning. Here they built their first town, which they called Kithenning, or Kittanning, literally, "Great-River-Town," or "Town at the Great River." By the Six Nations it was called Adego or Atiga. The route taken by the Delawares from Shamokin was in all probability the earliest important path between the Ohio and the main stream of the Susquehanna. It was travelled by Frederick Post, when he returned from his peace mission to the Ohio Indians in September, 1758. It was also followed by Bishop Ettwein and two hundred Christian Delawares of the Moravian missions in 1772. But game was scarce along this route and the way was rough and difficult.[1] A few years after 1724

---

[1] "Some [white families] have settled almost to the head of Joniady river, along the path that leads to Ohio. The Indians say (and that with truth) that that country

there were shorter and easier paths from Shamokin to Allegheny, which makes it probable that the long and difficult one by way of the West Branch must have been the first path traced by the Indians; and hence the one used in their first emigrations to the westward from Pennsylvania.

Kittanning, the first settlement made by the Delawares on the Allegheny, was located near the western terminus of this path, and nearly twenty miles above the terminus of the Frankstown Path, although connected with the latter by an intersecting trail. This fact, also, suggests the inference that the path by way of Chinklaclamoose was the oldest one between the Susquehanna and the Allegheny.

In a conference with the chiefs of the Six Nations at Albany, July 3, 1754, Conrad Weiser, the interpreter from Pennsylvania, told them: "The road to Ohio is no new road; it is an old and frequented road; the Shawnese and Delawares removed thither above thirty years ago from Pennsylvania, ever since which that road has been travelled by our Traders at their invitation, and always with safety, until within these few years, that the French sent armies there."

This fixes the date of the removal of the Delawares to the Allegheny as the year 1724 or earlier. But the Shawnees, perhaps, did not go so soon as Mr. Weiser said. In a deposition made by Jonas Davenport, an Indian Trader, at Philadelphia, October 29, 1731, he stated, "that last spring was four years, as he remembers, a French gentleman, in appearance, came down the river to a settlement of the Delaware Indians on the Ohio River, which the Delawares call Kithanning, with an intention, as this Examt. believes, to enquire into the numbers of English Traders in those parts, and to sound the minds of the Indians; that the said French gentlemen spoke the Shawanese language, with whom this Examt. has conversed; but that *few of the Shawanese being then there*, nothing of moment passed." Edmund Cartlidge, another Trader to Allegheny, in his examination before one of the justices of Lancaster County, December 7, 1731, also declared: "That for these five years past except that of 1729, a French gentleman who calls himself Cavalier has made it his practice to come every spring among the Indians settled there, . . . and that it is generally believed by all the Traders at Allegeney, as well as by this Examt., that this Cavalier is the bearer of the Governor of Montreal's messages to the Indians in these parts, and is entrusted with negotiating several affairs between ye Governor and them; that after the treaty held at Conestogoe in the year 1728 between the Governor of Pennsylvania and the Delaware Indians, several Shawnees,

---

is their only hunting ground for deers; because farther to the north was nothing but spruce woods and the ground covered with palm brushes; not a single deer could be found or killed there."—Conrad Weiser to Governor Hamilton, April, 22, 1749.

who were settled at Allegeney, went to the Governor of Montreal, as this Examt. believes, to seek protection from the French against the Five Nations, who, they suspected, would hinder their settling at Allegheny."

The Marquis de Beauharnois was Governor of Canada at this time, and in his report to the Ministry at home, written October 1, 1728, he observes, that the late Marquis de Vaudreuil had adopted measures in 1724 to bring nearer to the Colony the nation of the Chaouanons, who were at that time between the Iroquois and the English (*i. e.*, on the Susquehanna). "This nation," he says, "which consists of over 700 Indians, has been much attached to the French, and was the first to ask to approach them, saying they were unhappy alongside the English. . . . These Indians have begun a village on the river Ohio, which already contains more than 150 men and their families. They have traded from all time with the French, and are a very industrious people, cultivating a good deal of land. . . . Cavillier is the name of the person whom M. de Beauharnois has permitted to return to the Chaouanons. He is understood and known by these Indians, and will probably negotiate this affair with success."

The negotiations between the Susquehanna Shawnees and the French of Canada had really been going on for a longer time than is indicated in this letter. At a meeting of the Pennsylvania Council held at Philadelphia, May 28, 1723, the Governor read a letter received from James Mitchell, a justice of Chester County, dated April 25, 1723, and containing an address from Ocowellos, "king of the Upper Shawanese on Susquehanna," in which that chief mentioned their past visits, and another which they intended shortly to make to the Governor of Canada, whom the Shawnees in this message called their Father. In response to this letter, the Governor and Council wrote Ocowellos, discouraging the proposed trip to Canada; and sent the Shawnees five gallons of rum, "to cheer their hearts at the hearing of his words."

Governor Gordon, of Pennsylvania, wrote to the Governor of Maryland, April 18, 1732, and in referring to the Shawnees, tells Governor Ogle, that "On the river Susquehanna and in other parts of this Province for above thirty years past, there have been some colonies seated of these natives called the Shawannese, who, unhappily, have of late years given some offence to those Five Nations or Minquays; and to avoid the consequences, within these three or four years they have retired to a branch of Mississippi called Ohio, which comes from within less than 250 miles of this place, to which a considerable number of our own [Delaware] Indians had repaired sometime before, for the benefit of the hunting, and there, some French spies falling in with them, prevailed with the Shawanese to throw themselves under the protection of Canada."

Four months after this letter was delivered, Governor Thomas Penn held a conference with the deputies of the Five Nations at Philadelphia (August 26, 1732) and asked them to compel the Shawnees to return from the Ohio. "We have held several treaties with those Shawanese," he told the Iroquois chiefs, "and from their first coming they were accounted and treated as our own Indians. But some of their young men, having between four and five years since committed some disorders, though we had fully made it up with them, yet, being afraid of the Six Nations, they had removed backwards to Ohio, and there had lately put themselves under the protection of the French." To this, Tyoninhogarao, a Seneca chief, answered, that the Iroquois never intended to hurt the Shawanese; that as they were coming hither they spoke to Kakowatcheky, an old chief of the Shawnees, and told him that he should not look to Ohio, but turn his face to them. The Seneca chief also agreed to send a deputation of their chiefs to Allegheny to recall the Shawnees.

The disorders committed by some of the young men of the Shawnees some four or five years before 1732, to which Governor Penn had here alluded, appear to have taken place in the early part of 1728, and really after the advance guard of the Shawnee emigration westward had already reached the Allegheny. Outbreaks occurred simultaneously among the Shawnees of Pequea, Peixtan, and Otzenachse (Chillisquaque), in Lancaster County, and those of the two Pechoquealin towns in the present counties of Warren, in New Jersey, and Monroe, in Pennsylvania.

From Lancaster, John Wright, of Hempfield, wrote James Logan, May 2, 1728, giving an account of a murder committed by two of the Shawnees near Conestoga, the victims being a man and woman of the Conestogas. Through the connivance of Peter Chartier, the Trader among the Shawnees on the opposite of the Susquehanna from Peixtan, and himself a half-blood Shawnee, the two murderers escaped. "This," says Mr. Wright, "the Conestogas resent so highly, they threaten to cut off the whole nation of the Shawnys; yesterday there came seventeen or eighteen of the young men, commanded by Tilehausey, all Conestoga Indians, painted for the war, all armed. . . . We, hearing the above report, are apt to think they are going against the Shawnys."

Four days after this letter was read in Philadelphia, Governor Gordon acquainted his Council that he was just setting out for Mahanatawny, on advice brought him by express that morning, that a party of foreign Indians had fallen upon the inhabitants in those parts, fired upon a party of twenty of the settlers, who returned the fire, and, it was believed, had killed their chief, who appeared to be a Spanish Indian. Ten days later (May 20th), the Governor was waited upon by John Smith and Nicholas Schonhoven, two Indian Traders from Pechoquealin, "near Durham

Iron Works," who delivered to him a verbal message from Kakowatcheky, chief of the Shawnees there, to the effect that he, "having heard that the Flat-heads [Catawbas, from Carolina] were come into this Province with a design to make war upon our Indians, he had sent eleven of his men, armed, to enquire into the truth of this report; with orders to assist our Indians in case the same should be true; that their provisions failed them, and they were obliged to get from our inhabitants wherewithal to subsist; but that they offered no rudeness until the white people used them ill, and fired upon them; that he is very sorry for what has happened, and that he has a great love for us all as his brethren; but that one of their number is wounded, and lost his gun; which he desires may be sent."

This expedition from Pechoquealin was of course the one which had gotten into trouble at Mahanatawny. The Shawnee warriors sent by Kakowatcheky from Pechoquealin were possibly on the way to Paxtang, to help their brethren there, who had been attacked or threatened by the Conestogas. The fiction about the Flatheads may have been used to cover up their real design; which was probably to fight off the Conestogas. Samuel Blunston writes to James Logan from Conestoga on May 12th, that "an old Indian is here, returned from the Five Nations; says some of their chiefs are coming to Philadelphia in about three weeks to renew the alliance; that they are of opinion the Indians who were at Manahatany have been put on by the French, to stir up mischief. Last week, eight of this [Conestoga] town, the king one of them, went out to war; the rest are at home."

On September 1st of the same year (1728), a paper was presented to the Governor and Council from two Indian Traders of Durham, in Bucks County, named Corse Froom and John Schonhoven, who delivered it in person. In this paper it was set forth that several Indians at Pechoquealin, above Durham, had collected skins for a present, desiring to meet the Governor at Durham Iron Works, for a treaty. They sent for Schonhoven that he might be the bearer of a message to the Governor for that purpose. While he was amongst them at Pechoquealin, an Indian came from the Susquehanna with a message, "upon receiving which, they [the Shawnees], with their wives and children, went off from Pechoquealing, leaving their corn standing; that the hurry these Indians seemed to be in gave these two Traders cause to apprehend some mischief was on foot; and that therefore, they had taken a journey hither to acquaint the Governor with it."

Upon receiving this information, the Council directed that a message be sent to Kakowatcheky, the chief of the Pechoquealin Indians, "to know why he had left that place, and his people afterwards removed so suddenly from thence."

The Site of the Shawnee Town of Wyoming.
From a photograph furnished by Mr. Oscar J. Harvey.

Kakowatcheky's clan had really made its first move in the direction of the Ohio; and it may be that many of them went there directly from Pechoquealin. The majority, however, seem to have gone only so far as the Wyoming Valley, where they seated themselves on the west bank of the Susquehanna (North Branch), at *Skehandowana* (Iroquois for "Great Flats"), a place subsequently known as Shawnee Flats, immediately below the site of the present town of Plymouth,[1] in Luzerne County. This continued to be an important town of the Shawnees until 1743. Between April of that year and April, 1744, Kakowatcheky himself, with some of his followers, removed to the Ohio and settled at Logstown, where he was visited by George Croghan as late as 1751. He is called "Cachawatkecha" by Governor Morris, August 20, 1755, and referred to as possibly still living at the Ohio. The Shawnee village of Wyoming was visited by Count Zinzendorf in September, 1742, when none but Shawnees and Mohegans seem to have been there. John Martin Mack was at Wyoming, April 13, 1744, and found but six or seven Indian cabins standing, the others having been pulled to pieces. Zinzendorf's son-in-law, Bishop Watteville, was there in October, 1748, but found few Indians of any other tribe than the Nanticokes, the Shawnees having mostly gone to Ohio; or perhaps to the West Branch of the Susquehanna, in the vicinity of Great Island. A few months later, however, many of them were living at Wyoming again, under their chief, Paxinosa,[2] who had come hither from Paxtang. Their town, called Wyoming, was visited by the sons of Weiser and Shekallamy in April, 1754, and by Andrew Montour and Scarrooyady in December, 1755. In April, 1757, Paxinosa lived at Otseningo (now Binghamton, Broome County, New York) on the North Branch. A year later, he was reported to be near Tioga (now Athens, Bradford County, Penna.) on his way to Ohio, "where he was born."[3]

The Shawnees at Otzenachse, on the West Branch of the Susquehanna, likewise left their village of Chillisquaque in the summer of 1728, and removed farther West. In April of that year, James Le Tort, the Trader from "Chenastry [Otzenachse], on the upper parts of the River Susquehanna," reported to Governor Gordon that Manawkyhickon, a Minsi Delaware chief who lived at Muncy Creek and Catawasse in that vicinity, and with whom he had consulted that Spring about making a trading trip to the Miamis, had discouraged him in his project, telling him that he might happen in his way to see some Whiteheads, who

---

[1] See plat of the survey of Sunbury Manor, in *Penna. Archives*, 3d Series, vol. iv. (No. 67).

[2] See *Penna. Col. Rec.*, vi., 35; vii., 52, 108; viii., 126; *Penna. Archives*, ii., 33; *N. Y. Col. Doc.*, vii., 246, 316–20.

[3] See page 155.

come to hunt, not for skins, but for flesh and scalps; and asked him if he did not know that all the Delawares who were hunting at Allegheny had been called home.

Le Tort said that he talked about the matter with Mistress Montour afterwards, who informed him that she could not accompany him to the Miami country, as she had promised to do, because she had heard some news that made it dangerous to take such a trip. This news was to the effect "that a Delaware Indian woman whose son had been killed by the Shawanese [at Conestoga?] had brought Manawkyhickon a long belt of black wampum of twelve rows, desiring that by means thereof her tears might be wiped away; that Manawkyhickon had sent this black belt to the Five Nations; and that the Five Nations sent the same to the Miamis, with a message, desiring to know if they would lift up their axes and join with them against the Christians; to which they agreed; that thereupon, Manawkyhickon had sent four belts of wampum to those of his nation who were abroad hunting, ordering them quickly to return home." Le Tort said that he questioned Manawkyhickon about the matter, and the latter admitted that it was true; that Manawkyhickon was a near relation of Wequela, an Indian who was hanged last year in New Jersey; that he much resented his death, and went immediately afterwards to the Five Nations, with whom he had long had an interest.

At a meeting of the Pennsylvania Council held September 1, 1728, it was observed that Manawkyhickon, in resentment for the death of Wequela, had been endeavoring to stir up not only the Twechtwese, or Naked Indians (Miamis), against the Christians, but likewise, if possible, to set the Five Nations at variance with the English.

The occasion of this remark was the news which Governor Gordon that day laid before the Council, of the interview he had had with the two Traders from Durham, who, as already stated, informed him that the Indians at Pechoquealin had received a message from Susquehanna during the past month, which caused them to take their wives and children and remove to Wyoming, leaving their corn standing. The Governor said he was not so much surprised at this, as the message from Susquehanna might be supposed to come from the chiefs of the Five Nations then said to be about Conestoga, and having great power over all the Pennsylvania Indians; but that he was more surprised at a letter he had read, written by Antony Sadowsky to John Petty, both Indian Traders. This letter, with the spelling corrected was in part as follows:

Adj. 27th August, 1728.

MR. PETTY:

SR.—This is to acquaint you that an Indian came to Oley, to Philip Kerwain, and brought news from Siamocon [Shamokin], that all the

Indians have removed from there, and none is there but Sam Siehan [Opekasset] and his family, and Alomapis; and also, said Indian told to said Philip, that at Sauanos, that is, Malson, the Sauanos [Shawnees] have hanged Timothy Higgins upon a pole of their cabin. And also, said Indian brought word that the Indians will come to Philadelphia about full of this moon; and it is feared that with the rest of the loaders [Traders' assistants] it is not well. . . . Moreover, the French woman that came from your house (Mingo's wife), told me not to go to Indians this Fall until by better understanding between the Christians and Indians; for their is a great dis-satisfaction amongst them. . . .

The Council decided that a message should be sent to Shamokin to learn why Allumapees and Opekasset had not kept their promise to come to Philadelphia; and to know of Kakowatcheky why he had left Pechoquealin; and "to acquaint Shikellima, that as he is appointed (as 't is said) by the Five Nations to preside over the Shawanese, it's expected he will give a good account of them."

The Shawnees at Ohio themselves, four years later, gave an explanation to the Governor of Pennsylvania as to why they had removed from the Susquehanna. Governor Gordon sent them a message in December, 1731, reminding them of their former benefits, received from William Penn and his successors, while they lived on the Susquehanna. To this message they returned an answer by Edmund Cartlidge, the Trader, the following June. This letter of the Shawnee chiefs at Allegheny to Governor Gordon (with the spelling corrected) was as follows:

The Chiefs of the Shawanese to the Honourable Governor of Pennsylvania:

We received your message by our friend, Edmund Cartlidge, and take it very kindly, and return you thanks for ye dram given us; and we hereby acquaint the Governor of the reason that we are come to settle here at Ohioh.

About nine years ago, the Five Nations told us at Shallyschohking,[1] we did not do well to settle there; for there was a great noise in the Great House [at Onondaga], and that in three years' time all should know what they [the Five Nations] had to say as far as there was any settlements or the sun set.

About ye expiration of three years aforesaid, the Five Nations came and said, "Our land is going to be taken from us. Come, brothers, assist us. Let us fall upon and fight with the English." We answered them, "No; we came here for peace, and have leave to settle here; and we are in league with them, and cannot break it."

About a year after, they, ye Five Nations, told the Delawares and us, "Since you have not hearkened to us nor regarded what we have said, now we will put petticoats on you, and look upon you as women for the future, and not as men, Therefore, you Shawanese, look back toward

---

[1] *i. e.*, Chillisquaque, a town of the Shawnee tribe, probably of the Chillicothe clan. It stood at or near the mouth of Chillisquaque Creek, on the north side.

Ohio, the place from whence you came; and return thitherward; for now we shall take pity on the English, and let them have all this land."

And further said, "Now, since you are become women, I'll take Peahohquelloman [Pechoquealin], and put it on Meheahoming [Wyoming]; and I'll take Meheahoming and put it on Ohioh; and Ohioh I'll put on Woabach; and that shall be the warriors' road for the future."

One reason of our leaving our former settlements and coming here is, several negro slaves used to run away and come amongst us; and we thought ye English would blame us for it.

The Delaware Indians some time ago bid us depart, for they was dry, and wanted to drink ye land away. Whereupon, we told them, "Since some of you are gone to Ohioh, we will go there also. We hope you will not drink that away, too."

And whereas, the Governor desires to see some of us at Philadelphia, we shall answer his request; for some of our chiefs will come this summer and pay him a visit; but how many of us or exact the time, we know not as yet. But when we are got so far as Peter Chartier's, we shall send word how many of us there is, and when we shall be there; and bring our friends, the Conestogas, along with us. In the meantime, we remain, your Friends and Brethren,

NOOCHICKONEH.
PAWQUAWSIE.
UPPOCKEATY.
QUEEQUEEPTOO.

Present:
JAMES LE TORT, Interpreter.
PETER CHARTIER.
Taken down by me, EDMUND CARTLIDGE.

Neucheconeh, or Noochickoner, the chief whose name appears at the bottom of this letter, was the head chief of the Shawnees at Allegheny at this time; although Ocowellos, "king of the Upper Shawanese on Susquehannah," was seated on the Conemaugh, with 200 men and forty-five families of his tribe, before 1731. Neucheconeh's name was signed to another letter sent to the Governor and Provincial Secretary some six years after the date of the letter printed above. In that one, written March 20, 1738, he signed as "Deputy King," his signature being preceded by that of "Loyparcowah, Opehassah's Son." Neucheconeh, therefore, seems to have acted as vice-regent during the young manhood of the heir of Opessa, the old sachem of the Shawnees at Conestoga, who came with his people into Pennsylvania from Cecil County, Maryland, about 1697.

The location of the Shawnee town, "Shallyschohking," mentioned in their letter from Allegheny, was, in all probability at the mouth of Chillisquaque Creek, on the east bank of the Susquehanna, in what is now Northumberland County. Phonetically "Shallyschohking," is about as near to "Chillisquaque," as early Indian names usually are to their modern forms; and it is nearer in sound than Chillisquaque to the

The North Side of Chillisquaque Creek, at its Mouth.

The course of the creek is indicated by the row of trees. The Susquehanna River flows along the foot of the hills.

Shawnee word, *Tsalachgasagi,* for which it was written. Conrad Weiser wrote the name "Zilly Squachne" at the time of his first visit in 1737. "Chillisquaque," itself, as has been already suggested, seems to be a slightly modified form of "Chillicothe," the name applied by the Shawnees to many of their villages.[1] That there was a Shawnee town at the mouth of the Chillisquaque is evident from a passage in Bishop Spangenberg's *Journal* of his trip to Onondaga in 1745. On June 7th of that year, he writes: "Began our journey [from Shamokin] to Onondaga. . . . Crossed the river [the North Branch of Susquehanna, at its mouth], and travelled up the West Branch. Passed Shawnee [Chillisquaque] Creek, and the site of the town that formerly stood there. Next, came to the place where Shikellimy formerly lived—it is now deserted [about one-half mile below the present town of Milton, Northumberland County]. . . . Our course has been several miles W., and then NW., until we reached Warriors' Camp [now Warriors' Run, a few miles above Chillisquaque Creek]." Conrad Weiser, in his journey to Onondaga in 1737, speaks of having been ferried across Chillisquaque ("Zilly Squachne") Creek, by an old Shawnee, who still lived there. Possibly, this was the seat of Ocowellos's clan, which had carried on a correspondence with the French before 1723; and had emigrated in a body to the Conemaugh before 1731.

[1] Gatschet and Mooney give *Tsalachgasagi* as the correct plural form of Chillcothe, citing a Shawnee MS. in the archives of the American Bureau of Ethnology.

CHAPTER VII

THE SHAMOKIN TRADERS AND THE SHAMOKIN PATH

IN Dr. William H. Egle's *History of Dauphin County, Pennsylvania,* is printed a sketch map of the country along the Susquehanna River, between Swatara Creek and the second Indian town on the West Branch, as it was about 1727. The author of that history incorrectly gives the date of this map as 1701. In a later communication, in *Notes and Queries* (i., 151), Dr. Egle explained that the copy of this draft was made by John Taylor in 1735, the original being "well-known to his [Taylor's] father fifty years before." Isaac Taylor, John Taylor's father, was surveyor of Chester County from 1701 to the time of his death in 1728. Dr. Egle has evidently mistaken ten for fifty; as the map bears evidence on its face that it pictures the country in the vicinity of Harrisburg as it was some five to ten years before 1735. In all probability its correct date is between the years 1725 and 1728. From this map, which is reproduced on the opposite page, it will be seen that nine Indian towns are located along the Susquehanna: one above Swatara Creek (Paxtang Town); one at the mouth of the Cheniaty, or Juniata; one on the island opposite; one between the Juniata and the "Sequosackoo"; one on the large island opposite; one below the forks of the Susquehanna, called "Mikquar Town"; two at "Chinasky," or "Shamokin," on the West Branch; and one town above. James Le Tort's store is shown, between the forks of the Susquehanna; and John Scull's store, between the "Quatoochatoon" (Mahantango) and the Mikquar Town. "S. E.'s store," at the mouth of the Juniata, may be intended for Simon Edgell's. He was an Indian Trader, noted in the records of 1747.

Shekallamy[1] or Shikellimy, the resident representative of the authority of the Five Nations over the Pennsylvania Indians, lived near a town called Shamokin in 1728, probably having settled there in that or the preceding year. According to John Bartram, who travelled with him from Shamokin to Onondaga in 1743, Shekallamy was a Frenchman, born in Montreal and taken captive in his youth by the Oneidas, among

---

[1] So spelled by James Logan. This seems to have been the name given him by the Delawares. His Oneida name was Ungquaterughiathe (*Penna. Col. Rec.*, iv., 584.) He was also called Swatane by the Iroquois.

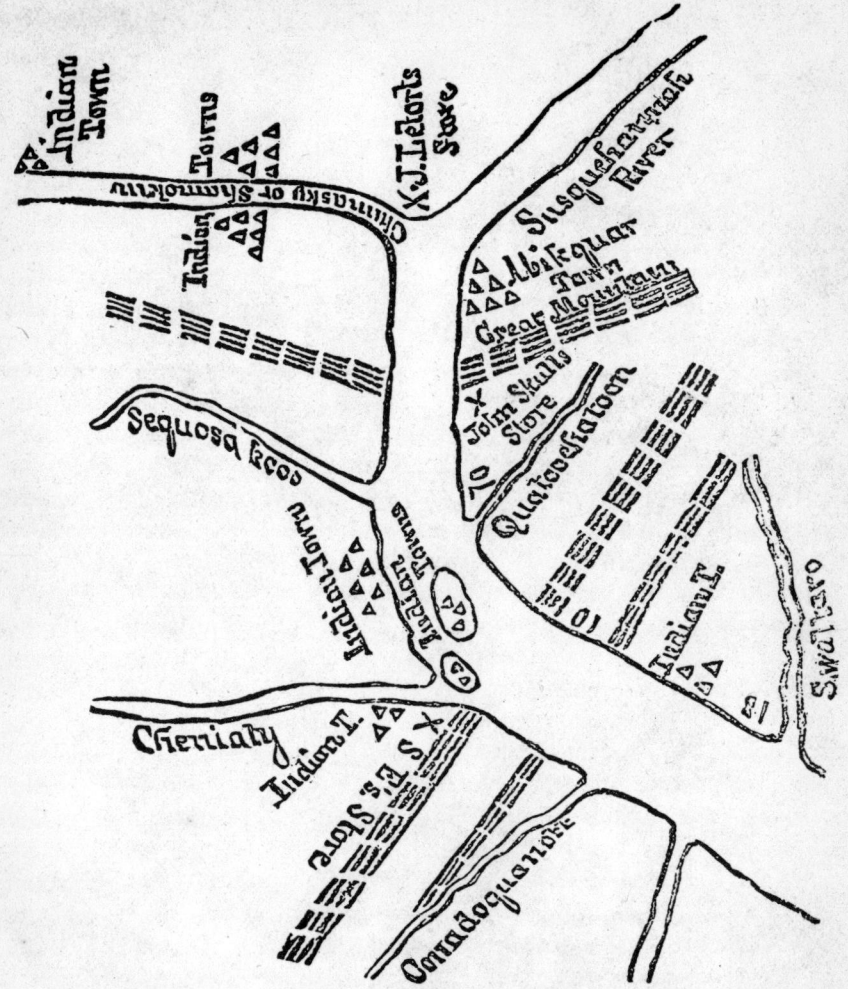

Taylor's Map of Shamokin and Vicinity, about 1727.

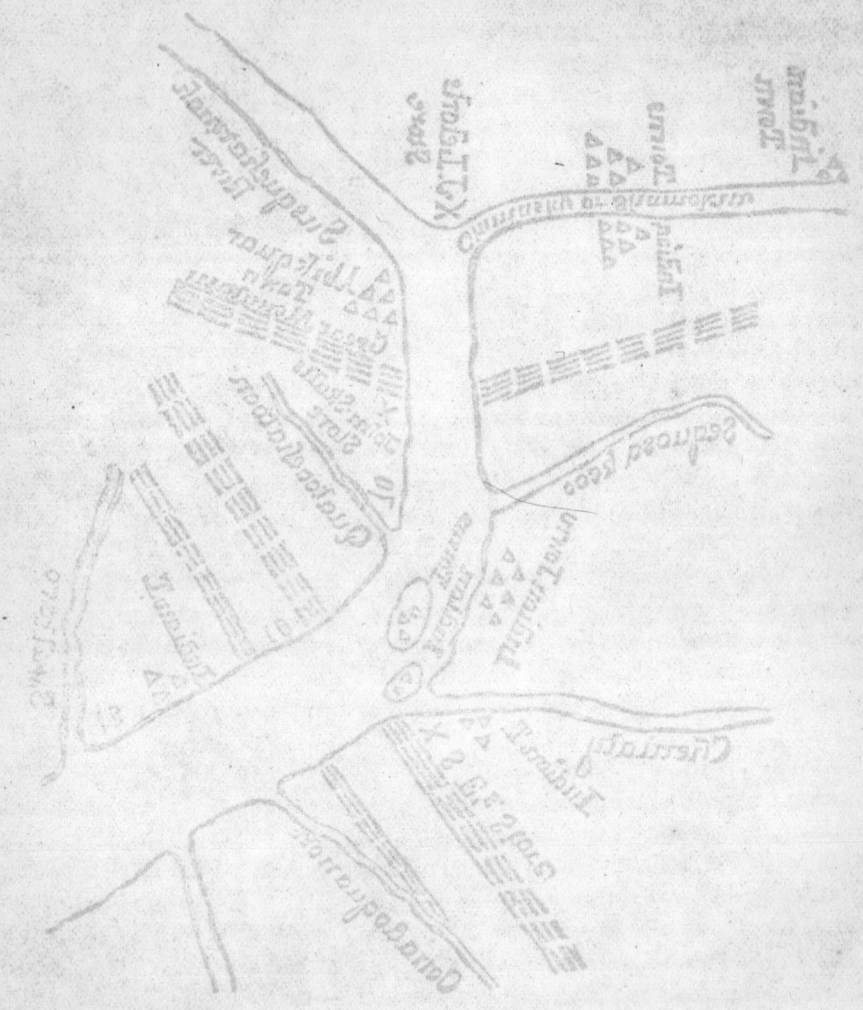

Taylor's Map of Shamokin and Vicinity about 1747

The Shamokin Traders and the Shamokin Path

whom he was reared, and among whom he attained the offices of Chief and Councillor. His second son was named after James Logan, Penn's Provincial Secretary, and later became prominent in Ohio history as Logan, the Mingo Chief.[1]

The Delaware term, "Shamokin" is probably derived from the circumstance that the place to which it was applied was the abode of their hereditary chief, or sachem.[2] It is apparently another form of the Algonquin word, 'Shackamaxon," the name applied to the residence of the sachem on the Delaware when William Penn first visited America. Allumapees or Sassoonan, the chief sachem of the Turtle tribe of the Delawares from 1715 to 1747, made Shamokin his residence as early as 1727, and probably was settled there before that date. In that year he sent the Governor a letter, dated at "Shahomaking." Conrad Weiser, who visited Shamokin first in 1737, and left a record of his visit, found the town then to be situated south of the mouth of the North Branch of the Susquehanna, near the site of the present town of Sunbury, and there it remained until it was deserted and burned by the Indians in 1756. At the time of his visit in 1737, Weiser describes the town where Shekallamy then lived, as being some distance north of Shamokin, and above Chillisquaque Creek. The site of Shekallamy's Town of that period has been thought by Mr. John Blair Linn to have been on the West Branch of the Susquehanna, at and opposite the mouth of Sinking Run, one-half mile below the village of Milton. The town was on the east side of the river, however, and not on the west side, as stated by Mr. Linn. This, the residence of Shekallamy, is probably the village marked "Shamokin" on the Taylor map; and the fact of its having been on the east side of the river explains why Conrad Weiser makes no mention in his *Journal* of having crossed the West Branch at that point. Chenasky, or Chenastry (now generally called Otzinachse, or Otzinachson), was a name also applied at that time to that part of the West Branch of the Susquehanna itself; although its original application may have been to Shekallamy's Town, lying on the east side of the stream. If Shamokin was a name also applied to this town in Isaac Taylor's time, it may have been so applied because here was for a time the residence of Shekallamy, the over-lord sent by the Five Nations. Later, both he and Allumapees, the Delaware sachem, lived together at the Shamokin below the mouth of the North Branch, which was the historic town of that name.

In April, 1728, as already stated, Governor Gordon reported to his Council that James Le Tort had lately come to town "from Chenastry, on the upper parts of the river Susquehanna," at which place he had

[1] Bartram's *Journal*, p. 17. See p. 381.
[2] Heckewelder gives a different and incorrect meaning.

made his preparations the Fall before to start on a trading trip westward to the country of the Twechtweys or Miamis; but was deterred from going by the reports he had received from Madame Montour, a French woman, who had married the Indian called Robert Hunter, or Carondowanna. She had formerly lived among the Miamis, and had a sister married to one of that nation. She told Le Tort that Manawkyhickon a Delaware "chief of note in those parts" (about Chenastry), had sent a black belt to the Five Nations, who had sent the same to the Miamis, desiring their assistance in taking up the hatchet against the English.

The Governor immediately sent messages and presents by Le Tort and John Scull who were about to return to their trading posts at "Chenasshy," and he instructed these Traders to deliver the same to Allumapees, to Mrs. Montour, and to Manawkyhickon. Reassuring answers came from two of these persons in response to the Governor's messages; and on May 15th, John and Nicholas Scull and Antony Sadowsky were despatched with additional presents for Allumapees, Opekasset, and Manawkyhickon. These offerings again brought favorable responses; but in the following August, Sadowsky sent a message to John Petty another Shamokin Trader, who was then in Philadelphia. This was to the effect that an Indian had come to Oley from Shamokin, and brought the news that all the Indians had removed from there but Sam Siehan and his family, and King Allumapees; and that "at Sauanos that is, Malson, the Sauanos [Shawnees] had hanged Timothy Higgins upon a pole of their cabin." "Moreover," Sadowsky adds, "the French woman [Madame Montour] that came from your house, Mingo's wife, told me not to go to Indians this Fall." Petty laid this information before the Council, and the Governor at once instructed him and Henry Smith, who were on their way to the Susquehanna, to carry friendly messages to Allumapees, Shekallamy, and other chiefs, and to Carondowanna and his wife. The latter chief was to be told that Jonah Davenport had never made complaints about him, and that therefore there was no occasion for his letter on that subject. On the 3d of the following month, Smith and Petty wrote the Governor, while on their way to Shamokin, that they had met Petty's man, Higgins, and the other Traders. Higgins, who "was thought to be hanged, escapt his life very narrowly. . . . We dare not take him [back to Shamokin], but ye Traders, we take them." The Governor laid this letter before his Council, with the added information, that "some little differences had accidentally arisen between the Traders and the Shawanese."

Shamokin, as generally known in Pennsylvania history, was located on the level ground south of the mouth of the North Branch, where Sunbury now stands. It was the largest and most populous Indian town of its time on the Susquehanna. Heckewelder, as we know, was a very

The Shamokin Traders and the Shamokin Path

unreliable authority on most Indian names (although followed by many writers as the prime authority), and he should not be accepted unless corroborated by other evidence. His editor's statement, however, that, according to Chief Shekallamy, the town the Delawares called "Shamokin" was by the Iroquois called "Otzenachse," is substantially true.[1] Count Zinzendorf, who travelled with Weiser and Shekallamy from Shamokin to Onondaga in September and October, 1742, relates in his *Journal* that, on fording the North Branch at Shamokin, "to the left of the path, after crossing the river, a large cave, in a rocky hill in the wilderness, was shown us. From it, the surrounding country and the West Branch of the Susquehanna are called Otzinachon, *i. e.*, "The Demon's Den"; for here the evil spirits, say the Indians, have their seats and hold their revels." In Taylor's map, reproduced on a preceding page, it will be noticed that the name "Shamokin or Chenasky," is applied to the district immediately north and west of the Susquehanna Forks. "Chenasky," or "Chenastry," James Le Tort's abiding place in 1727-28, was only another form of the word, Otzenachse or Otzinachon, which was applied as the name of the country about and above the Susquehanna Forks. Shamokin was the most important settlement south of Tioga Point, by reason of its strategic location near the intersection of the Catawba War Trail (which led from the Five Nations' country by way of Tioga, Lycoming Creek, Shamokin, and Tuscarora Valley) with the early path from Wyoming to Allegheny (which joined the Catawba Path below and near the site of Shekallamy's original town, located in Northumberland County, below the present village of Milton). For this reason, possibly, that location was chosen by Shekallamy as his seat, when he came into Pennsylvania in or before 1728 as the vice-regent of the Six Nations. If Otzenachse and Shamokin were Iroquois and Delaware words for the same district, and it seems probable that they were, then the town "Shamokin" in 1728 may have included Shekallamy's village at the intersection of the Catawba and Wyoming paths, between the mouths of Warrior's Run and Chillisquaque Creek. After Shekallamy removed to below the mouth of the North Branch (subsequent to 1737), the main path used by the Indians from Wyoming westward was one that joined the Catawba Trail at the mouth of Muncy Creek.

David Brainerd, a Presbyterian missionary, was at Shamokin in 1745, and wrote of it at that time: "The Town lies partly on the east and the west [southeast and northwest] shores of the river, and partly on the island. It contains upwards of fifty houses and three hundred inhabitants. The Indians of this place are accounted the most drunken, mischievous, and ruffian-like fellows of any in these parts; and Satan seems

---

[1] Heckewelder's *Narrative*, Connelley's edition, p. 554. See also, pp. 94, 187, 196, 209 of this volume.

to have his seat in this town in an eminent degree. About one-half are Delawares [under Allumapees]; the others, Senecas and Tutelars."

But Shekallamy's Town of 1728, as we have seen, was opposite the mouth of Sinking Run, or Shekallamy's Run, as it was formerly called, and less than a mile below the present town of Milton, in Northumberland County. In that location it was a few miles north of the Shawnee town at the mouth of Chillisquaque Creek. Governor Gordon, on sending his message to Shekallamy at the time of the disturbances with the young Shawnee braves who went on the war-path in the Spring of 1728, told the Traders, Henry Smith and John Petty, to "tell Shekallamy particularly that he is set over the Shawanah Indians." It will be remembered that in the letter sent by Antony Sadowsky to John Petty, dated August 27, 1728, he wrote: "At Sauanos, that is Malson, the Sauanos have hanged Timothy Higgins upon a pole of their cabin." The name, "Malson," is evidently a misprint for the term applied to the locality afterwards called "Otzinachson," which latter, at another place in the *Colonial Records*, is called by Conrad Weiser, "2 Machson."[1] It may have referred to the Shawnee town at Chillisquaque; although that town, as we have seen, was called by the Shawnees themselves, "Chillisquaque," or "Shallyschohking." There is a possibility that Malson was the Shawnee town on Big Island, at the mouth of the Juniata; or that it may have been the name of the town where Shekallamy first settled in 1728 and lived at the time of Weiser's visit in 1737. But it is most probable that it was an incorrect form for Otzenachse. In the *Journal* of his first visit to this place, Weiser writes: "27th February, 1737, left home for Onondaga. 1st March, left Tolheo, which is the last place in the inhabited part of Pennsylvania. On the 4th we reached Shamokin, but did not find a living soul at home who could assist us in crossing the Susquehanna River. On the 5th we lay still; we had now made about eighty miles. 6th, we observed a smoke on the other side of the river [North Branch], and an Indian Trader came over and took us across. We again lay still today. On the 7th we started along one branch of the river, going to the northwest. An old Shawano, by name Jenoniawana, took us in his canoe across the creek at Zilly Squachne [Shallyschohking, or Chillisquaque]. On the 8th we reached the village where Shikelimo lives, who appointed to be my companion and guide on the journey." In his notes to Heckewelder, Dr. Reichel, quoting Pyrlaeus, states that "Otzenachse" was a Mohawk name applied by Shekallamy to Shamokin in 1745.

Conrad Weiser made another trip to Onondaga in July, 1743. In

[1] *Col. Rec.*, vi., 35. "I arrived at Shamokin the 20th of April [1754]. Found that two of the Shickcalamys being about thirty miles off on the northwest branch Susquehanna, commonly called 2 Machson."—Weiser to Governor.

Conrad Weiser.
From a portrait in possession of his family.
Photograph furnished by Miss Frances
Weiser Shiffner, a descendant.

The Shamokin Traders and the Shamokin Path 197

his *Journal* of that visit, he gives no account of the journey from Shamokin to Onondaga. But John Bartram and Lewis Evans, who accompanied him, have both left a record of the early part of their travels; the latter in his map of 1749, and the description of the same; and the former, in his *Observations*, made on this journey. Under date of July 10, 1743, Bartram writes: "We departed [from Shamokin] in the morning, with Shickcalamy and his son,[1] he being the chief man in the town, which consisted of Delaware Indians. He was of the Six Nations, *or rather, a Frenchman, born at Montreal, and adopted by the Oneidoes, after being taken prisoner;*[2] but his son told me he [the son] was of the Cayuga nation, that of his mother, agreeable to the Indian rule. . . . Our journey now lay through very rich bottoms to a creek, six miles from Shamokin [Chillisquaque Creek], a great extent of fruitful low ground still continuing. Here we found a fine meadow of grass on our right, and rich dry ground on the left. . . . Our way from thence lay through an old Indian field of excellent soil, where there had been a town, the principal footsteps of which are peach-trees, plumbs, and excellent grapes. . . . And now leaving the river, we held a new course over a fine level, then down a rich hollow to a run, where we saw a summer duck; and so down the run. A little beyond this turns a path to Wiomick, a town on the East Branch. Hence N. N. E., then N., after W., to a rich bottom near the river, where Shickcalamy formerly dwelt."

Following these travellers over much the same route, Bishop Spangenberg, in 1745, also accompanied Conrad Weiser to Onondaga. His *Journal* from Shamokin commences: "June 7, 1745, began our journey to Onondaga. Our company is composed of Spangenberg, Conrad Weiser, John Joseph, David Zeisberger, Shikellimy, his son, and Andrew Sattelihu [Montour], seven in all. Crossed the river and travelled up the West Branch. Passed Shawnee [Chillisquaque] Creek, and the site of the town that formerly stood there. Next came to the place where Shikellimy formerly lived—it is now deserted. The land is excellent in this vicinity, the equal of which is seldom found. Our course has been several miles W., and then N.W., until we reached Warriors' Camp [now Warriors' Run, which empties into the river at Watsontown], where we passed the night. . . . June 8, our course was N.W. We crossed a creek near the Susquehanna, called Canachriage [now Muncy Creek].

[1] One of Shekallamy's sons was named John Petty after the Shamokin Trader of that name. Another was named James Logan, after the Provincial Secretary.

[2] Dr. Crantz, in his *History of the Brethren* (London, 1780), writes of Shekallamy: "When he was spoken to concerning baptism he said he had been baptized in his infancy . . . We were informed afterwards, that he was born of European parents in French Canada, taken prisoner when a child of two years old, and brought up among the Indians. He was so much altered in his way of life that he was hardly to be distinguished from other savages."

". . . At noon we reached Otstonwakin. The Indians here treated us very well; boiled meat and placed it before us in a large kettle. In the afternoon we proceeded on our journey, and at dusk came to the 'Limping Messenger,' or Diadachton Creek [now Lycoming Creek—although the true Didachton Creek was what is now known as Pine Creek, farther west], and encamped for the night. Observations—On our route we passed the Shawanese town [on the 7th, or 8th?]"

In the Spring or Summer of 1729, Carondowanna, Madame Montour's husband, was killed while on a war expedition against the Catawbas of Carolina; and in August of that year the Governor sent messages of condolence and presents to his widow and to "Shekallamy and Kalaryonacha [misprint for Kataryonacha, Madame Montour's son-in-law] at Shamokin."

Madame Montour and her son, Andrew Montour, were the most picturesque characters in the colonial history of Pennsylvania. We first learn definitely of her family in a letter written from New York, August 20, 1708, by Lord Cornbury, then Governor of that Province, to the Lords of Trade in London. Cornbury speaks of having been at Albany during the past month, and of twelve of the Far Nations of Indians who came there to trade with the Dutch and English. "There are two nations of them," he adds, "who are called Twigtwicks [Miamis] and Dinnondadoes [Wyandots]; the nearest of their castles is eight hundred miles from Albany. . . . I did in a letter of the 25th day of June last, inform your Lordships that three French soldiers, who had deserted from the French at a place called by them Los Destroit, were come to Albany. Another deserter came from the same place, whom I examined myself. . . . Besides this deserter, there is come to Albany one, Montour, who is the son of a French gentleman, who came above forty years ago to settle in Canada; he had to do with an Indian woman, by whom he had a son and two daughters. The man I mention is the son. He had lived all along like an Indian. Sometime ago, he left the French, and had lived among the Far Indians; and it is chiefly by his means that I have prevailed with those Far Nations [the Miamis and Wyandots] to come to Albany."

In 1694 the father of Madame Montour was severely wounded by the Mohawks near Fort La Motte on Lake Champlain. Possibly at this time, or thereabouts, the daughter (then ten years of age, and said to have been living among the Hurons or Wyandots) was captured by the Five Nations, taken to their country, and brought up by them. Buell and Reid both say that she was captured and reared by the Senecas, but it is possible that she lived with the Oneidas; for, on reaching maturity, she was married to Carondowanna, or Robert Hunter. He was a war-captain of that nation, who, in compliment to Robert Hunter,

Colonial Governor of New York from 1709 to 1719, had taken that official's name as one of his own. His wife first appeared as an interpreter, August 25, 1711, in a conference between Governor Hunter and the chiefs of the Five Nations at Albany.[1]

In November, 1709, the Marquis de Vaudreuil, Governor of Canada, wrote to the Minister that the Sieur de Joncaire, a lieutenant in the Canadian army, had been dispatched to the Senecas the Spring before, and that while on this mission, "he had made his men kill one Montour, a Frenchman by birth, but entirely devoted to the English, and in their pay, who was endeavoring for the last two years to attract to them all the Upper Nations, exerting himself to make them declare against us." De Vaudreuil also wrote, in 1721, that he would have had Montour hanged in 1709 if it had been possible to capture him alive. Mr. William M. Darlington and some other writers, have applied these references to John Montour, the brother of Madame Montour; but the present writer is of the opinion that Montour, the father, was the man killed by Joncaire; for the reason that the son, John Montour, was alive in 1733, as will be shown hereafter.

Mr. Benjamin Sulte, of the office of "Militia and Defence," for the Dominion of Canada, communicated a genealogy of the Montour Family to Egle's *Notes and Queries* in 1895 (Fourth Series, ii., 327), from which it appears, that, on April 16, 1647, at Three Rivers, about midway between Montreal and Quebec, Father Ragueneau, a Jesuit, solemnized the marriage of Pierre Couc, dit La Fleur, son of Nicholas Couc and Elizabeth Templair, of Cognac in France, with Marie Metiwameghwahkwe, of the Algonquin Nation. The children of Pierre Couc, by his Indian wife, were all born in Three Rivers between 1657 and 1673, and were as follows: I. Jeanne, born 1657, assassinated in 1679; II. Louis, born 1659, the first of his family to take the name Montour; III. Angelique, born 1661, married to M. St. Corney, of Three Rivers, August 4, 1692; IV. Marie, born 1663; V. Marguerite, born 1664, married Jean Lafart, dit Laframboise, of Three Rivers; VI. Elizabeth, born 1667; VII. Madeleine, born 1669; VIII. Jean, born 1673.

[1] In one of Cadwallader Colden's letters to his son (1759), on Smith's *History of New York*, he writes: "As I have no thoughts of mentioning anything particularly of the Indians during Mr. Hunter's administration, it may be proper to observe that he had so great a diffidence of all the people at Albany that at the public meeting with the Indians he had allwise a French woman standing by him, who had married one of our Indians, to inform him whether the interpreters had done their part truely between him and the Indians, notwithstanding that Col. Schuyler was present at the same time. This woman, commonly called Madame Montour, had a good education in Canada before she went among the Indians, and was very useful to Mr. Hunter on many occasions, for which reason she had a pension, and was sometimes admitted to his table in her Indian dress."— *N. Y. Hist. Soc. Coll.*, i., 200.

Louis Couc, the half-breed son of Pierre Couc, took the name of Montour, and, about 1683, married a Sokakis, or Saco, Indian girl, whose Christian name was Madeleine. The missionaries wrote his name, "Louis Couc, surnomme Montour," until after 1700. He lived for a time at St. François du Lac (Lake St. Peter).

From this information, it would appear that the first of the Montours, the father of Madame Montour, was Louis, the half Indian son of Pierre Couc. As we have seen, he was killed by the elder Joncaire in 1709, leaving at least three children by his Sokakis squaw, Madeleine. Madame Montour and her brother and sister, therefore, were three-quarters Indian in blood.

Madame Montour, as she continued to be called after her marriage with Carondowanna, had a sister married to one of the Miami Indians; and she herself, as her father had before her, lived a portion of her life among the people of that nation, prior to 1728, according to James Le Tort's statement to the Governor. In 1712, she and her husband accompanied Colonel Peter Schuyler as interpreters, to the Onondaga country, whither he was sent on a mission to dissuade the Five Nations from joining the Tuscaroras in their war against the government of North Carolina.

Afterwards, the influence of Madame Montour over the Five Nations became so great, and was used so much to the detriment of the French, that the Canadian Governor tried repeatedly to draw her to the French interest. In 1719, he sent her sister to try to persuade her to remove to Canada; but the New York Indian Commissioners offered her a man's pay to remain, and she remained.

We have seen from the report made by James Le Tort to the Governor in 1728, that Madame Montour was settled at Chenastry, or Otzinachson, on the West Branch of the Susquehanna, as early as the Fall of 1727. Her residence in 1734, and probably since before 1728, was at the mouth of Loyalsock Creek, opposite the site of the present town of Montoursville, Lycoming County The name of her town was Otstonwakin, or Otstuago. It was sometimes called "French Town," and is so named on Lewis Evans's map of 1749. Conrad Weiser visited Otstuago on his first trip to Onondaga, in 1737. "It is so-called," he wrote in his *Journal*, "from a high rock which lies opposite. We quartered ourselves with Madam Montour, a French woman by birth, of good family; but now in mode of life a complete Indian."

An interesting contemporary description of Madame Motour is to be found in the *Journal* of Mr. Witham Marshe, who acted as Secretary to the Commissioners of Maryland in an important conference held at Lancaster in the summer of 1744, between the representatives of Pennsylvania, Maryland, and Virginia, and a number of the chiefs of the Six Nations. Under date of June 28, 1744, Marshe writes: "I went to a cabin where I heard the celebrated Mrs. Montour, a French lady (but now, by having lived so long among the Six Nations, is become almost an Indian) had her residence. When I approached the wigwam, I saluted her in French, and asked her whether she was not born in Canada; of what parents; and whether she had not lived a long time with the Indians. She answered me in the same language, very civilly, and after some compliments were passed betwixt us, told me in a polite manner, 'that she was born in Canada, whereof her father (who was a French gentleman) had been governor,[1] under whose administration the then Five Nations of Indians had made war against the French and the Hurons of that government (whom we call the French Indians from their espousing their part against the English, and living in Canada); and that in the war she was taken by some of the Five Nations' warriors, being then about ten years of age, and by them was carried away into their country, where she was habited and brought up in the same manner as their children. That when she grew up to years of maturity, she was married to a famous war-captain of those Nations, who was in great esteem for the glory he procured in the wars he carried on against the Catawbas, a great nation of Indians to the southwest of Virginia; by whom she had several children; but about fifteen years ago he was killed in a battle with them, since which she has not been married. That she had little or no remembrance of the place of her birth, nor, indeed, of her parents, it being near fifty years since she was ravished from them by the Indians.'

"She has been a handsome woman, genteel, and of polite address, notwithstanding her residence has been so long amongst the Indians; though formerly she was wont to accompany the several chiefs who used to renew treaties of friendship with the Proprietor and Governor of Pennsylvania, at Philadelphia, the metropolis of that Province; and being a white woman was there very much caressed by the gentle women of that city, with whom she used to stay for some time. She retains her native language by conversing with the Frenchmen who trade for fur-skins, &c. among the Six Nations; and our language she learned at Philadelphia, as likewise of our Traders, who go back into the Indians' country. In her cabin were two of her daughters by the war-captain, who were both married to persons of the same station, and [their husbands] were then gone to war with the Catawbas before mentioned. . . . Madame Montour has but one [?] son, who, for his prowess and martial exploits was

[1] Buell, in his *Life of Johnson*, says: "Catharine [Madeleine?] Montour was a daughter of the Count de Frontenac by a Huron woman. She was born at Fort Frontenac about 1692 [1680–84, or earlier], and her name figures in a curious old document called 'Accusation against Louis de Buade, Comte de Frontenac,' in which, among other things, he is charged with 'debasing the morals of the Colony by propagating more than sixty half-breeds.'"

lately made a captain, and a member of the Indian Council; and is now gone to war against the Catawbas, with her sons-in-law."

Sometime prior to 1752, Madame Montour became blind; but she was still sufficiently vigorous to ride on horseback from Logstown on the Ohio, to the home of her relative, Nicholas, at Venango, in less than two days, a distance by the Path of over sixty miles. Her son, Andrew, travelled with her on foot, leading her horse all the way.[1]

John Harris, in January, 1753, wrote: "Madame Montour is dead."

Madame Montour's brother was named Jean or John Montour. James Logan, in 1728 sent him a blanket as a present from the Proprietary Government; and in 1729 he was sent by the Governor as a messenger to the Six Nations. His wife, named Anameakhickam, in the year last named, tried to sell to the Proprietaries some land at Lechay (Forks of the Delaware), "which," says James Logan, "she pretended to own." On August 22, 1733, Logan gave Montour a letter to Governor Thomas Penn, introducing him as "John Montour, brother to Madame Montour."[2]

Of Madame Montour's sister we have no information beyond the facts stated by James Le Tort, that she was married to one of the Miami Indians, and that both sisters had lived among that people before 1728. The sister married to the Miami presumably continued to live there after that date. In March, 1754, Andrew, son of Madame Montour, informed the Pennsylvania Governor that he had a cousin, Nicholas, who lived at Venango. This may have been the son of Madame Montour's sister who had married a Miami; or it may have been Nicholas, the son of French Margaret, of whom Conrad Weiser wrote to Secretary Richard Peters in May, 1755: "French Margaret, with some of her family, is gone to the English camp in Virginia; and her son, Nicklaus, is gone to the French fort. I suppose they want to join the stronger party, and are gone to get information."

Of Madame Montour's children, we know the names of two of her sons; and Marshe's *Journal*, quoted above, indicates that she had two married daughters with her at Lancaster in 1744. One of them, probably, was French Margaret. Her most noted son was named Andrew, or Sattelihu. He was sometimes called Henry, as at the great conference at Easton, in 1758, when he is referred to under both names; and in a land patent of 1785, a copy of which is printed in Meginness's *History of the West Branch Valley* (p. 323). Another son was named Louis or "Tan-Weson."[3] He acted as interpreter at Philadelphia, December 4, 1759, and is said to

[1] *Penna. Col. Rec.*, v., 762.
[2] *Penna. Archives*, 2d Series, vii. 156.
[3] *Penna. Col. Rec.*, v., 685.

have been afterwards killed in the French War. In the early winter of 1751–52, Andrew Montour told Captain Thomas Cresap that he then had a brother at the Ohio who had formerly been interpreter for the French at Fort Detroit. This brother was Louis Montour.

Buell, in his *Life of Johnson* gives the name and some account of another Montour, John, whom he asserts was a son of Madame Montour. He was a war-captain of the Senecas, and a faithful adherent of Sir William Johnson, with whom he fought at the battle of Lake George in 1755, and at Niagara in 1759. A Michael Montour, "son of Montour the Indian," is also mentioned in the Minutes of the New York Council in October, 1726, the Council voting that the expenses for his care should be paid.

Mary, one of Madame Montour's grand-daughters is mentioned by Zeisberger as being a sister of Andrew and Catharine Montour. She lived at the Moravian mission of New Salem, Ohio, on January 4, 1791. David Zeisberger speaks of her in his *Journal*, under that date, and adds that "she knows, too, how to speak many languages; for example, Mohawk, her mother tongue, Wyandot, Ottawa, Chippewa, Shawano, English, and French. Her sister, Catharine, and several of her friends, live not far from Niagara, over the Lake." Mary and Catharine were the nieces of Andrew Montour, being the daughters of French Margaret, by her Mohawk husband, Peter Quebec, or Katarioniecha.[1] Mary is said to have married Kanaghragait, generally called "The White Mingo." He is said by Mrs. Murray to have died on the site of Fort Wayne in 1790.[2]

French Margaret is called both the niece of Madame Montour and the sister of Andrew Montour, by the Rev. John Martin Mack, who visited her in 1753. At Philadelphia, June 18, 1733, Chief Shekallamy told Governor Gordon some news of a plot on the part of the whites to cut off the Indians, which he had received from "an Indian who lives in his neighborhood, named Katarioniecha [or Peter Quebec], who is married to one, Margaret, a daughter of Mrs. Montour." Shekallamy's account must be taken as the more correct.

Then, or later, French Margaret lived at what was known as French Margaret'sTown, near the mouth of Lycoming Creek, where Martin Mack visited her in 1753. Spangenberg, Zeisberger, and Mack met her and her

---

[1] See *Penna. Col. Rec.*, ix., 499, 500.

[2] *Old Tioga Point*, p. 109. He was not "John Cook" (as stated by Mrs. Murray), "the White Mingo" who was killed by Frederick Stump on Middle Creek in 1768; but he seems to have been identical with Conengayote, or Canigaatt, a well-known Six Nations chief whom the whites called "White Mingo," and who lived at Fort Pitt from 1759 until after 1777. See *Penna. Col. Rec.*, vi., 784; viii., 293; ix., 470. Dr. Thwaites (*Revolution on Upper Ohio*, p. 27) says that he died in 1777; but Simon Girty met him in November of that year at Conewago on the upper Allegheny (Darlington's *Gist*, p. 214).

brother on Shamokin Island in 1745, while she was on her way from Allegheny to Philadelphia. Christopher Gist, a surveyor in the employ of the Ohio Company, travelled from the Potomac, by way of Logstown on the Ohio to the mouth of the Scioto and beyond in November and December, 1750. He was at an Ottawa town on the Tuscarawas River on the 9th of December, when he wrote: "Set out down the said Elk's Eye [Tuscarawas] Creek, S. 45 W. 6 M., to Margaret's Creek, a branch of the said Elk's Eye Creek." On the 19th of January, 1751, he reached "Hockhockin, a small town with only four or five Delaware families." This town was on the site of what is now Lancaster, Fairfield County, Ohio. It is called French Margaret's Town on Evans's and Mitchell's maps of 1755. As Gist had crossed French Margaret's Creek in 1750, the time of her residence in Ohio was of course earlier than that date; and as Spangenberg and his companions met her on Shamokin Island in 1745, on her way from Allegheny to Philadelphia, she may have spent a portion of her life before that time on the Hocking and Muskingum. Madame Montour, herself, it will be remembered, lived among the Miamis before her first appearance on the pages of Pennsylvania history in 1727. The Ohio French Margaret, however, may have been Madame Montour's sister, and not her daughter.

Martin Mack, the Moravian missionary, who visited French Margaret's Town on the site of what is now Williamsport, Lycoming County, Pennsylvania, August 28, 1753, thus speaks of the ruler of the town in his *Journal:* "Towards nine A.M. we came to a small town where Madame Montour's niece, Margaret, lives, with her family. She welcomed us cordially, led us into the hut, and set before us milk and watermelons. Brother Grube told her that Mack had come from Bethlehem especially to visit her. 'Mother,' said Mack, 'do you know me?' 'Yes, my child,' she replied, 'but I have forgotten where I saw you.' 'I saw you,' he said, 'eight years ago, on the Island at Shamokin, when you were living with your brother, Andrew Sattelihu,' [Sattelihu was Andrew Montour's Indian name]. Hereupon, she bethought herself, that at that time she had come from the Allegheny, and was on the way to Philadelphia. . . . We had a long conversation with her on many subjects, and she spoke particularly of Andrew Sattelihu, and her husband, who for six years has drunk no whisky, and who had prevailed upon two men from drinking. . . . August 29. As to Andrew Sattelihu, he is now interpreter for Virginia, and receives a salary of £300, and has been twice this summer to Onondaga. He is now absent, to bring Margaret's relatives, who live in French Canada, to her. The French have set £100 on his head. The Governor of Virginia has also appointed him a Colonel [Captain], and presented to him a fine tract of land on the Potomac. He is a friend of the Moravians, and still remembers how, eleven years ago, he travelled with a great gentleman [Count Zinzendorf, on his journey to Wyoming in 1742]. The Six Nations have expressed themselves to this effect, that whatever nation should kill him, they would at once begin war—he is held in such high esteem among them."

If French Margaret was the niece of Madame Montour she may have been the daughter of Madam Montour's sister who lived with the Miamis. The sister's name was probably Margaret, and Madame Montour's own name, either Madeleine[1] or Catharine. Most writers speak of her as Catharine Montour, due, possibly, to the error of early historians in confusing her with her grand-daughter, Queen Catharine.

In July, 1754, the records of the Moravians refer to French Margaret with her Mohawk husband and two grandchildren, as having halted a few days at Bethlehem on her way to New York, "travelling in a semi-barbaric state, with an Irish groom and six relay and pack-horses." Her husband's name was Katarioniecha, alias Peter Quebec. He was regarded as a man of good character. Two of their daughters, as already stated, were named Catharine and Mary, both living at French Margaret's Town in 1760. A son was killed while on an expedition against the Creek Indians in 1753. Conrad Weiser, in 1754, speaks of meeting Andrew Montour and Nicholas Quebec at Harris's Ferry, both of whom accompanied him to Aughwick, to attend the Indian conference there. Another daughter was named Esther, known in Revolutionary history as "Queen Esther." She has been confused with her sister, "Queen Catharine," by Lossing and other writers.

In May, 1760, Frederick Post and John Hays found French Margaret living between Tioga and a town north of there, called by Hays "Asinsan," of which her son-in-law Eghohowen, a Minsi Delaware, was the chief.

Queen Esther was the most infamous of all the Montours. She became the wife of Eghohowen (or Echogohund), mentioned as chief of the Minsi Delawares at Asinsan above Tiaoga in 1756 and 1760;[2] and after his death Esther ruled as chieftainess of her husband's tribe. Her residence in 1772 was at Sheshequin, six miles below Tioga Point on the site of what is now Ulster, in Bradford County, Pennsylvania. About that time she removed six miles north and founded a new town known as Queen Esther's Town, opposite the southwestern shore of Tioga Point. In Butler's Wyoming Expedition of July, 1778, Queen Esther is said to have headed a company of warriors, and at the massacre on the third of

[1] As we have seen, Madame Montour's mother's name was Madeleine. Andrew Montour's daughter was also named Madelina. See *Penna. Col. Rec.*, iii., 287; vii., 95; *Archives*, i., 211

[2] See Journal of John Hays, *Penna. Archives*, iii., 740; also, *Col. Rec.*, viii., 176, 209, 435, 750.

that month she was reputed to have been "the most infuriated demon in that carnival of blood." Her son is said to have been killed at Exeter shortly before, which naturally would increase her desire for vengeance. She beat to death more than a dozen of the white prisoners.[1] In the Fall of the same year, Colonel Thomas Hartley destroyed her village above Sheshequin; and she afterwards settled and died near the head of Cayuga Lake.

Catharine Montour, daughter of French Margaret, was only a little less prominent than her sister, "Queen Esther. She married Telenemut, one of the less noted of the Seneca chiefs. Her husband's English name was Thomas Hudson, and they were both present at the treaty of Easton held in October, 1758, when she is spoken of as a married daughter of French Margaret, who was also present at the treaty, with her husband, Peter Quebec. Catharine Montour was then accompanied by five or six of her children. Her village, three or four miles south of the head of Seneca Lake, and not far from the site of the present village of Havana, was known in Revolutionary times as "French Catharine's Town." It contained thirty houses, and was destroyed by General Sullivan, September 2, 1779. "Queen Catharine" herself fled towards Niagara; and as we have seen, was living near there, on the north side of Lake Erie, in 1791. Two of her daughters are referred to in one of the Journals of Sullivan's Expedition as being "handsome women" in 1779. A son, Amochol, was living at New Salem, Ohio, in 1788. Roland, John, and Belle Montour, by some writers called children of Queen Catharine, were related to her, but it is undetermined whether or not they were her children.[2] Two of these brothers held commissions from the British and took an active part on their side in the war of the Revolution.

Another Catharine Montour was the second wife of Andrew Montour.[3] The career of Andrew Montour, the most famous of Madame Montour's children, will be outlined in a later chapter.

From what has been related in the early part of the present chapter, it will be seen that among the pioneer Indian Traders at Shamokin were included James Le Tort, John Scull, Nicholas Scull, Antony Sadowsky, John Petty, Timothy Higgins, Henry Smith, and Jonah Davenport. A letter written to the Governor of Pennsylvania by the "Chiefs of ye Delawares at Alleegaeening, on the Main Road," April 30, 1730, gives us

---

[1] Harvey's *Wilkes-Barre*, ii., 984, 1018.

[2] Egle's *Notes and Queries*, iii., 127; Harvey's *Wilkes-Barre*, i., 207; Mrs. Murray's *Old Tioga Point*, p. 109.

[3] *Penna. Archives*, 3d Series, i., 240. His first wife was a grand-daughter of the Delaware sachem, Allumapees, by whom he had two children, a son (John Montour) and a daughter. The daughter was named Madelina, possibly after his mother. See *Penna. Col. Rec.*, vii., 95.

Tioga Point, from the Southeast.
From a photograph by I. K. Park, furnished by Mrs. Louise Welles Murray.

the names of two more of the Shamokin Traders. This letter was written to explain the cause of the death of one of these Traders. In it, the subscribing chiefs "Do hereby certify to the Governor as far as we know concerning the death of one white man last Fall, and another shot through the leg and broke it. None of us being present at ye actions; but have made due inquiry, and find thereon, that some of our people was going down this river a hunting. Two of the Shoahmokin Traders, viz., John Fisher and John Hart went along; and when they was got above a hundred miles down [the Ohio, below Kittanning], our people proposed to fire-hunt, by making a ring. The white men would go along. Our people would have dissuaded them from it, alleging that they did not understand it, and might receive some harm. But they still persisted in it, so all went together; wherein ye said John Hart was shot in at ye mouth, and ye bullet lodged in his neck, and so was killed; but by whom we cannot learn; which we believe to be accidental, and not on purpose."

In the early maps of the Ohio River, from Evans's map of 1755 down to the close of the eighteenth century, a noted point on the river is that called "Hart's Rock," situated between the mouths of Little Beaver Creek and Cross Creek. "Hart's Rock" may be identical with that which was described by Chaussegros de Lery in 1739 as the "Portrait Rocks," in the channel of the Ohio at the mouth of Little Beaver Creek near what is now Smith's Ferry. These rocks are visible only at low water stages. They are covered with rude inscriptions made by the Indians and are in that part of the river lying between Smith's Ferry and Georgetown, in Beaver County.[1] The name, "Hart's Rock," perpetuates the memory of the hapless Shamokin Trader, who joined the Delawares in their fire-hunt on that fatal day in the Autumn of 1729. It may also, possibly, mark the vicinity of the scene of the fire-hunt; as the mouth of Little Beaver Creek is nearly fifty miles below the Forks of the Ohio; and Kittanning about the same distance above.

Of the Shamokin Traders whose names are given above, we know that Le Tort, Sadowsky, Smith, and Davenport, in addition to Hart and Fisher, extended their trade to the Allegheny. Other Traders who traded from Shamokin to Allegheny were Thomas McKee, John Armstrong, Alexander Armstrong, Woodworth Arnold, and James Smith. John, or "Jack" Armstrong, with his two servants, Arnold and Smith, were murdered by three Delaware Indians, in April, 1744, at a gorge which the Juniata makes through the mountains. This gorge has ever since been known as "Jack's Narrows."

Another very early Trader at and above Shamokin was William

[1] See Chapter VI., Vol. II. In a note to his *Fort Pitt*, Mr. Darlington identified Hart's Rock with McKee's Rock, two miles below Pittsburgh, but fails to give any authority for his statement.

Wilkins. When John and Edmund Cartildge were tried at Conestoga in March, 1722, for the killing of the Seneca Indian at Monocacy Creek, the Commissioners, Logan and French, reported that they had been unable to examine one of the witnesses, William Wilkins, as he "was one hundred and fifty miles up Sasquehannah, trading for his master, and therefore too far out of reach."

Thomas McKee was the most noted of the later Shamokin Traders; and we have records of his trading expeditions as far west as the Ohio.[1] His son, Captain Alexander McKee, afterwards became well-known at Fort Pitt, and rendered himself notorious in Border history by deserting to the British during the time of the Revolutionary War, and carrying over to that interest a great many Indians whom he had befriended during his service as Deputy Indian Agent under the Crown.

The career of Thomas McKee, the father, was highly romantic, and a consideration of the same will enable us to understand why his son at the time of the Revolution should seek more congenial company among the Ohio Indians and in the service of his King, than he had found among the American forces at Fort Pitt, who were enemies of both.

Dr. Egle has stated that Thomas McKee was a son of Patrick. He may have been; although it is possible that he was the son of a certain Alexander McKee, who died in Donegal Township, Lancaster County, in May, 1740, leaving a son, Thomas, who was the executor of his will. A contributor to Egle's *Notes and Queries* (second series, p. 265) relates a traditionary account of Thomas McKee's marriage, which had been told to him in boyhood by his father, a native of the Susquehanna Valley. This was to the effect that McKee, in his younger days, began trading with the Indians, and after learning the language of the Delawares, established a trading post amongst them, in the vicinity of Shamokin. While trading up the river, he ventured into a camp of strange Indians, who stole his goods, drank his rum, and then becoming incensed at the resistance he made to their proceedings, bound him as a captive, and decided to burn him at the stake the following day. During the night, an Indian maiden came to the wigwam where he was bound, released him, and they fled from the camp together. McKee, from gratitude, made the girl his squaw and they lived together during the remainder of their lives as man and wife. This makes a pretty story; but probably it is not a true one. The real facts of this adventure, as related by Thomas McKee himself, while perhaps not so exciting, are quite as romantic and interesting.

Whether Thomas McKee took to wife an Indian squaw or a white woman will be left for the reader to determine; but for the sake of correct history, and to set at rest conflicting stories which are still current among the neighbors of his worthy descendants, who to this day reside in the

[1] *Penna. Col. Rec.*, v., 762.

The Shamokin Traders and the Shamokin Path

vicinity of McKee's Rock, a few miles below Pittsburgh, the following facts may be stated.

Edward Shippen, writing to Governor Morris, April 19, 1756, observes that he has been to Captain McKee's fort, where he found about ten Indians, among them, John Shekallamy. The latter, he adds, "let me know, that he wished the Indians would be moved down to Barny Hughes, where Captain McKee's woman and children live."

On May 20th, of the same year, in a conference held at the Lower Mohawk Castle, between Sir William Johnson and Canaghquiesa, an Oneida chief, the latter told Colonel Johnson of the result of a mission to the hostile Shawnees of northern Pennsylvania. "One of the Skanoadaradighroonas who lives near the aforesaid Indians," he said, "had applied to the Delawares to accompany them to the proposed meeting at Onondaga; which they refused to do, saying that one, Thos. McGee, who lives upon the Susquehanna, and is married to a Shawanese squaw, had told them that in ten days' time an army of the English would come and destroy them."

McKee may possibly have been the Trader referred to in the following letter, written by the Rev. Gideon Hawley, from Aughquagey, to Sir William Johnson, Dec. 27, 1755:

The sachems who went from hence with your message to the Delawares just now return from Trizaoga [Tioga], and desire me to pen the following letter to Your Honor in which you have a brief account how the quarrel between the English and Delawares began. . . . :

Brother Johnson—We have been to Trijaoga upon your affairs. In the first place, we relate what news we hear. The Indians there inform us that about two months ago, there was a party of English at Tsnasogh [Otizinachson], alias Shamokin, upon a scouting design; and that while they were there, news came that there was a party of French and Indians from Ohio about there, and that Scarouyady advised the English party to turn back, and by all means to keep on the east side of the river. They took his advice, 't is said, and returned, but went the west side of the river; and that before they had gone far, a French party came upon them, fired, and drove them into the river, where four of the English were drowned [this was the attack on John Harris's party, near Shamokin, October 25, 1755]. Not long after this, that an Englishman came to Scahandowana, alias Wioming, and, as he used to trade upon this river, the Indians asked him whether he had brought any goods with him. He said, "No; but I have brought my body, my flesh, and you may do what you please with me. It 's you," said he, "and the Six Nations, who killed our people t'other day. I was there,[1] I know your language; it was certainly you that did the mischief. And now," said he, "you and the English will fight. Maybe you think that you and your uncles, the Six Nations, are able to stand the English. I tell you," said he, "that

---

[1] See *Penna Archives*, ii., 459; iii., 633.

we can pinch you between our fingers. I shan't cheat you, and act in the dark and underhand, as you do; but tell you plainly that the English are going to fight you." The Englishmen returned to the white people, and informed them that a great multitude of Indians, of all nations, were gathered at Wioming. . . . The Indians at Wioming, it's said, were fully concerned after the Englishman had been there, and kept scouts out to see if any English were coming against them. At last, they saw a single white man coming. The Indians went to the white man, and asked him whether he was alone. He told them that three more, who were gentlemen, were coming to have a treaty with them. They soon arrived, and called the Indians together; and informed them that they were sent to treat with them about building a fort there, that their squaws and children might be protected from the French. The Indians desired to see their commission. They produced a certificate of it in writing. The Indians objected against their not having wampum. With that, they produced another paper. Now, the old man, who had been taken by the English, and made his escape, said to the Indians. "Don't you believe these men. They only mean to deceive you, and make you prisoners, or put you to the sword." At that, the Indians took their hatchets, and knocked them all in the head, except the Indian Trader who came there before, and was now with these gentlemen, that made his escape. . . .

The Moravian Bishop, Camerhoff, visited Captain Thomas McKee's trading post in 1748. In his *Journal* of that visit, he writes, under date of January 13th: "We have before us twenty long miles to Shamokin; also, two bad creeks, and the narrowest passes along the river to pass. At nine-o'clock we reached Thomas McKee's, the last white settlement on the river, below Shamokin.[1] McKee holds a captain's commission under the government; is an extensive Indian Trader; bears a good name among them; and drives a brisk trade with the Allegheny country. His wife, who was brought up among the Indians, speaks but little English. They received us with much kindness and hospitality."

Thomas McKee's "woman," "squaw," or "wife," as referred to by Edward Shippen, Chief Canaghquiesa, and Bishop Camerhoff, respectively, in the light of what has been related above, may have been the same, possibly, who assisted him to escape from an unfriendly party of Indians in the early winter of 1743. The details of this adventure are set forth in an affidavit which McKee made before Governor Thomas at Philadelphia, January 24, 1743. In this deposition, he states, that "Being concerned in the Indian trade, he has a store settled at an Indian town on the South Branch Sasquehanna river, near an Island called

---

[1] Thomas McKee had two posts on the left bank of the Susquehanna, both of which are shown on Scull's map of 1759. His lower store was below the mouth of the Juniata, not far from Big (now Halderman) Island; while the upper store was at the site of the village of Georgetown, Northumberland County, and also opposite a large island, on which some Indians lived.

the Big Island,[1] inhabited by the Shawna Indians; and that on the 12th or 13th of this instant, January, about seven o'clock in the morning, the Indians of the Town came to this Deponent's store, and told him they had heard the Dead Halloa, and were much surprised at it. And soon after, the same halloa, as from the Big Island, was repeated in the hearing of this Deponent. Whereupon, he, with a servant of his, took a canoe and went over to the Island, and in his passage, heard the Indians belonging to the Town call over to those on the Island, and ask them what was the matter. To which they answered, that the white men had killed some of their men. And on this Deponent coming to them on the Island, he saluted them according to the usual way, saying, 'How do you do, my friends?' At which they shook their heads, and made no answer; but went over to the Shawnas' town. And this Deponent further saith, that there were ten in number of those Indians, and that they belonged to the Five Nations; and on their coming to town, immediately a council was called; and this Deponent attended at the Council House, and was admitted."

At this council, the leader of the Iroquois war band informed the Shawnees that his party had come down from Onondaga the previous Fall, proposing to travel through the back parts of Maryland and Virginia, on a war expedition against some Southern Indians. While camping on the Shenandoah river, they had been attacked by a party of Virginians and four of their party had been killed. McKee proceeds to relate that this speech was delivered in the Mingo language, and interpreted to him in Shawnee, which he well understood. Whereupon, he addressed the Council, and reminded them that none of the disorders of which the Indians complained had happened in Pennsylvania. One of the Shawnees observed that the white people were all of one color, and in case of war would assist one another. Another Shawnee asked the warriors if they had met McKee's men, who had been sent out to Chiniotta (Juniata) for skins. "They could not have met them," replied a third "for if they had, they would have cut them off." "On hearing these discourses," adds McKee, "he [McKee] rose, up, and called out an old Shawna, with whom he was best acquainted, and took him to his store; made him a present of two or three twists of tobacco, and desired him to press to the Indians in Council their treaty of peace with Pennsylvania, and the ill-consequences of breaking it in cutting him off, as he apprehended he had great reason to fear they intended. That some short time after, the same Indian called this Deponent from his store, and told him that he had offered in Council what he had requested, and it was approved, though it seemed disagreeable to some of the Shawnas. And in a short time after, this Deponent was informed by a white woman, who had been taken prisoner

[1] Now known as Halderman Island, at the mouth of the Juniata River.

by the Indians in their Carolina wars, that it was left to the Shawnas to deal with him as they pleased; and that they were gone to hold a council concerning him at some distance from the town; and that if he did not make his escape, he would certainly be cut off. Upon which last information, together with some observations he had made of their behavior, he thought it not safe to trust his life in their hands, and notwithstanding a considerable quantity of goods which he had carried up there to trade, he determined to withdraw, and leave his effects among them; and accordingly communicated his designs to his man; and they came off privately, travelling by night and day through the uninhabited parts of the country, till they apprehended themselves to be out of danger, being out three days and three nights."

Captain Thomas McKee was in command of McKee's Fort, at Hunter's Mills, near the place where the Susquehanna passes the Blue Mountain, in 1756. He died near McKee's Half Falls, on the site of Georgetown, in 1772, leaving two sons, Alexander and James McKee. The former was then at Fort Pitt, where he was an assistant to George Croghan, the Deputy Indian Agent for the Crown; and where he owned a large tract of land at the mouth of Chartier's Creek, including McKee's Rock, still a noted landmark on the Ohio River, just below Pittsburgh. When he joined the British, in 1777, his possessions in Pennsylvania passed to his brother, James McKee, whose descendants are still living in Allegheny County.

If the woman Captain Thomas McKee had made his wife before 1748 was the white woman who had been captured by the Shawnees in one of their raids in Carolina, and who had been adopted into their tribe and reared among them, it is not hard to understand why her son, Alexander McKee, the renegade, should have inherited a half-savage nature which was developed by the long residence of his father among the Indians as a Trader, and by his own life-long association with the forest braves. This would be even more true if his mother was a Shawnee squaw.[1] His adherence to the British Government when the Revolution came, a Government which had so long been his paymaster, is less to be wondered at than his temporary defection therefrom during the first two years of the struggle.

Two early travellers over the Shamokin Path have left us a record of their journeys to the Allegheny. The first of these was Frederick Post, who left Fort Augusta, near the site of Shamokin,

---

[1] In the *Journal* of the Rev. David Jones, a missionary who visited the Shawnee towns on the Scioto in January, 1773, he states, on the 23d of that month, that he "went to see Captain [Alexander] McKee, who lives about three miles, about west and by north from Chillicaathee, in a small Town called Wockachaalli. . . . Here the Captain's Indian relatives live."

The Shamokin Traders and the Shamokin Path 213

on July 27, 1758; and reached the Allegheny, opposite Venango Fort, on August 7th. The second traveller was the Rev. John Ettwein, a Moravian missionary, who led a party of Delaware Christian Indians, from Wyalusing, on the East or North Branch of the Susquehanna (in Bradford County), by way of Muncy Creek and the Shamokin Path to a point on the Allegheny eight miles above Kittanning. Ettwein's party departed from Wyalusing on June 11, 1772, and arrived at the Allegheny July 29th. There were over two hundred Indian men, women, and children in the party.

Frederick Post's *Journal* is in part as follows:

July 27th, 1758. They furnished us here [at Fort Augusta] with every necessary for our journey, and we set out with good courage. After we rode about ten miles [along the east side of the Susquehanna West Branch], we were caught in a hard gust of rain.

28th. We came to Wekeeponall, where the road turns off for Wyoming [at the mouth of Muncy Creek], and slept this night at Queenashawakee [on or near the site of Linden, six miles west of Williamsport].

29th. We crossed the Susquehanna over the Big Island [at what is now Lock Haven, Clinton County]. My companions were now very fearful, and this night went a great way out of the road to sleep, without fire, but could not sleep for the musquitos and vermin.

30th. and 31st. We were glad it was day, that we might set out. We got upon the mountains, and had heavy rains all night. . . . [The path[1] here led up the valley of Bald Eagle Creek to Marsh Creek, thence westward through Marsh Creek Valley, and across what are now Liberty, Curtin, Boggs, and Snowshoe townships, Centre County, described as a tract of wild, broken, mountainous country.]

August 1st. We saw three hoops [for drying scalps] on a bush. To one of them there remained some long white hair. Our horses left us, I suppose not being fond of the dry food on the mountains. With a good deal of trouble we found them again. We slept this night on the same mountain.

2d. We came across several places where two poles, painted red, were stuck in the ground by the Indians, to which they tie the prisoners, when they stop at night, in their return from their incursions. We arrived this night at Shinglimuhee [Chinklaclamoose, now Clearfield], where was another of the same posts. . . . [The path led westward from Moshannon Creek, in what is now Snowshoe Township, Centre County, across the townships of Morris, Graham, Bradford, and Lawrence, Clearfield County.]

3d. We came to a part of a river called Tobeco [Little Toby Creek], over the mountains, a very bad road. [From Chinklaclamoose, Post took a northwestern branch of the main path, which led him across Clearfield, Jefferson, and Clarion counties].

4th. We lost one of our horses, and with much difficulty found him, but were detained a whole day on that account. . . .

5th. We set out early this day, and made a good long stretch,

[1] It is shown on Scull's map of 1770.

crossing the big river Tobeco [Clarion River], and lodged between two mountains. . . .

6th. We passed all the mountains, and the big river, Weshawaucks [East Sandy Creek], and crossed a fine meadow, two miles in length, where we slept that night, having nothing to eat.

7th. We came in sight of Fort Venango, belonging to the French, situate between two mountains, in a fork of the Ohio River.

The Rev. John Ettwein's party of Indian converts which left Wyalusing on June 11, 1772, reached the West Branch of the Susquehanna at a point about five miles above the mouth of Muncy Creek. They remained in camp here until June 23d. From that date, Ettwein's *Journal* proceeds:

June 23d–24th. Broke up camp and moved on. Passed the Loyalsock at the place where Count Zinzendorf visited thirty years ago, and Lycoming Creek, which marks the boundary line of land purchased from the Indians. At both places we found white settlers. One mile above the Lycoming stood formerly the town of Quenischaschacki [Linden]. . . . We encamped above Larry's Creek [one mile east from Jersey Shore] . . .

June 25th. We encamped opposite Long Island [on or near the site of Lock Haven, opposite what is usually called Big Island]. . .

June 26th. To-day I assembled the men, told them that we had progressed but thirty miles during the past week, and that if we failed to make more rapid headway, our large company would come to want. . . . . . It was furthermore decided that the strongest of our party should proceed in five canoes, with the baggage of the women, as far as Chinklacamoose.

June 27th. Arrived at Campbell's, where we met Mr. Anderson, who dissuaded us from attempting to embark in canoes, stating the water was too shallow for navigation. . . .

June 28th, Sunday. By request I preached in English to a goodly audience of assembled settlers from the Bald Eagle Creek and the south shore of the West Branch. . . .

June 29th. . . . We set out from the Island by land. . . . Travelled fourteen miles to Beech Creek, on the Path agreed on. After encamping here, the men returned with horses to fetch up the baggage. This they did daily, and thus were compelled to travel the road three times [June 30th and July 1st and 2d].

July 3d. In company of Cornelius and William I advanced early in the morning. Up to this time we had passed only through a beautiful and fertile region of country, but now our way led across the mountains. . . .

July 4th. . . . We proceeded four miles into the mountains. . . .

July 7. Moved on six miles to a spring. . . .

July 8. Advanced six miles to the West Moshannok [a stream emptying into the Susquehanna between Clearfield and Centre counties], over precipitous and ugly mountains, and through two nasty, rocky streams. . . .

July 9. Advanced but two miles, to a run in the swamp. . . .

July 10. Lay in camp, as some of our horses had strayed. . . .

July 11. . . . We moved eight miles to an old beaver-dam. . . .

July 13. Proceeded six miles to a spring, in a beautiful, widely expanded mountain meadow. . . .

July 14. Reached Clearfield Creek, where the buffaloes formerly cleared large tracts of undergrowth, so as to give them the appearance of cleared fields; hence the Indians called the creek Clearfield. . . .

July 16. . . . Journeyed on with a few of the men two miles in a pelting rain to the site of Chinklacamoose, where we found but three huts and a few patches of Indian corn. The name signifies, "No one tarries here willingly." It may, perhaps, be traced to the circumstance, that some thirty years ago an Indian resided here—a hermit life upon a rock—who was wont to appear to the Indian hunters in frightful shapes. Some of these too, he killed; others he robbed of their skins; and this he did for many years. We moved on four miles and were obliged to wade the river three times, here rapid and full of ripples.

July 17. Advanced only four miles to a creek that comes out from the northwest [Anderson's Creek, in Pike Township]. . . .

July 18. . . . Here we left the West Branch three miles to the northwest up the creek, crossing it five times. Here the Path went precipitately up the mountain to the summit, to a spring, the first waters of the Ohio [probably the source of the north branch of Mahoning Creek, which rises in Brady Township, Clearfield County, and empties into the Allegheny, ten miles above Kittanning]. . . .

July 19 (Sunday). . . . We passed a quiet day and dried our effects. In the evening the *ponkis* were excessively annoying, so that the cattle pressed towards and into our camp, to escape their persecutors in the smoke of the fires. This vermin is a plague to man and beast, both by day and night. But in the swamp, through which we were now passing, their name is legion, and hence the Indians call it, *Ponks-utenink, i. e.*, "the Town of the Ponkis." . . .

July 20. We travelled on through the swamp, and after five miles crossed the Path that leads from Frankstown to Goshgoshink [the site of Tionesta, Forest County], and two miles beyond this point, encamped at a Run. . . .

July 21. . . . We proceeded six miles to the first creek, and camped.

July 22. We journeyed on four miles to the first Fork, where a small creek comes down from the north.

July 23. Again, to-day, four miles to the second Fork—to a creek coming in from the south-east.

July 24. The Path soon left the creek, over valleys and heights to a spring. We now had left the swamp and were free from the plague of *ponkis*. Huckleberries were found in abundance, which were enjoyed. Our to-day's station was five miles, and about so far we advanced on—

July 25th, and encamped at a salt lick, where we kept a religious service, three miles from the large creek, which runs in a horse-shoe, and which is navigable for Canoes when the water is high. It is a four days' journey by water to this point, where the Ohio is struck, whereas, by land, the point can be reached in one day. . . .

July 27. We proceeded over a long mountain to Tschachat, four miles to where the Path from Ligonier passes north, then four miles over a mountain to a creek coming from the southwest, and then one mile to a small run.

July 28. Advanced eight miles over hill and valley to a bad spring. Here we were met by the Indians from Kaskaskia, en route for Shemung.

July 29. With sunrise we were again on the way, as we desired to-day to strike the Ohio, and in the evening we arrived there without mishap... We came to eight miles above Kittaning, not far above Kawuntschhannink, down a very precipitous mountain (so much so that we were compelled to take off our shoes to effect the descent), to the Ohio, which here is not quite so broad as the Delaware at Easton, and scarce reached to our horses' bellies as we forded it.

Marie Le Roy and Barbara Leininger, who were captured by the Delawares a few miles below Shamokin, October 16, 1755, were carried to Kittanning over the Shamokin Path. Their Narrative gives the following account of their journey to the Allegheny:

The next day the whole troop divided into two bands, the one marching in the direction of the Ohio, the other, in which we were, with Galasko, to Jenkiklamuhs [Chinklaclamouche], a Delaware Town on the West Branch of the Susquehanna. There we staid ten days, and then proceeded to Puncksotonay, or Eschen Town. Marie Le Roy's brother was forced to remain at Jenkiklamuhs.

After having rested for five days at Puncksotonay, we took our way to Kittanny. . . . The month of December was the time of our arrival, and we remained at Kittanny until the month of September, 1756.

Chinklaclamouche, the Delaware town on the West Branch of the Susquehanna, to which Marie Le Roy refers under the name of "Jenkiklamuhs," seems to have been a temporary village, erected by a band of Delawares on one of their migrations from East to West. No Traders' accounts of, or references to, this Indian Town have come down to us, so far as the writer is aware, and it is uncertain whether it was built during the time of the westward movement of the Delawares (1724–44), or after 1750. It is certain, however, that there was such a town at the time of the capture of the Le Roy and Leininger girls in 1755; and that it had ceased to be a town at the time of Post's visit in 1758. It stood on the site of the present Clearfield borough, the county-seat of Clearfield County. The name was spelled in a great many different ways.

In a letter written by Governor Denny to the "Proprietaries" of Pennsylvania in London, dated April 9, 1757, he says:

In my last [written November 4, 1756] I mentioned that the Augusta Battalion were employed in building and carrying on the works at that Fort, their duty and labour very severe. Even under these circumstances of the garrison, I ordered a strong detachment under Col. [William] Clapham towards the Ohio, to act offensively, and if possible, destroy an Indian Town. But intelligence arriving before these orders could be carried into execution, that a large body of French and Indians was coming to besiege the Fort, they were obliged to lay the expedition aside.

This account proving false, Col. Clapham, who was employed in finishing the Fort, sent out a Captain's Command, to attack an Indian Town called Shingleclamouse, situate near the head of the West Branch of Susquehannah, where was supposed to be a great resort of Indians. Capt. [John] Hambright entered the Town [probably under orders issued by Col. Clapham, November 4, 1756[1]], found the cabins all standing, but deserted by the Indians. Agreeably to his orders, he did not touch anything, nor destroy the Town, in hopes the Indians would come to settle there again. This was the only Indian Town could be attacked; and we found by a second expedition that they had returned, set their Town on fire, and were retired to Venango, situate where the River *au Boef* runs into the Ohio. Since the affair of Kittanning, the Indians on this side the Ohio have mostly retired with their wives and children under the French forts on that River.

On April 7, 1757, Colonel James Burd, then in command of Fort Augusta (which stood near the site of the Indian Town of Shamokin), detached Captain William Patterson, (afterwards the son-in-law of John Finley, the Trader), with ten men, to go up the West Branch in quest of intelligence of the enemy, "as far as Shinglaclamush." On the 25th of the same month, "at noon, Capt'n Patterson arrived [back at Fort Augusta] with his party, all well. They came down the river upon rafts. Capt'n Patterson reports. . . . that he march't to Shinglacamuch; saw no Indians or French, either upon his march or at the Town. The road that leads from Buckaloons passes along by Shinglaclamuch and forks on the south side of Susquahanna River at the distance of abo't 40 miles from that Town; one road from that Fork leads to Fort Augusta, and the other to Cumberland County; that both these roads were very much frequented, and it appeared to him the enemy used them constantly when they came to make their incursions upon this Province; that the cheeff part of the houses at Shinglaclamuch were burnt down, and he immajn'd that no Indians had lived there a long time; that he was obliged to return from Shinglaclamuch, not being able to proceed for want of provisions, he and his party having lived upon walnutts for three days. The country there was so excessively mountainous that they could not find any game to kill."

On July 15, 1758, Colonel Bouquet wrote General Forbes from Raystown: "The settlement of Shingle Clamasche is a chimera, there being no one there."

The Shamokin Path to Allegheny, which the Indian captives and Post and Ettwein travelled, was followed more by the Indians than the Traders. Until the War broke out, it was little used by either after 1745. The Traders generally preferred the Frankstown or Raystown Paths, while the Pennsylvania Indians sometimes made use of another Path,

[1] *Penna. Arch.*, iii., 42.

which led through the country of the Senecas. The Minsis, who emigrated from the vicinity of Tioga Point to the Allegheny after 1764, probably used this path. Post and Hays tried to follow it in 1760, but were turned back by the Indians at Pasigachkunk, who told them that no white men were allowed to travel over that Path. It was doubtless used by the Minsi Delawares in making their journeys from Minisink to the Seneca country when going to pay tribute to their conquerors. On such a journey it formed part of the route between the Delaware River and the Allegheny.

There were three main Indian paths between the Susquehanna and the Delaware in use prior to the Revolutionary War. The shortest path led from the Great Bend of the Susquehanna, in what is now Harmony Township (Lanesboro Post-office), Susquehanna County, across the northern corner of Wayne County, to Stockport, on the Delaware. The distance between the two rivers by this route was about twenty miles. This Portage Path is shown on the Adlum-Wallis map of Pennsylvania (1792). A second path, long, rocky, and little used, was that which led directly westward from Minisink Island, across the stony hills of the present Pike County, crossing Shohola Creek near the Falls, Wallenpaupeck Creek below the junction of its West and South branches, thence to the upper waters of Lackawanna Creek, and down that stream to its mouth. This path was exceedingly difficult, and but little travelled except by the Minsis, who used it in passing from Minisink on the Delaware, to their town of Hazirok, at the mouth of the Lackawanna.

A third path, and the one that was travelled most, was the Path from Wyoming to the Delaware Water Gap. This led directly from the Susquehanna to the Shawnee Town of Pechoquealin, a short distance above the Water Gap. In all probability, it was the path used by some of the first of that tribe into eastern Pennsylvania. The fact that the advance guard of Arnout Viele's Shawnees passed by the Minisinks on the way to Albany in 1694, is almost positive proof that they came eastward from the Susquehanna by the southernmost path; and the fact that their first town was built at the Delaware extremity of this path, some twenty-five miles south of Minisink Island, makes the proof somewhat more conclusive. We know positively that the first Shawnees to come to Minisink in 1692 came with Martin Chartier into Cecil County, Maryland, before reaching the Delaware.

All three of these Indian paths are shown on Reading Howell's 1792 map of Pennsylvania; but the best map of the Wyoming Path is that which accompanies the *Journals of General Sullivan's Indian Expedition of 1779*, published by the State of New York in 1887. Map No. 1 of the collection in that volume is reproduced from the survey made by Lieut. Benjamin Lodge. It covers the road from Easton to Wyoming,

The Shamokin Traders and the Shamokin Path 219

a distance of some sixty-five miles. That part of Sullivan's route from Easton through the Wind Gap of the Blue Mountains, was not over the main trail. Twenty-two miles north of Easton, the road followed by the army joined the ancient Path which led from Pechoquealin, past what was known as Stroud's Settlement (now Stroudsburg), to Wyoming. Three miles farther, the Path crossed Pocono Creek; thence, to the head of that stream; around the eastern spur of Pocono Mountain, to Pine Swamp; thence ten miles through the Great Swamp,[1] crossing Tobyhanna Creek and the head of the Lehigh; thence four miles, to the Shades of Death, another deep swamp, two miles across; thence, two miles to Bear Swamp and across the "North branch of the Schuylkill" (really Bear Creek branch of the Lehigh); and thence over Moosic (now Wyoming) and Susquehanna (now Wilkes-Barre) mountains, nine miles farther, to Wyoming.

The trail up the Susquehanna from Wyoming to Tioga Point followed the east bank, after crossing at Hazirok; thence up the Tioga (Chemung) River to the mouth of Cowanesque Creek, in Tioga County, Pennsylvania; up that stream to its sources in what is now Potter County; across the country three or four miles, to the heads of the Genesee River; thence, six or seven miles farther, ascending nearly four hundred feet, to the heads of the Allegheny.

This was probably the route taken by Arnold Viele on his journey to and from the Shawnee country in 1692 and 1694.

David Zeisberger, the Moravian missionary, travelled over this path in 1767 from Friedenshutten on the Susquehanna, near what is now Wyalusing, Bradford County, to Goschgoschunk, at the mouth of Tionesta Creek, on the Allegheny, in what is now Forest County. Proceeding up the Susquehanna, accompanied by two Indian converts and a packhorse, he reached the Minsi Town of Assinissink, on the Chemung, October 3d. This stood on or near what is now Painted Post, Steuben County, New York. "Here," wrote Zeisberger, "the Tioagee [Chemung] divides itself into two branches; one goes toward the north, into the land of the Senekas, while the other, along which we pursued our way, extends to the west. We passed Gachtochwawunk and Woapassisqu, two old Indian Towns. The way was very wild and difficult. We camped for the night on the west branch of the Tioagee [Cowanesque Creek branch]. Oct. 4th. To-day it rained; however, we continued our journey, having a great deal of trouble in following the Path, which often could not be recognized. . . . Oct. 5th. We met an Indian, accompanied by two women, who came from Goschgoschingh, from which place they set out eleven days ago. . . . Towards evening we again crossed a plain, and encamped for the night on the west branch of the Tioagee.

[1] For an account of the route through the Great Swamp see Rev. Wm. Rogers's "Journal of the Sullivan Expedition." *Penna. Archives*, Second Series, xv., 258.

Oct. 6th. Before noon we arrived at Pasigachkunk,[1] an old deserted Indian Town. It was the last on the Tioagee. Here [Frederick] Post, during the last war, while on the way to the Allegheny, had to turn back; because the Indians would not allow him to proceed any farther.[2] It is possible to travel to this point on the waters of the Tioagee. When we left this place, we took the wrong path. Seeing that the route went too far south, we halted, and John struck into the woods towards the north in search of another path. He found one which we thought would be the correct one. We soon left the Tioagee altogether, and entered the great swamp above the place where the Tioagee has its source; for we had to travel until dark before we found water. It rained hard. . . . Oct. 7th. It continues to rain; still we pushed forward, and came across a large creek, called Zoneschio [Genesee], which flows into the lands of the Senecas (where I had been before, with Brother Camerhoff), and from there runs into Lake Ontario. We again travelled until late at night, and found no water. We pitched our camp, and John walked a great distance in the night and brought back a kettle full of water, so that we had at least something to drink. Oct. 8th. After we had crossed a slight elevation, we arrived at the source of the Allegheny, which is here no larger than Christian's Spring [at Bethlehem]. Here I had the pleasure of seeing the first fir grove in America. My two Indian brethren did not know what kind of wood it was, as they had never seen this kind before. They had a great deal of trouble in finding the way to-day, for often, for miles, there is no sign of a person ever having travelled this way before. We occasionally came across the footprints of deer. . . . They make a path wherever they go. We thus thought we had come upon the right path. But the tracks led us into a terrible wilderness, so we had to stop and wait until John had scoured the forest and found the right path. In the evening we arrived at the Allegheny, being very tired; for both yesterday and to-day we had to work our way through the wildest woods and densest underbrush imaginable. To my two Indian brethren, who are otherwise accustomed to underbrush, it seemed

---

[1] At the examination of Henry Hess, a returned captive, in 1756, he called this place Little Shingle (from the Lenape, *pasikachk*, "a board"), and stated that Teedyuscung and the Delawares went there from Tioga in the spring of 1756 to plant their corn. *Penna. Archives*, iii., 56; also pp. 44 and 46.

[2] Frederick Post and John Hays, in company with Teedyuscung, the Delaware chief, started from Wyoming, May 17, 1760, on a mission to the Ohio Indians. See Hays's Journal, *Penna. Archives.*, iii., 735–741; also, *Penna. Col. Rec.*, viii., 469. Under date of June 7, 1760, Hays writes: "Arrived at Paseckachkunk, about four o'clock, after crossing the River five times. This Town stands on the south side of the River, and is in two parts, at the space of a mile distance, where there is two sorts of people. The nearest part is peopled with Wonamies [Delawares]; Quitigon is their chief. The Upper Part is Mingoes, which commands all that country."

The STATE of PENNSYLVANIA reduced (with permission) from Reading Howell's Map by SAMUEL LEWIS

remarkably wild. The day has been passed in quite rapid travelling. At this place the Allegheny is fully twice as broad as the Maukosy at Bethlehem, and is navigable for canoes. Here also the Indians make canoes, in order to go down the stream. Of this we saw signs quite often. Canoes of bark as well as of wood are found. From Wayomink, therefore, the best route would be by water as far as Passiquachkunk, then two days overland to the Allegheny, where canoes can again be made to travel down stream.

"October 9th. We travelled along the Allegheny, keeping it to our left. This evening we came out of the thickest and densest swamp in which we had travelled four days. It cannot be surpassed in wildness. . . . Oct. 10th. At noon we arrived at a town of the Senecas, and consequently had a way before us which admitted of better travelling. . . . As we continued our journey, a Seneka mounted his horse and rode to the next town, which is at least thirty miles distant. . . Oct. 11th. At noon we arrived at the last mentioned town, Tiozinossongachta."

This town probably stood near the site of the present town of Cold Spring, Cattaraugus County, New York. Reading Howell's 1792 map of Pennsylvania names the creek which flows into the Allegheny at this point, the "Inshaunshagota"; and on the Adlum-Wallis map of Pennsylvania of about the same date, "Teushanushsonggoghta Town" is located at the mouth of this stream, which is now known as Cold Spring Creek. On Lewis Morgan's map of the Iroquois country in 1720, that writer locates the village of Deonagano ("Cold Spring") at this point.

Zeisberger reached Goschgoschunk (now Tionesta, Forest County, Penna.) on October 18th. He remained there but a few days, as the Indians had made threats against his life; and started on his return trip October 23d. On the evening of the next day the party arrived at "a town which is called Panawakee, where we remained over night, as we had the time before." This must have been the old Seneca town of Canawako, or Canawagy, or Conewango, visited by Celoron in 1749; which stood on the site of Warren, Pennsylvania.[1] On the 26th, Zeisberger advanced as far on the homeward trip as Tiozinossongachta, "the most central of the Seneca towns." At noon of the next day he passed through "the last Seneka town, Tiohuwaquaronta." On Guy Johnson's map of the country of the Six Nations[2] (1771), the town of "Tioniongarunte" is placed at the mouth of what appears to be intended for the stream now called Olean Creek; although on the Adlum-Wallis map (about 1792) "Ichsua Town" is located at this point, now the site of the town of Olean.

[1] Beauchamp calls it Panawakee or Ganawaca, and states that the latter form is the correct one, referring to *rapids*. This identifies it with the town at the site of Warren.
[2] *Doc. Hist. N. Y.*, iv., 1090.

Three beautiful maps, accompanying the reports of the Boundary Commissioners of New York and Pennsylvania, are printed in volume xi. of the *Pennsylvania Archives*. These show the surveyed boundary line between the two states. Tushanushagota Indian Town is located a mile or two above the mouth of Cold Spring Creek, which stream bears the same name as the town. Eighso Indian Town is placed at the mouth of the present Olean Creek. The head of canoe navigation on "Cawenisque" Creek is given as seventeen miles from the Tioga; while the head of navigation on the Oswaya branch of the Allegheny, is forty miles farther west, and eighteen miles west of where the Genesee River crosses the Pennsylvania line.

On October 29th, Zeisberger arrived "at the Forks" (the mouth of Oswayo Creek) and on the 30th, "to the end of the Allegheny." At night on October 31st, the travellers reached "Passigachgungh" again, on Cowanesque Creek; and thence via Assinissink, Willewane, and Sheshequin, to Friedenshutten, where they arrived November 5th.

CHAPTER VIII

ANDREW MONTOUR, "THE HALF INDIAN"

ANDREW HENRY MONTOUR,[1] or Sattelihu, as he was known to the Indians (and Eghuisera, when he became a Councillor of the Six Nations), was the oldest son and the most noted of the children of Madame Montour. He first appears in the Colonial history of Pennsylvania in February, 1743, when he served as an interpreter to the Delawares for Conrad Weiser at a conference held at Shekallamy's house in Shamokin. In 1744, while serving as captain of a party of Five Nation warriors, marching against the Catawbas of Carolina, he fell sick on his way to the James River, and was obliged to return to Shamokin. Two years before this, however, Count Zinzendorf, the Moravian, had visited Otstonwakin, the town of the Montours at the mouth of Loyalsock Creek; and that nobleman has left us a pen picture of Madame Montour's son, which is interesting and unique. "On September 30th, 1742," Zinzendorf writes, "as we were not far from Otstonwakin, Conrad [Weiser] rode to the village. He soon returned, in company with Andrew, Madame Montour's oldest son. Andrew's cast of countenance is decidedly European, and had his face not been encircled with a broad band of paint, applied with bear's fat, I would certainly have taken him for one. He wore a brown broadcloth coat, a scarlet damasken lapel waistcoat, breeches, over which his shirt hung, a black cordovan neckerchief decked with silver bangles, shoes and stockings, and a hat. His ears were hung with pendants of brass and other wires plaited together, like the handle of a basket. He was very cordial; but on addressing him in French, he, to my surprise, replied in English."

In May, 1745, Montour went with Conrad Weiser and Chief Shekallamy to Onondaga, as messengers from the Governor of Pennsylvania to the Six Nations. They were accompanied by the Moravians, Spangenberg, John Joseph Schebosh, and Zeisberger. In June, 1748, Montour was introduced by Mr. Weiser to the President and Council of Pennsyl-

---

[1] See *Penna. Archives*, 3d Series, i., 240, where an entry in the *Minutes* of the Board of Property refers to him as "Henry Montour, who is also called Andrew Montour."

vania at Philadelphia, Weiser informing them that he had employed Andrew in sundry affairs of consequence, and found him faithful, knowing, and prudent; "that he had, for his own private information, as Andrew lives amongst the Six Nations, between the branches of Ohio and Lake Erie, sent a message to him in the winter, desiring him to observe what passed amongst those Indians on the return of Schaiohady, and come down to his home in the spring; which he did." The Council voted Montour a recompense for his trouble and expense, and employed him to go to meet a deputation of Shawnee chiefs then on their way to Philadelphia from Allegheny. He assisted Weiser as interpreter in a conference held with these chiefs and others of the Six Nations and Twightwees at Lancaster, July 19–29, 1748. Some two weeks later, he accompanied Weiser and George Croghan to the Ohio River, where they were sent by the Government to carry a considerable present to the Indians at Logstown.

In May, 1750, he came from Allegheny to George Croghan's house in Pennsboro Township, Cumberland County, and joined in the conference held on the 17th with some chiefs of the Six Nations and Conestogas. On the 7th of the following June he took part in another Indian conference at Croghan's house, at which were present Canajachrera, or "Broken Kettle" (also written, Conajarca, Canajacharah, Canante-chiarirou, Canajachreesera, etc.), the principal Seneca chief at Kuskuskies near the Ohio, and two other chiefs of that nation from the same district. At the time of this conference, which was attended by Richard Peters, Secretary of the Province, Montour told the Secretary that messages had been received by the Ohio Indians the Fall before, desiring them to come to the headquarters of the Ohio Company at Thomas Cresap's house on the Potomac, to treat with the Virginia Traders, who promised to sell the Indians their goods at lower prices than they usually paid to the Pennsylvania Traders. Montour was present at the meeting of the Council, July 31st, when the report of this conference was read, and he informed the Governor then, that within the past two years two or three Traders from Pennsylvania or Virginia had been killed by the Indians at the Ohio.

On August 8th, Governor Hamilton sent a message to the Assembly, in which, after giving the Indian news he had received from Montour and others, he went on to state, that when Mr. Weiser had returned from the Ohio in September, 1748, he had left there several matters of consequence to Andrew Montour, finding that the Indians esteemed him and placed great confidence in him. "This gave him a sort of public character," the Governor adds, "which has put him to some trouble and expense. . . . I therefore recommend it to you that you will be pleased to make Mr. Montour a suitable recompense for his services . . . and as he resides at Ohio, he will, I am persuaded, upon a proper recompense, be always ready and willing to serve this Province to the utmost of his power."

In November of the same year, Montour accompanied George Croghan to Logstown, and from thence by way of the Lower Shawnee Town to the Miami village of Pickawillany, on a mission to strengthen the alliance between the Ohio Indians and the English. They returned the following Spring, and were sent again in May, 1751, to carry a present to the Indians settled at Logstown and elsewhere.

Croghan and Montour reached Logstown on May 18th. Two days later, Joncaire and another Frenchman, with forty Six Nations warriors arrived from the head of the Allegheny. Joncaire held a conference with all the Indians assembled there on the 21st, at which Croghan and Montour were present. He endeavored to persuade the natives to turn away the English Traders and prevent them from coming there in the future; threatening them with the displeasure of the French Governor of Canada in case of their refusal. Immediately one of the resident chiefs of the Six Nations arose in Council and answered Joncaire: "Fathers, I mean you that call yourselves our fathers, hear what I am going to say to you. You desire we may turn our brothers the English away, and not suffer them to come and trade with us again; I now tell you from our hearts we will not, for we ourselves brought them here to trade with us, and they shall live amongst us as long as there is one of us alive."

Perhaps the knowledge that Croghan and Montour had brought a present of goods and supplies for the Indians from the Pennsylvania Government, to the value of seven hundred pounds, had something to do with quickening the affection of their chiefs for the English on this particular occasion. The presents were given to the Indians on the 28th, and on that day, Croghan writes in his report of the proceedings: "The speaker of the Six Nations made the following speech to Monsieur Ioncœur in open Council; he spoke very quick and sharp, with the air of a warrior— 'Father, how comes it that you have broke the general peace? Is it not three years since you, as well as our brothers, the English, told us that there was a peace between the English and French; and how comes it that you have taken our brothers as your prisoners on our lands? Is it not our land? (stamping on the ground, and putting his finger to John Cœur's nose). What right has Onontio [the Governor of Canada] to our lands?'"

On the following day the Six Nations chiefs requested of Croghan that the Pennsylvania Government build a "strong house on the river Ohio," as a protection for the Traders and for their own families in case of war.

Croghan and Montour returned to Pennsboro in the early part of

June, 1751; and on the 10th instant, the former wrote the Governor, enclosing a *Journal* of their transactions at Logstown. In this letter he said: "Mr. Montour has exerted himself very much on this occasion, and as he is not only very capable of doing the business, but looked on amongst all the Indians as one of their chiefs, I hope your Honor will think him worth notice, as he has employed all his time in the business of the Government. . . . Mr. Montour is at my house, and will wait on your Honor when you please to appoint the time."

Montour returned to the Ohio in the Summer or Fall of 1751; and remained there until near the beginning of the following year. In an undated letter written by Colonel Thomas Cresap to Governor Dinwiddie in the early winter of 1751-52, and which Dinwiddie answered January 23d, Cresap gives a lengthy account of Indian affairs in Ohio, which he had just received from Andrew Montour, "who is on his journey home from the Ohio, and who is the proper person to be our [the Ohio Company's] interpreter, having a good character, both amongst white people and Indians, and very much beloved by the latter."

A few days before Montour had left Logstown seven French Traders had come there with their goods, and invited the Indians to a council. Very unwillingly the Traders admitted Montour to this council, as the Indians insisted upon having him for an interpreter. The Traders brought a message from the Governor of Canada, desiring a conference with the Shawnees at Logstown during the following spring. Montour also informed Cresap that he had a brother [Louis] who had acted as interpreter between the French and Indians at Fort Detroit for some time past; but who had now left them, and come to the Ohio; where he informed Andrew that the French had built a fort at a place called Kyhogo, on the west side of Lake Erie. Andrew Montour also gave an account of an unsuccessful expedition gotten up by the Canadian Governor against the Miami Indians of Pickawillany in the early fall of the year then ended. Cresap adds, further, that "one James [John?] Finley and another are suspected to be taken and carried off by the French, who make a practice of taking off our men [Traders] every year."

On August 4, 1748, Conrad Weiser, on the eve of his departure for Logstown, wrote to Secretary Richard Peters from Lancaster: "Andrew Montour has pitched upon a place in the Proprietor's Manor at Canataqueany [Conodoguinet, in Cumberland County]. He expects that the Government shall build him a house there, and furnish his family with necessarys. In short, I am at a loss what to say of him. I am much concerned about him. He seems to be very hard to please."

Montour, as we have seen, spent most of his time between 1748 and 1750 at the Ohio. On April 18, 1752, he was granted a license by Governor Hamilton to select a place of residence for himself and family at such a point north of Kittochtinny mountain and west of the Susquehanna, as he might think proper. He accordingly chose a tract of 143 acres of land lying on what is still called Montour's Run, near its junction with Shearman's Creek. His house was half a mile west of what is now Landisburg, in Tyrone Township, Perry County. This land he sold before 1763. It was on the other side of the mountain from George Croghan's house in Pennsboro township, and some twenty miles distant therefrom. In 1761, 1500 acres were granted to him by the Government, on Kishacoquillas Creek, near the Juniata. In the papers connected with this grant he is called both Andrew and Henry Montour.

In April, 1752, on the same day that Montour received his first land grant from the Governor, he requested permission of that official to interpret for the Governor of Virginia at a treaty which was to be held at Logstown the following June. Governor Dinwiddie and his friends were stockholders in the Ohio Company, which in 1748 had received a grant from the King of a large extent of territory lying on the east side of the Ohio River. The object of the treaty at Logstown was to induce the Six Nations chiefs to release their claims to this land. Messrs. Joshua Fry, Lunsford Lomax, and James Patton attended as Commissioners for Virginia, together with Christopher Gist, George Croghan, and Andrew Montour. The latter acted as interpreter. The Ohio Company allowed him thirty pistoles for his services, and offered to give him title to a thousand acres of land if he would remove to Virginia and settle within the Company's grant.

Montour was addressed by the Six Nations Indians at Logstown as one of their Councillors in June, 1752; and early in 1753 he visited the Onondaga Council at the instance of Governor Dinwiddie, to invite the Six Nations to hold a treaty with the Virginia Government (in the interest of the Ohio Company) at Winchester. August 27, 1753, John Fraser wrote from his trading-post at the Forks of the Monongahela, that Captain William Trent had been there, viewing the ground on which the fort projected by the Ohio Company was to be built; and that he had left for Virginia the day before, taking with him French Andrew and chiefs of the Six Nations, Picts, Shawnees, Wyandots, and Delawares.

In September of the same year, a treaty was made with these chiefs at Winchester, Colonel Fairfax representing the Virginia Government, and Andrew Montour interpreting. Christopher Gist, George Croghan, and William Trent were present.

After this treaty, the Indians proceeded to Carlisle, Pennsylvania, where (October 1st to 4th) they made another treaty with Commissioners Richard Peters, Isaac Norris, and Benjamin Franklin, representing the Pennsylvania Government. The Indian name of Andrew Montour's brother, Louis, who had accompanied the party from Ohio, is given in the list of Six Nations chiefs present at this conference. It was Tanweson.

Towards the close of the conference, the leading speaker, Scarrooyady, an Oneida chief, presented a large belt of wampum to Andrew, and addressing the Commissioners, said: "Since we are now here together, with a great deal of pleasure, I must acquaint you that we have set a horn on Andrew Montour's head; and that you may believe what he says to be true between the Six Nations and you, they have made him one of their Counsellors, and a great man among them and love him dearly."

After this conference the Indians returned to the Ohio, accompanied by Louis Montour. Andrew proceeded to his home in Shearman's Valley, and remained in that vicinity until the early part of November. There he was joined by his brother Louis, who had brought two messages from the Indian chiefs at Ohio, one for the Governor of Pennsylvania, and the other for Governor Dinwiddie, of Virginia. After a consultation with George Croghan, at Aughwick, Andrew started off express, to carry the Virginia message to its destination. Louis Montour brought the other message to Governor Hamilton at Philadelphia. It was dated at "Old Town, October 27, 1753"; signed by the Half King, Monacatootha, and Jonathan, the Deer; and witnessed by five Indian Traders. Louis Montour explained that "Old Town" meant Shanoppin's Town, three miles above the Forks of the Ohio. In this message the Indians said: "We depend that you and the Governor of Virginia will join hands and be as one; and we, the Six Nations, will be the third brother; and as for the French, our enemy is at hand, with a Tomhock in their hands, holding it over our heads to us, to take hold of it, or else to be struck with it, and to take it to strike our own flesh, we think it very hard. As for you, they have already struck, and openly declare they will clear this river of the English and all others that will not join them. So now we beg our Brother's assistance with quick despatch."

Governor Hamilton replied to this letter on November 20th, informing the Indians that he would communicate at once with Governor Dinwiddie, and endeavor to carry out their wishes so far as he had the power. This message he sent to Andrew Montour and George Croghan, to be carried by them to the Ohio. He wrote in the letter that on the recommendation of these chiefs when at Carlisle, he had appointed Croghan and Montour to attend to all the Indian transactions of the Government, as he could place confidence in what they might say or do. The Governor also sent John Patten, another Indian Trader, to accompany Croghan and Montour to Logstown, instructing him to inquire into the operations of the French on the Ohio, and the attitude of the Indians toward the English.

On the thirteenth of the following January, Mr. Croghan reached

Shanoppin's Town, where he was overtaken by Montour and Patten. The party proceeded to Logstown the next day, where they found all the Indian men drunk, and met a detachment of French soldiers, who placed Patten under arrest; but afterwards released him. Montour and Patten returned to Philadelphia after February 3d, leaving Croghan at Logstown to interpret for Captain William Trent, who had "just come out [on February 3d] with ye Virginia goods, and has brought a quantity of tools and workmen to begin a fort." Montour and Patten arrived in Philadelphia February 20th, and underwent a close examination by the Governor and Assembly in regard to the courses and distances of the road, and the relative locations of Shanoppin's Town, Logstown, and Venango. In these examinations they proved that these towns were all within the limits of the Province. But the Assembly discredited their evidence; refused to accept the report of its own committee as to its conclusiveness; decided that the encroachments of the French on the Ohio River did not concern Pennsylvania any more than they did Virginia; and sent a message to the Governor which concluded as follows:

The Governor is pleased to inform us that he had undoubted assurance that part of His Majesty's dominions within this government is at this time invaded by the subjects of a foreign prince, who have erected forts within the same, and calls upon us, pursuant to His Majesty's orders in the present emergency, to grant such supplies as may enable him to resist those hostile attempts, and repel force by force; but as it appears to us the Governor is enjoined by the Royal Orders not to act as principal beyond the undoubted limits of his government, and as by the papers and evidence sent down and referred to by the Governor, those limits have not been clearly ascertained to our satisfaction; we fear the altering our connections with His Majesty's colony of Virginia, and the precipitate call upon us as the Province invaded, cannot answer any good purpose at this time; and therefore we are now inclined to make a short adjournment.

Andrew Montour returned to his home on Shearman's Creek, from whence he wrote Secretary Richard Peters on May 16, **1754**:

Sir—I once more take upon me the liberty of informing you that our Indians at Ohio are expecting every day the armed forces of this Province to their assistance against the French, who, by their late encroachments are like to prevent their planting, and thereby render them incapable of supporting their families; and you may depend upon it as a certainty that our Indians will not strike the French unless this Province or New York engage with them; and that by sending some number of men to their immediate assistance. The reasons are plain, to-wit., that they don't look upon their late friendship with Virginia as sufficient to engage them in a war with the French. I therefore think, with submission, that to preserve our Indian allies this Province ought instantly to send out some men, either less or more, which I have good reason to hope would have the desired effect. Otherwise, I doubt there will in a little time be an entire separation, the consequence of which you are best able to judge. . . . I have delayed my journey to Ohio, and waited with great impatience for advices from Philadelphia; but have not yet received any. I am now obliged to go to Colonel Washington, who has sent for me many days, to go with him to meet the Half King, Monacatootha, and others, that are coming to meet the Virginia companies, and, as they think, some from Pennsylvania. . . .

One month before this letter was written, Ensign Edward Ward had surrendered to Contrecœur the little fort begun by Trent at the Forks of the Ohio.

On May 13th, Governor Dinwiddie left Williamsburg in Virginia, and proceeded to Winchester, that he might be in closer communication with Colonel Washington, who had left Will's Creek for the Redstone about the first of May, with the wholly mercenary and entirely laudable purpose of protecting the property and trade of the Ohio Company. Dinwiddie remained at Winchester for about a month, and on June 17th, two days after his return to Williamsburg, wrote Governor Hamilton, giving him an account of the success of the Virginians under Washington at the battle of Great Meadows, May 27th. He added that while at Winchester he saw George Croghan, whom he employed to go to Washington's camp as an interpreter; and that he had given Andrew Montour a Captain's commission, "to head a select company of friendly Indians, as scouts, from our small army."

Captain Montour did not organize a company of Indians from those who accompanied Washington's little army, but as there were a great many Traders and woodsmen gathered at Winchester, who had been driven out of the Ohio country on the approach of the French, he proceeded to organize a company of scouts or rangers from his friends among them, and from Croghan's Aughwick followers. His company consisted of eighteen men, enlisted for six months from May 26, 1754. With these Traders Montour and Croghan preceeded to the Monongahela; and there on the 9th of June they joined Washington. Montour and his company fought in the battle of Fort Necessity, where two of his men were taken prisoners, whose names are mentioned by Captain Robert Stobo in his letters from Fort Duquesne.[1]

On the 1st of August, Governor Dinwiddie wrote Colonel James Innes, at Winchester, "I have ordered Andrew Montour, with a company of Indians to you; if they come, show him and them a regard." The Governor was not then aware that Montour's company was made up of white Traders. Montour had already been at Winchester for

---

[1] Daniel Laferty and Henry O'Brien were taken prisoners. John Meinor was another member of Montour's company. See *Penna. Col. Rec.*, vi., 141, 145, 161.

some two weeks before this letter reached there; for on July 21st he had written from that town to Governor Hamilton that the Half King and Monacatootha, with a body of the Six Nations from Ohio had gone to Aughwick to settle (at George Croghan's settlement).

It was not until the following December that Dinwiddie learned that Montour's company was made up of white men. Governor Sharpe, of Maryland, wrote him on December 10, 1754; that "while in camp at Will's Creek, Gist acknowledged to me that he had received £45 for Andrew Montour, but Montour did not receive a farthing thereof, by which he complained to me that his private affairs and credit received no small detriment; wherefore, I was induced to advance him £25, his salary as Indian interpreter, and £20 towards defraying the expense of the eighteen men raised by your order and supported from the 26th of May to the 26th of November. . . . His behavior while I was at the camp prejudiced me in his favor, and as I esteem him a very useful person, I will endeavor by all means to keep him firm in our interest."

Dinwiddie, in answer to this letter, wrote, December 17th: "Mr. Montour's account is very unfair. He had no orders to raise the men charged. He had the commission to protect him in case he should fall into the hands of the French; as he is proscribed by them. . . . After the skirmish at the Meadows, he went home from the camp; and yet charges his men's pay till the 26th of last month. The account is made up for him by some of the woodsmen, who are a very bad set of people. He may be a very useful man if kept from these wretches." Sharpe wrote in reply: "I did not know that what you mention was the intent of giving Montour a commission, and indeed, I question whether the man did not misapprehend the purpose of it himself; otherwise I think he would not have proceeded to raise any men for the service; which that he did Mr. Washington can inform you, whose order Montour and his Company were attendant on at the time of the engagement."

Dinwiddie wrote Sharpe on the subject again on January 7th: "The commission to Montour was to command a party of Indians as scouts; which you will see by the como.; and indeed to protect his person. I never did hear before I received your letter that he had a company of white people; and indeed I suspect it's a trick of the woodsmen, who are always plotting for more. After the skirmish at the Meadows, he went to his own house; and if the people he says he listed had remained with the others, they might have claimed their provisions; but keeping them, as he alleges, so long in pay, and providing them with provisions, appear to me an imposition from the Traders and woodsmen."

August 31, 1754, Montour met Conrad Weiser at Harris's Ferry, and accompanied him to the Indian conference at Croghan's in Aughwick Valley. Weiser wrote privately to Secretary Peters that on this occasion

Montour became intoxicated several times, and abused him, the Governor, and the Secretary, for not paying him for his trouble and expenses. "I reprimanded him when sober," Weiser added; "he begged pardon, desired me not to mention it to you; but did the same thing again at another drunken frolic. . . . I left him drunk at Acwick; on one leg he had a stocking and no shoe; on the other, a shoe and no stocking. From six of the clock till past nine, I begged him to go with me; but to no purpose. He swore terrible when he saw me mount my horse. I went that day over Tuscarora Hill to Jacob Piat's in a very great rain; and over Kititany Hill the next day, to James Dunning. On the 10th, on nine of the clock in the morning, I came to Carlisle, light at William Buhanon's, where I found Andrew M. He welcomed me with shaking hands, called me a one side, asked pardon for offense given. He was arrived there the day before. He never stopped at his own house but for an hour, for fear of failing in meeting me. He is now gone to Virginia."

Montour probably remained in Maryland or Virginia until about the middle of December; or else he returned there again before that time; as Governor Sharpe wrote of his presence in the camp at Will's Creek (Cumberland), on December 10th. Before the end of that month, however, he was back at his home in Shearman's Valley, near Harris's Ferry. John Harris wrote to Edward Shippen from Paxtang, December 28, 1754: "This week Captain Andrew Montour has made his interest so good with my Bro. William Harris as to persuade him to go with him to our camp [at Will's Creek], and engages that he shall receive a lieutenant's commission under him. . . . Their company of white men I expect to have completed by Monday next, or day following. They expect to march for Will's Creek by the way of Oughwick, in order to take a number of Indians with them. Some Indians that's here leaves their families and sets off with them with all cheerfulness imaginable; and I'll assure you upon my brother's inclining to go, the young men about here enlisted immediately, with the small encouragement I gave them, which was but my desire; and I hope that this company will act their part so well as to be a credit to our River Men, which almost the whole consists of." Two days later, Captain Montour himself sent a letter to Secretary Peters, written for him by the hand of John Harris, in which he said: "I design to-morrow to march with my company, men raised here, for Will's Creek, by the way of Oughwick. I leave under the care of John Harris two Indian families. . . . All the men of the above said Indian families goes to the Camp with me cheerfully, and are of the Mingoes; and were at the Skirmish when La Force was taken [the first battle of Great Meadows] and his men."

How long Andrew Montour remained at Will's Creek is not certain; but he was there again in the spring, and on General Braddock's arrival at the camp at Fort Cumberland, May 10, 1755, that personage found Montour there; and Croghan, with about fifty warriors, soon afterwards joined the army. Braddock wrote Governor Morris, May 20th, that he had taken Croghan and Montour into the service, and had engaged the Indians to go over the mountains with him. Before the march began from Fort Cumberland, Croghan commanded forty-four Indians; but when the army reached Little Meadows, there were but seven in his company, the remainder, having been dismissed by Braddock, had gone with their families back to Aughwick, or proceeded to Allegheny and elsewhere.

Montour and Croghan marched with Braddock, and both took part in the disastrous defeat at the mouth of Turtle Creek. The seven Indians who fought with the English in that battle, received the thanks of the Governor and Council at Philadelphia in August, 1755. Their names were: Scarrooyady, Cashuwayon, Froson, Kahuktodon, Attschechokatha Kashwughdaniunto (or The Belt of Wampum), and Dyioquraio. The Governor addressed them all as Indians of the Six Nations. They accompanied Montour to Philadelphia in August, arriving there on the 13th. Montour and Weiser acted as interpreters at several conferences held with these Indians, and also with a number of Owendats (Wyandots), who had come to Philadelphia on August 8th, carrying messages of friendship from their old men, who lived "on this side Lake Erie, at a place called Deonandady." After the Wyandots had started for home, Scarrooyady, the Oneida chief, informed the Governor, through Wesier and Montour, why the most of the Indians had left Braddock before he had reached the Monongahela. "Brother, the Governor of Pennsylvania," began his message, "and all the English on this Continent; it is now well known to you how unhappily we have been defeated by the French near Minongelo. We must let you know that it was the pride and ignorance of that great general that came from England. He is now dead; but he was a bad man when he was alive; he looked upon us as dogs; would never hear anything that was said to him. We often endeavored to advise him, and to tell him of the danger he was in with his soldiers; but he never appeared pleased with us, and that was the reason a great many of our warriors left him, and would not be under his command. Brethren: We would advise you not to give up the point; though we have in a manner been chastised from above. But let us unite our strength. You are very numerous, and all the English governors along your seashore can raise men enough. Don't let those that come from over the great sea be concerned any more. They are unfit to fight in the woods. Let us go ourselves, we that came out of this ground. We may be assured to conquer the French."

Montour and Scarrooyady, after leaving Philadelphia, proceeded by way of Harris's Ferry to Shamokin; from which place the latter sent a message to the Governor on September 11th, telling him that the Six Nations had sent a large black belt of wampum to the Delawares at Shamokin, ordering them "to lay aside their petticoats, and clap on nothing but a breech-clout," and come with speed to their assistance, in the war against the French; and farther, that he, Scarrooyady, was gathering a company of Indians to go against the French, and had enlisted as his lieutenants, among others, John, James-Logan, and John-Petty, the three sons of Shekallamy. Andrew Montour also, according to a report received from Washington, joined this party.

On October 15th or 16th, a party of fourteen Delaware Indians from Kittanning at Allegheny, under the lead of Kickenepaulin, fell upon Gabriel's settlement at Mahanoy Creek, on the west side of the Susquehanna River, five miles below Shamokin, where they killed or carried off some twenty-five persons, and destroyed their houses. John Harris raised a company of forty-six men, and, on October 23d, they proceeded up the river, for the purpose of burying the dead. Learning that they had already been buried, the company went on to Shamokin, where they spent the night of the 24th. "They were seemingly well received," wrote Conrad Weiser to the Governor, six days later, "but found a great number of strange Indians, though Delawares [from the Ohio], all painted black, which gave suspicion. Thomas McKee told his companions that he did not like them, and the next morning, that is, last Saturday, he got up early, in order to go back, but they did not see any of the strangers; they were gone before them. Andrew Montour was there, *painted as the rest*. He advised our people not to go the same road they came, but to keep this side of the Susquehanna and go the old road; but when they came to the parting of the roads, a majority was for going the highest and best road, and so crossed the Susquehanna, contrary to Andrew Montour's counsel, in order to go down on the west side of that river as far as Mahanoy. When they came to John Penn's Creek, in going down the bank, they were fired upon from this [the south] side by Indians that had waylaid them. Some dropped down dead; the rest fled and made towards the Susquehanna, and came to this side and so home as well as they could. Twenty-six of them were missing and not heard of as yet, last Monday evening." [1]

John Harris sent the Governor a report of this expedition, dated, "Paxtang, ye 28th October, 1755," in which he wrote:

The Indians on the West Branch of the Susquehanna certainly killed our inhabitants on Penn's Creek; and there are a hatchet and two English scalps sent by them up the North Branch, to desire them to strike with them, if they are men.

[1] See also, *Penna. Archives*, ii., 459.

The Indians are all assembling themselves at Shamokin to counsel; a large body of them were there four days ago. I cannot learn their intentions, but seems Andrew Montour and Monacatootha [Scarrooyady] are to bring down the news from them. There is not a sufficient number of them to oppose the enemy; and, perhaps, they will join the enemy against us. There is no dependence on Indians, and we are in imminent danger.

I got certain information from Andrew Montour and others that there is a body of French, with fifteen hundred Indians, coming upon us —Picks, Ottaways, Orandox, Delawares, Shawanese, and a number of the Six Nations,—and are now not many days' march from this Province and Virginia, which are appointed to be attacked. At the same time, some of the Shamokin Indians seem friendly, and others appear like enemies.

Montour knew many days ago of the Indians being on their march against us before he informed; for which I said as much to him as I thought prudent, considering the place I was in.

In a letter written the next day by Harris to Edward Shippen, at Lancaster, the former states, that "Andrew Montour and others, at Shamokin, desired me to take care; that there was a party of forty Indians out many days, and intended to burn my house and destroy myself and family."

On November 2d, Colonel John Armstrong wrote from Carlisle to Secretary Peters: "There are no inhabitants on Juniata, nor on Tuscarora, by this time; my brother, William, being just come in. Montour and Monaghatootha are agoing to the Governor. The former is greatly suspected of being an enemy in his heart. 'T is hard to tell. You can compare what they say to the Governor with what I have wrote."

Montour and Scarrooyady were at Paxtang November 1st, and delivered a message to John Harris and others, who forwarded it to the Governor. Among other things, the message contained the information that "about twelve days ago the Delawares sent for Andrew Montour to go to the Big Island, on which, he [Scarrooyady, or Monacatootha] and Montour, with three more Indians, went up immediately, and found there about six of the Delawares and four Shawanese, who informed them that they had received a hatchet from the French, on purpose to kill what game they could meet with, and to be used against the English if they proved saucy." On the 8th, Montour and Scarrooyady were at Philadelphia, and gave the Governor further details of their trip to the Big Island. On the afternoon of the same day, the Oneida chief appeared before the Governor, his Council, and the Provincial Assembly, and told them of his journey up the North Branch of the Susquehanna, "as far as where the Nanticokes live," which journey he had taken in the interest of the English. It was at this meeting that Scarrooyady threw his belts down upon the table before the coldly indifferent members of the Quaker Assembly, and told them that if they would not fight with the Six Nations, the latter would go somewhere else for protection.

Whether he meant that they would go to the French or to one of the other colonies, is not certain; but, possibly, the latter; as Montour by this time had doubtless received the following letter, written to him from Winchester by Colonel George Washington, October 10, 1755:[1]

> DEAR MONTOUR—I wrote some time ago a letter of invitation from Fort Cumberland desiring yourself, your family, and friendly Indians, to come and reside among us; but that letter not coming to hand, I am induced to send a second express with the same invitation, being pleased that I have it in my power to do something for you on a better footing than ever it has been done. I was greatly enraptured when I heard you were at the head of 300 Indians on a march towards Venango [from Big Island], being satisfied that your hearty attachment to our glorious cause, your courage, of which I have had very great proofs, and your presence amongst the Indians, would animate their just indignation to do something noble, something worthy themselves, and honourable to you. I hope you will use your interest (as I know you have much), in bringing our brothers once more to our service. Assure them, as you truly may, that nothing which I can do shall be wanting to make them happy. Assure them also, that as I have the chief command, I am invested with power to treat them as brethren and allies, which, I am sorry to say, they have not been of late. Recommend me kindly to our good friend, Monocatootha, and others; tell them how happy it would make Conotocaurious [Washington's Indian name] to have an opportunity of taking them by the hand at Fort Cumberland, and how glad he would be to treat them as brothers of our Great King beyond the waters. Flattering myself that you will come, I doubt not but you'll bring as many of them with you as possible; as that will afford me what alone I want; that is, an opportunity of doing something equal to your wishes. I am, Dear Montour,
> Your real Friend and Assur'd H'ble Servant,
> GO. WASHINGTON.
> N. B. I doubt not but you have heard of the ravages committed on our frontiers by the French Indians, and, I suppose, French themselves. I am now on my march against them, and hope to give them cause of repenting their rashness.

In the middle of November, Montour and Scarrooyady started from Philadelphia, making their way up the North Branch of the Susquehanna to Onondaga, on a mission from the Governor to the chiefs of the Six Nations. They journeyed with Conrad Weiser as far as Tulpehocken, at which place they were threatened with death by the Germans who had gathered there for defense. Their errand was to ascertain the sentiments

---

[1] This letter is in the handwriting of Kirkpatrick, the secretary of Washington, but is signed by the latter. Washington wrote to Dinwiddie on the following day, enclosing a copy of this letter, which, he said "favours a little of flattery, &c., but this I hope is justifiable on such occasions."

of the Indians along the river toward the English, and to persuade the Six Nations to take forcible measures for bringing back the Delawares and Shawnees to their allegiance. They reached Oghquaga (now Windsor, Broome County, New York), on the Upper Susquehanna, January 4th, from which place they sent messages to Governor Morris, written for them by the Rev. Gideon Hawley, a missionary among the Six Nations at that point. In Mr. Hawley's letter, they informed the Governor that with much difficulty they had come through the settlements of the Delawares along the Susquehanna, and barely escaped with their lives. Montour added, that if the Delawares had known their business to the Six Nations, Scarrooyady and he would never have gotten through.

Governor Morris sent a copy of their message to Conrad Weiser on February 2d, and wrote to him: "I was glad to find that instead of their having deserted our interest and gone over to the enemy, as was most falsely reported, they had faithfully pursued their journey and delivered their message, like the trusty, honest friends we always looked upon them to be; and I desire you will, as soon as you can, write to some proper persons in Lancaster, Cumberland, and York counties [*i.e.*, to Armstrong, Harris, and others], to let them know this, in order to remove the bad impressions and prejudices that have prevailed there against them."

The two messengers returned from the country of the Six Nations by way of Albany and New York, reaching Philadelphia on the 21st of March, 1756. Six days later, they appeared before the Provincial Council, and made a report of their mission. They had gone from Tulpehocken by way of Thomas McKee's trading-post to Shamokin; thence through Laughpaughpitton's Town and Nescopeck to Wyoming. Here they found a large number of Delawares, with some Shawnees, Mohicans, and Six Nation Indians. Twelve miles above Wyoming (now Plymouth), they came to Asserughney, a town of the Delawares. This was doubtless Hazirok,[1] the town of the Minisink Delawares, also called by them Lechaweke, which was visited by David Zeisberger in October, 1753. It was located on the north side of the Lackawanna River, at its mouth. Some twenty miles farther up Susquehanna was another town, called Chinkanning (Tunkhannock), where they found Teedyuscung, with some Delawares and Nanticokes. Teedyuscung, they reported, had been made a king, or sachem, since his visit to Philadelphia the summer before. Fifty miles above Chinkanning, the messengers came to Diahogo (Tioga), a town of Mohicans, Delawares, and Minsis; there they found ninety men. Twenty-five miles beyond was the deserted Indian town of Owegy; and thence, twenty miles, Chughnut. Otseningo was five miles above Chughnut, and at the former place they found thirty cabins and about

[1] Pronounced *Asserughney*, or *Hazirok*, by the Iroquois; *Solocka* by the Delawares.

sixty men, Nanticokes, Conoys, and Onondagas. Fourteen miles more brought them to Oneoquague [Oghquaga], where they had sent the message to the Governor written by the hand of the Rev. Gideon Hawley. From thence they proceeded through Teyonnoderre (thirty miles), and Teyoneandakt (thirty miles) to Caniyeuke, or Teyeondarago, the Lower Mohawk Town, about two miles from Fort Johnson and thirty-eight miles from Albany. While at Wyoming, their lives were threatened by a party of eighty Delaware warriors, who came after their arrival. "All the way from Wyoming to Diahogo, a day never passed," said Scarrooyady, "without meeting with some warriors, six, eight, or ten in a party; and twenty under command of Cutfinger Pete, going after the eighty warriors which we saw at Wyoming. We believe Diahogo is about eighty miles by the way we went from Wyoming, and all the way we met parties of Delawares going to join the eighty warriors there."

As a result of the conference with Scarrooyady and Montour, the Governor and Council made a declaration of war against the Delaware Indians, and offered rewards for Indian scalps. The Assembly requested the Governor to make the messengers aware of its gratitude for the services rendered by them.

Scarrooyady went from Pennsylvania to the Oneida country a few days after this meeting, whither he was accompanied by Montour. The latter appeared as interpreter May 10, 1756, at a meeting at Fort Johnson, between Scarrooyady and other Oneida chiefs and Sir William Johnson. In June, he was at the camp on Lake Onondaga as an interpreter. On July 25th, at Fort Johnson, the hatchet was given to some chiefs of the Six Nations, Shawnees, and other tribes, by Sir William Johnson, who desired that some of the Six Nations should make use of it in Canada. Montour was appointed a captain. With some of the other chiefs, he sang the war-song. Some warriors joined his party, and the war-dance began. In the celebration which followed, some of Montour's warriors sold their weapons and clothes to the Tuscaroras and Mohicans for peltries with which to buy more rum. Sir William Johnson was obliged to equip them a second time. On September 10th, Montour appears again as interpreter at Fort Johnson. On the 20th, Sir William, with Croghan and Montour, and all the Indians they could assemble, marched to the relief of the army, besieged at Fort Edward. He was ordered back by General Webb, and reached Fort Johnson November 2d.

A conference was held at Fort Johnson, November 17 to 23d, with sundry chiefs and warriors of all the Six Nations, at which Montour appeared as interpreter.

Another conference was held at the same place, June 13, 1757, at which an Onondaga chief spoke of Sir William Johnson having sent Captains Montour and Butler to the Onondaga Castle during the past winter, to let the Six Nations know that he expected they "should use the hatchet against the French."

Montour acted as interpreter at Fort Johnson, September 12, 1757, at a meeting between five chiefs of the Mohawks and Senecas, and four deputies from the Cherokees, to all of whom Montour tendered the calumet of peace.

After the burning of the settlement at the German Flats, in the Mohawk Valley, by the French, November 12, 1757, General Johnson despatched George Croghan and Montour to the Oneida Castle, to ascertain why the Oneidas had not given the English notice of the enemy's approach. They met the principal chief of the Oneidas at Fort Herkimer, November 30th, who informed them, and the German officers present, that the Oneidas had sent a warning to the settlers at German Flats some fifteen days before, but that it had been received with indifference.

Sir William Johnson set out for Lake George with two hundred Indians in the latter part of June, 1758, for the purpose of joining General Abercrombie in his attack upon the French fort of Ticonderoga. From his "Camp in the Woods within ten miles of Fort Edward," Johnson wrote Abercrombie on the morning of July 5th: "I arrived here last night with near two hundred Indians. Mr. Croghan and some of the Indian officers are within a day's march of me with about one hundred more, as I hear by letters from him." As Montour was a Captain in Johnson's service at this time, it is probable he was in the Croghan party. The Indians under Johnson took part in the attack, and witnessed the cowardly retreat of Abercrombie and his army.

Captain Montour attended with George Croghan at the great Council at Easton, October 8th to 26th, between the Governors of Pennsylvania and New Jersey, and the chiefs of the Six Nations, Delawares, Nanticokes, Tuteloes, and other tribes. Under the name of Henry Montour, he is referred to in the minutes of the meetings as interpreter in the Six Nations and Delaware languages.

At the close of this treaty, Croghan and Montour left at once for the Ohio. The French burned and abandoned Fort Duquesne on November 24th, and General Forbes's army occupied its site the next day. On the 27th, Croghan and Montour crossed the Allegheny River, and went to Logstown the day following. On the 29th, they reached Sauconk, the Delaware Town on the Ohio, one mile below the mouth of Big Beaver Creek. Here they were joined by some Delaware Indians from Kuskuskies, accompanied by Frederick Post and Lieutenant Hays. Croghan's Journal of this visit is printed in the third volume of the *Pennsylvania Archives* (First Series, pages 560–563); but it is erroneously headed "Journal of Frederick Post." He states that, "at Beaver Creek [Sauconk] there is thirty-eight houses, all built by the French for the Indians, some with stone chimneys."

Captain Montour, who now went by the name of Henry Montour, acted as interpreter at a conference between Colonel Bouquet and the Delaware chiefs at Fort Pitt on the 4th of December.

He returned to Philadelphia with Croghan and was present as interpreter at a conference held there on February 8 and 9, 1759, between General Forbes and some Indians from Buccaloons or Canawago Town on the Allegheny ("about ninety miles above Venango"). On the 20th, Montour reported to the Governor that these Indians were dissatisfied with the answer they had received from General Forbes, and desired Andrew himself to return with them to their Town. Montour told them that he was an officer, and subject to the General's orders.

Croghan wrote to Captain Horatio Gates from Bedford, May 25th, that he had sent off Captain Montour with three Indians, to collect all the Indians he could, for the purpose of meeting Croghan in council at Pittsburgh.

On July 11th, George Croghan, as Sir William Johnson's deputy, held a conference at Pittsburgh with a number of the chiefs of the Six Nations, Delawares, Shawnees, and Wyandots, at which Montour acted as interpreter. Similar conferences were held at the same place by General Stanwix, on October 24, 1759, and by General Monckton on August 12, 1760.

Monckton wrote from Fort Pitt to Bouquet at Presqu' Isle, August 23, 1760: "Croghan proposes to send Montour up soon. If kept sober, he will do well."

Montour went with Chief Shingas to Presqu' Isle in the first part of September, and in company with Major Robert Rogers and George Croghan, started for Detroit, November 4th, at the head of a small army, to take possession of the Western posts, which had been surrendered by the French. The army was divided into two bodies, one, occupying nineteen batteaux, sailed over Lake Erie; the other, composed of about eighty men, marched by land. Croghan commanded one of the boats; Montour headed a land party, composed of twenty Indians of the Six Nations, Shawnees, and Delawares. They occupied the post of Detroit on November 29th. Croghan's Journal of the expedition is printed in one of the volumes of Thwaites's series of *Early Western Travels*. On December 8th, Croghan writes: "Major Rogers set off for Misselemachinack, with whom I sent Captain Montour and four Indians who were well acquainted with the country and the Indian nations that inhabit it." They passed up the west side of Lake Huron, about ninety miles, but were unable to proceed farther without snowshoes, or to cross the lake, on account of the ice; and so they returned, reaching Detroit on December 21st Croghan had started for Fort Pitt ten days before. Rogers set out with his Rangers for the same place on December 23d, and was doubtless accompanied by Montour. Rogers's Journal of this march will be given in a later chapter. He arrived at Fort Pitt on January 23, 1761.

On the 22d of May, two Delaware war chiefs from Ohio, Grey-Eyes (later known as White-Eyes), or Coquetakeghton, and Winghynunt (Wingenund), met Governor Hamilton in Council at Philadelphia. They were sent by their chief men at Ohio, Tamaqui, or King Beaver, and Netalwalemut (Netawatwes, or New Comer). Andrew Montour acted as one of the interpreters at this conference. In August and September he accompanied Sir William Johnson from Niagara to Detroit, and narrowly escaped being drowned by the upsetting of his boat while crossing Lake Erie.

Lieutenant Mayer, Commandant at Fort Sandusky, on Lake Erie, wrote Bouquet at Fort Pitt, September 30th: "Montour, left here by Croghan as interpreter, is tired of the post."

George Croghan wrote Johnson from Fort Pitt, May 10, 1762, that he had advanced £80 and "engaged for as much more," to Captain Montour. On July 10th, he wrote again, stating that he had drawn on Johnson for Captain Montour's pay and his own, and that he was then setting out for the meeting at Lancaster.

Governor Hamilton met 557 Indians, chiefs and warriors of the Six Nations, Shawnees, Miamis, Delawares, and others, in a great Council at Lancaster in 1762, which lasted from August 12th to 29th. Montour was one of the interpreters.

On May 5, 1763, Sir William Johnson wrote Henry Montour, instructing him to proceed to Chilliequagey (Chillisquaque, on the West Branch of the Susquehanna), and endeavor to allay the fears of the Indians there about their lands, co-operating for that purpose with Mr. Thomas McKee, Assistant Deputy Indian Agent. On July 3d, John Harris wrote to Colonel Bouquet, at Carlisle, stating that Andrew Montour had arrived at Paxtang from the Upper Susquehanna; that he had been through the Indian villages, and found the Indians "inveterate and inclined for war"; that he would have Montour proceed to Carlisle and give Bouquet the information in person. Bouquet wrote to the Governor from Carlisle the next day that Andrew Montour reported that when he left Sir William Johnson, nothing was known there of the insurrection. His Indian family and other Indians asked Bouquet to be allowed to come to the settlements during the war. Montour was at Fort Augusta (Shamokin) on his way up the West Branch, July 23d. He returned August 7th, bringing news of the attacks on Fort Pitt and Fort Ligonier.

In the narrative of a participant in the battle of Muncy Hill, printed by Loudon in the second volume of his *Indian Narratives*, the narrator tells, that "in September, 1763, about one hundred of us went to take the Indian town at the Great Island, and went up to Fort Augusta, where we sent a man forward to see whether Andrew Menture was there; but he was not. He asked where he was, and was told he had gone to the plantation. We had apprehended that Menture knew of our coming and had gone to inform the Indians at the Town called Great Island, or Monsey Town. . . . When we had crossed the River [North Branch], we saw Menture coming down [the West Branch] in a canoe, with a hog and some corn which he had brought from his plantation. When he came near, we called to him, upon which he landed and enquired our business; which we told him, and asked his advice, whether it was proper to proceed or not. He said that they were bad Indians, and we might use them as we pleased. We went that night to Menture's plantation [near the mouth of Chillisquaque Creek], and next morning crossed the Monsey Hill."

Croghan wrote to Johnson from Philadelphia, December 15th, giving him an account of Andrew Montour's distressing circumstances, and praising his integrity and faithfulness. On the 19th, five days after the murder of the Conestoga Indians by the Paxtang Boys at Lancaster, Captain Montour delivered to the newly arrived Governor, John Penn, an address of welcome from the Conestoga Indians of Conestoga Town, sent a few days before their massacre.

January 20, 1764, Ferrall Wade, of Philadelphia, wrote Johnson, complaining of Montour's refusal to honor a draft. On February 9th, Johnson sent instructions to Montour to lead a party of Indians against the town of Kanestio, and destroy it. Twelve days later, Henry Montour, William Hare, and John Johnston, Indian officers, wrote Sir William from Kaun au Wau Roharie, asking for money to pay for a feast to their Indian warriors, and telling of the opposition of some Indians of Old Oneida to their expedition. On the same day, Johnson wrote to Montour, urging him to begin vigorous hostilities, and offering bounties to Indians for the persons or heads of two Delaware chiefs. February 28th, Montour and his brother officers wrote from Auqvage (Oghquaga) on the Upper Susquehanna, relating the success of their expedition against Kanestio, and the capture of twenty-nine of the enemy, who were on their way against the English settlements. Three days later, they wrote again, telling of the departure of the Oneidas with their prisoners for Johnson Hall, condemning Captain Bull (a son of Teedyuscung), and his warriors among the captives to severe punishment, and asking for a reinforcement of white men and Indians, in order to destroy the Indian settlements along the "Dioaga" River. The war party reached Johnson

Hall, March 9th, with forty-one Delaware prisoners, including Captain Bull, who were chiefly from Kanestio. Captain Bull and thirteen of his warriors were sent to New York and confined in jail, the remainder of the prisoners being distributed among the Six Nations' castles to take the places of deceased relatives.

On April 7th, Montour, Hare, and Johnston wrote from "Diogoa," reporting that the Delawares had fled before their arrival at Kanestio, but that they, with 140 warriors, had destroyed three large Delaware towns, all the out villages, and 130 scattered Indian houses, very large and well built, together with horses and cattle; and that they had made "peaceable times" in that country.

Johnson wrote Captain Montour, April 28th, instructing him to take his Indian party to Niagara, by way of Oswego; to guard the Carrying Place, as well as Navy Island and the vessels; to co-operate with Colonel Bradstreet's expedition, taking command of all the Indians connected with it; and to require of all friendly nations the delivery of "all whites, negroes, and French amongst them." On the same day he wrote to Governor Colden, announcing that Captain Montour had arrived at Johnson Hall with some of his party the day before, and brought the scalp of the Delaware chief's nephew; that on the first instant, "Captain Montour, with 140 Indians and some white men had set out from Oghquaga, and on arriving at the first of the enemy's towns, found the same abandoned, which he burned; it consisted of 36 houses, built of square logs, with good chimneys; from thence he went to and burned another of 30 houses, with four villages, and then proceeded to Kanestio, which he likewise destroyed; it consisted of sixty good houses, with three and four fire-places in each of them; here and at the other towns he found a large quantity of Indian corn, which he destroyed, as also a great number of implements, which they had taken from the inhabitants, with several new saddles, etc., several horses, horned cattle, and swine, the most of them in such a poor condition that he killed them all, but about a dozen, which they carried off with them."

In the *Journal* of Captain John Montresor there is an entry made under date of June 13th, while he was at the Niagara portage, stating that the "Indians got drunk in their encampment, and were going to kill Montour."

Bradstreet's army reached Detroit on August 27th, and left a garrison there. The main body of the troops began their return by way of Lake Erie on September 14th. On the 29th, a court of inquiry was held at the encampment near the Carrying Place at Sandusky Lake, before Lieut. Colonel Israel Putnam, and Majors Daly and Le Hunte, for the examination of Henry Montour and John Johnston, Captains in the Indian service, regarding instructions given them by Sir William Johnson. Captain Montresor states in his *Journal*, that their answer was, "to make peace with all those that shall offer it, and comply with the same terms proposed them by Col. Bradstreet; if not, to carry on the war against them."

Daniel Campbell wrote Johnson from Schenectady, December 16th, that Captain Montour had drawn a bill on him.

The *Calendar* of the Johnson Manuscripts shows but three references to Andrew Montour during the next three years, and these refer to his accounts. John Johnston wrote to Sir William Johnson on April 13, 1765, regarding the accounts "of Johney Montour's Father." Francis Wade wrote from Philadelphia, March 17, 1766, regarding Montour's draft; and Thomas McKee sent Johnson from Fort Augusta (Shamokin), October 3, 1766, a bill for articles delivered to a party of Tuscaroras and to Captain Henry Montour.

The *Journal* of Zeisberger and Schmick, kept at Friedenshutten, or Wyalusing, on the North Branch of the Susquehanna, states, under date of April 28, 1766: "Andrew Montour passed through." Under date of May 26th, Zeisberger (who had set out for Onondaga) writes: "To Oweke, an outpost of the Cayugas [Owego, at the mouth of Owego Creek], where they keep a chief posted as a sentinel. . . . Met Andrew Montour, en route for the Ohio, thence to go with Croghan to the Western Indians."[1]

While there are no records to show it, it is probable that Montour accompanied Croghan and his party from Fort Pitt down the Ohio River to Fort Chartres and thence down the Mississippi to New Orleans, in the Summer and Fall of 1766. Croghan's party returned by way of New York.

A Council was held at Fort Pitt from April 26 to May 9, 1768, between George Croghan, Deputy Agent for Indian Affairs, John Allen and Joseph Shippen, Commissioners for the Province of Pennsylvania, the Commandant and officers of the Fort, and 1103 chiefs and warriors of the Six Nations, Delawares, Munsies, Shawnees, Mohickons, and Wyandots, besides their women and children. Henry Montour acted as interpreter.

A great Council or Congress was held at Fort Stanwix, October 24th to November 5th by Sir William Johnson, the Governor and the Chief Justice of New Jersey, Commissioners from Virginia and Pennsylvania, Croghan and Claus, Deputy Indian Agents, and some 2200 Indian chiefs and warriors, including those of the Six Nations, Delawares, Shawnees, and all the chiefs of the Upper Nations. Andrew Montour, John Butler, and Philip Phillips acted as interpreters. At this Congress a definite boundary line was established between the lands of the whites and the Indians. This line extended from the point where Canada Creek

[1] Egle's *Notes and Queries*, ix., 206, 211 (1897).

flows into Wood Creek (a short distance west of Fort Stanwix), south along Tianaderha (Unadilla) Creek and to the Mohawk Branch of the Delaware, down that branch to a point directly east of Owegy (or Oswegy) on the Susquehanna, thence to Owegy and down the North Branch of Susquehanna to Awandae (Towanda) Creek, thence up that Creek and along the north side of Burnett's Hills to the head of Tiadaghton Creek, thence down that Creek and along the south side of the West Branch to its head nearest, in a direct line, to Adigo or Kittanning, thence to Adigo, thence along the south side of the Ohio River to the mouth of Cherokee (now Tennessee) River.

On the 22d of January, 1769, James Tilghman wrote to Sir William Johnson from Philadelphia, expressing a desire to purchase the land at French Margaret's on the north bank of the West Branch, which Andrew Montour held under a "writing of preference." This land comprised 880 acres, covering the site of the present Montoursville, in Lycoming County, Pennsylvania, at the mouth of Loyalsock Creek. It included land on both sides of that Creek, and was granted to Andrew Montour, October 29, 1768. The land was surveyed November 3, 1769, as "Montour's Reserve."

A certificate in the records of the Pennsylvania Land Office, made by John Lukens, Surveyor General, June 17, 1785, recites the survey of this land, for Andrew Montour, and adds: "and whereas, the said Andrew, by the name of Henry Montour, by deed dated 12th Augt., 1771, conveyed the same to Robt. Lettes Hooper," etc.

On December 22, 1761, Governor James Hamilton issued a warrant to the Surveyor General to lay out a tract of land for Andrew or Henry Montour, in Sackson's Cove, between Kishacoquillas Creek and Juniata River, to contain fifteen hundred acres. Another tract, containing 820 acres, was surveyed for Montour on the head of Penn's Creek, above the Great Spring, the return bearing date May 19, 1767, and the tract given the name, "Succoth." Another tract was returned on the same day, as having been surveyed for Montour. It was called "Sharron," and contained 1710 acres. In April, 1769, there was also granted to Henry Montour a tract of land called *Oughsaragoh*, containing 300 acres, situated on the south side of the Ohio River, "including his improvement opposite to the Long [Montour's] Island, about nine miles below Fort Pitt. The name "Oughsaragoh" means "the place of Oughsara," or "Eghisara," Montour's Iroquois name.

From this time on, Andrew Montour's life seems to have been passed in obscurity. In an affidavit made by one Richard Brown before Arthur St. Clair, at Fort Pitt, September, 7, 1771, he mentions that Andrew McConnell had recently seen and talked with Andrew Montour at Fort Pitt concerning a murder of two Indians by a white man.

If, as Mrs. Murray states, in her *Old Tioga Point*, Mary Montour, Andrew's niece, was the wife of the White Mingo, a Six Nations chief, who lived at Fort Pitt from 1759 to 1777, it is possible that Andrew Montour spent his latter years at their house. It stood at the mouth of Pine Creek, on the east side, and was known in 1769 as the "White Mingo's Castle."[1]

Andrew Montour died prior to 1775, and Dr. Egle quotes Isaac Craig[2] as saying that tradition gave the place of his death as being on Montour's Island. "I have always been told," writes Craig, "that Andrew Montour died there, and have had his grave pointed out. Although I have no written authority for it, I am certain that the tradition must be true."

Captain Andrew Montour was twice or thrice married, first to a grand-daughter of Chief Allumappees, hereditary sachem of the Delawares; and second, to an Indian woman whose English name was Sarah. At one place in the Pennsylvania records, his wife's name (in 1768) is given as Catherine.[3] An entry in the Minutes of the Provincial Council under date of April 21, 1756, recites that: "On the 20th, the Indians [Scarrooyady, Montour, Newcastle, and others] had a long conference with the Governor. They put Andrew Montour's children under his care, as well the three that are here, to be independent of the mother, as a boy of twelve years old, that he had by a former wife, a grand-daughter of Allomipis. They added that he had a girl among the Delawares, called Kayodaghscroony, or Madelina, and desired she might be distinguished, enquired after, and sent for, which was promised."[4] John Montour, the oldest son of Andrew, was born about 1744. He was educated by Provost Smith at the Philadelphia Academy, and seems to have lived with his father at Fort Pitt at the time of the latter's death. He took part in the Dunmore War of 1774; and in 1775, as Captain John Montour, asked compensation for the lands of his father. He served in the Revolutionary Army, in the West, and commanded a company of Delaware warriors in 1782, under Colonel Brodhead, being distinguished for his valor and his friendship to the American cause. He resided on Montour's Island for a time, and was living as late as 1789. Isaac Craig may possibly have confused John Montour with his father in stating that the latter died on Montour's Island.

---

[1] Darlington's *Gist*, p. 189.
[2] Egle's *Notes and Queries*, Second Series, 441; Third Series, i., 124.
[3] *Archives*, Third Series, i., 240.
[4] *Penna. Col. Rec.*, vii., 95.

CHAPTER IX

THE FRANKSTOWN PATH

IN a preceding chapter it has been pointed out that the earliest path used by the Pennsylvania Indians in their journeys from the Susquehanna to the Ohio was probably the trail that led by way of the West Branch Valley, Bald Eagle Creek, Chinklaclamouche, and Punxsatawney. At certain seasons of the year it was possible to cover part of this route by the use of canoes, the West Branch of the Susquehanna being navigable in high water as far up as the point marked on early maps "Canoe Place," in the northwest corner of the present county of Cambria, not far from Grant Post-office. Near the mouth of Loyalsock Creek, where now stands the village of Montoursville, in Lycoming County, this trail was joined by the Sheshequin Path, which came from the northeast. That was the path used by the Iroquois warriors when coming from the Onondaga country by way of Tioga (now Athens), on their war expeditions to the south and southwest.

A second route westward by way of the Susquehanna was the one which led up the Chemung River from Tioga Point in Bradford County, to the mouth of Cowanesque Creek, thence up that stream to its head, across the plateau forming the present county of Potter to one of the heads of the Allegheny River (probably Oswayo Creek); and thence following the course of that River to the south and west.

Another and more important path to the west, which, if not quite so ancient a trail as the former two, became the principal one soon after the Pennsylvania Traders began to cross the Alleghanies, led from the mouth of the Juniata, along the north side of that stream to what is now Mifflintown, in Juniata County. Here it was joined by the southern Shamokin Path, which came from Shamokin in a southwesterly direction, through the present county of Snyder, crossed West Mahantango Creek at what is now the village of Richfield, and continued on through the present townships of Monroe, Fayette, and Fermanagh, in Juniata County, to the Main Path running westward along the north side of the Juniata.

This path along the Juniata, as used by the Traders, seems to have had several starting places, at points on the west side of the Susquehanna, between Paxtang and Shamokin. One branch may have led directly up the River from the Shawnee towns on Big Island (now Halderman Island), and on the mainland, opposite, at the mouth of the Juniata. If so, the first stage may have been by canoes, as the River, from the Island to what is now the village of Newport, is hemmed in in some places by mountains. Bishop Camerhoff, who travelled along the east bank of the Susquehanna from Paxtang to Shamokin in the winter of 1748, notes in his *Journal*, that, after crossing to the north side of Wiconisco Creek, near its mouth, on January 12th, he came to a house a short distance beyond, where he halted. Here his host informed him that on the west bank of the Susquehanna, opposite to his house, "began the Great Path to the Allegheny country, estimated to be three or four hundred miles distant." This terminus of the Juniata Path to Allegheny must have been in what is now Buffalo Township, Perry County. Some eight to ten miles further up the Susquehanna, on the site of what is now the village of Georgetown, in 1742, Thomas McKee had his upper trading-post, opposite the mouth of West Mahantango Creek. A third branch of the Juniata Path, which was known after 1744 as McKee's Path, led from the Indian village on the west bank of the Susquehanna, opposite McKee's post, in a westerly direction across the present townships of Susquehanna, Greenwood, and Delaware, to the Main Path along the Juniata at what is now Thompsontown, all in Juniata County. The Shamokin branch of this Path, as already stated, crossed the Susquehanna near the site of Sunbury, and ran in a southwestern direction, joining the Main Path at the present Mifflintown. The Juniata Path proceeded thence westwardly over the mountains and through the valleys lying to the north of the Juniata River, to what is now Lewistown, in Mifflin County. Here, in 1731, and for some years before, at the mouth of Kishacoquillas Creek, stood the Shawnee village of Ohesson, of which Kishacoquillas was the head man. The town is called Kishacoquillas Town on Evans's map of 1749, after the name of its chief. This chief died in August, 1754, at the house of Thomas McKee, the Trader. In 1731 the village of Ohesson contained twenty families and sixty men. Robert Buchanan is said, by local historians, to have located at this point before 1755, and established a trading-post. If this tradition be true, he was forced to retire during the period of the French War; but he returned after that war, for he was there in 1762, and obtained a warrant for the land on which Lewistown was afterwards built. He died about 1780.

Rev. Charles Beatty visited the settlements along the Juniata in 1766, on his way, as a missionary, to the Ohio Indians. On Monday, August 25th, of that year, he set out from Captain William Patterson's

Shadow of Death Gap, Looking West.
From a photograph made by the Author in September, 1909.

house, which stood near the site of the present town of Mexico, in Juniata County. His description of the Path westward along the Juniata at that time is as follows: "We travelled up Juniata river eight miles, through a bad road, to a place called the Narrows [now Lewistown Narrows], where a rocky mountain bounds so close upon the river as to leave only a small path along the bank for the most part; and this, for about ten miles, very uneven; at this time also greatly encumbered by trees fallen across it, blown up from the roots some time ago by a hard gale of wind; so that we were obliged to walk some part of the way, and in some places to go along the edge of the water. After riding about twenty-one miles, we came to Mr. Thomas Holt's, much fatigued, where we rested an hour or two, and refreshed ourselves and fed our horses. Not far from his house stood Fort Grenville, erected there the last war, and garrisoned by a small number of provincial troops [one mile west of the present borough of Lewistown]."

Other Traders besides Thomas McKee and Robert Buchanan, who travelled the paths between Shamokin, Wiconisco, and Ohesson, have been referred to in the chapter on the Shamokin Traders.

The Juniata Path proceeded westward from Ohesson, and just before entering Jack's Narrows (the pass through Jack's Mountain), a short distance above the present village of Mount Union, it was joined by the path from Harris's Ferry, or Paxtang, which reached the Juniata by way of Aughwick Valley.

The Paxtang end of the Frankstown, or Juniata Path was by far the most important and most frequently travelled. It must have been used by the Traders as early as 1730–33, when settlements were first begun in the Cumberland Valley, and possibly was used many years before 1730; as the Shawnees who removed from that Valley to the Allegheny from 1727 to 1730, may have travelled by this route. This course of the Path soon became the Main Road from the settled parts of Pennsylvania to the Great West; and for some twenty-five to thirty years it was travelled, back and forth, by the Traders with their pack-horses and by the Indians on their hunting trips or their migrations. In 1756 it was used by Col. John Armstrong in his expedition against the Delaware Indian town of Kittanning, on the Allegheny; and its importance as a main artery of communication between the East and the West ceased only with the construction, in 1758, of the Forbes military road along the course of the more southerly Raystown Path.

Three or four itineraries of the "Main Path to Allegheny" have been preserved, which were made by persons who travelled from Harris's Ferry to Logstown on the Ohio before 1754. Conrad Weiser, the Indian interpreter for Pennsylvania, passed over the road August 11 to 27, 1748, and a Journal of his trip may be found in the *Pennsylvania Colonial*

Records, volume v., pages 348 to 358. Hugh Crawford began trading with the Indians as early as 1739[1]; and George Croghan began before 1742. Hugh Crawford and Andrew Montour gave an account of the road from Philadelphia to the country of the Twightwees, to the Pennsylvania Council, April 16, 1752.[2] Croghan wrote to Secretary Richard Peters on March 23, 1754, giving some of the courses and distances on the road. John Harris, who afterwards founded the city of Harrisburg, carried a message from the Governor of Pennsylvania to George Croghan at Pine Creek, near Logstown, in May, 1753, arriving there on the twelfth of that month. He made the most detailed account of the stations and distances along this Path of any who have written of it; and on his account will be chiefly based the description of the road to be given in this chapter.

First, let us peruse Conrad Weiser's itinerary of the Allegheny Path, written by him five years before Harris's journey. It is as follows:

Augst. 11th, 1748. Set out from my house [he lived about one mile east of Womelsdorf in what is now Berks County], and came to James Galbreath that day, 30 miles.

12th. Came to George Croghan's, 15 miles.

13th. To Robert Dunning's, 20 miles.

14th. To the Tuscarora Path, 30 miles [now Path Valley, Franklin county; through which ran the Tuscarora Path, north and south].

15th and 16th. Lay by, on account of the men coming back, sick, and some other affairs hindering us.

17th. Crossed the Tuscarora Hill, and came to the sleeping-place called the Black Log, 20 miles.

18th. Had a great rain in the afternoon; came within two miles of the Standing Stone, 24 miles.

19th. We travelled but 12 miles; were obliged to dry our things in the afternoon.

20th. Came to Frank's Town; but saw no houses or cabins; here we overtook the goods, because four of George Croghan's hands fell sick; 26 miles.

21st. Lay by, it raining all day.

22nd. Crossed Allegheny Hill and came to the Clear Fields, 16 miles.

23rd. Came to the Shawonese Cabins, 34 miles.

24th. Found a dead man on the road, who had killed himself by drinking too much whiskey. The place being very stony, we could not dig a grave. He, smelling very strong, we covered him with stones and wood, and went on our journey. Came to the Ten Mile Lick, 32 miles.

25th. Crossed Kiskeminetoes Creek and came to Ohio that day, 26 miles.

26th. Hired a canoe; paid 1,000 black wampum for the loan of it to

---

[1] *Magazine West. Hist.*, v., 455.
[2] *Penna. Archives*, ii., 133; *Votes of the Assembly*, iv., 298.

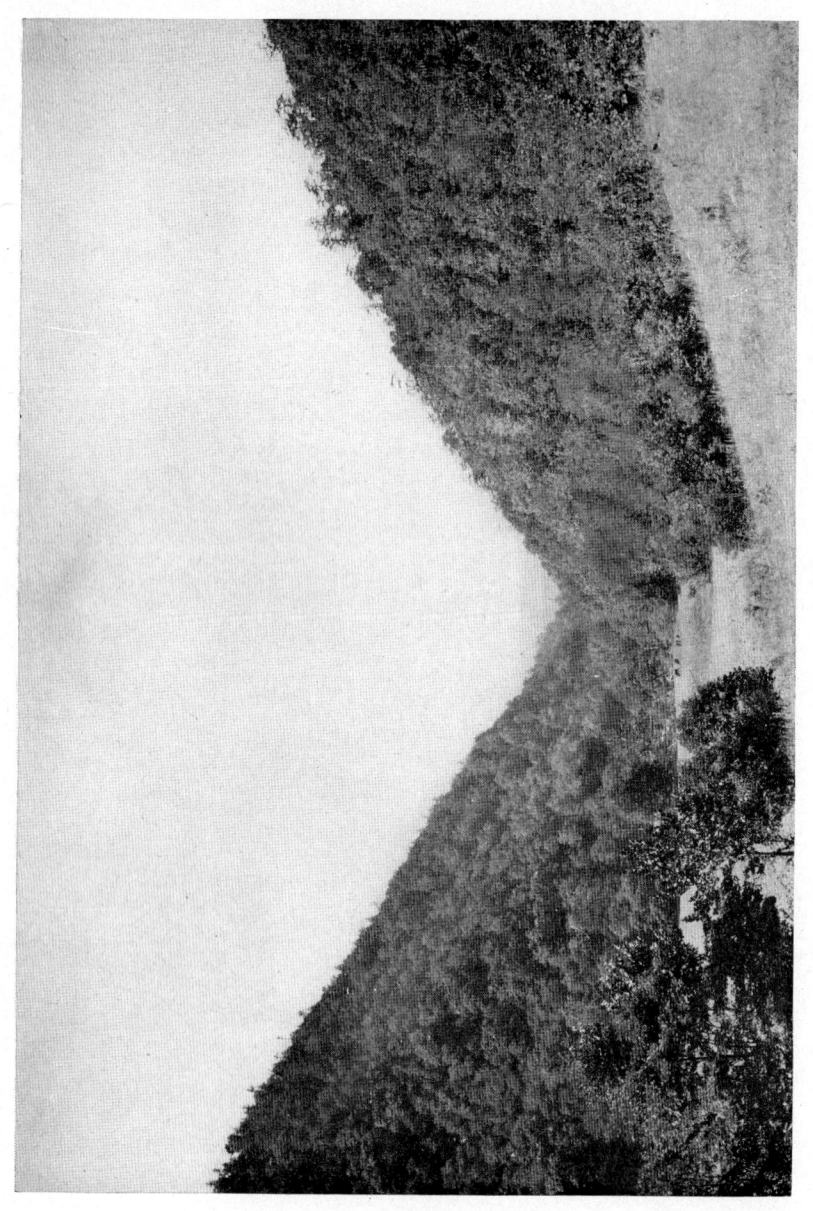

Black Log Gap, Looking West.
From a photograph made by the Author in September, 1909.

Logstown. Our horses being all tired, we went by water; and came that night to a Delaware town. The Indians used us very kindly.

27th. Set off again in the morning, early. Rainy weather. We dined in a Seneka town, where an old Seneka woman [Queen Alliquippa] reigns with great authority. We dined at her house, and they all used us very well. At this and the last mentioned Delaware town, they received us by firing a great many guns; especially at this last place. We saluted the town by firing off four pair of pistols; arrived that evening at Logs Town, and saluted the town as before; the Indians returned about one hundred guns; great joy appeared in their countenances. From the place where we took water, *i.e.*, from the Old Shawones Town, commonly called Chartier's Town, to this place, is about 60 miles by water, and but 35 or 40 by land.

Mr. Weiser finished his mission at Logstown and began his return journey from there, by horseback, September 19, 1748. He rode almost directly east from Logstown, crossing the head waters of Pine Creek, in what is now Allegheny County, near which stream he encamped for the night. His *Journal* proceeds:

20th September, 1748. Left a horse behind that we could not find. Came to the river [the Allegheny, at Chartier's Old Town]. Had a great rain; the river not rideable.

21st. Sent for a canoe, about six miles up the river, to a Delaware town.[1] An Indian brought one; we paid him a blanket; got over the river about twelve o'clock. Crossed Kiskaminity Creek, and came that night to the Round Hole, about twelve miles from the river.

22nd. The weather cleared up; we travelled this day about 35 miles. Came by the place where we had buried the body of John Quen; but found the bears had pulled him out, and left nothing but a few naked bones and some old rags.

23rd. Crossed the head of the West Branch of the Susquehanna; about noon came to the Cheasts [the two Chest Creeks, in what is now Cambria County]. This night we had a great frost; our kettle, standing about four or five feet from the fire, was frozen over with ice, thicker than a brass penny.

24th. Got over Allegheny Hill, otherwise called mountains, to Frank's Town, about 20 miles.

25th. Came to the Standing Stone. Slept three miles at this side; about 31 miles.

26th. To the Forks of the Road [*i.e.*, where the Frankstown and Raystown Paths diverged], about 30 miles. Left my man's horse behind, as he was tired.

27th. It rained very fast; travelled in the rain all day; came about 25 miles.

28th. Rain continued. Came to a place where white people now begin to settle; and arrived at George Croghan's, in Pennsbury, about an hour after dark. Came about 35 miles that day, but we left our baggage behind.

[1] Probably at the mouth of the Kiskiminetas.

29th and 30th. I rested myself at George Croghan's. In the meantime, our baggage was sent for, which arrived.

1st October. Reached the heads of Tulpenhocken.

2nd. I arrived safe at my house.

The distances over this same path, and beyond Logstown as far as Pickawillany (a Miami town, situated on the west bank of the Great Miami, about two miles north of the present town of Piqua, Ohio), as given by Hugh Crawford, an Indian Trader, and Andrew Montour, to the Governor and Provincial Council of Pennsylvania, April 16, 1752, were as follows:

Distances from Philadelphia to Twightwees [Miamis]:
From Philadelphia to George Croghan's, 100 miles.
From George Croghan's to Auchquick, Three Springs, 60 miles.
To Furthermost Crossing of the Juniata, 20 miles.
To Frank's Town, 20 miles.
To Clear Fields, 18 miles.
To the Head of Susquehanna, Chelisquaqua Creek,[1] 25 miles.
To the Two Licks, 25 miles.
To the Round Holes, 25 miles.
To the River Ohio, or Allegheny, 17 miles.
To the Logstown (250), 30 miles.
To the Kusk-Kusks, 30 miles.
To Tuskerawas, 60 miles.
To Muskinong, 40 miles.
To ye Three Licks, 30 miles.
To Hockhockon, 50 miles.
To the Lower Shawenese Town (270½), 60 miles.
To the first Pict Town, on a branch of Ohio, 180 miles. Total, 800 miles.

John Harris journeyed from his ferry at Paxtang (now Harrisburg) to Logstown in May, 1753. He may have made later trips over the Path, as his account of the road published in the *Pennsylvania Archives* (ii., 135–6), is headed, "An Account of the Road to Logs Town on Allegheny River, taken by John Harris, 1754":

Let us follow John Harris on one of his trips to the Ohio country:

"FROM MY FERRY TO GEORGE CROGHAN'S, 5 MILES."

Harris established the town of Harrisburg on the site of his ferry landing in 1785. George Croghan, from before 1747 to 1753 lived near

---

[1] This name, being the same as Chillisquaque Creek in the present Northumberland County, near the mouth of which the Shawnees had a village in 1728, and the name "Shawnee Cabins," mentioned by Weiser as being thirty-four miles from the "Clear Fields," indicate the temporary residence, near the head of the West Branch, of the Shawnees from Chillisquaque.

The Site of Aughwick Old Town and Croghan's Fort.
From a photograph made by the Author in September, 1909.

Silvers's Spring in Pennsboro (now Silvers's Spring) Township, Cumberland County. Owing to the losses he sustained by reason of the French attacks on his trading-posts in the Ohio country, from 1750 to 1754, he became bankrupt; and in order to escape imprisonment for debt, was obliged to remove from Pennsboro Township. He crossed Tuscarora Mountain in 1753, and settled at the site of a former Indian village, called Aughwick Old Town, in the present county of Huntingdon.

"TO THE KITTITANY MOUNTAINS, 9 MILES."

The main Allegheny Path in 1754 led from George Croghan's house to the northwest, crossing the Kittochtiny, or North, Mountain through Croghan's (now Sterrett's) Gap. Prior to 1747-48, the route of the Path from Croghan's house was down the Cumberland Valley to Robert Dunning's, as noted in Weiser's Journal. Dunning lived in West Pennsboro Township, a few miles beyond Le Tort's Spring, the site of the present city of Carlisle. From his house, the earlier Path proceeded along the south side of Conodoguinet Creek, through the Big Spring settlement, across Hopewell and Lurgan townships, and through the mountain by way of McAllister's Gap,[1] west of the present Roxbury post-office; thence up Path Valley to the pass through Tuscarora Mountain at the present village of Concord. At this point, the "New Road," by way of Croghan's Gap, travelled by John Harris in 1753, joined the old one. Thomas Cookson, a commissioner sent by the Governor to Cumberland County about the time of its erection, to recommend a proper site for the county-seat of the new county, in his report, dated March 1, 1750, wrote as follows about the site which was finally selected: "The next situation is on Le Tort's Spring. This place is convenient to the New Path to Allegheny, now mostly used, being at the distance of four miles from the Gap [Croghan's, or Sterrett's] in the Kittochtinny mountain."

On Lewis Evans's map of 1749, the trail by way of McAllister's Gap is called the "Allegheny Path"; while the one by way of Croghan's Gap is called the "New Path."

[1] Rev. David McClure, who made a missionary journey to the Ohio country in 1772, has left the following record of the road through McAllister's Gap: "August 12, 1772. We set out from Mr. Cooper's [at Shippensburg], and in two hours arrived at the foot of the North Mountain, which is the first of the Appalachian. We passed through McAllister's Gap. The road was dismal. It was hollow through the mountain about six miles, rough, rocky, and narrow. It was a bed of stones and rocks which, probably, the waters falling from each side had washed bare. In about two hours we passed through the Gap, having walked almost the whole way. On the western side, the descent into Path Valley was steep and stony, and so continued more than a mile. Leading our horses down, they came near falling upon us several times."

"TO GEORGE COWEN'S HOUSE, 6 MILES."

In Franklin Ellis's *History of the Susquehanna and Juniata Valleys*, the author of the histories of Spring and Carroll townships, Perry County, states that "the road across Sterrett's Gap to-day marks the line of the Indian trail, which then followed along the bank of the [Shearman's] Creek to Gibson's [near the line of Spring and Carroll townships], where it crossed. Marks of the old trail can still be seen." George Cowen's house probably stood near the point where the path crossed Shearman's Creek, the George Gibson house (of Revolutionary times) being about six miles northwest from Sterrett's Gap. The Path probably crossed Shearman's Creek south of Dromgold post-office, thence following the north bank of that stream through the gap which separates Pisgah from Rattlesnake Mountain.

"TO ANDREW MONTOUR'S, 5 MILES."

As we have already seen, Andrew Montour settled on Montour's Run, near its junction with Shearman's Creek, in 1752. His house stood between the present towns of Landisburg and Loysville in Tyrone Township. Conrad Weiser, the Provincial interpreter, while on his way to Aughwick to hold a conference with the Indians from the Ohio, stopped at Montour's in 1754. In his *Journal*, under date of September 1st, he writes: "I thought best to alter my route, and not go along the great road [by way of McAllister's Gap], for some particular reason [Montour had been drinking too much rum]; took, therefore, the road to George Croghan's Gap and Shearman's Creek, and arrived that day at Andrew Montour's, accompanied by himself, the Half King and another Indian, and my son. I found at Andrew Montour's about fifteen Indians, men, women, and children; and more had been there, but were now gone. Andrew's wife had killed a sheep for them some days ago. She complained that they had done great damage to the Indian corn, which was now fit to roast; and I found that there were most every day Indians of those that came from Ohio with some errand or another, which always wanted some victuals in the bargain. I gave them ten pounds of the Government's money."

"TO THE TUSCARORA HILL, 9 MILES."

William, Thomas, and Robert Robinson, three brothers, settled near what is now Centre post-office, Madison Township, Perry County, before 1756. Close to the old grave-yard of Centre Presbyterian Church, they built a strong house of logs, which was known in 1756 as Robinson's Fort. "This fort," says Mr. Flickinger, in his *History of Madison Township*, "was on the line of the Trader's Path, from Harris's Ferry westward. From the best information obtainable, it is almost certain

Jack's Narrows, Looking West.

that this path crossed the Conococheague [hill] near the [present] Sand-Hill road; thence to 'Mitchell's Sleeping-Place,' in Liberty Valley, the site of the old Meminger place; and from that point by Bigham's Gap into Juniata County. There is a tradition that this Path crossed the Conococheague Hill farther west than Sandy Hill, somewhere between Andersonburg and Blain [in Jackson Township]; but it seems improbable that a crossing so difficult would be selected, when Nature had provided an easier passage at a point almost as direct." Conococheague Hill is divided from Tuscarora Hill by the narrow vales known as Horse Valley and Liberty Valley.

"TO THOMAS MITCHELL'S SLEEPING-PLACE, 3 MILES."

From the quotation just given, it will be seen that this sleeping-place was located on what was known in 1885 as the "old Meminger farm." A deed on record in Perry County, executed in 1811 by the owner of this land, mentions it as formerly the location of "Mitchell's Sleeping-Place." Thomas Mitchell was an unlicensed Trader in 1747. He is referred to in the minutes of the Provincial Council for November 15, 1753, as a man of no character. His "sleeping-place" was nothing more than a rude shelter or shack, made of bark, branches, saplings, or logs; or, possibly, a natural shelter of some kind, such as a hollow log, where the Traders who happened along that part of the Path in the evening, could spend the night. It took Mitchell's name from the fact that he either improvised it, or else was the first to discover and use it as a place of lodging when along that part of the road. A number of similar "sleeping-places," named from other Traders, were known and used by travellers along the Allegheny Path. They usually consisted of a hollow log, a bark hut, or an abandoned Indian cabin. After leaving Andrew Montour's house on his way to Aughwick, September 2, 1754, Conrad Weiser wrote in his Journal: "We sat out from Andrew Montour's without any provision; because he told me we should be at Aucquick before night. We rid six hours before noon, and three hours after; took up lodging in the woods. 3d. We sat out by six o'clock, and by eight we came to the Trough Spring; by nine, to the Shadow of Death; by eleven to the Black Log; and by twelve, arrived at Aucquick."

"TO TUSCARORA, 14 MILES."

This was probably a point on Tuscarora Creek, near the present post-office of Blair's Mills in Tell Township, Huntingdon County, just west of the Gap through Tuscarora Mountain, at the eastern opening of which is the present Concord post-office, Fannett Township, Franklin County. The cabin of the Trader, Jacob Pyatt, indicated on the early maps, stood near the site of Concord.[1] The Old Path from Harris's Ferry through the Cumberland Valley came through this gap, and on the west side of the mountain was joined by this new section of the path which has just been described. Edward Shippen, writing to William Allen from Lancaster, July 4, 1755, of the danger from Indian incursions to which the inhabitants of Shippensburg would be exposed, in case of the failure of Braddock's Expedition, said: "They [the enemy] can march through the woods undiscovered within twenty miles of Shippensburgh; and they can come that twenty miles one way on a path, leaving Jacob Pyatt's (near the Tuscarora Mountain) on the right hand, and see but two houses, till they are within two miles of my place [at Shippensburg]."

"TO THE COVE SPRING, 10 MILES."

Weiser calls it "Trough Spring," in his Journal quoted above. It is probable the Path followed up the Trough Spring Branch of Tuscarora Creek to its source, above the present post-office of McNeal, in Tell Township, Huntingdon County, which is seven miles by road above Blair's Mills.

"TO THE SHADOW OF DEATH, 8 MILES."

This is now known as Shade Gap, which, at the present post-office of the same name in Dublin Township, Huntingdon County, crosses Shade Mountain into Black Log Valley.

"TO THE BLACK LOG, 3 MILES; NOW THE ROAD FORKS TOWARDS RAY'S TOWN AND FRANK'S TOWN."

The Black Log was at the gap (of the same name) through Black Log Mountain just east of Orbisonia, Cromwell Township. The road forked in Aughwick Valley on the west side of Black Log Mountain.

"NOW, BEGINNING AT THE BLACK LOG, FRANK'S TOWN ROAD: TO AUGHWICK, 6 MILES."

Shirleysburg, Huntingdon County, now occupies the site of Aughwick. George Croghan retired to this spot from the Cumberland Valley in 1753, about the time when he feared bankruptcy. It was then called "Aughwick Old Town," having been abandoned by the Indians who formerly lived there, possibly Tuscaroras. A fort was built here by Croghan, in October, 1755, which was afterwards strengthened and called Fort Shirley, being made one of a chain of forts for the protection of the

[1] Conrad Weiser wrote to Richard Peters from the "Tuscarora Path" while on his way to the Ohio, August 15, 1748, stating that "one Jacob Biat [Pyatt] is now here to choose a place."

Looking down the Juniata (East) from the Mouth of Water Street Branch.

frontiers. Col. John Armstrong rendezvoused here with his troops in the latter part of August, 1756, while on the march to Kittanning. On the 15th day of October, 1756, Governor Denny announced to his Council that Fort Shirley had been evacuated by his orders.

"TO JACK ARMSTRONG'S NARROWS, 8 MILES; SO-CALLED FROM HIS BEING THERE MURDERED."

Reference to the killing of Jack Armstrong and his two servants by three Delaware Indians in 1744 has already been made in the chapter on the Shamokin Traders. The gap where the Juniata River breaks through Jack's Mountain is still called Jack's Narrows. The Path crossed the Juniata to its north bank at the Narrows, a short distance above the present town of Mount Union; and joined the Juniata Path, whence it continued westward. Another crossing of the Juniata, below this one, was at the mouth of Aughwick Creek, whence a branch path led from the Juniata Path up Aughwick to Aughwick Old Town.

"TO THE STANDING STONE, 10 MILES; (ABOUT FOURTEEN FEET HIGH; 6 INCHES SQUARE;) AT EACH OF THESE LAST PLACES WE CROSS JUNIATA."

This Standing Stone was a noted landmark of those Juniata River Iroquois who may have been identical with the Black Mingoes. At one time it was covered with inscriptions, and venerated as a sacred totem pole. It stood within the limits of the present borough of Huntingdon. Rev. Philip Vickers Fithian made a preaching tour of the country in this vicinity in 1775; and under date of August 23d, he writes: "I had almost forgotten to tell the person who shall read these papers a couple of hundred years hence that there is now standing in a garden at Huntingdon a tall stone column or pillar, nearly square, which has given to the town and valley the name of 'Standing Stone Valley'. The column is seven feet above the ground."

The old Iroquois term for standing stone, as rendered by the Dutch, and marked on the Visscher maps of 1655 and later, was *Onojutta* (pronounced "Onoyutta"). From this term, the modern word, "Juniata," is corrupted. "Oneida" is another form of the same word, having the same meaning. Hugh Crawford, an Indian Trader, and George Croghan's chief lieutenant in his trading operations, made an improvement here in 1753 or 1754, and in 1760 conveyed the land on which Huntingdon now stands to Croghan.

"TO THE NEXT AND LAST CROSSING AT JUNIATA, 8 MILES."

From Standing Stone, the Path led directly west over the top of Warriors' Ridge and crossed the river between what are now the villages of Petersburg and Alexandria. The former town, standing at the mouth of Shaver's Creek, on the north side of the Juniata, six miles above Huntingdon, commemorates the settlement here before 1754, of Peter Shaver, a noted Indian Trader from 1733 to 1755. He was reported in October of the year last named to have been killed by the Indians near the Tuscarora Valley.[1] Alexandria, about five miles west of Petersburg and above the point at which the Trail crossed to the north side of the river again, was known in John Harris's time as "Hart's Log." It took its name from the fact that John Hart (either the John Hart who was killed near Hart's Rock on the Ohio in 1729, or the John Hart who was licensed as a Trader in 1744) on one of his trips westward had here hewed out a large log, so as to make a feeding-trough, for the purpose of salting and feeding his pack-horses. Joshua Elder made a deposition, May 27, 1795, to the effect that he had made a survey of the Hart's Log tract of land for John Gemmill, June 6, 1768, and that he "well remembers to see the log which was troughed or dug out at the time he made the survey, where, it was said, the old Indian Trader, John Hart, usually fed and salted his horses."

A warrant for 400 acres of land at this place was granted to James Sterrat, February 3, 1755, "including the bottom at the Sleeping-Place, called John Hart's Log." Hart's Log, of course, was at the disposition of all travellers along that Path who might wish to use it. It took its name, no doubt, from the Trader who set it up; but there is no ground for assuming, as the local historians have generally done, that Hart settled at this spot or established a trading-post there. Both the Harts traded at Allegheny. The name, "Hart's Log," was afterwards applied to the valley in which the log trough lay, and is borne by it to this day, as well as by a small stream in Porter Township. The story told by U. J. Jones in his *History of the Juniata Valley*, about the visit of hostile Indians to Hart's cabin at Hart's Log, is all pure fiction, with no foundation in fact whatever.

"TO WATER STREET (BRANCH OF JUNIATA), 10 MILES."

The name, "Water Street," was applied by the Traders to that part of the channel of the Water Street Branch of Juniata, which lies in the gap through Tussey's Mountain, east of the present Water Street village, Morris Township, Huntingdon County. The pass was so narrow and the mountains so steep on either side that the Traders found the best road through the gap to be on the bottom of the stream, and that was the course they travelled. The present post-office of Water Street is less than four miles above Alexandria; so that the Water Street point ac-

[1] "A letter from Conegochieg, dated the 31st ult., mentions that Peter Shaver, an old Indian Trader, and two other men in the Tuscarora Valley, have been killed by the Indians, and their houses, &c., burnt."—*Penna. Gazette*, Nov. 13, 1755.

(1) Looking down Water Street Branch of the Juniata (East) from Water Street Village.
(2) Water Street Village.

cording to John Harris would be some miles beyond what is now Water Street post-office. The Juniata begins to penetrate Tussey's Mountain from the west side nearly three miles south of Water Street and runs north, parallel with the centre of the mountain, for that distance, when it turns sharply to the east and comes out of the mountain about one mile east of Water Street post-office. Harris's account of the distance between the Last Crossing of Juniata and Water Street seems to have been about five miles too great. He gives the total distance between the Last Crossing and Frankstown as twenty-five miles. Hugh Crawford's account gives this distance as twenty miles; and Weiser's account about the same. The distance by rail from Alexandria to Frankstown is 21.4 miles. Water Street Creek, which is but little more than a mile in length, rises in Canoe Valley, flows through the west ridge of Tussey's Mountain, and enters the Juniata east of Water Street village.

"TO THE BIG LICK, 10 MILES."

From the west end of "Water Street," the Path crossed Canoe Valley, over the site of the present Yellow Springs village, and passed around the lower end of Canoe Mountain into what is now Frankstown Township, Blair County. On February 3, 1755, a land warrant was issued to Edward Johnston for 100 acres at and "including the Sleeping-Place at the Big Spring, at Frankstown Hill." This was probably identical with John Harris's "Big Lick." Mr. Johnston's land seems to have been located close to a tract of land for which a warrant was issued the same day to Alexander Lowrey, the Indian Trader, for 257 acres "at and below the mouth of Canoe Creek." The "Big Lick" is known to-day as Flowing Spring, and is situated near the south bank of the Juniata River about half a mile southeast of Canoe Creek post-office, Frankstown Township, Blair County, and six miles east of Frankstown.

"TO FRANK'S (STEPHENS') TOWN, 5 MILES."

Ever since Jones's fabulous and harmful *History of the Juniata Valley* appeared in 1856, all writers on the early history of this district have followed his false stories about an imaginary "old German Trader named Stephen Frank." No such individual ever existed outside of Mr. Jones's imagination; and it is needless to say that none of his adventures, as recorded by Jones, ever took place.[1] Frank's Town was a name given by the Traders to the old town of the Delawares and Shawnees at this point, known in 1731 as Assunepachla. At that time its population consisted of twelve families and thirty-six men, all Dela-

[1] At a later date (1763), there were three Lancaster Traders named Franks —Moses, Jacob, and David. See Egle's *Notes and Queries*, ii., 458; *Calendar Johnson Manuscripts*, 109, 177, etc.

wares. It received its English name from Francis, or Frank, Stevens, a Trader at Allegheny as early as 1734. Owing to the misplacing of an apostrophe in the printed account of John Harris's description of the road to Allegheny, Jones assumed that "Frank's (Stephens') Town," as written by Harris meant Stephen Frank's Town. As late as 1772, the Reverend David Jones, a Baptist missionary, on his way to preach to the Ohio Indians, met a Frank Stephens at the mouth of Captina Creek (on the west side of the Ohio River, twenty miles below Wheeling). This man was an Indian, who had received his English name from that of Frank Stevens, the Trader. Possibly, he may have been a half-blood son of the Trader. Contrary to the statements of local historians of Frankstown, the Indians had abandoned their settlements there a number of years before the time of Braddock's defeat. We have already seen, that when Conrad Weiser passed over the Path in 1748, he "came to Frank's Town, but saw no houses or cabins."

"TO THE BEAVER DAMS, 10 MILES."

This was probably a point on what is to this day called the Beaver Dam Branch of the Juniata, which joins the Frankstown Branch at the city of Hollidaysburg. Possibly, the Beaver Dams may have been on Burgoon's Gap Run, which unites with Hill Run and Sugar Creek, near El Dorado post-office, to form Beaver Dam Creek. The Rev. Charles Beatty is said to have preached to the troops of Col. John Armstrong, while encamped here, a few days before Armstrong's attack on Kittanning, in September, 1756.

"TO ALLEGHENY HILL, 4 MILES."

The Trail ascended the Alleghany Ridge by Burgoon's Run Gap to the mouth of Kittanning Run, thence, by way of Kittanning Run Gap, it crossed the divide and came down on the west side. To-day, Kittanning Run flows under the "Horseshoe Curve" of the Pennsylvania Railroad, almost directly beneath Kittanning Point station, and, joining Burgoon's Run, furnishes the water supply for the city of Altoona.

Jones, the romancer on the history of the Juniata Valley, while his statements as to historical facts can never be taken unless authenticated by documentary proof, may partly be trusted in his topographical descriptions of this part of the Valley, with which he was familiarly acquainted as a resident. At any rate, certain parts of his account of the course of the Traders' Path over Alleghany Mountain may be given without serious perversion of the truth. He writes: "This Path, traces of which can yet [1856] be plainly seen in various places, and especially in the wilds of the mountains, must have been a famous road in its day. It commenced . . . on the Allegheny river, and crossed the Alleghany

Looking up the Juniata (South) from the Mouth of Water Street Branch

Mountains in a southeastern direction, the descent on the eastern slope being through a gorge, the mouth of which is five or six miles [north-] west of Hollidaysburg, at what is well-known as Kittanning Point [the Trail is crossed by the Pennsylvania Railroad in rounding the Horseshoe Curve]. From this, it diverged in a southern direction, until it led to the flat immediately back of Hollidaysburg; from thence east, wound around the gorge back of the Presbyterian grave-yard, and led into Frank's Old Town. From thence it went through what is now called Scotch Valley, Canoe Valley, and struck the river at Water Street. From thence it led to Alexandria, crossed the river, and went into Harts' Log Valley. [Mr. Jones then gives an erroneous description of the course of the Trail eastward from Hart's Log.]

"At Kittanning Point, this Path, although it is seldom that the foot of any one but an occasional hunter or fisher treads it, is still the same Path it was when the last dusky warrior who visited the Juniata Valley turned his face to the West, and traversed it for the last time. True, it is filled up with weeds in the summer-time, but the indentations made by the feet of thousands upon thousands of warriors and pack-horses which travelled it for an unknown number of years are still plainly visible. We have gone up the Kittanning Gorge two or three miles, repeatedly, and looked upon the ruins of old huts and the road, which evidently never received the impression of a wagon-wheel, and were forcibly struck with the idea that it once must have been traversed, without knowing at the time that it was the famous Kittanning Trail. In some places, where the ground was marshy, close to the Run, the Path is at least twelve inches deep, and the very stones along the road bear the marks of the iron-shod horses of the Indian Traders. . . . The Path can be traced in various other places, but nowhere so plain as in the Kittanning Gorge. This is owing to the fact that one or two other paths led into it, and no improvement had been made in the Gorge east of 'Hart's Sleeping-Place,' along the line of the Path."

"TO THE CLEAR FIELDS, 6 MILES."

The Path across the plateau forming the present county of Cambria proceeded in a northwestern direction along the course now followed, west of Ashville, by the Dry Gap Road, which runs between the townships of Clearfield and Alleghany, crosses the northeast corner of Carroll Township, the extreme southwest corner of Elder Township, and thence diagonally across Susquehanna Township, to Cherry Tree (Grant post-office), Indiana County.

The term "Clear Fields," simply meant an open meadow space in the woods with which the top of the mountain was covered. It might have been cleared by a forest fire, or by the hands of the Red Men, at some remote period in the past.¹ It was perhaps near the line between the present townships of Alleghany and Clearfield, a mile or two east of what is now Chest Spring post-office. Harris estimates the total distance on the Path between Frankstown and the Clear Fields to be twenty miles. Conrad Weiser called it sixteen miles on his first trip westward in 1748; and twenty miles on his return trip. Hugh Crawford and Andrew Montour, in 1752, gave the distance as eighteen miles.

"TO JOHN HART'S SLEEPING-PLACE, 12 MILES."

This station was located in what is now Carroll Township, about a thousand yards southeast of the southwest corner of the present township of Elder, in Cambria County; and not far from the site of St. Joseph's Roman Catholic Church, which is some two or three miles north of Carrolltown. It was named for John Hart, the Indian Trader, who had erected the watering-trough at the point known thereafter as "Hart's Log."

"TO THE HEAD OF SUSQUEHANNA, 12 MILES."

This was not literally at the head of the Susquehanna West Branch, but meant the head of canoe navigation on that stream, which began near what is now the northwest corner of Cambria County. "Canoe Place" (*i. e.*, the place where canoe navigation of the West Branch began) is the name used on Scull's and Howell's maps to designate this point. It is now called Cherry Tree, or Grant post-office, in Indiana County. Harris's "Head of Susquehanna," may have been two of three miles farther up the stream than the site of Cherry Tree village.

About four miles beyond the "Head of Susquehanna," the Path forked, one branch leading northwest to Venango,² and the other southwest to the Forks of the Kiskiminetas and Kittanning paths. The parting of the Main and the Venango paths was on a tract of land lying along Cush Cushon Creek, between the present post-offices of Beringer and Cookport, in Green Township, Indiana County. This tract was warranted July 23, 1773, to Samuel Caldwell, a settler, and was "situate on the road leading from Frankstown to Kittanning, at the Forks of the Road, about four miles from Owens's Camping Ground, including several Indian cabins." Mr. Caldwell, in his *History of Indiana County*, says

¹ Rev. John Ettwein wrote in 1772 that the clearing had been made by buffaloes. See chapter vii.

² The Venango, or Shenango, Path led northwest across the waters of the Little Mahoning, "where the path from Frankstown to Chenango crosses the same," at or near "a large Indian camp on the bank of said creek"; which was at the mouth of Ross Run, thence to the forks of the Big and Little Mahoning, where it crossed the Chinklaclamoose Path from Shamokin to Kittanning; thence across the present counties of Armstrong, Clarion, and Venango to the mouth of French Creek on the Allegheny.

Kittanning Gap, Looking North from the Mouth of Kittanning Run.
At Kittanning Point Station on the Pennsylvania Railroad.

it was at this point Col. John Armstrong's little army encamped on the night of September 5, 1756, about sixty hours before his attack on Kittanning. In Robert Robinson's *Narrative*, it is called the "Forty Mile Lick,[1] where the Indians trimmed [plucked] the hair of their prisoners [before reaching the Kiskiminetas]." "Owens's Camping Ground" was probably another name for the sleeping-place called by Harris, "Head of Susquehanna."

"TO THE SHAWANA CABINS, 12 MILES."

The tract of land immediately above these cabins was surveyed June 29, 1773, and the Allegheny Path is shown on this survey. The tract is on the south branch of Two Lick Creek, about half a mile above its junction with the north branch. The cabins were located in the "Shawanese Bottoms," and were called, "the Spruce Camp, or the Old Shawnee Cabins"; about a mile southwest from what is now Cookport, Indiana County.

"TO P. SHAVER'S SLEEPING-PLACE, AT TWO LARGE LICKS, 12 MILES."

From the last named point, the Path passed close to the sites of Diamondville and Greenville. Peter Shaver's Sleeping-Place was situated about half a mile above the mouth of what is now known as Ramsey's Run. The "Two Large Licks" are located on a tract of land warranted in the name of Elijah Brown.

"TO THE EIGHTEEN-MILE RUN, 12 MILES."

Probably so-called because it was eighteen miles from Kiskiminetas Indian Town. From Shaver's Sleeping-Place, the Trail bore to the northwest, passing by "Shaffer's" or "Shaver's Spring," within what is now Indiana Borough; thence to a tract of land which, in May, 1785, was surveyed to William Armstrong, described as being situated on the waters of Crooked Creek, "to include the crossings of the Kiskiminetas and Kittanning Paths." Crooked Creek may have been the same stream called by Harris and the Traders, Eighteen-Mile Run. The parting of the roads was at a point a mile or two southeast of what is now Shelocta post-office, Indiana County. From here, the Path to Kittanning led over the site of Shelocta, passing an old Indian field near that point; and thence near the forks of Plum Creek and Crooked Creek, to the south of the present Blanket Hill post-office, and on to Kittanning. The old Indian field near Shelocta was the site of an earlier Indian town, called Tohoguses Town (at the mouth of Plum Creek) on Scull's map of 1770; and described in George Campbell's application for a tract of land on Plum Creek, dated April 3, 1769, as "James Litart's Town, an Indian."

[1] Within forty miles of Kiskiminetas Town or Kittanning?

See Caldwell's *History of Indiana County*, p. 132. This description marks it as the site of one of James Le Tort's early trading stations during a portion of the decade, 1730–40.

The Kiskiminetas, or Main Path proceeded in a southwestern direction, perhaps along the ridge between the sites of the villages of South Bend and West Lebanon, to the "Ten Mile Lick."

Col. John Armstrong, with about 300 men, recruited from among the Scotch-Irish of the Cumberland Valley, left the Main Path at this point in September, 1756, proceeding by night to the large Delaware town of Kittanning, on the Allegheny, some twenty miles distant, which he attacked and destroyed at daybreak. While Armstrong's references to the Trail, in his Journal of this expedition, are not so explicit as might be wished, they are inserted here because of their interest:

We marched from Fort Shirley [Aughwick] August 30th, and on Wednesday, the third instant, joined our advanced party at the Beaver Dams, a few miles from Frankstown, on the North Branch of Juniata [Beaver Dam Branch]. . . . Next morning, we decamped, and in two days came within fifty miles of the Kittanning [probably at the point where the Venango trail branched off from the Main Path]. It was then adjudged necessary to send some persons to reconnoitre the town. . . . The day following, we met them on their return.

We continued our march, in order to get as near the town as possible that night; so as to be able to attack it next morning about day-light; but to our great dissatisfaction, about nine or ten o'clock at night, one of our guides came and told us that he perceived a fire by the roadside, at which he saw two or three Indians, a few perches distant from our front. Whereupon, with all possible silence, I ordered the rear to retreat one hundred perches, in order to make way for the front, that we might consult how we could best proceed without being discovered by the enemy.

Soon after, the pilot returned a second time, and assured us from the best observations he could make, there were not above three or four Indians at the fire; on which it was proposed that we should immediately surround and cut them off.

But this was thought too hazardous; for if but one of the enemy escaped, it would be the means of discovering the whole design; and the light of the moon, on which depended our advantageously posting our men, and attacking the town, would not admit of our staying until the Indians fell asleep.

On which it was agreed to leave Lieutenant Hogg with twelve men, and the person who first discovered the fire; with orders to watch the enemy, but not to attack them till break of day; and then, if possible, to cut them off. It was also agreed (we believing ourselves to be but about six miles from the town) to leave the horses, many of them being tired, with what blankets and other baggage we then had [Blanket Hill post-office, in the present township of Kittanning, Armstrong County, marks the spot where these horses and blankets were left], and to take a circuit off the road, which was very rough and incommodious, on account of the

The Site of Kiskiminetas, Looking West.

The railroad runs through the village site. The old Path to Chartier's Town may still be traced along the top of the hill seen on the left.

From a photograph furnished by Mrs. Howard L. Bodwell.

stones and fallen timber, in order to prevent our being heard by the enemy at the fire-place.

This interruption much retarded our march, but a still greater loss arose from the ignorance of our pilot, who neither knew the true situation of the town, nor the best paths that lead thereto. By which means, after crossing a number of hills and valleys, our front reached the river Ohio, about one hundred perches below the main body of the town, a little before the setting of the moon; to which place, rather than by the pilots, we were guided by the beating of the drum and the whooping of the warriors at their dance.

It then became us to make the best use of the remaining moon-light; but ere we were aware, an Indian whistled in a very singular manner, about thirty perches from our front, in the foot of a corn-field. Upon which we immediately sat down, and after passing silence to the rear, I asked one, Baker, a soldier, who was our best assistant, whether that was not a signal to the warriors of our approach. He answered "No," and said it was the manner of a young fellow's calling a squaw, after he had done his dance; who accordingly kindled a fire, cleaned his gun, and shot it off before he went to sleep.

All this time we were obliged to lay quiet and hush, till the moon was fairly set. Immediately after, a number of fires appeared in different places in the corn-field, by which, Baker said, the Indians lay, the night being warm; and that these fires would immediately be out, as they were only designed to disperse the gnats.

By this time, it was break of day; and the men, having marched thirty miles, were mostly asleep; the time being long, the three companies of the rear were not yet brought over the last precipice. For those, some proper hands were immediately dispatched, and the weary soldiers being roused to their feet, a proper number, under sundry officers, were ordered to take the end of the hill at which we then lay, and march along the top of said hill at least one hundred perches, and so much further (it then being day-light), as would carry them opposite the upper part, or at least the body of the town. For the lower part thereof, and the corn-field, presuming the warriors were there, I kept rather the larger number of the men, promising to postpone the attack in that part for eighteen or twenty minutes, until the detachment along the hill should have time to advance to the place assigned them.

In the *Narrative* of Robert Robinson, who accompanied this expedition, and was wounded in the battle, that soldier states that the whites brought away with them fourteen Indian scalps. "As for our retreating from Kittanning," he adds, "we met no opposition. Only a few Indians on this side of the town fired on us. They shot about two hundred yards, and shot Andrew Douglas through both ankles. . . . We had no more injury done until we came to this side of the Alleghany Mountain; when one, Samuel Chambers, having left his coat at the Clear Fields, desired leave of Colonel Armstrong to go back for his coat, and to bring three horses, which had given out. Colonel Armstrong advised against it, but Chambers persisted in going; and so went back.

When he came to the top of the mountain a party of Indians fired on him, but missed him. Chambers then steered towards Big Island. The Indians pursued; and, the third day, killed him in French Margaret's Island; so the Indians told Captain Patterson."[1]

"TO THE TEN MILE LICK, 6 MILES."

By reference to Hugh Crawford's description of the road, it will be seen that he mentions a station on the Path some twenty-five miles west from Two Licks, or Shaver's Sleeping-Place, which he calls "The Round Holes." Conrad Weiser, also, on his return journey from Logstown, states that he came to the "Round Hole," after crossing Kiskiminetas Creek, at a distance of about twelve miles from the river. According to John Harris, the Ten Mile Lick was ten miles away from Kiskiminetas Town. It was probably identical with the "Round Hole." The latter is now known as "Boiling Spring," the land on which it is situated having been taken up by John Steel before the organization of Armstrong County. The "Round Hole" is referred to in Steel's survey of this tract. It is in Kiskiminetas Township, Armstrong County, at Spring Church post-office.

"TO KISKEMENETTES TOWN, ON THE CREEK, RUNS INTO ALLEGHENY RIVER, SIX MILES DOWN (ALMOST AS LARGE AS SCHUYLKILL), 10 MILES."

The Trail crossed Kiskiminetas Creek at the mouth of Carnahan's Run, and perhaps, also, at a point about one mile below the present village of Apollo, near the outlet locks. Apollo was formerly called Warren. The fact that the name was permitted to be changed shows a lamentable lack of taste on the part of its inhabitants. This town as originally laid out was partly on the upper portion of a tract of 500 acres of land (five miles from "Boiling Spring" or the "Round Holes,") surveyed to John Montgomery and Alexander Stewart on an application dated February 9, 1769, and designated in the survey as "Warren's Sleeping-Place." In other applications for the same tract, it is described as "Warren's Sleeping Ground" and "Warren's Sleeping Groves."[2]

Local historians have incorrectly assumed that "Warren" was the name of an imaginary Indian chief; and that the tract contained the

---

[1] Chambers was said by Colonel Armstrong himself to have been killed at Alleghany Hill. See *Penna. Archives*, iii., 148.

[2] See *Penna. Archives*, Third Series, i., 287; ii., 460. Benjamin Austin, who made application for the same tract, April 7, 1769, describes it as "including Warren's Sleeping Place, about fifteen miles below Black Legs Town" (now Saltsburg). Francis Silver applied for the same tract, April 3, 1769, describing it as "including, or near Warren's Sleeping Ground, about or near three miles from Kiskiminetas Old Town." See Caldwell's *Indiana County*, p. 132.

burial place of that chief. This assumption, like many other local traditions as to the origin of names along the Allegheny Path is based wholly upon imagination. Edward Warren, whose sleeping-place on the Allegheny Path was near where that Path crossed the Kiskiminetas, was himself an Indian Trader at Allegheny before 1732. In a deposition made by Thomas Renick, January 18, 1732, Warren is referred to as a hired servant of one Peter Allen, and as one who had then lately come to "Pextan" from Allegheny, "a place where our Indian Traders resort." Warren brought a report that some French from Canada were then engaged in building a log fort near the Ohio.

Kiskiminetas Indian Town was on the south bank of the stream of the same name, opposite the mouth of Carnahan's Run, and about two miles below the present town of Vandergrift. Carnahan's Run is designated on Reading Howell's map of 1792, as "Old Town Run," taking its name from the old Indian town of Kiskiminetas which had formerly stood on the opposite (south) bank of Kiskiminetas River. John McCullough, who was captured by the Indians in Franklin County in the summer of 1756, has left an interesting narrative of his experiences while in captivity, in which he refers to this town. "I must pass over many occurrences that happened on our way to [the site of] Pittsburgh," he says, "except one or two. The morning before we came to *Keesk-ksheeman-nit-teos*, which signifies 'Cut Spirit,' an old town at [below] the junction of Laelhanneck [Loyalhanna], or Middle Creek, and Quinnimmoughkoong, or Cannamaugh, or Otter Creek, as the word signifies; the morning before we got there, they pulled all the hair out of our heads, except a small spot on the crown, which they left. We got to the Town about the middle of the day."[1]

In the examination of James Le Tort and Jonah Davenport, Allegheny Traders, before Governor Gordon at Philadelphia, October 29, 1731, they made a report of the Indian settlements at Allegheny. On the Conemaugh (which is now called Kiskiminetas Creek, or River,

---

[1] McCullough, as we see, translates Kiskiminetas, "cut spirit." Heckewelder says the word means, "make daylight." In the Delaware language, the term, "Gisckhschummen," means, "to cut with a knife." "Gischachsummen" means "to make light, or to enlighten," from "Gischapan," "day-light." "Manitto," or "Manitou," is the Indian word for "spirit." The reader can decide for himself as to whether either McCullough or Heckewelder has given the proper meaning of the compound. J. N. B. Hewitt says the meaning of the term is, "plenty of walnuts." A second "Kishkeminetas Old Town," is located by Lewis Evans, on his map of 1755, as lying on the west bank of the Ohio, some miles above the mouth of the Great Kanawha. Old Town Creek and Island, in the present county of Meigs, Ohio, near what is still called Le Tort's Rapids, Creek, and Island, probably perpetuate its site and also establish the fact that James Le Tort traded there. The site of Keckenepaulin's Old Town was at the junction of the Loyalhanna and the Conemaugh when Post passed there in 1758.

below the mouth of the Loyalhanna), they locate one town of the Delawares, containing twenty families and sixty men; and three towns of the Shawnees, containing forty-five families and two hundred men, under the rule of a chief named "Okowela," or Ocowellos. The town opposite the mouth of Carnahan's Run, usually called Kiskiminetas Town, was, possibly, the one inhabited by these Delawares. Weiser, however, does not mention any town here in the record of his trip to Logstown in 1748. One of the Shawnee towns stood at the mouth of the Kiskiminetas. Post passed over its site on his second mission to the Ohio Indians, November 12, 1758, and refers to it in his Journal as "an old Shawano town, situated under a high hill on the east [of the Allegheny River], opposite an island of about one hundred acres." Another was that known as "Black Legs Town," just below and opposite the mouth of the Loyalhanna, at the mouth of Black Legs Creek, which enters the Kiskiminetas to the west of the present town of Saltsburg, Indiana County. Black Legs Town was situated near the site of Saltsburg in what is now Conemaugh Township, Indiana County. Its site is indicated on Scull's map of 1770. A cross Path connected it with the Frankstown Path, on the north, and the Raystown Path on the south. Post travelled over this connecting Path from the south (Fort Ligonier) at the time of his second journey to the Ohio, to which reference has just been made. After leaving the advanced outpost of Forbes's army, on Breastwork Hill, November 10, 1758, he travelled with his company down the west bank of Loyalhanna Creek, and encamped beside that stream for the night. The next morning, "we started early" he writes, "and came to the old Shawanese Town called Keckeknepolin, grown up thick with weeds, briars, and bushes, that we scarcely could get through. [This would indicate that this town stood on the south bank of the Kiskiminetas.] Pesquitomen led us upon a steep hill, that our horses could hardly get up. . . . It happened we found a Path on the top of the hill. At three o'clock, we came to Kiskemeneco, an old Indian town, a rich bottom, well timbered, good fine English grass, well watered, and lays waste since the war began."

Post met a chief named Kehkehnopalin at Kuskuskies, September 3, 1758, when on his first peace mission to the Delawares and Shawnees. From his account of the conference in which this chief took part, it would seem that the latter must have been a Delaware Indian; although the same writer, in the *Journal* of his second visit to the Ohio Indians, refers, as we have just seen, to Keckeknepaulin's Town at the mouth of the Loyalhanna as "the old Shawanese Town." On the Raystown Path to Allegheny, which will be made the subject of the next chapter, one of the stations at the eastern base of Laurel Ridge Mountain, and on or near the Quemahoning Fork of the Conemaugh, in what is now Jenner Township, Somerset County, is called by John Harris, "Kickeney Paulin's (Indian)

House," or cabin. Post calls the stream on which this cabin stood (probably Picking's Run, of the present day, near its junction with the Quemahoning), "Kekempalin's Creek," although his translator has mistaken Post's German "K" for the English "R," which it so nearly resembles, and rendered the word, "Rekempalin," instead of "Kekempalin," as Post wrote it. Sherman Day, in his *Historical Collections of Pennsylvania*, states that Johnstown, in Cambria County at the forks of Quemahoning and Conemaugh creeks, "occupies the site of an old Indian town called Kickenapawling's Old Town." This may possibly be true; but it is not improbable that the local historians of Cambria County have confused the town lower down the Conemaugh, at the mouth of the Loyalhanna, or else Keckenepaulin's Cabin, on the Quemahoning, above Johnstown, with the location at the site of that city. "Conemach Old Town" is marked at this point on Scull's map of 1770. The land on which Joseph Johns laid out Johnstown in 1800 was patented to James McLanahan, April 26, 1788, as the "Conemaugh Old Town Tract." If there was an Indian town there in early colonial times, it may have been the third Shawnee Town on the Conemaugh noted by Le Tort and Davenport in 1731. Christopher Gist, who travelled over the Raystown Path in the fall of 1750, camped during the night of November 9th at "Kehkehnopalin's Cabin." He travelled fourteen miles westward during the next four days, crossing the Laurel Ridge on the 12th, and halting the whole of the following day, detained by rain and snow. On the 14th, Gist "set out N. 45 W., 6 miles, to Loyalhannan, an old Indian town on a creek of Ohio called Kiscominatis; then N. 1 mile, NW. 1 mile, to an Indian's camp on the said creek." Loyalhanna was on the creek of the same name, a stream which unites with the Conemaugh to form the Kiskiminetas as it is known at the present day. Ligonier, in Westmoreland County, now occupies the site of this old Indian town; and it is more probable that that old town was the third Shawnee village "on the Conemaugh" in 1731 than that Kickeny Paulin's Town ever stood on the site of the present Johnstown.

The "Shawnee Cabins" mentioned by Weiser, Crawford, and Harris, and located on Two Lick Creek in what is now Indiana County, near the Head of Susquehanna, may also have been at the site of one of the Shawnee towns on the Conemaugh, referred to by Le Tort and Davenport in 1731.

"TO THE CHARTIER'S LANDING ON ALLEGHENY, 8 MILES."

This point was almost due west from Kiskiminetas Indian Town, and about eight miles below the mouth of Kiskiminetas River. Chartier's Town stood on the west bank of the Allegheny (probably at the mouth of Bull Creek), and on or near the site of the present borough of Tarentum,

Allegheny County. It was about one mile below where Chartier's Run flows into the Allegheny from the east. Lewis Evans, in the *Analysis* of his map of 1755, writes: "In this part of the river [at Toby's Falls] are several fording places; but they are the more rare as you come lower down. That at Chartier's Old Town is the best; which, as soon as the Rock appears above the water, is passable above it. At Shanoppen's [now Pittsburgh] is another, in very dry times, and the lowest down the river. This part [between Chartier's and Shanoppin's], which is very crooked, has seldom been navigated by our people, because the great number of horses necessary to carry their goods to Ohio serve also to carry them there from place to place; and the little game that way [down the river] makes it but little frequented."

An extended account of Chartier's Town will be found in a later chapter.

"TO KITTANNING TOWN, UP THE RIVER, 18 MILES."

An account of this place will be given in a separate chapter. It occupied the site of the present town of the same name.

"TO VENANGO, HIGHER UP ALLEGHENY, 70 MILES."

Captain Pierre Joseph Celoron (usually called Celoron de Bienville),[1] accompanied by two of the brothers Joncaire, commanded an expedition of Canadians and Indians who descended the Allegheny and Ohio in canoes, from Lake Chautauqua to the mouth of the Great Miami, in July and August, 1749. On the 3d of August, they passed a village of nine or ten cabins of Senecas, and perhaps, also, of Muncys, at the mouth of the River aux Bœufs (or French Creek, as it was called by Washington, when he visited the commander of the French garrison there in December, 1753). The Indian name for this village was "Ganagarahhare," and it was also called Venango. Celoron thus refers to it in his Journal: "August 3, 1749. I set out on the route. On the way, I found a village of ten abandoned cabins; the Indians, having been apprised of my arrival, had gained the woods. I continued my route as far as the village at the River aux Bœufs, which is only of nine or ten cabins. As soon as they perceived me, they fired a salute. I had their salute returned, and landed. As I had been informed that there was at this place a blacksmith and an English merchant, I wished to speak to them; but the English as well as the Indians had gained the woods. There remained only five or six Iroquois, who presented themselves with their arms in their hands." The English merchant Celoron speaks of was

[1] He was the son of Jean Baptiste Celoron, Sieur de Blainville. His younger brother seems to have inherited the title "de Blainville." "De Bienville" may have been a courtesy title, taken from Jean B. LeMoyne, Sieur de Bienville, Governor of Louisiana, under whom Pierre Joseph served in the Chickasaw campaign of 1739-40.

McKee's Rock, from the South.

From a photograph taken by the Author. The rock is rapidly being quarried away.

John Fraser, the Trader, who had established here a trading-post and a gunsmith's shop, where he repaired the guns and weapons of the Indians. He was driven out by the French, when they came here to build Fort Machault in the summer of 1753; and retired to his lower post, at the mouth of Turtle Creek, on the Monogahela, near the point where Braddock's catastrophe occurred some eighteen months later.

"DOWN THE RIVER FROM CHARTIER'S LANDING TO PINE CREEK, 14 MILES."

Pine Creek flows through the present townships of Pine, Richland, McCandless, Hampton, and Shaler, in Allegheny County, and enters the Allegheny River at the borough of Etna. The original Trail from Chartier's Town to Logstown may have crossed Pine Creek at some distance above its mouth, possibly at the intersection of the Path leading north from Shanoppin's Town (which was within the limits of the present city of Pittsburgh), to Venango. But in 1753 the Path probably crossed Pine Creek near its mouth. George Croghan, William Trent, Robert Callender, Michael Taafe, and several other Traders were at "Pine Creek," May 7, 1753, when they received a letter from John Fraser, then at Venango, announcing the approach of the French from Niagara. John Harris joined them at Pine Creek, with advices from Governor Hamilton, when Croghan and the other Traders named above summoned the Half King and Monacatoocha, and other Indian chiefs of that vicinity; with whom they held a Council at Pine Creek, for the purpose of learning whether or not the Indians would oppose the French; and whether it would be safe for the English Traders to continue among the Indians.

In 1753–54, George Croghan and William Trent, partners in the Indian Trade, had a storehouse above the mouth of Pine Creek, also fenced fields of Indian corn and numbers of large canoes and batteaux all of which were seized by the French in April, 1754.[1]

The Venango Path, leading from Shanoppin's Town (the Delaware village at the mouth of Two Mile Run in what is now the Twelfth Ward of the city of Pittsburgh) to Venango, crossed the Allegheny River at the mouth of that Run, and led northwest, probably up Girty's Run, through the present townships of Shaler, Ross, McCandless, Franklin (or Pine), and Marshall, in Allegheny County; Cranberry, Jackson, Forward, Connoquenessing, Franklin, Brady, Slippery Rock, and Mercer, in Butler County; and Irwin and Sandy Creek, in Venango County. The intersection of this Trail with the original (1743) Path which led from Chartier's Old Town, by way of Pine Creek, to Logstown, may possibly have been, therefore, near the west line of McCandless Township,

[1] MS. affidavit of Croghan and others at Carlisle, 1756.

Allegheny County and perhaps not far south from the present post-office of Keown, in the same township. If there was such a path, it had probably been superceded before 1753 by the one which followed the north bank of the river.

A few miles below the mouth of Pine Creek, on both banks of the Ohio, stood for some twenty years before 1750, "Queen Alliquippa's Town." It was adjacent to what was known in 1750 as the Written Rock, now McKee's Rock, which lies at the mouth of Chartier's Creek (called Alliquippa's Creek prior to 1759)[1]; and on and opposite the island in the Ohio now called Brunot's Island, which was called Alliquippa's Island in the early surveys. The location of this village is indicated on the map prepared for the Ohio Company from surveys made in April, 1750-52, which is published in volume two. A Seneka Town is also marked on Mitchell's map of 1755, on the north side of the Ohio, but *above* the mouth of the Monongahela. Conrad Weiser visited this town August 27, 1748, and speaks of it as "a Seneka town, where an old Seneka woman reigns supreme." Celoron was here nearly a year later. He passed Shanoppin's Town (within the present limits of Pittsburgh) August 7, 1749; which he refers to as a "village of the Loups [Delawares]." From that Town, his *Journal* proceeds: "I re-embarked, and visited the village which is called the 'Written Rock.' The Iroquois inhabit this place, and it is an old woman of this nation who governs it. She regards herself as sovereign. She is entirely devoted to the English. All the savages having retired, there only remained in this place six English Traders, who came before me trembling. . . . This place is one of the most beautiful that until the present I have seen on La Belle Riviere. I left this camp, and slept nearly three leagues below. As soon as I had disembarked our savages told me that on passing, they had seen writing on a rock [McKee's Rock]. As it was late, I could not send there until the next day. I appointed R. P. Bonnecamps and M. de Joncaire to go there, with the idea that these writings could give me some light. They were there early in the morning, and reported that it was some English names written with charcoal. As I was only two leagues from Chininque [Logstown], I dispersed as much as possible the men of my detachment, to give them a greater appearance, and arranged everything so as to arrive in good order at this village; which I knew to be one of the most considerable on La Belle Riviere."

Messrs. Patton, Fry, and Lomax, Commissioners sent by Governor Dinwiddie, of Virginia, to treat with the Ohio Indians, were at Shanoppin's Town on May 30, 1752. After leaving that place, they crossed the

[1] In the Narrative of Marie Le Roy and Barbara Leininger, who escaped from the Indians at Muskingum in 1759, they state that, "on the last day of March, we came to a river, Alloquepy, about three miles below Pittsburg." *Penna. Magazine*, xxix., 416.

McKee's Rock, from the East.
From a photograph taken by the Author in September, 1909.

Allegheny to the "opposite shore, where Queen Alliquippa lives," visited her, and presented her with a brass kettle and other articles.[1]

From Celoron's account, it would appear that Alliquippa's Town was on the south bank of the Ohio in 1749, at McKee's Rock, below the mouth of Chartier's Creek. In the Traders' Map of the Ohio country (of about 1753), reproduced in the second volume from the original in the Library of Congress, Alliquippa's Town is shown on the south bank of the Ohio, below the mouth of Chartier's Creek. But the Ohio Company's map of 1750–52,[2] and Mitchell's map of 1755, locate her village on the north side of the Ohio; and it would appear that she was there in 1752, when the Virginia Commissioners visited her. In December, 1753, when Washington visited her, she lived at the mouth of the Youghiogheny.

"TO THE LOGS TOWN, 17 MILES."
Logstown will be described in a later chapter.

[1] *Virginia Mag. of Hist. and Biog.*, xiii., 157.
[2] Also reproduced in the second volume.

CHAPTER X

THE RAYSTOWN PATH

THIS Trail left the Frankstown Path at the Black Log, as stated by John Harris in his itinerary of the road from his ferry at the Susquehanna, to Logstown, which is given in the preceding chapter. From Harris's Ferry, it will be remembered, the Path to Allegheny led by way of George Croghan's, the Kittochtinny Mountain, George Cowen's House, Andrew Montour's, the Tuscarora Hill, Thomas Mitchell's Sleeping-Place, Tuscarora Creek, the Cove Spring, and the "Shadow of Death," to the Black Log Mountain, a distance, according to John Harris's estimate, of seventy-two miles.

At about the same time Harris gave his information about the Allegheny Path to the Pennsylvania authorities, John Pattin, or Patten, an old Indian Trader, and Andrew Montour, appeared before the Governor and Council, with a map of the Indian country, on which they had laid off the courses and distances of the Path from Carlisle, by way of Ray's Town, to Shanoppin's Town (now Pittsburgh). Their examination before the Governor took place on March 2, 1754; and they were called before the Assembly some four days later for further information about the road. The distance as given by them on the Path from Carlisle to Three Springs, was sixty miles, as follows:

"From Carlisle to Major Montour's, 10 miles.

"From Montour's to Jacob Pyatt's, 25 miles [Pyatt lived near what is now Concord post-office, Fannett Township, Franklin County].

"From Pyatt's to George Croghan's at Aucquick Old Town, 15 miles.

"From Croghan's to the Three Springs, 10 miles."[1]

---

[1] The remainder of Patten's "Computed distances of the Road" is as follows:
"From the Three Springs to Sideling Hill, 7 miles.
From Sideling Hill to Contz's Harbour, 8 miles.
From Contz's Harbour to the top of Ray's Hill, 1 mile.
From Ray's Hill to the 1 Crossing of Juniata, 10 miles.
From the 1 Crossing of Juniata to Allaguapy's Gap, 6 miles.
From Allaguapy's Gap to Ray's Town, 5 miles.
From Ray's Town to Shawonese Cabbin, 8 miles.
From Shawonese Cabbins to the Top of Allegheny Mountain, 8 miles.

The Black Log was between Croghan's and Three Springs. "At the Black Log," says John Harris, "now the Road forks, towards Ray's Town and Frank's Town; we continue Ray's Town Road to Allegheney."

"TO THE THREE SPRINGS, 10 MILES [FROM BLACK LOG]."

This was at or near the present post-office of the same name, in Clay Township, Huntingdon County. A committee of the Pennsylvania Assembly, appointed for the purpose of determining whether or not the Forks of the Ohio were within the bounds of the Province, reported to the Assembly, March 7, 1754, that Three Springs was thirty miles north of the western extremity of the temporary Maryland boundary line, which extremity was about 144 miles west of Philadelphia. The report of the Committee then proceeds as follows: "And, that the several computed distances from the Three Springs to Ohio, laid before the Committee, are as follows:

"Hugh Crawford and Andrew Montour, on their examination before the Governor, April 10, 1752, make the said Road, through Frank's Town to the Ohio, 150 miles.

"William West, who travelled thither in 1752, makes the road from the Three Springs, through Ray's Town, to Shanopin's Town, on Ohio, 145 miles.

"John Harris, who travelled thither in 1753, makes the Ray's Town Road, to Shanopin's, from said Springs, 148 miles; and the Frank's Town Road from ditto, 151 miles.

"John Pattin, just returned, makes the Ray's Town Road from ditto, 140 miles.

"Which computations, nearly agreeing, do, at a medium, make about 147 miles; to which, the length of the temporary line, 144 miles, being added, make 291 miles; that, by the certificate of Theophilus Grew and Nicholas Scull, mathematicians, a degree of longitude, in Lat. 40, is fifty-three statute miles, accounting sixty-nine miles and a half to a degree of the equinoctial; and, if so, the extent of this Province, east and west, in that latitude, should be but 265 miles; which is short of the above sum 26 miles.

"That all the several accounts which speak of the course of the Road, do agree, that it is very winding and crooked in many places, to avoid creeks and swamps; and very uneven, as it passes through a mountainous country; and Pattin's map of the Road, laid before us, makes it in a

---

From Allegheny Mountain to Edmund's Swamp, 8 miles.
From Edmund's Swamp to Cowamahony Creek, 6 miles.
From Cowamahony Creek to Kackanapaulin's, 5 miles.
From Kackanapaulin's to Loyal Hannin, 18 miles.
From Loyal Hannin to Shanoppin's Town, 50 miles."

straight line from the Three Springs to Shanopin's, but eighty-three miles; which map, however, we do not understand to have been made from actual mensurations; but by taking the course from one known mountain to another with a compass, and computing the distance by the common methods of estimate used by travellers on horse-back.

"Andrew Montour and John Pattin say, that the Road is very crooked, and that having, by the Governor's direction (to said Pattin) observed the courses and distances with all the exactness in their power, it cannot, in their judgment, on a straight line, exceed eighty-five miles; by which estimation sixty-two of the travelled miles are lost in the crooks between the Three Springs and Shanopin's.

"William West saith, likewise, that the Road is very crooked, and that in many places, travelling several miles produces but a few miles westing; particularly, between the Shawana Cabins and Kekinnypalin's, computed near thirty miles, he thinks, would not make more than ten miles westing."

"TO THE SIDELING HILL GAP, 8 MILES."

The Road through Sideling Hill Mountain by this Gap was nearly identical with the present north line of Fulton County, near Waterfall post-office, at the northern extremity of the division line between Taylor and Wells townships. Sideling Hill Gap is still called by that name, and lies between Dublin Mills post-office, in Taylor Township, and New Granada post-office, in Wells Township. John Patten and Andrew Montour, in their table of distances, estimated the distance from the Three Springs to Sideling Hill to be seven miles; (*i.e.*, by the Traders' Path) or, by the compass, five miles; course, S. 70 W. After passing through the Gap, the Path proceeded up Wells Valley in a southwesterly direction. Near Sideling Hill Gap, in March, 1765, James Smith and ten of his companions, disguised as Indians, attacked a convoy of Traders' goods, killed and wounded six of their horses, and burned sixty-three loads of goods.

"TO JUNIATA HILL, 8 MILES."

Patten's account of this portion of the Road reads: "From Sideling Hill to Contz's Harbor, 8 miles; from Contz's Harbor to the top of Ray's Hill, 1 mile." Juniata Hill was better known as Wray's Hill; or Ray's Hill, as Patten spelled it. "Contz's Harbor" was probably in the southwestern corner of what is now Wells Township, Fulton County. The Trail may have crossed the Mountain about three miles west of the present Wells Tannery post-office, entering what is now Bedford County by way of Wray's Cove, in East Providence Township.

"TO JUNIATA CREEK, AT YE CROSSING, 8 MILES."

Patten's account reads: "From Ray's Hill to the first Crossing of Juniata, 10 miles." From the top of Wray's Hill, the Trail led down Tubmill Creek, to a point above its mouth, where, in later years, James Martin established a ferry, at what is now Breezewood post-office, about one mile west of the village of Ray's Hill. From this point westward the route followed by the Traders' Path was the same as that over which, a few years later, Burd's Road and Forbes's Road were built.

"TO THE SNAKE'S SPRING, 8 MILES."

Patten's account reads: "From the First Crossing of Juniata to Allaguapy's Gap, 6 miles." The Snake Spring was in the present township of the same name, in Bedford County, just west of Warriors' Ridge (also called Tussey's Mountain, on Scull's map of 1759). Alliquippa's Gap intersects the Mountain at this point, and its eastern opening is just west of the village of Everett. This place is located on Bloody Run. Everett itself was called Bloody Run prior to 1873. It was an important point in the early history of the Indian migrations; for it was here that the great north and south Trail known as the Warriors' Path, crossed the east and west Trail. Bloody Run, itself, is said by Samuel Evans, a writer on Lancaster County history, to have been so-called from the fact (?) that in the summer of 1763 a party of Indians who had joined in the conspiracy of Pontiac, is said to have attacked a party of Traders at this point, killed a number of the pack-horse drivers, destroyed all the goods they could not carry off; and pursued the fleeing Traders over several of the Mountain ranges to the banks of the Susquehanna.[1] The only attack on Traders near this point known to history was that of James Smith and his "Black Boys," at Sideling Hill in 1765. One of the Traders, present at the time the 1763 attack took place, Mr. Evans says, was Alexander Lowrey, of Donegal. Others, who were either present, or had sent goods with the caravan in 1765, or had made losses elsewhere (most of them in 1763), were William Trent, Robert Callender, David Franks, Joseph Simon, Levy A. Levy, Phillip Boyle, John Baynton, Samuel Wharton, George Morgan, Joseph Spear, Thomas Smallman, John Welch, Edmund Moran, Evan Shelby, Samuel Postlethwait, John Gibson, Richard Winston, Dennis Crohon, William Thompson, Abraham Mitchell, James Dundas, Thomas Dundas, and

---

[1] Dr. John Ewing, who took observations in southwestern Pennsylvania to determine the boundary line, in June, 1784, writes in his *Journal* that Bloody Run was so called because of "the murder of a number of people sent to escort provisions to Mr. [William] Buchanan, who was surveying ye roads to Bedford in ye year 1755." *Penna. Archives*, 6th series, xiv., 7.

John Ormsby. These Traders claimed to have lost goods by this and other attacks in 1763 to the value of 80,862 pounds sterling, which was probably a grossly exaggerated claim. It is true that claims for all the goods lost by these and other Traders on the frontier, during the course of Pontiac's War, as well as those destroyed by James Smith and the "Black Boys" in 1765, were included in their bill for damages.[1] The chiefs of the Six Nations agreed with Sir William Johnson in April and May, 1765, to cede the Traders certain lands between the Ohio and the Alleghany Mountains in compensation for their losses in 1763; and on November 4, 1768, at Fort Stanwix, the Six Nations deeded to the twenty-three Traders whose names have been printed, all that part of the present state of West Virginia lying between the Little Kanawha, Laurel Hill, the Monongahela, the southern line of Pennsylvania, extended to the Ohio, and along that river to the mouth of Little Kanawha. William Trent and his associates organized the Indiana Land Company, and gave the name of Indiana to their grant, which is so called on Hutchins's map of 1778. The Virginia Legislature refused to confirm the grant from the Indians, however; and the Traders eventually suffered the additional loss of all they had paid for securing and protecting this grant.

The name, "Allaquapy's Gap," applied to the pass through the Mountain at this point by John Patten, so early as March, 1754, is an indication that Queen Alliquippa may have lived for a time in that vicinity, prior to her removal to the Ohio, before 1731. In later years, as we have seen, Alliquippa's Town was located on both banks of the Ohio River, below Pittsburgh, opposite McKee's Rock and Brunot's Island. Brunot's Island itself was formerly called Alliquippa's Island,[2] and Chartier's Creek, which flows into the Ohio opposite this Island, is called "Alloquepy River, three miles below Pittsburgh," in the narrative of the captivity of Marie Le Roy and Barbara Leininger, 1755 to 1759.

In December, 1753, Washington visited Queen Alliquippa at her cabin near the Forks of the Youghiogheny. On June 1, 1754, accompanied by Tanacharison, or the Half King, and some twenty-five to thirty families of Mingoes and Delawares, Alliquippa joined Washington's camp at Fort Necessity. Between the time of his defeat there and Braddock's rout at the Monongahela a year later, it is probable that she retired to the English camp at Fort Cumberland. At any rate, she was reported, at a meeting of the Pennsylvania Council, August 22, 1755, as then living near Ray's Town; and Colonel James Burd dated a letter[3] from "Allogueepy's Town," near Raystown, June 17, 1755. She had probably

[1] See *Virginia State Papers*, i., 273; *Publications of the Lancaster County (Penna.) Historical Society*, ix., 305; *Mass. Hist. Coll.*, Fourth Series, ix.
[2] Craig's *Olden Time*, ii., 403.
[3] *Penna. Col. Rec.*, vi., 435.

gone back to her former home at "Allaguapy's Gap" sometime in 1754.

"Allaquippa's Town" is mentioned and included in a patent to a tract of land situated near Mount Dallas, on the south side of the Juniata, in the present Snake Spring Township, the title to which was obtained by Elizabeth Tussey, widow, in 1769. Her improvements dated from before the year 1763. Tussey's house is shown on Scull's map of 1759, at the western opening of Alleguippy's Gap; and that part of Warriors' Ridge Mountain to the eastward which is north of the Gap, is called Tussey's Mountain on Howell's map of 1792. A score or more of Indian graves marked the site of Alliquippa's Town at the time of the settlement there by the whites, some of which graves were opened in 1855. It is not unlikely that Queen Alliquippa herself may have died and been buried here very soon after her return from the Monongahela.

"TO RAY'S TOWN, 4 MILES."

Patten's account reads: "From Allaguapy's Gap to Ray's Town, 5 miles." The Snake Spring of John Harris's account, therefore, was one mile west of Alliquippa's Gap. Ray's Town, like Frank's Town, was named for an Indian Trader; and it also marked the site or propinquity of an early Indian settlement. The city of Bedford stands on the spot at the present day; but all efforts of its local historians, heretofore, have failed to discover why the first English settlement at this place was named Ray's Town. So far as the records show, Garret [Gerard] Pendergrass was the first known white man to settle here, he having built a cabin on the site of Bedford in 1752,[1] by permission of the Six Nation chiefs. The locality was even then known as Ray's Town, as shown by these accounts of John Harris and John Patten; although for some years before Pendergrass's settlement there, it contained no houses nor inhabitants. Christopher Gist passed over the Path at this point in the early part of November, 1750, but makes no reference to it by name or otherwise in his *Journal*. The Indian town or towns which once existed in its vicinity probably stood there before 1730, and may have remained until some five or ten years after that date. The next station on the Path west of Ray's Town, as noted by both Harris and Patten, was that of the Shawnee Cabins. These cabins, of course, marked the residence, for a more or less protracted period, of Shawnees in the vicinity. If they were standing in 1754, as to which we have no knowledge, they could hardly have been erected so early as 1730. But the name, Alliquippa's Gap, applied to the mountain pass five miles to the east of the site of Ray's Town, would suggest the possibility that she and some of her tribe may have lived there prior to 1731. Her town was on the Ohio in

---

[1] *Penna. Archives*, Second Series, vii., 306. William West called the place Pendergrass's or Ray's Town in March, 1754, *Col. Rec.*, v., 761.

that year. If there was a settlement of Alliquippa's followers on one side and a Shawnee village on the other, Ray's Town might have been an appropriate place for an English Trader to establish his trading-cabin; and undoubtedly one of them did so, at this point. His name was John Wray; and from him Ray's Town, Ray's Hill, and Ray's Cove have all taken their names. We first come across John Wray's name in the Minutes of the Pennsylvania Provincial Council, under date of September 2, 1732; when he was called upon to assist Conrad Weiser as interpreter, at a conference held by the Governor with a number of the chiefs of the Senecas, Cayugas, and Oneidas. Wray had therefore traded with the Mingoes, possibly the Conestogas, and was familiar with the Iroquois speech. After this conference, he may have started immediately towards Allegheny; for he is reported in the records under date of September 30, 1732, as having come down from there with two Shawnee chiefs, who formerly had lived at Potomac, and who arrived in Philadelphia on September 28th. John Wray acted as interpreter for these Indians, with Edmund Cartlidge and Peter Chartier, at a conference held with them by the Governor and Council, September 30th. Wray was paid five pounds for his services. Ray's Town was on the direct Path from Old Shawnee Town on the Potomac to the Allegheny; and it is well within the bounds of probability to say that John Wray may have traded with the Shawnees at Opessa's Town on the Potomac while he was living at Ray's Town, and before they had emigrated to the Ohio.

It is possible that the stations on the Trading Paths known as Ray's Town, Frank's Town, etc., may have been facetiously so-called, by the early Traders passing along the Trail, merely because at these points the Traders whose names they were given had there made their sleeping-places, or temporary camps, on one or more occasions, during their trips back and forth between the Susquehanna and the Allegheny. Stations of this kind were numerous, such as Hart's Log, John Hart's Sleeping-Place, Thomas Mitchell's Sleeping-Place, Edward Warren's Sleeping-Place, James Dunning's Sleeping-Place, Peter Shaver's Sleeping-Place, etc. In the case of Ray's Town, however, this does not seem probable; for the reason that John Wray's name was applied not only to his "Town," but also to Ray's Hill, Ray's Cove, Ray's (or Ray's Town) Branch of the Juniata, etc.; all of which would go to indicate that Wray's residence at Ray's Town was more than a transitory one.

Dunning's Creek and Dunning's Mountain, immediately to the north of Raystown, are both shown on Reading Howell's map of 1792. These were both so named for another Indian Trader, James Dunning, the same who was robbed by Peter Chartier and his band of Shawnees, while returning up the Ohio River from a trading expedition, April 18, 1745.

Alliquippa's Gap, from the East.
The Indian village was built on the bottom and terraces south of the Juniata.

"TO THE SHAWANA CABBINS, 8 MILES."

In his account of the Road, John Patten gives the distance the same as above. The Shawnee Cabins stood a mile and one-half east of the present town of Schellsburg, in Napier Township, Bedford County. As stated in the preceding section, the cabins may not have been standing in 1754; but of course they stood there when the name was first applied to that point on the route. Whether they once marked the site of an established Indian village or were merely temporary huts, erected for a night's or a season's shelter, during the hunting or migratory trip of some roving band of Shawnees from the Potomac or Susquehanna, it is impossible at this date to determine.

"TO ALLEGHENY HILL, 6 MILES."

Patten's account of the Road reads: "From Shawonese Cabbins to the top of Allegheny Mountain, 8 miles." The Trail crossed Alleghany Ridge from the northern corner of what is now Alleghany Township, Somerset County; and proceeded thence in a northwestern direction, its course being approximately identical with the present boundary line between the townships of Shade and Stony Creek.

"TO EDMUND'S SWAMP, 6 MILES."

Patten's account gives the distance as eight miles. Edmund's Swamp, like Ray's Town, was named for a Trader—Edmund Cartlidge, one of the first of the Conestoga Traders to reach the Allegheny. The fact of his name being given to one of the halting-places along the route of the Raystown Path suggests that he may have used this southern Path on some of his earliest trips westward. He began trading with the Delawares at Allegheny as early as 1727; and his journeys over this Trail were perhaps contemporary with those of John Wray and James Dunning. Buckstown, Shade Township, stands to-day over what was known in Cartlidge's time as Edmund's Swamp.

"TO STONY CREEK, 6 MILES."

Patten's account reads: "From Edmund's Swamp to Cowamahony Creek, 6 miles." The Path crossed the Stony Fork of Quemahoning Creek at a point just east of the present village of Stoystown, Quemahoning Township, Somerset County. Christopher Gist, who travelled over this Trail in the first week of November, 1750, records in his *Journal*, under date of November 4th and 5th: "Crossed the Juniatta and went up it S. 55 W., about 16 miles. Sunday, 5. Continued the same course, S. 55 W., 6 miles, to the top of a large mountain, called Allegheny Mountain. Here our Path turned, and we went N. 45 W., 6 miles. Here we encamped."

"TO KICKENEY PAULIN'S HOUSE (INDIAN), 6 MILES."

Patten's account of the Road reads: "From Cowamahony to Kackanapaulin's, 5 miles." Gist's account of the same part of the Path was as follows: "Set out N. 70 W., about eight miles. Here I crossed a Creek of Susquehanna, and, it raining hard, I went into an old Indian cabin, where I stayed all night." Frederick Post travelled over the same Path, then widened to a wagon road, with Forbes's army, November 6 and 7, 1758. He makes the following entries in his *Journal* under those dates: "We set off [from the western base of Alleghany Mountain], and found one of the worst roads that ever was travelled, until Stony Creek. . . . We lodged this night at Stony Creek. 7th, We arose early, and made all the haste we could on our journey. We crossed the large Creek, Kekempalin,[1] near Laurel Hill. Upon the hill we overtook the artillery, and came, before sunset, to Loyal Hanning."

Kickeney Paulin's, or Keckenepaulin's Cabin stood on a tributary of Quemahoning Creek, probably that now known as Picking's Run, near Jenner Cross Roads, Jenner Township, Somerset County. The Indian chief for whom the Cabin and the stream were named, was the same individual whose name was also applied in Post's time to the site of a former Shawnee Town at the mouth of Loyalhanna Creek. Keckenepaulin was a Delaware captain, or minor chief, whom Post met in Council at Kuskuskies, September 3, 1758. We first read of him in the narrative of Barbara Leininger and Marie Le Roy, two girls who were taken prisoners by some Delaware Indians of Kittanning, October 16, 1755, at the time of the attack on the settlers at John Penn's Creek. In their *Narrative*, these two girls state: "That they were both inhabitants of this Province, and lived on John Penn's Creek, near George Gabriel's; that on the 16th of October, 1755, a party of fourteen Indians fell upon the inhabitants at that Creek by surprise, and killed fifteen, and took and carried off prisoners, examinants and eight more. . . . The names of the Indians were Kechkinnyperlin, Joseph Compass and young James Compass, young Thomas Hickman, one Kalasquay, Souchy, Machynego, Katoochquay. These examinants were carried to the Indian Town Kittanning, where they staid till September, 1756, and were in ye fort opposite thereto when Col. Armstrong burned it; thence were carried to Fort Duquesne, and many other women and children, they think an hundred, who were carried away from ye several provinces of Pennsylvania, Maryland, and Virginia. Six hundred French and one hundred Indians at Fort Duquesne. They staid two months, and then were carried to Saucany, twenty-five miles below, at ye mouth of Big Beaver

---

[1] In all the editions of Posts' Journals which have come under the notice of the writer, this name is spelled "Rekempalin." The error was caused by the translator of Post mistaking his German "K" for an "R."

Creek. In ye spring, 1757, they were carried to Kuskusky, up Beaver Creek twenty-five miles, where they staid till they hear ye English were marching against Duquesne; and then ye Indians quitted Kuskusky, and took these examinants with them to Muskingham, as they think, 150 miles. On the 16th March [1759], made their escape, and got into Pittsburgh on the 31st."[1]

Major George Armstrong, in command of an advanced detachment of Forbes's army, wrote Colonel Bouquet from "Kickeny Pallan's," July 26, 1758, that this point "is the best place for a deposit [of supplies] between the Alleghanies and Laurel Hill." He wrote Bouquet again the following day, from "Drunding Creek," and explains in his letter that "Drounding Creek," is another name for "Kickeny Pallen's."

"TO THE CLEAR FIELDS, 7 MILES."

Patten's account reads: "From Kackanapaulin's to Loyal Hanning, 18 miles." Loyalhanna was the third stopping place beyond Keckenepaulin's. Gist left the latter place on Sunday, November 11, 1750. He writes: "Set out late in the morning, N. 70 W., 6 miles, crossing two forks of a Creek of Susquehanna. Here, the way being bad, we encamped and I killed a turkey. Monday, 12—Set out N. 45 W., 8 miles, crossed a Laurel Mountain." On August 23, 1758, Sir John St. Clair, who was building the road towards Loyal Hanna in advance of Forbes's army, wrote to Colonel Henry Bouquet: "I wrote you yesterday . . . that three waggons have got to this place; the road not so good as I shall make it. . . . I hope to get to Kikoney Pawlin's to-morrow night; if not, shall do it next day." That evening, he wrote again, from "Kikoney Paulin's": "It is impossible for me to tell you any more than I have done about the road to L[oyal] H[anna]. I required 600 men to make the road over the Laurel Ridge in three days, on condition I was to see it done myself, and perhaps I might reach L. H. the third day. I expect to get the road cleared as far as the Clear Fields, a mile from the foot of L[aurel] R[idge], on this side, by the time the army comes up."[2] This extract fixes the location of the Clear Fields as from one to two miles west of the present village of Jennerstown, Somerset County.

"TO THE OTHER SIDE OF THE LAWREL HILL, 5 MILES."

The Road took a winding course over the Mountain, and descended to its western base at a point about three miles east of the present village of Laughlinstown, Ligonier Township, Westmoreland County.

---

[1] *Penna. Archives*, iii., 633; a fuller account of their captivity, with the names of other captives at Kittanning, is given in the Second Series of the *Archives*, vii., 427–438.
[2] Hulbert, *The Old Glade Road* 145.

"TO LOYAL HANING, 6 MILES."

Patten, as we have seen, gave the distance from "Kackanapaulin's to Loyal Hannin," as 18 miles. The distance by compass (*i.e.*, the airline distance), he estimated as twelve miles, west. Gist's *Journal* relates under date of November 14, 1750: "Set out N. 45 W., 6 miles, to Loyalhannan, an Old Indian Town, on a Creek of Ohio called Kiscominatis; then N. 1 mile, N.W. 1 mile, to an Indian's camp on the said Creek." The Revs. Charles Beatty and George Duffield passed over the Raystown Road to Fort Pitt in August and September, 1766, on a mission to the Ohio Indians at Muskingum. In Beatty's *Journal* of their travels, he relates that they left Bedford on Tuesday, September 2d, on their way to Fort Pitt. "After riding about fifteen miles," he proceeds, "we came to the foot of Alleghany Mountain, and having fed our horses, we began to ascend the steep, which is about two miles from the foot to the top of the Mountain. We travelled about eight miles farther, along a bad road, to Edmund's Swamp, and lodged at Mr. John Miller's. 3d, Wednesday, Sat out early this morning, having had but poor lodging; went about five miles, to Stony Creek, and breakfasted. From thence we went to the foot of Lawrel Hill, eight miles; crossing which, we arrived at Fort Ligonier, thirteen miles."

Just six years later, the Revs. David McClure and Levi Frisbie travelled over the same road, on a like errand. They arrived, on August 13, 1772, at Bedford, which, McClure writes, "lies in an extensive and fertile valley." "The next day," he adds, "we rode across the valley, and had before us the sublime prospect of the Alleghany Mountain, which we soon began to climb. . . . This mountain is eleven miles over; in some parts so steep that we were necessitated to hold by the tails of our horses, and let them haul us up. . . . Arriving at the summit we were agreeably surprised to come upon a verdant plain, about half a mile in width. . . . The eastern side of the Alleghany is steep; but the westward descends with a gentle slope. . . . We descended, and at the setting of the sun, came to the house of a Mr. Millar, twenty-five miles from Bedford. August 15th—Saturday morning, ascended a steep hill, and descending a valley, came to Stoney Creek. . . . Rode to McMullen's, nine miles, and to McClee's, one mile further, where, resting awhile, we began to ascend the Laurel Hill; which is as deserving of the more exalted name of Mountain as several of its fellows. It is about nine miles over; although not so steep or high as the Alleghany. . . . At sunset, we arrived at Ligonier, and put up at the house of the Widow Campbell's. From Wednesday morning to Saturday evening, we have been clambering mountains; the most of the way was through a zigzag or serpentine horse-path. . . . The country before us was plain and fertile, about fifty miles to Pittsburgh."

The Raystown Path

Fort Ligonier was erected on the site of the Old Indian Town of Loyalhanna by the advanced detachments of General Forbes's army in September and October, 1758. The town of Ligonier now occupies the spot. Its annals from 1758 until after the close of the Revolution are more or less familiar to many students of American history; and those of few other towns in America exceed them in interest.

"TO THE BIG BOTTOM, 8 MILES."

"TO THE CHESTNUT RIDGE, 8 MILES."

"TO THE PARTING OF THE ROADS, 4 MILES; THENCE ONE ROAD LEADS TO SHANOPPIN'S TOWN, THE OTHER TO KISSCOMENETTES OLD TOWN."

There is some uncertainty as to the course of the Path from Loyalhanna Indian Town to the Parting of the Roads. Patten's account makes the distance between the two points, by compass, or in a direct line, ten miles; while John Harris gives the distance by the Path as twenty miles. Harris's estimates of these distances are evidently excessive. Evans's map of 1755, Scull's map of 1770, and Hutchins's maps of 1764 and 1778, all show the course of the road along the south side of Loyalhanna Creek. After crossing that stream at what is now Ligonier, the Path as shown on these maps, crosses Four Mile Run, Nine Mile Run, and Twelve Mile Run, all tributaries of the Loyalhanna from the south side. In a note to Gist's *Journals*, Mr. William Darlington, the editor, makes the following statement: "The Path here [at Loyalhanna Indian Town] left the Loyalhanna, and by a *northwest* course, passed through the Chestnut Ridge at the Miller's Run Gap, and reached the Creek again at the Big Bottom, below the present town of Latrobe." A road following this course is shown on Reading Howell's map of 1792, parallel with and north of the road along the southern side of Loyalhanna Creek. Post's *Journal* for November, 1758, states that the writer of the *Journal* left the English camp at Fort Ligonier on the 9th of that month, on his way to the Delaware towns in the vicinity of Fort Duquesne. Post then writes: "We passed through a tract of good land about six miles, on the Old Trading Path, and came to the creek again, where there is a large fine bottom, well-timbered; from thence, we came upon a hill, to an advanced breast-work, about ten miles from camp, well situated for strength, facing a small branch of the aforesaid creek; the hill is steep down, perpendicular about twenty feet, on the south side, which is a great defence; on the west side, the breast-work, about seven feet high; where we encamped that night." Mr. Dallas Albert, in his articles on Fort Ligonier (*Frontier Forts of Pennsylvania*, ii., 260), states that Breastwork Hill is still easily located, being on the Nine Mile Run, in Unity Township, Westmoreland County, about a mile and one-half south-east of Latrobe. "The hill has always been known as Breast-work Hill," he adds. Possibly, Forbes's army may have followed the route to the north of the Loyalhanna, in its march from Ligonier to Fort Duquesne; crossing the Loyalhanna a mile or two below the present town of Latrobe; although in Albert's volume on the *Frontier Forts of Western Pennsylvania*, the map bound in at page 65, indicates that this course was the route taken by Major James Grant on his retreat, after the disastrous engagement before Fort Duquesne. But it is most probable that the Old Traders' Path led in a *southwesterly* direction from Loyalhanna Indian Town, crossing Chestnut Ridge some two or three miles south of Loyalhanna Creek, and came to the creek again by way of the Nine Mile Run, northwest of the present post-office of Youngstown. Gist travelled over this path from Loyalhanna Indian Town ten miles, on November 16, 1750, on a course which he described as "S. 70 W."

The "Forks of the Road" were probably near the west bank of Twelve Mile Run (this Run was supposed to be twelve miles from Fort Ligonier), and not far from what, since 1772, has been known as Unity Presbyterian Church, the centre of the first considerable English settlement west of the Laurel Ridge Mountain.

"TO THE BIG LICK, 3 MILES."
"TO THE BEAVER DAMS, 6 MILES."

The Big Lick was probably one of the head springs of Fourteen Mile Run, a stream shown on Reading Howell's map of 1792.

The Beaver Dams may have been on the head waters of Jack's Run, a mile or two northwest of the present Greensburg, Westmoreland County, and near the site of what, in 1773, was known as Hannastown, the first county-seat and the point where English courts of justice were first established west of the Alleghanies. "Beaver Run and Beaver Dam," says Mr. Dallas Albert, in his *History of Westmoreland County*, "landmarks on Jack's Run, were evidently named after the presence of these rodents, which in early times, were numerous in all our streams. Their 'slides' have been seen at Beaver Dam by many persons still living." The Traders' Path here followed the divide, afterwards traversed by Forbes's army of occupation, lying between the heads of a number of small streams which flow towards the Allegheny on the north and towards the Monongahela on the south. On May 4, 1764, one, Jacob Myers, with Andrew Byerly and twelve others,[1] "lately betwixt Legonier and Fort Pitt; being all drove from our habitations by the savage enemy in the latter end of May last, 1763; our homes and furni-

[1] The names of the other twelve were Robert Creighton, John Fields, Samuel Shannon, Frederick Seever, Isaac Stimble, Andrew Bonsure, Michael Rutter, Robert Laughlin, Michael Kaufman, John Long, Robert Rodgers, and Robert Atkins. See Bouquet Papers, in the Canadian Archives at Ottawa, Series A, xxviii., 109.

ture being all burned, and our crops all destroyed," petitioned the "Commissioners at Carlisle" for relief. It is probable that Jacob Myers's settlement was on what was afterwards the site of Hannastown. The latter place was built on the head of one of the branches of Crabtree Creek which is known to this day, and since 1769, as "Miers's Spring." Like Andrew Byerly at Bushy Run, Jacob Myers may have had here a station for the purpose of supplying food, shelter, and forage to expresses travelling back and forth between Forts Pitt and Ligonier. The "Miers's Spring" tract of land came into the possession of Lieut. Colonel John Wilkins, who was in command at Fort Pitt in the summer of 1768. From him, it passed to Robert Hanna,[1] who secured title from the Proprietors in 1769, built a tavern, laid out a village site, and had the place established as the county-seat when Westmoreland County was erected in 1773. The town was burned by the Indians under Guyasutha, July 13, 1782; and never rebuilt.

"TO JAMES DUNNING'S SLEEPING-PLACE, 8 MILES."

The Trader for whom this stopping place was named was the same who was plundered of his peltries by Peter Chartier and his band of Shawnees, while returning up the Allegheny River in a canoe, April 18, 1745. His name is variously spelled in the Colonial Records as Dunning, Denning, Dennin, and Denny. On July 9, 1747, there was laid before the Pennsylvania Council the report of a number of conferences held by Conrad Weiser, at Chambers's Mill, near Paxtang, with Shekallamy and other Six Nation chiefs. In the course of this report, Weiser writes: "I am sorry to add, that there are great complaints against two of our Traders. One is James Dunning, who is accused to have stolen forty-seven deerskins and three horses (or mares), upon the heads of Joniady River. The circumstances are very strong. The Indian from whom the skins and horses have been stolen is a Delaware Indian, a sober, quiet, and good-natured man. . . . James Dunning is gone down Ohio River, and will stay out long. The Indian was content that I should inform the Council of his misfortune. He not only lost his skins and horses, but pursued James Dunning, in vain, to the place called Canayiahagen [Cuyahoga], on the south side of Lake Erie; from thence back again to the place where he left the skins; and from thence again to Ohio; but all in vain, for he could not find or come up with James Dunning. The other complaint was made by the same Indian against John Powell, a liver on Sasquehanna River, on the Indians' land, above the Endless Mountains; who

[1] Simon Girty procured deeds to this tract from Jacob Myers in 1773 and 1774. See his deposition, made at Niagara, May 12, 1788. *Ontario Archives*, 1904, pp. 988, 1282.

is accused of stealing two bundles of skins from the same Indian, while he was pursuing James Dunning."

James Dunning's Sleeping-Place, on the Raystown Path, was probably located on the head waters of Brush Creek, in what is now Penn Township, Westmoreland County, near Harrison City, and not far from the battle-ground of Bushy Run, where Colonel Bouquet defeated the Delawares and Shawnees in August, 1763.

"TO COCK-EYE'S CABIN, 8 MILES."

In his *Journal*, under dates of November 16 and 17, 1750, Gist writes: "Set out [from the Indian Camp, one mile west of Loyalhanna Indian Town] S. 70 W., 10 m. Nov. 17, the same course (S. 70 W.) 15 m., to an old Indian's Camp." Mr. William Darlington, in his notes to Gist's *Journal*, says that this camp was Cock-Eye's Cabin; and its owner, a Delaware Indian, well-known to the Traders. He adds: "It was on Bushy Run, a branch of Turtle Creek, near the place of the two days' battle between the army under Colonel Bouquet and the Indians, led by Guyasutha, August 5th and 6th, 1763, about three miles north of Penn Station, on the Pennsylvania Railroad, and twenty-three miles east of Pittsburgh." If this was the case, there is considerable discrepancy between the accounts of John Harris and Christopher Gist. Harris makes the distance between Loyalhanna Indian Town and Cock-Eye's Cabin, forty-five miles; and from thence to Shanoppin's Town (now Pittsburgh), twenty-three miles. Gist states that the distance from Loyalhanna to the Indian Camp was twenty-six miles; and from thence to Shanoppin's Town, twenty miles. The Bushy Run branch of Brush Creek is about thirty miles west of Ligonier by the road to-day. After the occupation of Fort Duquesne by the English in 1758-59, and before 1763, Andrew Byerly, with the permission of the commanding officer, settled on a tract of land near where the Road crossed Bushy Run, and established a station, for the accommodation of expresses and soldiers travelling between Ligonier and Pittsburgh. On May 29, 1763, during the siege of Fort Pitt by the Indians, Commandant Ecuyer wrote to Bouquet from that post: "The Indians have told Byerly [at Bushy Run] to leave his house within four days, or he and all his family would be murdered." Byerly received the warning, but his family was in no condition to be removed, as his wife had just been confined. One night, while the husband was absent, having gone with a small party to bury some persons who had been killed at some distance from his station, a friendly Indian came to his cabin and informed the family that they would all be killed if they did not make their escape before daylight. The mother arose from her sick-couch, and wrote the information on the door of the cabin, that her husband might get it on his return. A horse was then saddled, and the mother mounted, with her three days' old babe at her breast, and another infant tied on behind. Her two older sons, both mere children, followed on foot; and together during the whole of the night and a part of the succeeding day, the family struggled through the wilderness over the Path to Fort Ligonier, thirty miles to the east; where they all managed to arrive in safety.

"TO THE FOUR MILE RUN, 11 MILES."

This was probably the stream known in Pittsburgh for more than a hundred years as Negley's Run; which is about four miles east of the next station of John Harris's itinerary.

"TO SHANOPPIN'S TOWN, 4 MILES."

On November 15, 1753, Louis Montour informed the Governor and the Speaker of the Assembly that Shanoppin Town was situated about three miles above the Forks of the Monongahela, and contained about twenty men. John Hogan, who was taken prisoner at the destruction of Fort Granville, and carried to Fort Duquesne in August, 1756, in a deposition made by him in the following June, stated, that, "at about two miles distance from Fort Duquesne, there was an Indian Town, containing fifty or sixty natives, of whom twenty were able to bear arms." Shanoppin's Town, according to George Croghan, was situated on the south bank of the Allegheny, nearly opposite what is now known as Herr's Island, at the mouth of the Two Mile Run,[1] in what is now the Twelfth Ward of the city of Pittsburgh. Shanoppin's name appears signed to letters from the Indians at Allegheny as early as April, 1730. He died between 1748 and 1751. If his town was the same as that called "Senangel's Town" by Le Tort and Davenport in their examination before Governor Gordon, October 29, 1731, it contained sixteen families and fifty men, of the Delaware tribe, at that time.

"TO THE LOGS TOWN, DOWN THE RIVER, 16 MILES."

Christopher Gist left Shanoppin's Town for Logstown, Saturday, November 24, 1750, swimming his horses across the Allegheny and riding thence west and northwest along its right bank a distance estimated by him to be twenty-one miles. Cumming's *Western Pilot* (1834) estimates the distance from the steamboat landing on the Monongahela River at Pittsburgh, to Economy, which is about a mile above the site of the Old Logs Town, as twenty-two and one-half miles. By the Pennsylvania Railroad the site of Logstown is just eighteen miles from the railroad station in Allegheny City.

Logstown will be made the subject of a later chapter.

[1] See Peyton's *History of Augusta County, Virginia*, p. 75.

CHAPTER XI

THE TRADERS AT ALLEGHENY ON THE MAIN PATH; WITH SOME ANNALS OF KITTANNING AND CHARTIER'S TOWN

READERS of American Colonial history are more or less familiar with the account of the destruction of Kittanning Indian Town in September 1756, by Colonel John Armstrong's command of three hundred troopers recruited from the Scotch-Irish of Cumberland County. Few readers, however, are aware of the importance of this town in Indian and frontier history some twenty-five years before that date.

Known to the French under its Seneca name of Attigue, Atiga, or Adigo,[1] it was the first and chief settlement made by the Delawares when they began to migrate westward from the Susquehanna in 1723-24; and for fifteen years or more thereafter, it was the most important Indian centre west of the Alleghany Mountains. A few years after it came into existence, the Susquehanna and Potomac Shawnees took up their belongings and followed the Delawares over the mountains, establishing themselves a few miles below Kittanning, on the Allegheny, and along its tributary, the Conemaugh, or Kiskiminetas. What became known after its abandonment by them as Chartier's Old Town, at the mouth of Bull Creek, near the present borough of Tarentum, Allegheny County, seems to have been the principal village of the Shawnees during the decade from 1735 to 1745. This town and Kittanning, with two or three smaller villages between, and three or more along the banks of the Kiskiminetas, constituted a centre of Indian population and influence

---

[1] The name appears as "Adjiego" in 1735 (*Penna. Archives*, i., 454); Conrad Weiser wrote it "Adeeky on Ohio," Sep. 12, 1755 (*Col. Rec.* vi., 614). See John Trotter's Deposition, *Penna. Archives*, ii., 131. See also, *N. Y. Col. Doc.*, v., 789; vii., 728, 735; viii., 557; ix., 1035; x., 901, 956; Parkman's *Montcalm and Wolf*, i., 440. Otego Creek in Otsego County, New York, was called Adigo Creek on De Witt's 1790 map of the Upper Susquehanna.

The Delaware Indian name *Kittanning* means "at the Great River," great river being the equivalent of the Iroquois word *Ohio*. As the Great River of the Senecas, the name, Ohio, was at first applied to this river by the Iroquois from the sources of the Allegheny to the mouth of the Mississippi. The secondary meaning of *io*, as "grand," or "beautiful," came to be applied to the Ohio only after the discovery of the upper Mississippi by the French.

known for many years in Pennsylvania Colonial history as "Alleghenia," or "Allegheny on the Main Road." Just what was the "Main Road" at the time the term was applied to distinguish the settlements thereon cannot now positively be asserted. In all probability, however, it was the road which later was known as the Frankstown Path, leading along the Juniata to the Alleghany Mountain, thence across the present counties of Cambria and Indiana; and thence, by two different branches, to Kittanning and to the Shawnee town afterwards called Chartier's Town. The original path to Kittanning from Shamokin by way of the West Branch of the Susquehanna, Bald Eagle Creek, Chinklaclamoose, and Punxsatawney, was so difficult and barren as to be almost entirely destitute of game for man, or fodder for beast; so that it could never have been a much travelled route. The southern Pennsylvania, or Raystown Path, in the opinion of the writer, was, at first, only a westward branch of the great Warriors' Path which led south from what is now Lock Haven, Pennsylvania, up Bald Eagle Valley, through Frankstown, along the valley to the east of Warriors' Ridge, in the present Bedford County, thence down Old Town Run to Old Shawnee Town, on the Potomac (Opessa's Town), where Captain Thomas Cresap had settled, perhaps as early as 1742. Cresap's settlement is referred to in Engineer Harry Gordon's *Journal* of the Braddock Expedition,[1] as "on the track of Indian warriors, when going to war, either northward or southward." The Shawnees who emigrated from Opessa's Town on the Potomac to the Allegheny before 1732 were probably the first of whom there is any record in history to use this Path westward. Christopher Gist, who travelled from Cresap's house to the Forks of the Ohio in 1750, went over the same Path, and has left us a detailed account of the route. An intersecting path from Harris's Ferry through the Cumberland Valley, westward, joined the Warriors' Path at some point near the crossing of the Raystown Branch of Juniata. That this Lower Path from the Susquehanna to the Allegheny was used by the Traders at a comparatively early date seems evident from the fact that one of the noted landmarks along the Path, after it crossed the Alleghany Mountain, was called "Edmund's Swamp," after Edmund Cartlidge, one of the first of the Conestoga Traders to venture westward of the Mountains. Nevertheless, it is probable that the earliest "main road" to Allegheny was the more central Frankstown Path; as it was more direct and easier to travel over. It is now followed for most of the way by the Pennsylvania Railroad.

The first definite reference by the English authorities to the Indian settlements and trade at Kittanning, and the adjacent villages on the Allegheny, to be found in the Colonial Records of Pennsylvania, appears under date of July 4, 1727. In a Council held that day at Philadelphia

[1] See Hulbert's *Braddock's Road*, pp. 80, 89.

between Governor Patrick Gordon and some chiefs of the Five Nations and the Susquehannocks, Madame Montour, "a French woman, who had lived long among these people, and is now interpretress," acted in that capacity. At this conference, the Indians "desire there may be no settlements made up Susquehanna higher than Pextan [now Harrisburg], and that none of the settlers thereabouts be suffered to sell or keep any rum there, for that being the road by which their people go out to war [with the Southern Indians], they are apprehensive of mischief if they meet with liquor in these parts. They desire also, for the same reasons, that none of the Traders be allowed to carry any rum to the remoter parts where James Le Tort trades (that is, Allegheny, on the branches of the Ohio)." The Governor promised them that the sale of rum should be prohibited, both at Pextan and at Allegheny; and Secretary Logan issued letters of instruction to that effect, addressed "To the several Traders of Pennsylvania with the Indians at Allegheny, and the other remote parts in or near to the said Province."

An earlier reference than this, however, to the Allegheny settlement is to be found in the Minutes of the New York Provincial Council, under date of September 7, 1726. On that day Governor Burnet attended an Indian Council at Albany, where he met twelve chiefs of the Iroquois, two from each of the Six Nations.

The Governor asked the chiefs whether they knew of a war hatchet having been given by the French against the Six Nations. The Indians replied, "That they had heard that the Governor of Canada, by two of his interpreters, had given a hatchet of war to the Indians living to the southward [Okowela's clan?], near a branch of Susquehanah, on a branch [Conemaugh] of a river called Adiego, which vents into the Great River, Mississippi. Some of their people who were out fighting came to their habitation, who acquainted them that two Frenchmen had given a hatchet of war, by order of the Governor of Canada, against the Six Nations; which those Indians refused, and said they were a joint of the said Nations, and possessed part of their land; and if any people made war against them, they were to assist them. But when the French saw that those Indians would not accept the hatchet of war, they desired them not to speak of it to the Six Nations; for it was concluded by the French and English to cut them off; and gave them a bundle of papers to be carried to Philadelphia, and from thence to New York, and thence to Albany, and thence to Montreal; and when that arrived there, and the Fort at Niagara was built, then would be the time when the Six Nations were to be cut off. But their warriors happened to get that packet, and burned it."

On the page of the manuscript volume containing this speech of the Indians (*N. Y. Council Minutes*, xv., 92) there appears the following marginal note opposite the word, "Adiego": "Called by the French Olio [Ohio]." This seems to be conclusive proof, in connection with what has already been given, that the word, "Adiego," written by the French, "Adigo," "Atiga," "Attique," etc., was simply another rendering of the Seneca word, "O-hee-yo," the meaning of which is the "Great River," the name applied by the Senecas to the Ohio. It was later localized by the Traders among the Iroquois to the town of Kittanning, and the French erroneously applied it to two or three different tributaries of the Ohio,[1] when it really meant to the Iroquois that River itself. On Bellin's map of Louisiana, printed by Charlevoix, an Indian village on French Creek is called Atigua, and Kittanning, Atiga. On Bonnecamps's map of Ohio, Kittanning is called Atigue. On D'Anville's 1746–55 map, the Kiskiminetas is called the Atigue.

In a letter received by the author from the Rev. William M. Beauchamp, that gentleman writes: "Adiga Creek of 1790 is 'Atage' on a map of 1826, and is equivalent to 'Otego' of the present, and 'Wauteghe' of 1753—dropping the prefix. Bruyas (1670) defines *Ategen* 'to have fire there.' Schoolcraft's Mohawk word for 'fire' is *yotekha*. Cornplanter's lower village on the Allegheny [*Jennuchsadaga*] was called 'burned houses,' the latter part of the name being *adaga*. In Iroquois usage the word for river is to be expressed or understood, the word in question meaning the place where there was a fire—town, houses, or otherwise. *Kittany* is simply 'great,' and might be applied either to the river or mountains; usually to the former, when used for a place. Allegheny probably means the same. While Ohio is usually translated 'beautiful,' it also implies greatness, as in *Onondio*, 'great mountain'; *Ontario*, beautiful or great lake. The proper equivalent would be 'fine,' combining the two."

The Seneca pronunciation of the Iroquois word for "fire," as given to the writer in 1909 by a number of living Senecas from the Tonawanda Reservation, is *O-day-kah;* which is not, as Dr. Beauchamp suggests it might be, synonymous in sound or meaning with the word which the English and French spelled Adiego, Attigue, or Attiga.

The word *Ohio* was formerly applied by the Iroquois to a number of other rivers besides the one which bears that name to-day, and it is significant that anciently it was usually written with the locative suffix *ge* or *gue*. Father Jogues, the French Jesuit martyr-missionary, wrote in 1646, *Oi-o-gue*, as the Huron-Iroquoian name of the Hudson River, given to him at Sarachtoga, with the connection, "at the river." *Ohioge* "at the river"; *Ohioge-son*, "the length of the river," wrote Bruyas. The author of the *Journal of a Journey into the Mohawk Country* (erroneously attributed to Arent van Curler) wrote the same name in 1634, *Oyoge*,

[1] To the Kiskiminetas, the Loyalhanna, the Riviere aux Bœufs, etc.

and gave it as that of the Mohawk River, changing the spelling in his vocabulary to *Oyoghi*, "a kill, or small river." "It is an Iroquoian generic," writes Ruttenber, "applicable to any principal stream or current river, with the ancient related meaning of 'beautiful river.'"[1]

On April 30, 1730, Mukqun, Keakeenhoman, Shawannoppan, Quoowahaune, Lamoohan, and Queekockahwin, "the chiefs of ye Delawares at Alleegaeening, on the Main Road," as Edmund Cartlidge wrote their names, sent a letter to the Governor of Pennsylvania, explaining the circumstances attending the death of John Hart, one of the Shamokin Traders, and the wounding of David Robeson, another Trader, by the Indians, in the Fall of 1729. This letter was interpreted for the Indians by James Le Tort, taken down in writing by Edmund Cartlidge, and witnessed by Jonas Davenport. It concluded with the suggestion, "for to prevent any further misfortunes for the future, we would request that the Governor would please regulate the Traders, and suppress such numbers of them from coming into the woods: and especially from bringing such large quantities of rum." This letter was probably carried to Philadelphia by Cartlidge and Davenport, for those two Traders, about the time of its delivery, presented to the Governor a Memorial on the Indian Trade, signed by themselves and Henry Bailey, a third Trader. The signers of this memorial petitioned the Governor to limit the number of Traders. The condition of the trade at that time was set forth in the following preamble:

Whereas, the promotion of ye European trade is chiefly held up by making immediate returns to Great Britain in skins, furs, &c., and your petitioners for some years past have had a considerable share in promoting that branch of trade, by venturing themselves and goods further than any person formerly did; whereby they got large quantities of skins and furs, and disposed of more goods than had been for many years before, to ye great advantage of ye trade; and this lay chiefly betwixt your petitioners for about three years; and as ye trade in that place, viz.: Alleganeeing, consists in giving large credit to ye Indians in the Fall of the

[1] *Ohyo-hi-yo-ge*, large, chief, or principal river (Hewitt), is also cited by Ruttenber in his *Indian Geographical Names*, pp. 12 and 189, *N. Y. State Hist. Assoc. Coll.*, vol. vi. Horatio Hale writes (*Iroquois Book of Rites*, p. 14): "Cusick, however, does not know it [the Allegheny River] by this name. He calls it the Ohio,—in his uncouth orthography and with a locative particle added, the *Ouau-we-yo-ka*,—which, he says, means 'a principal stream, now Mississippi.' This statement, unintelligible as at the first glance it seems, is strictly accurate. The word *Ohio* undoubtedly signified, in the ancient Iroquois speech, as it still means in the modern Tuscarora, not 'beautiful river,' but 'great river.' It was so-called as being the main stream which received the affluents of the Ohio Valley. In the view of the Iroquois, this 'main stream' commences with what we call the Allegheny River, continues in what we term the Ohio, and then flows on in what we style the Mississippi—of which, in their view, the upper Mississippi is merely an affluent."

year; which, while ye trade lay betwixt us, they would honourably pay in the Spring; till several new Traders, such as had been your petitioners' servants, and other idle fellows, set up for trade, and there brought a small parcel of goods and large quantities of rum in the Spring of ye year, when we should have received our pay, and thereby underselling us in their goods, and so debauching them with rum hindered us from getting our pay, as usually; so that now the Indians stand indebted to us near two thousand pounds worth of peltry, which renders and makes us uncapable of making returns to discharge our merchants, as formerly.

On August 8, 1730, Anthony Sadowsky, John Maddox, and John Fisher, three Traders at Allegheny, complained to Governor Gordon that they had been robbed of a hundred pounds worth of goods by the Indians at Allegheny in June, 1729, and asked that a demand for satisfaction be sent through the Delaware chiefs, "Allumapees, at Shackachtan [Shamokin], and Great Hill, at Allegheny." The Governor accordingly wrote a letter about the matter to Allumapees and Opekasset, at Shamokin, and Mechouquatchugh, or "Great Hill," at Allegheny; but it availed nothing; as Maddox stated in a letter written two years later that he was still without recompense for his stolen goods.

On the 9th, of October, 1731, Governor Rip Van Dam, of New York, wrote to Governor Gordon, enclosing to him a copy of the minutes of a meeting held at Albany, September 25th, by the Indian Commissioners for that Colony. These minutes set forth that Johannis Wendel and Isaac Kip had brought news from Canada to the effect that "John Cour [Joncaire] was gone out to bring over to the interest of the French a new settlement of Indians, above Najagera [Niagara], who have been in commerce with the inhabitants of the Province of Pennsylvania." This information led Governor Gordon to seek for direct news from Allegheny; and on the 29th of October, Jonah Davenport and James Le Tort, two Traders who had lately returned from there, appeared before him, and gave a detailed account of the condition of the Indian settlements at Allegheny. Davenport stated that he had "lately come from Allegeney, where there are Indian settlements consisting of about three hundred Delawares, two hundred and sixty Shawnees, one hundred Asswekalaes, and some Mingoes; that last spring was four years as he remembers, a French gentleman in appearance, with five or six attendants, came down the river to a settlement of the Delaware Indians on Ohio River, which the Delawares call Kithanning, with an intention, as this Examt. believes, to enquire into the numbers of the English Traders in those parts, and to sound the minds of the Indians; that the said French gentleman spoke the Shawanese language, with whom this Examt. has conversed; but that few of the Shawanese being then there, nothing of moment passed." In the spring of 1730, and again in 1731, however, Davenport adds, a number of the Shawanese accompanied the French gentleman to Montreal to meet the French Governor.

James Le Tort, in his examination, states that he "is lately come from Allegeny, where there are several settlements of Delaware, Shawanese, Asswikalus, and Mingoe Indians, to the number of four or five hundred; that for these three years past, a certain French gentleman, who goes by the name of Cavalier,[1] has made it his practice to come every spring amongst the Indians settled there, and deals with them but for a very small value; that he particularly fixed his abode amongst the Shawanese, with whom he holds frequent Councils; and, 't is generally believed, with a design to draw them off from the English interest." Le Tort also speaks of visits made to Montreal by the Shawanese in the early part of the years 1730 and 1731.

Davenport and Le Tort, at the time of their examination, furnished the Governor with an estimate of the number of Indians located at the various towns of the Allegheny settlement, and the names of their chiefs, which was as follows:

"Connumach: 20 families; 60 men; Delawares. Kythenning River, 50 miles distant: 50 families; 150 men; mostly Delawares. Chiefs: Capt. Hill, a Alymaepy; Kykenhammo, a Delaware; Sypous, a Mingoe.

"Senangelstown, 16 miles distant: 16 families; 50 men; Delawares. Chief: Senangel.

"Lequeepees, 60 miles distant: Mingoes, mostly, and some Delawares; 4 settled families, but a great resort of these people.

"On Connumach Creek there are three Shawanese Towns; 45 families; 200 men. Chief: Okowela; suspected to be a favourer of the French interest.

"Asswikales: 50 families; lately from S. Carolina to Ptowmack, and from thence thither; making 100 men. Aqueloma, their chief, true to the English.

"Ohesson upon Choniata, distant from Sasqueh., 60 miles: Shawanese; 20 families; 60 men. Chief: Kissikahquelas.

"Assunepachla upon Choniata, distant, about 100 miles by water and 50 by land from Ohesson: Delawares; 12 families; 36 men."

Senangel's Town, a settlement of the Delawares, is said in the above account, as printed in volume 1 of the *Pennsylvania Archives*, to be sixteen miles distant from the Conemaugh (or Kiskiminetas); while Kittanning is put down as at a distance of fifty miles. It is possible that the latter statement is incorrect, and perhaps the result of a

[1] Two interpreters of a similar name (Louis and Toussaint), appeared at conferences held in Canada in 1748 and 1756. See *N. Y. Col. Doc.*, x., 187, 328, etc. Cavalier was the family name of La Salle. Could this French interpreter who spoke Shawnee have been a member of his family?

typographical error. If we transpose the respective distances from the Conemaugh to Kittanning and Senangel's Town, making the former sixteen and the latter fifty miles from the Conemaugh, then it may be that by Senangel's Town is meant the Delaware village afterwards known as Shanoppin's Town, near Two Mile Creek, occupying a part of the site of the present city of Pittsburgh. If Senangel's Town was really but sixteen miles from the Conemaugh, then it may have been located in what is now Indiana County.

"Captain Hill," mentioned above as the head chief of the Delawares at Kittanning and Conemaugh, is spoken of as an "Alymaepy." This means that he was of the Turtle Clan of the Delawares, of which Allumapees, then living at Shamokin, was the hereditary sachem, or great civil chief. Captain Hill was addressed by Governor Gordon as "Mechouquatchugh," in a letter written to him by that official August 20, 1730; the Delaware term for "Great Hill" being *Mechek-Wachtschu*, according to Dr. Brinton's Lenape Dictionary.

The Conemaugh Town of the Delawares may have been at the mouth of the Kiskiminetas, on the south side, nearly opposite what is now the town of Freeport; or, it may have been opposite the mouth of Carnahan's Run, in the present township of Allegheny, Westmoreland County, a town which, twenty years later, was well known to the Traders as Kiskiminetas Indian Town. Or, possibly, it may have been what in 1758 was called Keckenepaulin's Old Town.

"Lequeepees" is clearly a variation for Alliquippa's Town, which, in 1752, was situated on the north side of the Ohio, from one to three miles below the Forks. Queen Alliquippa was generally spoken of as a Seneca woman; but she was probably a Mohawk; as her son later became a chief of the Mohawk tribe. Washington visited her at the Forks of the Youghiogheny in December, 1753. After the English were driven from that vicinity she settled near Raystown (now Bedford). She was the widow either of a former Conestoga chief, or of a Seneca chief who had settled among the Conestogas; and she accompanied her husband to Newcastle, Delaware, in 1701, to bid farewell to William Penn at the time of his final departure for England.

Reference has already been made to the three Shawnee towns on the Conemaugh. One of them, possibly, was what was afterwards known as Keckenepaulin's Old Town, at the mouth of the Loyalhanna. One is called Black Legs Town on Scull's map of 1770, and placed at the mouth of Black Legs Creek, on the north bank of the Conemaugh. Keckenepaulin's Town, however, stood on the south bank of that river; and Keckenepaulin, himself, seems to have been a Delaware.[1] Another town, either of the Shawnees or Delawares, was probably the one

---
[1] See Post's *Journal*, Nov. 11 and 17, 1758.

shown on Scull's map of 1770 as Conemaugh Old Town, on the site of the present Johnstown. The Shawnee chief, Okowela, reported to be in the French interest, was none other than Ocowellos, "king of the upper Shawanese on Susquehanna," who in the early part of 1723 had sent a disquieting message to the Governor, mentioning his past visits to the Governor of Canada. Another town near the site of the present Shelocta, in Indiana County was known as "James Le Tort's Town." It was probably occupied by Shawnees. The "Shawnee Cabins" on Two Lick Creek in what is now Indiana County, likewise marked the site of a former residence place of Shawnees.

The name of the Asswikales Indians who came from South Carolina has been preserved to the present day under the form of Sewickley—a name now applied to two creeks, forty miles apart, one on the east and the other on the west side of Pittsburgh. Sewickleys' Old Town is shown on Lewis Evans's map of 1755 and also on the 1770 map of Scull, erroneously located north of the mouth of Dick's Creek, and a short distance below Chartier's Old Town (which stood on or near the present village of Tarentum, Allegheny County). Croghan's deed of 1749 mentions a "Sewichly Old Town" on the Youghiogheny. This probably stood at the mouth of the present Big Sewickley Creek of Westmoreland County.

In James Adair's *History of the American Indians in the South*, written by a man who had traded with the Southern Indians as early as 1735, the author, in describing the territories of the Creek Indians in what is now the state of Georgia, writes: "The upper part of the Musckogee Country is very hilly—the middle, less so—the lower Towns, level. These are settled by the remains of the Oosecha, Okone, and Sawakola nations. With them is also one Town of the Shawano."[1] Sawakola, or Sawokli, appears to be the original form of the word "Asswikale," or "Sewickley."

Ohesson upon Juniata was at the mouth of Kishacoquillas Creek, on or near the site of the present Lewistown. It is called Kishacoquillas's Town on Evans's map of 1749. Assunepachla was the Delaware name for the Indian town which the Traders afterwards called Frank's Town, or "Frank Stevens's Town."

On the 7th of December, 1731, Edmund Cartlidge, the Trader, was examined before Justice John Wright at Pequea, in Lancaster County, and his information was forwarded to the Governor. He stated that "about two months since, he left Allegeney, where there are settlements of Delawares, Shawanah, Asseekales, and Mingoe Indians to the number of about five hundred; that for these five years past, except that

---

[1] In his *Migration Legend of the Creek Indians*, Gatschet describes two of these towns among the Creeks under the name of Sawokli and Sawanogi (pp. 142–43).

of 1729, a French gentleman, who called himself Cavalier, had made it his practice to come every spring among the Indians settled there, and brings with him a small quantity of goods, with which he deals for furs; that he keeps a store, as this Examt. is well informed, at the head of the Ohio River, and every year goes to Montreal; that he appears to be a man of good sense and understanding; and that it is generally believed by all the Traders at Allegeney, as well as this Examt., that this Cavalier is the bearer of the Governor of Montreal's message to the Indians; . . . that after the treaty held at Conestoga in the year 1728 . . . several Shawnese who were settled at Allegeny went to the Governor of Montreal, as this Examt. believes, to seek protection from the French against the Five Nations, who, they suspected, would hinder their settling at Allegeny; . . . that Mr. Cavalier frequently holds consultations with the Shawanese, and this last spring, when he was among them, he delivered a message to them, as this Examt. is well informed, from the Governor of Montreal, with a present of some powder; that the Shawanese king, or chief, Paguasse, with seven or eight more of the Shawanese, went to Montreal to answer the Gov'er's message, etc."

On January 18, 1732, Thomas Renick appeared before Governor Gordon, and made an affidavit to the effect that some three weeks before, while at "Pextan," in company with William Jamieson and Edward Warren, hired servants of Peter Allen, an Indian Trader, who had lately returned from Allegheny, they told him that when they left Allegheny, some French people from Canada were building a log fort near the Ohio River; and that the English Traders in those parts seemed to be under great apprehensions on this account.

Further details of the coming of the French to Allegheny were given to Thomas Penn and Governor Gordon at Philadelphia August 25, 1732 by Hetaquantagechty, a chief of the Senecas. He stated that "last Fall, the French Interpreter 'Cahictodo' came to Ohio River (or Allegheny) to build houses there and to supply the Indians with goods, which they no sooner understood than they went out to forbid him, telling him the lands on Ohio belonged to the Six Nations; that the French had nothing to do with them; and advised him to go home; but he, not regarding their advice, proceeded, upon which they sent to the French Governor to complain; but their messengers were not returned when they came from home."

Meanwhile Edmund Cartlidge had returned to Allegheny in the winter of 1732; and made a second trip in the spring, carrying a message and present to the Delawares, from the Governor of Pennsylvania. He wrote to the Governor from Allegheny May 14th, announcing that the French had come again, and were going to settle there. He also stated that, in the preceding February, a Trader named John Kelly, in the employ of John Wilkins, had told the Shawanese at Allegheny that the Five Nations were ready to eat them all, and drive away the French, if the English Governor should say the word. This information put the Shawanese into such a state of alarm and anger that they were about to begin war on the English Traders at once, and were only restrained by the efforts of Peter Chartier and the French, who persuaded them that the news was false.

This letter was followed on June 7th by a message to the Governor from the chiefs of the Shawnees, themselves, interpreted and reported by Chartier, Cartlidge, and Le Tort. This message has already been printed in the sixth chapter. On August 8, 1732, Quoowhoune, Oppohwhyeckun, Queekoikahwin, Mechegoakehuk (or "Great Hill"), Shawanoppan, Allemykoppy, and Ohahmondamaw, "chiefs of the Delaware Indians at Allegaeening," also wrote to Governor Gordon, acknowledging the receipt of his message and a cask of rum, and stating that they would not be able to visit him in Philadelphia until the next spring.

On a preceding page, it has been pointed out that Beauharnois wrote to the French Ministry in October, 1728, calling attention to the steps taken by his predecessor, De Vaudreuil, as early as 1724, to bring the Shawnees nearer to Canada; and stating that the writer had permitted his representative, Cavillier, to return to them in the village they had begun on the Ohio River, which already contained more than 150 men and their families. One year later, Beauharnois reported the success of his measures, and notes that during the past summer Cavelier had brought four of their deputies with him to Montreal, who assured him of their entire fidelity and attachment to the French. In October, 1731, the Canadian Governor wrote again, of having sent Sieur de Joncaire among the Senecas in a former year; and during the past summer, he adds, he had sent that officer's son to the Senecas again, he having resided a long time among those Indians. "He went there with his father, who is to leave young Joncaire at the Seneca village, and to proceed himself to the Chaouanons, whither I have dispatched him to place those Indians in the location proper for the proposed purpose." For a number of years the French unavailingly tried to induce the Shawnees to remove to the upper Wabash and the Maumee, where they would be away from the sphere of English trade and influence.

In response to the letter of Beauharnois last quoted, the King wrote from Versailles, April 22, 1732, that, "he has learned with pleasure that the Chaouanons had come down to Montreal last summer to demand of the Marquis de Beauharnois the place where he wished to locate them. He has approved his sending Sieur Joncaire with them, to locate them on the north [west] bank of the River Oyo, with a view to approximate them to the Colony, and to detach them from the English." Beauharnois wrote the Minister again in October that Joncaire had reported to him last spring that the Chaouanons were settled in villages on the other side [*i.e.*, the east or south side] of the Beautiful River, six leagues below the River Atigue; that there had been some negotiations between the Chaouanons and the Hurons, Miamis, and Ouiatanons, to induce the Chaouanons to light their fire in that place; that the Hurons (Wyandots) told them if they located on the west side of the Ohio, they would encroach upon their own hunting grounds, and that it would be better if they remained where they were (on the east side of the river), where they would interfere with no others in their hunting.

In his report to the Ministry dated October 7, 1734, Beauharnois writes: "The Sieur de Beauharnois also sent the Sieur de Joncaire, the elder, to the Chaouanons, to continue to watch their actions, and to maintain them in the favorable dispositions that they felt in previous years. We have received no news concerning them that can lead us to suspect their faithfulness. That officer is charged with the duty of maintaining them in it, and of inducing them to form a village with the Miamis or Hurons, so as to keep them away from the snares that the English might set for them."

On October 12, 1736, Beauharnois writes again to the ministry on the same subject: "Sieur de Joncaire, commandant among the Chaouanons, has written Sieur de Beauharnois that his Indians continued to reject the evil advice of the Iroquois, and were disposed to follow their Father's pleasure; that they were about sending deputies to Detroit, to visit their brothers, the Hurons, and that they would come down to Montreal next Spring, to hear Sieur de Beauharnois's word and obey it. They have added, that as he had located them on the Beautiful River, they would not, without his orders, abandon the fire he had lighted for them at that place."

From what appears in this correspondence, we cannot determine whether or not the French succeeded in removing the Shawnees even to the west bank of the Ohio before 1734. If not, the occurrences of that year at Allegheny doubtless brought about that removal, and saw the start of "Chartier's Town."

In the latter part of August, 1732, five or more chiefs of the Senecas, Cayugas, and Oneidas came to Philadelphia in response to an invitation sent them by the Governor the fall before. Thomas Penn, one of the proprietors of Pennsylvania, having arrived in the Province a few weeks earlier, a meeting was held at Philadelphia on August 23d, at which the Proprietor suggested to the representatives of the Six Nations, that they compel the Shawnees to return eastward from the Allegheny, and locate themselves on a reservation which had been surveyed for them in their former place of residence, the Cumberland Valley. To this, the Iroquois chiefs agreed to do their best towards bringing the Shawnees back. Hetaquantagechty, a Seneca Chief, was the principal speaker at these conferences, which lasted for more than a week.

In October, 1734, Hetaquantagechty returned to Philadelphia, and told the Governor that the Six Nations had sent messengers to the Shawnees, to prevail upon them to leave Ohio, or Allegheny, and return to the Susquehanna. The Shawnees answered, that they would remove farther to the northward, towards the French country; whereupon, some chiefs of the Six Nations set out to speak with them, and they met together; but Hetaquantagechty had not yet learned the result of this meeting.

Eleven months later, however, Hetaquantagechty again returned to Philadelphia, accompanied by Shekallamy. He then informed the Governor and Council that the mission of the Iroquois chiefs to the Shawnees at Allegheny had been without success. The Shawnees had refused to leave that place, which they said was more commodious for them. He added, that one tribe of these Shawnees had never behaved themselves as they should, and the Six Nations were not satisfied with them, as they seemed to harbor evil designs. This tribe was called the Shaweygira, and consisted of about thirty young men, ten old men, and several women and children. When the Six Nation chiefs reached the Allegheny, they met there a great man of the Senecas, named Sagohandechty, who lived on that river. He accompanied the other chiefs to the Shawnee villages, to prevail with the Shawnees to return. He was the speaker, and pressed them so closely that they took a great dislike to him; and some months after the other chiefs were returned, the Shaweygira Shawnees seized on him, and murdered him cruelly. The tribe then fled to the southward, and it was supposed they were then "returned to the place from whence they first came, which was below Carolina."[1]

Hetaquantagechty also delivered a letter from the Seneca chiefs, written "in Sinnekes Land," July 29, 1735, by Abraham Wendall. Wendall states that he is sent to Seneca Land by the Government of New York, and the Indians there have divers times desired him to write what follows:

They tell me, that, according to your order, they have been to a place called Adjiego [*i.e.*, Atiga], and done their endeavor to live in peace and quietness with those Indians, and desired them to come and live here. But they will not hearken; but at last promised they would come and see the place. But when these had been about four months from thence, those living at Adjiego have murdered one who was a great man, and an Indian that was of good intention towards you. Howbeit, we have heard there is a number of them departed down the river, and they are

[1] *Penna. Col. Rec.*, iii., 660.

those who have little goodness in them, and the same who murdered the great man. . . . Brother, you may ask your children if we have not done our part at Adrego [misprint for Adjiego or Adiego], or the Handsome River [*i. e.*, the Ohio, or Beautiful River]; and we desire to know so soon as possible, where those people are travelled to.

John and Thomas Penn, in their answer to this letter from the Seneca chiefs, wrote that they understood that those who murdered the Mingo chief at Allegheny came there about four years since from the westward or southward to Ohio; but they did not know from whence they came, nor to what parts they had gone.

Dr. Daniel G. Brinton, in an article on the Shawnee Migrations, written for the *Historical Magazine* in 1866,[1] was of the opinion that the Shaweygira band of Shawnees "left the South in 1730, and having come as far north on the track of their predecessors as the region now occupied by Clark County, Kentucky, there divided, a portion of them, known as the Shaweygira band, thirty warriors in number, continuing north to western Pennsylvania, where they arrived in 1731; while the remainder established the town of Lulbegrud." This opinion of Dr. Brinton does not seem to be borne out by the facts. The identity of this band of Indians will be discussed later.

When they fled south from Atiga after the murder of the Mingo chief in 1734, it is possible the Shaweygira may have stopped on the west bank of the Ohio, between the mouths of the Hocking and the Kanawha, and established the Shawnee Town at the mouth of what is now known as Old Town Creek, near Le Tort's Rapids, where, in all probability, James Le Tort, many years before 1740, carried on a trade with the Shawnees who did settle there. It is more probable, however, that the Shaweygira band travelled as far down the river as the mouth of the Scioto, and built the town there, well known in Colonial and Revolutionary history as the Lower Shawnee Town. It is certain that that town was established before 1739; for Celoron states that Longueuil held a council with the Indians at Scioto in that year, while on his way down the Ohio River from Montreal to join the Louisiana expedition against the Chickasaws.

Sieur de Vincennes, who commanded at the French post on the Wabash, afterwards called by his name, reported to Bienville, Governor of Louisiana, the condition of Indian affairs at his post in 1734. Bienville's letter to the French Ministry, transmitting this report, bears date July 27, 1734. Vincennes states that the Piankeshaws, who were settled near his post, desire to draw to them a village of the same nation which is sixty leagues higher up the river. Two reasons make him favor this design; the first, to strengthen the French establishment, and the second,

[1] Vol. x., p. 1.

to take from the upper village the opportunity for trading with the English, "who have two warehouses at the home of the Shawnees on the Ohio River." Vincennes adds, that it will not be difficult to win over the Shawnees themselves, as they give the English the preference only because they are not urged to supply their needs from the French, as they are by the English. He states that one part of the Shawnees intend to withdraw to Detroit, and the other to come near to him. While it is possible that "the home of the Shawnees on the Ohio River" to which Vincennes referred in 1734 may have been what was later known as Lower Shawnee Town, at the mouth of the Scioto, it is more probable that he referred to the Shawnees who built what was later known as Chartier's Town, on the right bank of the Allegheny, below the mouth of the Kiskiminetas.

At a meeting of the Pennsylvania Council held at Philadelphia October 12, 1736, James Logan laid before the members a letter received by Edward Shippen from George Miranda, one of the Traders at Allegheny, giving an account of a quarrel that had taken place there between Solomon Moffat, a blacksmith, and an Indian of the Six Nations, or Mingoes, as a result of which the Indian had died. Moffat, fearing the vengeance of his family, had fled towards Virginia.

Beauharnois wrote to the Ministry October 1, 1740, stating that the Shawnees had not yet been prevailed on to remove to Detroit. "In the Memorial to the King," the Governor adds, "we had the honor of telling you the reasons that prevented the Chaouanons from coming down this year. They are to come next spring. I have sent an answer to the messages they sent me, by Vincent Poudret, who will start from Montreal shortly, to take it to them. I shall know what I am to think with regard to their migration. What the Sieur de Noyan writes me, that as soon as the Hurons leave, the Chaouanons will come and take their place, leads me to hope that I shall have no difficulty in inducing them to do so; as they are very docile, and the individual named [Pierre] Chartier seems very well disposed."

At a meeting of the Council held August 10, 1737, Mr. Logan laid before the members certain papers and letters received by the Proprietor, one of which was a communication from George Clarke, Governor of the Province of New York, informing Penn that the Mohawks (on June 25th) had told him that some 130 of the Shawnees then settled on the Susquehanna [Allegheny?], above Shamokin, were planning to remove to the vicinity of Detroit, and accept the protection of the French.[1] A second letter was also read, which had been received by the Proprietor from the Shawnees at what was later known as Chartier's Town on the Allegheny. In this letter, the Shawnees state that they are strongly

[1] See *New York Col. Doc.*, vi., 99.

solicited by the French, whom they call their fathers, to return to them; that every year the French send them powder, lead, and tobacco, to enable them to withstand their enemies, the Southern Indians, by whom they have often suffered, and were last year attacked in one of their towns; that they are got so far back that they can go no farther, without falling into their enemies' hands or going over to the French, which they say they would willingly avoid; that if they should return to Susquehanna, as the Pennsylvania Government has often pressed, they must starve, there being little or no game to be met with in those parts; therefore, they request that they be furnished with some arms and ammunition, for their defence against their enemies, and to secure their continuance at Allegheny.

The Council was of the opinion that a small present should be sent to the Shawnees, and their chiefs invited to visit Philadelphia, with a view to renewing their treaties; which was done accordingly.

The town of the Shawnees which the Allegheny chiefs of that tribe wrote Thomas Penn had been attacked by their southern enemies, the Catawbas, the year before (1736), may have been the town which we know was in existence at the mouth of the Scioto in 1739. If so, then its beginning was some years before 1739; and it may have been built by the Shaweygira band of Shawnees when they fled south from Allegheny in 1734-35. Possibly, it was the location of one of the two English warehouses, which Vincennes, in 1734, reported as being established at the home of the Shawnees on the Ohio River. At any rate, there is some reason to believe that the Lower Shawnee Town, on the Scioto, was started as early as the middle of the decade, 1730-40.

On March 20, 1738, the Shawnees at "Alegania" wrote an interesting letter to Thomas Penn and James Logan, which was signed by three of their chiefs: "Loyparcowah (Opessa's Son), Newcheconner (Deputy King), and Coycacolenne, or Coracolenne (Chief Counseller)." They acknowledge the receipt of a present from Penn and Logan of a horseload of powder, lead, and tobacco, delivered to them by George Miranda; state that they have a good understanding with the French, the Five Nations, the Ottawas, and all the French Indians; that the tract of land reserved for them by the Proprietary Government on the Susquehanna does not suit them at present; that they desire to remain where they are, gather together and make a strong town, and keep their young men from going to war against other nations at a distance. The Indians then add, that "After we heard your letter read, and all our people being gathered together, we held a council together, to leave off drinking, for the space of four years. . . . There was not many of our Traders at home at the time of our council, but our friends, Peter Chirtier and George Miranda; but the proposal of stopping the rum and all strong liquors was made to the rest in the winter, and they were all willing. As soon as it was concluded of, all the rum that was in the Towns was all staved and spilled, belonging both to Indians and white people, which in quantity consisted of about forty gallons, that was thrown in the street; and we have appointed four men to stave all the rum or strong liquors that is brought to the Towns hereafter, either by Indians or white men, during the four years." This letter was accompanied by a pledge, signed by ninety-eight Shawnees and the two Traders named above, agreeing that all rum should be spilled, and four men should be appointed for every town, to see that no rum or strong liquor should be brought into their towns for the term of four years.

On July 27, 1739, Cacowatchike, Newcheconneh, Tamenebuck, and Meshemethequater, chiefs of the Shawnees, with others of that nation to the number of twenty-one, came to Philadelphia from Wyoming and Allegheny, and held a council with Governor Thomas Penn. Secretary Logan told them, "since your nation first left their settlement near Pextang, on the west side of the Susquehanna, and retired to so great a distance as the River Ohio, or Allegheny, this Government has ever been desirous of a conference with some of your chiefs. Some of your older men may undoubtedly remember that about forty years ago a considerable number of families of your nation thought it fit to remove from the great river that bears your name, where your principal correspondence was with those of the French nation." The Indians were then reminded of the obligations entered into between their chief, Opessa, and William Penn, in 1701, and the treaty of that year was read to them. In their reply, the Shawnees acknowledged that they were scattered far abroad, "from the Great Island to Allegheny," and promised to tell the reasons for their going so far off. In answer to a question, they said that they were then at war with the Catawbas and the Catewas (Cherokees) in Carolina, who had detained some of their people who had been sent to them four years ago. A new treaty of alliance and friendship was concluded at this council, in which it was set forth that the Shawnees had removed westward to the Allegheny from their former home on the Susquehanna, for the benefit of the hunting. This treaty was signed on behalf of the Shawnees by Kaashawaghquillas (Kishacoquillas), Palakacouthater, Moreottawcollo, representing the Shawnees on the Juniata and Susquehanna; by Kaycowockewr (Kakowatcheky), chief of those at Wyoming; and by Newcheconner and Tomenebuck, for the Shawnees of Allegheny.[1]

[1] Meshemethequater, or Big Hominy, was also named with the other Shawnee chiefs as one of the parties to this treaty, but his signature does not appear in the printed copy. Tomenebuck is described in this paper as "a Mingo." A chief named Tawnamebuck, or Keightighqua, or Comblade, was one of the hostages offered to Bouquet by the Shawnees at the Forks of Muskingum, November 14, 1764.

During the first week of August, 1740, Sassoonan, or Allumapees, and Shekallamy, with sundry Delaware and Mingo Indians from Shamokin and Allegheny, held a council with Governor Thomas at Philadelphia. The Allegheny Delawares were represented by two of their chiefs, Mechouquatchugh, or Captain Hill, and Shanoppin. Other Delawares were present from Otzenaxa, Conestoga, and Brandywine. The Allegheny chiefs told the Governor that two of their nation had been taken prisoners by the Catawbas about six years ago, and carried away to the southward. They asked that the Governor make inquiry for them, and endeavor to secure their release.

Peter Chartier, the half-breed French-Shawnee Indian Trader of the Cumberland Valley, who formerly lived among the Shawnees on the Susquehanna, opposite Harris's Ferry, began trading at Allegheny as early, at least, as 1732. Some time after that year, he joined a band of Shawnees who were already on the Allegheny, or else who had accompanied him thither from the Cumberland Valley; and had built the village which later took his name, at this place. Chartier himself appears to have become either a chief or a very influential leader of this band.

On May 14, 1732, the Quaker Trader, Edmund Cartlidge, wrote to Governor Gordon from Allegheny in these words: "I find Peter Chartiere well inclined, and stands firm by the interest of Pennsylvania, and very ready on all accounts to do all the service he can. And, as he has the Shawnise tongue very perfect, and well looked upon among them, he may do a great deal of good." On the 7th of the following month (June, 1732), the chiefs of these Shawnees at Allegheny had Cartlidge write a letter for them to Governor Gordon, in which they said: "Whereas, the Governor desires to see some of us at Philadelphia, we shall answer his request, for some of our chiefs will come this summer and pay him a visit; but how many of us, or exact the time, we know not as yet. But when we are got so far as Peter Chartiere's, we shall send word how many of us there is, and when we shall be there; and bring our friends, the Conestogoes along with us." This allusion would seem to indicate that Chartier had not, up to that time, permanently removed from his post near the mouth of Yellow Breeches Creek, in what is now Cumberland County, to the Allegheny.

Reference has already been made to a letter written by Beauharnois, Governor of Canada, October 1, 1728, to the Ministry, in which he stated that the Shawnees had begun a village on the Ohio, which then contained more than 150 men and their families. The French Governor also wrote in this despatch that "two families have already removed from this village to the vicinity of Lake Erie. There is another small lake in a tongue of land situate between Lake Erie and the River Ohio, which divides into two branches, whereof, one falls into the River Ouabache, and the other flows towards Lake Erie. The latter is not very navigable. It is in this tongue of land that the Chaouanons desire to settle. This settlement will not be at most over twenty-five leagues from Lake Erie, opposite a place called Long Point. Cavillier is the name of the person whom M. de Beauharnois has permitted to return to the Chaouanons. He is understood and known by these Indians, and will probably negotiate this affair with success."

On the 15th of October, 1732, Beauharnois wrote to the Comte de Maurepas as follows:

Sieur de Joncaire, whom I sent last year to the Chaouanons, has reported to me this spring that these Indians were settled in villages on the other side of the Beautiful River of Oye, six leagues below the River Atigue; that there had been some negotiations between this nation, the Hurons, Miamis, and Ouiatanons, to induce the first to light their fire in that place; that the Hurons, among other things, had represented that, as they were disposed to live with them as brethren, if they located themselves on this side, they would injure their hunting grounds, and that it would be better they were in a place where they could not injure anybody. The Ouiatanons, who are their nearest neighbors, have expressed the joy they felt on the occasion, and matters have been harmoniously arranged in that way among these tribes. They continue apparently resolved not to suffer the English to come to trade in those parts; I have sent back Sieur de Joncaire there, with a view to encourage them in these dispositions. They number two hundred persons, exclusive of women and children, and are distant, the one from the other, only some four or five leagues; the greatest portion of them are six leagues below the River Atigue.

Atigue, Attique, Adigo, or Adjiego, was an early form of the Seneca name "Ohio" and the French name for the Indian Town which the Delawares called Kittanning. The "River Atigue" referred to above, was probably the Kiskiminetas[1]; although the site of Chartier's Town is not more than three (Old French) leagues below its mouth instead of six leagues. Montcalm, writing to the Marshall de Belle Isle from Montreal, November 15, 1758, says: "We have just received news from Fort Duquesne of the 23d of October, Captain Aubry, of the Louisiana troops, has gained a tolerably considerable advantage there on the 15th. The enemy lost on the occasion a hundred and fifty men; they were pursued as far as a new fort, called Royal Hannon [Loyalhanna; now Ligonier], which they built at the head of the River Attique."[2]

The district called "Allegheny" by the Traders, from 1727 to 1737, or later, embraced the Delaware and Shawnee villages on the Kiskimine-

---

[1] The Riviere aux Bœufs or French Creek is also called the Atigue on some of the early French maps.

[2] *N. Y. Col. Doc.*, x., 901; *ibid.*, vii., 728. See, also, Parkman's *Montcalm and Wolfe*, i., 440; *Historical Researches in Western Pennsylvania*, i., 20, 25–29; ii., 105, 106.

tas, or Conemaugh, and those above and below its mouth, on the Allegheny River, from Kittanning to Chartier's Town. It is thus correctly designated on Mitchell's map of 1755.

On April 24, 1733, the Shawnee chiefs at "Allegania" wrote Governor Gordon, stating that they had received by Peter Chartier the present the Governor had sent them; and complained of the number of new Traders who came amongst them, bringing nothing but rum. "We therefore beg," they add, "thou would take it into consideration, and send us two firm orders, one for Peter Cheartier, the other for us, to break in pieces all the cags so brought; and by that means the old Traders will have their debts, which, otherwise, never will be paid."

On May 1, 1734, the Shawnee chiefs dictated a letter to the Governor and Council of Pennsylvania, regarding the characters of the various Traders who came among the Indians at Allegheny. The letter was written by one of the four Traders who signed the same as witnesses—probably by Davenport, and read as follows:

MY BRETHREN:

Sometime ago Edmund [Cartlidge] brought a letter amongst us, and withal advised me to mind and be careful of my people; and if we wanted any assistance, we might expect it from you; which we are very glad to hear. As for ye belt of wampum you sent by ye Five Nations, we have not yet had, though so often mentioned.

Edward Kenny, Jacob Pyatt, Timy. Fitzpatrick, Wm. Dewlap, and Jno. Kelly of Donegal, come trading with us without license; which is a hindrance to ye licensed Traders.

Charles Poke and Thos. Hill are very pernicious; for they have abused us; and we gave them a fathom of white wampum, desiring them by that token to acquaint you how they had served us.

And at a drinking bout, Henry Bayley, Oliver Wallis, and Jno. Young, took one of our old men, and after having tied him, abused him very much. Jas. Denning was among them, and abused us likewise. Such people, we think, are not proper to deal with us.

Jno. Kelly of Paxtang has made a great disturbance by raising false reports among us; and Timy. Fitzpatrick, Thos. Moren, and Jno. Palmer quarrel often with us; therefore, we desire those four men may be kept particularly from us.

Jonas Davenport, Laz. Lowrey, Jas. Le Tort, Fras. Stevens, Jas. Patterson, Ed. Cartlidge, we desire, may have license to come and trade with us; as also, Peter Cheartier, who we reckon one of us; and he is welcome to come as long as he pleases.

Likewise, we beg at our Council, that no Trader above mentioned may be allowed to bring more than thirty gallons of rum, twice in a year, and no more; for by that means, we shall be capable of paying our debts and making our creditors easy; which we cannot do otherwise. And that every Trader may be obliged to bring his rum in ye cabin where he lives, directly, and not to hide any in ye woods; but for P. Cheartier to bring what quantity he pleases; for he trades further yn. ye rest. And that every Trader bring his license with him.

And for our parts, if we see any other Traders than those we desire amongst us, we will stave their cags, and seize their goods, likewise.

We also beg, every Trader may be obliged to bring good powder.

And, if we are indebted to any of those we desire may not be admitted to trade with us, if they will come without goods or rum, if we have it by us, we will pay them their due.

We also hope no hired man will have liberty to bring any rum with him.

We are, your friends and brethren.
                         NECHIKONNER, OPOCKEETOR,
                         CAWKECAWLEN, OLANAWKANOR,
                                  MEELATAINEN.

Teste—Jonah Davenport, James Le Lort,
        Larey Lowrey, Peter (P.) Cheartier.

From the foregoing citations, it would appear probable that Chartier removed permanently to Allegheny between the years 1734 and 1738; and that he had made trading trips to some distance beyond the Allegheny before 1734.

At a meeting of the Pennsylvania Council held June 6, 1743, Governor Thomas informed the Council that Robert Dunning, John Canon, and Esther Harris, were waiting at the Council door, in order to lay before the Governor a deposition made by one James Hendricks, servant to an Indian Trader at Allegheny, who had deposed, "that he had seen the Indians there in pursuit of some of the Traders, and that he had heard the discharge of two or more guns, from whence he verily believed that the pursued Traders were murdered." Thereupon, the messengers were admitted to the Council, and Hendricks's deposition was read, as well as those of two other Traders, who stated that they had been advised by some friends of theirs among the Indians at Allegheny to make the best of their way out of that country, in order to avoid being murdered by the Indians, who had come to the resolution of cutting off all the white people. Dunning and his companions were examined, and told the Council of some "insinuations" which had been put forth by one Peter Chartier, an Indian Trader. The Governor concluded, after the examination of the witnesses, that there was no disposition on the part of the Indians to begin a war, "that the information given by Hendricks and the rest was the effect of fear, and Chartier's villainous reports." He advised the messengers to return to their homes in Lancaster County, and to prevail on their neighbors to disperse and remain quiet.

On September 29, 1744, Conrad Weiser wrote James Logan: "The day before yesterday, I came back from Shohomokin. . . . Shickelimy informed me that the Governor of Canada hath sent an embassy to Onontago. . . . The French embassy also informed the Counsel of the

United Nations of a treachery which the Shawanese formed against them, with the Ionontatech-Roanu [Wyandots] and Cheestagech-Roano [Missisagas], Indian Nations about the Lakes of Canada, in order to make war against the 6 Nations. Now Cheekano [Neucheconno], the Shawano chief, is suspected to be the author of it. A message of the United Nations is gone to him."

At another meeting of the Pennsylvania Council held April 25, 1745, Governor Thomas laid before the Board a deposition made by one James Cunningham, a servant to Peter Chartier, the Indian Trader at Allegheny, which was to the effect that Chartier had accepted a military commission under the French King, and was going to Canada. On the same day the Governor sent a message to the Assembly regarding this piece of news and other Indian affairs, in which he referred to Chartier as follows:

I have just received information that Peter Chartier, after disposing of his effects in this Government, has gone over to the enemy. His conduct for some years past has rendered him generally suspected; and it seems my reprimanding him for some very exceptionable parts of it is made use of, among other things, to excuse his infidelity. Had he been punished, as he deserved, for the villainous report he spread two years ago among the back inhabitants, in order to spirit them up against such of the Six Nations as travel through those parts of the country, he would not have been at this time with the enemy; but an apprehension that the Shawnese (whose perfidious blood partly runs in Chartier's veins), might resent upon our Traders any severities to him, restrained me from making use of such, and induced me to choose the gentle method of reproof, which his brutish disposition has construed into an affront.

I am likewise informed that he had persuaded a considerable number of the Shawnese to remove from their old town to a greater distance upon another river; and it is not to be doubted that a person of his savage temper will do us all the mischief he can.

At a meeting of the Pennsylvania Assembly, held July 23, 1745, a petition from James Dinnen (Dunning) and Peter Tostee, two Indian Traders, was presented to the House, and read. This paper set forth that, on the 18th day of the April preceding, as Dunning and Tostee were returning up the Allegheny River in canoes from a trading trip, with a considerable quantity of furs and skins, "Peter Chartier, late an Indian Trader, with about 400 Shawnese Indians, armed with guns, pistols, and cutlasses, suddenly took them prisoners, having, as he said, a captain's commission from the King of France; and plundered them of all their effects, to the value of sixteen hundred pounds; by which they are become entirely ruined, and utterly uncapable to pay their debts, or carry on any further trade."

Chartier and his band of Shawnees, headed by Chief Neucheconno, had fled from "Chartier's Old Town," and started down the Ohio, when they met and robbed these two Traders. They continued on down that river until they reached the mouth of the Scioto, where another Shawnee settlement had been established, probably ten years before, known among the Traders for many years afterwards as the Lower Shawnee Town. The Marquis de Beauharnois, Governor of Canada, wrote to De Maurepas, in France, on October 28, 1745, as follows, in relation to Chartier's band of Shawnees: "The emigration of the Chaouanons has at length taken place; they have removed from their former location to the place I have allotted them at the Prairie of the Maskoutins [the writer of the letter was misinformed on this point]; they have even tied and plundered the English Traders on La Belle Riviere to the number of eight, and advised M. de Longueuil to send in search of them. But the detachment of fifteen or sixteen Canadians sent thither by that officer discovered only one, and the Chaouanons have said that they had carried the others along with them to their winter quarters, and would bring them to me themselves next year." Chartier and his band did not proceed to Canada on this occasion, as Beauharnois had written; but after remaining at Scioto for a short time, most of them took the Warriors' Path towards the Catawba country, and began their wanderings in the southern wilderness, which were destined to continue for three or four years.

In James Le Tort's report of the Indian settlements at "Allegheny," which he made to Governor Gordon, October 29, 1731, he also included the "Asswikales, fifty families, lately from S. Carolina to Ptwomack, and from thence thither, making one hundred men; Aqueloma [or Achequeloma], their chief; true to the English." Edmund Cartlidge, a few weeks later, mentioned them as the "Asseekales."

James Adair, the Trader who operated in South Carolina from 1735 to 1773, in his book on the Southern Indians, speaks of having once visited the remnant of the Sawakola nation, in the Upper Muskogee country, in what is now the state of Georgia; and states that with them was one town of the Shawnees.

On Lewis Evans's map of 1755, Sewickley Old Town is located on the west bank of the Allegheny, close to and below Chartier's Old Town. If it stood there, it was between the mouths of what are now known as Bull and Deer creeks. The same location is given on Scull's map of 1770, and on Hutchins's map of 1778, except that on the last, the Sewickley Old Town is placed above Chartier's Town. The true site of this town, however, seems to have been elsewhere, unless there were two towns of that name between 1731 and 1735, which seems unlikely.

In a deed executed by the chiefs of the Six Nations to George Croghan in 1768, confirming a former deed, which he claimed had been made to him in 1749, "Sewichly Town" is described as being located on the Youghiogheny River. And in Commandant Ecuyer's *Journal* of the Siege of Fort Pitt, the following entry occurs under date of May 29, 1763: "At break of day this morning, three men came in from Colonel [William] Clapham's, who was settled at the Sewickley Old Town, about 25 miles from here, on the Youghyogane River, with an account that Colonel Clapham, with one of his men, two women, and a child, were murdered by Wolfe and some other Delaware Indians, about two o'clock the day before."[1]

At the present time there are, in the vicinity of Pittsburgh, two streams known as Big Sewickley Creek, one entering the Youghiogheny from the east, two to three miles below the village of West Newton, in Westmoreland County, and the other entering the Ohio from the north, about two miles above Logstown Bar, and forming a part of the boundary line beween the counties of Allegheny and Beaver. Near the mouth of the former stream was probably the site of the Sewickley Town mentioned in the deed to Croghan.

In the earlier part of this chapter, reference has been made to the killing of a Seneca chief at Allegheny in 1734 or 1735, by a tribe or sept of the Shawnees who had come from the South four years before, consisting of thirty warriors and ten old men, with their families. After this murder, it will be remembered, the members of this clan fled to the southward, and it was supposed they had returned to the place from which they came, "which was below Carolina." Hetaquantagechty, who gave the news of this murder to the Governor and Council at Philadelphia, was a Seneca chief. He said that the name of the tribe which had committed the murder was Sha-weyg-i-ra.

In the Seneca language there is no sound equivalent to that represented by the letter "l." In the Delaware and Shawnee languages, the "r" sound is so rare as to be practically unused. Accordingly, words which in English contain an "r" sound, would be pronounced by an Algonquin, usually, as if spelled with an "l"; while words containing an "l" sound, would be pronounced by a Seneca as if spelled with an "r." A familiar example of this occurs in the name of the Siouan tribe of early Carolina and Virginia which was known to the Algonquins as Tutelo, and to the Senecas as Totero.[2]

This being the case, we have a simple explanation of the identity of this mysterious Shaweygira band, which has so long aroused the curiosity of students of the Shawnee Indians. The Sha-weyg-i-la, or

[1] Darlington's *Fort Pitt*, 85.
[2] Another instance is in the case of the Iroquois word, *Tuscarora*, which was pronounced "Tuscalawa" by the Delawares.—See Beatty's *Journal*, p. 37.

Sha-weyg-i-ra, is synonymous with the Sawakola of Adair, and the Asswikales or Se-wick-a-leys of Le Tort and Evans,[1] who were reported in 1731 as having come "lately from S. Carolina to Ptowmack, and from thence thither [to Allegheny]."

[1] There were two "Sawokli" towns among the Lower Creek villages on the Chatahuchi River before 1773, the inhabitants of which spoke the "stinkard" (*i.e.*, alien) language. Gatschet gives the derivation of *Sawokli* as from the Hitchiti words, *sawi*, raccoon, and *ukli*, town. See *Creek Migration Legend*, 144; Bartram, 462.

CHAPTER XII

THE OHIO MINGOES OF THE WHITE RIVER, AND THE WENDATS

PIERRE JOSEPH DE CELORON, Commandant at Detroit in 1743, wrote in the month of June of that year to Beauharnois, the Governor-General of Canada at Quebec, respecting some Indians "who had seated themselves of late years at the White River." These Indians, he reported, were Senecas, Onondagas, and others of the Five Iroquois villages. At their urgent request, Celoron permitted some residents of Detroit to carry goods thither, and had recently sent Sieur Navarre to the post, to make a report thereupon. Navarre's account was transmitted to Quebec with this letter. Celoron's letter has been printed in the *New York Colonial Documents*, but the accompanying report of Sieur Navarre has not heretofore been published. Following is a portion of that report:

"Memoir of an inspection made by me, Navarre,[1] of the trading post where the Frenchman called Saguin carries on trade; of the different nations who are there established, and of the trade which can be developed there. . . .

"The tribe of the Senecas, who had come to ask for Saguin, has fulfilled its promises. Since last autumn, they had told the English who traded in their territory that they did not wish them to return; that they [the English Traders] should confine themselves to their trade among their own Shawnees. . . . This had been told to the English at Saguin's

[1] Robert Navarre, Intendant at Detroit from 1730 to 1760, was born at Villeroy, in Brittany, 1709, of an illegitimate branch of the royal house of Navarre. He died at Detroit in 1791, leaving nine children.

The town of Navarre, in Stark County, Ohio (established about 1839), is not far from the centre of the district which was served by Saguin's post. Peter Navarre, son of Robert (1739–1813) and grandson of the above named Robert Navarre, died in Toledo, Ohio in 1874 (?), at the age of eighty-eight. He was a noted frontiersman of his time, lived many years among the Indians, and served as scout to General Harrison in the War of 1812. For some years before his death he was President of the Maumee Valley Pioneer Association. See Waggoner's *History of Toledo and Lucas County*, p. 657; Howe's *Historical Collections of Ohio*, ii., p. 152; Denissen, *Family of Navarre* (Detroit, 1897); Hamlin, *Legends of Detroit* (Detroit, 1884).

House in the autumn of 1742; a Frenchman who lived among the English acting as interpreter.

"There are ten different tribes settled upon that river, numbering altogether about five or six hundred men, namely, the Senecas, Cayugas, Oneidas, Onondagas, Mohawks, Loups, Moraignans, Ottawas, Abenakis of St. Francis, and Sauteux of the lower end of Lake Ontario. Forty leagues from the French house, going down towards the River Oyo (because by this river one reaches the Mississippi, as by the Miamis River, it is the same thing) there is an English blacksmith, whom five or six families of the Loups have stopped. This blacksmith was afraid to settle there, as much on account of the French as on account of the English governor, whose instructions were, not to go farther than the Shawnee settlements. These English Traders have themselves admitted the fact, and say, moreover, that if their expeditions were known, they would be punished. Upon which Saguin told them: 'You are then trying to get yourself plundered by the French.' To this, the English replied: 'If they plunder us here, we shall be well able to revenge ourselves upon the French [Traders] among the Shawnees.' It is difficult to pursue these Woods Traders, because they are all scattered among the winter quarters of the Indians; as soon as spring comes, they start for their cities, and their governors or masters think they come from points within the Shawnee territories.

"M. de Noyans had sent a notice to the English governor in a letter, to inform him of the behavior of his people. This letter was never delivered; the bearer, knowing it to be injurious to himself, had destroyed it. One named Maconce[1] offered to deliver a letter to the English which we might wish to entrust to him, and bring back an answer, provided he was paid for it.

"The number of Indians who have settled on this river increases every day; since hunting there is abundant; while on the other hand, at their former homes, there is no more game.

"The powder and balls which Saguin asks that we send him, are very necessary, as ammunition is scarce at this time, when deer hunting begins; while besides, there have come from afar some Indians loaded with peltries, in order to buy powder from Saguin. He made them wait, telling them that some was then coming from Detroit, where he had written for it.

"As soon as the people knew of my arrival, they hurried in to ask if I had brought powder. Saguin answered them that I had brought nothing; for the letter which he had sent to Detroit by an Indian never

---

[1] See page 334. One Maconse acted as guide to a party of French and Indians from Fort Machault (Venango) who attacked the Susquehanna settlements in September, 1757. See *Penna. Archives*, iii., 295.

was delivered. That if they would wait several days longer, I would inform M. de Celoron of their wants, and entreat him to permit powder to be brought to them. They have all besought me not to forget them; as, otherwise, they would buy from the English as soon as they should arrive; that to go to Niagara was too long and too difficult a voyage for them.

"Saguin knows well how to conduct himself towards these tribes. He understands them perfectly, and his good conduct towards them causes them to gather in increasing numbers, which will render this post a considerable one. And it would be grievous if the English should come and profit from the work of Saguin, through the little regard the French may have for the place.

"It would be necessary for the maintenance of this post that we should send two canoes of merchandise each year.

"We cannot with reason reproach the Senecas for having failed to keep their word to M. de Celoron; for they were not powerful enough to drive away the English. If they tell the English to leave, another tribe will tell them to stay. The Indian is never provoked by seeing merchandise abundant where he lives, knowing that it will enable him to buy cheaper; besides, they are no more culpable than the Hurons of Detroit, who do not scruple to go for the English and guide them as far as their winter quarters [at Sandusky Bay], to trade with them.

"Last spring, as Saguin did not sow corn, as was his wont, some Indians asked him his reason for not cultivating his field, as usual; and he answered them that he hesitated to work on it, fearing that he might not be allowed to come back. The chiefs assembled, in order to discuss the matter, saying, that 'if we find you are not to come back, we will start at once for Detroit, and tell M. de Celoron . . . "you have given us our brother, Saguin, and now you call him back to you again." . . . So, Saguin, our brother, work your field, we will guard it while you are going to Detroit. It is necessary that you should cultivate the land, because we are not able to furnish you with grain for the sustenance of yourself and the Frenchmen who live with you. If we sell you our grain, our wives and children, with the old people, whom we leave behind in summer, in going to war, would run the risk of dying of hunger; so do not count on us for grain. . . .'

"Saguin makes his arrangements in order to return to Detroit in accordance with M. de Celoron's order. However, he charges me to represent clearly that it is a great hardship to him to [be obliged to] abandon his building and his post, which have cost him so much. The rum which is on the way from Oswego will place his goods in great risk. The drunkards break everything. The English will arrive from the Shawnees during his absence, and will insinuate that the French are abandoning them. Saguin says further, if we do not want him to return there to trade, we should send another Frenchman; that he would not, like the people of Detroit, be angry at seeing one established there.

"The merchants of Detroit have made a great mistake in accusing Saguin of trying to gain over the Ottawas of Detroit. There was found there of that nation five or six cabins, who have asked the Iroquois Senecas for a small piece of land, in order to light a little fire; which has been granted them. The greater part of these Ottawas are bad people who only established themselves in this place in order to be able to go more easily to Choueghen [Oswego trading post]. No one can prevent them. The people of Detroit to whom they owe money can never catch them to make them pay. Besides, the road from there is very much shorter. It is this which likewise causes a part of the Hurons to remain in their village of Sandoske.[1] On returning from Saguin's place we have seen their preparations for their voyage to the English."

In June, 1744, the Chevalier de Longueuil, who, several months before, had succeeded Celoron as Commandant at Detroit, gave the war hatchet to the four nations of Indians seated near that post—the Ottawas, Hurons (Wyandots), Pottawattomies, and Mississagas, and incited them to make war against the English Traders of the White River. "It is neither to Montreal nor his territory that I direct your first steps against him. It is in your own immediate vicinity, where he for several years hath quietly made his way with his goods. It is to the White River or to the Beautiful [Ohio] River that I expect you will immediately march in quest of him and when you destroy him, you will seize and divide all his goods among you." On the 19th of the same month Longueuil sent a similar message to the chiefs of the post of the White River: "Children, I answer your speech and send Saguin back to you, with some Frenchmen, who convey your necessaries to you. . . . Your brothers at Montreal, as well as those at Detroit, are ready to start, tomahawk in hand, to go and avenge the insult the English have offered me. It is for you to imitate them, in order to parry and anticipate the blows Assaregoa[2] wishes to give me. Wait not till he strikes you first. Commence by

[1] This sets back the date of the Huron settlement at Sandusky three years before 1745—the date usually given. It really began before 1739. See *Wis. Hist. Collections*, xvii., 286, 287, 333.

[2] *Assarigoa*, usually translated "long knife," was an Onondaga term, meaning "big knife" (Zeisberger spells it *Asharigoua*), first applied by the Five Nations to Lord Howard, the Governor of Virginia in 1684, and to all the Provincial Governors of Virginia who succeeded him. In the minutes of a Council held by Governor Spotswood with the chiefs of the Five Nations at Albany, September 6, 1722, it is explained that "Assarigoa is the name of the Governor of Virginia, which signifies a simeter, or cutlas, which was given to the Lord Howard, Anno 1684, from the Dutch word, *Hower*, a cutlas."— *N. Y. Col. Doc.*, v., 670.

binding and pillaging all the English who will come to your parts and to the Beautiful River; divide the goods among you, and bring the men here to Detroit; let your warriors penetrate even as far as the land of Assaregoa himself. Toyaraguindiague and Canante-Chiarirou[1] chiefs of the nations of the White River, I rely on you, and on the promise you have given me of your fidelity and attention for the success of the good work."

Longueuil wrote to Beauharnois again in September, 1744, that, "on receiving intelligence of the arrival of several Englishmen at the White River, he immediately raised a party of thirty-five picked Ottawas to plunder and kill them, or to fetch them prisoners to him; and they set out on the 17th of September with every desirable demonstration of joy." Longueuil adds, "that he is much the more determined to urge on this party, as he is informed that the English were loaded with powder and ball, and were resolved to annihilate the French Traders who were going to that quarter; that he also sent messages[2] to the Indians seated on this White River, in answer to their request to him to send them back some Frenchmen, and that they would not suffer any Englishmen there; whereby he prevails on them in like manner, to take up the hatchet and join their brethren of Detroit."

The result of this expedition does not appear in any of the contemporary documents that the writer has been able to discover; but that the English were not driven away from the White River permanently is evidenced by the fact that Beauharnois wrote to Longueuil so late as the fall of 1746, recommending him to induce his Indian allies "to make some incursions during the winter, against the settlements the English have made in the direction of the Beautiful River and of the White River."

Meanwhile, Beauharnois had written as follows to the Ministry at home (October 14, 1744), concerning the Indian settlements on the White River:

With regard to the settlement established by a number of Indians of different nations in the region of the White River, and about which, Monseigneur, you have deigned to inform us regarding the intentions of his Majesty, it appears to us, as we have had the honor to explain it last year, that it is more suitable to the interests of the Colony to let it exist, rather than to attempt to break it up by compelling the Indians to

---

[1] Canante-Chiarirou was evidently the same chief who was known to the English from 1747 to 1754 as Canajachrera, Conagaresa, Onidagarehra, Connageriwa, Canajackanah, Conajarca, and Canajachreesera. His hostility to the French will be shown in the course of the present chapter. He was one of three "chiefs of the Seneca Nations settled at Ohio," who attended a conference with Secretary Richard Peters at George Croghan's house in Pennsboro Township, Cumberland County, June 7, 1750. See *Penna. Archives*, i., 742; ii., 59; *Penna. Col. Rec.*, v., 358, 438, 531, 686; *Doc. Hist. N. Y.*, ii., 750, 757.

[2] On the 19th of June, as stated above.

return to their villages. Indeed, besides that one cannot hope to succeed in this, there can result no advantage to the Colony; neither by commerce, which the French might be permitted to continue to carry on there; nor by the [probability of the] Indians being induced, not only to drive away the English, as they even this year reiterated to M. de Longueuil, but also to make raids on the settlements which they have in the vicinity of the White River.

We enclose the words of these Indians, which M. de Longueuil has addressed to M. de Beauharnois, through which Monseigneur will be able to judge, so far as it is possible to count on them, as to their situation, and of which M. de Beauharnois will do the most he possibly can to make them feel how grateful they should be for the attentions shown them in supplying them their necessaries. For this purpose, there will be sent two licenses every year, based upon those of Detroit, counting from next spring, and amounting to five hundred livres each, for the profit of his Majesty. This appears to us even now as advisable to put in practice, until the circumstances and advantages which can be derived from this post demand that there should be a larger number of licenses.

On the second day of November, 1747, Captain Raymond, an officer at Quebec, also wrote to the French Ministry concerning the reports which had been previously sent "that the Hurons of Detroit and the Yrocois at the outlet of La Riviere Blanche have killed some Frenchmen at Sandoske." He adds: "As your Grace must have remarked in the Memorial I had the honor of sending you from Niagara on this subject in 1745, in which I took the liberty of pointing out to you all the evil there was to fear for the Upper countries from the English Traders, who were allowed to establish themselves at La Riviere Blanche, in the vicinity of Detroit and of other posts, that the English would infallibly corrupt and win over the savage nations that live with them on that River. And this has not failed to happen as I had predicted to you. They have succeeded so well in making them their devoted creatures that it is these same savages who, at their instigation, have killed the French at Sandoske; who wished to surprise Detroit, to put these same English there. . . . I beg you to observe, Monseigneur, that the cause of all the ills and agitation of the Upper country is due to the English who have been left in peace at La Riviere Blanche; and that all that evil was fomented there."

Where was the White River, on which these Indians were settled?

The Marquis de la Jonquiere, who became Governor-General of Canada in 1749, in a letter to Governor Clinton of August 10, 1751, refers to a certain Huron or Wyandot Town on Sandusky Bay, as "Ayonontout, the place selected in 1747 by Nicolas, the rebel Huron Chief, as his stronghold, near the little lake of Otsanderket [misprint for Otsandesket, *i. e.*, Sandusky], that is to say, within ten leagues of the town of Detroit." This town was identical with that called "Junundat" (*i. e.*, Wyandot) on Lewis Evans's map of 1755, and located on the east side of the Sandusky River, a short distance from its mouth.[1] The Indian Town of "Sunyendeand" or "Junqueindundeh," where James Smith lived during a part of the year 1756, was above the site of the other village. Longueuil's letter from Detroit of October 22, 1747, contains "news brought from Ostandousket 20th October, by two Hurons, deputed by the sachems." One item of this news was to the effect "that fear of the Iroquois war party has obliged the Hurons of Sandusky to collect together at the White River, twenty-five leagues from Detroit, to entrench themselves there, and examine in safety the conduct of the Iroquois."

A very circumstantial account of some of the leading incidents of the conspiracy of Nicolas has been written by Mr. Alfred T. Goodman in his history of the Miami Confederacy, printed in 1871 as an introduction to that writer's edition of the *Journal of Captain William Trent from Logstown to Pickawillany A. D. 1752*. This account has been followed by Mr. Butterfield in his *History of Ohio*,[2] by Mr. Knapp, in his *History of the Maumee Valley* and by many other writers since.[3] Both Goodman and Butterfield have made the mistake of giving as the dates

[1] Darlington thinks Nicolas's town was between Sandusky River and Green Creek. See Darlington's *Gist*, p. 110; also *Journal* of Sir William Johnson, Sep. 22d, 1761 (in Stone's *Life*, ii., 466), who visited two Wyandot towns, one nine miles west and the other three miles south of Fort Sandusky. In Appendix IV. of Smith's *Historical Account of Bouquet's Expedition* are given the distances on the Trail from Ft. Pitt to Junqueindundeh, as follows: From Ft. Pitt to the mouth of Big Beaver Creek, 25 miles; to Tuscarawas, 91; to Mohickon John's Town [in what is now Mohican Township, Ashland County], 50; to Junundat or Wyandot Town [meaning the town on the site of what is now Castalia, Erie County], 46; to Sandusky [now Venice, Erie County], 4; to Junqueindundeh [now Fremont, Sandusky County], 24; total, 240 miles. While this location of Junundat four miles south of the English Fort Sandusky may be the correct one, I am inclined to think the earlier site, or at least the site of Chief Nicolas's stronghold, was the Wyandot village visited by Sir William Johnson in 1761 on the southwest shore of the bay, nine miles west of Fort Sandusky. Major Robert Rogers and his Rangers, also, on their return from Detroit in January, 1761, in crossing Sandusky Bay from the north, arrived at a town of the Wyandots on the south shore, and thence proceeded southeast seven and one quarter miles to "a small Indian Town at a large bubbling spring," being the same town three or four miles south of Fort Sandusky, which is called Junundat in Smith's *Bouquet*. Ayonontout, like Junundat, may have been a synonym for Wyandot, or, possibly for Anioton, the name of a Huron chief who was associated with Nicolas in his rebellion, and whose name was applied to the village of Nicolas on Sandusky Bay by the French of Detroit.

[2] *Magazine of Western History*, vols. iv., v., and vi.

[3] Mr. Charles E. Slocum, in his recent *History of the Maumee Basin* (Defiance, Ohio, 1905), also follows the same inaccurate account of Goodman. Dr. Thwaites, likewise, in volumes xvii., and xviii., of the *Wisconsin Historical Collections*, attempts to make various identifications of La Riviere Blanche of 1745 with the White River of Indiana, White Oak Creek, the Little Miami, and the Sandusky; neither one of which is correct, although the same name was applied to a stream near the Wabash by Beauharnois so early as 1733—a stream on which some of the Miamis had settled.

of two of the principal occurrences of that little war, the dates of the letters from the Detroit Commandant reporting those occurrences. Both writers have likewise made the serious mistake of locating the White River district in Indiana, when it was really the seat of the most important early eighteenth century Indian settlements in Ohio. It is possible that these writers have also made other mistakes in their accounts of the operations of Nicolas's band. Mr. Goodman's account may be summarized as follows:

In 1745 [before 1740], a large, powerful, and unscrupulous body of Huron Indians, belonging to the tribe of the war chief Nicolas, removed from the Detroit River to the lands on the north [southwest] side of Sandusky Bay. Late in the same year, a party of English Traders from Pennsylvania visited the village of Nicolas, who had become an implacable enemy of the French; and he permitted the Traders to erect a large block-house, and to remain and dispose of their stock of goods. Once located, the English established themselves at the place, and acquired great influence with Nicolas and his tribe.

On the 23d of June, 1747,[1] five Frenchmen with peltries arrived at the Sandusky Town from the White River, a small stream falling into the Wabash [Lake Erie] nearly opposite the present town of Mt. Carmel, Ill.[2] They were received by Nicolas with pronounced evidences of hostility. The English Traders, noticing this feeling, urged the chief to seize the Frenchmen and their peltries. This was accomplished on the afternoon of the day of their arrival. Nicolas condemned them to death, and they were tomahawked in cold blood. Their peltries were sold to the English Traders, and by the latter disposed of to the Senecas.

On the 7th of April, 1748,[3] Nicolas destroyed his village and forts, and on the following day, at the head of 119 warriors and their families, left for the White River[4] in Indiana [Ohio]. Soon after, they removed to the Illinois [Allegheny] Country, locating on the Ohio, near the In-

---

[1] Longueuil's report of the massacre was of that date; the French Traders were killed more than a month before.

[2] French Traders on their return from Indiana posts to Detroit descended the Miami (Maumee) River from Fort Miami, the present site of Fort Wayne, to the Maumee Bay, and thence northwards along the west coast of Lake Erie to Detroit River. Sandusky Bay is some forty miles east of the outlet of the Maumee; so that it is very improbable that any French Trader on his return trip to Detroit with peltries from an Indiana post would go so far out of his way to the east as Sandusky would be. The village of Nicolas, however, was on the direct trail *westward* from the White River to Detroit.

[3] The messenger who brought the news from Sandusky to the French reached Detroit on that date; the migration had taken place before.

[4] The White River of Indiana is called the *Oiapikaming* on Franquelin's map of 1684 (which see, in vol. ii.). The first two syllables of this word are the French equivalent for what would be written in English, *wapi*, or *wabi*, the Algonquin term for "white"; but the White River of Indiana was not the White River to which Nicolas retreated.

diana line [on the Shenango branch of Beaver Creek, which latter stream flows into the Ohio at Beaver, Pennsylvania, near the Ohio State line].

Now, let us see if a closer examination of some of the contemporary documents relating to this occurrence will not make it appear that Mr. Goodman's account will have to be still farther corrected.

The killing of the French Traders, for which Nicolas was blamed, may have been in part due to the instigation of George Croghan. This man was an Irish Trader from Pennsylvania, of scanty education but great natural abilities, whom this episode now, for the first time, brought to the notice of the Provincial authorities of that Colony. He was a strong and fearless man, and during the ten years following 1742, his active and unceasing efforts to push and develop his trade with the Ohio River and White River Indians, did more than any other one cause to extend and increase the English influence far to the westward of the Alleghanies. In trade, Croghan competed with, rivalled, and outstripped the French on their own ground. In diplomacy, he was more than a match for the younger Joncaire, the astute, insinuating, and highly trusted Indian agent of the Canadian Government. In results, the effect of Croghan's commerce and intercourse with the Ohio Indians between 1741, the time of his first appearance on the pages of American history, and 1752, were so far-reaching and important as to cause the Governor-General of Canada to report to the French Ministry, three years before Braddock's defeat, "that the Indians of the Beautiful River are all English, for whom alone they work; that they are all resolved to sustain each other; and that not a party of Indians goes to the Beautiful River but leaves some there to increase the rebel force."

George Croghan wrote from his house in Pennsboro to the Provincial Secretary of Pennsylvania, May 26, 1747: "I am just returned from the Woods, and has brought a letter, a French scalp, and some wampum, for ye Govenor, from a part of ye Six Nation Ingans that has their dwelling on ye borders of Lake Arey. Those Ingans were always in the French interest till now, but this spring almost all the Ingans in the Woods have declared against ye French; and I think this will be a fair opertunity, if purshued by some small presents, to have all ye French cut off in them parts; for the Ingans will think a great dail of a little powder and lead att this time; besides, it will be a mains of drawing them that has nott yett joyned."[1]

The letter which Croghan brought with him from the "Woods," was dated May 16, 1747, and signed by three chiefs of the Mingoes (as the western Iroquois were called by the Traders). The names of these Six Nations' chiefs were Canajachrera, Sunathoaka, and Conaroya.

[1] This was during the progress of the *Old* French War, of 1744–48.

Canajachrera, the chief first named, is the same as one of the two "chiefs of the French Post at the White River" in 1744, to whom Longueuil sent a message, quoted above, on June 19th of that year; the French spelling of this chief's name in that document being *Canante-Chiarirou*. Through an error on the part of the editor of the *New York Colonial Documents*, this message of Longueuil, sent by him from Detroit on June 19, 1744, to the White River Indians, as well as the account of his conference with the Four Nations' chiefs at Detroit, instead of being printed in connection with Beauharnois's letter of November 7, 1744 (which appears on pages 1111,1112, vol. ix., of the *Colonial Documents*, and in which reference is made to the message), have been wrongly dated as of the year 1700, and printed among other papers of that year, on pages 704 to 708 of the same volume.

The letter of the Mingo chiefs, Conajachrera (he was a Seneca), Sunathoaka, and Conaroya, to Governor Thomas of Pennsylvania, was written from near "Canayahaga" (now Cuyahoga), and transcribed for these chiefs by the hand of George Croghan. After correcting Mr. Croghan's eccentric spelling, this letter reads as follows:

May ye 16th, 1747.

BROTHER ONASS[1] GIABOGA:—

Last fall, when our kings of the Six Nations were down at Albany, you and our brother of New York gave them ye hatchet, to make use of against ye French; which we very willingly and with true hearts took hold of, and has now made use of it, and killed five of ye French hard by this Fort, which is called Detroat; and we hope in a little time to have this Fort in our possession. We can assure you, Brother, we shall take all methods to cut off all ye French in these parts. We are likewise joined by ye Missisagas and Tawas, which are all as one with us. We now take this opportunity of presenting you by ye bearer, one of those Frenchman's scalps, assuring you it shall not be ye last of them. You shall see more of them as soon as we have completed a victory over them all in these parts, which we hope will be very soon done. We hope, Brother, you will consider that we shall be in need of some powder and lead, to carry on ye expedition with a vigor. We hear you have sent an army against Canada, to reduce it, which army we wish may have as good success as that you sent against Cape Breton. In assurance of our sincere wishes for ye success over all your and our enemies, we present you this string of wampum, and remain ye everlasting Brothers.

CONAGARERA,[2]
SUNATHOAKA,
KINNERA.

[1] *Onas*, an Iroquois word, signifying a "quill," or "pen," was the name given by the Five Nations to Governor William Penn, and to all the Provincial Governors of Pennsylvania succeeding him. See *Penna. Arch.*, iii., 199.

[2] *Penna. Archives*, i., 741 (where, in one place, it is misprinted "Conagaresa"), 751; ii., 59; *Penna. Col. Records*, v., 86, 136, 148, 150, 151, 189, 358 (where it is written

Endorsed—"Letter from the Indians, dated May 16th, 1747; an Indian Nation on the borders of Lake Ery. Conajachrera, in English: 'A Broken Kettle.' Conaroya. Read in Council, 8th June, 1747."

In a letter written by Anthony Palmer, President of the Pennsylvania Council, to Governor Gooch, of Virginia, January 25, 1748, he states that the foregoing letter from the Indians was sent to the Pennsylvania Government "by some of the Six Nations and other Indians seated at Canayahaga, a place on or near the River Conde,[1] which runs into the Lake Erie."

On July 9, 1747, the Provincial Secretary had laid before the Pennsylvania Council a number of letters he had received from Conrad Weiser, in which the latter relates the details of several conferences held by him on June 17th and following, with Shekallamy and Scaientes, two Iroquois chiefs, at the house of Joseph Chambers in Pextang. "The five French Indian Traders," writes Weiser, "that were killed on the south side of Lake Erie, have been killed by some of the Six Nations (there called *Acquanushioony*, the name which the Six Nations give their people—signifys, a confederate). Another French Trader has since been killed in a private quarrel with one of the Jonontatichroanu [Wyandots], between the River Ohio and the Lake Erie—the Frenchman offering but one charge of powder and one bullet for a beaver skin to the Indian; the Indian took up his hatchet and knocked him on the head." In this correspondence Weiser also reports that he is sorry to add that there are great complaints against James Dunning and John Powell, two of the Pennsylvania Traders. Dunning was accused by the Indians of having stolen forty-seven deer-skins and three horses from a Delaware, living on the heads of the Juniata. "James Dunning," continues Weiser, is gone down Ohio River, and will stay out long. The Indian was content that I should inform the Council of his misfortune. He not only lost his skins and horses, but pursued James Dunning in vain to the place called Canayiahagen, on the south side of Lake Erie; from thence back again to the place where he left the skins; and from thence again to Ohio; but all in vain, for he could not find or come up with James Dunning."

Conrad Weiser also, in a letter to the Provincial Council written from Tulpehocken, October 15, 1747, reports, that either the Zisgechas

---

"Oniadagarehra"), 438 (where it is misprinted "Canajachanah"), 531, 686. *Dinwiddie Papers*, i., 191; *N. Y. Col. Doc.*, v., 800; vi., 391, 706; vii., 330 (printed "Connageriwa"), 423.

[1] La Hontan's map depicts the River Conde as flowing from the southeast and emptying into Lake Erie along its southeastern coast. There is no large stream flowing into the Lake along that part of the coast. La Hontan may have meant to describe the Cuyahoga or the Grand River in Ohio. President Palmer's idea of the location of the Conde was indefinite, but he knew it was near the eastern end of Lake Erie.

(Mississagas) or the Jonontadys (Wyandots) had sent a large black belt of wampum to all the Delawares and Shawnees of the Ohio and Susquehanna, inviting them into the war against the French; that "100 men of the Delawares were actually gone to meet the Jonontadys about Deoghsaghronty,[1] where seventy or eighty of the Six Nations living at Canoyinhagy were also expected; they intend to cut off a French settlement to the south of Lake Erie."

Besides the above accounts of the killing of the French Traders, which Croghan and Weiser sent to the Pennsylvania Council, we have the official French version of the same; as well as an account carried to New York by an Iroquois warrior, who was an eye-witness, and may have been also a participant therein. These relations are, briefly, as follows: Longueuil writes from Detroit on the 23d of June, 1747, that "some Hurons of Detroit, belonging to the tribe of the war chief Nicolas, who, some years since, had settled at Sandoske, have killed five Frenchmen who were on their return from the post at the White River, and stolen their furs; that all the Indians of the neighborhood, except the Illinois, had formed the design to destroy all the French of Detroit on one of the holidays of Pentecost; but that some Hurons having struck too soon, the plot had been discovered by a Huron squaw."[2] "This conspiracy," he adds, "is the fruit of the belts the English have had distributed among all the tribes by the Iroquois of the Five Nations." Other Hurons, belonging to the tribes of the two friendly chiefs, Sastaretsy and Taychatin, came to Detroit to assure the Commandant that they had no share in the misconduct of Nicolas's people; "meanwhile, asking pardon, they endeavor to exculpate themselves, and propose settling near Detroit. Nicolas's tribe continues, nevertheless, to reside at Sandoske, where they doubtless expect not only to maintain themselves, but even to harass Detroit by small war parties. They have attached to them several families of vagabond Iroquois, Loups, &c. 'T is even asserted that there are some Saut Indians among them." In transmitting this intelligence to France, in the "Journal of Occurrences in Canada, 1746–47," the Governor-General adds: "Private letters mention the murder of the five Frenchmen with circumstances which show that the Hurons of Sandoske have perpetrated the greatest cruelties on this occasion."

In a conference held at Albany on July 17, 1747, between Governor Clinton and some of the Six Nations' chiefs, the latter informed the Governor, "that one of their Indians, in his way down from the Quitways [either the Quatoghees, *i.e.*, Hurons, or, more probably, Twightwees, *i. e.*, Miamis], met with three other different nations at Kichaga [Cuyahoga],

---

[1] Detroit; see *N. Y. Col. Doc.*, v., 694, 709.
[2] See *N. Y. Col. Doc.*, x., 83.

where they lodged all together. As they lay there, came a battoe with nine Frenchmen, and landed near them. After they had landed, a nation called Younondadys[1] called a council of all that were present, and told them they knew the Five Nations had taken up the axe against the French from our Governor, but that they had not taken the axe, but desired to use their own weapons; which was granted by the rest of the nations then present. Then they immediately killed eight [five], and took the commander prisoner, whom they have resolved to return in the place of a great Trader from Philadelphia, who was killed two years ago by the French, or his directions[2]; and the scalps they resolved to send where his Excellency, our Governor, had hung over the war kettle, in order to see if they would not give the broth a good relish to the pleasing of his Excellency's palate. The Ottawauways and other nations thanked them, and said they intended in a short time to make tryal, if they could not boil the same broth."[3]

Longueuil writes again from Detroit, August 24, 1747, that "the Hurons of Sandosket, and of Nicolas's band, continue insolent; this chief not ceasing in his efforts to gain allies. The same Nicolas sent back the people of the White River who were on their way to Detroit, on account of the death of the five Frenchmen killed by the Hurons. He likewise persuaded twenty-seven Shawnees to turn back, who were coming to answer M. de Longueuil's message; and as the sole result of the expenses incurred for that nation (of the village of Sonnioto)[4], he [Longueuil] saw one Shawnee arrive on the 23d of August." Kinousaki, an Ottawa chief attached to the French interest, informed the Detroit Commandant that no matter how things might turn, the Shawnees could not be induced to leave their village of Scioto and settle nearer the French. At the same time, from another source, the Commandant learned that two Englishmen had come to Sandosket, with ammunition for Nicolas and his men. Six months later, in February, 1748, Longueuil again informed the Governor of Canada that the Pennsylvania Traders had visited Nicolas twice during the winter, to trade, and were well received. He writes, finally, on June 5th of the same year, that Kinousaki, the friendly Ottawa chief, had returned, on the 7th of April, 1748, from the lower end of the Miami,[5] whither he had gone to bring back the Hurons

[1] Wyandots, or Hurons; their town, *Ayonontout* of the French, *Junundat* on Lewis Evans's map of 1755, was named for the tribe.
[2] Possibly, by the Ottawa war party sent from Detroit by De Longueuil in September, 1744 (see *ante*); or by Peter Chartier's Shawnee band.
[3] Captain Raymond wrote the French Minister from Quebec, November 2, 1747: "The Hurons of Detroit and the Yricois at the outlet of La Riviere Blanche have killed some Frenchmen at Sandoske."
[4] Scioto; near the present town of Portsmouth, Ohio.
[5] Now called Maumee, a corruption of Miami.

and Ottawas who had deserted from the village of Ostandosket. This messenger reported that "Nicolas, with 119 warriors of his nation, men, women, and baggage had taken the route to the White River, after having burnt the fort and cabins of the village." At the same time, two Hurons, who had been sent by Sastaredzy, the Huron chief of a loyal tribe, returned to Detroit, confirming the departure of Nicolas and his people "for the White River, to seek shelter among the Iroquois there, or among the Mohegans who are near Orange; and that *only seventy men* of all their nation would come back. The scalps of the Frenchmen who were killed by Nicolas have been conveyed to the Mohegans."[1]

From Longueuil's correspondence it will be seen that in the early spring of 1748, some 119 warriors of Nicolas's band, with their families and belongings, had left Sandusky for the White River, in order that they might be nearer the tribes there, who were in the English interest. Seventy more warriors of the same band, partly Ottawas, had previously deserted from the Sandusky village, and taken up their residence at the lower end of the Maumee.

On September 8, 1748, Pierre de Celoron arrived at Quebec, on his return from Detroit, whither he had conducted a convoy sent to that post. From his information, and from letters received, La Gallissoniere, the Governor, concluded, that "the Hurons who are at Point Montreal appear again too convenient to Nicolas, who has removed to the Beautiful River." The Governor accordingly writes to the Commandant at Detroit (October 3d) that "though we be at peace, every attempt of the English to settle at River a la Roche [the Great Miami], White River, the Beautiful River, or any of their tributaries, must be resisted by force."

In June of the following year, Celoron, with a force of about two hundred and forty men, started on his expedition down the Ohio, going by way of Lake Chautauqua. His purpose was to drive off the English Traders; but he found the Indians along the Ohio and Miami so friendly to the English that he was unable to accomplish it.

Let us turn again to Croghan's correspondence with the Pennsylvania Government in behalf of the Six Nations Indians of Cuyahoga, who had requested that powder and lead be sent them, to enable them to continue their war against the French. Croghan, September 18, 1747, wrote his factor, Thomas Lawrence of Philadelphia, a member of the Provincial Council, telling him that one of his men, who had just come "down from ye Woods," informs him that the Indians at this side of the Lake Erie are "making war very briskly against the French, but is very impatient to hear from their brothers, ye English, expecting a present of powder and lead; which, if they don't get, I am of opinion, by the best accounts, that

[1] One or more of the scalps, as we have seen, was conveyed to Pennsylvania by George Croghan and others. See *Penna. Archives*, i., 742; *Col. Rec.*, v., 138.

they will turn to the French. . . . If there be nothing sent, I will not send out any goods or men this year, for fear of danger."

On November 11, 1747, ten Indian warriors from Ohio arrived in Philadelphia, and at a conference held with the Governor and Council two days later, they informed the English that they had taken up the hatchet against the French in their behalf. Their speaker, Canachquasy, the son of old Queen Alliquippa, addressed the Council as follows: "We who speak to you are warriors living at Ohio, and address you on behalf of ourselves and the rest of the warriors of the Six Nations. . . . You know when our Father, the Governor of Canada, declared war against our brethren, the English, you . . . sent to inform the Council at Onondago of it, and to desire that they would not meddle with the war. . . . But some time after this, messengers were sent to Onondago by all the English, to tell us that the French had begun the war on the land in the Indian countries, and had done a great deal of mischief to the English; and they now desired their brethren, the Indians, would take up the hatchet against the French. . . . The old men at Onondago, however, refused to do this, and would adhere to the neutrality. . . . At last, the young Indians, the warriors and captains, consulted together, and resolved to take up the English hatchet against the will of their old people. . . . This the young warriors have done—provoked to it by the repeated applications of our brethren, the English. And we are now come to tell you that the French have hard heads, and that we have nothing strong enough to break them. We have only little sticks and hickories, and such things that will do little or no service against the hard heads of the French. . . . When once, we, the young warriors, engaged, we put a great deal of fire under our kettle, and the kettle boiled high; and so it does still, that the Frenchmen's heads might soon be boiled, but when we looked about us to see how it was with the English kettle, we saw the fire was almost out, and that it hardly boiled at all, and that no Frenchmen's heads were like to be in it. . . . This has not a good appearance, and therefore we give you this string of wampum to hearten and encourage you, to desire you would put more fire under your kettle."

The Indians were encouraged to continue the war against the French, and told that a present had been prepared for them and for the Canayiahaga (Cuyahoga) Indians. Canachquasy then thanked the Council in behalf of the Indians present, and for the Canayiahaga Indians, "who, being their own flesh and blood, they were pleased for the regard shown to them."

Acting on Croghan's information, the Council had purchased some £200 worth of goods for the Indians in November, and sent them by wagon carriage as far as John Harris's Ferry on the Susquehanna, where they were held until the following spring. Additions having been made thereto, so as to bring their total value up to about £1000,[1] arrangements were made to have Conrad Weiser accompany the convoy to Logstown, carry a message to the Indian nations of the Ohio, and deliver to them the present of goods. Weiser was delayed in setting out until August, 1748; so that George Croghan was sent to Logstown in April, with a portion of the goods, to the value of £200. In Council with the Indians at Logstown May 28, 1748, Croghan announced that he had been sent by the Pennsylvania authorities to return thanks to the Indians for the French scalp they had sent down in the spring of the year before, and to bring to them sufficient supplies to enable them to kill meat for their families until the rest of the goods could be brought out. As he found some 1500 Indians about Logstown in great want of powder and lead, and the present sent by the Province was insufficient to supply half of them with ammunition, Croghan was obliged to supplement it by adding goods from his own storehouse at that point, to the value of £169 more.

Weiser set out from his house in Tulpehocken August 11th, and reached Logstown on the evening of the 27th inst. His *Journal* of the trip out and back has been printed in a preceding chapter. On the 30th, he went to Beaver Creek Village (afterwards known as Sauconk, at the mouth of the Beaver), eight miles beyond Logstown, and lodged there at George Croghan's trading house. His companion, Andrew Montour, in the meanwhile had gone to carry a message to Coscosky (Kuskuskies), a large Indian Town about thirty miles from Logstown, which was the seat of the Six Nations regency in those parts. On September 3d, Weiser, having returned to Logstown, relates that he "set up the Union flagg on a long pole, treated all the company with a dram of rum; the King's health was drank by Indians and white men. Towards night, a great many Indians arrived to attend the Council. There was great firing on both sides; the strangers first saluted the Town at a quarter of a mile distance, and at their entry the Town's people returned the fire; also, the English Traders of whom there were above twenty."

On September 8th Mr. Weiser held a council with the "Wondats, otherways called Ionontady Hagas. . . . Enquired their number, and what occasioned them to come away from the French. . . . They informed me their coming away from the French was because of the hard usage they received from them; that they would always get their young men to go to war against their enemies, and would use them as their own people; that is, like slaves; and their goods were so dear that they, the Indians, could not buy them; that there was one hundred

---

[1] £200 had been contributed meanwhile by the Government of Virginia.

fighting men that came over to join the English; *seventy were left behind at another Town a good distance off, and they hoped they would follow them.*" Further on in his *Journal*, Weiser says of the Wyandot chiefs with whom he conversed, "They behaved like people of good sense and sincerity; the most of them were grey headed." On the day of this conference with the Wyandots, he requested "the deputies of all the Indians settled on the waters of Ohio" to give him a list of their fighting men. "The following is their number," Weiser writes, "given to me by their several deputies in Council, in so many sticks tied up in a bundle: the Senecas, 163; Shawonese, 162; Owendaets, 100; Tisagechroanu, 40; Mohawks, 74 (among whom were 27 French Mohawks); Mohichons, 15; Onondagers, 35; Cajuckas, 20; Oneidos, 15; Delawares, 165; in all, 789."

From the foregoing, it is apparent that when Nicolas's band of 119 warriors left their village at Sandusky in the early spring of 1748, and took the route for the White River, leaving seventy of their companions at another town a good distance off, who had previously deserted from the village, and whom Sastaredzy's messengers reported as being willing to return to Detroit, the larger party travelled eastward from Sandusky, and some finally settled on an eastern branch of the Beaver River, above what is now Newcastle, Pa. This "Owendoes" village is located on the Shenango in Dr. John Mitchell's map of 1755, a short distance northeast of "Kuskuskies,"[1] and was probably identical with the "Shaningo's Town" of Lewis Evans's map of the same year.[2] At Logstown, as we have seen, Weiser found that this village of the Wyandots contained 30 (?) warriors; and that the Wyandots had left seventy of their men behind in another town some distance to the westward. The location of that town will be considered in a subsequent chapter. Nicolas's band did not long remain at the White River, by the French account, it will be remembered; but located at the Ohio.

[1] See Everts's *History of Lawrence County, Penna.*, p. 120; Darlington's *Gist*, p. 108; De Schweinitz's *Life of Zeisberger*, p. 361; Loskiel's *Mission of the United Brethren*, part iii., ch. iii; Smith's *Bouquet*, App. iv; Darlington's *Ft. Pitt*, p. 84.

[2] Hutchins (maps in Smith's *Bouquet* and Darlington's *Ft. Pitt*) locates Shaningo Town in 1764 as a little more than half way between the Kuskuskies Town at the mouth of the Shenango and Pymatuning Town at the mouth of a creek of the same name which enters the Shenango Creek near Clarksville Station, Pymatuning Township, Mercer County, Penna. This would place Shaningo Town in the present township of Shenango, Mercer County. Mr. Darlington in his *Gist's Journals* (p. 108) states that an old Wyandot Town stood on the site afterwards occupied by Zeisberger in 1770 for his Indian village of Friedenstadt. This is still the site of Moravia post-office in Taylor Township, Lawrence County, on the east bank of the Beaver three miles below the mouth of the Shenango. Mr. Darlington thought that wherever the name "Chenango" occurs on an early map it marks the site of a Wyandot settlement or of a place where the tobacco plant was largely cultivated.

The truth seems to be, that the term, "White River," as used by the Detroit commandants from 1743 to 1749, really applied to the district in which the "Indians of the White River" were settled; and that the exact identity or location of that stream was not very clear in the minds either of Longueuil or Celoron.

Longueuil, as we have seen, wrote in 1747 that the menaces of the Iroquois had obliged the Hurons "to collect and entrench themselves at the White River, twenty-five leagues from Detroit," probably meaning the Cuyahoga terminus of the White River portage route.

Celoron while on his expedition down the Ohio River in August, 1749, applied the name, White River, to the Little Miami, and that stream is called *Riviere Blanche* on the map of Father Bonnecamps, the geographer of that expedition: both of them evidently taking it for the stream that led to the Ohio from the White River country, and not knowing that the Muskingum, or, as they called it, the *Yanangue*, was really that stream. The territory of what is now northeastern Ohio, Bonnecamps states, "is all unknown."

Baron de Longueuil, acting Governor of Canada, in a letter written to the Ministry in the spring of the year 1752, refers to a report received from the Commandant of the Miamis [Maumee] Fort, in which that officer tells of his unsuccessful efforts at bringing back a revolted band of Miami Indians from the White River, referring either to the band of *La Demoiselle*, who had built the large town of Pickawillany, on the Great Miami, or to the band of Le Baril, whom Celoron found located near the mouth of the Little Miami (by him then called the White) River in 1749.[1]

D'Anville, in his 1746 map of North America, applies the name "Riviere des Femmes Blanch" to the Muskingum; and in his map of 1755, he calls the Sandusky the White River; as does also Dr. John Mitchell, in his London map of the same year, which was largely copied from maps of the French, and particularly from that of Robert de Vaugondy (1755). Mitchell, following Vaugondy, locates "Canahogue" as the district between the Sandusky (which they both call "River Blanche") and the "Gwahage" (Cuyahoga); and he calls it "the seat of

---

[1] In J. N. Bellin's 1755 map of the Western Part of New France, the Little Miami is called the Riviere Blanche, and the Great Miami, the Riviere a la Damoiselle, the village of Le Baril being located at the mouth of the former, on the east bank, and the village of La Damoiselle on the west bank of the stream of the same name. Mr. Berthold Fernow, in his *Ohio Valley in Colonial Days*, refers to another of Bellin's maps of 1755, in which he locates the village of Le Baril at the mouth of White Woman's Creek, thus erroneously applying two names (White River, and White Woman) to the Little Miami, one of which seems to have belonged to the present Walhonding or White Woman's River, the stream that unites with the Tuscarawas at Coshocton, Ohio, to form the Muskingum.

war, the mart of trade, and chief hunting grounds of the Six Nations on the Lake and the Ohio." Vaugondy locates the Iroquois village of "Gwahago" on the Cuyahoga River a short distance above the mouth of a tributary which seems to be the stream now known as Tinker's Creek.

Broadly speaking, the White River country was really that between Lake Erie, the Forks of the Beaver, and the Upper Muskingum. The term, "White River," apparently, was applied to include not only the Cuyahoga, but also, at times, the Mahoning, the White Woman (or Walhonding) and Tuscarawas branches of the Muskingum, the Sandusky, and the Huron. The Cuyahoga connected almost directly with the Upper Tuscarawas by means of a portage (in what are now Portage and Coventry townships, Summit County),[1] and with the Mahoning Branch of the Beaver; while the Sandusky, the Huron, and the White Woman rivers were connected by similar portages in what are now Plymouth and Sharon townships, Richland County, Ohio.

The 1755 map of Lewis Evans was the first approximately correct map of the Ohio country ever made. It shows a "French House" twenty-five miles below (north of) the portage, on the left bank of the Cuyahoga River. There was no house standing there at the time Evans made his map; because James Smith, the Indian captive, travelled up and down the Cuyahoga in the winter of 1756–57; and makes no mention of any French post or Indian village on the river at that time. Lewis Evans says the information in his map concerning "the routes across the country, as well as the situation of Indian villages, trading places, the creeks that fall into Lake Erie, and other affairs relating to Ohio and its branches, are from a great number of informations of Traders and others, and especially, of a very intelligent Indian called The Eagle, who had a good notion of distances, bearings, and delineating." The "French House" on Evans's map could have been none other than the approximate site of Saguin's trading post, referred to in the report of Navarre, in 1743. A short distance south of this post, on the same side of the Cuyahoga, Evans shows a Mingo, or Seneca, Town; while, on the opposite bank of the river from the "French House," he locates a town of the Tawas (Ottawas). Mr. Charles Whittlesey, in his *Early History of Cleveland*, identifies the latter point with the "site of the old Ottawa Town," on which site, on Sunday, June 18, 1786, David Zeis-

[1] The Portage Path between the Cuyahoga and Tuscarawas in 1797, as surveyed by Moses Warren in that year, left the Cuyahoga at the point where it crosses the line between Northampton and Portage townships, proceeding thence southwards to a point on the Tuscarawas nearly opposite the mouth of the outlet of Long Lake, in Coventry Township. In 1797, this trail measured 8 miles, 4 chains, 55 links, in length. See map in Hulbert's "Indian Thoroughfares of Ohio," *Ohio Arch. and Hist. Soc. Publications*, vii., 291.

berger and John Heckewelder settled, with their Christianized Delaware Indian followers, on their return to Ohio from Detroit. The point at which they located was on the east bank of the Cuyahoga, just north of the mouth of Tinker's Creek, in what is now Independence Township, Cuyahoga County. On the opposite, or west, side of the river, they found a plat of good cleared ground, covered with a dense growth of rank weeds, where they tilled and planted. This was very probably the site of Saguin's house,[1] and as, in the early part of the eighteenth century, the main trail from the Forks of the Ohio westward led to the portage between Cuyahoga and Tuscarawas, it will be seen that his location was near the centre of the Indian settlements in Ohio in 1742.

Proceeding southwards, up the Cuyahoga, from Saguin's house to the portage, crossing thence to the head waters of the Tuscarawas, and down that stream past the site of the present town of Navarre, in Stark County, Lewis Evans depicts, on his map of 1755, the Indian Town "Tuscarawas," as between the forks of that stream and the Big Sandy Creek. Christopher Gist, the surveyor in the employ of the Ohio Company, who visited this town, December 7, 1750, found it at that time to be "a Town of the Ottaways, a nation of French Indians; an old Frenchman, named Mark Coonce,[2] who had married an Indian woman of the Six Nations, lived here." The town of Bolivar, Tuscarawas County, on the west bank of the Tuscarawas River, nearly opposite the mouth of Big Sandy Creek, is just below the former site of Tuscarawas Town, as located on the 1764 and 1778 maps of Thomas Hutchins, the geographer of Bouquet's expedition to the Forks of the Muskingum in

[1] Gen. L. V. Bierce, in his *Historical Reminiscences of Summit County* (Akron, Ohio, 1854), refers to a former Seneca village as having been located near the north line of Boston Township, Summit County, on the east side of the Cuyahoga; and to another former Indian village, known as "Ponty's Camp, about half a mile northwest, on the west side of the river." He also refers to an Ottawa Town, in what is now Northampton Township, and on the opposite, or west, side of the river, a Mingo Town. General Bierce adds, "If there is any correctness in Evans's map, the French House there laid down was undoubtedly Ponty's Camp." It is quite possible that one of the sites mentioned by General Bierce, on the west side of the Cuyahoga, may have been that of the "Mingo Town" of Evans. One of the two sites on the east bank was that of the "Cayahoga Town," of Hutchins's maps of 1764 and 1778. Saguin's house and the Tawa Town were farther down the river (north), as already shown.

[2] This man was probably the "Maconce" of Navarre's Memoir; and he may have been the French interpreter for the English Traders at Saguin's House, referred to in that Memoir, who had lived among the English. One, Maconse, guided a party of French and Indians from Fort Machault to the English settlements on the Susquehanna in the summer of 1757, he having a brother living among the English at that time. It is uncertain whether he was a Frenchman or an Indian, however, the Chippewa name for "bear cub" being *makons*, or *mackconce*. It may have been that that was the Indian name for the Frenchman whom Gist found at Tuscarawas Town in 1750. See *Penna. Archives*, iii., 294, 304; *Long's Voyages*, Thwaites's edition, 241.

The Site of Saguin's Trading House on the Cuyahoga River. Looking West from the Mouth of Tinker's Creek.

From a photograph furnished by Mr. Charles Starek.

October, 1764. In 1764, the Indian village was called "King Beaver's Town at Tuscarawas," and it was then occupied by Delaware Indians, who had removed from the vicinity of Fort Duquesne before the time of its evacuation by the French in 1758.[1] King Beaver's Town stood on the west bank of the Tuscarawas, nearly opposite the mouth of Big Sandy Creek.

Evans's map of 1755 does not show any portage between the Cuyahoga and the West Branch of Beaver (Mahoning); but it does show a land trail leading eastward eighty miles, from the French House on the Cuyahoga (Saguin's) and the "Mingo Town," to "Kishkuskees" Indian Town, below the mouth of the Mahoning, on the Beaver. A trail thirty-five miles long, running along the south bank of the West Branch of Beaver, is also shown, leading from Kishkuskees to the "Salt Spring," a locality within the present township of Weathersfield, Trumbull County, Ohio, still known by that name down to the time of its first settlement by the Connecticut pioneers.

The true "White River" of New France in the fourth decade of the eighteenth century therefore, was the Cuyahoga. The district called "Canayahaga" or "Canahogue" was that part of the present state of Ohio lying south of Lake Erie, and almost entirely surrounded by the Cuyahoga River. That river, it will be remembered, rises not far from the mouth of the Grand, and after flowing south and west, doubles on itself, and flows north into Lake Erie, at a point farther south than its source. The peninsula formed by the stream includes the greater part of Geauga County, the northwest corner of Portage, the northeast corner of Summit, and the eastern half of Cuyahoga counties. Flowing north through the centre of this peninsula is another small river, the eastern branch of which heads near the sources of the Cuyahoga itself. This second river has been incorrectly named on the maps during the past hundred years as the "Chagrin" River.

On Rufus Putnam's 1804 map of Ohio, the name "Shaguin," from which Chagrin has been corrupted, is correctly given, although Putnam applied it to a river which really never existed. Putnam copied this portion of his map from that of Thomas Hutchins, made in 1778; and the latter may have copied it from the French (1754) and English (1764) accounts of the stream which was the true Shaguin River.

But Hutchins and Putnam both made the mistake of applying the name to an imaginary river between the Riviere La Biche (*i.e.*, Elk, now the Chagrin) and the Cuyahoga, instead of to the Cuyahoga itself, to which latter stream the name Saguin, Shaguin,[2] or Sequin had been

---

[1] See *Penna. Col. Rec.*, vii., 381; *Penna. Archives*, iii., 81.

[2] "In Iroquois, *s* frequently sounds like *sh.*"—Horatio Hale, quoted by Ruttenber in *New York State Hist. Assoc. Collections*, vi., 183.

given by the French of Detroit after 1742, to commemorate the residence there of the French Trader, Saguin.

On both Hutchins's and Putnam's maps, three rivers are shown between the Cherage, or Grand, and the "Cayahoga," all bearing their French names—Biche (or Deer, or Elk), Shaguin, and Roche (or Rocky), and all east of the Cuyahoga. Inasmuch as the Rocky River is some half a dozen miles *west* of the Cuyahoga, it is plain that these cartographers, being ignorant of the fact that Shaguin was a French name for the same stream of which the Indian and English name was Cuyahoga, imagined a river to lie between the Biche, or Elk (the present Chagrin River), and the Cuyahoga, to which belonged the name Saguin or Shaguin; and so they inserted at this place on their maps a river which never existed. And further, knowing from their accounts of the shore of Lake Erie that the Rocky River was the stream next west of the Saguin, Hutchins and Putnam made the second mistake of placing the Rocky River east of the Cuyahoga, instead of making the Saguin identical with the Cuyahoga, and the latter east of the Rocky, as they should have done. The river now doubly miscalled the Chagrin, Hutchins and Putnam both called by its French name, *Biche*, meaning Deer, or Elk, River.

Lewis Evans's map of 1755 gives a true representation of these various rivers, and shows only three streams (the Cherage or Grand, the Elk, and the Cayahoga), where Hutchins and Putnam show five. Evans gives an Indian name to the Grand River, calling it "Cherage." This is the same stream which Major Robert Rogers called the "Chogage" in 1760; which Parkman, in his *Pontiac*, erroneously identified with the Cuyahoga; and from the Indian name of which comes the word, "Geauga," the name of an Ohio county to-day, in which the Grand River has one of its sources. "Cherage" is a variant of the Onondaga word, *tsho-eragak*[1] meaning "raccoon." From this word seems to have been derived the name Eriga, or Erighek, which the Iroquois applied to the people who lived or hunted on the banks of the Cherage, and who were known to the French and English as the Eries, or Nation of the Cat.

The Chagrin River, which Evans called Elk Creek, now bears a name which is simply a corruption of Saguin, a Detroit French name for the Cuyahoga. The river Cuyahoga Evans called "Cayahoga" (its Indian name), he not being familiar in 1755 with the personal name

---

[1] Zeisberger's *Onondaga Dictionary*. Mr. Gatschet, in his article on the Massawomekes (Peet's *American Antiquarian*, iii., 323), gives *tchu-eragak* as the Onondaga word for "wild-cat." This is the definition given in the *Onondaga-French Dictionary* of the seventeenth century, and definitely fixes the Cherage of Evans's map, now the Grand, as the River of the Raccoon, or Cat, or Erie Tribe, in whose country it was.

which had been applied to it some ten years before by the French settlers at Detroit, to commemorate Saguin's trading post, established on its banks by one of their fellow citizens about the year 1742.

However, the Shaguin River on Putnam's map perpetuated, until 1804, the name of the French Trader, Saguin, whom Navarre visited at his trading post on the Cuyahoga in 1743. The name, "Chagrin," as now applied to what Thomas Hutchins and Rufus Putnam called the Biche River, is a corruption and a misnomer, and wholly devoid of the historical significance attached to the true name of the French Trader, Saguin or Shaguin, which the Connecticut pioneers corrupted and erroneously applied to this river[1] instead of to the Cuyahoga where it originally belonged.

Lieutenant John Montresor, who accompanied Colonel Bradstreet's army from Fort Erie to Detroit, August 8th to 27th, 1764, has left a very complete *Journal*[2] of the movement of the army along the south shore of Lake Erie. Under date of August 14th he writes: "The whole set sail for Presque Isle . . . and arrived there at nine—twelve miles. Halted a short time, and continued to the Carrying Place, being four miles further, and there encamped." On the 16th, the army proceeded on its voyage, and encamped at "La Riviere de Villejoint—seventeen miles." On the 17th, the expedition started at six o'clock in the morning, and arrived in the evening at "La Grand Riviere, or Cayahuga, sixty-two miles." This was the present Grand River, and not the present Cuyahoga. Montresor's estimate of the distance covered that day was much too large.

"18th. The whole proceeded at seven o'clock this morning. . . . The canoes with the Indians not arrived. Detained till this hour by frivolous excuses of the savages, in which they are never wanting. At nine o'clock the wind sprang up at NNEt. The whole fleet set sail. After some time the wind rose at NW. by N. and blew fresh, the sea running high, and the whole bore away into the River de Seguein [Cuyahoga or Saguin], with a little difficulty, as there is a spit off the entrance, but no bar in the mouth of it. This is a remarkable river, where the Upper Nations hunt, and also paddle six leagues up this river, land on the east side, and from thence march loaded to Fort Duquesne, now Fort Pitt, in six days. Great party of the Ottawas hunted and saved corn here last year. Gained thirty-six miles this day. The River Assequesix [*au Seguein*] is navigable for birch canoes sixty miles up.

"19th. Continued our route at daylight. The wind moderate, but rose with a fresh swell. Signals were made for making a harbor.

[1] "All of the parties [of surveyors, in 1796], when they reached the Chagrin, supposed they were at the Cuyahoga."—Whittlesey, *Early History of Cleveland*, p. 213.
[2] *New York Historical Society Collections*, vol. xiv.

The whole bore away into the River de Roches [Rocky River]—the wind at NE.—seven miles one-half from the last encampment.

"21st. At six o'clock this morning orders were given for the whole to proceed. Arrived at La Riviere de la Culiere, twenty-one miles, and there halted. At two o'clock this afternoon continued to the Riviere de Vermillion, thirteen miles further; thirty-four miles this day."

The detachment of troops accompanied by Lieutenant Montresor to Detroit left there to return to Sandusky on September 14th. On the 18th of that month the army left Sandusky for Niagara. Montresor writes: "This morning, at half-past eight o'clock, the whole decamped and embarked for Niagara, consisting of 1400 men, besides 150 Indians —59 long boats, one barge, and nine birch canoes. . . . Continued this whole day on Lake Erie. Passed by the Rivers Huron, Vermillion, and Culiere, and encamped on a sandy beach to the westward, one mile off the Riviere au Roche. . . . 19th. . . . Offered my services this morning to Colonel Bradstreet to command and conduct a party to Fort Pitt, as provisions was so scarce—the route by the portage from the River de Seguein. . . . 21st. . . . At twelve o'clock opened the dam and all the boats proceeded, being thirty-six in number, and arrived at the River de Seguein at two o'clock. . . . 22d. At seven o'clock a detachment of three hundred and eighty men, with two days' provisions marched off for the River au Biche [Deer or Elk River], and if they should not find our boats there, to continue their route to Grande River, as per written instructions. At eight o'clock this morning continued our route (the same number of boats). . . . Attempted to disembark on a sandy beach, but found it not practicable, being in danger every instant of filling by a prodigious surf. Could not enter into the River au Biche, so were obliged to keep the sea and push for Grande River, which we reached about two o'clock. . . . 23d. . . . I went up the Grand Riviere, or Cayahage Creek to discover how far it was navigable; found it so for five miles for a barge at a place called *le petit rapide*. Arrived, the party that marched from the River de Sequein."

These extracts from the Journals of Montresor thus afford absolute proof of the identity of the White River (on which Saguin's Trading House stood in 1742) with the Cuyahoga River of to-day.

The last reference to this White River contained in the records of the English colonies appears to be that found in a letter from one Smith, transmitted by Governor William Shirley, of Massachusetts, to the Governor of Pennsylvania in March, 1754. Smith's letter to Governor Shirley was written from Cape Cod, December 24, 1753. He had left Quebec on the 18th of the preceding August. Mr. Smith writes: "September the

29th, 1752, the Castor or Beaver Company of Quebec petitioned the Governor and Council of Canada to have a Fort erected on or near a river called by the French, La Riviere Blanche, for the support and strength of their Indian commerce, which they alleged was encroached upon by the English Traders. This was forthwith granted by the Governor and Council, and an army of six thousand men to be [raised] forthwith, and ready to march by the first of January, 1753. . . . They were to be divided into three parties, and to march as follows, the first party . . . on the first of January, 1753; . . . the second party . . . to be ready on the first of March; . . . and the third party, consisting of the regulars and the rest of the militia to be ready to embark at Quebec on board of boats which were to be provided for them by the first of May.[1] . . . The first party began their march on New Year's Day, 1753; the second party in March; and the remainder I saw embarked at Quebec on the first of May, on board 100 flat-bottomed boats built for the expedition. . . . The Indian Traders with whom I conversed inform me that La Riviere Blanche is 500 leagues from Quebec, and that it is in the British territories."

This was the expedition sent by Governor Duquesne in the spring of 1753 to build the French forts on the Ohio, three of which were nearly completed when Washington carried Governor Dinwiddie's letter to their commander in December of that year. These were Forts Presqu' Isle, Riviere aux Bœufs, and Venango. A fourth fort—Duquesne—was built during the next spring; and with the completion of these posts, the efforts which the French had been making for the past ten years to drive the English Traders away from the country of the White River and La Belle Riviere, were finally, for a brief period, successful.

[1] See deposition of J. B. Pidon, a French deserter, in *Penna. Archives*, ii., 124.

CHAPTER XIII

KUSKUSKIES ON THE BEAVER

KUSKUSKA, Kishkuskes, Kishkuske, Kuskuskies, the Cuscuskoes, Coscosky, the Kaskuskies, Kuskusky, Cushcushking, Cuscuskey, Kiskuskis, Cascaski, Kaskaskunk, Cachekacheki, etc., as it was variously spelled by George Washington, Lewis Evans, Thomas Hutchins, John Mitchell, George Croghan, Conrad Weiser, Christopher Gist, Richard Peters, Frederick Post, William Irvine, John Armstrong, John Heckewelder, David Zeisberger, and the Marquis de Vaudreuil, was not one town, but three or four contiguous towns of the Mingoes, located along the Beaver River, at and above the junction of its east and west branches—the Mahoning and the Shenango. This being the case, the writer prefers the plural form of the name, as given by Evans, Mitchell, Croghan, Gist, and Armstrong; that is—Kuskuskies. In Durant's *History of Lawrence County, Pennsylvania* (the site of the town is in that county), the author erroneously assumes that Kaskaskunk (a Delaware form of the word), and Kushkushkee were two distinct names for different localities, instead of being, as they were, two forms of the same word, which was originally applied to three or four contiguous towns of the Mingo or Six Nations Indians along the Beaver,[1] occupied by the Delawares from Kittanning after 1756.[2] Mr. Durant writes: "Two villages . . . were in this locality: one at the mouth of Mahoning River, called Kas-kas-kunk; the other upon the site of Newcastle, and called New Kas-kas-kunk. . . . Another famous Indian town was located on the Mahoning, near to the present town of Edenburg, and known as Kush-kush-kee. . . . There are various opinions as to the location of this village. Some authorities locate it at the mouth of the

---

[1] It is unfortunate that the National Bureau of Ethnology has made a similar mistake, in its map of the "Indian Cessions in Pennsylvania to the United States," published in the Bureau's Eighteenth *Report*. This map locates "Kaskaskunk" in what is now Butler County, twenty miles east of its true site; while "Kushkushking" is placed several miles above "Kaskaskunk," and likewise within the territorial limits of Butler County.

[2] *Penna. Col. Rec.*, vii., 515.

The Site of Old Kuskuskies. Looking East from the Pennsylvania Railroad Station at Edenburg.

Mahoning, on the Big Beaver, and others still farther down, between that and Moravia. But the evidence points strongly to the site of Edenburg as the location of this once famous Indian town. It is at least certain there was a village where Edenburg stands, which was divided into two parts, one a short distance farther up the river than the other. . . . In the vicinity have been picked up gun-flints, oxidized bullets, flattened and battered, old gun-locks and gun-barrels, bayonets, etc. . . . Many bones have also been found. Near the Town was a burial ground, containing, among other relics, an interesting mound, originally some fifty feet in circumference, and about six feet high. This mound was examined some years since, and found to contain several layers of human skeletons; flag-stones were placed in regular order around the bodies, and the whole covered with earth. Nearby were quite a large number of bodies, buried separately. Large numbers of flint chips and arrow-heads have been picked up in the vicinity. The location of the village was on the south side of the Mahoning, the principal part being below the present village of Edenburg, and close to the river. . . . In 1770, at the request of Pakanke, the Moravians removed from their settlement on the Allegheny River, and settled on the Big Beaver, five miles below Newcastle, near the present site of Moravia Station." DeSchweinitz, in his *Life and Times of David Zeisberger* states that in 1770, old Kaskaskunk (of the Delawares) was at the confluence of the Shenango and Mahoning, which form the Beaver; while New Kaskaskunk stood near, or perhaps on, the site of Newcastle, at the mouth of the Neshannock. In Mathews's *History of Butler County* the site of Cushcushkunk, or Koshkoshkung, is fixed as at Newport, Lawrence County (about two miles below Moravia).

Frederick Post, in his *Journal* for August 14 and 17, 1758, writes of this place at that time (then occupied by the Delawares): "Cushcushking is divided into four towns, each at a distance from the others, and the whole consists of about ninety houses and two hundred able warriors . . . . The Frenchmen came and would speak with me; there were then fifteen of them building houses for the Indians; the captain is gone with fifteen to another town." In his *Journal*, under date of November 16, 1758, Post writes: "Went down a long valley [McKee Run Valley?] to Beaver Creek, through old Kushkushking, a large spot of land, about three miles long." This was the extensive bottom lying in what is now Taylor Township, Lawrence County, on the east side of the Beaver, between the present East Moravia and Newcastle Junction. Anyone who has seen the wide, flat valley along the Tuscarawas River in Coshocton County, Ohio, or the "Great Plain called Maguck," (Pickaway Plains) on the Scioto, in Pickaway County, Ohio, both formerly most populous centres of the Indian races in that State, will readily understand from Post's description of the approach to Old Kuskuskies, why it should be a favored spot of residence for the red man. On the 20th of November, Post speaks of attending a Council with the Delawares in "the middle town" of the Kuskuskies.

Thomas Hutchins, in his *Topographical Description of Virginia, Pennsylvania, Maryland, and North Carolina*, writes of Beaver Creek that "at Kishkuskes (about fifteen miles up) are two branches of this Creek, which spread opposite ways; one [Shenango] interlocks with French Creek and Cherage [the Grand River, in Ohio]—the other [Mahoning], with Muskingum and Cayahoga; on this Branch, about thirty-five miles above the Forks are many Salt Springs. It is practicable with canoes about twenty miles farther."

General William Irvine, who made a survey of Western Pennsylvania in the summer of 1785, writes of the Beaver Valley: "From where McLane's Line strikes the . . . Beaver, I continued exploring the country up the several western branches of the Beaver, viz., the most westerly, and two branches denominated the Shenango. The distance from the above named line to an old Moravian Town is three or four miles; from thence to Shenango, two and a half miles; thence to a Fork, or second Branch [Neshannock]; two miles; from the mouth of Shenango to Cuscuskey on the West Branch [Mahoning] is six or seven miles; but it was formerly all called Cuscuskey by the natives along this Branch, as high as the Salt Springs, which is twenty-five miles from the mouth of Shenango."

Another Kuskuskies town, perhaps, was the one called Mahoning on Hutchins's map of 1764. This is supposed to have been located at or near where the city of Youngstown, Ohio, now stands. John McCullough, a captive among the Indians at Sauconk at the mouth of the Beaver, after 1755, writes in his *Narrative*, that at about the time Forbes occupied Fort Duquesne, the Indians to whom McCullough belonged removed from Shenango (or from Logstown) to the Salt Licks, on the West Branch of the Beaver, "where they were settling a new town, called *Kseek-heoong*, or Salt Licks"; and from thence, the following spring they removed to a town about fifteen miles farther up, called Mahoning. This latter town is probably the same as that shown as "Old Mahoning Town" on Heckewelder's map of 1796. It was located on the west bank of the Mahoning, near the boundary line between the present counties of Trumbull and Mahoning—probably on or near the site of Newton Falls. After the battle of Bushy Run, in August, 1763, John McCullough's master took him from Mahoning to "Cayahawge, a town not far distant from Lake Erie." Hutchins's "Mahoning Town" is located by him as being below the Salt Lick Town.

General William Irvine wrote to Washington, January 27, 1788,

Looking down Big Beaver Valley.
From a point opposite the mouth of Mahoning River.

regarding a water communication between the Ohio and Lake Erie. Of the portage between the Beaver and the Cuyahoga, he says: "From a place called Mahoning, on the Big Beaver, to the Falls of Cuyahoga, it is about thirty miles. . . . The Cuyahoga above the great falls is rapid and rocky, and is interrupted by several lesser falls on the branch which leads towards that part of the Big Beaver, called Mahoning. This information I have from an intelligent person, then loading a sloop at the mouth of the Cuyahoga for Detroit. He added, that an old Indian assured him it was only fifteen miles across from the Mahoning to a navigable creek, a few miles east of the Cuyahoga. . . . Captain Brady, a partizan officer, informed me that the sources of the Big Beaver, Muskingum, and a large, deep Creek, which emptied into Lake Erie fifteen or twenty miles above Cuyahoga, are within a few miles of each other (perhaps four or five). . . . Following the Indian path, which generally keeps in the low ground along the river, the distance from the mouth of the Big Beaver to Mahoning, is about fifty miles; which, with the computed distance thence to Cuyahoga, gives eighty miles in all."

In the *Narrative* (written in 1826) of the captivity of Hugh Gibson, who was taken at Robinson's Fort by the Delawares in July, 1756, he states that he lived, in the spring and fall of 1757, at "Kuskuskin, or 'Hog Town,'[1] on the Mahoning, a considerable distance above its confluence with the Big Beaver."

While this was the meaning of a Delaware word somewhat resembling *Kuskuskies* in sound, the latter name probably means "at the falls," from the Seneca, *koskohsh-ehtoh* " by the falls, or rapids."[2] In this case the Falls of the Big Beaver were meant.

John Mitchell's map of 1755 places Kuskuskies opposite the mouth of the Shenango, and calls it, "the chief town of the Six Nations on the Ohio."

In his comments on the report which Pierre de Celoron wrote to Beauharnois from Detroit in June, 1743, respecting the Indians who had seated themselves of late years at the White River, Beauharnois says: "These Indians are Senecas, Onondagas, and others of the Five Iroquois villages. They have earnestly asked that officer for some Frenchmen to supply their wants, under promise that if their request be granted, they would drive off the English from that quarter, and

[1] Heckewelder gives the same meaning to "Cushcushing" (which he writes "Goschgoshing"), the name of an old Indian town seventeen miles above the mouth of Oil-Creek on the Allegheny, where the Minsis settled about 1765. It is called Kushkushing on Hutchins's map of 1778. It consisted of three villages, and was near the site of the present town of Tionesta, Forest County, Pennsylvania.

[2] Zeisberger gives *quis-quis* as the Onondaga word for "hog," and *goschgosch* as the Delaware word. The *French-Onondaga Dictionary* gives the same word as *kouichkouich*, in Onondaga.

have no dealings with them; whilst, if refused, they would be under the necessity of inviting them thither. . . . By this report it will be seen that those different tribes may amount to about six hundred men; that they seem to feel a sincere desire that the French should go to trade with them; and that they are equally disposed to keep the English at a distance; that game is abundant in the place where these Indians are seated; but that they are in want of ammunition and merchandise, some of which they would assuredly obtain from the English, should the French not carry any to them."

In the fall of 1749, Thomas Cresap, the agent of the Ohio Company, (in which Governor Dinwiddie and other prominent Virginians were interested), invited some of the Mingo chiefs at Ohio to come down to his storehouse on the Potomac, with a view to making a trade treaty, Cresap proposing to let the Indians have goods at much cheaper prices than the Pennsylvania Traders charged. In accordance with this invitation, "Canajacharah," or "Broken Kettle," and two other "Chiefs of the Seneca nations settled at Ohio," came over the Frankstown Path in June, 1750, as far as George Croghan's house near Carlisle, where they stopped awhile before proceeding to Cresap's; and there Richard Peters, the Provincial Secretary, held a conference with them, on the 7th of that month.

Among other things, Canajachrera informed the Provincial Secretary, that "We were sent from Ohio about six years ago [1744?] to Canada, to desire the French to supply us with goods; and they could not supply us. When we returned, our council determined to send a string of wampum to the Governor of Pennsylvania, to desire that the English Governors would send their Traders with goods among us; which string was sent by James Lowrey."

Canachquasy, Queen Alliquippa's son, afterwards called by the English, Captain Newcastle, led a party of ten young Mingo warriors from the vicinity of Kuskuskies to Philadelphia in November, 1747.

Conrad Weiser met Canajachrera (whose name Weiser wrote "Oniadagarehra"), September 19, 1748, at Logstown, to which place he had accompanied the Mingoes from Kuskuskies who were to receive from Weiser a portion of the present sent by the Pennsylvania Government.

George Croghan and Andrew Montour carried a present from the Pennsylvania Government to the Indians at Logstown in the spring of 1751; and in Croghan's *Journal* of the expedition, he writes, under date of May 23d: "Conajarca, one of the chiefs of the Six Nations, and a party with him from Cuscuskie, came to Town to wait on the Council; and congratulated me upon my safe arrival in their country."

In a "List of the names of the Chiefs now entrusted with the Conduct of Public Affairs among the Six Nations, delivered by Mr. Conrad Weiser [November 1, 1753] for the use of the Government," Canajachreesera, or Broken Kettle, Deharachristion (Tanacharison), or Half King, Scarrooyady, and Kachshwuchdanionty (Belt of Wampum), are named as the chiefs at Ohio.

The English meaning of Canajachrera's name as translated by the Pennsylvanians, was "Broken Kettle."[1] By the Virginians, he was called "Big Kettle." Washington mentioned him under this name (which the French translator rendered "Grand-Chaudiere") in his *Journal* of 1754, under date of June 3d. He writes: "The Half-King assembled the Council and informed me that he had received a speech from Big Kettle, in answer to the one he had sent him." Washington wrote to Dinwiddie the same day, enclosing this speech, of which he says: "The French, early in the Spring, sent a speech to the Wayandotts, Twigtwees, and their allies, and desired them to take up the hatchet and start to Ohio, and there cut off the inhabitants, with all the English thereon. This, the Big Kettle acquainted the Half-King with, and at the same time assured him with their good intentions." The "speech" which Big Kettle forwarded is headed "The answer returned by the Big Kettle to a speech, sent by him from the Six Nations to the Vendates [Wyandots], letting them know how near the danger was, and what they intended to do; . . . delivered to the Big Kettle to be sent to the Six Nations, English, and Delawares."[2]

The location of the town of the Wyandots (the remnant of Chief Nicolas's band) from which this message came, and its contiguity to Kuskuskies, the town of which Canajachrera was chief, are shown approximately by Mitchell's map of 1755; on which Kuskuskies is located on both sides of the Beaver, immediately below the confluence of the Mahoning and Shenango; while the "Owendoes' first settlement on the Ohio" is located on the west bank of the Shenango below the mouth of a stream intended for the Pymatuning.[3] The location of

[1] *Penna. Archives*, i., 741; *Penna. Col. Rec.*, v., 438, 686.

[2] *Dinwiddie Papers*, i., 191; *Virginia State Papers*, i., 250. O. H. Marshall refers (pp. 351, 353) to a Seneca Indian known as Big Kettle, or Kanajowaneh, who died in 1839; also to one "Black Kettle," an Onondaga, whose Indian name was Kanajeagah. Therefore "Broken Kettle" was probably the correct meaning of Conajachrera's name. In one conference, held at Carlisle in 1750, his name is written "Canajachanah, alias Broken Kettle"; while the true translation of that word would be Big Kettle (*kuwaunah*, big). Zeisberger gives *tiochriro* as the Onondaga word for broken.

[3] "The Wyandots were called Tionontaties or Petuns, *i. e.*, Tobacco Indians, from their industrious habit of cultivating that plant; *Petun* (obsolete French for tobacco, derived from the Brazilian) being a nickname given to them by the French Traders. In the Mohawk dialect of the Iroquois the name for tobacco is *o-ye-ang-wa*. . . . It is probable that wherever the name Shenango occurs in early times or on early maps it indicates the site of a town of the Tobacco Tribe—Wyandots—or of a place

Pymatuning Town is shown more accurately on Reading Howell's map of 1792. It stood within the Big Bend of the Shenango, above the mouth of Pymatuning Creek, in what is now Delaware Township, Mercer County. Mitchell's map also shows an Iroquois town located on the Gwahago (Cuyahoga), midway between its source and mouth; as well as the district known as "Canahogue" (called by Weiser and the Pennsylvanians, "Canayiahaga"), which he places between the Cuyahoga and the Sandusky, and describes as "the seat of war, the mart of trade, and chief hunting grounds of the Six Nations on the Lake and the Ohio." The Sandusky, Mitchell calls "River Blanc."

All efforts on the part of the writer to find any further reference to the chief, Canajachrera, subsequent to the time he sent the friendly message from the Wyandots to Washington in June, 1754, have been unavailing. Possibly, he may have been killed by the French after they secured control of the Ohio. More probably he retired toward the country of the Senecas on the Upper Allegheny in 1756, when the Indians of the Six Nations at Kuskuskies were largely replaced by the Delawares, some of whom removed from the Susquehanna in that year. Dumas wrote to Vaudreuil on August 14th, that "the Iroquois of the vicinity of Fort Duquesne have almost all retired to M. de la Chauvignerie, at the mouth of the River au Bœuf [Venango], on a belt from the Five Nations."[1] Post found Sauconk and Kuskuskies inhabited almost entirely by Delawares when he came there in August, 1758.[2]

From what has been set forth in the preceding chapter, it appears that Canajachrera was identical with that Indian chief whom Longueuil addressed in 1744 as "Canante-Chiarirou, Chief of the Nations of the White River"; and it can be positively asserted that the "Nations of the White River," who caused so much trouble and uneasiness to the French commandants at Detroit from 1743 to 1747, were none other than the Mingoes and their neighbors, of the Cuyahoga, the Mahoning, the Big Beaver, and the Tuscarawas; whose capital was Kuskuskies.

On October 20, 1748, William Trent wrote from George Croghan's house in the Cumberland Valley, to Secretary Richard Peters, giving him an account of an affair which had taken place at Kuskuskies. "Last night," he said, "came here from Allegheny one John Hays, who

---

where Indian tobacco was cultivated."—Darlington's *Gist*, 106, 108. Pymatuning may be another form of "Petun Town," or Wyandot Town, and Shenango Creek is the name of the stream on which this band of the Tobacco people, or Wyandots, lived. Darlington, following Loskiel and DeSchweinitz, states that " there was a Wyandot town on the Big Beaver, on the east side, nineteen miles above its mouth. On its site the Moravians, in 1770, erected their town of Friedenstadt."—*Gist's Journals*, 108.

[1] *N. Y. Col. Doc.*, x., 408, 436.

[2] See his *Journal, Penna. Archives*, iii., 520–544; also, in the same volume, pp. 560–565, George Croghan's (wrongly headed Post's) *Journal*.

informs us that the night before he left it, the Indians killed one of Mr. [Hugh] Parker's hands. It was owing to ill usage Mr. Parker [the factor of the Ohio Company] and his hands gave them that day, and his being a Maryland Trader, who the Indians don't care should come amongst them. Mr. Parker had a large quantity of liquor up with him, which he was tying up in his goods, in order to send to the Lower Shawna Town; and the Indians kept pressing into his house, and he unwilling that they should see what he was about. Some he turned out, and others, as they came in, he pushed the door in their faces; upon which they were determined to take his liquor, unless he would let them have it at the price settled at the treaty. They brought him wampum, and offered to leave it in pledge; but he refused to let them have it; upon which they took a quantity from him. A great many of them got drunk, who then insisted upon revenge for the ill-treatment he gave them; and accordingly took Parker prisoner and tyed him, and determined to scalp him. But the rest of the whites who were in the town rescued him.

"He immediately went off about two miles from the town, where some of his people lay, and got a horse, and rid that night thirty miles, bare-backed, to the Logs Town. The Indians imagined that he was gone into his house. One of them laid wait for him at the door, with his gun. At last, one Brown, one of Mr. Parker's hands, came out, with a white match-coat round him; which the Indian took for Parker (as he was in his shirt at the time they had him tyed); and shot him down. This happened at Coscoske."

In a conference held at George Croghan's house in Pennsboro Township by Richard Peters and the Seneca chiefs from Kuskuskies and Logstown, June 7, 1750, the Indians stated, that in the fall of 1749, one, "Barny Currant, a hired man of Mr. Parker," brought them a message from Colonel Thomas Cresap, the agent of the Ohio Company of Virginia, to the effect that he and Mr. Parker, the Trader at Kuskuskies, would sell them goods at rates very much less than those charged by the Pennsylvania Traders—a match-coat for a buckskin; a strowd for a buck and a doe; a pair of stockings for two raccoons; twelve bars of lead for a buck; and other articles at proportionately low prices.

It will be remembered that James Le Tort, on October 29, 1731, furnished Governor Gordon with a list of the Indian settlements at Allegheny. In this list, he included "Lequeepees, sixty miles distant [from the Conemaugh]; Mingoes, mostly (and some Delawares); four settled families; but a great resort of these people." This was the Seneca or Mingo town known for twenty years afterwards as "Alliquippa's town," on both banks of the Ohio, at and opposite the mouth of Chartier's Creek and what is now called McKee's Rock.

Brunot's Island, between McKee's Rock and the present city of Allegheny, was formerly called Alliquippa's Island. Weiser visited Queen Alliquippa at her town here in the summer of 1748; and Celoron was there a year later. When Gist travelled along the north bank of the Ohio, from Shanoppin's Town to Logstown, in November, 1750, he made no entry in his *Journal* of any habitation between; but we have seen that Messrs. Fry, Lomax, and Patton, the Virginia Commissioners, visited Alliquippa at her cabin nearly opposite Shanoppin's Town, while on their way to Logstown in June, 1752.

The date of the settlement of the Mingoes at Kuskuskies, therefore, was between the decade 1731-1741. So late as 1750 the Iroquois chiefs of the Great Council at Onondaga informed Conrad Weiser at a Council fire which he attended at Oneida on September 17th of that year, that "the Ohio [Mingo] Indians were but hunters, and no counsellors, or chief men; and they had no right to receive presents that was due to the Six Nations, although they might expect to have a share; but that share they must receive from the Six Nations chief under whom they belong."

After the defeat of Washington at Great Meadows in July, 1754, upwards of a hundred Mingoes, with their chiefs, Tanacharison, Scarrooyady, Kashwughdaniunte (Belt of Wampum), Tokaswayeston, and Seneca George, retreated to George Croghan's post at Aughwick. Of the remainder of the Iroquois, as has been stated, Dumas wrote Vaudreuil, between May and August, 1756, that they had almost all retired from the vicinity of Fort Duquesne to M. de la Chauvignerie, at the mouth of the River au Bœuf [Venango], on a belt from the Five Nations. When Frederick Post reached Kuskuskies in August, 1758, the Indians he found there were principally Delawares and some Shawnees. The largest one of their four Kuskuskies towns which Post mentions at that time was probably New Kaskaskunk, on the west bank of Shenango, opposite the mouth of the Neshannock, where the city of Newcastle now stands.[1] Doubtless it was built for the Delawares by the French upon the departure of the Mingoes from the villages referred to in this chapter as Old Kaskaskunk (at the confluence of the Shenango and Beaver), the Kususkies town six miles higher up on the Mahoning, and the other Kuskuskies towns along that stream.

The Five Nations were called Iroquois by the French, Maquas by the Dutch of New York, Five Nations by the English, Minquas by the Dutch on the Delaware, Senecas by the Marylanders, and Mengwe[2] by the Swedes and the Algonquin Indians. The Pennsylvanians, changing

---

[1] DeSchweinitz, *Zeisberger*, 361, 708; Darlington calls this the Old Kuskuskies Town.
[2] Captain John Smith found an Iroquoian tribe living southwest of the Powhatans,

the appellation, "Minquas" or "Mengwe," which they had heard used by the earlier settlers, called the Indians of the Six Nations, "Mingoes." Accordingly, the various bands of the Senecas, Onondagas, Cayugas, Oneidas, and Mohawks (of whom the greater part were Senecas), who settled along the Cuyahoga, the Beaver, and the Mahoning during the two decades before 1750, usually went by the name of Mingoes.

The route of the trail leading from the mouth of the Beaver westward, as shown on Evans's map of 1755, has been referred to in a preceding chapter. A later description of this path was given to Henry Howe in 1846 by James Hillman, of Youngstown, Ohio, an Indian Trader, who had made several trips over the route in 1786. In the spring of that year, Mr. Hillman was employed by Messrs. Duncan & Wilson, Indian Traders of Pittsburgh, who were then engaged in forwarding provisions and supplies across the country to the mouth of the Cuyahoga, to be shipped thence to Fort Detroit. During the summer of 1786, Mr. Hillman made six trips over this path, his caravan consisting of ten men and ninety pack-horses. He stated that, "they usually crossed the Big Beaver four miles below the mouth of the Shenango, thence up the left [west] bank of the Mahoning, crossing it about three miles above the site of Youngstown, thence by way of the Salt Springs in the present township of Weathersfield, Trumbull County, through what are now Milton and Ravenna townships, crossing the Cuyahoga at the mouth of Breakneck Creek, and again, at the mouth of Tinker's Creek [at the site of the Ottawa village of Saguin's time], in Bedford Township, Cuyahoga County, and thence, down the Cuyahoga to its mouth." The trail between the Salt Springs, in Weathersfield Township, Trumbull County, and the mouth of Breakneck Creek at Kent, in Franklin Township, Portage County, passed to the southwest, through Lordstown and Newton townships, Trumbull County, near the present village of Newton Falls, in Trumbull County, thence westward through the northern parts of Palmyra and Edinburg townships, Portage County, crossing Silver Creek in Edinburg township, one and one-half miles north of the centre road, thence through Ravenna and Franklin townships, where it crossed the Cuyahoga at a point where a "standing-stone" once marked the ford, above the site of the present village of Kent, which lies below the mouth of Breakneck Creek. From here, one branch of the trail led directly west, through Stow and Northampton townships, Summit County, to the Mingo village noted on Evans's map, which

---

which was known to them as the "Mangoacs" (*i.e.*, "stealthy ones"). Their country had been visited by the English settlers at Roanoke Island as early as 1586. They were the Tuscaroras of later history.

stood, probably, on the west bank of the Cuyahoga, in the present township of Northampton. The path from the mouth of Breakneck Creek to the mouth of Tinker's Creek, as noted by James Hillman, was the earliest Main Trail to Cuyahoga, and thence, by way of Lake Erie, to Sandusky and Detroit.

John McCullough, who was a captive among the Delaware Indians along the Beaver and Mahoning from 1756 to 1764, has given some brief notices of the settlements along the latter stream in his *Narrative*. "We lived about two years and a half in Shenango," he writes. "We then moved to where they were settling a new town, called Kseek-he-oong, that is, a Place of Salt, a place now well known by the name of Salt Licks, on the West Branch of Beaver [in Weathersfield Township, Trumbull County, Ohio]; where we lived about one year. We moved there about the time that General Forbes took Fort Duquesne from the French. . . . The next spring [probably in 1759 or 1760], we moved to a town about fifteen miles off, called Mohoning, which signifies, a lick. . . . We remained in Mohoning till shortly after the memorable battle at Brushy Run [1763]; we then moved to Cayahawge. . . . We stayed but a short time in Cayahawge, then moved across the country to the Forks of Mooshkingoong [Muskingum]."

In May, 1760, Frederick Post and John Hays left Easton with the intention of journeying up the North Branch of the Susquehanna, in company with Chief Teedyuscung, thence, by way of the Chemung and its tributaries to the Allegheny, and thence to Ohio, where a great Indian Council was to be held, "at some principal Indian Town over the Ohio." They were joined at Wyoming by Teedyuscung, and the party proceeded up the Susquehanna as far as Pasigachkunk, on Cowanesque Creek. Here they were stopped by the Mingoes, and the white men were turned back and obliged to retrace their steps, "for," says Mr. Hays, "there was an old agreement that no white men should pass through their [the Senecas'] country, for fear of spies to see their land." Teedyuscung, however, continued on, accompanied by some of his Indian followers, and attended the Great Council in Ohio. He returned in the course of the summer, and, on September 15th, met Governor Hamilton in a Council at Philadelphia, and related to him the results of his mission. He said: "I have been a long way back, a great way indeed, beyond the Allegheny, among my friends there. When I got as far as Salt Lick Town, towards the head of Beaver Creek, I stopped there, and sent to the chiefs of all the Indians in those parts, desiring them to come and hold Council. It took three weeks to collect them together." Teedyuscung then related the speeches which had been made at this Council, and stated that he had seen and consulted with the Nelametenoes, or Owendats (Wyandots), the Twicktwees, the Shawonese, the Chippeways, the Tarons,[1] all the tribes of the Delawares. and others, to the number of ten nations.

Salt Lick Town and Cayahoga Town are both shown in their correct locations on Hutchins's map of 1764. Mahoning Town is shown on Heckewelder's map of 1796. Hutchns locates a Mahoning Town east of Salt Lick Town. This was probably the village which stood on or near the site of the present Youngstown. Hutchins's map of 1778, however, places the Salt Lick Town on the north side of the Mahoning. The famous Salt Spring itself, known to the whites years before any settlements were made in Ohio, is situated about one and one-half miles south of the Mahoning, and a mile west of the present village of Niles.[2] It is shown in this locality on Evans's map of 1755.

[1] Could *Taron* be a misprint for *Tawa* (Ottawa); or is it the same as the Huron word. *tiron, i. e.*, "raccoon," the name applied to the animal which the French called *chat sauvage*, or "wildcat," and from which the Eries got their tribal name of the Cat Nation, or Raccoon Nation? See pp. 8, 9, 336.

[2] Williams's *History of Trumbull and Mahoning Counties, Ohio* (Cleveland, 1882) i., 221.

CHAPTER XIV

LOGSTOWN ON THE OHIO

ON July 31, 1744, Governor Thomas sent a message to the Pennsylvania Assembly, transmitting the treaty made with the Six Nations at Lancaster during the month of June. In the Governor's message, he observes that there was but one of the Shawnees from their principal town on the Ohio present at the treaty; and that he had since been informed that the Six Nations and the Shawnees were far from being on good terms. The latter had been endeavoring to draw the Delawares from Shamokin to Ohio and the Six Nations feared that in case they themselves were involved in the war which had begun between the English and French, they would be obliged to fight the Shawnees, and perhaps the Delawares also. The Governor adds, "indeed, it is observable that the closer our union has been with the Six Nations, the greater distance they [the Shawnees] have kept from us. I wish any method could be fallen upon to secure them effectually to the British interests, as they lie upon one part of our frontiers, and *our most valuable trade for skins is with them;* but considering their frequent intercourse with the French, and their inconstancy, I almost despair of it."

The principal town of the Shawnees on the Ohio at this time, to which Governor Thomas referred, was Neucheconneh's Town, known to the Traders as Chartier's Town, from the fact that Peter Chartier, himself a half-breed Shawnee-Frenchman, was the most influential resident Trader among the Shawnees at "Allegheny" between 1733 and 1745. This town was situated near the site of the present Tarentum in Allegheny County, opposite to and about a mile below the mouth of a stream called to this day Chartier's Run.[1]

It will be remembered that in the report made by James Le Tort and Jonah Davenport to the Pennsylvania Council, October 29, 1731, it was stated that there were then three towns of the Shawnees on the Conemaugh River, in which lived two hundred men and forty-five

[1] The Shawnees near Paxtang were the first of their tribe to follow the Delawares to the Allegheny. *Penna. Col. Rec.*, iv., 337.

families, all under the chieftainship of Okowela. Okowela or Ocowellos was from the Upper Susquehanna. About the same time, the Shawnees from Opessa's Town on the Potomac removed to the Allegheny; and they were followed during the years 1731, 1732, 1733, and 1734 by the greater part of the Pequea Shawnees then living in the Cumberland Valley, especially by those living near what is now the village of New Cumberland, on the right bank of the Susquehanna, a few miles below Harrisburg. The latter were accompanied by Peter Chartier, who had been a Trader amongst them for many years, since the death of his father, Martin Chartier. The father led some of these Indians, or their parents, from Fort St. Louis to Cecil County, Maryland, in 1692.

Neucheconneh, one of their chiefs, with Pawquawsie, Uppockeaty, and Queequeeotoo, wrote a letter to the Governor of Pennsylvania, June 7, 1732, explaining why the Shawnees left the Susquehanna. They stated that some of them would pay the Governor a visit during the summer, and when they got as far on their way as Peter Chartier's trading house below Harris's Ferry, they would notify him of their coming, and bring their friends, the Conestogas, along with them from the Susquehanna. Some six years later, Newcheconneh's name again appears as one of the signers of an agreement made by the Shawnees at "Alleghenia," to the effect that any rum brought thereafter into their towns at that place should be "broak and spilt in the presence of the whole Townes, wheresoever it is brought, and four men is appointed for every Town to see that there is no rum or strong liquor brought into our Townes, and to have it for the term of four years from date" (March 15, 1738). This paper was signed by "Newchuonner," as Deputy King, "Laypareawah [or Loyparcowah], Opehasas' Son," and nearly a hundred more of the Shawnees.

At a meeting of the Pennsylvania Council, held at Philadelphia, August 10, 1737, President James Logan laid before the Board a message which had been sent to the Proprietor from the chiefs of the Shawnees at Allegheny, which was, in substance, that they were strongly solicited by the French, whom they called their fathers, to return to them; that every year the French send them some powder, lead, and tobacco, to enable them to withstand their enemies, the Southern Indians, by whom they have often suffered and by whom they were last year attacked in one of their towns (probably one of the towns near the mouth of the Great Kanawha); that the Shawnees have now gotten so far to the westward that they can go no farther without falling into the hands of their enemies or going over to the French, which, they say, they would willingly avoid; and that if they should return to the Susquehanna, as the Government has often pressed, they must starve, little or no game being to be met with in those parts; therefore, they request that the Government furnish them with some arms and ammunition for their defence against their enemies, and to secure their continuance at Allegheny.

On February 4, 1743, Conrad Weiser held a council at the house of Shekallamy in Shamokin, with some chiefs of the Delawares, Shawnees, and Tuscaroras. Fearing attacks by the Shawnees on the English Traders at Allegheny, Weiser gave the Shawnee chief, Missemediqueety, or Big Hominy, some strings of wampum, which the Shawnees undertook to "send immediately to the Great Island and Allegheny in favor of the Traders." Weiser returned to Shamokin again in April, and held a conference with some of the same Indians. Sachsidowa, a Tuscarora chief, who in the interim had attended an Iroquois Council at Onondaga and received his instructions from that Council, acted as speaker for the Indians.

When the Council at Shamokin came to consider the messages sent by Weiser to the Shawnees, "then the speaker, in behalf of Cachawatsiky [Kakowatcheky] the Shawonese chief at Wyomink, and of Nochecouna, the Shawonese chief at Ohio, related their answers to two messages that were sent with some strings of wampum by the Council held at Shamokin the first time Conrad Weiser was there. He began with Nochecouna's answer, directed to the Governor of Pennsylvania:

"Brother, the Governor of Pennsylvania:
"I live upon this River of Ohio, harmless, like a little child. I can do nothing; I am but weak; and I don't so much as intend mischief. I have nothing to say and do; therefore, send these strings of wampum to Cachawatsiky, the chief man, again. He will answer your message, as he is the older and greater man."

In a private conference held in Philadelphia at the house of Governor Thomas on August 25, 1744, between the Governor, Conrad Weiser, Shekallamy, and four or five of the Delawares from Shamokin, the former told the Indians, "that, having heard some of the Shawnese from Hohio had been with them, and invited them to remove from Shamokin to Hohio, he was desirous to know the truth of it." Quidahickqunt, the speaker for the Delawares, answered, "That the Shawnese at Hohio had indeed invited Cacawichiky and the Shawnese Indians at his town [Wyoming] to Hohio, and that they had removed thither; and, that their uncles, the Mingoes, had sent a messenger to Cacawichicky, with a belt of wampum, to know the reason of their removal, and to invite them back again to their former settlement; to which no answer was yet come."

It will be remembered that, in 1742, the Delawares living between the Forks of the Delaware had been ordered by the Six Nations to depart from there immediately, and to seat themselves either at Wyoming or Shamokin. Many of these Indians seem to have settled at Wyoming during the next two years; and as game there became less plentiful, in consequence, it is probable that this was the chief reason why the remainder of Kakowatcheky's band removed to the Ohio.

As a matter of fact, they removed in the summer or fall of 1743. The Moravians, Mack and Froehlich, visited Wyoming April 13, 1744. In his *Journal*, Mack writes: "We found few Indians there, and those who remained there looked much dejected. They were in number only seven men. There has been a surprising change in Wayomick since two years ago . . . about six or seven cabins are left; the others are all pulled to pieces."[1]

On April 25, 1745, Governor Thomas sent a message to the Pennsylvania Assembly, informing it that he had just received word that Peter Chartier, after disposing of his effects in the Province of Pennsylvania, had gone over to the French. The Governor adds, that he is "likewise informed that Chartier has persuaded a considerable number of the Shawnese to remove from their old Town to a greater distance upon another river."

From the citations given above, it will be seen that Kakowatcheky's band left Wyoming after April, 1743, and had settled on the Ohio before August 25, 1744. The desertion of Chartier and his band took place in April, 1745. After that date, the site of the former village of Chartier's Shawnees was known to the Traders and has been marked on the early maps as "Chartier's Old Town." Celoron stopped at this place August 6, 1749, and wrote to the Governor of Pennsylvania, heading the letter "From our Camp on the Beautiful River at *un ancien Village des Chaouanons*."

The Shawnees who were with Peter Chartier came mostly from the Cumberland Valley, the Potomac, and the West Branch of the Susquehanna, and they were probably for the most part the descendants of the first band of Shawnees who had followed Martin Chartier into Cecil County, Maryland. Kakowatcheky's clan was from the settlement first made above Delaware Water Gap, from whence it had removed to Wyoming in 1728, and thence to the Ohio.

Those Shawnees from Wyoming who removed with Kakowatcheky to the Ohio in 1743–44 probably at that time, or certainly not later than the time of Chartier's flight down the river (1745), settled on the right bank of the Ohio, about eighteen miles below the Forks and just below the site of the present village of Economy in Beaver County, Pennsylvania. Here with the co-operation of the Ohio Mingoes, they built a village, which, during the next ten years, became the most important

[1] Harvey's *Wilkes-Barre*, i., 215.

centre for the fur trade of the Pennsylvania Traders. Dr. Thwaites states that the name the Indians gave to this village was Maughwawame.[1] By the French the name was written Chiningue,[2] which has the same pronunciation as Shenango in English. The English Traders themselves called the village Logstown, and it was known by that name in Pennsylvania history during the next half century. It appears as Logstown for the first time on the minutes of the Pennsylvania Council, June 23, 1748, when it is described as "the first of the Indian towns on the Road from Lancaster to Allegheny." George Croghan visited it as the bearer of gifts and messages from the Pennsylvania Government in April and May of the same year.

Conrad Weiser also visited Logstown as the bearer of additional presents and messages from the Governor and Legislature in the following August. The *Journal* of his proceedings during this visit reads in part as follows:

"August 27, 1748. Arrived that evening at Logstown, and saluted the town as before. The Indians returned about one hundred guns. Great joy appeared in their countenances. . . . The Indian Council met this evening to shake hands with me, and to show their satisfaction at my safe arrival. I desired of them to send a couple of canoes, to fetch down the goods from Chartier's Old Town, where we had been obliged to leave them on account of our horses being all tired. . . .

"29th. This day my companions went to Coscosky, a large Indian town, about thirty miles off.

"30th. I went to Beaver Creek, an Indian Town about eight miles off, chiefly Delawares, the rest Mohocks, to have some belts of wampum made. This afternoon rainy weather set in, which lasted about a week. Andrew Montour came back from Coscosky with a message from the Indians there, to desire me that the ensuing Council

[1] *Wis. Hist. Col.*, xviii., 42. Stone, in his *History and Poetry of the Wyoming Valley*, says that the Delawares who removed from the Lehigh Forks [in 1742-3] to the site of Wilkes-Barre, there "built the Town of *Maugh-wau-wa-me*, the original of Wyoming." As a matter of fact, the Valley was called by that name by the Delawares long before 1743. The Delaware letter from Allegheny, written in 1731, and printed in Chapter vi., gives the word as *Meheahoming*, Edmund Cartlidge's spelling. Heckewelder spelled the same word, *M'ch-cu-wa-mi*, and said that its signification is "extensive flats," (which is in accordance with the meaning of its Iroquois name), and that it is the Delaware word from which Wyoming has been corrupted. The description applies to the site of Logstown, and to the flat country on the opposite side of the Ohio, although these flats are not so extensive as those of Wyoming on the Susquehanna.

[2] Marshall states that he examined in Paris a copy of a Journal of Father Bonnecamps, in which the Jesuit mathematician is quoted as writing, "We called it Chiningue, from its vicinity to the river of that name." The *Journal* of Bonnecamps printed in the *Jesuit Relations* does not appear to contain this sentence.

The Site of Logstown, Looking North, down the Ohio.
From a photograph made by the Author in September, 1909.

might be held at their town. We both lodged at this town [Logstown or Sauconk?] at George Croghan's Trading House.

"31st. Sent Andrew Montour back to Coscosky with a string of wampum, to let the Indians there know that it was an act of their own that the ensuing Council must be held at Logstown. They had ordered it so last Spring when George Croghan was up; and at the last treaty at Lancaster the Shawanese and Twightwees have been told so, and they stayed accordingly, for that purpose; and both would be offended if the Council was held at Coscosky; besides, my instructions binds me to Logstown, and could not go further without giving offence.

"Sept. 1. The Indians at Logstown, having heard of the message from Coscosky, sent for me to know what I was resolved to do, and told me that the Indians at Coscosky were no more chiefs than themselves; and that, last Spring, they had nothing to eat, and expecting that they should have nothing to eat at our arrival, ordered that the Council should be held here. Now, their corn is ripe, they want to remove the Council; but they ought to stand by their word. We have kept the Twightwees here, and our brethren, the Shawonese, from below, on that account. As I told them the message that I had sent by Andrew Montour, they were content.

"2d. Rain continued; the Indians brought in a good deal of venison.

"3d. Set up the Union flag on a long pole. Treated all the company with a dram of rum. The King's health was drank by Indians and white men. Towards night a great many Indians arrived to attend the Council. There was great firing on both sides. The strangers first saluted the Town at a quarter of a mile distance, and, at their entry, the Town's people returned the fire; also, the English Traders, of whom there were above twenty."

On the 6th, 7th and 8th, Weiser held conferences with the Wondats (Wyandots); on the 9th with the Senecas; and on the 13th, the Wyandots were formally taken into the alliance with the English. Weiser, having asked the deputies of all the nations of Indians settled on the waters of the Ohio to give him a list of their fighting men, the following was the number of every nation, Weiser states, "Given to him by their several deputies in council, in so many sticks, tied up in a bundle: the Senecas, 163; Shawonese, 162; Owendaets, 100; Tisagechroanu, 40; Mohawks, 74; Mohickons, 15; Onondagers, 35; Cajukas, 20; Oneidos, 15; Delawares, 165; in all, 789."

Captain Pierre Joseph de Celoron (sometimes by courtesy called Bienville, possibly on account of his having assisted the Louisiana Governor of that name in his expedition against the Chicaksaws in 1739), visited Logstown in August, 1749, at the head of a party of two hundred and fifty Frenchmen, Canadians, and Indians.

"As soon as I was in sight of the village," writes Celoron, "I observed three French flags and one English. As soon as I was observed, salutes of musketry were sent from the village. . . . When disembarking, they drew on us a discharge of balls. This salute is made by all nations of the South; often accidents happen from it. . . . I told them, by M. de Joncaire, to cease firing in that manner, or I should fire on them. I told them at the same time, to lower the English flag, or I should pull it down myself. This was done instantly; a woman cut the staff, and the flag has not since appeared. I disembarked, and as the beach is extremely narrow and very disadvantageous in case the savages had evil designs, being at the base of a bluff which was more than thirty feet high, I immediately carried my canoes and the baggage up on the bluff, so as to place myself advantageously. Near the village, I established my camp, which I made to appear as extensive as possible. . . . The officers who were on guard had orders to make the rounds all night. These precautions prevented the savages from doing what they had projected. This M. de Joncaire discovered a short time afterward by means of some women of his acquaintance.

"This village is of fifty cabins, composed of Iroquois, Chaouanons, and of Loups, and a part of the men of the villages I had passed, who had come to seek refuge there, and to render them stronger. About five o'clock in the evening, the chiefs, accompanied by thirty or forty warriors, came to salute me, to compliment me on my arrival at their home."

The chiefs told Celoron, among other things, "It is a long time since we have had the satisfaction of seeing the French in our village."

Celoron spent the 8th, 9th, and 10th of the month in councils and speech making, and on the next day received the replies from the Indians and distributed his presents among them. He left Logstown on August 12th. "This village," he writes, on August 10th, "is composed of Iroquois, of Chaouanons, and of Loups, which caused the Council to last more than four hours. Besides these three nations there are in this village some Iroquois from Sault St. Louis, from the Lake of the Two Mountains, some Nepissingues, Abenakis, Ottawas, and other nations. This assemblage forms a very bad village, which, seduced by the bait of a cheap market given to them by the English, keeps them in a very bad disposition towards us.

"I had called before me the most considerable of the English Traders, to whom I gave a summons to retire to their own country with all their employes; as I had done to those whom I had met before. They replied, like the others, that they would do so; that they knew well they had no right to trade on La Belle Riviere. I added that their government was bounded by the mountains, and they should not pass beyond. . . .

"The 11th of August, the Indians came to give me their answer. . . . Their interest engages them to look with favor on the English, who give them their merchandise at so low a price that we have reason to believe that the King of England, or the country, bears the loss which the Traders make in the sale of their merchandise to attract the nations. It is true that the expenses of the English are not nearly so great as those which our Traders will be obliged to make, on account of the difficulties of the route. It is certain that we will never be able to reclaim the nations except by giving them merchandise at the same prices as the English. The difficulty is to find the means."

Father Bonnecamps, a Jesuit who accompanied Celoron's expedition as chaplain and geographer, wrote of Logstown: "*The village of Chiningue is quite new; it is hardly more than five or six years since it was established.* The savages who live there are almost all Iroquois; they count about sixty warriors. The English there were ten in number, and one among them was their chief. Monsieur de Celoron had him come, and ordered him, as he had done with the others, to return to his own country. The Englishman, who saw us ready to depart, acquiesced in all that was exacted from him—firmly resolved, doubtless, to do nothing of the kind, as soon as our backs were turned." Bonnecamps also states that, while at Chiningue, a savage came to tell Monsieur Joncaire that eighty warriors, starting from Kaskaske (Kuskuskies) were on the point of arriving; that they came, intending to aid their brothers, and to deal the French a blow.

George Croghan was sent by Governor Hamilton to Logstown in August, 1749, to learn the meaning of the march of this French expedition through the Ohio Valley. He arrived there a few days after Celoron had departed, and was met by Andrew Montour. The Indians told Croghan that Celoron's message to them was to the effect that the French were coming to trade with them again the following spring; that they were "now going down the river in order to whip home some of their children, that is, the Twitchwees and Wayndotts, and to let them know that they have no business to trade or traffic with the English." Celoron, they said, "desired them to hunt that summer and fall, and pay the English their debts; for the French would not suffer them to come there to trade after that winter." Croghan adds, that to this speech the Indians paid little or no heed, but only gave the French to understand that the land was their own, and while there were any Indians in those parts they would continue to trade with the English; "to separate them from their brothers, the English, would be like cutting a man in two halves, and then expecting him to live."

At the Indian Treaty at Fort Stanwix, November 4, 1768, the chiefs of the Six Nations, in presence of the representatives of New York,

Connecticut, Virginia, New Jersey, and Pennsylvania, executed a deed to George Croghan, confirming the sale to him of two hundred thousand acres of land at the Forks of the Ohio, which he claimed had been granted him by three chiefs of the Six Nations at Logstown in August, 1749. This deed is on record in Augusta County, Virginia. It sets forth that, "Whereas, Johonerissa [Tanacharison], Scaroyadia, Cosswentanica, Chiefs or Sachems of the said Six United Nations, did, by their deed duly executed, bearing date the 2d day of August, 1749, for and in consideration of the following goods and merchandise being paid and delivered to them at a full Council of the Six United Nations, Delawares, and Shawanese, held at Logstown, on the River Ohio, on the 2d of August, 1749, etc." The deed then goes on to recite the consideration, and follows with the description of a second and third deed executed at the same time and by the same parties. It may be remarked that the dates of these purported deeds are given as August 2, 1749. We have just seen that Celoron and his followers did not leave Logstown to proceed down the Ohio River, until August 12th; and that Croghan did not get there until a day or two after Celoron had departed. The dates of Croghan's deeds, however, may have been written in before he left his home in Cumberland County.

The full consideration named in these deeds which Croghan claimed were executed by the Six Nations chiefs at Logstown in August, 1749, was as follows: 476 pieces of strouds, 800 Duffield blankets, 919 pairs of half thick stockings, 400 shirts, 40 pieces of calico, 32 pieces of callimancoe, 40 pieces of embossed serge, 100 pounds of vermillion, 82 gross of gartering, 100 pieces of ribbon, 100 dozen of knives, 1000 pounds of gunpowder, 2000 of bar lead, 5000 gun-flints, 100 pounds of brass kettles, 406 pounds of thread, 2000 needles, 20 dozen jews-harps, 30 dozen tobacco tongs, and 200 pounds of tobacco.

The first of the three 1749 deeds conveyed 100,000 acres of land on the south side of the Monongahela, "beginning at the mouth of a Run nearly opposite to Turtle Creek, and then down the River Monongahela to its junction with the River Ohio, computed to be ten miles"; thence down the Ohio to the mouth of Raccoon Creek; thence up that creek, ten miles; thence in a straight line to the place of beginning. The second deed conveyed a tract of land fifteen miles in length by ten miles in breadth, to contain, by estimation, 60,000 acres, and to be located by Croghan on both sides the Youghiogheny River, either up or down, but so as to include "the Indian village called the Sewichly Old Town."[1] The third deed conveyed 40,000 acres, "beginning on the east side of the River Ohio, to the northward of an old Indian village

[1] At or near the mouth of Big Sewickley Creek, near the present West Newton, Westmoreland County.

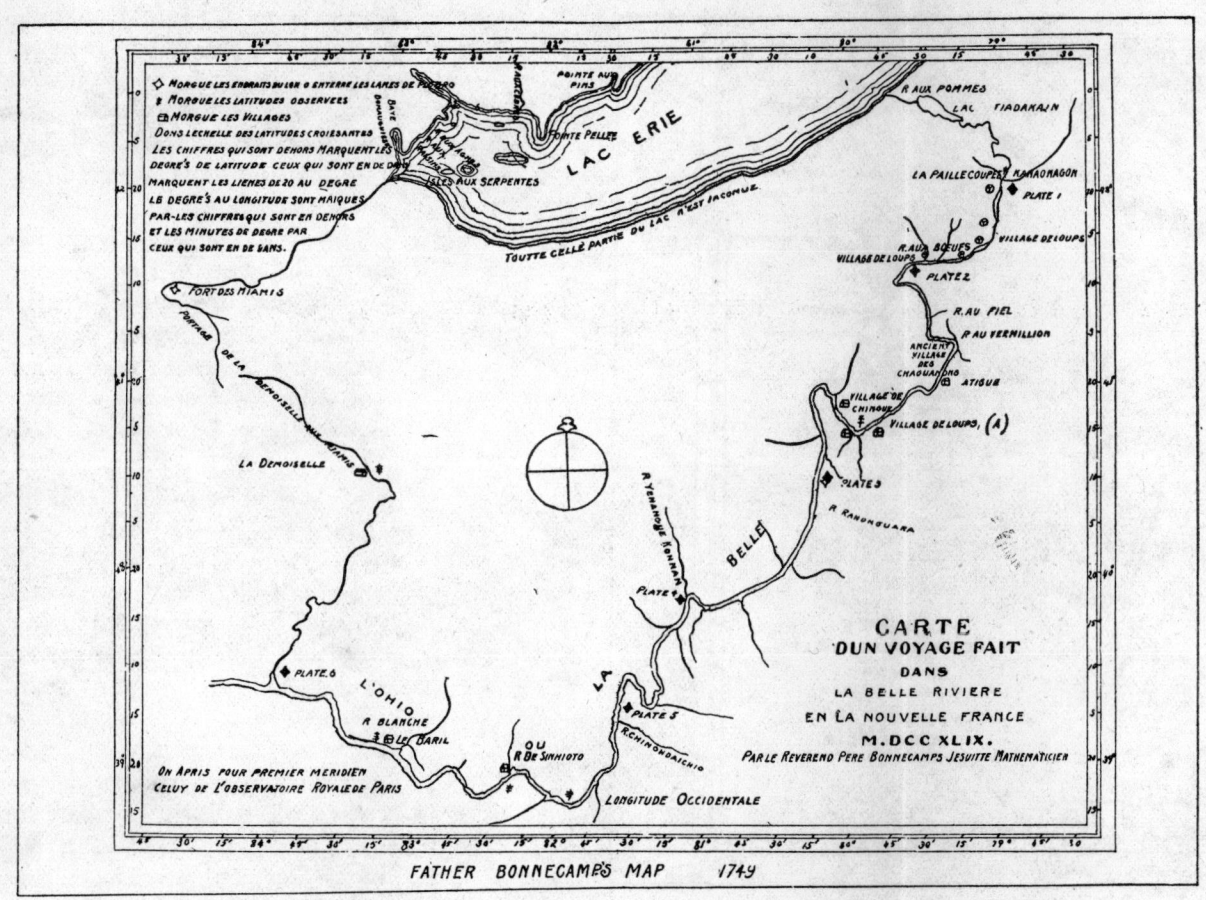

Bonnecamps' 1749 Map of the Ohio River.

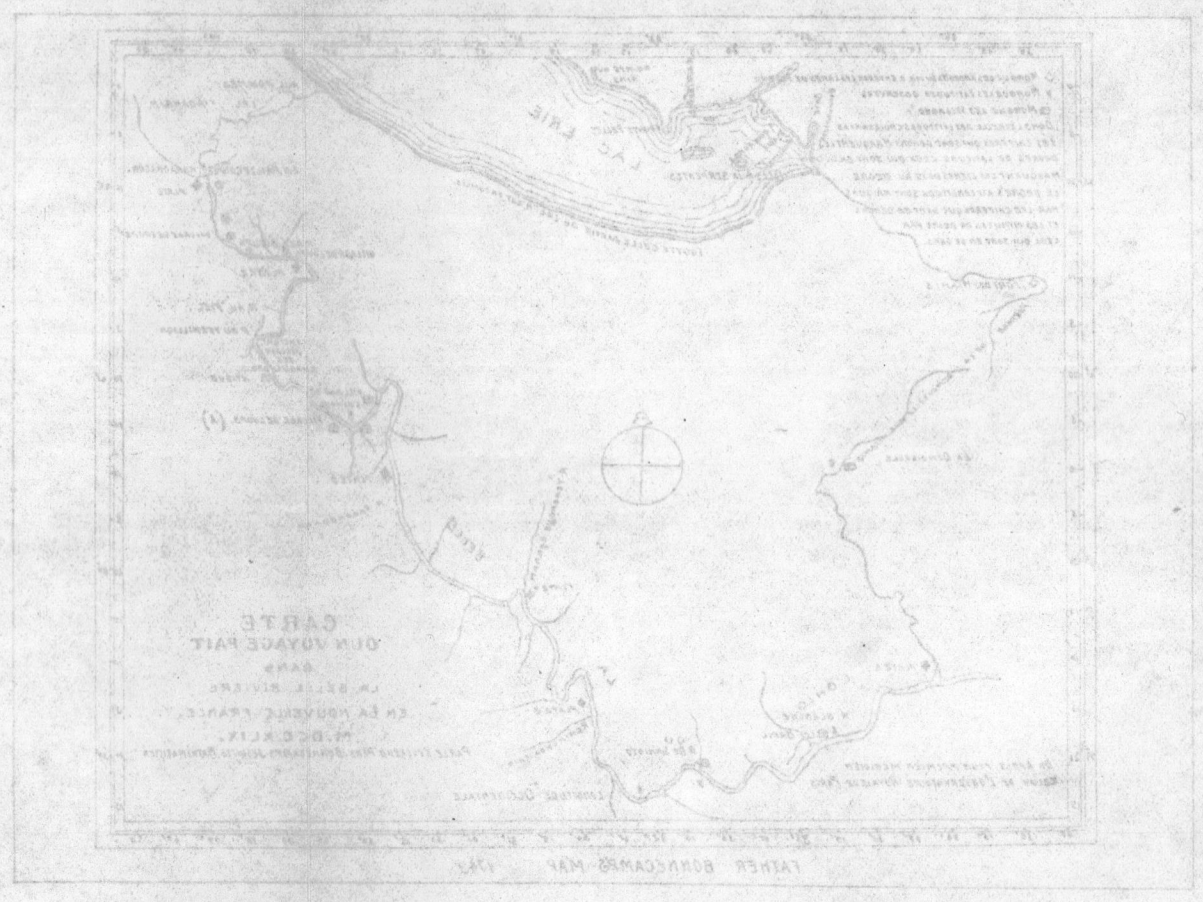

Bonnecamps, 1749 Map of the Ohio River.

called Shanopin's Town, at the mouth of a Run called the Two Mile Run; then up the said Two Mile Run [to] where it interlocks with the heads of the Two Mile Springs, which empties into the River Monongahela; then down the said Two Mile Springs to [by] the several courses thereof unto the said Monongahela"; then up the said River Monongahela to the mouth of Turtle Creek; thence by that creek to the head of Plum Creek, down the latter stream to the Allegheny, and down that river to the place of beginning.

Croghan was in Logstown again in November, 1750. He wrote to Governor Hamilton from there on the 16th: "Yesterday, Mr. Montour and I got to this Town, where we found thirty warriors of the Six Nations going to war against the Catawba Indians. They told us that they saw John Cœur [Joncaire] about one hundred and fifty miles up this River at an Indian Town, where he intends to build a Fort if he can get liberty from the Ohio Indians. He has five canoes loaded with goods, and is very generous in making presents to all the chiefs of the Indians that he meets with. . . . We have seen but few of the chiefs of the Indians, they being all out a hunting; but those we have seen are of opinion that their brothers, the English, *ought to have a fort on this River to secure the trade,* for they think it will be dangerous for the Traders to travel the roads, for fear of being surprised by some of the French and French Indians, as they expect nothing else but a war with the French next Spring."

Christopher Gist, a surveyor in the employ of the Ohio Company of Virginia, made a tour of exploration through Ohio and Kentucky in 1750-51. He reached Logstown a few days after Croghan had left. His *Journal* reads, under date of November 25, 1750: "In the Loggs Town I found scarce anybody but a parcel of reprobate Indian Traders, the chiefs of the Indians being out a hunting. Here I was informed that George Croghan and Andrew Montour, who were sent upon an embassy from Pennsylvania to the Indians, were passed about a week before me. The people in this town began to inquire my business, and because I did not readily inform them, they began to suspect me, and said, I was come to settle the Indians' lands, and they knew I should never go home again safe. I found this discourse was like to be of ill consequence to me; so I pretended to speak very slightingly of what they had said to me, and enquired for Croghan (who is a mere idol among his countrymen, the Irish Traders) and Andrew Montour, the interpreter for Pennsylvania, and told them I had a message to deliver the Indians from the King, by order of the President of Virginia, and for that reason wanted to see Mr. Montour. This made them all pretty easy (being afraid to interrupt the King's Message) and obtained me quiet and respect among them; otherwise I doubt not they would have contrived some evil against me. I immediately wrote to Mr. Croghan by one of the Traders' people. Monday, 26th. Tho' I was unwell, I preferred the Woods to such company, and set out from the Loggs Town down the River NW 6 M. to Great Beaver Creek, where I met one Barny Curran, a Trader for the Ohio Company, and we continued together as far as Muskingum."

The Pennsylvania Assembly sent a second present of goods to the Indians on Ohio in May, 1751, by George Croghan and Andrew Montour. Croghan's *Journal* of the proceedings attending the delivery of this gift reads in parts as follows:

"May the 18th, 1751. I arrived at the Logs Town on Ohio with the Provincial Present from the Province of Pennsylvania, where I was received by a great number of the Six Nations, Delawares, and Shawonese in a very complaisant manner, in their way, by firing guns and hoisting the English colors. As soon as I came to the shore their chiefs met me, and took me by the hand, bidding me welcome to their country.

"May the 19th. One of the Six Nations kings from the head of Ohio came to the Logstown to the Council. He immediately came to visit me, and told me he was glad to see a messenger from his Brother Onas on the waters of Ohio.

"May the 20th. Forty warriors of the Six Nations came to Town from the heads of Ohio, with Mr. Ioncœur and one Frenchman more in company.

"May the 21st, 1751. Mr. Ioncœur, the French interpreter, called a Council with all the Indians then present in the Town, and made the following speech:

"'Children—I desire you may now give me an answer from your hearts to the speech Monsieur Celoron (the Commander of the party of two hundred Frenchmen that went down the River two years ago) made to you. . . .' And to enforce that speech he gave them a very large belt of wampum. Immediately one of the chiefs of the Six Nations got up and made the following answer:

"'Fathers—I mean you that call yourselves Fathers, hear what I am going to say to you. You desire we may turn our Brothers, the English, away, and not suffer them to come and trade with us again. I now tell you from our hearts, we will not; for we ourselves brought them here to trade with us; and they shall live amongst us as long as there is one of us alive. You are always threatening our Brothers what you will do to them, and in particular, to that man (pointing to me); now, if you have anything to say to our Brothers, tell it to him if you be a man, as you Frenchmen always say you are, and the Head of all Nations. Our Brothers are the people we will trade with, and not you. Go and tell your Governor to ask the Onondaga Council if I don't speak the minds of all the Six Nations.' And then returned the belt.

"I paid Cochawitchake, the old Shawonese king, a visit; as he was rendered incapable of attending the Council by his great age. . . .

"May the 22d. A number of about forty of the Six Nations came up the River Ohio to Logstown to wait on the Council. . . .

"May the 23d. Conajarca [Canajachrera], one of the chiefs of the Six Nations, and a party with him from the Cuscuskie, came to Town to wait on the Council, and congratulated me upon my safe arrival in their country.

"May the 24th. Some warriors of the Delawares came to Town from the Lower Shawonese Town, and brought a scalp with them. They brought an account that the southward Indians had come to the Lower Towns to war, and had killed some of the Shawonese, Delawares, and Six Nations, so that we might not expect any people from there to the Council.

"May the 25th. I had a conference with Monsieur Ioncœur. He desired I would excuse him, and not think hard of him for the speech he made to the Indians, requesting them to turn the English Traders away and not suffer them to trade; for it was the Governor of Canada's orders to him, and he was obliged to obey them; altho' he was very sensible which way the Indians would receive them; for he was sure the French could not accomplish their designs with the Six Nations, without it could be done by force; which, he said, he believed they would find to be as difficult as the method they had just tried, and would meet with the like success. . . .

"May the 27th. Mr. Montour and I had a conference with the chiefs of the Six Nations, when it was agreed upon that the following speeches should be made to the Delawares, Shawonese, Owendatts, and Twightwees, when the Provincial Present should be delivered them."

On May 28th the various speeches were read to the Indians, and the presents distributed. "Then," says Croghan, "the Speaker of the Six Nations made the following speech to Monsieur Ioncœur in open Council. He spoke very quick and sharp, with the air of a warrior:

"'Father—How comes it that you have broke the general peace? Is it not three years since you, as well as our Brothers, the English, told us that there was a peace between the English and French; and how comes it that you have taken our Brothers as your prisoners on our lands. Is it not our land (stamping on the ground, and putting his finger to Ioncœur's nose)? What right has Onontio to our lands? I desire you may go home directly off our lands and tell Onontio to send us word immediately what was his reason for using our Brothers so, or what he means by such proceedings, that we may know what to do; for I can assure Onontio that we, the Six Nations, will not take such usage. You hear what I say; and that is the sentiments of all our nations; tell it to Onontio that that is what the Six Nations said to you.'

"Gave four strings of black wampum."

In the letter which Croghan wrote from Pennsboro, June 10, 1751, enclosing the *Journal* of these proceedings to Governor Hamilton, he says that, "the Indians in general expressed a high satisfaction at having the opportunity in the presence of Ioncœur of expressing their hearty love and inclinations towards the English, and likewise, to assure your Honor what contempt they had for the French; which your Honor will see by the speeches they made. Ioncœur-Ioncœur has sent a letter to your Honor, which I enclose here." Joncaire's letter was dated, "De Chininque, le 6 de Juin, 1751," and he reminds the Governor of the promises made by the English Traders to Celoron two years before to withdraw from the Beautiful River, and give up their trade there.

The Indian Traders present at this Council, as given by Croghan, were, Thomas Kinton, Samuel Cuzzens, Jacob Pyatt, John Owens, Thomas Ward, Joseph Nelson, James Brown, Dennis Sullavan, Paul Pearce, and Caleb Lamb.

In the early part of January, 1752, Captain Thomas Cresap wrote from Old Town, Maryland, to Governor Dinwiddie, giving him important news from the Ohio country, a part of which was as follows: "Having just now received the following acct. from Mr. Andrew Muntour, who is on his journey home from the Ohio, and who is the proper person to be our interpreter, having a good character both among White People and Indians, and very much beloved by the latter, I thought proper to communicate it to your Honor's consideration, which is as follows: That a few days before he left the Logs Town, there came several French Traders with a parcel of goods, and invited the Indians to a Council. . . . They produced a string of wampum, which they said they brought from the Governor of Canada as a token of his friendship, and to invite the Shannah Indians to a Council to be held at the Loggs Town early in the Spring, when sundry matters of consequence are to be communicated to them from the said Governor, and also a present to be delivered from him to them. . . . One, James [John?] Finley and another are suspected to be taken and carried off by the French, who make a practice of taking off our men every year. Therefore, I think it highly necessary to take the French that are at the Loggs Town, and detain them till those of ours taken last year as well as those suspected to be taken this year, are restored, and restitution made for the goods taken with them. Mr. Muntour tells me the Indians on Ohio would be very glad if the French Traders were taken, for they have as great a dislike to them as we have, and think we are afraid of them, because we patiently suffer our men to be taken by them, without making reprisals of them the same way."

In June, 1752, a treaty was made at Logstown between Messrs. Fry, Lomax, and Patton, Commissioners from Virginia, and the Indians. Andrew Montour, George Croghan, Christopher Gist, William Trent, and other Traders were present.

The Commissioners arrived at Shanoppin's Town, on the site of Pittsburgh, May 28th, where they remained two days, holding a Council with the Delawares living there. On the 30th, they started for Logstown. From this date the *Journal* of the Commissioners' Proceedings[1] reads:

"Saturday, May the 30th, 1752. The goods being put on board four large canoes lashed together, the Commissioners and others went on board also, to go down the River with colors flying. When they came opposite the Delawar Town they were saluted by the discharge of fire-arms, both from the Town and opposite shore, where Queen Alliquippa lives; and the compliment was returned from the canoes.

"The Company then went on shore to wait on the Queen, who welcomed them, and presented them with a string of wampum, to clear their way to Logg's Town. She presented them also with a fine dish of fish, to carry with them, and had some victuals set, which they all eat of. The Commissioners then presented the Queen with a brass kettle, tobacco, and some other trifles, and took their leave.

"The weather being very wet the Commissioners went on shore to a Trader's house, secured their goods in the canoes by covering them in the best manner they could, and lay there that night.

"Sunday, May the 31st. They set off with the canoes and arrived at Loggs Town, where they were saluted by the firing of small arms, both from the Indians and English Traders residing there; and the Commissioners were met by the chiefs of the Indians on the shore, and welcomed."

The Commissioners exchanged some speeches with the Indians on the following day and told them they would await the arrival of other chiefs who were on their way before asking for a general council.

"On Thursday, June the 4th, Thonariss, called by the English the Half King, with a sachem deputed by the Onondaga Council, and others, came down the River, with English colors flying, to Loggs Town; and the following days they were employed in their own business till the 10th, when a Council was appointed for treating with the Commissioners of Virginia. . . .

"After the speeches had been spoke and interpreted, the Commissioners, in his Majesty's name, delivered the present of goods to the

[1] Published in the *Virginia Historical Magazine*, xiii., 143–174.

Half King and the other chiefs of the Indians, who thankfully received them and appointed some of their men to make a division of them; which they did without the least noise or disorder, on the spot, among the several nations, whose representatives respectively took charge of their parts, to be subdivided when they carried them home."

The Half King then made speeches to "Eghisara,[1] which is Mr. Montour's Indian name," and to "our brother, The Buck (meaning Mr. George Croghan)."

"Thursday, June 11th. . . . Afterwards, the Half King spoke to the Delawares: 'Nephews, you received a speech last year from your brother, the Governor of Pennsylvania and from us, desiring you to choose one of your wisest Councillors, and present him to us for a King. As you have [not] done it, we let you know it is our right to give you a King, and we think proper to give you Shingas for your King, whom you must look upon as your chief, and with whom all public business must be transacted between you and your brethren, the English.'

"On which the Half King put a laced hat on the head of The Beaver, *who stood proxy for his brother, Shingas*, and presented him with a rich jacket, and a suit of English clothes which had been delivered to the Half King by the Commissioners for that purpose.

"The Commissioners, addressing themselves to the Shawnees, acquainted them that they understood that their chief, Cockawichy [Kakowatcheky], who had been a good friend to the English, was lying bed-rid, and that, to show the regard they had for his past services, they took this opportunity to acknowledge it by presenting him with a suit of Indian clothing.

"Then the Half King spoke as follows: 'Brother, the Governor of Virginia. . . . We are sure the French design nothing else but mischief, for they have struck our friends, the Twightwees. We therefore desire our brethren of Virginia may build a strong house at the Fork of the Mohongalio, to keep such goods, powder, lead, and necessaries as shall be wanting; and as soon as you please.'"

On June 13th, the Commissioners presented to the chiefs for their signature a written instrument, confirming and ratifying the treaty held at Lancaster in the year 1744, and giving their consent and permission to the English to make settlements on the south and east of the Ohio River. This instrument was executed by the Six Nations chiefs present at the Council, and signed by them as follows:

"Conogariera [Canajachrera], Cheseago, Cownsagret, Enguisara [Montour], Tegrendeare, Thonorison, sachems and chiefs of the said United Nations."

[1] Also written Eghnisara and Enguisara. It likewise appears as Ecknisera in the treaty made with the Twightwees at Lancaster, July 23, 1748.

Captain William Trent, George Croghan's partner in trade, was then in the employ of the Ohio Company of Virginia and accompanied the Commissioners to Logstown. On June 21st, he left Logstown, in company with Andrew Montour, under instructions from the Virginia Commissioners, to carry a present from them to the Twightwee or Miami Indians, whose principal town, known as Pickawillany, on the Great Miami River, two miles above the present town of Piqua, Ohio, had been visited by Christopher Gist in 1751, in the interest of the Ohio Company.

Captain Trent's *Journal* of this expedition will be found in the chapter on the Pickawillany Path.

The minutes of the Provincial Council of Pennsylvania for May 30, 1753, contain the following important news from Logstown:

"Mr. James Galbraith, one of the Justices of Lancaster County, Mr. John Harris, who keeps the Ferry over Susquehanna at Pextang, Messieurs Michael Taafe and Robert Calendar, partners in the Indian Trade, came to Town from Ohio and waited on the Governor. Their intelligence, which, by his Honor's order was put down in writing by Robert Calendar, is as follows, vizt.:

"That on the 7th of this inst., May, he was at Pine Creek, a place about twenty miles above the Logs Town [Pine Creek rises in the northern part of Allegheny County, and flows through the borough of Etna just before entering the Allegheny River, nearly six miles above the mouth of the Monongahela], in company with Captain Trent, Mr. Croghan, and several other Traders. They received a letter the same day from John Fraser, a Trader who lives at Weningo [Venango] on the Ohio, about one hundred miles above the Logs Town. He wrote that he was informed by some of the Mingos that there were then, and had been since March last, one hundred and fifty French and Indians at a carrying place which leads from Niagara to the heads of the Ohio, building canoes and making other preparations for the reception of a large body of French and Indians who were expected there every day with eight pieces of brass and a large quantity of ammunition and provisions.

"That on the 8th of May they received a full confirmation of the above account by two Indians who were sent by the Council at Onondaga to give the Ohio Indians notice of the preparations the French were making to attack them.

"When our Indians received this notice, one of the Mingoes went to a French Trader [La Force] at the Logs Town and told him of it, and said that he had amused them with fine stories this last year, as sweet as if his tongue was sweetened with sugar; that if the French made any attempt to attack them or the English, he might depend he should be the first man killed.

"Mr. Croghan and the other Traders, upon this intelligence, thought it advisable to send for the Half King, to inform him of it. He arrived the same day, and seemed much concerned at the news. He said he expected Monighotootha [also called Scarrooyady] every day up the River, and that as soon as he arrived they would call a Council and see what ought to be done. *Monighotootha is deputed by the Six Nations to look after the Shawonese.*

"The twelfth of May, John Harris arrived, with the advices from his Honor the Governor [letters from Governor Clinton and Colonel William Johnson, enclosing accounts of a large French and Indian armament having passed Fort Oswego destined for the Ohio]. Monighotootha arrived the same day. There were messengers immediately despatched to the Logs Town, etc., to the Delawares and Shawonese, to invite them to Council. But they, being all drunk, none of them came. . . . That, when he went away, the Shawonese and Delawares had not delivered an answer to the message sent by the Mingoes, as they were not all quite sober; but several of their chief men declared they would agree to what the Half King had said."

On June 23, 1753, Tanacharison (the Half King) and Monakatootha (the Delawares' name for Scarrooyady) wrote to Governor Dinwiddie from Logstown: "We send you this by our brother, Mr. Thomas Burney [a blacksmith then living at Logstown], to acquaint you that we, your brethren, together with the head men of the Six Nations, the Twightwees, Shawonese, and Delawares, were coming down to pay you a visit, but were prevented by the arrival here of four men, two Mingoes and two Delawares, who informed us that there were three hundred Frenchmen and ten Connewaugeroonas within two days' journey of this place, and we do not know how soon they may come upon us. Therefore, our request is, that you would send out a number of your people, our brethren, to meet us at the Forks of Mohongiale, and see what is the reason of their coming."

This letter was copied by Edward Shippen while Thomas Burney, its bearer, passed through Lancaster County on his way to Williamsburg. Governor Hamilton laid the copy before the Pennsylvania Council August 7th; and on the same day informed its members that Mr. Richard Peters had written him from Carlisle that he had seen Andrew Montour after his return from the Onondaga Council, where he had gone as bearer of a message from the Virginia Governor. Montour told him that the Six Nations were against both the English and French building forts and settling lands at Ohio, and desired that they might both quit that country, and send only a few Traders with goods sufficient to supply the wants of their hunters; that they did not like the Virginians and Pennsylvanians making treaties with these

Indians, whom they called Hunters, and young and giddy men and children."

Governor Hamilton reported that on the 31st of July Andrew Montour came to town and delivered a message from five chiefs of Onondaga. In this message the Onondaga Councillors thanked the Governor for his interest in their young men at Ohio. "They stand in need of your advice," add the chiefs, "for they are a great way from us. . . . It is an hunting country they live in, and we would have it reserved for this use only, and desire no settlement may be made there; though you may trade there as much as you please; and so may the French. We love the English and we love the French, and as you are at peace with one another, do not disturb one another. If you fall out, make up your matters among yourselves. You must ask the French what they intend to do, and endeavor to preserve the peace. We would not have you quarrel, but trade with us peaceably, one as well as another. But make no settlements. If our Indians should be struck, it will be very kind to help them. It is better to help them than us, for we are near New York, and can be supplied easily from thence. But our young men at Ohio must have their supply from you. We therefore heartily thank you for your regards to us and our Hunters at Ohio."

Major Edward Ward made a deposition at Pittsburgh in 1777 regarding the Indian towns above and below the Forks of the Ohio in 1754, at which time he was an Ensign, in command of the Virginians engaged in building a fort at the mouth of the Monongahela. In this he stated, "that in the year 1752, and before his surrender to the French, there was a small village inhabited by the Delawares on the southeast side of the Allegheny River [Shanoppin's Town], in the neighborhood of that place [Pittsburgh]; and that old Kittanning on the same side of the said River, was then inhabited by the Delawares; that about one-third of the Shawnees inhabited Loggs Town, on the west side [right bank] of the Ohio, and tended corn on the east side of the River; and the other part of the Nation lived on the Scioto River; that the Deputies of the Six Nations, after the surrender, joined the Virginia forces, commanded by Colonel George Washington, who was then on his march, at Little Meadows, and continued with him, in the service of Virginia till after the defeat of Monsieur La Force and a party of French troops under his command. And the Deponent further saith, that subsequent to the defeat of Col. Washington at the Great Meadows, the Shawanese, Delawares, many of the western tribes of Indians, and an inconsiderable number of renegades of the Seneca tribe, one of the Six Nations, joined the French."

Duquesne wrote the French Ministry from Montreal, August 20, 1753: "The letter I received on the 12th of January last from M. de

Joncaire, has obliged me to proceed to force to obtain provisions from the farmers to enable me to oppose the projects of the English, who, he advised me, had sent smiths to Chinengue and the River au Bœuf where they were even settled; and that there was a terrible excitement among the Indians, who looked upon it as certain that the English would be firmly settled there in the course of this year."

On September 21st the following letter, written by John Fraser to his partner in the Indian Trade, was laid before the Pennsylvania Council by the Governor, and ordered to be entered on the records:

[MONONGAHELA] FORKS, August 27, 1753.

MR. YOUNG:

I have sent the bearer in all haste, to acquaint you what a narrow escape William made from the French at Weningo. I had sent him off there the same time that you ordered him, and from that time until he ran away he only sold eight bucks worth of goods, which Custologo [a Delaware chief] took from him, and all his corn, when he was making his escape in the night. He is made a captain by the French; and next morning after William's escape, he delivered John Trotter and his man [James McLaughlin] to the French, who tied them fast, and carried them away to their new Fort, that they made a little from Weningo, at a place called Caseoago, up French Creek.

The night that William ran away, that afternoon two Frenchmen came to Weningo, who told William that there was no danger. But William, being a little afraid, got all ready that night, and came as far as Licking Creek, and there staid till break of day, and then came by land to the top of the hill against my house, where he saw about one hundred of the French dogs, all under arms; and had Trotter and his man then tied.

Fourteen of them followed William, but, it being a foggy morning, he outrun them; so that there is nothing lost yet, only those eight bucks and all the corn. . . .

I have not got any skins this summer, for there has not been an Indian between Weningo and the Pict country hunting this summer, by reason of the French.

There is hardly any Indians now here at all, for yesterday there set off, along with Captain Trent and French Andrew [Montour], the Heads of the Five Nations, the Picts [Twightwees, or Miamis], the Shawonese, the Owendats, and the Delawares, for Virginia. And the Half King set off to the French Fort with a strong party, to warn the French off their land entirely, which, if they did not comply to, then directly the Six Nations, the Picts, Shawonese, Owendats, and Delawares, were to strike them without loss of time. The Half King was to be back in twenty days from the time he went away. So were the Indians from Virginia.

Captain Trent was here the night before last, viewed the ground the Fort is to be built upon, which they will begin in less than a month's time. . . .

The captain of the Fort that took John Trotter from Weningo

was the White Frenchman that lived last winter at Logstown [La Force.][1]

The Indians under Scarrooyady who had set off for Virginia, reached Winchester, and met Colonel William Fairfax there in September, with whom they made a treaty. Messrs. Croghan, Gist, Trent, and Montour were present with them. After the close of this Council, they proceeded to Carlisle, in Pennsylvania, where they were met by Richard Peters, Benjamin Franklin, and Isaac Norris, Commissioners appointed by Governor Hamilton to treat with them. At this conference, a letter from the two Traders, Michael Taafe and Robert Callendar, was handed to the Commissioners by William Buchanan, and by them read to the chiefs. It greatly alarmed them, and they set off for Logstown as soon as the conference was over.

The letter read as follows:

SHAWONESE CABBINS, September 28, 1753.
SIR:

This day met with Joseph Nelson, coming from Ohio, and brought the news, which I believe to be true, which I am sorry for, of the French coming down; and all the English have come off the River Ohio and have brought their goods with them.

The Half King went to the French Fort to know what was their reason for coming to settle the lands of Ohio. The Commander told him the land was theirs, and discharged him home; and told him he was an old woman, and all his nation was in their favor only him; and if he would not go home, he would put him in irons.

He came home and told the English to go off the place, for fear they should be hurt—with tears in his eyes.

Sir, we are on our journey to the River to see the Half King, and to talk to him; but durst not take our goods over the [Alleghany] Hill. Pray, Sir, keep the news from our wives, but let Mr. Peters know of. it, as we understand he is to be in Carlisle.

Remain your friends and humble servants,
CALLENDAR AND TAFFE.

To Mr. WILLIAM BUCHANAN.

The Carlisle Council came to an end on October 4th, and the Indians returned to the Ohio. On the 15th of the following month, Governor Hamilton informed his Council that Louis Montour, a brother to Andrew Montour, had come express from Ohio, bringing with him a message from the Half King, Monakatootha, and Cayenquilaquoa, written for them at Shanoppin's Town on their return, by five Traders there, whose names were signed as witnesses—Thomas Mitchell, Joseph Campbell, Reed Mitchell, Thomas Mitchell, Junr., and William Campbell. This message said, among other things: "We depend that you

[1] *Penna. Col. Rec.*, vi., 22.

and the Governor of Virginia will join hands and be as one, and we, the Six Nations, will be the third brother; and as for the French, our enemy is at hand, with a Tomhock in their hands, holding it over our heads to us to take hold of it, or else to be struck with it; and to take it to strike our own flesh, we think it very hard. As for you, they have already struck, and openly declare they will clear this River of the English and all others that will not join them. So now, we beg our brothers' assistance with quick despatch."[1]

Governor Hamilton, in a letter dated October 30th, communicated this news to Governor Dinwiddie, of Virginia, who wrote in reply, on the 24th of the following month, that he had "sent a person of distinction to the Commander of the French forces on the Ohio, to know his reasons for this unjustifiable step in invading our lands. . . . The messenger has been gone three weeks. When he returns, I shall acquaint you of his proceedings, reception, and answer of the French officer."

This messenger whom Governor Dinwiddie had sent to the Ohio was Major George Washington, then a young man of twenty-one. Washington left Williamsburg, October 31st, and proceeded to Alexandria, where he equipped himself for the journey. From Alexandria he went to Winchester. At this place he engaged Christopher Gist as a guide, and hired for other assistants Barnaby Curran and John McGuire, Indian Traders, with Henry Stewart and William Jenkins.

The party left Winchester, November 15th, and reached the house of John Fraser, the Trader, at the mouth of Turtle Creek, on the Monongahela on the 22d. From there Curran and Stewart started down the river in a canoe, with the goods, while the others proceeded on horseback. About two miles below the Forks of the Ohio "on the southeast side of the River, at the place where the Ohio Company intended to erect a Fort [McKee's Rock, 2750 feet below the mouth of Chartier's Creek], lives Shingiss, King of the Delawares," wrote Washington in his *Journal*. "We called upon him, to invite him to a Council at the Loggs Town. . . . Shingiss attended us to the Loggs Town, where we arrived between sun-setting and dark, the 25th day after I left Williamsburg. . . .

"As soon as I came into Town, I went to Monakatoocha (as the Half King was out at his hunting cabin on Little Beaver Creek, about fifteen miles off), and informed him by John Davison, my Indian Interpreter, that I was sent a Messenger to the French General; and was ordered to call upon the sachems of the Six Nations, to acquaint them with it. I gave him a string of wampum and a twist of tobacco, and desired him to send for the Half King; which he promised to do by a

[1] See Egle's *Notes and Queries*, Third Series, iii., 116, for an interesting letter of Secretary Richard Peters on this message.

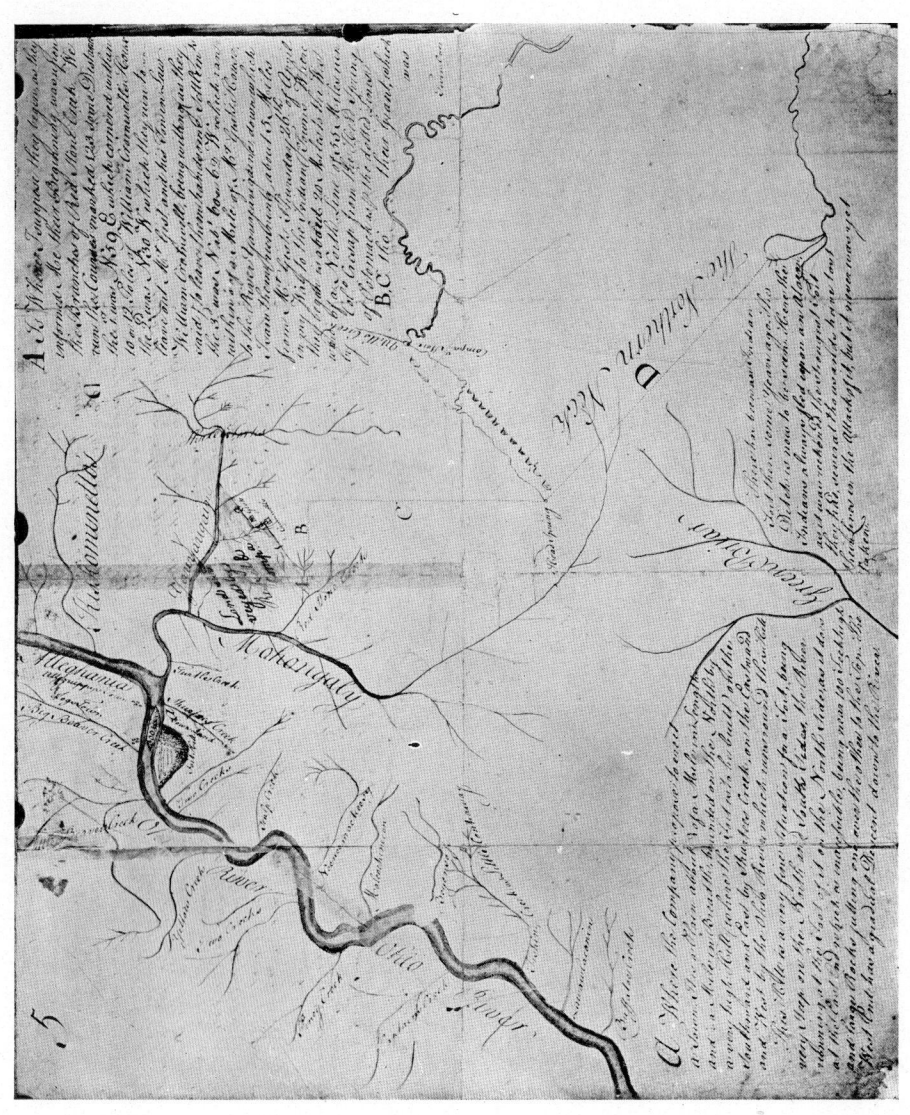

The Ohio Company's Map of the Forks of the Ohio, about 1752.
From a photograph furnished by Mr. Archer Butler Hulbert.

runner, in the morning, and for other sachems. I invited him and the other great men present to my tent, where they stayed about an hour and returned. . . .

"25th. Came to Town four Frenchmen, who had deserted from a Company at the Kuskuskas [Kaskaskia], which lies at the mouth of this River. . . . These deserters came up from the Lower Shannoah Town with one Brown, an Indian Trader, and were going to Philadelphia. . . . About three o'clock this evening the Half King came to Town. . . .

"26th. We met in Council at the Long House about nine o'clock, where I spoke to them."

The Half King promised that they should set out for Venango three nights later. The *Journal* of Christopher Gist (Washington's guide) for the next week reads as follows:

"Tuesday, 27th. Stayed in our camp. Monacatoocha and Pollatha Wappia gave us some provisions. We stayed until the 29th, when the Indians said they were not ready. They desired us to stay until the next day, and, as the warriors were not come, the Half King said he would go with us himself, and take care of us.

"Friday, 30th. We set out, and the Half King and two old men and one young warrior went with us [Washington gives their names as Jeskakake, White Thunder, and the Hunter (Guyasutha)]. At night we encamped at the Murthering Town, about fifteen miles, on a branch [Connoquenessing]of Great Beaver Creek. Got some corn and dried meat.

"Saturday, 1st December. Set out, and at night encamped at the crossing of Beaver Creek from the Kaskuskies to Venango, about thirty miles. The next day, rain; our Indians went out a hunting; they killed two bucks. Had rain all day.

"Monday, 3d. We set out and travelled all day. Encamped at night on one of the head branches of Great Beaver Creek, about twenty-two miles.

"Tuesday, 4. Set out about fifteen miles, to the town of Venango, where we were kindly and complaisantly received by Monsieur Joncaire, the French interpreter for the Six Nations."

Washington and Gist returned from the French forts to Virginia by way of Shanoppin's Town.

After Washington's return to Williamsburg, Dinwiddie wrote to Governor De Lancey, of New York, the results of his mission. "On his arrival," Dinwiddie says, "he found that the French had taken a post on a branch of the River Ohio, and built a Fort. . . . and that they had in readiness materials for other forts, which they declared their intentions to erect on the River, and particularly at Logstown, the place destined for their chief residence, as soon as the season would permit them to embark."

On the 5th of December, 1753, Governor Hamilton laid before the Pennsylvania Council a message he had prepared, to be sent to the Half King, to Scarrooyady, and to other chiefs of the Six Nations at Ohio; and also a copy of the instructions he proposed to give to John Patten, a Trader, who was to proceed to Logstown in company with Andrew Montour and deliver the Governor's message to the Indians. Patten and Montour did not get started on their journey until after the first of January, 1754. George Croghan left Aughwick for Logstown a day or two in advance of them, and reached Shanoppin's Town, January 13th, where Patten and Montour overtook him. He had stopped at John Fraser's house, at the mouth of Turtle Creek, the day before, and learned from Mr. Fraser that Washington had returned from the French forts and departed for Virginia; and that the French General had told him that his orders were to take all the English Traders he found on the Ohio, which orders he was determined to obey.

Croghan's *Journal* then proceeds: "On the fourteenth we set off to Log's Town, where we found the Indians all drunk. The first salutation we got was from one of the Shawonese, who told Mr. Patten and myself we were prisoners, before we had time to tell them that their men that were in prison at Carolina were released, and that we had two of them in our company. The Shawonese have been very uneasy about those men that were in prison, and had not those men been released it might have been of very ill consequence at this time; but as soon as they found their men were released they seemed all overjoyed, and I believe will prove true to their alliance.

"On the fifteenth five canoes of French came down to Log's Town in company with the Half King and some more of the Six Nations, in number an ensign, a serjeant, and fifteen soldiers.

"On the fifteenth, in the morning, Mr. Patten took a walk to where the French pitched their tents, and on returning back by the officer's tent, he ordered Mr. Patten to be brought in to him; on which word came to the Town that Mr. Patten was taken prisoner. Mr. Montour and myself immediately went to where the French was encamped, where we found the French officer and the Half King in a high dispute. The officer told Mr. Montour and me that he meant no hurt to Mr. Patten, but wondered he should pass backward and forward without calling in. The Indians were all drunk, and seemed very uneasy at the French for stopping Mr. Patten; on which the officer ordered his men on board their canoes and set off to a small town of the Six Nations about two miles below the Log's Town, where he intends to stay till the rest of their army come down. . . .

"By a Chickisaw man who has lived among the Shawonese since he was a lad, and is just returned from the Chickisaw country, where he had been making a visit to his friends, we hear that there is a large body of French at the Falls of Ohio, not less, he says, than a thousand men; that they have abundance of provisions and powder and lead with them; and that they are coming up the River to meet the army from Canada coming down. He says a canoe with ten Frenchmen in her came up to the Lower Shawonese Town with him, but on some of the English Traders threatening to take them, they set back that night without telling their business.

"We hear from Scarrooyady that the Twightwees that went last Spring to Canada to counsel with the French were returned last Fall; that they had taken hold of the French hatchet, and were entirely gone back to their old towns among the French.

"From the sixteenth to the twenty-sixth we could do nothing, the Indians being constantly drunk. On the twenty-sixth the French called the Indians to Council, and made them a present of goods. On the Indians' return, the Half King told Mr. Montour and me he would take an opportunity to repeat over to us what the French said to them.

"On the twenty-seventh we called the Indians to Council, and clothed the two Shawonese [prisoners] according to the Indian custom, and delivered them up to Council, with your Honor's speeches sent by Mr. Patten. . . .

"On the twenty-eighth we called the Indians to Council again, and delivered them a large belt of black and white wampum in your Honor's and the Governor of Virginia's name, by which we desired they might open their minds to your Honor, and speak from their hearts and not from their lips. . . . After delivering the belt, Mr. Montour gave them the goods left in my care by your Honor's Commissioners at Carlisle."

On the 31st a signed speech addressed to the Governor of Pennsylvania and Virginia was delivered by the chiefs, the Half King, Scarrooyady, Newcomer, Coswentannea, Tonelaguesona, Shingas, and Delaware George. In this message the Indians said: "You desire we may inform you whether that speech sent by Louis Montour was agreed on in Council or not, which we now assure you it was, in part; but that part of giving the lands to pay the Traders' debts, we know nothing of it; but we earnestly requested by that belt, and likewise we now request, that our Brother, the Governor of Virginia may build a Strong House at the Forks of the Mohongialo, and send some of our young brethren, the warriors, to live in it. And we expect our Brother of Pennsylvania will build another House somewhere on the River, where he shall think proper, where, whatever assistance he will think proper to send us may be kept for us, as our enemies are just at hand, and we do not know what day they may come upon us. We now acquaint our brethren that we have our hatchet in our hands to strike the enemy as soon as our brethren come to our assistance." Croghan's *Journal* proceeds:

"February the Second. Just as we were leaving the Log's Town, the Indians made the following speech: 'Brethren, the Governors of Pennsylvania and Virginia, We have opened our hearts to you and let you know our minds; we now, by these two strings of black wampum, desire you may directly send to our assistance, that you and we may secure the lands of Ohio; for there is nobody but you, our brethren, and ourselves, have any right to the lands. But if you do not send immediately, we shall surely be cut off by our enemy, the French."

In a letter to the Governor accompanying this report, Croghan writes: "Your Honor will see by ye Indians' speeches that they are in high spirits and very willing to defend themselves from the enemy, provided the English governments, whom they depend upon, will assist them. They expect your Honor will immediately order a House built, to keep necessaries in, to enable them to carry on a war against their enemy, who had already invaded their country. . . . The Indians all intend, as soon as your Honor and the Governor of Virginia begins to build, to gather all their warriors to ye places where you 'll build, and not suffer ye French to come down ye River. As for what French is amongst them already, as soon as they hear of ye army coming down they say they will secure them. I would awaited on your Honor in company with Mr. Montour and Mr. Patten, but that Mr. Trent is just come out with ye Virginia goods, and has brought a quantity of tools and workmen to begin a Fort; and as he can't talk ye Indian language, I am obliged to stay and assist him in delivering them goods, which is Mr. Montour's advice."

The story of Captain Trent's unsuccessful attempt to build a fort at the mouth of the Monongahela, and of the driving off by the French of his ensign, Edward Ward, and the men he had at work upon the structure, is all familiar history to the reader, and need not be repeated here. The Virginia expedition, sent by Governor Dinwiddie under command of George Washington for the purpose of re-inforcing Captain Trent, left Will's Creek, Maryland, in the latter part of April, 1754. On June 26th, while the little army was at work on the road between Fort Necessity and the mouth of Redstone Creek, Washington records in his *Journal*, "An Indian arrived, bringing news that Monacatoocha *had burned his village, Logstown*, and was gone by water with his people to Red Stone, and might be expected there in two days." Monacatoocha, or Scarrooyady (also called Scruneyattha), it will be remembered, was the Oneida chief who was delegated by the Onondaga Council to be the overlord of the Shawnees, and for that reason his residence was fixed at Logstown, their chief town.

This was the end of the Old Logs Town.[1] About two hundred of the Six Nations, Shawnees, and Delawares living there removed, after the defeat of Washington at Great Meadows, to Fort Cumberland, and thence to Aughwick,[2] where they were cared for during the winter of 1754–55 by George Croghan. In the spring of 1755, some of the Six Nations left Aughwick for their own country in New York; some of them, with many of the Shawnees and Delawares, returned to the Ohio; while a few of them, with some of the Shawnees, removed to Otstuagy or French Town, on the West Branch of the Susquehanna, about forty miles above Shamokin, on the site of the present village of Montoursville.

Before March, 1755, the French at Fort Duquesne rebuilt Logstown for the Shawnees who still remained in that vicinity. Frederick Post was there in August, 1758, and again in December of the same year. In his *Journal*, under date of December 2d, he writes: "I, with my companion, Kekiuscund's son, came to Logs Town, situated on a hill. On the east end is a great piece of low land, where the Old Log's Town used to stand. In the New Log's Town, the French have built about thirty houses for the Indians."

At a meeting of the Pennsylvania Council held at Carlisle, January 13, 1756, George Croghan informed Governor Morris that he had sent a friendly Indian to the Ohio for news, who had returned to his house five days before. He informed Croghan that "from Kittaning he went to the Log's Town, where he found about one hundred Indians and thirty English prisoners, taken by the Shawonese living at the Lower Shawonese Town, from the western frontier of Virginia, and sent up to Logstown. He was told the same thing by these Shawonese that the Beaver had told him before respecting their striking the English by the advice of some of the Six Nations."

In November, 1756, William Johnson, a native of Pennsylvania, who had been made a prisoner at Fort Cumberland while in company with a party of Indians sent to attack the inhabitants near there, was examined before Governor Sharp at Annapolis. He stated that, "about six weeks or two months since, when this informant was at the Logs Town, he heard Teedyuscung's son and several other Indians say that they, the Delawares, were about to offer terms to the inhabitants of Pennsylvania."

Croghan reported to Sir William Johnson that on May 8, 1757, three of the messengers he had sent to Ohio had returned. They told him, among other things "that the Ohio Indians are much afraid of the Southern Indians, having been struck three times by them this Spring—

[1] *Penna. Col. Rec.*, vi., 198.
[2] *Ibid.*, vi., 149.

twice near Fort Duquesne, and once at the Logs Town; and that the Indians are moving fast up the Ohio toward the Senecas."

An Indian prisoner, taken near Raystown, was examined at Fort Littleton May 12, 1757. He reported that "He left the French Fort [Duquesne] about the 22d of April last; that there was then in the said Fort about one hundred French and forty Indians; that there were about eighty Delawares at the mouth of Beaver Creek, one hundred at Kuskushing, one hundred at Shenango [Logs Town?], and about ten at Venango."

In the *Narrative* of Marie Le Roy and Barbara Leininger, who were captured by Delaware Indians at Mahanoy Creek, a few miles below Shamokin, October 16, 1755, the captives relate that they were carried to Kittanning, and thence to Sauconk, and Kaschkaschkung. They state that while they were living there, "last summer the French and Indians were defeated by the English in a battle fought at Loyal-Hannon, or Fort Ligonier [probably the engagement of October 12, 1758, at the "Breastworks" a few miles west of Ligonier]. This caused the utmost consternation among the natives. They brought their wives and children from Locks Town [Logstown], Sackum, Schomingo, Mamalty, Kaschkaschkung, and other places in that neighborhood, to Moschkingo, about one hundred and fifty miles farther west."

On November 24, 1758, the French abandoned Fort Duquesne, and on the following day the army of General Forbes occupied its site. Two days later, George Croghan and Andrew Montour proceeded down the river to treat with the Indians at Shingas's Town, one mile below the mouth of the Beaver. In his *Journal*, under date of November 28th, Croghan writes: "Set off at seven o'clock, in company with six Delawares, and that night arrived at Logs Town, which we found deserted by its late inhabitants. On inquiring the reason of their speedy flight, the Delawares informed me the Lower Shanoes had removed off the River up Sihotta, to a great plain called Moguck, and sent for those that lived here to come there and live with them, and quit the French, and at the same time the deputies of the Six Nations, which I had sent from Easton, came and hastened their departure. In this Town is forty houses, all built for them by the French, and lived here about one hundred and twenty warriors."

In a conference held by Sir William Johnson with some chiefs of the Six Nations and Delawares at Johnson Hall, May 2, 1765, Johnson reminded the Indians of the losses suffered by the English Traders at the time of Pontiac's conspiracy. "You know," he told them, "the treacherous and cruel part acted by some of your people at Logs Town and about the Ohio two years ago. You then plundered numbers of the Traders who were supplying you with goods. Some of them you promised to protect and save their effects, but you did not keep your words. Several of these unhappy sufferers are thereby reduced to great necessity, some of whom are thrown into Gaol because they could not pay their debts."

In the *Journal* of Bouquet's expedition against the Ohio Indians in 1764, it is stated that the army left Fort Pitt on October 3d, and marched about eleven miles on that day and the next. The *Journal* then proceeds: "Friday, October 5th. In this day's march the army passed through Loggs-Town, situated seventeen miles and a half, fifty-seven perches, by the Path, from Fort Pitt. This place was noted before the last war for the great trade carried on there by the English and French; but its inhabitants, the Shawanese and Delawares, abandoned it in the year 1750 [misprint for 1758]. The Lower Town [*i.e.*, the Old Logs Town] extended about sixty perches over a rich bottom to the foot of a low steep ridge, on the summit of which, near the declivity, stood the Upper Town [built with the assistance of the French after Scarrooyady had burned the Old Town in 1754], commanding a most agreeable prospect over the Lower, and quite across the Ohio, which is about five hundred yards wide here, and by its majestic easy current adds much to the beauty of the place."

In 1765, George Croghan started down the Ohio River with a party, in order to visit the Indian tribes on that stream and the Wabash. His *Journal* of this trip begins as follows:

"May 15th, 1765. I set off from Fort Pitt with two batteaux, and encamped at Chartier's [now Brunot's] Island, in the Ohio, three miles below Fort Pitt.

"16th. Being joined by the deputies of the Senecas, Shawnesse, and Delawares, that were to accompany me, we set off at seven o'clock in the morning, and at ten o'clock arrived at the Logs Town, an old settlement of the Shawnesse, about seventeen miles from Fort Pitt, where we put ashore, and viewed the remains of that village, which was situated on a high bank, on the *north*[1] side of the Ohio River, a fine fertile country round it. At eleven o'clock we re-embarked and proceeded down the Ohio to the mouth of Big Beaver Creek, about ten miles below the Logs Town. . . . About a mile below the mouth of Beaver Creek we passed an old settlement of the Delawares, where the French, in 1756, built a town for that nation. On the north side of the River some of the stone chimneys are yet remaining."

The Revs. Charles Beatty and George Duffield made a missionary journey to the Ohio Indians in 1766, arriving at Fort Pitt on the 5th of September. From there Beatty's *Journal* proceeds:

"9th, Tuesday. Having sought direction of Heaven and the

[1] So written by Croghan, though usually misprinted *south*.

Divine Presence, we resolved to attempt a journey to Kighalampegha [New Comer's Town], an Indian Town about 130 miles from here. This place we fixed upon because . . . the king or head man of the Delaware nation lived there. . . . We were much engaged this day in preparing for our journey, and received much assistance from the gentlemen of this place. Mr. [John] Gibson, a Trader here, who was taken prisoner last war by the Indians, and was adopted into one of their chief families, and was well respected by them, recommended us to one of the chiefs by a letter. . . .

"10th, Wednesday. . . . We crossed the Allegheny River in a canoe, swimming our horses along side of it. We then proceeded on our journey down the River Ohio about five miles, having on our right hand a high hill, and encamped upon the bank of the River. . . .

"11th, Thursday. Sat out in the morning, the weather dull and gloomy, and after travelling nine or ten miles, most part along the River side, we came to an old Indian Town, now deserted, called by the Traders, Log Town, situated on a fine, rich, high bank, covered with fine grass, commanding a most beautiful prospect both up and down the River Ohio."

When Washington went down the Ohio River in October, 1770, he speaks of having breakfasted at the Logs Town with Colonel Croghan, Alexander McKee, and another person, who had accompanied him that far on his voyage from Fort Pitt, and there separated from him to return.

Rev. David McClure was at Fort Pitt in the early part of September, 1772, preparing for a missionary journey to the Indian towns on the Muskingum. On the 5th, he rode with John Gibson, a Trader, "to his house in Logs Town, which was the only house there." "The greater part of the Indian Traders," wrote McClure, "keep a squaw, and some of them a white woman, as a temporary wife. Was sorry to find Friend Gibson in the habit of the first."

Gibson's Indian wife was a Shawnee woman, sister-in-law to Logan, the Mingo chief,[1] who lived, in 1773, at a small Mingo village called Logan's Town, at the mouth of Beaver Creek. In April, 1774, Logan was living at the mouth of Yellow Creek, with some relatives, while a party of whites, headed by Daniel Greathouse, were on the opposite side of the river. Logan's brother and sister (or sister-in-law) and four or five other Indians crossed the river, and after drinking became involved in an altercation with the whites. Three or four of the Indians were killed, including Logan's brother and sister and perhaps another woman. On the back of one of the women was an infant. Its mother (probably Logan's sister-in-law) attempted to escape, but was shot down. She lived long enough to beg mercy for her child, telling her

[1] *Penna. Archives*, iv., 499.

Looking down the Ohio River from the Site of Logstown.
From a photograph made by the Author in September, 1909.

murderers that its father was a white man. The babe was sent to John Gibson, as the father.[1] These murders were the cause of the Indian outbreak of 1774, generally called Lord Dunmore's war. John Gibson, the white man who wrote down Logan's famous speech, had the same reason to feel embittered against the Virginians that Logan had; so that it is altogether probable that that speech was as much the expression of Gibson as of Logan.[2]

In July, 1773, John Lacey travelled with his uncle, Zebulon Herton, from Chester County to the Muskingum, Herton having been sent on a mission by the Quakers to the Ohio Indians. On the 18th of the month, they arrived at Pittsburgh, and put up at Samuel Semple's tavern. The next day they had a conference with Captain White Eyes, the Delaware chief, who informed them that John Gibson, the Trader, had set out that morning for New Comer's Town, and advised them to endeavor to overtake him. Lacey's *Journal* then proceeds:

"20th. We had made preparations to set out early this morning, in order to overtake the Indian Trader; but, upon inquiry, learned that he had returned and said that John [James] Logan,[3] a Mingo Indian, was lying in wait to kill him. He had returned to Town, among the Indians, for protection. He got Gayashuta, a Mingo Chief, and Captain White Eyes, to agree to go and see what was the matter with Logan, and endeavor to pacify him. White Eyes said he would attend us all the way to New Comer's Town; he thought the behavior of Logan would make us afraid, as he should be, were he in our place.

"They set out in a canoe, and we, with a Delaware Indian, by land. We crossed the Allegheny branch in a canoe; and our horses swam by the side. When we came near to a place called Logstown, where Logan lay, our guide stopped and hearkened very attentively, though we could not tell what he was listening at; but before we had proceeded much farther, we heard a great noise. Our guide, who could not speak one

---

[1] The best account of this transaction is that received by Alexander McKee from Major William Crawford and Captain John Neville May 3d, and transmitted by McKee to Sir William Johnson. It is printed in *N. Y. Col. Doc.*, viii., 464.

[2] See also *West Va. Hist. Mag.*, iii., 152.

[3] The names of Shekallamy's three sons were "John," or *Taghneghtoris* (or *Tachnechtoris*); "James-Logan," or *Soyeghtowa*, or *Sayughtowa* (who was also called "Shekallamy's lame son"); and "John-Petty," or *Sogogeghyata*. See *Penna. Archives*, iii., 776; iv., 91. Many writers confuse Taghneghtoris with "Logan." See *Penna. Col. Rec.*, vi., 616. Some of the Moravian accounts state that Logan's wife was a Mohican woman. She is generally thought to have been a Shawnee. Possibly, one of her parents was a Shawnee, and the other, a Mohican. Her sister, John Gibson's squaw, was always called a Shawnee. See *Otzinachson*, p. 131. According to Dr. Lyman C. Draper, Logan's Indian name was "*Tah-gah-jute*, or 'short dress.'" (Brantz Mayer's *Logan and Cresap*, p. 32). This was the Delaware name for Logan, apparently; and it means, not "short dress," but "short foot," referring to his lameness.

word of English, made motions to us to stop and retire. He took us up a hollow to some water, where we stayed while he went to the camp from whence the noise proceeded. He, for our safety, secretly informed George Girty, a Trader, where we were. He immediately came to us and conducted us around the camp to the River side. He told us that an Indian had got drunk, and fell in the River, and was drowned; and that Logan suspected Gibson of making him drunk and killing him. Soon after we came to the River, Captain White Eyes and our Indian guide came with canoes; and we again swam our horses by the side, over the River, to the house of John Gibson. Gayashuta was left to pacify Logan, who was very drunk. White Eyes and our two guides returned to Logan's camp, where they stayed all night, leaving us at Gibson's.

"21st. In the morning, White Eyes came over to us, and wanted us to proceed on our journey, as he was ready to go with us, and Logan had become somewhat quieted; but Uncle Zebulon being a little unwell, and White Eyes pretty merry, we thought it best, as Gibson was to go next day, to remain where we were. White Eyes soon fell asleep. About eleven o'clock, Logan, Gayashuta, and several more Indians, came over to Gibson's. They soon began to talk very loud; while all the others stood around them, with their tomahawks in their hands. However, their differences were soon made up.

"22d. We set out; crossed the Ohio with Gibson and White Eyes; came to a Mingo Town, where they had Logan shut up in a house. An old Indian advised us to go on; but before we could get off, Logan broke down the door and came to us in a very good humor, expressing a great deal of sorrow for what he had said yesterday.[1]"

The next visitor to the site of Logstown whose account has been preserved was Arthur Lee, one of the Indian Commissioners of the Confederated Colonies, who visited Fort McIntosh on the Beaver in 1784. In his *Journal,* Commissioner Lee writes, under date of December 17th: "We embarked on the Monongahela, and soon entered the Ohio, on our way to Fort McIntosh. . . . Four miles down the River brings you to Montour's Island, which is six miles long and about a half mile broad on an average [now Long, or Neville's Island]. . . . The next place is Loggstown, which was formerly a settlement on both sides of the Ohio, and the place where the treaty of Lancaster was confirmed by the Western Indians. From Logstown to the mouth of Beaver Creek is [seven to eight] miles, and from thence to Fort McIntosh, one mile."

In September, 1787, Isaac Melcher, of Philadelphia, laid out a town on the site of Logstown, which he called "Montmorin." His description of the place is as follows: "This town . . . is delightfully situated on the north bank of the Ohio River, on a beautiful plain, that is not liable to be overflowed, in a healthy and fertile country, about

[1] Dawson's *Hist. Mag.,* Sec. Ser., vii., 104.

eighteen miles below Fort Pitt, on the road to Fort McIntosh, . . . and at the ancient settlement formerly called Logstown, which was abandoned previous to the peace of 1763, where an extensive trade was carried on many years."

General Anthony Wayne established a drill-camp on or near the site of Logstown, where he trained his troops from November 30, 1792, to April 30, 1793, preparing them for the successful campaigns which he later made against the Indians of Ohio and Indiana. This camp was called Legionville; and that name has been perpetuated to the present day by a station on the Pittsburgh, Fort Wayne & Chicago Railway, about one mile below Economy; which thus marks the site of Wayne's Camp and of the historic Logstown.

The writer visited the site of the Old Logstown in September, 1909, and found nothing there but a ploughed field, with an abandoned oil-well near the foot of the bank ascending to the second level, on which the later town was built.

Before leaving the subject of this chapter it will be well to refer at some length, to the activities of the white man who was most intimately connected with the history of Logstown. This man was George Croghan. His experience as an Indian Trader and agent, as negotiator and diplomat, would furnish material for a great many interesting volumes; and the value of his work in getting the Western Indians into the English alliance was greater than that of all others combined. Though at times unjustly an object of suspicion to the authorities of Pennsylvania and the neighboring Colonies, his services in the French War were of much value to that Province; and had his efforts and advice previous to that war been properly recognized and followed by the Quaker Assembly, probably there would have been no French war. No adequate account of this man can be given in a few chapters, and all that will be attempted here is to present the briefest record of his movements while he was in Pennsylvania and New York.

The Journals of Croghan's Indian transactions and treaties in the years 1750, 1751, 1754, 1756, 1760–61, and 1765, are printed together in the first volume of Thwaites's *Early Western Travels*. Other Journals and many letters are printed in the volumes of the Pennsylvania *Colonial Records* and *Archives*, in Craig's *Olden Time*, and in the New York *Colonial Documents* (vol. vii.) There are also a great many unpublished letters and accounts in the Johnson and Bouquet Manuscripts.

END OF VOLUME I.